The British School at Athens

KNOSSOS:
POTTERY GROUPS OF THE OLD
PALACE PERIOD

KNOSSOS:

POTTERY GROUPS OF THE OLD PALACE PERIOD

J. A. MacGillivray

BRITISH SCHOOL AT ATHENS
STUDIES 5

Published and distributed by
The British School at Athens
Senate House, Malet Street, London WC1E 7HU
©The Managing Committee, the British School at Athens

First published in Great Britain 1998

ISBN 0 904887 32 4

This book is set in Ehrhardt 11/12 pt
Camera-ready copy prepared by Rayna Andrew
Printed in Great Britain by Technical Print Services Ltd, Nottingham

Contents

List of figures

List of plates

List of abbreviations

AM   Ashmolean Museum, Oxford
BM   British Museum, London
DB   Daybooks, or excavation notebooks, kept by Duncan Mackenzie and Sir Arthur Evans, currently in the library of the Ashmolean Museum
E   east
EBA   Early Bronze Age
EM   Early Minoan
F.   Phaistos inventory numbers as published by Doro Levi in *Festos e la Civiltà Minoica*. Wherever possible all references to finds from Phaistos are cited using the inventory number alone. For a list with context, type, page number and illustration see Levi 1976, 809–55. For a list by context see Levi and Carinci 1988, 353–79

HM   Herakleion Museum, Herakleion, Crete
K.   Knossos Inventory Number. See p. 19 and APPENDIX IV
KSM   Knossos Stratigraphical Museum, Knossos, Crete
LM   Late Minoan
MBA   Middle Bronze Age
MM   Middle Minoan
N   north
PB   Pottery notebooks kept by Duncan Mackenzie during the early years of excavations.
S   south
TP   Test pit(s)
W   west
KSM box number

Acknowledgements

It gives me great pleasure to record here my very deep debt of gratitude to the Managing Committee of the British School at Athens for the permission and encouragement to take on the study of the Middle Minoan pottery from Knossos while serving successive terms as Knossos Curator and Assistant Director of the School.

Generous awards from the Institute for Aegean Prehistory and the Knossos Donated Fund of the British School at Athens helped cover the expenses of vase mending, drawing and photography and the last year of writing up. I was fortunate to receive the Vans-Dunlop Scholarship of the University of Edinburgh to support the first stage of writing up this research into a Ph.D. submitted in 1986. A Junior Faculty Development Leave from Columbia University in 1991 allowed for continued study at Knossos.

The initial impetus for this study came in 1982 when I struggled to fix the dates for Cycladic pottery in Crete and Mervyn Popham suggested that 'Someone must come to grips with the MM pottery from Evans' excavations', in the same way he had dealt with the LM III pottery from Knossos. Throughout the many years since the first box of sherds was poured out onto a strewing table in the Stratigraphical Museum to their description and interpretation in this text I have benefited from the kindness, knowledge, expertise and patience of very many scholars and friends whom I wish to acknowledge here with my warmest gratitude.

Peter Warren and Petros Petrakis taught me how to study pottery in the Stratigraphical Museum at Knossos where Pat Cameron, Christine Morris and Alan Peatfield assisted with the nuts and bolts of working there. Henry Davis helped with the strewing and marking of sherds and Jeff Clarke drew the majority of the examples illustrated in PLATE 130. The typology figures in Chapter 2 are by Alesia Margolis, the patterns are my own.

Work in the Herakleion Museum was facilitated by the permission of the Greek Ministry of Culture, the successive Ephors, Professor Iannis Sakellarakis and Dr. Charalambos Kritsas, who provided the assistance of Alexandra Karetsou, Nota Dimopoulou, Giorgos Rethemiotakis and Antonis Papadakis. In the Ashmolean Museum, Ann Brown and Michael Vickers kindly dismantled the pottery display (on more than one occasion) for me and provided the photographs from the Evans Archive reproduced here by kind permission of the Visitors of the Ashmolean Museum. Chris Mee alerted me to some surprises in the Merseyside and County Museum in Liverpool and facilitated their study. Anna Collinge brought to my attention relevant material in the Irish collections, as did Leslie Fitton in the British Museum. I benefited from the warm hospitality of Rachael and Sinclair Hood and Jeff Clarke in Oxford, Christa and Chris Mee in Liverpool and Pat Cameron in London.

Putting the work together was greatly assisted by Douglas Babbington-Smith and Sheila Raven with the plates and Ann Aertssen who helped compile the concordances.

During the course of the museum study and subsequent write-up I profited much from discussions with the 'Knossians' of the School, especially Gerald Cadogan, Nicolas Coldstream, Vronwy Hankey, Sinclair Hood, Colin Macdonald, Nico Momigliano, Mervyn Popham, Hugh Sackett and Peter Warren and with many colleagues who shared their discoveries and ideas over the years, most notably Stelios Andreou, Dorothea Arnold, Maria Avgouli, Robin Barber, Phil Betancourt, Filipo Carinci, Hector Catling, Stella Chrysoulaki, Ellen Davis, Jack Davis, Peter Day, Nota Dimopoulou-Rethemiotakis, Jan Driessen, Doniert Evely, Lisa French, Olga Hadjianastasiou, Robin Hägg, Peter Jablonka, Richard Jones, Athanasia Kanta, Alexandra Karetsou, Bobby Koehl, Manfred Korfmann, Ariane Marcar, Nanno Marinatos, Marisa Marthari, Jean-Pierre Olivier, Angelia Papagiannopoulou, Olivier Pelon, Ingo Pini, Edith Porada, Jean-Claude Poursat, Giorgos Rethemiotakis, Iannis and Efi Sakellarakis, Metaxia Tsipopoulou, Iannis Tzedakis, Lucia Vagnetti, Henri Van Effenterre, Sarah Vaughan, Vance Watrous, Malcolm Weiner, Judith Weingarten, Ian Whitbread, David Wilson and Carol Zerner. To all I am grateful.

The relative chronology proposed here owes a very great deal to the Knossos 'Sherd Nerds' who met at Nico Momigliano's instigation in the Stratigraphical Museum at Knossos in July 1992 to review pottery groups of the EM and MM periods at Knossos (Cadogan et al. 1993). The methods we employed persuaded me to alter the terminology for certain groups discussed below and, I trust, helped to correct serious errors in previous versions of this work and relevant publications (MacGillivray 1984*a*; 1990). Colin Macdonald generously shared his knowledge of the MM pottery from his recent excavations in and around the palace at Knossos. Nota and Giorgos Rethemiotakis kept me informed of their findings in Lasithi and were always ready to discuss the significance of the Knossos-Lasithi link. Ken and Diana Wardle very kindly shared their discovery in 1995 and 1996 of a deposit very similar in context and composition to the Early Chamber beneath the West Court and convinced me that it really does represent a distinct style and period in the Knossian sequence.

The absolute chronology owes a very great deal to Vronwy Hankey who provided an advance copy of K. A. Kitchen's latest dates and to Sturt Manning who provided advance copies of his new ideas combining C-14 and dendrochronology to allow for the ancient history that concludes Chapter 3. The review of Creto-Egyptian relations owes much to Dorothea Arnold, Leslie Fitton, Christine Lilyquist, Vronwy Hankey and Stephen Quirke.

The concentrated effort necessary to revise and complete this manuscript was made possible by a Visiting Fellowship at All Souls College in Oxford in 1995–96 and I am most grateful to Warden Davies and the Visiting Fellows Committee for their confidence.

Nico Momigliano and Sturt Manning read and sent detailed comments on the latest draft, which was then whipped into its present shape by Bill Cavanagh, Rayna Andrew, Doniert Evely and Holly Parton. I am deeply grateful to all for their time and energy spent correcting my grammar and oversights.

Finally, I am most indebted to Robin Barber and Sinclair Hood who supervised the earlier version of this work into a PhD thesis and without whose constant encouragement (and gentle pressure) it never would have been completed. It gives me the greatest pleasure to dedicate these fruits of my labours to those who planted the seeds and trimmed the branches.

Oxford, June 1996

Preface

In 1900 Sir Arthur Evans began large scale excavations into the tell site of Tseleve he Kephala at Knossos. During the succeeding five years he cleared much of an Aegean Bronze Age structure he identified as the palace of the legendary King Minos. Tests beneath the floors and paved areas of the Late Bronze Age complex revealed a long, complex history of occupation on the tell, much disturbed by the Middle Bronze Age foundations and early floors of the palace. Evans, with his field director Duncan Mackenzie, paid close attention to the stratigraphy in the tests. In 1905 he proposed an outline for a chronological scheme of the Bronze Age in Crete that he called Minoan: 'As indicating the probable duration of successive dynasties of priest-kings, the tradition of which had taken abiding form in the name of Minos' (1905*b*). In the absence of written history but in imitation of the Egyptian dynastic sequence, Evans set out three broad periods of Early, Middle and Late Minoan with a further sub-division of three, to reflect historical events and changes as extrapolated from the archaeological record.

The MBA walls and floors on the tell became known as the 'Old Palace', the later repairs and newer walls and floors became the 'New Palace'. The most distinctive pottery found in Old Palace levels was a finely made polychrome decorated ware very much like that found in earlier excavations in the Kamares Cave (Mariani 1895; Myres 1895), and so, during the early years of excavation, the period of the Old Palace was referred to as the 'Kamares Period' and the fine pottery called 'Kamares Ware'. In Evans' Cretan Bronze Age sequence the Old Palace was seen to belong to the Middle Minoan period, more specifically to MM I B, II A and II B, and the New Palace, constructed late in MM III, belonged essentially to the Late Minoan period.

Evans' Minoan chronological framework soon became the standard for all prehistoric sites in the Aegean, and attempts were made to set the historical sequences elsewhere in a similar order, on the basis of ceramic imports from Crete. It was not long before problems in synchronization became apparent and the stratigraphy observed at Knossos called into question. Joseph Hatzidakis suggested that Evans' Early and Middle Minoan periods should be combined because he had found pottery from both periods together at Gournes and Tylissos (1918, 56–7; 1934, 75). Andonis Zois later re-studied the material and concluded that it belonged to various apparently unrelated deposits and ranged in date from the EM II to MM I B periods (1969, 34). In 1933 Nils Åberg dismissed much of the evidence observed by Evans and Mackenzie and grouped the three phases of the Old Palace period into one that he called the 'Kamares Phase' (1933). Åberg's proposal was soon refuted by John Pendlebury who re-affirmed the validity of the stratigraphic sequence at Knossos as he himself had observed in his own excavations there (1939, xxxi–xxxii).

Problems arose again in the 1950's when a previously undiscovered wing of the Bronze Age palace at Phaistos was cleared by Doro Levi. Previous excavations at Phaistos by Federigo Halbherr and Luigi Pernier, carried out at the same time as Evans' major work at Knossos, had uncovered a contemporary palace and a sequence of construction and destruction horizons similar to those described by Evans at Knossos (Pernier 1935; Platon 1949*a*). Levi's excavations revealed an undisturbed wing of the MBA in which he defined four ceramic phases, none of which appeared to correspond to Evans' MM III A period. He concluded that the period did not exist at Knossos either and further speculated that the Old Palace at Knossos had been destroyed in MM III B and not MM II B as Evans and Pernier had suggested (Levi 1960).

Nicolas Platon (1962; 1968) and Andonis Zois (1965; 1968) were quick to criticize Levi's interpretation of the levels at Phaistos. They suggested that two of Levi's periods, Ib and II, belonged to the same phase and represented upper and lower floors of a single destruction event. They also felt that the newly discovered wing had suffered the same fate as the previously excavated areas of the palace at Phaistos, but failed to agree between them on the date. Zois proposed that the destruction took place during his 'Ripe Classical Phase' which corresponds to Evans' MM II A period. Platon compared the material from the final destruction to MM II B at Knossos and suggested that both palaces suffered the same fate at the same time (1962, 127). Gisela Walberg has reviewed the Phaistos stratigraphy, for her study of the Middle Minoan pottery from the site, and accepts Levi's interpretation of the stratigraphy so that her 'Classical Kamares' stage may be seen to include three of Evans' ceramic periods (1976, 96–125; 1988).

An alternative to Levi's interpretation of the Phaistos stratigraphy was put forward by the excavation's architect, Enrica Fiandra (1962, 1980). Fiandra also proposed four periods, called 1 to 4, but compared them closely to Evans' Knossos sequence. I have found that Fiandra's architectural and ceramic phasing makes the most sense both in terms of Levi's observations at Phaistos and my own impressions of Knossos, so references to comparative material and events at Phaistos in the following pages are given using Fiandra's periods and not Levi's.

One of the major stumbling blocks towards a consensus on the problem of Middle Minoan chronology is understanding the definitions of Evans' ceramic phases at Knossos. He used less than 100 vases and only a few groups of sherds to illustrate the characteristic ceramics of the Old Palace period, and there are several instances, when he changed his mind on the dating of certain pieces. The resulting discord, then, is hardly surprising.

This book presents the first results of over a decade of research, initially conceived to refine the chronology of the appearance of Middle Minoan pottery in the Cycladic islands and Cycladic products in Crete. The first has since been admirably studied and published by Angelia Papagiannopoulou (1991) and one aspect of the other side of the coin by myself (1984a). At an early stage of the research it became apparent that the Cycladic framework I sought to clarify could not be considered without a full re-investigation of the Knossos stratigraphy and a new study of Middle Minoan pottery. I changed the focus of the research design from the Cyclades to Crete and began the task of re-group-ing some of the main deposits assigned by Evans and Mackenzie to the Old Palace period at Knossos. The initial aim was to determine their stratigraphic position, and analyse the pottery groups from these deposits, to allow for a discussion of such basic issues as the relative chronology and early history of the palace at Knossos. Verification in the form of recent excavations at Knossos (Popham 1974; Catling *et al.* 1979; Warren 1980; Hood 1994), Archanes (J. and E. Sakellarakis 1991) and Kommos (Betancourt 1990), and a re-working of the well-published and indexed excavations at Phaistos (Levi 1976, 1980, Levi and Carinci 1988) all suggest that the sequence proposed by Mackenzie and Evans may continue to be acceptable with minor alterations. The following re-investigation of their work at Knossos illustrates not only their powers of observation and perception, but also the concern they took over accurate records and conservation with future generations of sceptical scholars in mind. Had they not stored the finds as they did in the Stratigraphical Museum at Knossos, the present study would not have been possible.

This study has one very limited aim: to place the ceramics from the first major period of the palace's history in a relative and continuous sequence, based on their immediate archaeological context here defined as stratigraphical/depositional, technical and stylistic. The suggested sequence is applicable to Knossos.

The deposits and pottery selected for this study reflect the specific aims stated above. Much material remains in the KSM and elsewhere for those who may have other questions to ask of it and are as privileged as I have been to work on it.

Oxford, June 1996

I

Re-investigation of archaeological contexts

INTRODUCTION

The early history of the palace at Knossos has been reconstructed on the basis of trials beneath the relatively well-preserved renovations of the New Palace period. Disturbances, probably caused by an earthquake and the subsequent re-building activities at the end of the Old Palace period, have made an overall understanding of the structure's initial appearance quite difficult. Nonetheless, Evans was confident about the early date of many of the foundations and included them in his schematic plan of the palace in its first phase, reproduced here in FIG. 1.1.

Fig. 1.1. Plan of Knossos showing conjectural arrangement at the end of the Old Palace period (Evans 1921, fig. 152).

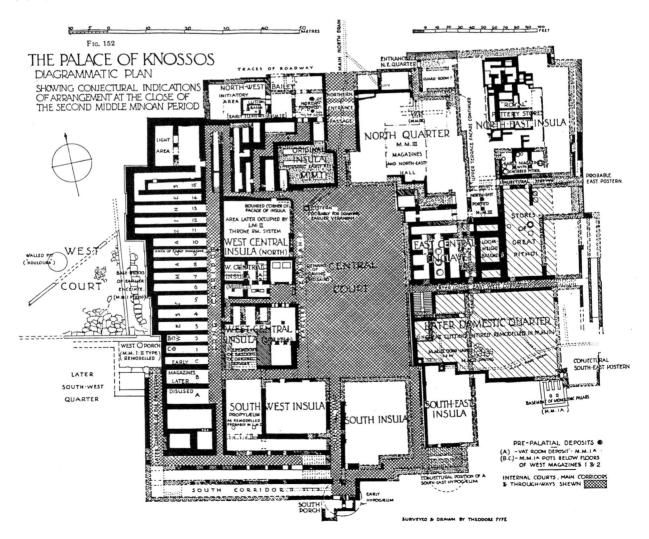

This chapter reviews the history and results of excavations into levels of the Old Palace period at Knossos. The primary aim of this re-investigation is to re-evaluate the early history of the palace and its relation to contemporary sites in central Crete. For this reason, only pottery is considered here and used as an indicator of relative date, interaction and change. The pottery, from a selection of the main deposits, assigned by Evans to the Old Palace period, is assembled into Groups A to P and used to suggest the relative dates of those groups. Deposits which had been assigned by Evans to the MM I period, and thus thought to be earlier than the first palace, were not included in the present study. Recent research by Momigliano (1991), however, has shown that many of these should have been treated. As these are published in detail by her, they will be referred to in summary and her conclusions incorporated into the discussion. Likewise, other relevant groups at Knossos not treated in detail are referred to only when considered to be relevant to the limited aims of this work.

The 16 groups of pottery discussed in detail below come from deposits excavated by Evans, Mackenzie and Pendlebury between 1901 and 1930. In the absence of detailed plans, photographs and true stratigraphic sections, it is not possible to know for certain how these deposits were formed. Some seem to represent primary deposits on floors, for example the Early Chamber beneath the West Court (Group A) and some floors in the rooms of the Royal Pottery Stores (Groups F to I). Others are cumulative deposits, that is an accumulation of material withdrawn from use over time, for example the North-West Pit (Group D), while others may comprise re-deposited material used as fill, for example the West and South Polychrome Deposits (Groups E and N). Given the additional possibility that the finds may have become contaminated during subsequent study and storage, or even during excavation, caution of the sort advised by E. French (1987) is exercised here and the material is re-assembled to form 'groups' rather than deposits or contexts.

The pottery groups are re-assembled by means of three sources of information:

- publications,
- the excavator's notebooks and photographs, and
- the pottery itself.

The first source includes detailed preliminary reports of the early campaigns (Evans 1900–1905a), summaries of the pottery from the same years (Mackenzie 1903, 1906), and the final reports (Evans 1921–35).

The second source includes the excavation notebooks, or Day-Books (DB) kept by Evans and Mackenzie, currently stored in the Ashmolean Library, Mackenzie's pottery notebooks (PB) in the library of the British School at Athens in Athens, and the photographs of groups of restored vases and sherds in the Evans Archive of the Ashmolean Museum. Mackenzie described a number of individual pieces in his pottery notebooks which can be identified in the material studied. Also, he and Evans occasionally wrote contexts on vases and sherds in a hard lead pencil, which remain legible and help to suggest the find spots for a number of vases, which otherwise would have been considered without provenance. Pendlebury also wrote on most of the whole vases. The relevant inscriptions are given in the catalogue entries in APPENDIX I and listed separately in APPENDIX III. In all cases the graffito confirms the suspected or published context of the inscribed piece. Evans' photographs of the pottery are useful in re-assembling groups, because many vases in a group photograph can be shown to come from the same deposit, and so allow for the suggestion that the others in the same photograph most likely come from the same context and should be included in the group. In the case of some vases, the photographs are the only record of their existence as they can no longer be traced.

As the interpretation of Evans' and Mackenzie's notes and publications has become rather like debating the meaning of holy scriptures, the third source, the pottery itself, is perhaps the most valuable. It was kept in separate lots in the storerooms of reconstructed areas of the palace and surrounding buildings, and formed the nucleus of the Knossos Stratigraphical Museum (KSM). Some of the pottery was mended for publication and sent to the Herakleion (then Candia) Museum. Some vases and a great number of fragments were sent to the Ashmolean Museum in Oxford, the Fitzwilliam Museum in Cambridge (Lamb 1936), the British Museum in London (Forsdyke 1925), the Liverpool Museum (Mee and Doole 1993) and the American School of Classical Studies at Athens. Subsequent exchanges have dispersed fragments to public collections in Sweden (Åström and Holmberg 1985), Ireland (Johnston 1973) and the Royal Museums of Art and History in Brussels (Laffineur 1976). The remaining vases and fragments were boxed by Pendlebury and arranged into the ordered system listed in his guide to the Knossos Stratigraphical Museum (1933). These were moved to the new Stratigraphical Museum near the Villa Ariadne in 1963–5 and re-boxed, labelled and shelved in Pendlebury's order, allowing them to be consulted with much greater ease than before (Popham 1970a, 12).

None of the deposits of the Old Palace period had been strewn or studied in detail, so this was the first step in the present re-investigation. As with Furness (1953) and Popham (1970a), it was found that there were errors in labelling, but that these could be corrected, when a complete deposit was studied. Some boxes were found to be unrelated to the others assigned to a given Group and had to be put aside. Others were found to join with Groups assigned to other areas. The contents and labelling of boxes has not been altered, but what are believed to be the correct groupings of boxes are listed in APPENDIX II.

Once the labelling problems were overcome, many 'new' vases were mended and fragments in the boxes were found to join published vases in other museums, either confirming a known context, or suggesting a likely find spot for some well-known pieces hitherto without exact provenance. A list of joins between museums is given in APPENDIX VI. It should be noted that these joins are suggested on the basis of photographs, drawings and tracings made of the sherds in the various museums. None of these joins has been physically executed.

Mackenzie began to inventory the pottery in 1902 with vases K.1 to K.29 (1902 PB (2), 68–76, 79–80). The present study takes on where he left off; vases and sherds have been marked with a series of numbers ending with K.1078. The inventory numbers were used to facilitate the cross-references of joins and parallels during the re-investigation. They are superseded here by the catalogue sequence in APPENDIX I; a concordance between catalogue and inventory numbers is given in APPENDIX IV.

In the following chapter the most complete and useful Groups from the Old Palace are described. Frequent reference to the types, wares and stylistic groups set out in Chapter 2 is necessary here, to allow for discussion of the likely relative date of each Group. The full catalogue of inventoried pottery is in APPENDIX I. It was not possible to catalogue all of the pottery. Some deposits are treated in full but others, that were considered to be badly mixed, have only a selection of vases in the catalogue. Some examples that could not be located but appear in Evans' photographs are included here because of their close resemblance to known types. Many examples could not be included because of the uncertainty of their find context. A number of pieces were selected for drawing (PLATE 130), because of their form or because they did not reproduce satisfactorily in photographs. The majority of the pottery is illustrated in photographs in PLATES 31–156. Only a very small percentage of the inventoried pottery is not illustrated, in most cases because close parallels could be cited among the other vases from Knossos, or because they have been well-illustrated elsewhere.

The likely contexts of the Groups are discussed and relative dates are suggested on the basis of their stratigraphic context, the analyses in Chapter 2, and comparison with reliable deposits at Phaistos. The meaning of the Groups can only be alluded to in some cases, because most were sorted by Mackenzie who rejected great quantities of both fine and coarse fragments, so that the true nature of the deposits cannot be known.

PART 1. THE EARLY HOUSES BENEATH THE WEST COURT

The West Court was identified and the S end partially cleared in 1900. It was then said to comprise 'Consid-

erable remains of irregular paving', and an altar base (Evans 1900, 9–10).

In 1904, Mackenzie supervised a series of stratigraphic trials including what Evans described as a 'Section beneath the court', in an area 6.50 m to the W of the first altar base, where the tops of walls had become visible, through weathering, since the area had first been opened four years earlier (Evans 1904, 6). The stratigraphic sequence revealed here was to become an important part of the standard framework for the relative chronology of the Cretan Bronze Age, and the notes kept were particularly detailed.

The area of the tests has been filled-in and no detailed plan survives. However, it is possible to suggest their approximate location using four sources:

- Mackenzie's description of the trials and his sketches (1904 DB, plans opp. 18, 32, 34),
- Pendlebury's sketch plan (1933, Plan 4),
- a photograph of the later trials in the West Court taken from horse-back shortly after 1930 (Pendlebury 1939, pl. XVI.3; Evans 1935, 61 fig. 36) and
- an aerial photograph also taken some time after 1930 (Evans 1935, opp. xxvi).

The information from these sources is used to place the likely locations of the trials as suggested in the sketch plan in FIG. 1.2.

The first test pit was sunk in an area about 15 m from the West Facade of the palace, FIG. 1.2, no. 1. The material from the upper levels contained mixed MM and EM pottery, but a floor at 1.60 m from the surface produced pottery of EM II A date (Wilson 1984, 31). A trial in this area in 1969 uncovered an EM terrace wall, FIG. 1.2, CC (J. Evans 1972, 116–17 fig. 1 Tr. 1). A modern fill was observed to the W of the wall and it was suggested that the fill may have been deposited in 1955, perhaps during N. Platon's programme of reconstruction work in the palace (Hood 1955, 16). It seems quite likely, then, that the W end of the 1969 trial cut into part of Mackenzie's first test pit of 1904, that had been backfilled in 1955. The location of the early TP suggested in FIG. 1.2 is partly based on this assumption.

TP 2 was located about two or three metres to the NE of TP 1, FIG. 1.2, no. 2. Here Mackenzie found a mixture of EM II and neolithic pottery. In the W side of the test there was a wall, on a roughly N–S axis, continuing to a depth of 0.70 m from the surface of the court, and built on top of an earlier wall on the same alignment. The later wall was probably EM II to judge from the associated pottery and may have been a continuation of the EM II A terrace wall found in the 1969 trial. This would explain why TP 2 entered EM II strata immediately below the surface of the court. The terrace was probably levelled and filled-in at the end of

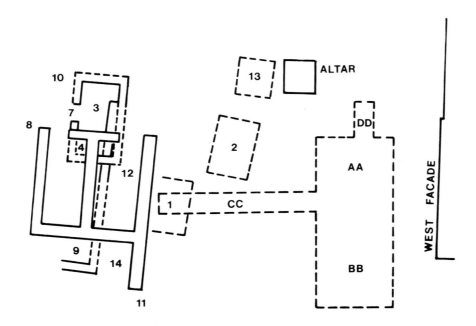

Fig. 1.2. Sketch plan of the early houses beneath the West Court with approximate locations of 1904–5 test pits (1–14) and 1969 trials (AA–DD). 1:200.

the EM II A period. It then seems to have served as an open space throughout the subsequent life of the site. This post-EM II A terrace may be the earliest ancestor of the West Court and suggests an open area in the EM II B period similar to, and contemporary with, that observed at Vasiliki (Branigan 1970a, 44).

TP 13 was located to the W of the altar base, probably to the N of TP 2, FIG. 1.2, no. 13. Here Mackenzie found EM II pottery in the first and second metres. This has since been more specifically assigned to the EM II A period and associated with the EM West Court House (Wilson 1984, 177). This test, like 1 and 2, seems to have entered the area of the EM terrace as no MM levels were found.

Most of the 1904 trials were located to the W of 1, 2 and 13, and produced quite different results. The suggested locations are given in FIG. 1.2. It was the results of these W trials that formed the basis for Evans' hypothetical West Court Section, reproduced here in FIG. 1.3. The aerial photograph of the West Court (Evans 1935, opp. xxvi) shows that the trials in this area were eventually merged. Rather than try to discuss the results of each separately, it may be more useful to summarize the sequence of phases observed as a whole.

Three phases of the MM period were noted with three associated architectural phases, which are referred to here as Structures 1, 2 and 3 in order of appearance from top to bottom.

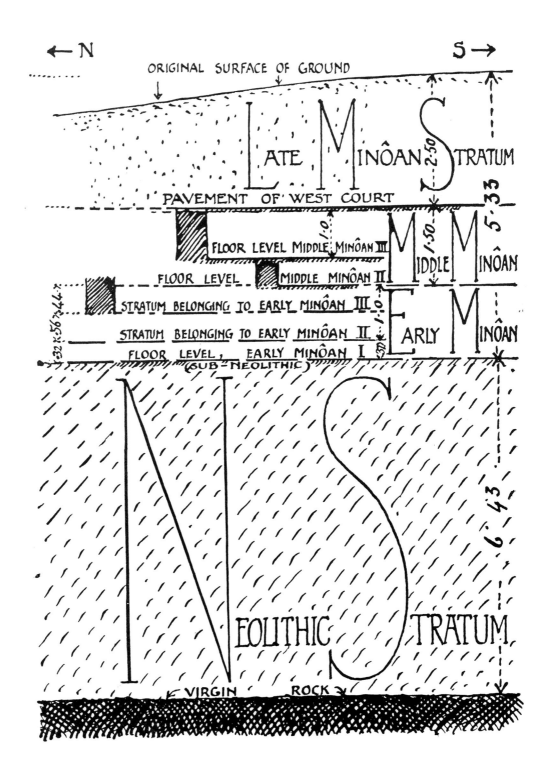

Fig. 1.3. The West Court Section; reconstructed on the basis of trials in 1904 (Evans 1921, 33 fig. 4).

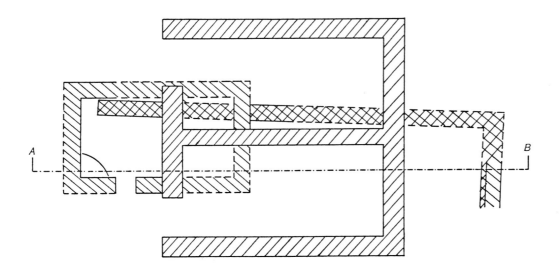

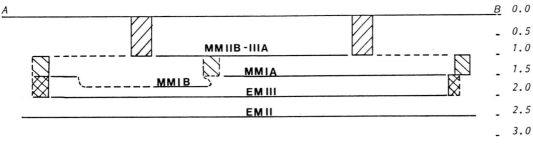

Fig. 1.4. Sketch plan and recon- structed section of building phases observed in 1904 trials beneath West Court (after Mackenzie 1904 DB (1), opp. 32).

STRUCTURE 1

STRUCTURE 2

STRUCTURE 3

Structure 1

The latest building, here called Structure 1, consists of two rectangular rooms 2.40 m wide and 5.00 m long with a common long wall and two separate doors at the N end, not E as reported (Evans 1904, 6). The E wall of the structure appears to continue S beyond the corner shown in Mackenzie's 1904 sketch, which is the basis for the sketch plan in FIG. 1.4 (1904 DB (1) opp. 32). The S continuation and apparent return to the E may have come to light in the 1905 trials, discussed below with Structure 2. This E wall seems to have remained visible until quite recently and is probably the wall shown in J. Evans' plan of the West Court in 1969 (1972, fig. 1). Only a trace remained when Hood and Taylor (1981) planned the West Court, but enough to allow it

to be linked to Mackenzie's sketch plan and to suggest the location of Structure 1 as shown in FIG. 1.2.

The walls of Structure 1 begin at the surface of the court, and go down to a depth of 1.00 m below the level of the court, stopping at a floor at this level. The floor levels associated with the structure were found at a depth of *c.* 1.00 m below the surface of the court in a number of tests. The absence of fine 'Kamares' pottery and the tendency toward monochrome decoration in the material led Mackenzie and Evans to date the build- ing to the MM III period (Mackenzie 1906, 266–7). This was supported by the discovery of a group of large, coarse, spouted jars, which they compared to similar shapes from the North-East Magazines. However, the jars were found at a depth of 1.35 m below the court and should be associated with Structure 2, discussed below.

The pottery from the first metre of deposit in TP 3 and 12, stored in the Knossos Stratigraphical Museum, is almost entirely plain wares and crude types of the MM II B–III A periods.

The pottery from the first two metres of TP 11 is for the most part very fine and can be conclusively assigned to the MM II B–III A periods, because it joins with material from elsewhere and forms part of the West Polychrome Deposits Group that belongs to the final phase of the early houses beneath the West Court (see below, Group E).

The exact location of TP 11 is uncertain. Pendlebury places it to the S of TP 9 (1933, Plan 4: B I 14). It was probably somewhere in the area NE of Kouloura 1 and SE of TP 9 against the S wall of Structure 1, as suggested here in FIG. 1.2. As there is no pottery later than the MM II B–III A periods associated with the building, it seems most likely that Structure 1 went out of use in MM III, probably early in the period at the same time as the filling operations that took place in the West Court, discussed below p. 33.

Structure 2/House C

Traces of an earlier structure, on the same alignment as the latest, were found in the 1904 TP 3, 4, 7, 9 and 12, FIG. 1.4. The tops of the walls of the lower building, here called Structure 2, appeared immediately beneath the floor of Structure 1 at 1.00 m and continued to a depth of 1.50 m below the court with associated floor levels found at depths of 1.35 m, in TP 7 and 12, and 1.50 m, in TP 4 and 9. Structure 2 consisted of a rectangular room, *c.* 2.00 m wide and 4.15 m long with a door on the W side. The floor at a depth of 1.50 m below the court in TP 9, to the S of Structure 2, was associated with wall 7, which is aligned with the structure and which Mackenzie felt belonged to it.

The 1904 report makes no mention of the finds from this building. No date was suggested and Evans referred to it as 'Some intermediate walls of no importance', which lay beneath the first building and above an important deposit at a depth of 1.75 m below the court (1904, 14 n.1). In his description of the pottery, Mackenzie lists a group of large spouted jars from the floor at 1.35 m in TP 12 and compares them with similar jars from the North-East Magazines (1904 PB (1), 47–8). Presumably because of the suspected late date for the pottery, Mackenzie associated it with the most recent structure, even though the deposit came from below the floors of Structure 1. On present evidence it would seem best to assign the Group to Structure 2.

In 1905 TP 9 was extended to the E as TP 14 and a deposit of MM I pottery was found on a floor level at a depth of 1.20 m below the court (Mackenzie 1907 DB, 1–6; Evans 1905*a*, 16 fig. 9). On the basis of the MM I deposit Evans subsequently called the walls House C, Houses A and B being the MM I A houses below the

Koulouras found by Pendlebury in 1930 (Evans 1935, 85 n.4). Andreou in his study of House C confirms Evans' MM I date for the deposit in TP 9/14 and demonstrates that the floor level, at 1.50 m below the court in TP 15 and TP 4, also contained contemporary material which he assigned to his Kouloura Group or the MM I A period (1978, 28). Momigliano recently re-investigated the 1904 and 1905 trials and speculated that the floors between 1.50 m and 1.20 m in TP 4, 9, 14 and 15 belong to within the EM III–MM I A periods (1991, 187, 191). To the same Group should be added the floor at 1.35 m in TP 12; the large spouted jars as described by Mackenzie are very similar to examples from Houses A and B below the Koulouras, which can be assigned with confidence to the EM III–MM I A periods (Momigliano 1991, 216 pl. 43.15, 226 pls. 51.65, 53.79–80).

Structure 2 and House C, therefore, seem to be the same building and belong within EM III–MM I A. The pottery from the floor deposit for the most part comprises types that are found in the EM III repertory, but there are at least two vases which indicate a later date. The first is a miniature angular bridge-spouted jar decorated with thick orange and thin white bands on the body and alternating white and orange vertical strokes on the rim, in a manner very similar to the decoration on a footed goblet from the area of House B (Momigliano 1991, 213 pl. 54 no. 121); this has close parallels among the sherd material from what is reported as the lowest level in the Monolithic Pillar Basement (Mackenzie 1906, pl. 7 nos. 14, 15). The second vase is a large jug with an elaborate design comprising a thick orange wavy line with vague diagonal motifs resembling double-axes outlined in white and red and filled with white dots on the shoulder (Evans 1905*a*, fig. 9.1; 1921, 174 fig. 123a). There are no exact parallels for the design, but the method of filling in a motif with carefully spaced white dots is found on sherds from the Monolithic Pillar Basement, in a style that might be called 'Polychrome Geometric', and which should be taken to represent the fine decorated pottery of the late MM I A period (Mackenzie 1906, pl. 7 nos. 3, 4; Evans 1921, 177 fig. 125 no. 5) (for a discussion of this style and its implications see Chapter 2, Part 4).

Momigliano points out that the jug was lifted and partially restored before being set back into place for a photograph of the floor deposit (1991, 190–1 pl. 32). This certainly seems to be the case and suggests that the location and exact context of the jug was 'fudged' for the photograph. However, the same cannot be said for the miniature bridge-spouted jar which appears unwashed and still filled with soil in the same photograph. The jug may have been encountered at an earlier stage of clearing the room, perhaps at the end of the previous day, and Evans felt justified to recompose it and set it in place when the full extent of the floor deposit had been cleared. In any case, the miniature jar alone confirms a *terminus post quem* late in the MM I A period for the deposit.

Structure 3

Traces of a third building, here called Structure 3, appeared in a few places under Structure 2. It consisted of one long N–S wall about 9.00 m in length with a doorway at the N end. The lower E–W wall at the N end of TP 3 was seen to belong to this building as well as wall 6, an E–W wall under wall 7 in TP 9, FIG. 1.4. The tops of the walls lie immediately below the floor of Structure 2 at a depth of 1.50 m and continue to an associated floor at a depth of *c.* 2.00 m from the court. Mackenzie described the pottery from the floor at 2.00 m as 'The early Minoan geometric pottery' (1904 DB, 42), a description frequently applied to the decorated wares of the EM III period. Structure 3 seems to be the building described by Evans in the 1904 report, although again he appears to have confused the points of the compass (1904, 18–20).

Andreou in his study of the material from the early floor encountered in TP 14 and 15, which seems to be associated with this structure, assigned it to his Upper East Well Group, which he regarded as characteristic of the EM III period (1978, 14). Momigliano's re-investigation concluded that there was no distinction between Andreou's EM III and pre-polychrome MM I A pottery groups and that they probably belong to one period, which she tentatively called EM III/MM I A (1991, 268). The most recent re-appraisal of Knossian ceramics of this period suggests that Andreou's Upper East Well Group should be regarded as stylistically earlier than groups with the first use of polychrome decoration, and may thus be equated with EM III (Cadogan *et al.* 1993, 24–5).

It is interesting to note that Structure 3 is aligned very closely with the walls of Houses A and B below the Koulouras. The floor level in the E room of House B is only 0.23 m higher than the floor in House A. The steps, leading to the E from the room with the central depression in House A, are preserved to a level less than 1.00 m apart from the floors in Structure 3; they may have continued for the necessary four steps to arrive at the same level, but were cut off when the second Kouloura was built. As Momigliano has shown that the pottery deposits from all three structures are contemporary, and the alignments are quite similar, Structure 3 and Houses A and B may be part of the same architectural complex. In any case, Structure 2/House C post-dates the EM III deposits in Structure 3 and in the Houses below the Koulouras.

Group A. The Early Chamber Beneath the West Court

Context

As luck would have it, the largest and most important group of pottery from the 1904 trials did not come from any of the floors encountered in the three structures described above. It came from a deposit at a depth of 1.75 m below the West Court inside the W room of Structure 1 in TP 4, but could not be linked with any of the architectural phases. The deposit consisted of over a hundred vases stacked and piled in order, as shown in the drawing in FIG. 1.5. It continued under the middle dividing wall of Structure 1 into the area of the E room, and was thus shown to be earlier than Structure 1. It also continued to the S under the S wall of Structure 2, and so seemed to be earlier than that building as well. At the time, the pottery was compared with that from the Royal Pottery Stores and assigned to the MM II period. The problem with the date was that it failed to explain how a MM II deposit might pass under the wall of a MM I house. Mackenzie resolved the problem by suggesting that the MM II floor cut into the earlier floor (1906, 256). Evans later revised the date of the deposit and called it MM I B, presumably on stylistic grounds (1921, 186 n. 3, 187–9). The change in thinking may have been possible because the wall that lay over the deposit was described as 'Consisting of rough foundation' (Mackenzie 1904 DB, 32), and Mackenzie later may have thought that it was not a wall but rather a line of tumble, which he had taken for a wall because of its alignment with Wall 4 in TP 12. However, it should be possible to accept it as an early wall that was undercut when the later floor was dug into the room.

A further problem arises with the material said to come from the second metre in TP 3. The pottery from this test stored in the KSM joins completely with the pottery from the floor 1.75 m from court in TP 4. It seems most likely that the pottery from the two tests comes from a single floor, cut into the earlier floor at 1.50 m, within the area of the room that is part of Structure 2. This would explain why the floor anticipated at 1.50 m was not observed in most places in the two trials, although it was shown to have existed by a fragment which remained *in situ* against the W wall N of the door. Outside the room the sequence fits nicely with the architecture and the three major floor levels associated with the structures described above. The MM I B deposit, within the room at a level lower than the MM I A floor, may have belonged to a cellar or pit cut into the earlier floor of the building. The MM I A floor at 1.50 m was found in one corner inside the room and immediately outside the room on the other side of Wall 4 in TP 12. It may be that the post-MM I A occupants of the area required more storage space, or may have been trying to hide the store of fine pottery that was stacked in this basement.

Re-assembly

This Group comes from the deposits from the floor at 1.75 m below the court in TP 3 and 4. The pottery from the two trials joins so completely, that they are considered here to belong to the same deposit. The Group was re-assembled by means of published illustrations (Evans 1904, 15 figs. 4, 5.2; 1921, 187 fig. 136;

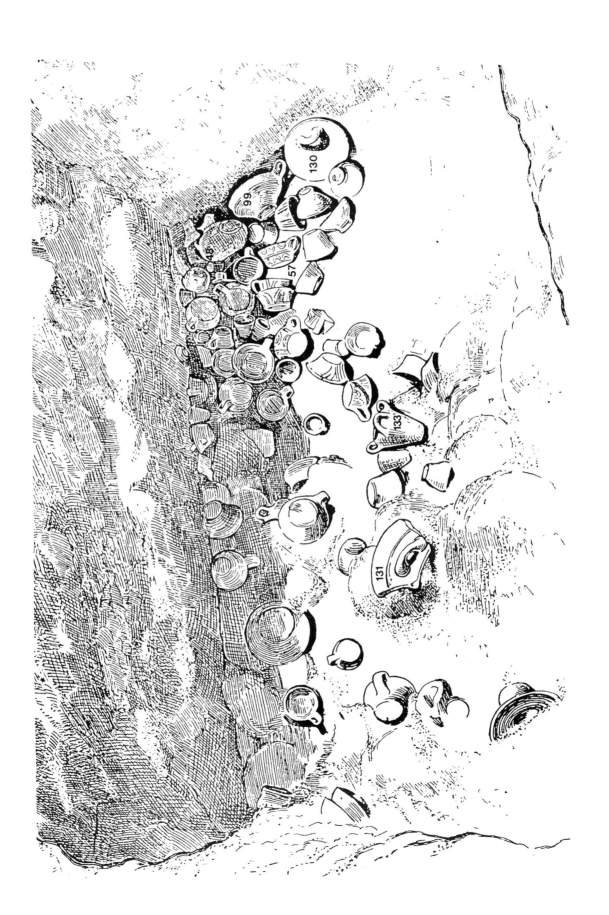

Fig. 1.5. Sketch of Group A in position (Evans 1905a, 15 fig. 8; 1921, 187 fig. 135).

Pendlebury 1933, pl. 17 2c, 3 and 4) and one unpublished photograph in the Evans Archive, reproduced here in PLATE 32. There is also a sketch of the deposit, which is sufficiently detailed to allow for pottery in the KSM to be identified and assigned to the Group, FIG. 1.5.

Most of the whole vases could be traced. The published pieces are in the HM and were probably sent as a group and inventoried as such, because they all belong within a close range of numbers in the HM catalogue. Some pieces from the Royal Pottery Stores, Groups F–J, seem to have been inventoried at the same time, but the numbers are generally earlier than those of Group A.

The pottery illustrated in PLATE 32 can be included in this Group for the following reasons:

- the finds are identified in the top right hand corner as coming from the North-West House indicating that they come from the West Court area,
- strainer **97** joins the rim of a cup from boxes in the KSM assigned to and joining Group A, and
- three of the vases shown, **50**, **74** and **145**, are inscribed with 'K.04 W Sq. T.P.3', or 'T.P.4' which records that they come from the same trenches as Group A.

The remaining pieces are all of types represented by other examples in the Group and thus most likely belong to it. Though some of the pieces could not be located, they are included in the catalogue because they are in recognizable types and are most likely of Fine Buff Fabric.

The relevant boxes of pottery from TP 3 and 4 in the KSM (APPENDIX II, B I 6 and 7) were strewn and sorted and in some cases mended. A total of 152 examples were inventoried, **1–152**, and are illustrated here in PLATES 1–6 and 31–47.

Relative date

The poor publication and changing attitudes towards this Group, more than any other at Knossos, are responsible for most of the confusion, that has arisen over the chronology of the early Old Palace period in central Crete. Mackenzie's first impression of the material's date was that it should be placed with the early floors in the Royal Pottery Stores and the North-West Pit and thus within the MM II A period (1906, 250, 256). Evans revised the date to the MM I B period (1921, 186–9), which was accepted by Pendlebury who used much of the material in this Group to illustrate the typical designs on MM I B pottery (1939, 109 fig. 17 pl. 17, 2–4). Warren and Hankey accepted the MM I B date and treated the Group as representative of the period (1989, 50). Walberg, however, assigned it to her Classical Kamares phase which she equated with Evans' MM II A–II B–III A (1976, 119). In recent work, I have followed Mackenzie's first instincts and placed Group A

in an early stage of the MM II A period (MacGillivray 1990), but now believe this must be revised.

Much of the pottery is handmade or proto-wheelmade and monochrome coated. The forms in Fine Buff Fabric are the Rounded Goblets of Type 1 (**1–7, 15–16**) Type 2 (**110**) and Type 3 (**111**), Straight-sided Cups of Type 2 (**20, 26–30, 37–41, 56–67**), Tall-rimmed Angular Cups of Type 1 (**31–4, 43** and **70**), Short-rimmed Angular Cups of Type 2 (**99–101**), Rounded Cups of Type 3 (**109, 125–6**) and Type 4 (**108**), Angular Bridge-spouted Jars of Type 1 (**36**) and Type 2 (**75**), all of which may be taken as typical of the MM I B period. There are also examples of Pared, Barbotine, Shallow Grooved and Early Printed Wares and pottery in the White-banded, Diagonal Red and White and Woven styles, all characteristic of the MM I B period. In Gritty Soft Buff Fabric there are Hand Lamps of Type 1 (**148–51**) which also occur in Groups G and L and may belong to both the MM I B and MM II A periods. There is a noteworthy lack of the characteristic Egg-shell Ware of the Royal Pottery Stores, Rounded Bridge-spouted Jars of Type 4 most common in Group L, and the early Crude Types that are so numerous in the MM II A destruction deposits in the E wing of the palace.

A large percentage of the pottery is handmade and there is a possibility that some pieces were manufactured in the MM I A period. For example, large spouted jar **146** is very similar to those we now assign to Structure 2/ House C. This may be regarded either as a survivor or as a mixture from the MM I A floor, into which this Group was cut. There are also handmade types such as the Shallow Bowls of Type 1 (**18, 24**) and Convex-sided Cups (**42** and **69**) which are found only in this Group and could belong to a late stage of MM I A or early MM I B.

It is quite certain that the deposition of Group A belongs to a period later than MM I A. As we must assign a date using the latest material in the Group, it should be considered MM I B, as concluded by Evans. It seems to belong to a time when there is evidence for a first horizon of destruction by fire in the palace, best demonstrated by the deposit in Early Magazine A at the SW Palace Angle (Catling 1974, 34; 1988, 68; Cadogan *et al.* 1993, 26) and before the second destruction by fire in the palace, which are taken here to mark the end of the MM II A period. A comparable phase at Phaistos is Fiandra's Period 1 which contains the closest comparanda for some of the examples in this Group. It is suggested below (Chapter 3, Part 3) that the term MM I B be retained at both sites.

Comment

The 1904 TP were designed to recover the earlier stratigraphy of Knossos and did so, although not perhaps as clearly as had been hoped for. The results of the 'section' through the West Court were presented as a reconstructed section showing MM III stratified above MM II which was above EM III, FIG. 1.3 (Evans 1904,

18 fig. 7). A revised version, based on the observations outlined above, is suggested in FIG. 1.4. It shows MM II B–III A stratified above MM I A and EM III with a cutting into part of the MM I A floor during the MM I B period. Given the complexities of the stratigraphy and problems involved with the manner in which the levels were excavated and the finds stored, this re-assessment must be treated as provisional until new trials may be undertaken in the West Court.

PART 2. THE NORTH-WEST TREASURY

In 1901 the clearing operations in the West Court were extended northward and the large, irregular structure which came to be known as the 'North-West Treasure House' or 'North-West Treasury', FIG. 1.6, was uncovered and a second altar base found nearby (Evans 1901, 5). The main floors of the house were seen to belong to the 'Mycenaean Period' but it was also observed that there were lower floors that were 'Of the pure Kamares Period' (ibid.).

Excavations were concentrated on the E slopes of the palace in 1902, but in 1903 were resumed in the North-West Treasury. Evans reports that the upper layers were found to contain pottery of 'the decadent style', characteristic of his period of 'partial occupation' (1903, 115). This could be a reference to the LM III B period, for which there is evidence of occupation in the form of two bowls and some sherds (Popham 1970a, 60–2). The next layers comprised clay flooring with Palace

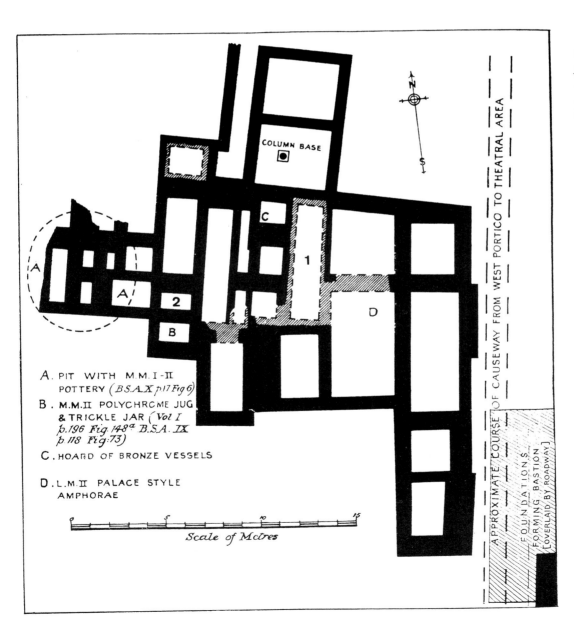

Fig. 1.6. Sketch plan of North-West Treasury (Evans 1928, 618 fig. 387).

COLUMN BASE

A. PIT WITH M.M. I-II POTTERY (*B.S.A.X p.17 Fig 6*)

B. M.M.II POLYCHROME JUG & TRICKLE JAR (*Vol I p.196 Fig. 148ª B.S.A. IX p.118 Fig.73*)

C. HOARD OF BRONZE VESSELS

D. L.M.II PALACE STYLE AMPHORAE

Scale of Metres

APPROXIMATE COURSE OF CAUSEWAY FROM WEST PORTICO TO THEATRAL AREA

FOUNDATIONS FORMING BASTION [OVERLAID BY ROADWAY]

Style amphorae at a depth of 2.00 m below the surface (ibid.). About 1.00 m below these was an earlier series of clay floors with 'Kamares' pottery, especially on the W side of the building, where the effects of later levelling were presumed to have been less destructive (Evans 1903, 115). Mackenzie, in his record of the excavation of the building, noted the sequence of strata, but also the general lack of good floor levels (1903 DB, 64–6). In one room the early floor yielded a 'Spouted two-handled jug' with 'obliquely arranged parallel systems of tooth-bands in relief alternating with similar bands in lustreless cream white and red on a lustrous glaze slip' (ibid. 64). The location is marked 1 on the plan in FIG. 1.6. The vase has not been identified, but the description is reminiscent of the bridge-spouted jars found on the early floor beneath the Room of the Olive Press and assigned to the MM II A period (Group L, **930–58**). The presence of the vase suggests the existence of a MM II A floor beneath the later room.

Group B. The Area of the Polychrome Jug

Context

In a small area to the W of the previous early floor a clay floor at a similar level produced a deposit of cups and jars including one large jar (**165**) which Evans regarded as 'The most elaborate vase of the polychrome style.' (1904, 18; 1921, 247 pl. III). The small room where the vase was discovered became known as the 'Area of the Polychrome Two-handled Spouted Jug'. Mackenzie identified the room as that shown in FIG. 1.6, no. 2. The location given by Evans and Pendlebury is the next room to the S, FIG. 1.6 B. The present study uses Mackenzie's location and, in any case, the exact location is of little importance.

Re-assembly

This Group has been re-assembled using two photographs published with Evans' report for 1904, reproduced here in PLATE 48. Four of the published vases could be found. Most of the others belong to recognizable types and so are included in the Catalogue. Sixteen vases were inventoried for this study: **153–68** illustrated in PLATES 48 and 49. Two cups (**155–6**) are in boxes #92 and #93 in the KSM along with published jugs (**154** and **164**) and numerous fragments of fine pottery. The large bridge-spouted jar (**165**) from which the deposit takes its name is in the HM along with **157**.

Relative date

Mackenzie's first impression was that this Group was contemporary with the Royal Pottery Stores (1906, 256). This was repeated by Evans who assigned jar **165** to the MM II A period (1921, 247). This date is re-affirmed by the present re-investigation.

The pottery includes Rounded Goblets of Type 2 (**162–3**) and Straight-sided Cups of Type 2 (**153, 155–6**) which are found in groups of the MM I B and MM II A periods. The small angular jug (**164**) is similar in profile to a jug from the floor in West Magazine 2 (Brown 1983, 68–9 AE 977), and may be related to the MM I B jugs with butterfly patterns on the shoulder from the Vat Room Deposit and the Area Encircling the Middle Kouloura, although these are in Fine Buff Fabric (Momigliano 1991, 171, 236).

The large bridge-spouted jar (**165**) is quite similar to early products in a similar tempered fabric from Phaistos, and may originate from there (Pernier 1935, pl. XVIa, b; F. 1400). The Phaistos examples belong to Fiandra's Period 2 which marks the end of the MM II A period. Jar **165** and Crude Goblets **158–60** are the latest objects in the Group and provide a likely date in the MM II A period for the deposit.

Group C. The Porcelain Deposit

Context

Pendlebury lists a group of material in the KSM as coming from the 'Porcelain Deposit' of the North-West Treasury but does not give a more detailed provenance (1933, 4 B I 17). There is no mention of this deposit in notebooks or publications, so nothing can be said of its context. However, it may be assumed that the pottery most likely comes from an early floor level beneath the North-West Treasury.

Re-assembly

The contents of the two boxes in the KSM are listed as coming from the 'Porcelain Deposit' in the area of the North-West Treasury (Pendlebury 1933, 5: A II 17). One box, #107, contains mixed pottery ranging from neolithic to LM III. The other, #106, contains numerous fragments of fine cups and bridge-spouted jars with polychrome decoration. Two vases whose profiles could be restored (**169** and **170**) are included in this study and illustrated in PLATE 50.

Relative date

170 is a Tall-rimmed Angular Cup of Type 4 with a close parallel in **656** from the Royal Pottery Stores. The decoration on **170** is very similar to that on a Rounded Bridge-spouted Jar of Knossian Type 4 from Phaistos, which belongs to Period 2 (F. 426). Group C, then, should be assigned to the MM II A period and may represent the contents of an early floor deposit similar to Group B.

Group D. The North-West Pit

Context

A large circular pit, filled with fragments of fine MM pottery, was discovered beneath the W rooms of the North-West Treasury and excavated in 1903. It became known as the North-West Pit and a small selection of finds was published (Evans 1904, 16–17 figs. 5i, 6; Mackenzie 1906, pl. VIII).

A preliminary examination of the pottery from the area of the pit, now stored in the KSM, shows that finds from the North-West Pit (A II 1, 2) join material from the West Rooms (A II 21) which were built over the pit, the Area s of the Polychrome Jar (A II 10), the West Border of the Area (A II 11) and the Area of the Walls (A II) to the W. These deposits are all in the immediate vicinity of the North-West Pit, and suggest that the pit may not have been a regularly shaped feature of one period, but rather an area to the W of the early house beneath the North-West Treasury. Here pottery could have been dumped over an extended period or perhaps thrown against the Western Enceinte Wall, which seems to have come into being at roughly the same time as the earliest pottery found in the North-West Pit (see below pp. 30–2). The area seems to have been used as a pottery dump up until the time of the major levelling operation in the West Court. It was then built over by the E rooms of the North-West Treasury in the neopalatial period.

Re-assembly
This Group is a selection of diagnostic fine decorated pieces from among the great quantities of sherd material kept in the KSM, HM, AM and BM, described by Evans as having come from the North-West Pit. The catalogue includes 90 examples: **171–261** illustrated in PLATES 7–8 and 51–60.

The Group has been re-assembled using the photograph published with Evans' 1904 report, reproduced here in PLATE 51, the colour drawing of fragments of decorated pieces used in Mackenzie's report on the MM pottery—the original photograph of which is reproduced here in PLATE 52 (1906, pl. VIII), and an unpublished photograph in the Evans Archive showing pieces said elsewhere to have come from the North-West Pit, PLATE 53. Also useful was Mackenzie's pottery notebook for 1903, that allowed for the inclusion of bridge-spouted jar **247**, still without catalogue number or provenance in the HM, but almost certainly the vase described as having come from the 'N. W. Kamares Area' (ibid., 1903 PB, 3 vase 8). A number of fragments in the AM were said by Evans to come from the North-West Pit; many of these join vases stored elsewhere, for example spouted jar **211**, of which most fragments are in the AM, has joining fragments in the BM, HM and in three boxes in the KSM. Cross-museum joins are most frequent within this Group, because Evans took it to represent the typical pottery of the MM II A period, and could illustrate the high quality of 'Kamares Ware' with samples removed and sent to the teaching collections of museums in Great Britain.

Most of the joins confirm known attributions, but some produce new and useful information, for example cup **239** is made up of fragments which had been illustrated as having come from the Gypsades Well (Evans 1921, 595–6 fig. 437a, b), but which join other fragments from boxes assigned to the North-West Pit

in the KSM, shown in PLATE 58. This effectively removes the only MM II B evidence from the otherwise neopalatial deposit in the well (*contra* Warren and Hankey 1989, 56).

Relative date
Mackenzie assigned the North-West Pit to the MM II A period, contemporary with the deposits on the early floors under the nearby North-West Treasury (1906, 256). The material illustrated by Evans could all be considered to belong to the MM I B and MM II A periods as defined in Chapter 2. Group D comprises much material of those periods, including Straight-sided Cups of Type 2 (**173–4, 178–88**) decorated in the Woven Style, and numerous fragments in a reserved style with added red and white, e.g. **203–20**, that are quite similar to a style common in periods 1 and 2 at Phaistos, but not later (F. 85, 1919, 1923, 2082, 2238, 2327, 3685, 5214a, 5330, 5957c; Pernier 1935, 378 fig. 226; Levi 1976, pl. LXIIIc, k, l). However, stored together in the KSM are also fragments of MM II B wares, styles and types such as **237**, a Rounded Cup of Type 5 in Precision Stamped Ware, **239**, a Rounded Cup of Type 6 decorated in the Wavy-line Style, and **240–1**, Rounded Cups in the Heavy Spiral Style, as well as many fragments of neopalatial pottery. Whether the pit had been a closed group prior to excavation, it is impossible now to know. The MM II B and later material may indicate that it was in use for a long time, perhaps for the duration of the Old Palace period and beyond.

Comment
In summary, there are at least three floor deposits of similar date and most likely at a similar level beneath the North-West Treasury. They indicate the existence of a building of the Old Palace period at the N end of the later West Court, although, until further excavation is conducted to the S, it remains to be seen whether the building was separate or part of an architectural continuum that stretched from the Koulouras to the later Theatral Area; the latter suggested in a sketch plan of the West Court following the 1930 excavations (Evans 1935, 51 fig. 30). What is clear is that the floor deposits point to a destruction in the area of the North-West Treasury at the end of the MM II A period contemporary with similar destruction in the Royal Pottery Stores, as suggested by Mackenzie (1906, 256). The majority of the material in the North-West Pit is contemporary with the destruction groups and could include the rubbish from the early house. The later rubbish may be associated with the levelling operations that took place in the West Court at the end of the Old Palace period, for which there is evidence from the S part of the court (see Group E below). It is also possible that the pit was not a pit at all, but re-deposited material from occupation and destruction levels within the building cut away when it was re-modelled in the early neopalatial pe-

riod. This would explain the presence of MM III B and LM I A pottery in the boxes in the KSM.

PART 3. THE KOULOURAS, SOUTH FRONT AND NORTH-WEST ACROPOLIS HOUSES

The Koulouras

Immediately S of the area of the 1904 TP a stone lined circular structure which Evans called a 'Kouloura', was discovered and cleared in 1907 (Karo 1908, 120–1). It was found full of fine pottery sherds assigned by Evans to the MM III period (1921, 554). An extended excavation campaign by Pendlebury in 1930, in the area to the W of the 1904 trials, revealed two more Koulouras and other important structures both contemporary and earlier (Payne 1930, 250–1).

The two additional Koulouras were laid out in a line to the W of the first, FIG. 1.7. The Central and Western Koulouras were built over West Court Houses A and B. Both houses were founded on neolithic levels, indicating that occupation in EM I and II either didn't exist here, or had been removed prior to construction. The lowest floor deposits have been re-examined by Momigliano who, by means of clever detective work, has rejected much later material previously thought to come from these floors and re-assembled their most likely contents (1991, 206–35). The remaining pottery belongs to the EM III or early MM I A periods.

In rooms 1 and 2 of House B, Pendlebury noted two distinct floor levels 0.50 m apart (1930, 58). While it was concluded that both floors belonged to the same ceramic phase, the upper floor was reported to contain polychrome decorated pottery while the lower floor did not (ibid., 60). Momigliano is unable to separate the sherd material which could have come from the upper floor, and rehearses a number of possible scenarios to explain the presence of later material among the stored pottery, finally suggesting that both floor levels belong to the 'EM III/MM I A' period, as Pendlebury had done (1991, 215). However, the polychrome pottery illustrated by Pendlebury and said to be from the upper floor, finds close parallels in the 'Polychrome Geometric' pottery from the lowest level in the Monolithic Pillar Basement which is characteristic only of the late MM I A period (Cadogan *et al.* 1993, 25–6). The second and final floor, then, may represent occupation late in the MM I A period contemporary with the floor at *c.* 1.50 m in Structure 2/House C to the E (see above p. 23). This would place the construction of the Koulouras at a late stage of the MM I A period or soon after. The material identified by Momigliano as having come from the 'Area encircling Kouloura II' may provide a construction date early in MM I B (1991, 236–8).

The cuttings for the Koulouras were all made to a uniform depth of *c.* 3.00 m below the level of the later West Court, presumably so that they would all have similar internal capacities. As the earlier architecture had been terraced down the slope from E to W, the East

Kouloura cut through and removed any prior structures, that may have existed. The Central Kouloura was cut down to a level that removed the E area of House A, but stopped before reaching the lower, S rooms. The Western Kouloura left House B, whose floors were 0.50 and 1.00 m lower than those preserved in House A, relatively undisturbed.

When the East Kouloura was built it must have stood at least 1.00 m above the contemporary floor and ground levels of the houses to the N of it, which at the end of the Old Palace period were still 1.00 m below the level of the later court, as shown by Structure 1 (above, p. 22). The Central and West Koulouras probably also stood partially above ground level and perhaps even more so than the East Kouloura, if the contemporary buildings to the N continued to be terraced during MM II. It is likely that during the Old Palace period all three structures stood higher than the 3.00 m preserved, but were cut off at the level of the West Court, when they were filled in and the court extended, early in the New Palace period.

The function of the Koulouras at Knossos and elsewhere has been much discussed. They have been interpreted as cisterns, as suggested for the eight similar round structures at Malia (Chapouthier *et al.* 1962, 17–19) and for the North-West Kouloura at Knossos (Evans 1935, 65–6), or as rubbish pits (ibid.), and granaries (Graham 1962, 134–5 n.11; Levi 1976, 352). Whatever the original purpose, the Koulouras were found filled with re-deposited rubble and pottery sherds.

Evans observed two stages of use in the East Kouloura. The later stage comprised material dumped in during MM III, the earlier use he put in MM II. He concluded that the Kouloura was cleared out at the end of MM II, or a slightly later date contemporary with the material in the other two. It was then used as a dumping place in MM III (1935, 64). Pendlebury tested this hypothesis by excavating the Central Kouloura stratigraphically. He dug the E half first in order to provide a section within the structure but concluded that 'The contents had been tipped over from the N–E corner' at one time (1930, 55 n.1). Pendlebury regarded the pottery as primarily MM II in date, but with admixtures of MM I B and MM III.

This re-investigation of the pottery suggests that the latest material can be assigned to the MM III A period, but there are numerous examples of MM II B types (see below, Group E). It also shows that the material from the three Koulouras joins so thoroughly that it should all be regarded as having been deposited at one time and coming from the same source. There is no late MM III material preserved from the East Kouloura.

The Western and Southern Enceinte Walls

Among the most important features to come to light during the 1930 season were the enclosure or 'Enceinte' walls, FIG. 1.7 (Evans 1935, 49–59 fig. 30). These walls enclosed the area of the later West Court. The Western

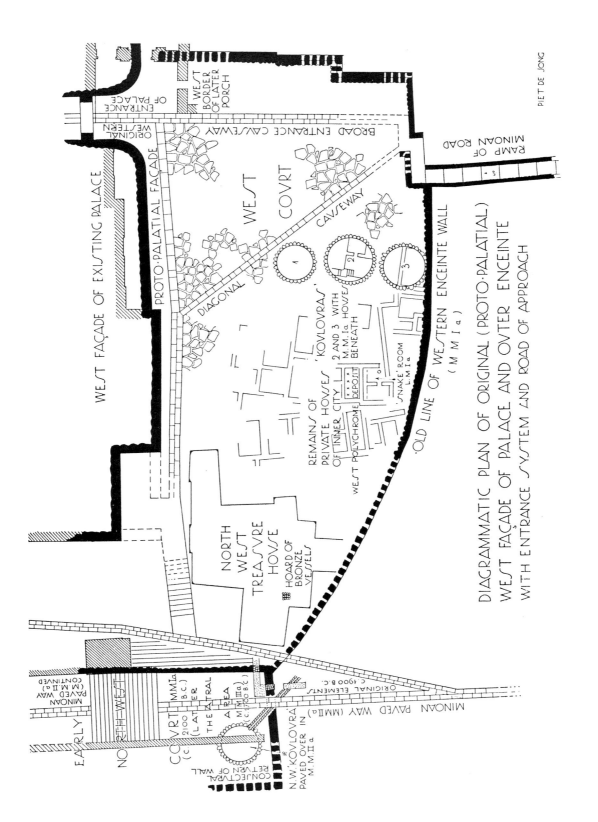

Fig. 1.7. Sketch plan of the West Court (Evans 1935, 51 fig. 30).

Enceinte was shown to begin at the SW corner of the later court and continue to the N as far as the Theatral Area where it was cut by a line of raised paving which Evans assigned to the MM II A period, the date of the first paving of the Theatral Area. The wall, therefore, was taken to be earlier than MM II A and so Evans placed it in the MM I A period (ibid., 54). The Southern Enceinte joins the W wall, at an abrupt angle at the SW corner of the court, and runs eastward to the area of the later West Entrance Porch. The S section was constructed with huge blocks apparently set on virgin soil (ibid., 57–9 fig. 35). There was no stratigraphy mentioned with the S wall, but it was assumed to be part of the same construction as the W wall and assigned likewise to the MM I A period.

The problem with a MM I A date for the Enceinte walls is that the W wall was built over the SW rooms of House B (ibid., 70 fig. 42), which seem to have gone out of use as late as the end of the MM I A period. Therefore, the wall's construction must post-date the MM I A period. Momigliano points out that rooms 5–8, previously assigned to the MM I phase of House B and whose construction appears to be contemporary with the Western Enceinte Wall, are stratigraphically later than the MM I house and contained pottery of what is considered here to be the MM I B period (1991, 210–2; see below. The argument for the early date is weakened further if we consider the section of raised paving, that intersects the Enceinte wall to the S of the Theatral Area, as part of the building programme that included the construction of the Theatral Area in MM III A, when the steps were built over the MM II paving and a new route to the N entrance of the palace was required (Damiani-Indelicato 1982, 60).

The Western and Southern Enceinte walls, then, seem to belong to the period after MM I A and before MM III A. A date in MM I B may be suggested on the basis of the W wall's connection with rooms 5–8 of House B. This would imply that the walls formed part of the programme of re-organisation in the area of the later West Court which may also have included the construction of the Koulouras.

The Southern Enceinte goes out of use following its destruction by earthquake (Evans 1935, 58). Although no stratigraphy or pottery is mentioned in connection with the destruction, Evans states that the South-West House, directly to the S of the wall, was built soon after the earthquake that 'Overthrew so much of the MM III Palace' (1928, 672; see also 390). Elsewhere he places the event in the MM III B period, but it is clear that he is referring to end of the Old Palace (ibid., 1930, 88). This may provide further evidence of the earthquake that marks the end of the Old Palace period, which this study places at the end of the MM II B period.

The Early South-West Houses

Excavation by C. F. Macdonald beneath the South-West House (abbreviated P/92) has revealed two successive buildings of the Old Palace period. The earliest is a rectangular structure with white plaster floors. The deposit on the floors was accompanied by substantial traces of burning. Material recovered includes a large quantity of pottery, horn cores cut from the skulls of bovid and ovicaprids, one nodulus, one possible basket sealing and one fragment of a clay tablet inscribed in the Linear A script (French 1993, 68; Weingarten 1994, 177–8). The pottery from the early floor has been assigned to the MM II A period. The event suggested by the burnt destruction could, therefore, be linked with the burnt deposit in the nearby West Magazine 2. A more substantial structure than the first was erected over the fill of the MM II A debris, during the MM II B period. The second building was also destroyed by fire, apparently at the end of the Old Palace period in MM II B (French 1994, 68).

The South Front

D. Wilson and N. Momigliano in 1993 conducted excavations on the South Front to help elucidate the history of settlement in the area prior to the construction of the palace (French 1994, 74–5). To the E of a house of the EM III period, called the 'S Front House', they found a level of paving, that sealed a large fill of the MM I B period. The paving may be associated with a ramp leading up the slope towards the South Front and so may be part of an early access to the palace. The sealed deposit, when fully studied, could help define the construction period of the earliest phase of the South Front.

The North-West Acropolis Houses

The Western Enceinte Wall enclosed a number of buildings known as 'the private houses of the inner city' or 'the North-West Acropolis Houses', FIG. 1.7 (Evans 1935, 51 fig. 30). There is no detailed report of these buildings, cleared by Pendlebury in 1930; no notebooks kept during their excavation have come to light and the walls are shown only in schematic plan. It is clear from the visible remains that there were at least two architectural phases (Hood and Taylor 1981, Plan, Early Houses).

Evans assigned the earliest material from this area to the MM I B period; there was also said to be a rich deposit of MM II pottery in one room, and later houses, contemporary with the New Palace, were constructed over the tops of some of the earlier ones on the W side and over the Western Enceinte Wall (Evans 1935, 76). Momigliano has shown that rooms 5–8 of House B are later than the MM I A period and so should also be included among the early houses of the Old Palace period (1991, 210).

The rich deposit of MM II pottery was called the 'West Polychrome Deposit', FIG. 1.7. The location given by Evans corresponds to that given by Pendlebury to a group of material from the 'Trench E. of later houses' in KSM boxes B III 8 (1935, 7 plan 4). The study of the pottery from this test shows that it joins with the pottery from the Koulouras and 1904 TP 11, and seems to be part of the large-scale filling operation that took place in the area of the West Court at the end of the Old Palace period. All the material from these deposits has been joined to form Group E, here called the West Polychrome Deposits, after the name given by Evans to the deposit in the North-West Acropolis Houses.

Group E. The West Polychrome Deposits

Context

Pendlebury's observation, that the pottery and rubble in the Central Kouloura had been tipped in from the NE corner, suggests that the structure was intentionally filled-in (1930, 55 n. 1). Given the fact that the pottery from the three Koulouras, the area to the N of the East Kouloura, 1904 TP 11, and from the room in the North-West Acropolis Houses (B III 8) joins and, therefore, is from the same source, its most likely interpretation is that the Koulouras were filled in with pottery and building materials re-deposited from destroyed structures nearby. A similar and contemporary re-deposition group in the area of the House of the Fallen Blocks, Group N, may also be interpreted as a filling operation and the nature of the destruction there suggests that it followed a major earthquake (see below p. 46). The North-West Acropolis Houses may also have been destroyed in the same earthquake, and the resulting debris pushed S into the Koulouras and used for levelling operations throughout the area. Shortly afterwards, the paving of the West Court was extended over the Koulouras and some of the early houses. This Group, then, comes from the time of the cleaning up and re-modelling of the area.

Re-assembly

Some of the pottery from Kouloura 1 was illustrated by Evans (1935, pls. XXIX, XXX), but only very little in relation to the amount recovered and photographed. This Group was re-assembled using photographs in the Evans Archive, reproduced here in PLATES 61–7, which illustrate vases and sherds recognised among the material from the Koulouras in the KSM. Most of the pots in the archive photographs could not be located, and could not be included in the catalogue because of uncertainty over their fabric and manufacturing techniques. The 347 vases included here, **262–608** illustrated in PLATES 9–21 and 61–99, are for the most part fragments from boxes in the KSM assigned to B I 14, 19, 20 and 21 and B III 8. Some are in the HM, and were recognised in the Evans Archive photographs, and others are fragments in the AM that join vases in the HM or KSM.

The material, found to be mixed with the EM III–MM I A pottery from the Houses below the Koulouras, but comprising primarily MM II B and MM III A types,

and recently published by Momigliano, should be considered as part of this Group (1991, 210, 235–6).

Relative date

The Fine Buff pottery is all wheelmade and in types, wares and styles that are not found in Groups A–C and the Royal Pottery Stores. There are many examples of the characteristic types of the MM II B period, as defined in Chapter 2, including Straight-sided Cups of Type 7 (**274, 303–5, 323, 329, 433**), Type 9 (**280, 284, 319–21, 326, 332, 335–7**), Type 10 (**273, 277, 293–8, 315–17, 322, 327–8, 331, 338–9**); Short-rimmed Angular Cups of Type 3 (**409–12**); Rounded Cups of Type 6 (**340–68**); Baggy-shaped Bridge-spouted Jars (**390–1**) and Rounded Bridge-spouted Jars of Types 5 (**379–88**) and 6 (**389**). Many types seem to span the MM II B and MM III A periods, including Straight-sided Cups of Type 8 (**275, 279, 300–2, 333 and 408**), Type 11 (**423–6**) and Type 12 (**404–7**); Rounded Cups of Type 5 (**285–6, 370–6, 417–21, 436–44**) and Type 7 (**413–6**); Rhytons of Types 1 (**395–7**) and 2 (**398–9**). The single MM III A type is Straight-sided Cup of Type 13 (**403**).

Examples of the characteristic wares are Precision Stamped (**433–4, 436–45**) and Late Printed Ware (**293–8**) of the MM II B period; and Precision Grooved (**408, 411–21, 430**) and Ridged Ware (**401–12, 423–6**) of both the MM II B and MM III A periods.

Examples of the distinctive styles are in the Sunrise, (**280–4, 336–7, 385–7**), Starburst (**274–7, 338**), Wavyline (**340–68**) and Spiral Band (**306, 309–31, 333, 372, 379–84, 390, 400**) styles of the MM II B period; and the White-spotted, (**299–305, 403–7, 409–16, 419–20, 423–6, 428–9**) and Heavy Spiral (**311, 332, 334**) styles of the MM II B and MM III A periods.

The Fine Buff pottery from the West Polychrome Deposits, then, consists for the most part of forms, techniques and styles of both the MM II B and MM III A periods, with no evidence of later material. Pottery sherds and a sheep-bell of the MM I A and possibly MM I B periods, grouped with some of this material, appear in the lower half of one of the Ashmolean Archive photographs, reproduced here in PLATE 67. These fragments may have been part of the fill, but may also have come from either the construction phase of the Koulouras or from the late MM I A floors in House B.

Evans regarded White–spotted Style pottery as characteristic of the MM III A period and assigned the latest use of Kouloura 1 to MM III on this basis, while suggesting an earlier use in MM II to explain the presence of polychrome decorated pottery which he felt should be earlier (1921, 554). The presence of great quantities of polychrome pottery in the second and third Koulouras caused him to place them earlier than the first. The present study suggests that much of the polychrome pottery should be regarded as MM II B in form and style, based largely on comparison with material from Phaistos. The two phases suggested for the East

Kouloura, then, are not necessary if it is accepted that the majority of the material is of MM II B date with some MM III A pottery mixed in during the Group's deposition.

Comment

There seems to have been a large-scale re-organisation of the West Court at the beginning of the MM I B period. The EM III–MM I A houses beneath the Koulouras were sacrificed for the large stone-lined Koulouras. Apparently at the same time the Enceinte walls were built, again cutting through earlier buildings. The collapsed rows of gypsum blocks from the S wall allow for the suggestion that both it and the W wall had impressive and high courses of gypsum blocks on their external facades, which had been removed or largely decayed by the time of their discovery. The walls must have been designed to control access to the Koulouras and associated buildings, and may have served as a boundary or defensive wall for the palace which came into being at this time.

The area was again re-modelled on a grand scale, following what appears to have been a seismic event. The debris created by the earthquake includes a great deal of fine pottery of the MM II B period, which may have come from nearby buildings or from the clearing out of the palace itself. This second remodelling most likely coincides with the renovations that mark the beginning of the New Palace period in MM III A. Significant at this time is the expansion of the West Court over the Koulouras, perhaps to enhance the monumentality of the newly restored West Façade, and the abandonment of the Enceinte walls in favour of permitting the 'invasion of parts of the Palace site by private persons' (Evans 1928, 672).

PART 4. THE WEST WING

Little of the early history of the West Wing survives intact, perhaps due to a major remodelling early in the neopalatial period. The reconstructions seem to have affected even the façades, though further re-investigation with new trials may be necessary before drawing any conclusions (Momigliano 1991, 169–71).

North Front, West Façade and Early Keep

S. Hood and J. Shaw conducted trials in 1973 to determine the construction date of the North-West Platform with its singular make-up of small rectangular stones (Catling 1974, 34). Hood directed further trials by A. Peatfield in 1987 (Hood 1994, 101–2). Both campaigns revealed the same result: the North Front was built during EM III well before the main palace structure. Though a function could not be suggested, Hood observed that during the early palace period the North Front continued to be used and there seemed to have been an entrance from the N that went out of use in MM I B or MM II A.

Evans' trials in the W wall of Magazine 12 indicated that the West Façade was built during MM I (1921, 129 n.2), although Momigliano points out that there is a problem as what he would have called MM I A others now call EM III (1992, 170). Hood and Shaw's 1973 trials in the walls of Magazines 11 and 14 to 18 seem to confirm Evans' early date, but until the pottery is fully published it may be most sensible to reserve judgment on the date of the West Façade, EM III or MM I A. Either way, the North Front seems to be the earliest architectural element to have been a part of the palace, perhaps followed soon after by the monumental West Façade.

To the E of the North Front, Evans discovered an early structure built of small stones, similar to those employed in the North Front, that contained six deep rectangular stone-lined cuttings he likened to dungeons (1921, 127–39; Branigan 1992). Evans assigned the construction date of the Early Keep to the MM I A period; but Branigan's re-investigation of the pottery from Evans' trials, to date the cuttings into neolithic and EM levels and the construction of the internal walls, shows that the latest forms are Rounded Goblets of Type 2 and therefore MM I B in date (ibid., 158 fig. 2.7–9). He ponders the late date for a 'carinated cup', that he feels should almost certainly be MM II; but this is not in conflict with his desired date as the illustration depicts a Short-rimmed Angular Cup of Type 2, a form that originates in the MM I B period (ibid., fig. 2.5). The Early Keep, then, seems to have been built early in the Old Palace period, but not as early as the North Front and West Façade.

The Vat Room Deposit

In 1903 Evans conducted a series of trials beneath the floors of the palace, which he felt had been erected on a flattened surface created by levelling the earlier tell. Immediately under the pavement of the entrance to the Room of the Stone Vats, he excavated a 'pit' about one metre in depth (1903, 94–8). Within the pit he reported two layers: a lower deposit of ceramic types he considered to be Early Minoan and a later deposit which he considered to belong at the beginning of the MM I period.

Momigliano's detailed re-investigation of the pottery has cast doubt on the stratigraphy within the pit, and shown that its contents belong to what is now regarded as the earliest stages of the Old Palace period (Momigliano 1991, 167–75). The pottery includes types that are found in both the MM I A and MM I B periods, such as a Shallow Bowl of Type 1 (ibid., no. 14), a Rounded Goblet of Type 1 (ibid., no. 1), a Convex-sided Cup (ibid., no. 9), and a Pedestalled Lamp of Type 1 (ibid., no. 49), but also a Conical Goblet of Type 1 in the Diagonal Red and White Style (ibid., no. 4)—a form and style of the MM I B period. The small jugs with butterfly pattern (ibid., nos. 17–24), are related in form to **164** in Group B and the small jug from the deposit below the floor in West Magazine 2, both Groups deposited in the MM II A period. The Vat Room juglets may be the late MM I A or early MM I B predecessors of the more angular forms of late MM I B or MM II A types.

The Vat Room Deposit, then, could have been formed at one time. There are pottery types that are found in both the MM I A and MM I B periods, and they allow us to conclude that the deposit was formed after the end of MM I A and during an early stage of MM I B, very early in the period of the first palace. It is tempting to suggest that the material was either the result of clearing up after a late MM I A destruction, in which case the associated pottery and finds would be assignable to the very end of the MM I A period, or a foundation deposit to mark the construction of this part of the West Wing early in the MM I B period.

West Magazines
During the first excavation season in 1900, Evans cleared the S part of the West Magazines. Beneath the floor of Magazine 2 he found an early deposit consisting of a large two-handled jar, the upper part of which had been cut away, filled with small pots and several clay nodules. He then reported that 'The older floor on which this vase stood apparently represents the original floor level' (Evans 1900, 21; Brown 1983, 68–9).

In 1901, Evans found a second early deposit beneath the West Magazines, this time 1.65 m from the W end of Magazine 1. He reported finding 'A wide mouthed Kamáres jar, broken at the rim, containing smaller vessels, among them some cups of exquisitely thin fabric' (Evans 1901, 48). He drew the comparison with the deposit in Magazine 2, and later drew the parallel both for the finds, particularly the tumblers in fine red mottled fabric, and the circumstance with the Vat Room Deposit (1921, 172). But, by 1921 he observed that both deposits 'Were contained in small pits excavated in the superficial neolithic stratum on which the floors of the later Magazines were laid' (ibid.), and concluded that they may have belonged to magazines of an earlier building, an idea later repeated (1928, 663).

Both early deposits were seen to belong to the same time as the Vat Room Deposit and thus assigned to the MM I A period. Momigliano's review of the contexts rejected Evans' date and suggested that both belonged in the Old Palace period (1991, 154–5). As the Vat Room Group now seems to have been deposited in MM I B, it may be necessary to consider the pottery in the Group beneath Magazine 1 to belong to the same period and perhaps, like the Vat Room Deposit, to have been a foundation deposit; though any further speculation without the original finds may be pointless. The Group beneath Magazine 2, though, seems to be of a later date.

The large jar is a handmade amphora decorated in a style reminiscent of the Polychrome Geometric Style of the late MM I A period (Brown 1983, fig. 36a). The contents included a Rounded Goblet of Type 2 (ibid., 36b, c), which can be both MM I B and MM II A, a small jug with angular profile like **164** (ibid.), and several Crude Goblets (ibid.), a diagnostic form of the MM II A period. This Group, then, could represent an original floor deposit in Magazine 2, as first suggested by Evans. The large amphora could have been an heirloom at the time of the destruction, which fired the clay nodules found inside it. The burnt deposit may relate to that found on the first floor in the nearby Early SW House, that also contained a fired nodulus.

The South-West Palace Angle
In 1973, S. Hood and J. Shaw opened a trial on the E side of room 17, immediately S of the West Magazines (Catling 1974, 34). They recovered a substantial pottery deposit that included burnt clay sealings. The remainder of the deposit was cleared by C. Macdonald in 1987, who found many more whole vases and three burned noduli stamped by the same seal (Catling 1988, 68; Hood 1994, 101). The pottery includes a large number of Early Palace forms and a collection of angular cups and bridge-spouted jars in the Diagonal Red and White Style of the MM I B period. Thus the deposit should be associated with the burnt destruction at the end of the MM I B period elsewhere in the palace and town.

PART 5. THE NORTH-EAST INSULA OR ROYAL POTTERY STORES

Excavations in 1902 were concentrated on the E slope of the Kephala hill, where Evans was surprised to find that the palace continued for a greater distance than previously thought. Mackenzie supervised the clearing of a long protuberance of land to the E of the North Entrance Passage known as the 'North-East Shoot'. Structures of the later palace period were almost entirely absent, for which a lime kiln was thought responsible (Mackenzie 1903, 117). At a depth of about 0.50 m from the surface, walls began to appear and soundings between them produced some of the finest pottery from the site. By the end of May the walls had become a defined architectural unit, FIG. 1.8. The area became known as the North-East Kamares Area and North-East Insula and finally, because of the high quality of the ceramics found, the Royal Pottery Stores.

There are many problems associated with the re-investigation of the Royal Pottery Stores. The absolute levels given by Mackenzie and Evans are from the surface, which almost certainly sloped eastward, making the cross reference of levels between the different rooms impossible. Also, Mackenzie recorded that he threw away great quantities, at least 93 baskets, of pottery from this area rarely specifying from which deposit (1902 PB (2), 34, 37, 50–8). The following Groups, then, must be taken as pre-selected and treated with extreme prejudice.

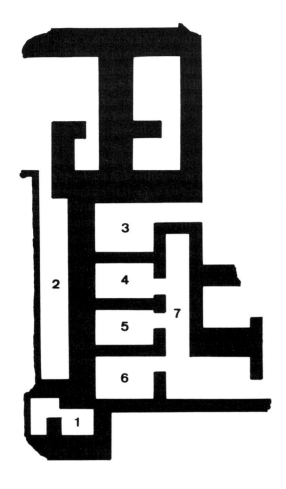

Fig. 1.8. Sketch plan of the Royal Pottery Stores (after Mackenzie 1902 DB (2); Mosso 1907, plan; Hood and Taylor 1981, plan).

Group F. The South-West Room

Context

The first deposit encountered was in a small space between two E–W walls, 0.90 m apart and closed off at the W end. The deposit was said to be 'Packed with Kamares potsherds some of them of fine quality' (Mackenzie 1902 DB (2), 81). The stratigraphy within the tiny enclosure was reported as follows:

> neolithic levels were encountered at 1.50 m from the surface; at a depth of 1.00 m lay the 'Kamares' deposit which continued to 0.50 m from the surface, above which was surface deposit (ibid.).

Along with the numerous ceramic finds reported from the 'Kamares' deposit were four terracotta figurines apparently of bulls.

The exact location of this space within the area of the Royal Pottery Stores is problematic, because no further reference was made to the deposit in the notebook, when other walls began emerging. There is a small space of similar dimensions in the rooms N of the Lime Kiln, but no finds were reported from there. At the S end of the long walls to the E of the Lime Kiln there is a small square space of 0.90 × 0.90 m, which fits Mackenzie's description, FIG. 1.8 no. 1. A Group of very fine pottery and four terracotta bulls in the KSM are said to come from the 'SW Room' of the North-East Kamares Area, and some of the pottery from here joins with published vases from the Royal Pottery Stores. Pendlebury locates the room as the southernmost of the four rooms on the E side of the Lime Kiln, but this does not explain why it was called the South-West Room (1935, 18 L III 1). Mackenzie's description of the room and its dimensions do not allow for it to be put in one of the four rooms E of the Lime Kiln. It seems most sensible to place the deposit in the tiny enclosure to the SW of the other rooms as the name suggests.

Re-assembly

The Group was re-assembled by means of illustrations published by Mackenzie (1903, 176 fig. 3 pls. V, VI. 1–3) and Evans (1921, figs. 178, 181, 184, pl. II) and two unpublished photographs in the Evans Archive, reproduced here in PLATES 70 and 71. A number of pieces were inscribed to show they came from here (listed in APPENDIX III). Most useful is Mackenzie's list of pottery from the 1902 excavations, which includes descriptions of many of the whole vases from this and other groups, and much of the sherd material as well (1902 PB (2), 65–80).

The pottery assigned to this Group in the KSM was problematic until it was realized that the contents of boxes #997 and #1197 had become switched. When #1197 was strewn with #996 and #998, L III 1 in the KSM Guide, a number of useful joins were made and the Group could be re-assembled. Joins were also found with material in the HM, allowing for the inclusion of jar **667**, and with the AM bringing in the unique cup **669**. Joins were also made with box #1198 which, like #1197, was meant to contain material from the Early Deposit beneath the Room of the Olive Press, Group L.

The catalogue includes 62 vases (**609–70**) illustrated in PLATES 22–4 and 100–10.

Relative date

There is some handmade pottery, but the majority of the Fine Buff Ware is wheelmade. There are examples of the Diagonal Red and White (**609–10, 613**) and Woven (**611–2, 614**) styles, which are characteristic of the

MM I B groups at Knossos, as are Straight-sided Cups of Type 2 (611–2). Forms, wares and styles that seem to span both the MM I B and MM II A periods are Conical Goblets of Type 1 (609–10); and Type 3 (651–2); a Tall-rimmed Angular Cup of Type 1 (613); Rounded Cups of Type 3 (618–23, 631, 643–6) and Type 4 (616–7, 642, 661); Barbotine Ware (613); Early Printed Ware (624–32) and pottery decorated in the White-banded Style (636, 648). Pottery of the MM II A period includes a Rounded Bridge-spouted Jar of Type 4 (665) and numerous examples of true Egg-shell Ware (615–23). The latest pottery, then, indicates that this Group was formed in the MM II A period. Pedestalled bowl 647 is of a type well-known at Malia, where it has been assigned to the MM II period (Pelon and Stürmer 1989).

Group G. The Area of the Lime Kiln

Context

Early walls were observed to continue beneath the later Lime Kiln, which was subsequently removed and the deposit beneath cleared. The result was that 'A good deal of Kamares pottery' was found (Mackenzie 1902 DB (2), 31). There is no mention of stratigraphy. Pendlebury locates the position of a group of boxes in the KSM labelled 'Lot from Area of Lime Kiln (N. E. Shoot)' in the long and narrow N–S passage directly beneath the Lime Kiln (1933, L III 16), which conforms with Mackenzie's description and is accepted here, as shown in FIG. 1.8 no. 2. This Group, then, represents the contents of the only floor deposit reported in the narrow corridor adjacent to the Small East Rooms.

Re-assembly

This Group comes from a series of boxes in the KSM labelled 'Lot from Area of Lime Kiln (N. E. Shoot)' (Pendlebury 1933: L III 16). The inventoried pottery, 671–753 illustrated in PLATES 121–27, is all from the KSM. The context for many of these pieces is confirmed by their description in Mackenzie's notebook (1902 PB (2), 39–44).

Relative date

The presence of types such as Crude Goblets (689–97) and Crude Cups of Type 2 (671–707) provide a date at the end of the MM II A period for the Group. Earlier elements that seem to have survived from the MM I B period are a Rounded Goblet of Type 2 (682); Straight-sided Cups of Type 2 (674–5); Short-rimmed Angular Cups of Type 2 (677–81) and examples of Pared Ware (671) and Woven Style (674–5).

Group H. The Small East Rooms

Context

The next deposit excavated was in an area defined by a N–S wall and two E–W walls 1.94 m apart. Mackenzie's sketch at the time of excavation shows the first room as being E of the Lime Kiln (1902 DB (2), 18). He reports that 'The space was packed full of Kamares pottery some of it of the very finest typical painted varieties' (ibid.).

The stratigraphy observed in the room is as follows:

- near the surface was a 'Clayey deposit with common Mycenaean and some Kamares pot sherds', continuing to a depth of 1.25 m from the surface,
- a dark stratum full of wood ashes 0.12 m thick, 'packed with common Kamares pot sherds',
- a pale, 'clayey', stratum 0.20 m deep with little pottery, and
- at a depth of 1.88 m from the surface was a 'dark stratum with wood ashes 0.45 m thick and crammed with Kamares pot sherds some of it of the finest painted varieties' (ibid., 18–19).

Evans repeated the description of this sequence in his report on the 1902 season, giving general hints about the relative dates of each level. He said the top level contained pottery as late as the 'Period of Re-occupation', the next layer contained pottery similar to that below the Room of the Spiral Fresco. The pottery from the third level was said to have the same general character as the second, and the lowest level, with a deposit resting on a clay floor, had Minoan vases 'Of the finest fabric' (1903, 118). This was repeated again in 1921 (240–1).

Re-assembly

There are two boxes of pottery in the KSM said to be from the 'Small rooms E. of Lime Kiln' (Pendlebury 1933, 19: L III 15). One of the boxes contains a mixture of all periods, and may represent the finds from the upper levels. The other contains a group of pottery typical of the MM II A period, including two examples, 755 and 758, that are described by Mackenzie as having come from here (1902 PB (2), 53). Mackenzie stated that 'There is no admixture of Mycenaean (LM) potsherds in the deposit proper, that is, in the stratum immediately above the floor', presumably the one at 1.88 m (1902 DB (2), 20). The labelling of the boxes in the KSM suggests that it may belong to more than one floor deposit, and could represent a collection of selected pots from the lowest floors of all four rooms to the E of the Lime Kiln, FIG. 1.8 nos. 3–6.

The inventoried pottery, 754–87 illustrated in PLATES 118–20, is from box #1071 in the KSM. Some of the pottery in Group J is quite similar and probably comes from these rooms, but cannot be included in this Group with confidence.

Relative date

The pottery is very similar to that from Groups G and L, although there is a marked lack of fine decorated examples. The Crude Goblets (763–5) and Crude Cups of Type 2 (766–71) place the formation of the burnt floor deposits in the MM II A period. Among the survivors from MM I B, or perhaps from an earlier floor, are a Rounded Cup of Type 1 (756) and an Angular Bridge-spouted jar of Type 1 (755).

Group I. The Room of the Jars

Context

East of the middle rooms to the E of the Lime Kiln, is another early room with a floor level at 1.15 m below the surface. On the floor were twelve large jars lying in rows on their sides with their tops to the S, after which the area became known as the Room of the Jars. Mackenzie likened the shape of the jars to an example with an inscription on its shoulder from the South-West Basement, but wrote that 'There is no doubt that the deposit belongs to the Kamares period like that adjacent W. Some fine Kamares fragments were found in the same deposit' (1902 DB (2), 19). Cleaning of the walls, late in the 1902 season, revealed that there were doors leading from the Room of the Jars into the two middle rooms to the E (ibid., 45). Pendlebury (1933: L III 8) located the Room of the Jars in a space that corresponds to Mackenzie's description as being to the E of the Small East Rooms, shown here in FIG. 1.8 no. 7.

Evans, perhaps influenced by Mackenzie's suggested parallels for the jars, associated them with the upper level in the Small East Rooms and stated that they were found 'Separated by layers of clay and burnt materials' from the MM II A material below (1921, 571). He suggested a MM III date for the jars and classified them with the 'rustic' ware of MM III, which included the elongated jars from the North-East Magazines. He also compared the shape with that of the inscribed jar from the South-West Basement (ibid., 572 fig. 416).

Re-assembly

The pottery from the Room of the Jars presented here represents only a very small selection of whole vases, included to allow for the date of the deposit to be discussed. Much more material from this area is stored in the KSM and will be published by Momigliano in due course. For the present study the jars published by Evans (1921, fig. 416), and three cups from the KSM are inventoried, 788–94, and illustrated in PLATES 121–23 including two photographs from the Evans Archive.

Relative date

The cups are Straight-sided Cups of Type 2 (789 and 790) and a Tall-rimmed Angular Cup of Type 1b (788) which are types of the MM I B period. The large jars are quite different from the example cited from the South-West Basement and are decorated in the White-banded Style, which is characteristic of both the MM I B and MM II A periods.

It seems most likely that this Group belongs to the MM I B period and may be earlier than the other groups in the Royal Pottery Stores, and not MM III B as reported by Warren and Hankey (1989, 62).

Group J. The Royal Pottery Stores in General

This Group is composed of vases, primarily in the HM, that are known to come from the Royal Pottery Stores but cannot be assigned to one of the specific locations described above. It also includes vases published by Mackenzie (1903, 180 fig. 6; PLATE 124), some of which could no longer be found.

Most of these examples probably belong either to Group G or H, as they are very similar to pottery in those Groups. 808, however, is much finer than pieces in those Groups and may have come from Group F. It was published by Pendlebury (1939, pl. XVII.2a) as having come from the West Court Basement, our Group A, but is inscribed with 'K.02 NEKA', which places it in the Royal Pottery Stores.

Comment

Mackenzie's first impression (1906, 256) was that the destruction deposits in the Royal Pottery Stores were contemporary with those below the later North-West Treasury (Groups B–C), the Early Chamber beneath the West Court (Group A), and the early floor beneath the Room of the Olive Press (Group L), and all belonged in the MM II period. It is suggested above, p. 26, that Group A was formed toward the end of the MM I B period.

Evans maintained that the pottery from the Royal Pottery Stores was characteristic of the MM II A period (1921, 231–47), and these Groups, F in particular, have become the standard reference for the ceramics of the period (e.g. Pendlebury 1939, 133; Warren and Hankey 1989, 52). The only opposing voices seem to be those of Betancourt, who assigns them to MM II B (1985a, 95), and Walberg, who regards them as part of her Classical Kamares phase which corresponds to Evans' MM II A–II B–III A (1976, 120–1).

This study recommends that the latest pottery from the Royal Pottery Stores should be retained as the standard reference group for the end of the MM II A period. It is primarily through comparisons with these Groups and the pottery of Fiandra's Period 2 at Phaistos that the definition for the MM II A period, outlined in Chapter 2, is suggested.

Group I, deposited in MM I B, is earlier than Groups F–H, but may be contemporary with early floors beneath those of the MM II A period. The existence of early floors could account for the intact MM I B pottery in the otherwise MM II A groups. Two burnt levels are reported in the Small East Rooms, Group H. The finds have not been kept separate, but it might be proposed that the pottery defined stylistically as MM

I B came from the floor at 1.88 m and that the MM II A floor was at 1.37 m.

Mackenzie (1906, 252–3) mentioned that further excavations, carried out in 1905 below the floors in this area, produced vases and sherds, which he likened to those from the Upper East Well, assigned to the EM III period (Cadogan *et al.* 1993, 25), but also to the earliest floor in the Monolithic Pillar Basement and the deposit from House C, which are taken here as belonging in the MM I A period (Chapter 2). Comparison was also made to the Group from the North Quarter of the City, which Momigliano has shown to contain a great deal of EM III pottery, but also MM I A and MM I B fragments (1991, 176–84). Until the material is identified and studied, we are not in a position to be more precise than EM III, MM I A or even MM I B.

The MM II A groups from the Royal Pottery Stores belong to destruction deposits, created during an event that left its mark elsewhere in the palace. The burnt layer in the Small East Rooms conforms with evidence from other deposits, and helps characterize the nature of this widespread destruction at Knossos, which is used to mark the end of MM II A period.

It is quite likely that the area was re-occupied, if only on a limited scale, after MM II A. Evidence for this may be provided by the upper floor with wood ash in the area of the Small East Rooms. The material from this floor could not be positively identified, but Evans compared it to the pottery from the Loomweight Basement, which is of MM II B–III A date.

The ravages of the later Lime Kiln may have removed any other evidence for the late Old Palace period here.

PART 6. THE EAST CENTRAL ENCLAVE

Excavations on the E side of the palace in 1901 uncovered a network of rooms, which included the Corridor of the Bays and associated storerooms, the School Room and the Room of the Olive Press (Evans 1901, 82–90 pl. I). Further investigations in 1902 revealed the existence of basement rooms with earth floors, lying almost 2.00 m below the ground floor levels. The basements were found filled with debris. In some cases the walls continued below the floor levels of the late palace basements to depths of over 4.00 m below the surface. Earlier floor levels with 'Kamares' pottery were found, and so the foundations for the system of walls was assigned to the Old Palace period and the area became known as the East Central Enclave, FIG. 1.9.

The Area of the Spiral Fresco

Group K. The Loomweight Basement

Context

Excavations in 1902, beneath the basements in the Area of the Spiral Fresco and the room to the S, revealed a depth of stratigraphic levels, described by Mackenzie

in detail in his excavation notebook for that year. In the area S of the Area of the Spiral Fresco, at a depth of about 4.00 m from the surface, a tumble of rough blocks was encountered. Beneath the tumble was a level of thickly packed 'Kamares' pottery and fresco fragments. Associated with the tumble in the NW corner was a deposit of loomweights, after which this area was named. Below the level of stone and loomweights, at roughly the same depth, were the fragments of two large spouted jars, reported to be at the top of a deposit of Kamares pottery. At the same depth there was a plaster platform and the remains of what was interpreted as a plaster chest in the SE corner (Mackenzie 1902 DB (1), 75). The plaster platform, or 'dais', continued under the wall to the N, into the space under the Area of the Spiral Fresco. Mackenzie recorded quantities of the 'Finer Kamares pottery' from the deposit (ibid., 75). The plaster platform, which was 0.19 m thick, was resting on a stratum of pottery sherds above a floor of rough plaster at a depth of 4.50 m below the surface. 'Accordingly', wrote Mackenzie, 'the platform cannot belong to the system of the floor but must be a later construction' (ibid., 77).

A test beneath the platform, going down to the level of the floor at 4.50 m below the surface, showed that the earlier level 'Contained large quantities of Kamares pottery some of it of very fine quality' (ibid. 1902 DB (2), 53).

In the next room to the N, the Area of the Spiral Fresco, the 'Kamares' deposit was also found at a depth of 4.50 m from the surface (1902 DB (2), 1–2). There was also a floor level, constructed of rough cement, found at a depth of 4.80–4.90 m from the surface. The lower floor was reported to have 'Above it a stratum in which Kamares pottery exclusively occurred' (Mackenzie 1902 DB (2), 11). In the NE corner, there were large fragments of wall plaster at depths of 3.40 to 3.60 m from the surface, in a deposit 0.50 m deep. The Kamares floor level was 0.60 m below the plaster level (ibid.). In association with the plaster was a raised platform, like that found in the room to the S (ibid., 14).

Evans' first report on the Loomweight Basement did not mention the two distinct levels, observed by Mackenzie, but described the finds as having come from a single deposit (1903, 23–7). He stated that hard cement floors occurred throughout the area, at a common depth of about 5.00 m below the datum, which was a triangular block in the wall between the E and W sections of the structure (1921, 249). There are problems with the absolute levels in this area because some are given as from the surface, others as from the LM I floor level and others as from the datum. The datum and surface are probably quite close. The LM I floor level seems to be an average of 0.50 to 0.70 m below the surface. This discrepancy might help to explain the difference of 0.50 to 1.00 m in the floor levels reported by Mackenzie in the Area of the Spiral Fresco and in the room to the S. Evans seems to have understood the problem and ig-

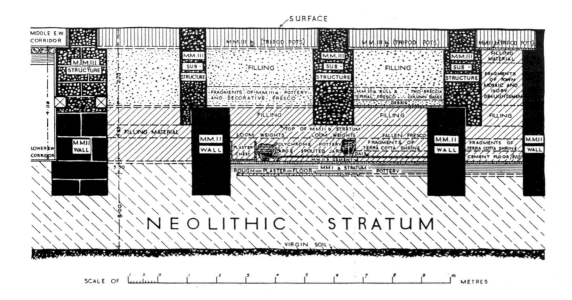

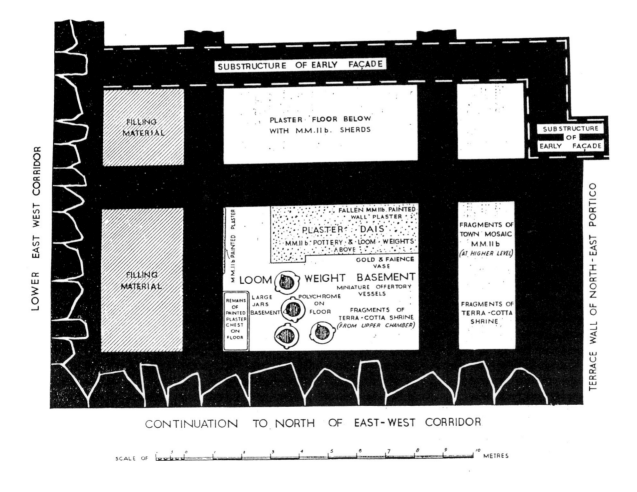

Fig. 1.9. Sketch plan and reconstructed section of Loomweight Basement and adjacent areas (Evans 1921, 250–1 fig. 187a, b).

nored the discrepancy in his reconstructed section of the area, reproduced here in FIG. 1.9.

Evans' cement floor, at about 5.00 m below datum, seems to correspond to Mackenzie's level at 4.00 m. The deposit includes the plaster platform or dais and everything above it, including the large amphora with palm tree decoration (Evans 1921, 253 fig. 190) and large spouted jars, FIG. 1.9. Evans also included the fragments underlying the dais in the 0.20 m of fill, that made up the platform (ibid., 251). Mackenzie's rough plaster floor, at 4.50 m, was given by Evans at a depth of 5.30 m below datum, and was assigned to the MM I A period (1921, 251 n. 1), instead of the 'Kamares' period, as Mackenzie had stated. The reason for the change may be due to the findings of supplementary excavations undertaken in 1920. Unfortunately, the material from the 1920 test cannot be checked; the box in the KSM, said to come from this test, contains material which clearly belongs to the Royal Pottery Stores (Pendlebury 1933, 20: M III 2a). There is no material of the MM I A period in any of the boxes attributed to the Loomweight Basement (Momigliano 1991, 204).

Re-assembly
This Group is composed of pottery illustrated as having come from the Loomweight Basement (Mackenzie 1903, 177 fig. 4, 178 fig. 5; Evans 1921, figs. 190, 191, 192a), now in the HM, AM and KSM. Mackenzie's notes on the kept pottery (1902 PB (2), 9, 12, 28, 79) confirm the attributions in published sources, and examples may be recognized from his descriptions of pottery in the boxes assigned to the 'Loom-weight Area S. of Area of Spiral Fresco' (M III 2 #1189–1194) in the KSM. Mackenzie also records that 22 baskets of sherds from this area were thrown out (1902 PB (1), 53). The inventoried pottery, 814–91, is illustrated in PLATES 25–6 and 126–32.

Relative date
Unfortunately, the finds from the two levels do not seem to have been kept apart. However, it is possible to suggest that the large jars in Tempered Buff Fabric (876–8) and the amphora with palm tree decoration (891) come from the level above the cement floor, as shown by Evans (1921, 251 fig. 187b and FIG. 1.9) and stated by Mackenzie for 878 at the time of excavation (1902 PB (2) 11). A date in MM II B may be suggested by comparisons with pottery from Group E. 877 is so similar in fabric, type and decoration to 585 that the two should be considered products of the same workshop. The decoration on 876–8 is closely related to the Spiral Band Style of Fine Buff Fabric and so Evans' date in the MM II B period should be maintained.

Amphora 891 does not have close parallels elsewhere, but has generally been regarded as a late element in the deposit; Hood assigns it to the MM III A period (1978,

36) while Warren and Hankey draw parallels with Phaistos phase III (1989, 52). It does not fit the central Cretan fabric groups and its shape is unique, which suggest that it was imported from elsewhere on the island. Given its association with 876–8, it seems most likely to belong to the end of the MM II B period.

Mixed with the pottery in this late MM II B level, were fragments of painted plaster dadoes, one of which could provide a link between wall painting, the ceramic Spiral Band Style (Evans 1921, 251 fig. 188), a small juglet of gold and faience (ibid., 252 fig. 189a; Foster 1979, 60–1 fig. 1 pl. I), and a shallow bowl with gold branches set on carbonized remains (Evans 1921, 252 fig. 189b), all of which Mackenzie mentioned at the time of excavation (1902 DB (1), 66–70; (2), 7, 49). Also from this level of fill, and found in all of the basement chambers including that below the Enamel Deposit, were fragments of a terracotta shrine with pillars, horns of consecration and birds, which Mackenzie felt belonged to a single shrine model (1902 DB (1), 85; (2) 1–2, 7–11, 14, 44, 49; Evans 1921, 251–2 figs. 188–9, 306 fig. 225; Schoep 1994). The loomweights, which numbered over 400, seem to have been found throughout the fill from the very top, overlying the first appearance of 'Kamares' pottery, down to just above the plaster platform (1902 DB (1), 75; DB (2), 53).

Most of the pottery in this Group may, on typological and stylistic grounds, be assigned tentatively to the level of fill above the cement floor: for example the Crude Cups of Type 3 (826–33) and Type 4 (834–9), the Hand Lamp of Type 2 (887) and Pedestalled Lamp of Type 2 (888) and the examples decorated in the White-spotted Style (818, 873), which are characteristic of the MM II B period.

It could be suggested that examples of earlier types could have come from the level below the cement floor, or the make-up of the plaster dais: for example the Tumbler of Type 3 (817), the jug with horizontal spout of Type 1 (825), cups (824 and 818), bridge-spouted jar (874) and the fragments of large jars (871–2) which are very similar to fragments 738–9 in Group G. These examples would suggest that the earlier rough plaster floor belongs within the MM II A period.

The material from the upper level became the standard reference for pottery of the MM II B period, which was equated with the destruction of the Old Palace (Evans 1921, 248–60; Pendlebury 1939, 137–8, fig. 23). This has been questioned in detail by Warren and Hankey, who conclude that it belongs within the MM III period (1989, 52–3). The conflict in dates may be averted, if we consider that the fill in the Loomweight Basement may have been deposited early in the MM III A period, though few of the forms classed as such have been identified from here; instead the Group seems to comprise primarily MM II B material from the destruction of the area at the end of the Old Palace period.

The nature of the upper deposits (which include both vases said to have been found *in situ* on the cement floor and pottery from the deep fill above the floor and below the early neopalatial floor with the Spiral Fresco), is quite similar to the West and South Polychrome deposits, which contain for the most part rubbish and building debris used as filling and levelling material following the earthquake, that marks the end of the Old Palace period.

The Enamel Deposit

The small area N of the Area of the Spiral Fresco was excavated as part of the 1902 campaign and the stratigraphy was found to be similar to that above the Loomweight Basement. Mackenzie recorded a floor at a depth of 4.40 m from the level of the late palace floor (1902 DB (2), 51). This 'cement' floor corresponds to that at a similar level in the adjacent Loomweight Basement. The reconstructed section shows a hypothetical continuation of the earlier plaster floor, found in the Loomweight Basement, FIG. 1.9. However, there is no mention of this earlier level in the sources.

Evans reported that the Town Mosaic and other fragments of faience enamelled plaques, from which the area takes its name, were found in a level of fill from a depth of 0.60 m to 2.10 m below the later floor. The fill was assigned to the MM III A period, and thus regarded as later than the 'MM II B' fill below and in the Loomweight Basement (Evans 1921, 301–2). Further fragments of the terracotta shrine were found at a fairly low level, in the area of the Enamel Deposit (Mackenzie 1902 DB (2), 44). Evans placed the shrine fragments at the same level as they occurred in the Loomweight Basement, that is the level of the plaster dais 0.60 m above the cement floor. The joins of the fragments of terracotta shrines, found in the lower fill of the Enamel Deposit, with those from above the cement floor in the Loomweight Basement, confirm that both fills are contemporary. Given the evidence from Group K, they most likely belong to a building operation after the end of the MM II B period. The upper fill, however, is not related, and could belong to a later stage of the early neopalatial period. It has a *terminus post quem* provided by the floor in the 'Room of Tripod Vases', which Evans assigned to the MM III B period, but Popham has shown belongs to an early stage of LM I A (1977, 192–3; Warren 1991a, 334). Evans certainly regarded the upper fill as later than the lower, and we may now state that it post-dates the end of the Old Palace period in MM II B and even the major reconstruction works in MM III A. It could be taken either as contemporary with the deposits, in which the spiral and bull frescoes were found at the same absolute level in the adjacent rooms to the W, or as part of a filling operation associated with the laying of the floor in the Magazines of the Tripods. In either case, it belongs to the neopalatial period, where the iconography of the Town Mosaic is far better suited than in the Old Palace period.

Group L. The Early Floor beneath the Room of the Olive Press

Context

In 1902, Mackenzie conducted a small sounding beneath the late palace floor in the NE corner of the Room of the Olive Press. A detailed re-evaluation of the excavation by Panagiotaki (1993a) outlines inconsistencies in depth and description of the various trials made in this area. I have found it most useful to accept Mackenzie's observations, as they seem to fit best the physical evidence of the pottery itself. At a depth of c. 3.30 m below the later floor level, there was an earlier floor approached by two sloping plaster steps. Wall plaster associated with the early floor was found in position on one wall, preserved to a height of 1.00 m above the floor (Mackenzie 1902 DB (2), 33). More of the early floor was cleared in 1903, and Evans reported that abundant 'Kamares' pottery and a number of clay sealings were found immediately above the floor level (1903, 19–22; 1921, 239–40).

Mackenzie referred to the early floor as a 'Landmark in the Minoan Epoch', because he felt it would allow for the differentiation between the pottery found above and below it (1903, 169). He studied the material in detail and recorded it in one of his pottery notebooks for the year (1902 PB (2), 17–28). His notes are summarized in his report on the pottery of Knossos (1903, 168–9).

The report refers to levels as 'metres' and two sets of levels are described. Below the 'Kamares' floor are four 'metres' which comprise chiefly neolithic material; but in the fourth metre, that immediately underneath the 'Kamares' floor, he mentions the occurrence of wheelmade 'Kamares cups', a likely reference to our Rounded Goblet of Type 2 or Momigliano's Footed Goblet of Type 4, which is found in her EM III groups and in House C (1991, 247–8 fig. 30). He also mentions the presence of 'painted geometric' sherds in this level 'Immediately underlying the Minoan floor' (1902 PB (2), 24; 1903, 169). He compares the pottery with that from the first floor in the Monolithic Pillar Basement, and cites a parallel with a fragment, published by Hogarth and Welch (1901, 97 fig. 31), which leaves no doubt that he is referring to our 'Polychrome Geometric' style of the late MM I A period (see pp. 93–4). The 'Kamares' floor, then, was most likely stratified above a level containing MM I A or early MM I B pottery.

The second set of levels, as described in the notebook, seems to count in the opposite direction, with the first 'metre' lying directly underneath the neopalatial floor in the Room of the Olive Press. The numbering used in the notes is inverted for the publication of the trial, so the lot, listed as the first 'metre' below the 'Mycenaean' floor in the pottery notebooks, is described as the third 'metre' in the publication (1903, 179).

The pottery from the 1903 excavations, below the Room of the Olive Press, is preserved in the KSM (Pendlebury 1933: M II 5). Four 'metres' of deposit are listed and numbered as they were excavated. Thus, the fourth 'metre' is the lowest and should correspond to the earliest use of the 'Kamares' floor at a depth of *c.* 3.30 m. Re-investigation of the kept sherds shows that the material from the fourth and third 'metres' joins so thoroughly, that they must be taken as part of the same deposit. Mackenzie had also observed this and suggested that the two related levels could represent a lower floor deposit mixed with material fallen from an upper floor (1903, 179). It could also be suggested that some of the material may have fallen from shelves along the walls of this basement room, on which the plaster was found preserved to a height of one metre.

The deposit contains a number of almost complete vases, that could be restored, and, when combined with the examples published by Evans, form quite a useful and diagnostic Group.

Re-assembly

The Group consists of four vases illustrated by Evans, **925–7** and **930**, and the pottery from boxes #1171 to #1182, in the KSM, assigned to the Olive Press Area, box #997 incorrectly assigned to the Royal Pottery Stores, and #1195–6 incorrectly assigned to the Loomweight Basement. Once the errors had been sorted out, it was possible to join together one of the finest groups of pottery of its period from the palace; **892–974** in the Catalogue, illustrated in PLATES 27–9 and 132–40. A jug in Liverpool is so similar to **928**, that it could well have come from here (Mee and Doole 1993, cat. no. 283).

Relative date

Evans described **926** and **927** as coming from a 'MM IIa deposit 3.20 metres down' (1921, 239–40 n.1; 1935, 134), but referred **930** to 'the earlier part of MM IIb' (1921, 270).

Pottery of the MM I B period includes Rounded Goblets of Type 1 (**892–7**) and Type 2 (**918–9**); a Straight-sided Cup of Type 1 (**900**); Rounded Cups of Type 1a (**902**); Angular Bridge-spouted Jars of Type 1 (**903–5**) and examples in Pared Ware (**892–7**) and the Diagonal Red and White Style (**899, 905**).

Forms, wares and styles that may be both MM I B and MM II A are a Rounded Goblet Type 3 (**925**); a Conical Goblet of Type 1 (**899**); a Tumbler of Type 1 (**898**); Short-rimmed Angular Cups of Type 2 (**909–17**); Rounded Cups of Type 3 (**921**) and Type 4 (**922**); Shallow Angular Bowls of Type 2 (**926–7**); a Hand Lamp of Type 1 (**971**) and examples of Barbotine Ware (**926–7**) and pottery decorated in the White-banded Style (**923–4**).

The latest pottery in the deposit are the Rounded Bridge-spouted Jars of Type 4 (**930–58**) and the Crude Bowls of Types 2 (**959–60**) and 3 (**961–3**), which place the formation of the Group in the MM II A period. Though the decoration on jars **957–8** is difficult to restore completely, the characteristic pattern of an undulating white band with one straight and one 'bumpy' edge with added thin red or orange lines on top is very close to that on a group of sherds from a closed form, most likely a bridge-spouted jar, from the channel beneath Vano LX at Phaistos (Fiandra 1980, 186–7 pl. 45.1, 10, 13). Also quite similar is the design on a fragment of a bridge-spouted jar from Haraga in Egypt (Kemp and Merrillees 1980, 299–301 Ha. 16). The Phaistos jar is from a deposit of Fiandra's period 2, which conforms with the MM II A date suggested here for **957–8**.

There are no examples of material in styles of the MM II B or MM III A periods.

The deposit included a number of sealings, including some with characters belonging to the Pictorial Script (Evans 1903, 20). A few attributions were made on the basis of similarities in colour, shape and condition (Gill 1965, 84–5). Evans assigned one of the sealings to MM I A because of its 'MM I associations' (1921, 201–2, fig. 151). This early date is not questioned by Yule, in his study of early Cretan seals, despite the close similarities between the sealing with the wild goat from here, and examples from the Hieroglyphic Deposit and the deposits of clay sealings at Phaistos, which he places at the end of MM II (Yule 1980, 122–3). Panagiotaki has convincingly re-assembled the sealings and repeats their association with the 'Thorne-vases'—our **926–7** (1993a, 34–5). When taken as part of the context of Group L, there can be little doubt that the sealings belong with the pottery, that is, at the end of the MM II A period and closely contemporary with the much larger groups of sealings from the burnt deposits that mark the end of Period 2 at Phaistos (see below, p. 101). The sealings are evidence that the deposit was formed during a destruction by fire.

The room was subsequently filled-in with debris belonging to the MM II B and MM III A periods. The first and second 'metres' of deposit from the 1903 excavations consist of numerous fragments of plain MM II B and MM III A pottery, primarily of large jars very similar to those from the South Polychrome Deposits, including similar types of imported jars (MacGillivray 1984a, 156 n. 20). Although no material is illustrated, the descriptions of the pottery include references to 'Wheelmade cups resembling the round Mycenaean type but large & more saucer-like'—a likely reference to the bowls with everted rim of the MM III period (Catling *et al.* 1979, 27 fig. 21 V.61–3), and fragments decorated with 'large spirals in opaque cream-white on purple black lusterless varnish'—surely a reference to one of the most characteristic styles of the MM III B or early LM I A periods (e.g. Warren 1991a, 322 fig. 6b pl. 76c, 330 fig. 8a–b pl. 78f–g). This level, then, seems to include material of the MM III B and LM I A periods, but perhaps also MM II B and MM III A. Mackenzie grouped the level with his deposits of the 'Closing period of the Middle Minoan Age' (1906, 264–5), which includes the North-East Magazines, Temple Repositories and other groups assigned by Warren to his MM III B/LM I A transitional period (1991a, 333–4).

The sequence beneath the Room of the Olive Press is similar to that in the adjacent Loomweight Basement, except that the early floor is about 1.00 m higher in the former and there is no mention of a corresponding floor level in the MM II B period. The early floor here seems to have belonged to the basement of the W room in a building which continued eastward under the North-East Portico.

The School Room Area

The School Room and adjoining rooms were first cleared in 1900 (Evans 1901, 96–7). Soundings throughout the area in 1913 produced evidence, that many of the walls were founded during the Old Palace period, FIG. 1.10. There was also evidence for at least two earlier floor levels beneath that of the later palace.

Court of the Stone Spout

A trial at the base of the S wall of the Court of the Stone Spout showed that the wall was built on top of an older

wall, which Evans assigned to MM III A. The older wall was built over the top of the base of a pithos standing on a plaster floor, which Evans put in MM II (1921, 362 figs. 262, 266).

Room of the Stone Pier

A trial along the E face of the wall at the back of the Room of the Stone Pier in 1913 produced a clear stratigraphic sequence. Evans described the levels from the top as follows: the first was patchwork gypsum paving, the second was a 'MM III B' deposit with shallow cups, the third was a floor of white beaten earth 0.70 m below the first, the fourth was a 'MM III A' deposit with taller cups than the second and fragments of dark-faced vases with white spots and broad plain pans, the fifth was a level of *kalderim* floor paving at a depth of 1.17 m below the first level (1921, 366 n. 2). The material from this trial could not be located, but the published illustrations provide some useful information.

The only pottery illustrated from the second level, that is the deposit above the floor at 0.70 m, are two plain cups which Evans likened to the conical cups of the LM I period (ibid., 588–9 fig. 432 bb). The published drawings do not allow for more specific comment on their chronology, although it should be noted that they bear a close resemblance in profile to our Crude Goblet which is a type-fossil of the MM II A period.

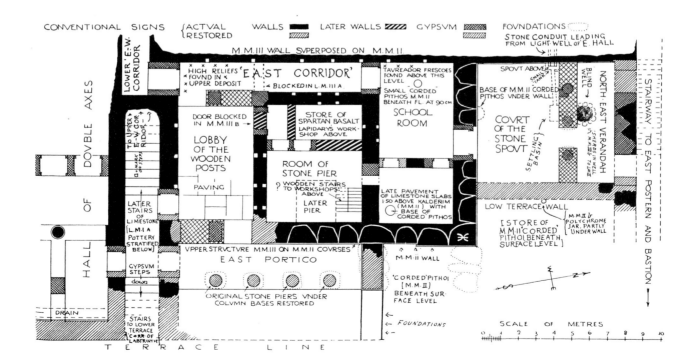

Fig. 1.10. Plan of School Room Area with features of Old Palace period (Evans 1930, 270 fig. 183).

The pottery from the fourth level, the stratum below the white clay floor and resting on top of the kalderim paving, seems to be that grouped in a photograph in the Evans Archive, reproduced here in PLATE 141, part of which was used to illustrate the finds from this level (Evans 1921, 589 fig. 433). Evident in the photograph are a Conical Goblet of Type 1 decorated in the Diagonal Red and White Style of the MM I B period, but also found in MM II A groups, and Pyxides of Types 3 and 4 which belong in the MM II A period; an open Spouted Goblet similar to 786–7 in Group H; and Crude Bowls of Types 2 and 3 which occur in both the MM II A and MM II B–III A groups. The deposit on the kalderim paving, then, should be assigned to the MM II A period.

The East Corridor

In the East Corridor, which was blocked off and used for storage in the New Palace period, Evans reported a MM II floor at depth roughly corresponding to that in the Loomweight Basement on the other side of the wall to the W (1921, 369 n.2). The level was also said to correspond with those of the early floor on the S side of the Court of the Stone Spout, which Evans called MM II, and the kalderim paving from the E borders of the School Room Area, which he assigned to MM III A but, as we have seen above, should be regarded as belonging to the MM II A period.

A small 'MM II' pithos with a triple line of handles and rope work decoration is the only vase reported from the early floor. Unfortunately, the vase was not illustrated and has not been found.

Comment

The earliest floors in the Loomweight Basement, Olive Press Area, Room of the Stone Pier and, most likely, the Court of the Stone Spout belong to the MM II A period. The presence of sherds of the late MM I A or early MM I B periods mixed with neolithic pottery, below the first floor in the Olive Press Area, suggests that the early floors and associated walls were constructed during the MM I B period or early in MM II A. The presence of accidentally fired sealings in the Early Olive Press deposit indicate a destruction by fire during the MM II A period, perhaps related to that in the Royal Pottery Stores.

The MM II A deposits were levelled and covered over with a 'cement' floor, found in the Loomweight Basement and Area of the Enamel Deposit. Above the 'cement' layers were floor deposits and deep levels of filling material with pottery of the MM II B and MM III A periods. This upper destruction and filling operation may be linked to the similar filling operations in the West Court (Group E) and houses near the SE angle of the palace (Group N), which mark the beginning of the New Palace period.

PART 7. THE SOUTH-EAST KAMARES AREA

On the SE slope of the upper plateau, on which the palace was constructed, Evans noticed an area of walls of the late palace period with earlier material between them. This area became known as the South-East Kamares Area, the location is given in FIG. 1.1 'Basement of Monolithic Pillars'.

Group M. The Monolithic Pillar Basement

Context

In 1900 Evans carried out a test between two early walls in the South-East Kamares Area. He found that the depth of deposit was 4.20 m and that, from a depth of about 3.00 m downwards, there was an accumulation of early painted pottery including a vase in the form of a dove, after which the sounding became known as the 'Dove Pit' (1900, 7). Further excavations in the area took place in 1902, when two cups with Linear A inscriptions on the interiors were found. The early building into which the Dove Pit had been sunk was found to consist of deep chambers and cell-like compartments. Again, at a depth of about 3.00 m large quantities of painted pottery of the MM period were found, and a variety of clay sealings, some with pictographic script (1902, 106–7 figs. 63–6, 70).

In 1903 the building was cleared and the following stratigraphic sequence observed: the tops of the walls started to appear at about 0.50 m below the surface; at 1.30 m below the tops of the walls was a floor level with a 'streaked' pithos and pottery of the 'Palace Style'; the two cups with painted Linear A inscriptions were said to correspond to this level (Evans 1921, 587–8, fig. 431). Below, there was a second architectural phase, 0.65 m in depth, then a basement chamber with walls preserved to a height of 2.10 m in places. 'Kamares' pottery was found associated with a floor level in the lower chamber, but there was also an earlier deposit of polychrome decorated pottery which could be seen to pre-date the fine 'egg-shell' ware (1903, 17–18).

Mackenzie described and illustrated the 'Kamares' pottery, which he assigned to MM II, and stated that it was associated with floors (1903, pls. 6.4, 7; 1906, 244, 246). He also described in detail and illustrated the earlier polychrome decorated pottery, which he reported lay in an early floor deposit beneath those of MM II (1906, 244, 246, 252 pls. 7, 9). Momigliano's re-investigation of the pottery from the earliest floor has led her to doubt the existence of the superimposed floors, and suggest instead that Evans invented the stratigraphy, to support his notions of stylistic development, and that the two groups presented by Mackenzie belong to one period (1991, 163–6).

The present study finds no reason to reject Evans' and Mackenzie's statements. While it is true that we are no longer in a position to re-examine the material as closed groups, most of the pottery from the earliest floor does not find close parallels with that of the Old Palace period, as stated by Momigliano. Rather, the best correspondence comes from the upper floor in House B, below the West Court. In both cases, the existence of whole vases confirms Mackenzie's and Pendlebury's statements that these were floor deposits, which, because of the quantities of pottery in the 'Polychrome Geometric Style' in both, may be placed late in the MM I A period.

The pottery illustrated from the second, or 'Kamares', floor is later in style than that from the earliest floor and corresponds with the earliest stages of the Old Palace period, the MM I B period (Mackenzie 1903, pl. VII). That there was a floor deposit of this period is confirmed by a number of fine, almost complete vases. On the basis of Evans' statement in 1902, it seems most likely that the sealings should be associated with this floor. This would indicate a destruction by fire.

The next floor in the stratigraphic sequence is that at 1.30 m below the tops of the walls, which belongs to a new architectural phase and contained, along with the two inscribed cups, pottery which Mackenzie placed at the end of the MM period (1906, 266), perhaps now to be assigned to the MM III B or early LM I A periods.

There are many fragments of MM II B and MM III A pottery from the area, which may come from a filling operation below the latest architectural phase, but such a fill is not recorded by the excavators.

Re-assembly

It was decided to include here only those pieces, inventoried or described by Mackenzie in his pottery notebooks for 1902 and 1904, and those, which appear with them in a photograph in the Evans Archive, reproduced here in PLATE 142. A great deal more sherd material exists in the KSM (O II 3, 4, 7, 8) and in the HM, AM and BM (Momigliano 1991, 164–5), but, as the boxes at Knossos are thoroughly mixed and the examples in other museums are without more specific provenance, further examples would be unlikely to assist with the chronological aims of this study. The inventoried pottery is **975–84** in APPENDIX I, illustrated in PLATES 29, 142–3.

Relative date

The pottery selected to make up this Group include a Squat Rounded Cup of Type 1 (**975**); a Rounded Goblet of Type 3 (**976**) and a Rounded Cup of Type 4 (**978**); and examples of Early Printed Ware (**976**) and 'Prickly' Barbotine Ware (**977**) which are found in groups of the MM I B and MM II A periods. The fragments illustrated by Mackenzie include examples decorated in the Woven Style of the MM I B period (1903 pl. VII. 1, 7). Although the evidence is not firm, it seems most likely that the 'Kamares floor' belongs in MM I B.

The Cypriot Red Polished III amphora from the Monolithic Pillar Basement (Catling and MacGillivray

1983) cannot be placed with confidence on any of the specific floors within the structure and could equally have been found on the first, late MM I A, or the second, MM I B.

Given Evans' statement that the sealings were found at a depth of about 3.00 metres with large quantities of painted MM pottery, it seems most sensible to associate them with the MM I B material, rather than with the late MM I A material, found below the 3.00 metre horizon. This would provide a relative date for the noduli and seals with Hieroglyphic signs, and a chronological association with the noduli from the S. W. Palace Angle and impressions from the Vat Room deposit (Weingarten 1994, 178–9).

Group N. The South Polychrome Deposits

Extensive excavations were undertaken in 1922 to the S and E of the SE angle of the palace where a large depression in the earth had been observed. Two small houses separated by a corridor with a drain were uncovered, FIG. 1.11. The house on the E side of the corridor had a deposit of large cut blocks in the centre and was given the name 'House of the Fallen Blocks'. The house on the W side contained among other things two skulls with horns and was called the 'House of the Sacrificed Oxen' (Evans 1928, 296–303). At the time of excavation the area was called the South Kamares Area.

Context

Two architectural periods were noted in the House of the Sacrificed Oxen. The first is represented by three bonded walls, associated with a 'clay plaster' floor beneath Room 1. Associated with the early walls was a group of pottery, from which Mackenzie described (1922 DB (1), 46, 79–80) and Evans illustrated (1928, 215 pl. IX d–f) a large spouted pithos, a flask and a bridge-spouted jar, our **1011**, **1003** and **1000**. Mackenzie stated that 'Taken together they form one of the most important polychrome groups at Knossos' (1922 DB (1), 80), which he assigned to 'the close of MM II or the very beginning of MM III A' (ibid., 79). This group from Room 1 was regarded as earlier than the main body of material and second architectural phase in the area. Evans published it as the 'South-East Polychrome Deposit' and placed it in the MM II A period on the basis of stylistic parallels with the Royal Pottery Stores (1928, 300). The present study agrees with Evans' date.

In Room 5 of the same house, an early deposit, built over by a wall of the second architectural phase, comprised a large jar and its contents, FIG. 1.11. The jar was not illustrated, but Evans mentioned that a goblet, likened to those from House C, was found inside it (ibid., 300–1). The goblet is not published; it could be a footed goblet of the EM III or MM I A periods, but could also be a Rounded Goblet of Type 2 which belongs in the MM I B and MM II A periods. The latter

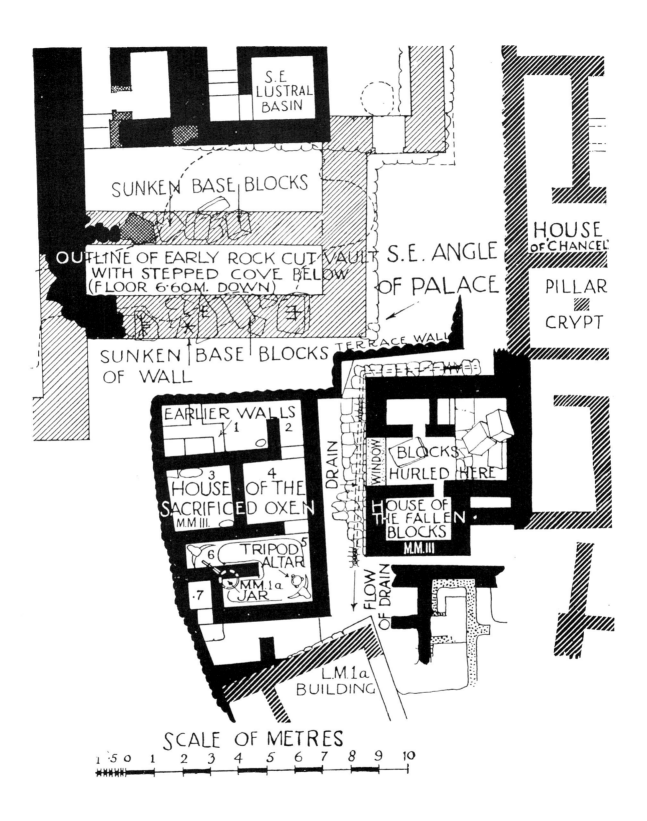

*Fig. 1.11. Plan of South Polychrome Area
(Evans 1928, 295 fig. 172).*

is suggested by the discovery of part of Cup (**995**) with the material said to come from Room 5 in the KSM. The cup is almost certainly the product of the same workshop that produced Bridge-spouted Jars (**947–952**) in Group L and therefore should belong in the MM II A period.

Both early deposits seem to represent layers of the final stages of the MM II A period, which pre-date the construction of the House of the Sacrificed Oxen.

Mackenzie recorded that:

> Some exceptional fragments of egg-shell texture with delicate feather-like motives…[were] found in the interval of the cutting made for the drain running East–West in the passage

to the N of the House of the Fallen Blocks (1922 DB (1), 60). This may be a reference to our **998**, and could indicate that the last use of the drain belongs to the MM II B period.

The main architectural period and most of the contents of the building belong to a subsequent and final stage. During the course of excavation Mackenzie frequently stated that 'There was no stratification in the deposits' (1922 DB (1), 63), and that:

> at first it seemed puzzling to find that the pottery did not change its character as one went down but it ultimately became apparent that this was not stratified and consisted of filling thrown in at the time the houses got ruined and were abandoned which seemed to be at the end of the Middle Minoan age (ibid., 44),

and that:

> taking the pottery from the different rooms in the 'House of Sacrifice' separately…all the different types of vessels domestic and other exhibiting different phases within MM III occur at all the levels and parts of the same vessel occur in different basements, sometimes as far apart as the North and South areas of the house (ibid., 71).

The same confusion was found in the House of the Fallen Blocks and the corridor between the two buildings.

With regard to chronology, Mackenzie stated that 'No LM I vases were found in these deposits' (ibid., 63), and that some of the decorated pottery pointed 'to the earlier rather than the later MM III period' (ibid.), but finally concluded, on the basis of comparisons with the pottery from the Temple Repositories and South-West Basements, that the filling took place at the end of MM III (ibid., 58). Evans later assigned the filling operation to the MM III B period (1928, 305).

Re-assembly

The quantity of pottery found in the two houses is enormous. Evans restored a large number of vases from the fill which were photographed as three groups, reproduced here in PLATES 144–5. A selection of these was drawn from the photographs and used to illustrate the domestic pottery from the fill (Evans 1928, 304 fig. 176). Only one of the illustrated vases, **1010**, could be located and included in the catalogue. The others could

not be included without information about their fabrics and techniques of manufacture. However, they can be compared typologically.

This Group is composed of pottery selected from boxes in the KSM from the 'House of the Fallen Blocks and Area' (R IV 2–6 #1527–1551) and from the 'House of Sacrifice' (R V 2, 4–6 #1553–1560). A preliminary examination of all the sherds from both houses shows that the material joins throughout, a confirmation of Mackenzie's observations at the time of excavation. It is also apparent that the finds from the two architectural periods were not kept apart. This Group, then, contains material that represents more than one period. The selected pottery is **985–1021** in APPENDIX I, illustrated in PLATES 30, 144–50.

Relative date

The earliest groups, from below rooms 1 (**1000, 1003** and **1011**) and 5 (**995**) may be assigned to the MM II A period. To the same period may belong **994, 1004** and **1008–9** which find close parallels in MM II A examples from Phaistos (F. 2516, 5291, 6269, 6271).

A few pieces may be assigned to the primary floor deposit of the latest architectural phase on purely stylistic grounds. **996** is in the Starburst Style, **997** is in the Spiral Banded Style and **998–9** are in the Wavy-line Style, and Short-rimmed Angular Cups of Type 3, **991–2**, all characteristic of the MM II B period. Perhaps also belonging to this period is the 'salt container' in PLATE 144, which is very similar to those of Periods 2 and 3 at Phaistos (Levi 1976, pl. 150). The position of the blocks, fallen from the SE angle of the palace, on the floor of the House of the Fallen Blocks indicates that the seismic event responsible for the displacement of the blocks took place before the filling operation in the house.

A great deal of the pottery assembled and illustrated by Evans was largely complete and so may have belonged to primary destruction deposits, formed within the houses. By the time of their excavation, they had become confused with fragmentary rubbish and fill, perhaps following the main destruction event. Evans suggested that certain rooms had been intentionally dug out, soon after the main event, in order to place the two skulls he had found in the corners of rooms 5 and 6, that gave the name to the House of the Sacrificed Oxen (1928, 295).

Much of the pottery most likely belongs to the post-destruction filling operation in the area, which may be placed in the MM III A period on the basis of **985, 989, 1002** and **1005**. There are also fragments of Straight-sided Cups of Type 12 with horizontal ridges, but none preserved sufficiently to be inventoried. There are no fragments of MM III B or later pottery from the fill.

Comment

The preliminary examination of the kept sherds, from both houses and the corridor in between, shows that the material joins throughout, and that it is exactly similar to the pottery from the filling-in of the Koulouras in the West Court, Group E. The latest elements in the pottery are MM III A and it seems most probable that the filling operation took place in that period.

The displaced masonry in the House of the Fallen Blocks is startling evidence of the force of the earthquake that destroyed the building. It is probably the most convincing evidence of the shock that severely affected the palace at Knossos. Evans distinguished between the event here and that in the area of the Loomweight Basement, dating them to the MM III B and MM II B periods respectively. The present study indicates that the two events are related and should be placed at the end of the MM II B period, marking the end of the Old Palace period at Knossos.

PART 8. THE EARLY TOWN AND ROYAL ROAD

The Town Drain and Early Houses

Excavations in 1926 in the area NW of the House of the Frescoes, to the W of the palace, brought to light parts of two houses that Evans felt represented typical town houses of the MM period, and a drainage channel, FIG. 1.12, (Evans 1928, 366–70).

Group O. The Town Drain

Context

The drain was earlier than the town houses, as it could be traced beneath House B and the Royal Road nearby. Evans reported that the drain was found filled with

Fig. 1.12. Plan of Town Houses and Early Drain (Evans 1928, 367 fig. 203).

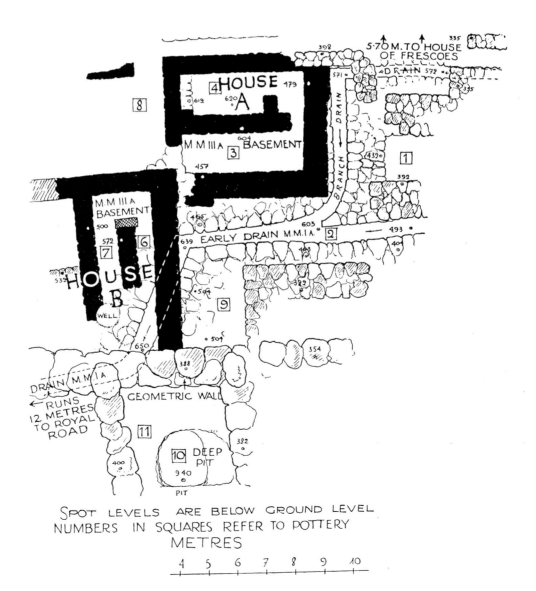

SPOT LEVELS ARE BELOW GROUND LEVEL
NUMBERS IN SQUARES REFER TO POTTERY
METRES

masses of MM I A pottery but that it went out of use at around the close of MM II (ibid., 368–9).

Re-assembly

Evans published one cup which he assigned to the group of pottery from the drain (ibid., 369 fig. 205). The cup, **1033**, was photographed together, PLATE 151, with two similar cups, **1030** and **1032**, and it is probable that all three were found together. The rest of this Group is early vases in the HM, inventoried at the same time as the three cups and the pottery in Group P. The evidence is very circumstantial, but the pottery seems to form quite a coherent chronological group.

Relative date

Evans first published **1033** as MM I A (1928, 369), but later revised it to MM I B, calling it a transitional piece (1935, 106 n.3). Given the fact that it is wheelmade and decorated with barbotine patterns, the later date seems more appropriate. A similar date could be suggested for **1030** and **1032**, on the basis of their crinkled rims and the fact that **1032** is a Tall-rimmed Angular Cup of Type 3.

The other pottery which may come from the drain includes Straight-sided Cups of Type 2 (**1022–24**) and (**1026–27**) in the Woven Style, and a Tall-rimmed Angular Cup of Type 2 (**1025**) which are also characteristic of the MM I B period.

Hogarth's Early Heap

At a point SW of the West Court, Hogarth excavated a deposit of early pottery that he found 'Heaped up between two houses' (1900, pl. XII 12; and Welch 1901, 80). Among the illustrated finds are a Straight-sided Cup of Type 2 in the Woven Style (1901, pl. VIIb) and a Jug with Cut-away Spout of Type 1 (ibid., pl. VIc). Though little more can be said about the deposit, the published examples suggest it belongs to the MM I B period.

Group P. The Early Town Houses

Context

Little stratigraphical information is given for the context of the pottery from the Town Houses, labelled A and B, other than the fact that it was found 'At a depth

Fig. 1.13. Drawing of selected pottery in Groups P and N (Evans 1928, 371 fig. 206): (a) 1048; (b) 1039; (c) 996; (d) 1043; (e) 1046; (f) 1035.

of between five and six metres' below the surface on the basement floors of both houses (Evans 1928, 369).

Re-assembly
This Group comprises material from the basement floor deposits in houses A and B built over the Town Drain. Evans illustrated some of the finds in a drawing, reproduced here in FIG. 1.13. There is also a photograph in the Evans Archive that identifies pieces in the HM as belonging to this Group, PLATE 155.

The material in the KSM, said to come from the area of the Town Houses and Drain (Pendlebury 1933: P III 5–7), appears to be mixed but contains much sherd material of the MM III A period. One cup (**1044**) could be mended from fragments in box #1484.

The other elements in the Group are vases in the HM, **1037**, **1040–1**, and **1047**, included because they were inventoried at the same time as the vases illustrated as having come from the deposits.

Evans restoration of the base in FIG. 1.13 *a* into an elongated amphora may be revised if we compare the preserved base with footed goblet **605** and similar contemporary goblets from Group N, **1006**. The inventoried pottery, **1035–49**, is illustrated in PLATES 154–6.

Relative date
The pottery includes a Straight-sided Cup of Type 12 (**1037**) and sufficient examples of White-spotted decoration to suggest that the Group belong in the MM III A period, as Evans proposed (1928, 369, 371 fig. 206).

Comment
Evans' typical town houses of the MM period could well have been built at the time of Old Palace, but the only evidence of their occupational history can be assigned to the MM III A period, after the events that mark the end of the Old Palace period.

Hogarth's Later Heap
At a point W of the West Court and most likely to the S of the Royal Road, Hogarth excavated what he regarded as the richest find of Kamares Ware he made in the town (1900, pl. XII 12; and Welch 1901, 80 figs. 7–9, 12, 18, 19). It was found as a 'heap about two metres in circumference' in the corner of a small yard on the S side of a house. The illustrated pottery includes two large jugs, that are quite close parallels for **1046** in Group P (1900, figs. 8 and 9), a juglet with plastic 'corn' decoration painted in the White-spotted Style (ibid., fig. 7), and two small jugs, one of which is a Jug with Horizontal Spout of Type 3 in the White-spotted Style (ibid., fig. 19). All are quite characteristic of the MM III A period as defined by Evans, who used this material with Group P to form his definition (1921, 415–6 figs. 299a, 300a–b), and suggest that this 'heap' may be part of a similar event.

Royal Road South/Basements
M. S. F. Hood conducted a series of stratigraphic excavations on the S side of the Royal Road in 1957 to 1961 (Hood 1962; 1966). In 1959 and 1960 he cleared the basement rooms of a structure, that contained three well-stratified floor deposits of the earlier part of the MM period (Cadogan *et al.* 1993, 26). Beneath the earliest was a 'deep fill of solid pottery' of the MM I A period (Hood 1959, 19–20; 1960, 23). The lowest floor contained numerous fragments of pottery in the Polychrome Geometric Style and seems to correspond to our late MM I A period. The middle floor included pottery in the Alternating Red and White, and White Banded Styles, and was compared to Levi's Phase Ia at Phaistos, thus closest to our MM I B. The latest floor contained Egg-shell Ware and the first appearance of Crude Ware, both of which are characteristic of the MM II A period in the palace. At the top of the latest floor deposit was an Egyptian scarab of late XIIth–early XIIIth Dynasty type (Hood 1959, 19 fig. 31; CMS II, 2, 34). The precise contents of the three floor deposits should go a long way to filling out the pottery descriptions in Chapter 2, as the Royal Road Stratigraphy should be much more reliable than the earlier efforts of Evans and his colleagues. Meanwhile, the preliminary results seem to confirm the earlier part of the sequence suggested for the palace deposits.

Further West Extension of Royal Road (SEX)
Excavations by Peter Warren in 1979 to 1982 on the site of the proposed Stratigraphical Museum Extension, abbreviated SEX, revealed a long historical sequence of the town's history beginning in the MM I A period.

In 1980 and 1981 he cleared a room in a structure apparently built in MM II. The room was reported to have contained:

> A substantial pottery deposit of *c.* 60 vases, mostly undecorated but ranging from large jars to tiny miniatures; there are bridge-spouted jars, a cylindrical pyxis, an imitation of a stone bowl, carinated cups and a metal-imitating chalice cup (Catling 1982, 53).

Nearby were other 'MM II' rooms that produced about 15 more vases. Warren and Hankey (1989, 57) add the detail that there were at least two examples of Straight-sided Cups in Ridged Ware with added white spots found in the MM II rooms. The Pyxis is very similar to **537** in Group E (Catling 1982, 53 fig. 116). The chalice is a reference to a Short-rimmed Angular Cup of Type 3. Associated stylistically with the 'MM II' pottery are the cups found in F/FG (Warren 1981, 74 figs. 3, 4). One is a Straight-sided Cup in Precision Stamped Ware, with shells as the motif; above and below are bands of interlocking reversed-S motifs in tiny white dots very similar to those on rhyton **395** (ibid., fig. 3). Another is a Crude Cup of Type 4 (ibid., fig. 4 right). On present evidence it seems that the primary floor deposits in SEX F/FG, assigned by the excavator to MM II, should be given the further precise designation of MM II B and perhaps associated with events at the end of the Old Palace period.

Villa Ariadne—North

Ken Wardle's excavations in the field to the N of the Villa Ariadne have revealed traces of an early building, beneath the Roman structures that are the focus of the fieldwork (French 1994, 75). A large deposit of over 60 vases or whole profiles, almost certainly signalling one event, contains numerous close parallels for Group A and Hogarth's pits on Gypsades, and thus seems to have been formed late in the MM I B period or early in MM II A. A more recent group with Crude Ware may be distinguished (Tomlinson 1996, 42).

Acropolis Houses (KSP 1975)

H. W. and E. A. Catling with D. Smyth conducted a rescue excavation on the plot of the Staphylakis family on the E slopes of the Acropolis Hill in 1975, abbreviated KSP 1975, (Catling *et al.* 1979). Despite the effects of deep agricultural ploughing, the excavators succeeded in isolating three architectural phases, which contained six deposits all belonging to the neopalatial period. The earliest deposits, A and B, are associated with the basement room of a structure, the remainder of which has not survived. Deposit A was interpreted as the material left in place, when the building was abandoned; Deposit B was seen to comprise material gathered up by the builders of the subsequent MM III building on the site, and used to level the terrace created by the early basement's walls (ibid., 78).

The pottery in Deposit A comprises a large percentage of Crude forms none of which corresponds to the MM II A and MM II B types described in Chapter 2, see below p. 82–5, but include the Everted Rim Bowl also found in period 4, and thus MM III, at Phaistos (ibid., fig. 16.3; Warren and Hankey 1989, 58). There is a single example of a ridged cup similar to Straight-sided Cups of Type 12 (Catling *et al.*, fig. 16.5), and several more in Deposit B, including five decorated in the White-spotted Style (ibid., fig. 18.49, 95–8; 19.52, 114, 116, 119). Deposit B also contains two rounded cups in the Heavy Spiral Style (ibid., fig. 18.91–2).

The pottery wares and styles in Deposits A and B were treated together, because of their close similarities to each other. Given the correspondences with Phaistos period 4, it seems most likely that the primary deposit A was formed after the end of the MM II B period, though probably after not too long an interval, as the close similarity of cups in the Heavy Spiral Style with those from Phaistos period 3, and the ridged cups of MM II B at Knossos and Archanes would seem to suggest. Deposits A and B fit well with Group P and

Hogarth's Later Heap to provide a ceramic definition of the MM III A period.

Trial KV

In 1969 M. Popham conducted a rescue excavation at a site called Sochara, on the slopes of the Acropolis due W of the palace, abbreviated Trial KV (Popham 1974). The trials revealed the basement rooms of a substantial building, perhaps part of a water system. The deposit in the central room was found in a state, that suggested a primary deposit created during the destruction of the room: some of the cups and bowls were found to have been stacked. Beneath the destruction level was a layer of silt belonging to the room's period of use prior to the destruction.

The silt layer contained five vases, including a Crude Bowl of Type 2 (ibid., 185 fig. 5.1), a Crude Pyxis (ibid., fig. 5.2) and a Crude Cup of Type 4; all types that seem to originate in the MM IIA period and continue into MM IIB.

The destruction deposit contained a large number of crude forms including Crude Bowls of Types 1 (ibid., fig. 6. 1–5), and 4 (ibid., fig. 6. 8); a Rounded Bridge-spouted Jar of Type 6 (ibid., 188 fig. 7. 2 pl. 29a), large jars decorated in the Spiral Band Style (ibid., pls. 30e; 32a), a Hand Lamp of Type 2 (ibid., fig. 8. 9) and a Pedestalled Lamp of Type 2 (ibid., pl. 32c), all of which strongly indicate a date in the MM II B period for the formation of the deposit, as suggested by the excavator (ibid., 191).

Gypsades Hill

In March of 1900, while Evans and Mackenzie began clearing the Kephala, D. G. Hogarth conducted a series of trial excavations in the surrounding valley (Hogarth 1900). On the E slopes of Gypsades, just to the W of the modern road, he cleared two houses of the neopalatial period, which have come to be known as 'Hogarth's Houses' (ibid., pl. XII. 6 & 7 'Early Houses'; Hood and Smyth 1981, no. 297). Trials nearby revealed a number of early contexts, likened to receptacles, numbered 58. No. 5 was a plastered pit 1.70 m deep (1900, 70 pl. VII 'cistern'). The pit or cistern was found to contain several almost complete vases including a three-handled jug in Barbotine Ware (Hogarth and Welch 1901, 79 pl. VI. 1), and 'Hundreds of fragments mostly unpainted cups of metallic type' (ibid.), a reference to Straight-sided Cups of Type 2. Near the cistern he:

Opened three circular excavations, sunk from 3 to 10 feet into the soft rock. They can have been neither wells, for their lowest point is far above the water level of the vicinity, nor cisterns, because not being plastered they would not have retained water. Possibly they were originally intended for the storage of grain; but more probably they were cut...to contain what was actually found in them namely a mass of broken...vases and other rubbish, evidently cleared out of the neighbouring houses when re-stored after the conflagration of which the large house [House A in Hogarth 1900, pl. III] shows traces (ibid.).

The pottery illustrated from these pits includes a Straight-sided Cup of Type 2 in the Woven Style (Hogarth and Welch ibid., pl. VIIa), and fragments decorated in a similar manner (ibid., pl. VII f, g, h).

To the N of 'Hogarth's Houses', S. Hood in 1958 excavated a 'Kind of rock-cut basement', in which he found two Straight-sided Cups of Type 2 and a spouted jar, all in the Woven Style of MM I B (1959, 19 fig. 29).

The cisterns and pits on Gypsades seem to have been filled at a time close to the formation of Group A and the similar deposit at Villa Ariadne North, all containing pottery of the MM I B period.

Mavrospilio Tombs

In 1926, Evans excavated six tombs on the W slopes of Aïlias below Mavrospilio. John Forsdyke was asked to continue the excavation in 1927, when the total of tombs was brought to 22, and publish the results (Forsdyke 1927). Few of the tombs were undisturbed and there is no single primary burial of the Old Palace period. There is, however, a context that may belong to one period. In Tomb XVII a pit had been dug into the floor at the S end of the chamber. The pit had been used as a receptacle, then covered over with pithos fragments and thus not disturbed by later burials. The pit contained skulls, bones, beads and pottery (ibid., 279–81 fig. 34). Among the pottery are a number of pieces that can be placed in both the MM II A and MM II B periods, but also a Crude Cup of Type 3 (ibid., pl. 23.24), and a Crude Jug of Type 2 (ibid., pl. 23.32), which belong only in the latter. The pit seems to have been used during MM II and sealed at some point in MM II B. If the 'corroded iron cube' was in fact sealed in the pit, as the report suggests, it would be the earliest piece of iron in the Aegean (ibid., 279, pl. 23.2).

The latest material from Tomb VI includes a large jug in the White-spotted Style (ibid., 295 fig. 49 left) and a conical cup with everted rim comparable to those from Deposit B in the Knossos Acropolis Houses (ibid., pl. 23 VI. 7). Though small and insufficiently published, the material from Tomb VI could be included in the groups formed during the MM III A period.

2

Pottery fabrics, wares and styles

INTRODUCTION

The pottery of the Old Palace period in Crete has been called 'Kamares Ware' since its discovery in the Kamares cave last century (Mariani 1895; Myres 1895). Unfortunately, the term lacks concise definition and seems to include all Cretan MBA pottery regardless of fabric, manufacturing technique, decoration or origin (Walberg 1976; MacGillivray 1984c, 250). At the turn of the last century, the term was even used to describe an entire period, despite the cautionary statement that it cannot be used for both a period and technique (Dawkins 1904, 192).

A possible definition of 'Kamares Ware' might include the pottery of the MM I B–III A periods made with the white clays of central Crete including the various tempered products; but this would still be largely stylistic, as the white clays of E Crete can only be distinguished from those of the centre with a comprehensive programme of petrographic and chemical analysis. Until there is a new definition of what 'Kamares Ware' might include, it remains an unsatisfactory designation and is not used here.

The first studies of the MM pottery of central Crete by Mackenzie (1906) and Banti (1940) were the standard introductory works until the analyses of Walberg (1976) and the comprehensive and detailed typology of Levi and Carinci (1988). None of these studies, however, analyses the pottery from a technological viewpoint and the last three deal primarily with the pottery of Phaistos, which does not include all of the forms, wares and styles that occur in N central Crete.

The pottery from the early levels of the palace at Knossos is as plentiful and varied in fabric and decoration as one would expect of a cosmopolitan centre. The present study is necessarily selective, as the intention is to define the most common types, and the wares and styles in which they appear, in order to outline a ceramic sequence at Knossos alone. The examples used are those which could be assigned with confidence to the Groups re-investigated in Chapter 1, although reference is made to occurrences of types, wares and styles from relevant contexts elsewhere.

The pottery is considered first from a technological point of view, as the first phase in the manufacture of any pot is the preparation of the clay paste. For this reason, the present analysis groups the pottery on the basis of macroscopic observations of its fabric and begins with the most common, Fine Buff, and continues with the minority, that is less frequent, fabrics.

The period treated here covers a time of major changes in ceramic technology. The most obvious change, but also one of the most difficult to detect and describe accurately, is the experimentation with and wide-spread adoption of the radial potter's wheel, evident in those examples with the grooves and texture of thrown pottery (Momigliano 1991, 247–9, 264–5; Gillis 1990, 6–7). There could have been a variety of techniques in simultaneous use that lie, technologically speaking, between forming a pot from coils and throwing it on the well-centred radial potter's wheel, to exploit the full force of a centrifuge. Those pieces that cannot be placed at either end are here classified under the deliberately ambiguous heading of 'proto-wheelmade', pending future analyses focusing on formation techniques.

PART 1. THE FINE BUFF POTTERY

The fabric used most commonly in the MM pottery of Knossos is based on a distinctive light coloured clay in a highly refined state, without obvious temper. Apparently dependent on firing conditions, the fabric may vary from light buff to grey in colour. Visually, the clay corresponds to Wilson's Buff Fabric of EM II A Knossos (1985, 307, 319) and Momigliano's Fabric I for the EM III pottery of Knossos (1991, 245). It may relate to the Fine Buff fabric of Kommos, although the Knossos fabric seems to be harder and more dense (Betancourt 1990, 5–9). One certain source for the clay is the region around the N, W and S slopes of Mt. Juktas, but similar clay beds are said to occur all the way from Juktas to the Mesara (Day 1988). Once refined, these are virtually indistinguishable to the naked eye, although there seems to be a greater tendency for the Phaistos pottery to fire grey. In the case of Fine Buff, then, we cannot at present give a more precise source than central Crete. This may explain why the fine wares of Knossos and Phaistos can be distinguished only stylistically, and even then, for the present, only in certain instances.

i. The Fine Buff Wares and Styles

The *ware* groupings proposed here are determined on the basis of techniques in the manufacture and decoration of the pottery. The content of designs or repeated use of similar motifs are the criteria for suggesting *stylistic* groupings.

Pared Ware

A distinctive group of handmade pottery is characterized by signs of paring, or the shaving away of clay with a cutting tool in downward strokes, on the lower exterior of the vase. The group includes Rounded Goblets of Type 1 with plain (1–7, 895), dark-on-buff sprayed (15–16, 892–4, 896–7), and monochrome coated (671) surfaces, Straight-sided Cups of Type 1 with plain surfaces, (8–14), and Tumblers of Type 1 with dark-on-buff decorated (898), or monochrome coated (17) surfaces. The examples are in Groups A, G and L, in types that belong in the MM I B period. This manner of finishing a vase is quite common in the MM I A pottery of Knossos where it is found on similar types (Momigliano 1991, 264). The MM I B examples may represent the last products in this ware, which seems gradually to have ceased with the adoption and popular use of the radial centered potter's wheel.

Barbotine Ware

Small dabs of clay or slurry, applied in relief to the surface of a vase to form part of the decorative pattern, characterize Barbotine Ware (Foster 1982). The examples employing this technique in Fine Buff Fabric have 'prickles' (see Betancourt 1985a, 83 fig. 58c), which are used to outline or give structure to the decoration or to accent the angle on an angular form. The barbotine technique is used in both handmade and wheelmade pottery on Tumblers of Type 4 (977), Rounded Goblets of Type 3 (226), Conical Goblets of Type 3 (227), Straight-sided Cups of Type 5 (117), Tall-rimmed Angular Cups of Type 1 (613), Short-rimmed Angular Cups of Type 2 (926–7), and other forms.

The examples are in Groups A, F, J, L, M, and O, and in types that belong in the MM I B and MM II A periods. The use of barbotine decoration begins in the neolithic period in Crete, is evident on the MM I A pottery of Knossos (Foster 1982, 147–8; Momigliano 1991, 267), but has come to be regarded as most typical of the MM I B period (Betancourt 1985a, 83). It may well be that the manufacture of most examples of Barbotine Ware should be assigned to the MM I B period, as numerous examples in Period 1 groups at Phaistos suggest (e.g. F. 61, 62, 2116, 2169, 2170); but it may have continued into MM II A, as the examples in Groups F, J and L and in period 2 contexts at Phaistos (Fiandra 1980, pls. 32.10, 35.2, 44.2, 49.2, 54.10, 55.10) suggest; a date in keeping with the example found at Haraga in Egypt (Kemp and Merrillees 1980, Ha.4). However, a much more detailed study is very much called for, building on the work of Foster by isolating the different types of 'barbs', both technologically and stylistically, within a framework of groups defined by chemical and petrographic analyses. Then the exact dates for the different classes within Barbotine Ware can be assessed.

Egg-shell Ware

The most distinctive and rarest of the palatial pottery is in 'Egg-shell Ware', so-called by Evans because the walls of vases are comparable in thickness to the walls of small birds' eggs (1921, 241). The term has been used, erroneously, to describe fine polychrome decorated MM pottery in general (for example Betancourt [1985a, 94] wrongly cites 926 as an example of 'Egg-shell Ware') but is restricted here to examples of Fine Buff Pottery with walls less than 0.1 cm thick. The technical feat represented by this ware may have been achieved by the careful shaving of a vase at high speed revolutions, as it would have been almost impossible to throw a pot of such extreme delicacy. Another possibility is that the body was moulded. A very thin sheet of highly refined clay could have been smoothed onto the inside of a mould, in effect taking the place of a metal sheet, as would have been the process for vessels in gold, silver or copper. One problem with this theory is that there are no traces of mould lines left on the vases.

We may assume that the aim of the potter, besides the obvious display of virtuosity, was to produce the ceramic equivalent to the fine, and presumably more valuable, metal wares. The only examples from Knossos come from the Royal Pottery Stores, Groups F and J, and are Straight-sided (615, 798), and Rounded (616–23, 799–801) Cups. There are also examples without specific provenance in the AM (1929.405; 1938.577). The limited repertory and extremely fine workmanship evident in these pieces may indicate that they were the products of a single, highly specialized workshop.

True Egg-shell Ware remains a hallmark of the MM II A period. It was certainly the finest pottery of its time and can hardly have been intended for everyday use. Nevertheless, a cup from Kato Symi may belong to this class (Lembesi 1994, 101 fig. 96) and two fragments are known from Palaikastro (MacGillivray, Sackett *et al.* 1992, fig. 14.3). Two cups were exported to Melos (Papagianopoulou 1991, nos. 348, 358), one to Kea (Overbeck 1989, 183 pl. 85 DG 20) and perhaps another to Israel (Yadin *et al.* 1960, 91 pl. 115.13).

The rounded cup form, mouldings and decoration on this ware link it directly to the cups and bowls of the 'Tôd Treasure', discussed in Chapter 3, Part x.

Shallow Grooved Ware

A small group of early wheelmade vases has thin horizontal incisions or rough grooves cut into the exterior of the body. These are distinguished from the incisions on the later Precision Grooved Ware by their shallowness and random displacement on the vase. The technique appears on Squat Rounded (**106**), and Angular (**93**, **95–7**) Cups and a Tumbler of Type 4 (**169**). Its occurrence in Group A allows the origin of this ware to be assigned to the MM I B period at Knossos and, perhaps, Juktas (Karetsou 1978, fig. 11.2). It may continue into MM II A as examples in similar forms are quite numerous in periods 1 and 2 at Phaistos (F. 397, 626, 2115, 2499, 3490a, 5022, 5273, 5606a, 5644, 6571; Fiandra 1980, pls. 36.4, 37.2, 9) and in MM II contexts at Kommos (Betancourt 1990, nos. 371, 383) and Malia (Stürmer 1993, nos. 2, 8, 9).

A related ware occurs in pottery of similar forms and date in Fine Red Fabric, see **141–2** below.

A clear link to metal originals is suggested by a cup fragment in this ware with spool handle in the AM (AE 839) (Evans 1921, fig. 183bi; Matthäus 1980, pl. 76.5). A stone equivalent to **95** is a cup from Myrtos-Pyrgos (Hankey 1980, pl. 76 MP 73/10).

Precision Grooved Ware

A number of fine wheelmade vases have distinctive, precision tooled and evenly spaced horizontal grooves cut in groups into their sides. These may represent a carefully measured successor to Shallow Grooved Ware. The technique is used on Straight-sided (**408**), Rounded (**413–21**, **430**, **987**, **1045**) and Short-rimmed Angular (**411–12**) Cups and a Jug with Horizontal Spout (**1042**). Many of the examples are decorated in the White-spotted Style which, along with the ware's frequency in Groups E, N and P and its use of late pottery types, indicates that its greatest popularity was at the end of the Old Palace period, perhaps originating during MM II B, as examples from period 3 at Phaistos suggest (F. 783, 3089, 6248; Fiandra 1980, pl. 42.1), and continuing into the MM III A period.

A very similar effect in silver may be seen on a cup from Enkomi in Cyprus (Matthäus 1980, pl. 76.3).

Stamped and Impressed Ware

A group of early wheelmade pottery has designs stamped or impressed into the side of the vase while still wet. The stamps are generally repeated horizontally in a haphazard manner. On some examples grooves are impressed to create a three-dimensional background to painted patterns. This class, called 'Stamped Ware' by Evans (1921, 242), includes rounded cups in Egg-shell Ware (**616**, **799–801**) and an angular cup (**233**). It is quite distinct from the later Precision Stamped Ware, which uses the stamps to form a coherent and measured decorative pattern and on which stamps are employed quite differently. Its presence in Groups F and J and its coincidence with Egg-shell Ware place this ware in the MM II A period. Other examples from Knossos are without exact provenance in the AM (AE 1627), BM (A528.3) and HM (4342), but may have originated in the Monolithic Pillar Basement or North-West Pit.

Examples of a very similar ware are quite common in period 2 at Phaistos (F. 359, 398, 865, 986, 5759; Fiandra 1980, pls. 35.4, 7, 44.13, 46.5, 47.2, 7, 48.4, 9, 49.8, 52.1, 4, 53.5, 11, 54.13, 15, 60.1, 2; Levi 1976, fig. 683, pl. LXII) and in MM II at Kommos (Betancourt 1990, nos. 108, 353, 375, 376, 380, 382, 1011). There are also examples from Kato Symi (Lembesi 1994, 101 fig. 96) and Phylakopi in Melos (Papagianopoulou 1991, nos. 347, 348, 358). An example from Haraga in Egypt helps to align MM II A with the middle of the XIIth Dynasty (Evans 1928, 211 fig. 119, 228; Kemp and Merrillees 1980, Ha.5)

It is evident, as Evans pointed out (1921, 242), that the stamps used here very likely imitate, or may even be the same as, those used on metal wares, which Egg-shell Ware certainly copies (MacGillivray 1987). The impressed lines could be compared to the chasing technique used in finishing metal products; perhaps the most accomplished examples of which are the gold cups and bowls in the 'Tôd Treasure' (see Chapter 3, Part x).

Precision Stamped Ware

A distinctive class of wheelmade vases, with a measured use of stamps, occurs in some quantity in Group E. This Precision Stamped Ware, like Stamped and Impressed Ware, employs dies, but instead of being pushed into the wall of the vase, the vase is pushed from within (leaving a fingerprint) into a form. The dies are now in the form of circles, star or sun motifs, spirals, concentric circles and shells, arranged in such a way as to be supplemented or connected with painted designs to form well ordered decorative patterns. The technique is used on Straight-sided (**433–4**), and Rounded (**237**, **436–44**) Cups and on a Bridge-spouted Jar (**445**).

The mixed context of Group E does not allow for a firm date in either the MM II B or MM III A periods in the palace, though a cup from a group near the North House on the Royal Road, deposited in MM II, suggests the former (Warren 1981, 74 fig. 3). This is firmly supported by a number of almost identical examples from Phaistos period 3 (F. 1041, 1477; Borda 1946, 21 pl. XI, 77406; Pernier 1935, pls. XXIVa, XXXb, XXXV), including one also decorated in the Sunrise Style (ibid., pl. XXXb), which place this ware in the MM II B period. Similar examples are known from Kommos (Betancourt 1990, nos. 378, 1159, 1160, 1191, 1209, 1307, 1589), Palaikastro (Bosanquet and Dawkins 1923, 16 fig. 11; Bernini 1995, 71 fig. 13.52) and Thera (Papagiannopoulou 1991, nos. 295–6), and a large closed vessel from Kea IV may be a Cycladic imitation (Overbeck 1989, 136 pl. 70 no. 26).

A silver cup from Byblos gives a good impression of what the metal inspirations for this ceramic class might have been (Montet 1928, pl. CXI; E. Davis 1977, fig. 64), as does the shoulder of a bronze jug with interlocking spirals (Matthäus 1980, no. 260).

The difference between Stamped and Impressed Ware of MM II A and Precision Stamped Ware of MM II B could reflect a change in the manufacture and decoration of metal wares; the earlier being stamped and chased, the later introducing the repoussé technique.

Early Printed Ware
The use of a device, perhaps of clay, wood, leather or sponge, dipped in paint and applied repeatedly, either directly onto the buff surface or a dark monochrome coat, to imprint a continuous pattern may be observed on a group of early wheelmade vases. The motifs employed are a sponge pattern, **114**, **1032**, a roughly circular sponge or dot pattern, **628–30**, likened by Mackenzie to 'brush dabs' (1902 PB (2), 69), a crescent or 'maggot-like' pattern, **624–7**, **798**, **976**, which continues to be used in Late Printed Ware, and irregular shapes, **631–2**.

This ware is represented by a Rounded Goblet of Type 3 (**976**), Straight-sided Cups of Type 6 (**624–30**) (Mackenzie 1902 PB (2), 68, mentions the bases of eleven other examples), a Rounded Cup of Type 3 (**631**), a Tall-rimmed Angular Cup of Type 3 (**114**), and a bridge-spouted jar (**632**). Its occurrence in Groups A, F, J and O and on early pottery types confirms that it begins during the MM I B period and continues to be made into MM II A.

A similar ware is found in periods 1 and 2 at Phaistos (F. 361, 418, 1926, 1941, 2175, 2314, 2315, 5479a; Pelagatti 1962, 111 and pl. 14 nos. 1 and 2; Fiandra 1973, pl. 23. 1,2), Kommos (Betancourt 1990, no. 1006) and the Porti tholos (Xanthoudides 1924, pl. VI no. 5069).

These ceramic prints should be viewed as part of a wider appeal in printed design, as seen in wall painting (Evans 1930, 362), and thus perhaps textiles during the early stages of the Old Palace period. We might wonder if printing and stamping in the design world may not have been inspired by the increase in the use of seals in administration early in the palace period.

Late Printed Ware
The successor to Early Printed Ware may be seen on a group of Straight-sided Cups of Type 10 (**223**, **293–8**), which have the crescent or 'maggot-like' pattern similar to that used in the early version, although no longer applied directly onto the buff surface of the clay. The patterns are now printed on a cream/white horizontal band as well as on a dark monochrome surface. The examples of this ware in Group E and its use of Straight-sided Cups of Type 10 indicate that it belongs in either the MM II B or the MM III A period. As it would be difficult to imagine that much time elapsed between the early and late versions of the ware, it could be suggested that the late examples were made during the course of the MM II B period; apparently, printing ceramics does not survive until the end.

A fragment of a large vase from a Group E context, in PLATE 63 upper right hand corner, appears to show the use of printed patterns on what may be a tempered fabric, though the fragment could not be located for verification.

Ridged Ware
One of the most distinctive wares is characterized by fine tooling to create evenly spaced, horizontal ridges giving an impression of stacked metal plates. This technique characterizes Straight-sided Cups of Types 11 (**423–6**), and 12 (**404–7**, **1037**, **1044**; and numerous uncatalogued sherds from Group E contexts in the KSM) and Short-rimmed Angular Cups of Type 3 (**409–12**, **991–2**). Fragments of a large bridge-spouted jar (**422**), are also in this ware. Its frequency in Groups E (**401–12**, **423–6**), N (**991–2**), and P (**1037**, **1044**), in late ceramic types, often decorated in the White-Spotted Style, and its appearance in Deposits A and B at the Knossos Acropolis Houses (Catling *et al.* 1979, V. 49, 95–8) places Ridged Ware in the MM III A period, although it may be unwise to discount an origin late in MM II B (see below, p. 58).

Ridged Ware seems to be a Knossian product, as there is only one possible example from Phaistos (Levi 1976, 477 fig. 730). Its export and imitation may be seen elsewhere in Crete at Gournia (Boyd-Hawes *et al.* 1908, 38 pl. VI.34), the Trapeza Cave (Pendlebury *et al.* 1936, 62–3 fig. 14. 548) and Palaikastro (MacGillivray, Sackett *et al.* 1992, fig. 14.2), and in the Cyclades at Phylakopi in Melos, Akrotiri in Thera (Papagianopoulou 1991, nos. 263, 340), Mikre Vigla in Naxos (Barber and Hadjianastasiou 1989, 107 fig. 22 no. 420) and Ayia Irini in Kea (Davis 1986, 81 pl. 28 U 79–82). A later survival may be seen in cups of the MM III B period from a cave shelter in Poros (Lembessi 1967, pl. 180b; Muhly 1992, nos. 35–7).

Pattern Painted Ware
A number of styles, defined on the basis of decorative patterns, may be observed in Pattern Painted Ware. Detailed analyses of the decorative styles on MM pottery have been published by Walberg (1976; 1983; 1992). However, as her classification fails to account for technical differences such as fabric and surface treatment, and uses broad, loosely defined chronological borders, it contributes little of use to the present study. Instead, I have chosen to describe some of the more striking styles, according to what the decorative motifs or patterns may represent.

White-banded Style. The simplest decorative style consists of one or more thick, white-painted bands applied horizontally on the dark monochrome surface of wheelmade vases. Single bands appear on Rounded Goblets of Type 2 (**110**, **162–3**, **682**, **918–19**). Single or multiple bands are found on a Rounded Goblet of Type

3 (111), Straight-sided Cups of Types 2 (789–90), 5 (112–13), and 6 (636), on pyxides (648, 683, 760, 806, 924), and on large jars (791–4).

The occurrence of this style in Groups A (110–13, 115), B (162–3), F (636, 648), G (682–3), H (760), I (789–94), J (806) and L (923–4) place it in the MM I B and MM II A periods. A single example from a period 2 context at Phaistos confirms the Knossian dates (F. 89), as do examples of a related style at Palaikastro (MacGillivray, Sackett *et al.* 1992, 133 figs. 11.1, 12.2). A close parallel for 113 is from Porti in the Mesara (Xanthoudides 1924, no. 5119).

The examples in Old Palace contexts may represent the end of a style begun in EM III and/or MM I A at Knossos (Momigliano 1991, 245–9).

Diagonal Red and White Style. A small group of handmade vases is decorated with pairs of red or orange lines outlined with pairs of white lines and placed diagonally or, in the case of goblets, spiraling outward from the base to the rim. This pattern is found on Conical Goblets of Type 1 (609–10, 899) and examples from the early floor beneath the Room of the Stone Pier in PLATE 141 (bottom, second from right) and the Vat Room Deposit (Momigliano 1991, 172 no. 4 pl. 23), a Conical Goblet of Type 2 (55), Tall-rimmed Angular Cups of Types 1 (613—where it is used on Barbotine Ware) and 2 (71–2), and an Angular Bridge-spouted Jar of Type 1b (905).

The occurrence of this style in Groups A (55, 71–2), F (609–10, 613), and L (899, 905), and its use on early ceramic types, place it for certain in the MM I B period, with the possibility that it continued into MM II A. The fact that the style appears on a restricted number of similar handmade forms suggests that the above examples may all be products of the same workshop, in which case the examples from Groups F and L could be taken either as survivors, or as indicators of earlier, MM I B, floors in the Royal Pottery Stores and Early Olive Press floor. The date in MM I B may be strengthened by examples of this style in the destruction debris at the SW Palace angle, see above Chapter 1.

Woven Style. A large number of handmade vases are decorated with patterns in thick, powdery white, red and orange paint on a thick, lustrous dark monochrome surface. The patterns may be horizontal, diagonal or vertical and employ linear, circular, interlocking and floral motifs in a complexity of designs, whose description lies beyond the scope of the present study; a selection is illustrated in FIGS. 2.1–3. The patterns are those that one might imagine to have been inspired by woven textiles, in that they are regularly laid out in measured, well-defined and geometrically spaced zones, and the colours are made to alternate within the designs; very similar to the Geometric and Deximata styles of traditional Cretan textiles (Charvalia and Antonopoulou 1986).

This style is found on Straight-sided Cups of Types 2 (31–47, 56–67, 155–6, 173–4, 178–88, 611–12, 674–5, 797, 1026–7), and 3 (68, 189–91), a Tall-rimmed Angular Cup of Type 1a (192), a Shallow Angular Bowl of Type 1 (50), Angular Bridge-spouted Jars of Type 2 (75, 193–7), Squat Rounded Bridge-spouted Jars (73–4), Rounded Bridge-spouted Jars of Type 2 (46–7, 76–7), a jug (200), and large jar (614).

The frequency of this style in Group A (37–41, 46–7, 50, 56–68, 73–7), and its occurrence in Groups B (155–6), F (611–12, 614), G (674–5), J (797), and O (1026–7), and its use on early ceramic types place it with some confidence in the MM I B period, but with the possible continuation into MM II A. Some of the motifs used in this style are also found on contemporary wheelmade pottery, for example similar dot rosettes also appear on 655, 662 and 942–4, and the row of white dots with superimposed red line on 183 is also found on 203, 211 and the 'Karmi Cup' (Stewart 1962).

This is very much a style of the Knossos region with examples from Juktas (Karetsou 1978, 247–9 figs. 11. 6, 7; 12.4), Phourni (J. and E. Sakellarakis 1972, pl. 5a), and Gournes (Zois 1969, 22 pls. 27 no. 7046, 28 no. 7014a). It is found rarely in E Crete (Bosanquet and Dawkins 1923, pl. IVg) and the Mesara (Vasilakis 1990, 44 fig. 14e), though there are several examples among the earliest Cretan exports to Phylakopi in Melos (Papagiannopoulou 1991, nos. 337–8, 382, 386). There is a closely related and contemporary style from period 1 at Phaistos (F. 62, 2029, 2171, 2276, 2315, 5398, 5473–4, 5482, 5939, 5946).

A predecessor to this style may be seen in the Polychrome Geometric Style of the MM I A period (Mackenzie 1906, 246), discussed in Part 4 below.

Sunrise Style. One of the most distinctive styles is set around a white design composed of two concentric semicircles with upright petals or rays above, possibly representing a stylized sunrise. The main motif alternates most frequently with red 'coralline' designs (Walberg 1976, 69) outlined in white, less frequently with vertical strokes and occasionally is represented on its own. Examples are 280–4, 336–7, 385–7.

All are from Group E and could thus belong in either MM II B or MM III A. The earlier date is strongly suggested by the popularity of this style in the destruction deposits of period 3 at Phaistos (F. 341, 441, 445, 801, 950a, 1358; Pernier 1935, 220 fig. 97, 262 fig. 145, figs. 150 left, 177 right; Borda 1946 pls. A top left, 9 second row left; Levi 1976, pl. 179 l). One example combines the style with Precision Stamped Ware of MM II B (Pernier 1935, pl. XXXb). 340 combines the defining motif of this style with the Wavy-line Style, also arguably MM II B. Two examples from Kommos should probably also be assigned to the MM II B period and not MM III A (Betancourt 1990, nos. 822, 1666).

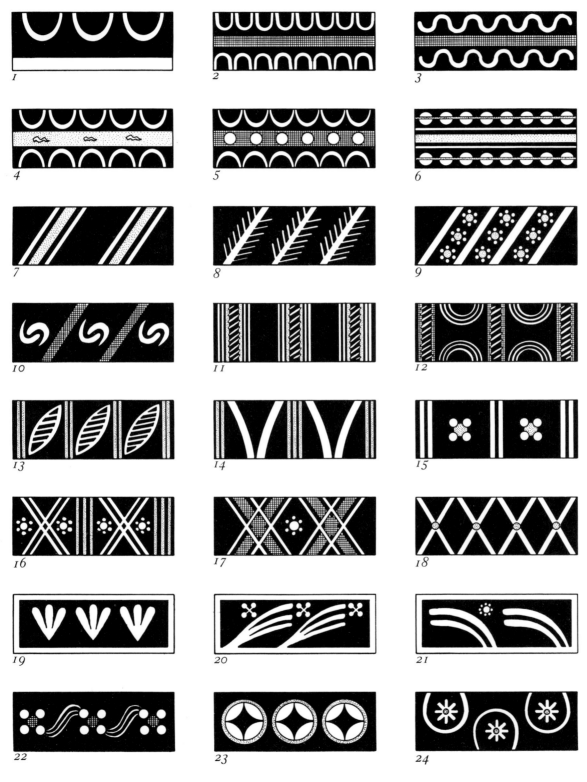

Fig. 2.1. Selection of designs in the Woven Style on Straight-sided Cups of Type 2: (1) 36; (2) 60; (3) 52; (4) 675; (5) BM A475; (6) 183; (7) 179; (8) HM 4383; (9) 181; (10) 1027; (11) 182; (12) BM A476; (13) 67, 797; (14) 63–5; (15) 56; (16) 674; (17) 1026; (18) 188; (19) 178; (20) Bosanquet and Dawkins 1923, pl. IVg; (21) 173; (22) 156; (23) 184; (24) 187.

Fig. 2.2. Selection of designs in the Woven Style on
Straight-sided Cups of Type 3: (1) 68; (2) AM AE960,
2; (3) 191; (4) 190.

Fig. 2.3. Selection of designs in the Woven Style on Angular
Bridge-spouted Jars of Type 2: (1) 196; (2) AM AE959;
(3) AM AE952; (4) 193.

*Fig. 2.4. Fine Buff
Fabric cup K.1010.*

Starburst Style. A small number of Straight-sided Cups of types 8 and 10 are decorated with a white-painted star or rosette as the central motif on two sides, with swirls and loops as frames. Examples are in Groups E (274–7, 338) and N (996) both containing material of the MM II B and MM III A periods. The earlier of the two dates may be indicated by the frequency of very similar types in a closely related style from Phaistos period 3 (F. 610, 700, 1040, 4076, 4941, 5083, 5541; Pernier 1935, 267 fig. 150 right, 381 fig. 228.2), and Kommos (Betancourt 1990, no. 1328). Betancourt illustrates the motif as typical of MM II B (1985 a, fig. 70 o).

    The Type 5 Bridge-spouted Jar from Abydos is decorated in a similar manner (Kemp and Merrillees 1980, 118–19 fig. 38 pl. 13), though the disc at the centre of the main motif is red, unlike those in the Starburst Style. Red discs at the centre of star or rosette motifs are found on a MM II A jar (956) where, however, the motif stands alone. The Abydos jar, then, could be placed somewhere after the end of the MM II A period and before the end

of MM II B. It probably comes from the same work-shop as K.1010, in FIG. 2.4. Unfortunately, K.1010 is not from a secure context (KSM box 1813) and so is not included in the inventory here.

Wavy-line Style. A highly distinctive and common style in the late groups is characterized by covering the body of Rounded Cups of Type 6 with either wavy-lines or scale patterns in white paint, and filling the interstices with white or polychrome patterns, often repeated in diagonal lines; a selection showing the variety of patterns is in FIG. 2.5. In most cases, the base of the cup is decorated with elaborate, dynamic polychrome patterns on the bottom and inside of the base, see PLATES 13, 74–5. In some ways, this style could be considered a successor to the Woven Style, as the patterns here could well be seen to reflect woven designs with tiny beads stitched-on in a variety of regular patterns.

    This style is quite common at Knossos with a number of examples from Group E (340–68) and N (998–9), and others in the AM (AE 826; 832.2; 968.2, 4; 1938.568) and BM (A 529). The contexts allow for dates in either the MM II B or MM III A period at Knossos. A strong argument for the earlier date may be put forward on the basis of very similar cups in this style from Phaistos period 3 (F. 527, 1430 Pernier 1935, pl. XXIa; Levi 1976, pl. 124 c, e, f, h), Kommos (Betancourt 1990, no. 517), and the primary destruction deposit at Anemospilia assigned by the excavators to the MM II B period (J.

and E. Sakellarakis 1991, 144 fig. 120; Warren and Hankey 1989, 47–52; MacGillivray 1995).

Exported examples at Phylakopi (Papagianopoulou 1991, nos. 346, 359, 361), Kea (Overbeck 1989, 182 pl. 85 DG. 16), Ugarit (Schaeffer 1949, 256 fig. 109A) and Tell el-Dab'a (Walberg 1991; MacGillivray 1995) testify to the popularity of this distinctive Knossian style overseas. A second cup from Ugarit has some of the

Fig. 2.5. Selection of designs in the Wavy-line Style on Rounded Cups of Type 6: (1) 343; (2) 344; (3) 352; (4) 353; (5) 355; (6) 358; (7) 360; (8) 363.

features of this style, including the pattern-painted base decorated in and out, the use of tiny white dots in the patterns and the cup's form (Schaeffer 1949, 256 fig. 109 pl. XXXVIII bottom); but the main motif, while constructed above and below an undulating line, incorporates an ivy pattern not seen in Crete until the LM I A period (Bernini 1995, 64 fig. 8E). One wonders if the cup could not have been painted over, at a time several generations subsequent to its manufacture.

A bridge-spouted jar decorated in a wavy-line pattern, quite closely related to that on cup **356**, was found with the MBA group in a tomb at Byblos (Baramki 1973, pl. IV.1). The group does not provide a firm chronological link, but the form of the jar, with slightly raised and flattened rim and elongated foot, resembles that of **1002** and so helps to confirm the rounded bridge-spouted jar typology outlined below.

An early version of the style may be seen in cup **642**, with simple scale pattern but lacking decoration on the base. A type of squat rounded cup, found in later deposits at Phaistos (F. 6018; Pernier 1935, 372 fig. 223; Borda 1946, pl. X. 3, 5), Kommos (Betancourt 1990, nos. 790, 1715) and Palaikastro (Bosanquet and Dawkins 1923, 16 fig. 10) painted with similar wavy-line designs with simplified motifs and in white only, may be a related style of the MM III A period. An example from Kastelli in Chania may be a W Cretan version of the early MM III style (Hallager and Tzedakis 1988, 20 fig. 6). It is possible to identify a further successor in the Finicky Style of the MM III B period, examples of which are found in the North-West Pit (PLATE 53), in a deposit near the North House on the Royal Road (Warren 1991, 330 fig. 10 C, M) and at Palaikastro (MacGillivray, Sackett *et al.* 1991, 138 fig. 14 centre right).

Spiral Band Style. One of the dominant styles on the decorated pottery in Group E is defined by the subdivision of the surface into horizontal zones, and the use of either a spiky foliate band or interlocking S-spirals running essentially unbroken around the vase. Forms are a small bowl (**306**), Straight-sided Cups of types 5–10 (**309–31, 333, 997**), a Rounded Cup of Type 5 (**372**), Rounded Bridge-spouted Jars of type 5 (**379–84**), a Baggy-shaped Bridge-spouted Jar (**390**), and a large bowl (**400**). Very closely related styles are found in Fine Soft Buff and Tempered Buff Fabrics.

The Group E context for the majority of the examples allows for a likely range of dates from the MM II B to MM III A periods at Knossos. The earlier date, which is the one suggested by Evans for the large jars **876–8** in a closely related style (1921, 251), is strongly supported by the frequency of examples in the destruction deposits of Phaistos period 3 (F. 305, 525, 782, 804, 806–7, 1359, 2585, 3059, 6144, 6150; Pernier 1935, 390 fig. 237). Further support may be the use of the spiky foliate band on Precision Stamped Ware Cup **433**. It is likely that the frequent occurrence of the main motifs in the

destruction deposits of Phaistos Period 3 led Betancourt to assign them to the MM II B period (1985 *a*, 97 fig. 70 K, AG).

An earlier, MM II A period, inspiration for the spiky foliate band may be seen in the elaborate bands at the centre of bridge-spouted jars (**930–41**). There is little evidence for the use of the continuous running band of interlocking S-spirals on pottery prior to its adoption, in MM II B, on two jars from the main Trial KV deposit (Popham 1974, pl. 30e, 32a). Its use as the only decoration on **157** may be its first appearance at Knossos. It becomes quite common only during MM II B when employed for this style. Variations in the interlocking spiral may be seen in the Heavy Spiral Style of MM II B and MM III A; during MM III B it becomes one of the dominant decorative patterns and is enlarged to exaggerated proportions (e.g. Warren 1991, fig. 6B).

A link between this style and wall-painting may be indicated by a fragment of painted plaster dado from the Loomweight Basement, with a possible row of crescents like those on **326**, and jars **876–8** (Evans 1921, 251 fig. 118b).

Heavy Spiral Style. A relatively rare but important style, it is distinguished by a heavy or 'weighted' spiral design, created by either thickening the outermost line or 'filling the angle' (Walberg 1992, 93) between the spirals. Within this style, an important distinction may be made between those composed of open running spirals (**332, 334**), and those with closed spirals resembling crashing waves (**240–1, 311**). The examples are straight-sided and rounded cups in Groups D and E and, thus, could be either MM II B or MM III A.

The style seems to originate in the MM II B period at Phaistos, where heavy open running spirals are combined with precision stamps on a bridge-spouted jar from a destruction deposit (Pernier 1935, pl. XXXV). Another jug from Phaistos combines heavy open running spirals on the body with pendant closed spirals on the shoulder, suggesting that closed spirals first appear at the very end of the MM II B period (Pernier 1935, 295 fig. 172). This is confirmed by a jug with closed heavy spirals from the primary destruction deposit at Anemospilia (J. and E. Sakellarakis 1979, pl. 183; 1991, fig. 120).

Closed heavy spirals continue to appear in the early stages of MM III on cups from Deposit B of the Acropolis Houses at Knossos (Catling *et al.* 1979, 28 fig. 18 V. 91–2) and from early neopalatial deposits at Phaistos (F. 354, 387; Borda 1946, 21 pl. XI 77437) and rounded bridge-spouted jars very much like Knossos type 6 at Phaistos (Pernier 1935, pl. XIX a, b).

White-spotted Style. This study uses the term 'White-spotted', as employed by Evans (1921, 417), to describe a style characterized by the use of consistent white spots on a dark ground, likened by Mackenzie to 'snow flake dots' (1901 PB, 51), applied with the tip of a fine brush so that there is rarely an overlap or running downward of the thick white paint. These may have been applied individually, as on **426**, or carefully sprayed as on **404–7**. Obviously, this definition can be problematic as sprayed, dabbed or otherwise applied white spots are found on pottery in many periods (Warren and Hankey 1989, 57). However, with caution and careful observation it is possible to distinguish those examples that Evans referred to and present a brief analysis.

This style is found on a Tumbler of Type 4 (**989**), Straight-sided Cups of Types 7 (**990**), 8 (**300–5**), 12 (**404–7, 423–6, 1044**), and 13 (**403**), Rounded Cups of Types 5 (**419–20, 1045**), and 7 (**413–16**), Short-rimmed Angular Cups of Type 3 (**409–10, 412, 991–2**), and a Jug with Horizontal Spout of Type 3 (**1042**). Its frequency in Group E (**299–305, 403–7, 409–16, 419–20, 423–6, 428–9**) and occurrence in Groups K (**818**), N (**989–93**) and P (**1042, 1044–5**) on late ceramic types, taken with its appearance in Deposits A and B at the Knossos Acropolis Houses (Catling *et al.* 1979, V. 49, 95–8) and in the group from an early excavation W of the palace (Hogarth and Welch 1901, 80 figs. 7–9, 12, 18–19), place this style largely in the MM III A period, as proposed by Evans (1921, 417). However, the examples from Group K and the Short-rimmed Angular Cups of Type 3 indicate that the style came into existence before the end of the MM II B period.

Rare in the Mesara (Betancourt 1990, no. 1796), examples were exported to Thera and Melos (Papagianopoulou 1991, nos. 278, 332).

Earlier pottery decorated with large white dots, (e.g. **630, 641**) or carelessly sprayed with white paint (e.g. **686**) are also distinct, but not sufficiently numerous to justify their being treated as a style. A possible survival into MM III B may be seen on three cups from Poros (Muhly 1992, nos. 35–7).

ii. A Formal Typology of the Fine Buff Pottery

A recent attempt at a typology of MM pottery (Walberg 1976) is based on variations in form and is practically useless to the archaeologist; for this reason no reference will be made to those types in this study. It is thought here to be more important to consider the function of a vase, rather than its overall form. Whether it was meant to pour liquids is given more relevance than whether it had a conical-ovoid shape. It has been shown

that the variations archaeologists frequently use to separate types of vases over centuries, can be accounted for in what time of day the pot was thrown. For example, a potter throwing rounded cups will begin with a freshly mixed batch of clay, and the earliest pots in the series will tend to sag and appear dumpy. As the clay dries out, the shape of the vase will become more firm and retain its intended shape (Van As 1984, 136). For this reason, the typology presented here pays little attention to minor variations in the form of a vase, but concentrates on similarities in production techniques, function and overall shape.

The following analysis applies primarily to the Fine Buff pottery of Knossos, although frequent reference is made to similar and related types at Phaistos from sound stratigraphical contexts. The object is to try to isolate 'type-fossils', that is distinctive and easily recognizable ceramic forms that occur most commonly in one archaeological period and can be used with the analyses of wares and styles to suggest relative dates for the Groups described in Chapter 1.

Shallow Bowl (FIG. 2.6)

The shallow bowl is relatively rare, occurring in only two types, one handmade the other thrown on the wheel. Both have a similar profile with outsplayed sides, flat rim and base.

Type 1 is handmade. The two examples in the catalogue (**18** and **24**) are 3.2 and 3.8 cm high; diameters are 9.4 and 16.0 cm at the rim and 5.0 cm at the base. One example is plain, the other monochrome coated. Both belong to Group A, which, taken with its occurrence in the Vat Room Deposit, suggests that this type may be assigned to the MM I B period at Knossos (Evans 1921, 167 fig. 118a.16; Momigliano 1991, 169, 173 fig. 4 pl. 24 no. 14). Similar bowls at Phaistos are most common in Period 1, contemporary with MM I B at Knossos (e.g. Levi 1976, pl. 36). However, the form originates in the EM II B pottery of Knossos and continues to be produced in EM III and MM I A and so cannot be taken as characteristic of any single period (Momigliano 1991, 252 Type 1).

Type 2 is a fine, wheelmade variant of Type 1 with slightly larger dimensions. There are two examples in the catalogue (**79** and **116**). Both are monochrome coated and **116** is also polychrome decorated. Both examples

Fig. 2.6. Fine Buff Shallow Bowl Types.

are in Group A and should be assigned to the MM I B period, though the sample is hardly enough to define the type as diagnostic. A common later variation of this type may be the Crude Bowl of Type 2 which begins in the MM II A period (see below p. 82).

Small Rounded Bowl with Tripod Feet
There are two examples of small, rounded, handmade bowls with a part of the rim pulled out to form a spout, two lugs on the rim and three bosses on the rounded underside that act as pods: **25** and **49**. Both examples are 4.5 cm high with diameters of 6.0 cm at the rim and 3.5 cm at the base. Both are monochrome coated and **49** is polychrome decorated. Both belong to Group A, and should be regarded as MM I B.

A possible later form of this type may be seen in a small spouted bowl with tripod feet of the MM II B period from the pit in Chamber Tomb XVII at Mavrospilio (Forsdyke 1927, 281 pl. 23 no. 27).

Rounded Goblet (FIG. 2.7)
A common form in the early deposits of the Old Palace is the Rounded Goblet, or 'Egg-cup', which occurs in three types.

Type 1 is handmade. It is formed by shaving or 'paring' the lower side and then attaching a rough strip of clay to form the base. The sixteen examples in the catalogue (1–7, **15**, **16**, **671** and **892–7**) are 6.0–7.0 cm high with diameters of 8.0 cm at the rim and 4.5 cm at the base. Eight examples have plain surfaces, five are dark-on-buff painted and three are monochrome coated. The type's frequency in Group A, and its use in Pared Ware suggest that it was in use during the MM I B period. This date is supported by an example from the Vat Room Deposit (Evans 1921, 167 fig. 118a.10; Momigliano 1991, 172 no. 1). The examples from Groups G and L could represent continued production in the MM II A period, or in the case of Group G could have come from an earlier, MM I B, floor. However, given the origins of Pared Ware in the MM I A

period, we must allow for the possibility of an earlier date for this type as well (Momigliano 1991, 264).

A related form, though lacking a foot, may be seen in some of the Period 1 'skutelia' from Phaistos (Fiandra 1973, 86–8 pl. 21; Levi 1976, pl. 35; Levi and Carinci 1988, pl. 99).

Type 2 has a wheelmade upper body attached to a handmade base. There are six examples in the catalogue (**110**, **162–3**, **682** and **918–19**, with heights of 7.4–7.8 cm, and diameters of 7.5–9.0 cm at the rim and 4.5–5.0 cm at the base. All the examples are monochrome coated on the upper part and have a distinctive thick white horizontal band added below the rim. The foot is plain but has drips of paint from the coating of the upper part. This type occurs in Groups A, B, G and L, which suggests that it spans both the MM I B and MM II A periods. Other examples are from the MM II A deposit in Early West Magazine 2 (Brown 1983, 68–9 figs. 36b, c).

Type 2 may be the successor to the EM III and MM I A footed goblet of Type 4 (Momigliano 1991, 247–8 n.285). It seems likely that it is the prototype for the Crude Goblet that becomes quite common during the MM II A period, see below p. 83.

Type 3 is the fine wheelmade variant of Types 1 and 2. None of the four examples in the catalogue (**111**, **226**, **925** and **976**) is complete, but the average dimensions of this type are likely to be 10.0–11.0 cm in height and diameters of 10.0–12.0 cm at the rim and 4.0–5.0 cm at the base. One example is monochrome coated and decorated in the White Banded Style, the others are in Pattern Painted Ware. There are also other decorated examples in the AM. The presence of two of the examples in Groups A and L and the use of this type in barbotine, **226**, and Early Printed Ware, **976**, indicate that the type begins in the MM I B period and likely continues into the MM II A period.

Two examples from Phaistos were found in what appear to be deposits of Period 2; one was below the floor in Vano CVII (F. 6506), the other below the floor in Room Gamma of Chalara South (F. 4378).

Fig. 2.7. Fine Buff Rounded Goblet Types.

The immediate predecessor for this type may be seen in goblets from House B beneath the West Court (Momigliano 1990, 483 fig. 1–4; 1991, pl. 54 no. 12) and the earliest floor beneath the Monolithic Pillar Basement (Mackenzie 1906, pl. 7 nos. 15 and 16), which may on stylistic grounds be assigned to late in the MM I A period. There is no comparable form from the later deposits at Knossos or elsewhere.

The Rounded Goblet is one of the characteristic forms found in the MM I B and MM II A deposits at Knossos. Hood (1971 a, 38 fig. 14) convincingly traces the development of the Minoan goblet from the EM I period; re-stated in detail by Momigliano (1990). The immediate predecessors of the goblets discussed here are the handmade dark-coated footed goblets of EM III and MM I A (Andreou 1978, 34–5; Momigliano 1991, 245–8). The example Hood uses to illustrate MM I B goblets is very similar to our Type 2 and thus could also be used to represent the form in MM II A.

Conical Goblet (FIG. 2.8)
Three types of goblet with conical profile of the body and pronounced outsplayed foot appear alongside the Rounded Goblets of the early stages of the Old Palace period.

Type 1 is handmade, but very fine. There are three examples in the catalogue (**609**, **610** and **899**). The average height is 6.0 cm, and diameters are 6.0 cm at the rim and 5.0 cm at the base. All three are monochrome coated and decorated in the Diagonal Red and White Style. Similar goblets are known from the Vat Room Deposit (Evans 1921, 167 figs. 118a.7, 120; Momigliano 1991, 172 pl. 23 no. 4), the Early Floor beneath the Room of the Stone Pier, PLATE 141, and there is an unpublished example from Knossos in the AM (1909.327). All are so similar that they must be the products of the same workshop. The examples in the catalogue belong to Groups F and L, which are primarily MM II A Groups with some earlier material. Given the relationship of this type to the following and the decoration on both, it would seem most sensible to place its manufacture in the MM I B period. A single conical goblet from Phaistos, decorated in rough barbotine, appears to be contemporary (F. 3014).

Type 2 is handmade and may be regarded as a large variant of Type 1. The lone example in the catalogue (**55**) is *c.* 21.0 cm high with diameters of 9.5 cm at the rim and 10.0 cm at the base. It is monochrome coated and decorated in the Diagonal Red and White Style like Type 1, and may come from the same workshop. It belongs to Group A and may be assigned to the MM I B period. The relative date may be confirmed by the discovery of a very fine goblet, probably of this type but decorated in horizontal zones, in the burnt MM I B deposit from the South-West Palace Angle (Catling 1988, 68—erroneously reported as MM II A egg-shell ware).

Two stone goblets with very similar profile, from Ayia Triada, are assigned to the MM III–LM I periods, but should perhaps now be regarded as survivors from MM I B (Warren 1969, 97–8).

Type 3 is wheelmade and quite fine. The three examples in the catalogue (**227**, **651** and **652**) are monochrome coated, with polychrome decoration. Although no complete example survives, the average height may be estimated at 11.0 and 12.0 cm, and rim diameters are 9.0 cm. The presence of two examples in Group F suggest a date within the MM II A period for this type.

The Conical Goblet may be taken as a 'type fossil' of the early stages of the Old Palace period, as it has no obvious immediate predecessors or successors.

Fig. 2.8. Fine Buff Conical Goblet Types.

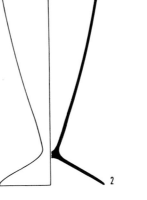
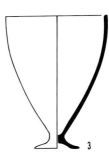

Momigliano suggests an origin for this type in the footed goblets of type 3 in the EM III pottery of Knossos (1991, 247), but the profile and foot construction are so distinct on the MM I B and MM II A examples, that the two types need not be related.

Tumbler (FIG. 2.9)
A common form in the deposits of the Old Palace period is the simple straight-sided tumbler, which occurs in four types.

Type 1 is handmade, occasionally with traces of shaving or paring on the lower exterior. The eight examples in the catalogue (**17, 52, 53, 175–7, 673** and **898**) are 3.0–7.0 cm high, with diameters of 4.0–8.0 cm at the rim and 2.0–3.5 cm at the base. Examples are dark-on-buff decorated, monochrome coated and monochrome coated with white and polychrome decoration.

This type may represent the continuation of the footless goblet of Type 1 of the EM III and MM I A pottery of Knossos (Momigliano 1991, 248 n.288). Its frequency in Group A, the use of the same reversed-3 motif on **53** and a jug from Period 1 at Phaistos (F. 2169), and the presence of an example in the Building 6/Tholos B deposit at Phourni (J. and E. Sakellarakis 1972, pl. 2 a) may indicate that this type was manufactured in MM I B; the isolated examples from Groups G and L being either survivors in MM II A contexts, or indicators of one or more MM I B floors in the Royal Pottery Stores. There are also three small examples from the deposit below the Room of the Stone Pier, but it is difficult to be certain of their fabric, as a very similar form occurs in Fine Red Fabric.

Type 2 is handmade and may be taken as the large variant of Type 1. There is a single example in the catalogue (**54**), which is incomplete but may have stood as high as 12.0 cm with a rim diameter of 8.0 cm. The surface is monochrome coated, with polychrome decoration. Its occurrence in Group A and its relation to Type 1 suggest that it should be assigned to the MM I B period.

Type 3 is the wheelmade version and likely successor to Type 1. The seven examples in the catalogue (**225, 633–5, 650, 807** and **817**) are 3.6–6.6 cm in height, with diameters 5.0–6.0 cm at the rim and 2.2–2.8 cm at the base. All are monochrome coated, with white or polychrome decoration. Evans assigned **807** to the MM I B period (1935, 98), but the presence of examples in Groups F and J may indicate a date within the MM II A period. This may also be the date for a similar example from Phaistos, although it comes from a mixed context (F. 4934).

Type 4 seems to be the wheelmade successor to Type 2 and the large equivalent for Type 3. The three examples in the catalogue (**169, 308**, and **989**) are 11.0–12.0 cm high, with diameters of 11.5 cm at the rim and 4.0–5.0 cm at the base. One example is decorated in the Polychrome Reserved Style. The others are monochrome coated, with white or polychrome decoration. The example from Group C is MM II A in date. **308** and **989** are from mixed contexts, which contain pottery of the MM II A period, but include later material and could represent the continuation of this type into MM II B.

The tumbler has a long history starting in the EM period (Warren 1972, fig. 53 P223–4). More common in Middle Minoan E Crete, where it was richly decorated (Bosanquet and Dawkins 1923, pls. IVa, c, X k–m; Betancourt 1983, fig. 19 no. 254; Walberg 1983, 8 form 38, 184 no. 203; MacGillivray, Sackett *et al.* 1992, 133 fig. 11.1–3; Stürmer 1993, no. 174), the form was simple enough to be copied by Knossian potters, although infrequently. The form also occurs in stone (Hankey 1980, pl. 76). A later development of Type 4 may be recognized in the 'chalice' form of the neopalatial period, well illustrated by MM III B examples from Palaikastro (MacGillivray *et al.* 1991, 135 fig. 12. 6–7).

Straight-sided Cup (FIG. 2.10)
The straight-sided, cylindrical or 'Vapheio' cup, most often with one vertical handle, is the most common

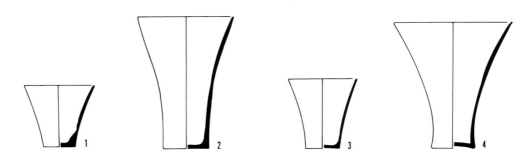

Fig. 2.9. Fine Buff Tumbler Types.

product of the central Cretan potters to be found in levels of the Old Palace period at Knossos. Among the numerous examples from Knossos, thirteen types may be distinguished on the basis of technological criteria and dimensions.

Type 1 is 'proto-wheelmade' with a strap handle and, in some cases, finished by shaving or paring the lower side. The eight examples in the catalogue (8–14 and 900) are 4.5–6.0 cm high, with diameters of 9.0–10.0 cm at the rim and 5.5–6.0 cm at the base. Seven examples are plain and one is smeared with dark paint. The frequency of this type in Group A suggests that it belongs to the MM I B period; confirmed by its frequency in the burnt deposit at the SW Palace Angle (Catling 1988, 68). Therefore, the single example in Group L should be regarded as a survivor in a MM II A context.

Type 2 is 'proto-wheelmade', with a slightly convex base and strap handle. There are forty-nine examples in the catalogue (20, 26–30, 37–41, 56–67, 153, 155–6, 173–4, 178–88, 611, 612, 674–5, 789, 790, 797, 1022–4 and 1026–7) and numerous others are known from Knossos. Examples are 3.05 cm high, with diameters of 5.0–9.6 cm at the rim and 4.0–7.0 cm at the base. They are buff-reserved decorated, monochrome coated, and monochrome coated, with white or polychrome decoration. The decoration is quite varied: it may consist of simple vertical or diagonal lines, wavy bands, or dot rosettes and floral motifs all in the Woven Style, a selection of which is given in FIG. 2.1. The fact that this type is proto-wheelmade, decorated in the Woven Style and found in great numbers in Groups A, I and O, strongly suggests that its period of manufacture was in MM I B. The examples in Groups B, F, G and J may indicate its continued production into the MM II A period.

Cups of this type have been found in the West Court (Momigliano 1991, 210 fig. 19 pl. 54 no. 123), the Northern Quarter of the City (ibid., 181, 184 fig. 6), the 'MM I Oikia' (ibid., 239–40 pl. 57 no. 1) and in Hogarth's Early Heap in the town of Knossos (Hogarth and Welch 1901, pl. VIIa, b). There were also examples from the rock-cut basement, to the N of a neopalatial house on Gypsades Hill, assigned to the MM I B period (Hood 1959, 19 fig. 29).

Elsewhere in central Crete similar cups are found at Phourni (J. and E. Sakellarakis 1972, pl. 5a) and Gournes (Zois 1969, pls. 27, 28a). The type is rare in the Mesara, there being only one example from Megaloi Skinoi (Vasilakis 1990, 44 fig. 14e) and one similar form, though in Barbotine Ware, from a period 1 context at Phaistos (F. 362). An example from Palaikastro had been assigned to the MM I A period (Bosanquet and Dawkins 1923, pl. IV g), and used to suggest an overlap between E Cretan MM I A and the early stages of the Old Palaces in Central Crete (Warren 1980, 491–2; Cadogan 1983, 513), but should now be regarded as belonging to

the MM I B or MM II A period at Palaikastro (MacGillivray and Driessen 1990, 399 n. 26). Examples from the Cyclades testify to Knossian products travelling far afield at this time (Papagianopoulou 1991, cat. 337–8).

Type 3 is 'proto-wheelmade' and serves as the large version of Type 2. The four examples in the catalogue (68, 189–91) are 6.5–9.0 cm in height, the diameters are 14.0–15.0 cm at the rim and 10.5–12.0 cm at the base. All are monochrome coated, with polychrome decoration in the Woven Style, of which a selection is given in FIG. 2.2, resembling those on Type 2 straight-sided cups. The similarity with Type 2 cups and the occurrence of one example in Group A suggest that this type belongs in the MM I B period.

Type 4 is fine and wheelmade, with a sharp edge at the base and lower side and no handle. The eight examples in the catalogue (80–6, 228) are 4.5–6.0 cm in height, diameters are 9.0–10.0 cm at the rim and 4.0–5.0 cm at the base. Seven examples are monochrome coated, one is monochrome coated, with polychrome decoration. The frequency of this type in Group A, and its absence in later groups, firmly place it in the MM I B period.

Type 5 is wheelmade and similar to Type 4, but has a strap handle added at the rim and lower side. The twelve examples in the catalogue (87, 112, 117, 269, 270, 281–2, 310–13, 653) are 5.0–7.0 cm in height, diameters are 8.5–12.0 cm at the rim and 5.5–11.0 cm at the base. One example is monochrome coated, the others are monochrome coated, with white or polychrome decoration. The occurrence of this type in Groups A, E, and F does not allow for a precise date, but indicates that the type came into being in the MM I B period and seems to have persisted without change throughout the Old Palace period.

Type 6 is wheelmade and the tall version of Type 5, having a similar strap handle attached at the rim and middle of the side. The 26 examples in the catalogue (88, 113, 118, 119, 229, 230, 263–6, 271–2, 278, 314, 318, 624–30, 636, 638–9, and 654) are 6.0–10.0 cm high, diameters are 8.0–13.0 cm at the rim and 5.0–7.0 cm at the base. Examples are dark-on-buff decorated, monochrome coated, and monochrome coated, with white or polychrome decoration. The occurrence of this type in Groups A, E and F, as with Type 5, allows for a long history beginning in the MM I B period to be suggested.

Type 7 is wheelmade with a slightly rounded profile at the base and lower side and strap handle attached at the rim and lower side. The ten examples in the catalogue (274, 303–5, 323, 329, 433, 990, 994, 1043) are 5.5–7.0 cm in height, diameters are 8.0–10.5 cm at the rim and 5.5–7.5 cm at the base. Examples are monochrome

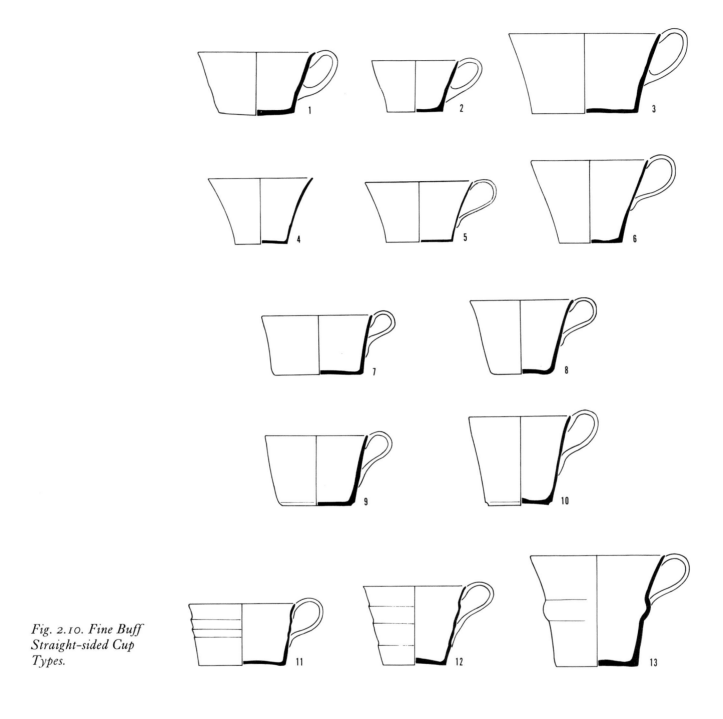

Fig. 2.10. Fine Buff Straight-sided Cup Types.

coated, with white or polychrome decoration. As most examples are from the mixed contexts of Groups E and N, the chronological position of this type could be MM II B or MM III A. Examples in the Starburst Style, (274) and the Spiral Band Style (323, 329) and its use by Precision Stamped Ware Cup (433), which also has a spiky foliate band, argue for its place in MM II B. The White-spotted Style decoration on 990 may be interpreted two ways: it could be used to argue for the continuation of this type into the MM III A period,

though there are no examples among the cups from the early deposits at the Knossos Acropolis Houses, or to suggest that the White-spotted Style originated in the MM II B period.

Type 8 is wheelmade and a tall counterpart for Type 7, having a slightly rounded profile at the base and strap handle at the rim and middle of the side. The seven examples in the catalogue (275, 279, 300–2, 333, 408) are 7.5–10.0 cm in height, diameters are 10.0–12.0 cm at the rim and 5.0–7.0 cm at the base. One example is monochrome coated, the remainder are monochrome coated and white decorated. All are in Group E and thus from a mixed context. However, many examples are decorated in styles that belong in the MM II B period: **275** is in Starburst Style, **333** is in the Spiral Band Style and **408** is in Precision Grooved Ware. Similar cups from Phaistos appear to come from Period 3 contexts and thus are contemporary (F. 1426, 1445, 1719, 1911, 2301a). **300–2** are in the White-spotted Style and can be compared with cups in Deposit B of the Knossos Acropolis Houses, most likely an indication that this type continues into the MM III A period (Catling *et al.* 1979, fig. 19 V. 53, 115).

Type 9 is wheelmade with a strap handle attached at the rim and lower side, and has a distinctive bevelled profile at the base and lower side. The 11 examples in the catalogue (**280, 284, 319–21, 326, 332, 335–7, and 1041**) are 6.0–7.0 cm in height, diameters are 8.0–12.5 cm at the rim and 5.0–6.0 cm at the base. All examples are monochrome coated and white or polychrome decorated. Most examples come from the mixed context of Group E. **280, 284** and **336–7** are decorated in the Sunrise Style most common at Phaistos on similar cup types in Period 2 (F. 441, 445, 801, 950a), but which may continue into Period 3 (F. 1911). **319–21** are in the Spiral Band Style and most likely to be placed in the MM II B period. K. 1010 is in the Starburst Style of MM II B. **332** is in the Heavy Spiral style, which originates in MM II B but becomes popular in MM III A.

This type, then, seems to have been most popular during the MM II B period. It may have been introduced during MM II A at Phaistos, as an example from Vano 11 shows (F. 443). There are no such early examples from Knossos, though the straight-sided cups, to accompany the Rounded Bridge-spouted Jars of Type 4, have not been found. An example from a well-stratified sequence of deposits at Palaikastro confirms that the type belongs to the later part of the Old Palace period in E Crete (MacGillivray *et al.* 1992, 136 fig. 13).

Type 10 is wheelmade with bevelled base and is the tall version of Type 9. The twenty examples in the catalogue (**223, 273, 277, 293–98, 315–17, 322, 327–8, 331, 338–9, and 996–7**) are 7.5–9.0 cm in height, diameters are 9.0–12.0 cm at the rim and 5.0–9.0 cm at the base. All are monochrome coated, with white or polychrome decoration. The numerous examples in Group E and the pair in Group N are from mixed contexts. However, **223** and **293–8** are in Late Printed Ware, which is most likely a direct development from Early Printed Ware and should be placed early in the MM II B period. This type is frequently decorated in styles of the MM II B period, for example **277, 338** and **996** are in the Starburst Style, **315–17, 322, 327–8, 331, 997** are in the Spiral Band Style. It is also a common type in the destruction deposits of Period 3 at Phaistos (Levi and

Carinci 1988, 205–11 pls. 88–9). The technique of tooling the base to create the bevel, however, may persist into the MM III A period, as examples from the Knossos Acropolis Houses show (Catling *et al.* 1979, fig. 18 V. 97, 19 V. 114, 118–19).

Type 11 is wheelmade with strap handle attached at the rim and lower side, and has horizontal grooves cut in the side creating ridges in the centre. The four examples in the catalogue (**423–6**) are 5.8 cm high, diameters are 9.2–9.5 cm at the rim and the base is 7.8 cm. All are monochrome coated and polychrome decorated in a manner very similar to each other and probably come from the same workshop. The four examples are in the mixed context of Group E. However, its close relationship to Type 12 cups and its decoration in the White-spotted style indicate that it belongs near the close of MM II B or early in MM III A.

A possible example of this type from Phaistos, unfortunately from a mixed deposit, would be the only instance of its occurrence outside of Knossos (Levi 1976, 477 fig. 730).

Type 12 is wheelmade with strap handle attached at the rim and middle of the side, and has a distinctive series of well-spaced horizontal grooves cut in the side at regular intervals, creating ridges. The six examples in the catalogue (**404–7, 1037, and 1044**) are 5.7–7.3 cm high, diameters are 9.0–11.5 cm at the rim and 5.6–8.0 at the base. All are monochrome coated with white or polychrome decoration. The type is very common in Group E, **404–7** represent only a fraction of the fragments from the context in the KSM, and to which might be added one in the AM (1938.458). **1044** in Group P, and the popularity of Ridged Ware and the White-spotted Style in the earliest deposits at the Knossos Acropolis Houses (Catling *et al.* 1979, fig. 18 V. 49 and 95–8; fig. 49 shape 17), place this type in the MM III A period. At least two examples, in a closed deposit near the Knossos North House, indicate that the type was first produced before the end of the MM II B period (Catling 1982, 53 fig. 116; Warren and Hankey 1989, 57). Some of the Group E examples, then, may be MM II B.

A cup very similar to Type 12 was found at Gournia and placed by the excavator 'On the borderline between Middle Minoan and Late Minoan times' (Boyd-Hawes *et al.* 1908, 38 pl. VI.34).

It is curious that this type does not occur in the Mesara—there is not a single example reported, yet the form is imported and imitated in E Crete and in Kea (Davis 1986, 81 pl. 28 U 79–82), Naxos (Barber and Hadjianastasiou 1989, 107 fig. 22 no. 420), Thera and Melos (Papagiannopoulou 1991, cat. no. 263, 340) in the Cyclades.

The metallic inspiration for the form may be best understood by comparing a gold cup from Grave Circle A at Mycenae with **407** (Hood 1978, 156 fig. 148 F; Matthäus 1980, pl. 75.9).

Type 13 is distinguished by a rounded horizontal bulge at the middle. The single example in the catalogue (**403**) comes from the mixed context of Group E. Its decoration in the White-spotted Style allows for a MM II B or MM III A date. However, its similarity to cups from a period 4 deposit in Vano LXXV at Phaistos (F. 3708) and from the Kamilari Tholos (F. 3202), which produced material of numerous periods including early MM III, make it most likely that the type was introduced in MM III A.

It is the obvious predecessor to the MM III B and LM I A 'Vapheio cup' with ripple decoration (e.g. Popham 1977, 193 fig. 1B; 1984, pls. 128a, 142 nos. 12–14; Catling *et al.* 1979, 41 fig. 27 V.186; Warren 1991a, fig. 9 K and L; Levi 1976, pl. 212r).

Convex-sided Cup
There are two examples of handmade cups with slightly convex profile, flat base and strap handle rising above the rim, **42** and **69**. They are 5.5 cm high, and diameters are 7.5 cm at the rim and 5.0 cm at the base. Both are monochrome coated and white or polychrome decorated, **69** with a pattern reminiscent of the Polychrome Geometric Style of late MM I A and **42** with a single closed spiral very similar to that on jug **48**. Both are in the late MM I B context of Group A, but may have been manufactured in the earlier stages of the period as suggested by examples from the Vat Room Deposit (Evans 1921, 167 fig. 118a.20; Momigliano 1991, 169, 173 fig. 4 no. 9), the Building 6/Tholos B deposit at Phourni (J. and E. Sakellarakis 1972, pls. D, Ea; 1991, 101 fig. 74), and Gournes (Zois 1969, pls. 27, 34).

The form is relatively unknown in S central Crete, there being only one example from the tomb at Tis Chatzinas to Liophyto, which contained pottery from the EM II to MM I B periods (Vasilakis 1990, 64–5 pl. 13b).

Tall-rimmed Angular Cup (FIG. 2.11)
Cups with high outsplayed rim and side, above a carination or angle near the base, are a feature of the earlier stages of the Old Palace at Knossos. Six types may be distinguished.

Type 1 is handmade and may be regarded as an angular companion to the Straight-sided Cup of Type 2.

Sub-class 1a has a flat base; 1b has a foot. The eight examples of Type 1a in the catalogue (**31–4**, **43**, **172**, **192**, **613**) are 4.0–5.0 cm high, diameters are 6.0–8.0 cm at the rim and 2.5–5.0 cm at the base. Examples are buff-reserved, monochrome coated and monochrome coated, with white or polychrome decoration. A reserved-painted example was found by Hogarth (Hogarth and Welch 1901, 90 fig. 20).

The three examples of Type 1b in the catalogue (**70**, **788**, **795**) are 4.5–6.2 cm high, diameters are 9.0 at the rim and 3.0–4.0 cm at the base. They are monochrome coated, and **70** has polychrome decoration and a pulled out spout at the rim. An example with two handles, from Hogarth's Early Heap in the town of Knossos, shows another variation of this type (Hogarth and Welch 1901, 91 fig. 21). Type 1 cups are found in Groups A, F, I and J and would appear to belong to both the MM I B and MM II A periods, although the examples in Groups F and J could well be survivors.

Examples from Phourni (J. and E. Sakellarakis 1972, pl. 5b) and Gournes (Zois 1969, pl. 28) most likely belong to the early stages of MM I B, while a very similar type from Phaistos comes from a Period 2, or MM II A, context (F. 3247).

Type 2 is handmade and is the large version of Type 1. There are four examples in the catalogue (**19**, **71–2**, **1025**), of which only the last is complete with foot, similar to that on Type 1b, perhaps indicating that this type needed such a support at the base. The average height is 7.0 cm, diameters are 11.0–13.0 cm at the rim and are 6.0 cm at the base. Examples are dark-on-buff, monochrome coated, and monochrome coated, with polychrome decoration. The occurrence of examples in Groups A and O, and the decoration on **71–2** in the Diagonal Red and White Style, suggest a date in the MM I B period for this type. A complete, undecorated example was found in the early MM I B deposit at Phourni (J. and E. Sakellarakis 1991, 101 fig. 74).

There are fragments of a very large version of the handmade tall-rimmed angular cup, in KSM #94 and HM 5738, but none could be restored to give an adequate profile. The fragments are decorated in a manner very similar to the Straight-sided cups of Type 3, for which they are most likely angular counterparts.

Type 3 is the wheelmade equivalent to Type 1. The two types are similar in profile, but the lower side of Type 3 is more often concave instead of the straight or convex profile of Type 1. The twelve examples in the catalogue (**89–95**, **114**, **231–2**, **756**, and **1032** are 3.5–6.1 cm high, diameters are 7.0–8.5 cm at the rim and 2.4–5.0 cm at the base. Examples are in Shallow Grooved Ware and monochrome coated, and monochrome coated, with white or polychrome decoration; **1032** has a crinkled rim. The form's occurrence in Groups A and O suggests that it belongs in the MM I B period. The example in Group H may be a survivor. An example from a group of sherds, used to date the construction of the Early Keep, was assigned by Branigan to the MM II period (1992, 160 fig. 2.5). However, it may now be accepted to belong with the rest of the material it was found with, and indicate that the cutting, into which the Early Keep was built, took place in MM I B.

There is an example in the early MM I B group at Gournes (Zois 1969, pls. 25–6), but similar cups at Phaistos seem to come from Period 2 contexts (e.g. F. 186, 405, 424, 430, 434, 695, 1397 a,b, 4935a, 4944a; Fiandra 1980, pl. 43.2) contemporary with MM II A at Knossos.

Type 4 is wheelmade, and distinguished by its very high upper side and rim as compared with the lower side. It has a strap handle probably rising above the rim and a flat base. The two examples in the catalogue (**170** and **656**) are 6.5 cm high, diameters are 9.0 cm at the rim and 3.5 cm at the base. Both are monochrome coated and polychrome decorated. The examples are in Groups C and F, and thus most likely belong in the MM II A period. The decoration on **170** is very similar to a rounded bridge-spouted jar like Type 4 from Phaistos (F. 426). Both pieces are probably contemporary and may even originate from the same workshop.

Similar cups are most often found in deposits of Period 2 at Phaistos (e.g. F. 398, 429, 435, 446, 447, 1427, 2297a, 2604, 4904, 5063, 5420) which complements the Knossos date and suggest a likely place of origin for **170** and **656** in the Mesara.

Type 5 is wheelmade with a distinctive convex profile on the lower side. The two examples in the catalogue (**907–8**) are *c.* 6.5 cm high, diameters are 11.0 and 13.0 cm at the rim and 4.2 and 5.3 cm at the base. Both are monochrome coated and belong to Group L, which should allow for this type to be placed in the MM II A period. A similar type in E Crete seems to occur at the same time (MacGillivray *et al.* 1992, figs. 10.1, 12.2–3).

Type 6 is a wheelmade counterpart to Type 2. It has an indented base, strap handle, attached at the rim and above the angle in the side, and a concave profile at the lower side. The two examples in the catalogue (**657–8**)

are monochrome coated, with polychrome decoration. The examples belong to Group F, which indicates that this type belongs in the MM II A period at Knossos.

Examples of this type at Phaistos appear to belong in Period 2 (e.g. F. 277, 399, 420, 436, 974, 1996, 3423, 5410; Fiandra 1980, pl. 38. 1–4), which conforms with the Knossos date for the type, and again suggests a likely origin for **657–8** in the Mesara, where their decoration would be more at home than at Knossos.

The Tall-rimmed Angular Cup belongs to the groups of the MM I B and MM II A periods at Knossos. Types 1–3 seem to belong, for the most part, in MM I B, while Types 4–6 belong to the MM II A period. There are no examples in the later groups, so the type may not have survived the MM II A destruction in the palace. A similar situation may be observed at Phaistos, though largely obscured by Levi's publication of the finds from the SW Block of the palace. The situation may be remedied by re-establishing the primary deposits using Fiandra's definitions of the periods (see below, pp. 99–102).

Short-rimmed Angular Cup (FIG. 2.12)
Cups, with angular profile and a short outsplayed rim above a high lower side, are found in three types.

Type 1 is wheelmade with a strap handle attached at the rim and angle and has a simple foot. The three examples in the catalogue (**98, 759** and **804**) are 3.7–5.3

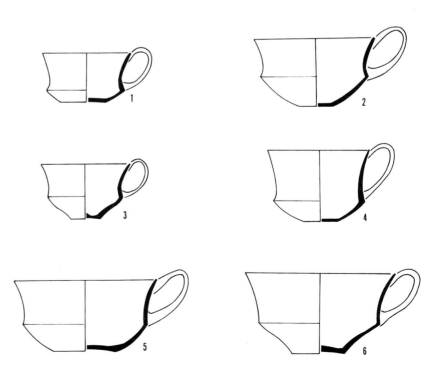

Fig. 2.11. Fine Buff Tall-rimmed Angular Cup Types.

cm high, diameters are 7.2–10.0 cm at the rim and 3.0–4.5 cm at the base. All are monochrome coated and two are also decorated in white. The example in Group A shows that the type begins in the MM I B period. Those in H and J could indicate that the type continues into the MM II A period, or could be survivors.

Type 2 is wheelmade with a strap handle attached at the rim and angle and a high foot. Two sub-types may be distinguished: 2a has a plain foot, 2b has a moulded foot. The twenty-four examples in the catalogue (**99, 100, 101, 203–07, 677–81, 802–3,** and **909–17**) are 4.5–8.0 cm high, diameters are 7.0–17.0 cm at the rim and 4.0–6.0 cm at the base. The five examples from Group D are buff-reserved decorated, the remainder are monochrome coated. The examples in Group A, and the frequent occurrence of this type in the burnt deposit at the SW Palace Angle (Catling 1974, 34; 1988, 68), indicate that this type begins in the MM I B period. The numerous examples in Groups G, J and L seem to show that it continued into the MM II A period, as does a related form at Phaistos (F. 187, 3520, 4358).

Type 3 is wheelmade with a strap handle attached at the rim and below the slight angle, formed by tooling. The six examples in the catalogue (**409–12, 991–2**) are 8.5–10.0 cm high, diameters are 10.0–13.5 cm at the rim and 4.5–5.0 cm at the base. All are monochrome coated and most are also decorated in the White-Spotted Style. The occurrence of this type in Groups E and N does not allow for a firm date. However, the quality of the surface treatment and the fine tooling, to create the ridge below the rim, are quite similar to those on Straight-sided Cups of Type 12; they give the impression of both types having been manufactured in the same workshop. The problems associated with dating the straight-sided cup are shared with this type, however, the mention of an example from a MM II deposit in the Stratigraphical Museum excavations (Catling 1982, 53), suggests that this type belongs in the MM II B period, contemporary with a closely related form in Period 3 at Phaistos (F. 534, 4687, 6054).

A formal development may be traced in the short-rimmed angular cup. Type 1 is characteristic of MM I B. Type 2 spans the MM I B and MM II A periods. Type 3 represents the latest version of the form in MM II B, as there seems not to be a MM III A successor.

It would be useful to try to place the Karmi Cup in this sequence (Stewart 1962, 202 fig. 8 pl. VIIa–d). None of the Knossian examples has barbotine on the angle, but the barbotine on the Shallow Angular Bowls of Type 2 is very similar, and the decoration on the Karmi Cup is quite similar to that on the fine Type 2 cups from the Group D, e.g. on **203** and **211**. It would best fit, then, in either MM I B or MM II A and is unlikely to be later, or earlier.

Squat Rounded Cup (FIG. 2.13)
Two types of wheelmade cup with squat rounded profile are found in the early groups.

Type 1 has a simple profile with slightly outsplayed rim, strap handle attached at the rim and lower side and flat base. The six examples in the catalogue (**104–6, 121–2, 975**) are 5.5–8.0 cm high, diameters are 6.5–9.5 cm at the rim and 2.5–5.0 cm at the base. Examples are buff-reserved decorated, monochrome coated and monochrome coated, with polychrome decoration. The five examples in Group A confirm that the type belongs in the MM I B period at Knossos.

Two very similar examples from Phaistos were found with material of Period 2 under Vano CVII, and may show that the type continued to the end of the MM II A period there (F. 6448, 6485).

There is a strong resemblance between this type and one of the cup forms in the 'Tôd Treasure' (Bisson de la Roque *et al.* 1953, pls. XII 70580, XIII 70583), see below pp. 103–04.

Type 2 is similar in profile to Type 1 but has a horizontal step or flange in the middle. The two examples in the catalogue (**107** and **123**) are 7.5 and 9.9 cm high, diameters are 7.5 and 8.3 cm at the rim and 4.5–5.5 cm

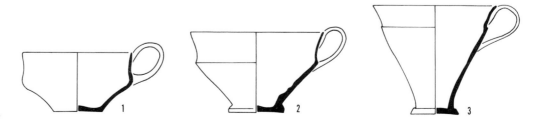

Fig. 2.12. Fine Buff Short-rimmed Angular Cup Types.

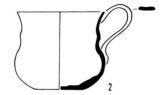

Fig. 2.13. Fine Buff Squat Rounded Cup Types.

at the base. Both are monochrome coated and **123** also has polychrome decoration. Both examples are in Group A, which shows that the type belongs in the MM I B period.

Rounded Cup (FIG. 2. 14)

The rounded, semi-globular or hemispherical one-handled cup enjoys a long history at Knossos and appears in six general types in the Old Palace period.

Type 1 is handmade, with simple profile and a strap handle attached at the rim, rising above it and connecting in the middle of the side. There are two sub-classes. 1a has a simple, flat base, 1b has a slightly raised and moulded base. There are three examples of Type 1a in the catalogue (**22**, **44** and **754**, that are from 5.2–5.8 cm high, diameters are 8.5–9.0 cm at the rim and 4.0–5.0 cm at the base. They are buff reserved decorated, monochrome coated and monochrome coated, with white decoration. Type 1b has two examples in the catalogue (**45** and **902**). They are 5.5 cm high, diameters are 8.0 and 8.3 at the rim and 4.5–5.2 cm at the base. One is dark-on-buff decorated, the other is monochrome coated, with white decoration. Hogarth found a third example of this sub-type in his Early Heap group in the town of Knossos (Hogarth and Welch 1901, 91 fig. 23). The occurrence of this type in Group A would suggest that it belongs in the MM I B period, perhaps to the earlier part of the period, as suggested by the presence of an example in the Building 6/Tholos B group at Phourni (J. and E. Sakellarakis 1991, 101 fig. 74). However, it is almost indistinguishable from the One-handled Cups of Types 1 and 2 from EM III and MM I A contexts at Knossos (Momigliano 1991, 249–51). The examples in Groups H and L may be regarded as survivors from the MM I period, or the last in a long line that saw very little change.

Type 2 is handmade, with offset rim, rounded bulge in the profile of the upper side, and a strap handle attached at the rim and widest part of the body. The only example in the catalogue is **35**, which is monochrome coated and belongs to Group A, suggesting a date in MM I B for the type.

This type is a direct descendant of the EM III–MM I A One-handled Cup of Type 5 (ibid., 251) and may be a handmade equivalent to the more common Rounded-cup of Type 3. The form in stone is illustrated by a serpentine cup from the Patema ossuary at Palaikastro (Warren 1969, 40 P227).

Type 3 is wheelmade and similar in profile to Type 2, but with a concave profile on the lower side and the base is usually indented. The 19 examples in the catalogue (**109**, **125–6**, **209**, **221**, **236**, **618–23**, **631**, **643–6**, **805** and **921**) are 6.5–8.0 cm high, diameters are 8.0–14.0 cm at the rim and 3.7–5.0 cm at the base. One example is buff reserved decorated, the others are monochrome coated, with white or polychrome decoration. Examples in Egg-shell Ware (**618–23**) and Early Printed Ware (**631**) and the occurrence of examples in Groups A, F, J and L indicate that the type spans the MM I B and MM II A periods, but does not continue into MM II B. This may also be the case at Phaistos, where the closest parallels for this type are from a Period 2 context in Room XCIV (F. 4817b, 5017, 5421a–d)

Type 4 appears to be the wheelmade variant and possible successor to Type 1, but with slightly out-turned rim. It is distinguished from Type 3 by the globular profile of the lower side. The 11 examples in the catalogue (**108**, **210**, **616–17**, **642**, **661**, **799–801**, **922**, and **978**) are 6.0–8.0 cm high, diameters are 8.8–12.5 cm at the rim and 3.5–5.5 cm at the base. One example is buff reserved decorated, the others are monochrome coated and most examples have white or polychrome decoration. The frequency of examples in Groups A, F, J, L and M indicate that it belongs in both the MM I B and MM II A periods, with the finest examples, **799–801**, occurring in Egg-shell ware.

Type 5 is wheelmade and appears to be a development of Type 3, with a less pronounced base and lower side, but retaining the same offset rim and rounded bulge in the profile of the upper side. The 30 examples in the catalogue (**237–8**, **240–1**, **285–6**, **370–6**, **417–21**, **436–44**, **987** and **1039**) are 5.0–8.0 cm high, diameters are 11.0–17.0 cm at the rim and 4.5–5.5 cm at the base. Examples are monochrome coated and monochrome coated, with white and polychrome decoration. The large number of examples attest to its popularity at Knossos. Most are from the mixed deposits of Groups D, E and N but, as examples are in Precision Stamped

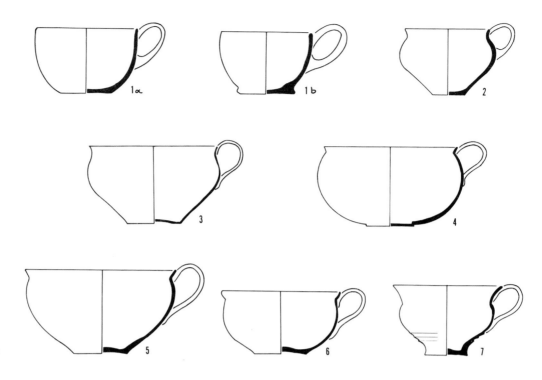

Fig. 2.14. Fine Buff Rounded Cup Types.

Ware (**237, 436–44**), Precision Grooved Ware (**987, 417–21**) and the Spiral Banded (**372**) and Heavy Banded (**240–1**) styles, the type can be assigned to the MM II B period, with the possibility of its continued use in the early stages of MM III A. Type 5, then, may be the MM II B successor to Type 3.

The striking similarity between **369–70** and cups from the final MM II B destruction in Vano VIII at Phaistos (Pernier 1935, 233 fig. 110) indicates that they almost certainly come from the same source, presumably somewhere in central Crete.

Type 6 is wheelmade and seems to be a development of Type 4. It continues to have a rounded profile on the lower side, but now has a slightly raised foot and wider mouth. The 32 examples in the catalogue (**239, 242, 340–68** and **998–9**) are mostly fragments. Diameters are 9.0–14.0 cm at the rim and 3.0–5.0 cm at the base. All are monochrome coated and decorated with wavy-lines and polychrome filling elements in the Wavy-line Style. A selection showing a variety of patterns is given in FIG. 2. 5. The numerous examples are from the mixed contexts of Groups E and N. However, very similar cups, with Wavy-line Style decoration, are found in the MM II B destruction deposits at Phaistos, and provide a firm date for both the type and the style (F. 521, 527,

1430, 6018, 6147, 6148; Pernier 1935, pl. 21a; Levi 1976, pl. 64). This is confirmed by an example from Anemospilia near Archanes (Sakellarakis 1979, pl. 183b; 1991, 144 fig. 120).

This 'wavy-line cup' may be the successor to the cups of Type 4 in Egg-shell Ware, which do not seem to have been produced after the MM II A period. A possible successor to this MM II B version may be seen in a MM III cup type from Kommos (Betancourt 1990, fig. 38 no. 790). Later still is the rounded cup, decorated in the Finicky Style of the MM III B period (Evans 1921, 595 fig. 437c–e), two examples of which are illustrated in PLATE 58.

These distinctive cups are one of the most popular central Cretan ceramic products to be exported during MM II B. Examples are found at Palaikastro (Bosanquet and Dawkins 1923, 16 fig. 10) Phylakopi (Papagiannopoulou 1991, nos. 346, 359, 361), Kea (Overbeck 1989, 182 pl. 85 DG. 16), Ugarit (Schaeffer 1949, 256 fig. 109A) and Tell el-Dab'a (Walberg 1991, 117 pls. 1–2; MacGillivray 1995).

Type 7 is wheelmade, has a sharply offset rim and stands on a raised base. The four examples in the catalogue (**413–16**) are 6.5 cm high, diameters are 9.0–10.0 cm at the rim and 4.0 and 4.6 cm at the base. All are from the mixed context of Group E, but are in Precision Grooved Ware and decorated in the White-spotted Style. The form is not found in the Period 3 deposits at Phaistos, but also does not appear in the MM III A groups from the town and acropolis at Knossos. It seems that this type was produced for a short time, either at the very end of the Old Palace period, or early in MM III A.

Shallow Angular Bowl
Two types of shallow bowl, with angular profile, vertical handles and spouts at either end, are found in the early groups of the Old Palace.

Type 1 is handmade, with loop handles and a raised outward splayed base. There is a complete example, **50**, and a rim fragment, **51**, that could come from this type of bowl. Both are monochrome coated and polychrome decorated, **50** in the Woven Style, and both belong in Group A, which suggests a date in MM I B for this type.

Type 2 is wheelmade with a crinkle rim, cylindrical lambda-shaped handles on the upper side and flat base. The three examples in the catalogue (**662, 926–7**) are 5.0–5.5 cm high, diameters are 14.0–16.0 cm at the rim and *c.* 5.5 cm at the base. All are monochrome coated and polychrome decorated, and **926–7** are in Barbotine Ware. The examples are in Groups F and L, which indicates a date in the MM II A period for this type, which may, therefore, be the successor to Type 1.

Pyxis
Small open vases, evidently designed to receive lids, are found in six types.

Type 1 is wheelmade with a simple straight-sided profile and flat base. There are two examples in the catalogue (**648–9**); both are monochrome coated, with white decoration, **648** in the White-banded Style, and belong to Group F, which supplies a date in the MM II A period for this type.

Type 2 is wheelmade, with a distinctive out-turned rim, a slight groove in the upper side below the rim and two horizontal handles at the middle of the side. The single example in the catalogue (**924**) is monochrome coated, decorated in the White-banded Style and belongs to Group L, all of which place it in the MM II A period.

Type 3 is wheelmade and has a distinctive angular profile, outward turned rim and two horizontal lugs on the side. The three examples in the catalogue (**676, 762** and **806**) are 5.5–6.3 cm high, diameters are 8.5–9.5 cm at the rim and 3.0–4.0 cm at the base. All are monochrome coated, with white or polychrome decoration, **806** in the White-banded Style. The examples are in Groups G, H and J and so the type belongs in the MM II A

period. A pyxis of this type, found on the early floor beneath the Room of the Stone Pier (PLATE 141), further confirms the MM II A date.

Type 4 is wheelmade, with a wide flat rim, two horizontal handles at the middle of the side and a slightly bevelled base. The two examples in the catalogue (**757** and **760**) are 5.2–5.5 cm high, diameters are 11.0–12.0 cm at the rim and 7.5–9.0 cm at the base. Both are monochrome coated and **760** is decorated in the White-banded Style. Both are from Group H and there is a third example from the early floor beneath the Room of the Stone Pier (PLATE 141), all of which suggest a date in the MM II A period for this type.

Type 5 is small and wheelmade, with a flattened, outsplayed rim, two imitation lugs on the side and an indented base. The two examples in the catalogue (**287–8**) are 3.3 and 3.5 cm high, diameters are 8.0 and 9.0 cm at the rim and 5.5 and 6.0 cm at the base. Both are monochrome coated and decorated with white horizontal lines. Both are from the mixed context of Group E and so difficult to date with certainty. However, the type's general resemblance to the Crude Pyxis of Type 1, a form of the MM II A period, and with a vase stratified below the MM II B destruction deposit in Trial KV (Popham 1974, 185 fig. 5.2), may indicate that it belongs near the end of the MM II A period.

Type 6 has a pronounced indent below the rim, two horizontal handles on the side and a bevelled base. It may be a developed form of Type 2. The lone example in the catalogue (**289**) is monochrome coated and decorated with horizontal white lines. It bears a resemblance to the Crude Pyxis of Type 2, but both forms belong to the mixed Group E and may not be dated conclusively. As it seems to be a developed form of Type 2, a date in MM II B may be put forward tentatively.

Angular Bridge-spouted Jar (FIG. 2.15)
Bridge-spouted or Hole-mouthed Jars with angular profile occur in two types in the early groups of the Old Palace period.

Type 1 is handmade with two cylindrical lambda-shaped handles on the shoulder. Two sub-types may be distinguished. Type 1a has a simple, tapering lower side and flat base. Type 1b has a moulded, slightly raised base. The two examples of Type 1a in the catalogue (**36** and **755**) are 10.0–10.3 cm high, diameters are 10.3–11.0 cm at the rim and 5.0–5.7 cm at the base. Both are monochrome coated. The four examples of Type 1b in the catalogue (**796** and **903–5**) are 9.8–13.5 cm high, diameters are 9.0–12.0 cm at the rim and 4.5–6.0 cm at the base. One is dark-on-buff decorated, the others are monochrome coated and **905** is decorated in the Diagonal Red and White Style. The occurrence of Type 1 jars in Groups A, H, J and L confirms that it belongs within the MM I B and MM II A periods.

Type 2 is handmade and a large version of Type 1, but with a distinctive thickened and flat rim. The six examples of this type in the catalogue (**75**, and **193–7**) are fragmentary, but the average dimensions may be roughly 17.0 cm in height with rim diameters 12.0–14.0 cm and base diameters 8.0–10.0 cm. All six examples are monochrome coated and decorated in the Woven Style, the variety of the decorative patterns is shown in FIG. 2.3. The almost complete example from Group A and the type's exclusive use of the Woven Style place it in the MM I B period.

There is a rim fragment from a jar of this type from the North Quarter of the City (Momigliano 1991, 181 fig. 6.36) and three fragmentary examples without specific provenance from Knossos in the Ashmolean Museum (AE 959 and AE 1032.1) and the British Museum (Forsdyke 1925, A486), also decorated in the Woven Style.

This type seems to be confined to the Knossos area, there being also at least one example from Juktas (Karetsou 1981 *b*, 144 fig. 8 nos. 6). Angular bridge-spouted jars are almost unknown in the Mesara; there being only one possible example from Phaistos (F. 264) as well as a stone variant (F. 6245). The examples from Phylakopi are, thus, quite likely to be Knossian in origin (Papagiannopoulou 1991, nos. 382, 386).

Squat Rounded Bridge-spouted Jar

There are two examples, **73–4**, of handmade bridge-spouted jars with rounded bulge in the profile of the lower body, giving a squat appearance, two cylindrical lambda-shaped handles and simple flat base. The one intact example (**73**) is 8.5 cm high with rim and base diameter of 7.5 cm. Both examples are monochrome

coated, decorated in the Woven Style and belong to Group A, which places them in the MM I B period.

Baggy-shaped Bridge-spouted Jar

Two fragments of bridge-spouted jars, with outsplayed and overhanging rims, cylindrical rounded handles and bag-shaped profiles, are in the catalogue (**390–1**). The shape of this type is reconstructed on the basis of close parallels from Phaistos (F. 806). Both Knossian examples are monochrome coated and polychrome decorated, **390** in the Spiral Band Style. They come from the mixed context of Group E, but the close correspondence to the Period 3 examples at Phaistos suggest a date in the MM II B period (F. 499, 806). An example in stone was found in a chamber tomb at Mycenae, where it was surely an heirloom (Xenaki-Sakellariou 1985, pl. 141 no. 4921).

Rounded Bridge-spouted Jar (FIG. 2.16)

Bridge-spouted jars with rounded profile occur in six general types.

Type 1 is a short, handmade jar with the spout pointing above the rim and cylindrical lambda-shaped handles. The single, well-preserved example in the catalogue (**157**) is 7.5 cm high with a rim diameter of 7.0 cm and base diameter of 8.7 cm. It is monochrome coated and white decorated and belongs to Group B, which suggests that this type should belong in the MM II A period.

Type 2 is handmade, with a tapering lower side, flat base, raised rim and spout rising above the rim. The handles were probably cylindrical and lambda-shaped. The only preserved height is 10.0 cm. Diameters are 8.0 and 10.0 cm at the rim and 5.5 and 10.5 cm at the base. The four

Fig. 2.15. Fine Buff Angular Bridge-spouted Jar Types.

examples in the catalogue (**46–7** and **76–7**) are mono-chrome coated and decorated in the Woven Style and, as they are part of Group A, should be assigned to the MM I B period.

Type 3 is an elegant, wheelmade equivalent to Type 2, with distinctive pointed handles that are triangular in section. There are two examples in the catalogue (**127** and **247**). The one restored example, **247**, is 12.0 cm high. Diameters are 8.8 cm at the rim and 6.7 cm at the base. Both examples are in Pattern Painted Ware. The fragmentary example in Group A may indicate the type's beginning in the MM I B period, though it seems to belong in both periods 1 and 2 at Phaistos (e.g. Levi 1976, 144 fig. 215; Levi and Carinci 1988, pl. 53) and so may have continued into MM II A.

Type 4 is a wheelmade jar, with tall tapering base, rounded shoulder, spout rising only slightly above the rim and thick, rounded handles with a roughly rectangular section. There are 33 examples in the catalogue (**290–1, 665, 688** and **930–58**). They are 13.5–15.5 cm high. Diameters are 7.5–9.5 cm at the rim and 5.0–6.0 cm at the base. Examples are monochrome coated and white or polychrome decorated. The frequency of examples in Group L and its occurrence also in Groups F and G indicate a MM II A date for the type.

Among the numerous examples in Group L, work-shop groups may be suggested (MacGillivray 1985). It is quite likely that this type and the next were fitted with lids, as seen on the stone copy from Mycenae (Xenaki-Sakellariou 1985, pl. 97 no. 3050). Lids similar to **684** would fit well on this type of vase.

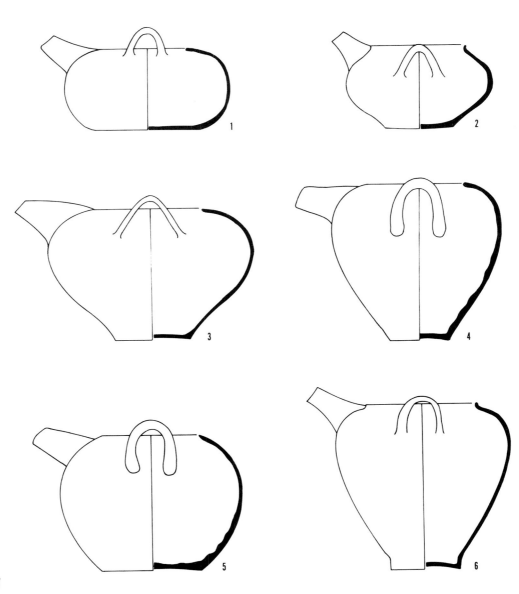

Fig. 2.16. Fine Buff Rounded Bridge-spouted Jar Types.

Type 5 is wheelmade with a bulbous profile, spout rising above the rim, and handles very much like those on Type 4. There are ten examples in the catalogue (379–88). They are 10.5–12.0 cm high. Diameters are 7.5–10.0 cm at the rim and 5.6 cm at the base. All are monochrome coated and polychrome decorated, and are from the mixed context of Group E. Its use with the Sunrise, 385–7, and Spiral Band, 379–84, styles indicates popularity during MM II B. A similar form decorated with sunrise motifs, from Context 19 at Kommos, could be a MM III A development to the type (Betancourt 1990, no. 822). Examples in stone, probably heirlooms and certainly imports, were found in chamber tombs at Mycenae (Xenaki-Sakellariou 1985, pls. 97 no. 3050, 141 no. 4922).

Type 6 is wheelmade, with a tall profile tapering towards the base, slightly raised rim, spout rising above the rim and handles like those on types 4 and 5. There are two examples in the catalogue (389 and 1002). They are 14.2 and 15.0 cm high, diameters are 9.8 and 16.5 cm at the rim and 6.5 and 6.6 cm at the base. Both are monochrome coated and polychrome decorated, but neither in any of the distinctive styles. The occurrence of these examples in Groups E and N place the type at the end of the Old Palace period, confirmed by a single example from the destruction deposit in Trial KV (Popham 1974, 188 fig. 7.2, pl. 29a). The very similar rounded bridge-spouted jar from a grave in Byblos, decorated in the Wavy-line Style, further confirms a MM II B date (Baramki 1973, pl. IV. 1).

In general, the rounded bridge-spouted jar of MM III stands on an elongated foot (Betancourt 1985 a, 106 fig. 77; Levi and Carinci 1988, pl. 58). Miniature jar 377 conforms to the MM III type and could be one of the latest items in Group E.

Jug with Cut-away Spout (FIG. 2. 17)

Four types of jug with cut-away spout may be distinguished.

Type 1 is handmade, with a squat profile and flat handle. There are three examples in the catalogue (23, 48 and 199). They are 10.0–11.0 cm high, with base diameters of 6.5 and 7.5 cm. They are buff-reserved decorated and monochrome coated, with white or polychrome decoration. The two examples in Group A suggest that this type belongs in the MM I B period. This is further confirmed by the presence of an example in Hogarth's Early Heap, S of the West Court (Hogarth and Welch 1901, pl. VIc). Hogarth's group also contained a Straight-sided cup of Type 2 (ibid., pl. VIIb). The decoration on Convex-sided Cup 42 and Jug 48 is so similar that they may come from the same workshop, thus suggesting that this type belongs early in MM I B.

Type 2 is wheelmade, with a large opening at the rim. There is one example in the catalogue (1034), which belongs to Group O. Another example was found on the early floor beneath the Room of the Stone Pier (PLATE 141 bottom, far right), which may place this type in the MM II A period.

Type 3 is wheelmade with a rounded body, tall spout and strap handle. There is one example in the catalogue (250) and the possible bases of others from the same context are visible in PLATE 51, top left. As the example belongs to Group D, it cannot be assigned to a specific period, though the majority of the material from the North-West Pit should be taken as MM II A on stylistic grounds.

The decoration on 250 is so similar to that on a Rounded Bridge-spouted Jar of Type 4 from Kahun that they should be regarded as products of the same workshop; in which case the most likely date for the type is in the MM II A period (Kemp and Merrillees 1980, 57–9 fig. 22 Ha. 1).

Type 4 is wheelmade, with a tall shape, tapering lower body and three strap handles attached at the rim and middle of the side. There are two examples in the catalogue (687 and 988). The restored example, 988, is 17.5 cm high, base diameters are 3.5 and 4.0 cm. Both examples are monochrome coated and white decorated. They belong to Groups G and N, which provides a date in the MM II A period for its start and the end of the Old Palace period for its finish, the latter confirmed by an example from Anemospilia (J. and E. Sakellarakis 1979, pl. 183). A possible third example, from the context of Group N, is shown in PLATE 144 *d*.

Jug with Horizontal Spout (FIG. 2.18)

There are three general types of rounded jugs with horizontal spouts.

Type 1 is wheelmade, with a long, cylindrical neck and rounded handle. There are three examples in the catalogue (685–6 and 825). They are 9.0–10.0 cm high. Diameters are 3.5–4.0 cm at the base and 2.9–3.8 cm at the rim. The examples are monochrome coated and white or polychrome decorated. The occurrence of this type in Group G suggests that it should belong in the MM II A period. The example from Group K, then, may belong to the early group of pottery from the Loomweight Basement, see above Chapter 1, Part 5.

Type 2 is wheelmade with a slightly squat rounded body and rounded handle pushed into the rim. There is one example in the catalogue (928) in Group L, suggesting that this type originates in the MM II A period. A similar jug, with very similar decoration, is known from

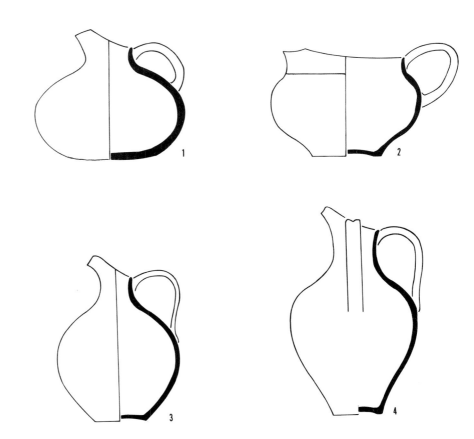

Fig. 2.17. Fine Buff Jug with Cut-away Spout Types.

Hogarth's Later Heap in the town of Knossos; it could be an heirloom or may show continuity of the type into the MM III A period (Hogarth and Welch 1901, fig. 18). A third example, in the Liverpool Museum, is from Knossos but without more detailed provenance (Mee and Doole 1993, no. 55.66.77).

Type 3 is wheelmade, with a tapering lower body and rounded handle pushed well into the rim of the spout, causing an indent. There are two examples in the cata-logue (**1040** and **1042**). They are 11.0 and 15.5 cm high, with base diameters of 3.3 and 4.5 cm. Both are mono-chrome coated and **1042** is decorated in the White-spot-ted Style. Both belong to Group P which places the type in the MM III A period. Further confirmation for the date comes from an example in the White-spotted Style, from Hogarth's Later Heap in the town of Knossos (Hogarth and Welch 1901, 90 fig. 19), and by the occurrence of a very similar form in Deposit C in the Knossos Acropolis Houses (Catling *et al.* 1979, 35 fig. 23 V.154).

Fig. 2.18. Fine Buff Jug with Horizontal Spout Types.

Rhyton

Fragments of two types of rhyton appear in the later groups from the Old Palace.

Type 1 is conical, with a flat rim, strap handle and metallic-like rounded additions at the rim. There are three examples in the catalogue (**395–7**). The height may be suggested by the reconstruction of **395** to be roughly 27.0 cm. Rim diameters are 7.5 and 8.0 cm. All three examples are in Pattern Painted Ware and from the mixed context of Group E. A MM II B date could be proposed because of the similarity of the decoration on **395** with that on a straight-sided cup in Precision Stamped Ware from a MM II floor deposit near the Knossos North House (Warren 1981, 74 fig. 3). However, very similar forms appear in Period 4 at Phaistos (F. 4263, 5778) and in MM III contexts at Kommos (Betancourt 1990, no. 652; 1985, 105 fig. 77; Koehl 1981, 180 fig. 1). Type 1, then, must be placed at the 'cusp' and regarded as one of the first conical rhytons in Crete.

Type 2 appears to be globular, but the examples preserve only the lower opening, so that no reconstruction of the middle and upper side is possible. There are two examples in the catalogue (**398–9**). The former has a well-defined flat, raised opening at the base, like Koehl's MM III A/B type, the later has a simple, pierced opening with slightly raised rim like Koehl's MM II B type (Koehl 1981, 180 fig. 1). Both examples are found in Group E and so are problematic. However, an example from Phaistos may give the complete profile for this type and suggests that it belongs in the MM II B period (F. 1036).

PART 2. THE FINE BUFF CRUDE WARE

i. Definition

A very distinctive class of wheelmade pottery appears at Knossos during the course of the Old Palace period. It consists of simplified versions of some types we have looked at in Fine Buff Ware, that are here 'Mass produced and clumsily made' (Popham 1974, 186), ignoring quality but with a view to quick and plentiful production, perhaps as containers used only once. This class is manufactured by centering a large cone or hump of clay on the potter's wheel and throwing small pots in rapid succession without having to re-centre a new measure of clay (Van As 1984, 150 fig. 5). This innovation was almost certainly learned from Egyptian potters and was retained by the Cretans into the MM III and LM I periods, to manufacture the conical cups that are found in such quantities that they have become subjects of some derision by Aegean archaeologists (Caskey and Huxley 1978).

There are fourteen forms manufactured in this manner in the Old Palace period. They are called 'Crude Types' here, meaning rough and hastily made—lacking in refinement, in order to distinguish them from the finer varieties of the forms.

ii. Typology

Crude Bowl (FIG. 2.19)

There are four types of bowls thrown off the hump that can be distinguished by differences in shape.

Type 1 is a shallow bowl with a very thick section, flat base and rounded rim. There are five examples in the catalogue (**446–50**), and others from the same context which could not be found (PLATE 61). They are 3.0–3.5 cm high with rim diameters 9.5–10.0 cm and base diameters 5.0–5.5 cm. All are plain and belong to the mixed context of Group E. A date in the MM II B period may be proposed, on the basis of close similarities with examples from the final destruction deposit in Trial KV at Knossos (Popham 1974, fig. 6.1–5), and perhaps by its absence from the earliest groups at the Knossos Acropolis Houses (Catling *et al.*, 1979, 21–5).

Type 2 is a shallow bowl, with wide flat base and simple outward splayed rim. There are 30 examples in the catalogue (**161, 451–6, 708–16, 772–6, 854–60** and **959–60**). They vary in height from 2.0–4.0 cm; diameters are 8.5–11.5 cm at the rim and 3.5–5.0 cm at the base. Examples are plain or sprayed with dark paint, but never otherwise decorated. The frequency of examples in Groups B, G, H, and L, and their occurrence in the early floor deposit below the Room of the Stone Pier (PLATE 141) suggest a MM II A date for the appearance of this type. Its continued production, without ob-

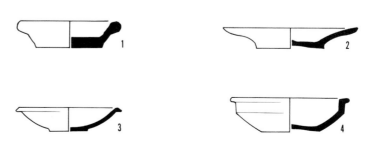

Fig. 2.19. Fine Buff Crude Bowl Types.

vious change, into MM II B is shown by its occurrence in Group E, the destruction deposit in Trial KV (Popham 1974, fig. 6. 6–7) and in the pit of Tomb XVII at Mavrospilio (Forsdyke 1927, 281 pl. 23 no. 23).

This type is the most obvious predecessor of the ubiquitous conical cup of the neopalatial period (e.g. Fiandra 1973, pl. 32; Catling *et al.* 1979, 23–4 fig. 21; Gillis 1990).

Type 3 is a shallow bowl, with distinctive, slightly rounded profile and flattened rim, with varying degrees of outward projection. There are 45 examples in the catalogue (**457–63, 467–9, 717–32, 777–82, 861–70** and **961–3**). They are 1.5–3.5 cm high, diameters are 8.5–10.0 cm at the rim and 3.5–5.5 cm at the base. Examples are plain, dark-sprayed, partially dipped in dark paint or monochrome coated. The frequency of this type in Groups G, H, and L, and in the early floor deposit below the Room of the Stone Pier (PLATE 141), indicate that it begins in the MM II A period. That it continues to be manufactured in MM II B is confirmed by its occurrence in Group E, the destruction deposit in Trial KV (Popham 1974, fig. 6. nos. 8 and 16) and the pit in Mavrospilio Tomb XVII (Forsdyke 1927, 281 pl. 23 nos. 19 and 20). There are also similar bowls from destruction deposits of Period 3 at Phaistos (Fiandra 1973, pl. 31; Levi 1976, pl. 143).

A later development of this type may be the everted rim bowl of the MM III A period (Catling *et al.* 1979, 27 fig. 21 V.61–3).

Type 4 is a shallow bowl, with distinctive angular profile and slightly flattened, out-turned rim. There are three examples in the catalogue (**464–6**). They are 3.2–3.4 cm high, diameters are 8.5–10.0 cm at the rim and 3.3–5.5 at the base. The occurrence of this type in Groups E and N (PLATE 144 *n*), and in the destruction deposit in Trial KV (Popham 1974, fig. 6 no. 8) provide a date in the MM II B period for the type.

Crude Pyxis (FIG. 2.20)
There are three examples of a deep, straight-sided form with horizontal groove below an out-turned rim (**470–1** and **735**), that are the crude equivalent to the Fine Buff Ware Pyxis of Type 5. They are 3.3–4.8 cm high, diameters are 8.2–8.9 cm at the rim and 5.0–6.0 cm at the base. All are monochrome coated. The example in Group G suggests that this type begins in the MM II A period. A contemporary parallel for **735** may be the example from the silt layer below the destruction deposit in Trial KV (Popham 1974, fig. 5 no. 2). The form's continued use, perhaps slightly deeper and with a more pronounced groove in the side, into the MM II B period is suggested by **470–1** from Group E.

Crude Goblet (FIG. 2.20)
There are seventeen examples of simple rounded goblets (**158–60, 689–98, 763–5** and **813**), that are the rough

version of the Rounded Goblets of Type 2 in Fine Buff Ware. They are 4.0–5.0 cm high with diameters of 8.5 cm at the rim 3.5–5.0 cm at the base. All are plain and their occurrence in Groups B, G and H suggests that they belong only in the MM II A period at Knossos; this is confirmed by their presence in the early floor deposit in Early West Magazine 2 (Brown 1983, 68–9 figs. 36b, c).

In the Mesara, a related type seems to have persisted into the MM II B period at Phaistos (Levi 1976, 274 fig. 431; Fiandra 1973), and Kommos where they are called 'conical cups' (Betancourt 1985a, 92–3 figs. 65–6; 1986, fig. 2 12–15).

Fig. 2.20. Fine Buff Crude Pyxis and Goblet Types.

Crude Cup (FIG. 2.21)
There are four general types of cups produced in this class of pottery.

Type 1 is a simple, straight-sided conical-shaped cup without handle. There are 22 examples in the catalogue (**472–91** and **699–700**). They are 5.0–6.0 cm high with diameters of 6.5–9.0 cm at the rim and 3.5–4.5 cm at the base. The examples in Group H suggest that the type was first produced in MM II A. It seems to have been more popular in the MM II B period, as shown by the numerous examples in Group E, the destruction deposit in Trial KV (Popham 1974, figs. 6 no. 10, 8 nos. 1, 4 and 7) and the pit in Mavrospilio Tomb XVII (Forsdyke 1927, 281 pl. 23 no. 25).

Type 2 is a straight-sided cup like Type 1, but with a vertical strap handle. It may be the rough equivalent to the Straight-sided cup Type 5 in Fine Buff Ware. There are 15 examples in the catalogue (**701–7, 766–71, 810** and **812**). They are 5.0–6.0 cm high with diameters of 8.5–9.0 cm at the rim and 4.4–5.0 cm at the base. All are monochrome coated. The occurrence of this type in Groups G, H and J of the Royal Pottery Stores suggests that it belongs in the MM II A period, for which it should be regarded as a type-fossil.

Type 3 is a one-handled straight-sided cup like Type 2, but the handle is smaller and rougher and, in most cases, too small to function as a handle; it is more like a grip in the shape of a handle. There are 17 examples in the catalogue (**492–500** and **826–33**, and others, that could

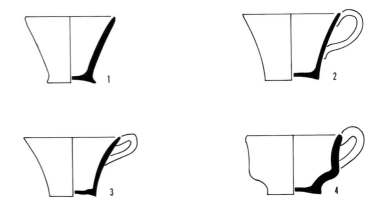

Fig. 2.21. Fine Buff Crude Cup Types.

not be found, from Group E (PLATE 61) and Group N (PLATE 144*f*) contexts. They are 5.4–6.8 cm high, with diameters of 8.5–9.5 cm at the rim and 4.2–5.0 cm at the base. All are monochrome coated. The occurrence of this type in Groups E and N and the presence of two examples in the destruction level in Trial KV (Popham 1974, fig. 6 nos. 11 and 13) and three in the pit in Mavrospilio Tomb XVII (Forsdyke 1927, 281 pl. 23 no. 24) place it firmly in MM II B.

Type 4 has a roughly angular profile, which in most cases has a small, rough handle or grip like that on Type 3. There are 23 examples in the catalogue (**501–16, 811** and **834–9**, and there are others, that could not be found, from Group E (PLATES 61, 64) and Group N (PLATE 144 *r*) contexts. They are 4.5–6.8 cm high, with diameters of 7.0–9.0 cm at the rim and 3.4–5.0 cm at the base. The numerous examples from Group E, Trial KV (Popham 1974, fig. 6 nos. 11–15), the pit in Mavrospilio Tomb XVII (Forsdyke 1927, 281 pl. 23 no. 26) and a MM II deposit in the town of Knossos (Warren 1981, 74 fig. 4 right) help assign this type in the MM II B period. The single example in Group J is problematic; it could indicate that this type begins in the MM II A period, or **811** may have been incorrectly recorded at the time of excavation.

Crude Amphoriskos (FIG. 2.22)
There are two examples, **519–20**, of small closed jars similar in profile to the crude juglet, but with two false handles represented by arched folds of clay on the sides.

Fig. 2.22. Fine Buff Crude Amphoriskos and Juglet Types.

Both are plain and part of Group E, and, in the absence of close parallels, could belong in either the MM II B or MM III A periods.

Crude Juglet (FIG. 2.22)
There are 22 examples (**521–6, 736–7** and **840–53**) of small juglets with horizontal spout and arched round handle in the catalogue, and a further three from Group E (PLATE 61). They are 4.7–8.1 cm high, with diameters of 2.5–4.0 cm at the rim and 3.4–5.0 cm at the base. Examples are sprayed with dark paint or monochrome coated. The two examples in Group G suggest a date in MM II A for the beginning of this type, which becomes quite common in the MM II B period, as shown by the examples from Group E, Trial KV (Popham 1974, fig. 6 nos. 23 and 25), the pit in Mavrospilio Tomb XVII (Forsdyke 1927, 281 pl. 23 no. 28) and Anemospilia (J. and E. Sakellarakis 1979, pl. 183).

The neopalatial successor to this form may be seen in deposits at the Unexplored Mansion (Popham 1984, pls. 131j, 137d, 143 nos. 15–17) and Stratigraphical Museum Excavations (Warren 1991*a*, 323 pl. 77G).

Crude Jug (FIG. 2.23)
There are two types of crude jug with cut-away spout.

Type 1 is a small slightly rounded jug, with rough handle or grip like those on Crude cups of Types 3 and 4. There are two examples in the catalogue (**527–8**). They are 7.0 and 7.8 cm high with base diameters of 3.0–4.0 cm. Both are plain and belong to Group E, which could indicate that they belong in the MM II B and/or MM III A periods. This type also seems to be a late occurrence at Phaistos (F. 4401; Levi 1976, 500 fig. 771).

Type 2 is a large rounded jug, with round handle and raised base. There are two examples in the catalogue (**529–30**). They are 10.5 and 10.7 cm high with base diameters of 5.0 and 5.5 cm. Both have the body coated in dark brown paint. Its occurrence in Group E and in the pit in Mavrospilio Tomb XVII (Forsdyke 1927, 281 pl. 23 no. 32) suggest a date in the MM II B period.

Fig. 2.23. Fine Buff Crude Jug Types.

Comment

This class of mass-produced or Crude Ware pottery was introduced to Crete during the MM II A period. There are no related products in the MM I A or MM I B groups at Knossos, nor do they occur in the Period I deposits at Phaistos.

The typology and chronology proposed here reflects manufacture and consumption at Knossos. Crude Ware seems to be very much a 'domestic' product. The equivalent wares in the Mesara seem to follow a consistent but different pattern, as do those in E Crete. For example, Crude Juglets similar to those in the MM II B groups at Knossos do not seem to appear in the Mesara until the MM III period (Betancourt 1985*a*, 107 fig. 79; Levi and Carinci 1988, pls. 36i, k, l, m, 38f; Betancourt 1990, no. 828). Also, the Crude Goblet, found only in MM II A at Knossos, continues to appear until the end of MM II B at Phaistos and Kommos. Regionalism continues to be a factor with the ubiquitous conical cups of the neopalatial period's crude pottery (Gillis 1990, 140).

An obvious source of inspiration for the manufacturing technique is found in Egypt, where the radial centred potter's wheel was introduced during the Vth Dynasty and where by the time of XI–XIIth Dynasty wheel thrown pottery was in the majority (Arnold 1993, 43). A clear depiction of throwing off the hump may be seen in the paintings, showing a potter's workshop, on the W wall of the Main Chamber of the tomb of the nomarch Amenemhat at Beni Hasan from the end of the reign of Senwosret I, *c.* 1908 BC, perhaps less than a generation before Crude Ware appears in Crete (Newbury 1893, pl. XI fourth register; Warren and Hankey 1989, 170 note 11). That the Cretans made the technique their own is shown by the forms they chose to produce: primarily bowls and cups, that had already been a part of their repertory.

PART 3. MINORITY FABRICS

A minority of pottery occurs in fabrics other than Fine Buff. These were sorted on the basis of macroscopic observation of their colour, texture and content. Noteworthy is the fact that the types noted in Fine Buff Fabric are not present in any of the minor fabrics.

i. Minor Buff Fabrics

A significant percentage of pottery was produced with the same hard pink to buff matrix as Fine Buff with varying concentrations of inclusions.

Semifine Buff

668, 738–41, 871–3 are in the same hard clay as Fine Buff, but with an uneven texture and reddish-brown flaky inclusions, which do not appear to have been added intentionally as tempering agents.

738–9 and 871–2 are fragments of closed jars, decorated with dark-on-buff patterns with added white paint. Although none could be restored, they resemble a class of large jars from the Royal Road at Knossos (Daux 1960, 834 fig. 1), Phaistos (e.g. F. 227, 1042, 1959, 4218, 5937) and Kommos (Betancourt 1990, nos. 1254–5).

Gritty Buff

130–6 are in Fine Buff clay but with dark and light rounded pebble-like inclusions giving it a gritty texture.

The radiating decoration on large jug 134 is very similar to that on a number of forms from Phaistos (e.g. F. 411, 473, 611, 4715, 4796, 5032) and on an amphora from Malia, which may be from central Crete (Pelagatti 1962, 110). Many of the parallels are decorated with dark-on-buff patterns, with added white paint, linking this class with Semifine Buff.

Tempered Buff

165, 255–61, 558–86, 670, 742–6, 875–9 and 1010–11 are in the same hard matrix as Fine Buff and resemble Gritty Buff, but have dark angular inclusions added as a tempering agent. This may correspond to the Tempered Buff fabric at Kommos (Betancourt 1990, 9–10), although the temper in the Knossos pottery is quite angular, as if it had been crushed before being added to the clay mixture. This fabric is indistinguishable macroscopically from the tempered buff pottery of Phaistos, where most of the closest parallels in form and decoration are found.

Two decorative styles are worth mentioning here. One uses the spiky foliate band and running S-spiral motifs, in a manner very similar to the Spiral Banded Style in Fine Buff Fabric, but on large jars (566, 585–6 and 876–8) and on the rims of large bowls (575–9). A second style features a large abstract floral motif in the centre of each side on large closed jars. 583–4 are two examples of large, horizontal-rimmed jugs with abstract floral motif on the shoulder, represented by numerous fragments of similar jugs and oval-mouthed amphorae in the same style among the sherd material from Group E in the KSM. A complete example of the type and decoration was found in the destruction horizon at Anemospilia (J. and E. Sakellarakis 1991, fig. 120). Evans published a restored drawing of an oval-mouthed amphora decorated in the same abstract floral style and said to be from the Temple Repositories (1921, 596 pl. VII). If the sherds he based the drawing on were in fact found in the Temple Repositories, they would consti-tute the only vase of the Old Palace period in an other-wise late neopalatial group. A firm date for the charac-teristic abstract floral decoration in the MM II B pe-riod is provided by the Anemospilia jug.

165, 582, 585–6 and 876–7 are large spouted jars of a type well-known at Phaistos (Levi and Carinci 1988, 110–16, pls. 49–52).

255 is fragments of a closed jar, most likely a jug of a type best known from Phaistos (e.g. F. 717, 5293) also found at Kommos (Betancourt 1990, fig. 13 pl. 3 no. 64, fig. 43 pl. 54 nos. 959–60).

259 and 260 are fragments of cylindrical spouted jars, quite similar to a common type from Phaistos (Levi and Carinci 1988, 137–8, pl. 59).

Offering tables (256–8, 670 and 746) find close par-allels in the Period 2 fruit-stands of Phaistos (ibid., 17–18 pl. 10; Fiandra 1980, pl. 38.5), but differ from those of Malia, for which our 647 is a close parallel (Van Effenterre 1980 a, 206 fig. 287).

Askoid jug 560 is one of the most characteristic forms at Phaistos (Levi and Carinci 1988, 85–7 pls. 40–1), and is decorated with dark-on-buff patterns outlined in white paint, which links this fabric to Semifine and Gritty Buff.

Large bowls 574–80 are closely related in form and decoration to examples from the end of the Old Palace period at Phaistos (e.g. F. 5186).

The few parallels cited here make it clear that the mi-nor buff fabrics, like Fine Buff, are most common in central Crete and originate either at Knossos or Phaistos; or, more likely, come from a small number of sources in N and S central Crete, which can only be identified through physical analysis of the pottery, in conjunction with geological prospection and petrographic analysis of the beds producing the white clays of central Crete.

ii. Soft Buff Fabrics

Pottery in a soft and porous buff coloured matrix, less dense than Fine Buff, follows roughly the same divi-sions into sub-groups on the basis of macroscopically visible inclusions.

Fine Soft Buff

129, 252–4, 531–45, 667, 874 and 1004–7 are in a well-levigated soft buff matrix.

Large jars 532–4 are decorated in a manner very simi-lar to the Spiral Banded Style of Fine Buff Fabric.

129, 535 and 537 are undecorated, straight-sided pyxides; 536 and 538 are lids that may belong to pyxides.

A similar form is found at Phaistos where, however, it also seems to be rare (Levi and Carinci 1988, 158 pl. 69e).

252–3 resemble in form the distinctive loop-handled bowls found at Phaistos (F. 4942, 5099; Levi and Carinci 1988, 172–3 pl. 75g, h), Kommos (Betancourt 1990, 159 fig. 52 pl. 69 nos. 1281-2) and Platanos (Xanthoudides 1924, 98 pl. IX no. 6859) in the Mesara, but are deco-rated very much like shallow rounded bowls from Palaikastro (Bosanquet and Dawkins 1923, 11–12 pl. VI B–D). This form is the closest ceramic parallel to the gold loop-handled bowl in the Tôd Treasure (Bisson de la Roque et al. 1953, pl. XVIII 70631; Hood 1978, 154 fig. 145 b).

Bridge-spouted jars 874 and 1004 are decorated with a similar pattern in a dark-on-buff style with added white paint. In a related style are 667 and 531. Jugs 540–1 are in a dark-on-buff style with added white, but have the additional use of orange paint.

Rhyta 539 and 1005 are both decorated with dark-on-buff ripple burnished patterns, anticipating the Tor-toise-shell Ripple ware of the MM III B period (dis-cussed below).

542–5 are a group of jugs, with distinctive beaked spouts, with lugs on the sides and neck mouldings. The spouts are coated in a creamy-white paint and deco-rated with vertical floral designs in red. Evans (1935, 120) referred to these jugs as his 'Creamy-bordered Class' (discussed below).

Gritty Soft Buff

148–52, 164, 598–603, 750–3, 886–8 and 971 are in a soft buff matrix with numerous sandy grits and tiny flecks of silver mica. Most examples are slipped red and burnished, and appear to imitate stone vases. This fab-ric was evidently used primarily for the manufacture of lamps, for which a basic typology is proposed here:

a. Hand Lamp Types (FIG. 2.24)

Small lamps with long handles opposite the opening for a spout or wick occur in two types.

Type 1 has an angular profile due to its incurving rim. There are seven examples in the catalogue (148–51, 751–2 and 971). They are 3.0–3.5 cm high, with diameters of 7.0–12.0 cm at the rim and 4.5–8.0 cm at the base. The occurrence of this type in Groups A, G and L sug-gests that it belongs in both the MM I B and MM II A periods. The early date is borne out by a similar type in a Period 1 context at Phaistos (F. 5321a).

Type 2 has an outsplayed profile, with flattened inward sloping rim. There are five examples in the catalogue (598–71 and 887). They are 3.0–3.7 cm high, with di-ameters of 10.0–11.5 cm. The examples are in Groups E and K and there is a further example from Group N in PLATE 114, and one from Trial KV (Popham 1974, fig. 8.9); all indicate a date in the MM II B period. A similar and contemporary type is found in deposits of Period 3 at Phaistos (Levi 1976, pl. 156 a–e, g; F. 4725, 6142, 1311, 4727).

Perhaps a later development of this type may be seen in the hand lamps from the MM III A and MM III B deposits B and C in the Acropolis Houses (Catling *et al.* 1979, 34–5 figs. 22.138, 23.161).

b. Pedestalled Lamp Types (FIG. 2.24)

Wide, shallow lamps, with at least two diametrically opposed spouts and standing on tall pedestalled bases, are found in two types.

Type 1 has a thick outsplayed profile and rounded rim. There are two examples in the catalogue (**152** and **753**). The average height is around 20.0 cm; rim diameters are 19.0 and 30.0 cm. Examples are from Groups A and G and the Vat Room Deposit (Evans 1921, 167 fig. 118a.12) giving a date in the early part of the Old Palace period at Knossos. The type may have begun earlier, as an example in stone found in a MM I A level on the Royal Road suggests (Warren 1969, 52 P292), though the publication of its associated context is pending. Related types at Phaistos seem to appear in Period 1 (F. 2313) and slightly later (F. 54, 381).

Type 2 has a thin profile with sharply downturned rim. There is one example in the catalogue (**888**) in Group K, which may indicate that this type belongs in MM II B. This date is supported by a lamp of this type in

Group E (PLATE 31), a short version in Group N (PLATE 114) and an example from Trial KV (Popham 1974, pl. 32.c). Comparable forms from Phaistos (F. 1567) and Palaikastro (MacGillivray, Sackett *et al.* 1992, fig. 12.10) may be contemporary.

The gritty sandy inclusions and burnished exterior link this fabric to the Lamp Fabric of Kommos (Betancourt 1990, 11–12, 156, no. 1072) though it is not considered local to the site. The contemporary lamps of Phaistos have been studied by Mercando (1980), Levi and Carinci (1988), and Speziale (1993), but the complexities of the Phaistos stratigraphy have produced typologies not quite compatible with Knossos.

Also in this fabric are a small angular jug (**164**) which finds a close parallel in a jug from Early West Magazine 2 (Brown 1983, 68–9 fig. 36), a bowl with internal tripartite divisions (**750**) and a large shallow tray coated with a thick white paint (**886**) similar to the Creamy-bordered class.

Tempered Soft Buff

546–57 and **1008–9** are in a soft buff matrix with numerous and varied angular inclusions. There is a resemblance to Tempered Buff, but without the characteristic density of dark angular inclusions.

546 and **1008** are amphoriskoi very similar to *unguentaria* from all stages of the Old Palace period at Phaistos (e.g. F. 5157, 5291, 6231). Lid (**1009**) which may fit the amphoriskoi, also finds close parallels at Phaistos (F. 2693, 6269).

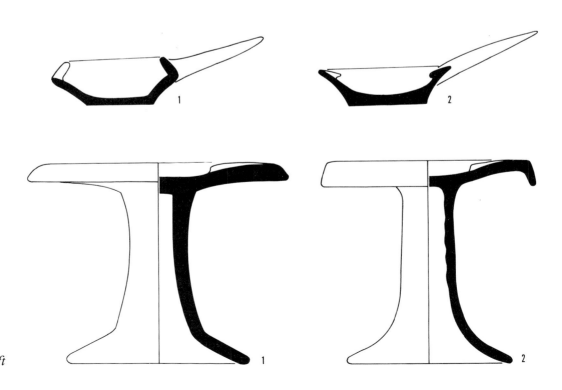

Fig. 2.24. Gritty Soft Buff Lamp Types.

548–51 are large bowls with stamped, incised or moulded decoration and belong to Evans' Creamy-bordered class, providing a link with Fine and Gritty Soft Buff. Similar bowls and stands are known from Phaistos (e.g. F. 480, 4928).

Large bowls (**552–5**) and a large jar (**557**) are decorated with dark-on-buff ripple burnished patterns, similar to those on rhyta (**539** and **1005**), providing another link with Fine Soft Buff. **555** also has a zone of featherwave design, as does basin **556** (discussed below).

Comment

Three decorative styles exist in the Soft Buff fabrics that are not found in Fine Buff.

Creamy-bordered Style. Evans' 'Creamy-bordered class' is identified by the technique of coating an extreme zone of a vase in thick creamy-white paint, but which also employs stamped, incised, moulded and modelled decoration, with motifs related to Precision Stamped Ware (Evans 1935, 120–2). Evans assigned this class to the MM II A period, but the Knossos examples are from Group E, and thus are more likely to belong in the MM II B or MM III A periods. Examples at Phaistos are found in the destruction deposits of Period 3 (F. 480, 1477, 1905). Betancourt assigns a lone example from Kommos to MM II B on stylistic grounds (1990, 162 fig. 53 pl. 71 no. 1341), but the style clearly continues into the MM III A period, as examples from Period 4 at Phaistos confirm (F. 4928; Pernier 1935, 371 fig. 222 top left). It is quite likely that some of the Knossos examples should also be placed in MM III A, for instance jugs (**542–5**) have red painted lugs on the sides of the spouts, very much like those on conical rhyta from Knossos (**395–7**) Phaistos (F. 4029, 4263) and Kommos (Betancourt 1990, 111–12 fig. 31 pl. 38 no. 652), which are MM III in date.

Related to the Creamy-bordered Style, and also in Soft Buff, are the terracotta shrine fragments found in the MM III fill in the Loomweight Basement, see above p. 41.

Tortoise-shell Ripple Style. A second decorative style is distinguished by the application, in horizontal zones, of vertical bands of dark paint on a buff ground smoothed horizontally, to create the well-known ripple burnished or Tortoise-shell Ripple Style. Examples are bowls (**552–5**), a large basin (**556**) and a large jar (**557**).

Evans illustrated part of a bowl with ripple burnished decoration, as an example of the style's early or MM II occurrence, since specimens were said to have been found in the Loomweight Basement (1921, 592 n.1 fig. 435). There were no examples among the sherds kept from the Group K context; the sherd illustrated by Evans may have come from one of the fill levels, above the floor deposit in the Loomweight Basement. As the examples in the catalogue are from the mixed MM II B and MM III A context of Group E, it is not possible to

support a firm MM II date for the first occurrence of the style at Knossos. Given its discovery in the early MM III contexts, 1518, at Kommos (Betancourt 1990, nos. 499–500, 582, 729, 797) and Phaistos (F. 5219; Levi 1976, pl. 212r), and what are most likely mixed fills of the late MM II B and MM III A periods at Palaikastro (Bosanquet and Dawkins 1923, 23–4 figs. 13–14), it seems most sensible, for the time being, to accept that the style first comes into existence after the end of the Old Palace period, perhaps early in MM III A. It then develops into the painted, not burnished, Tortoise-shell Ripple Style, most characteristic of the early neopalatial period (Betancourt 1985a, 113–14).

Feather-wave Style. A third class, related to Ripple Burnished, is the Feather-wave Style. This is created by smearing a thin solution of dark paint on a buff ground in an undulating pattern, looking as though the tip of a feather was used instead of a fine paint brush, **555** and **556**. Evans suggested that this style was created to imitate alabaster originals (1935, 122–4 figs. 91–4). Rare in central Crete, there being a few examples from Kommos (Betancourt 1990, nos. 590–1), the style may be more common in the E, where it is found in some quantity at Myrtos-Pyrgos (Cadogan 1978 a, 75 fig. 16, and personal communication) and examples are known from Priniatikos Pyrgos (Betancourt 1983, no. 23), Pseira (Seager 1910, 21), Palaikastro (Bernini 1995, 59–62 fig. 4F) and Kato Zakros (Forsdyke 1925, A692).

If the examples in Soft Buff are indeed all from the same source, it is difficult to suggest a likely place of origin. The parallels with similar forms from the Mesara are not as plentiful as with the Buff fabrics. There is a chronological problem as well. The amphoriskoi, lids and lamps belong to all stages of the Old Palace period; while the Creamy-bordered Style appears only at the end, and the Ripple Burnished and Feather-wave styles, after the end, of Old Palace period, during MM III A; at this time there are fewer comparable deposits in the Mesara. East Cretan links are suggested by the period III origin of the Feather-wave Style at Myrtos-Pyrgos, and the close similarity of bowls **252–3** with those found at Palaikastro.

While one suspects that Soft Buff forms a coherent group, representing the products of one centre of innovative potters, little more can be said about its location until the fabric has been fully analyzed.

iii. Red Fabrics

Fine Red

A number of small, open, wheel-made forms are in a brick red coloured matrix with tiny flecks of silver mica. The surface is often slipped deep red-brown. Examples are in Group A (**138–45**), Group E (**587–90**), Group F (**669**) and Group G (**749**) and so span the Old Palace period. The fabric is very similar to Momigliano's Fabric

III for the MM I A period pottery at Knossos (1991, 261–2). Examples of tumblers and other small, fine forms in this fabric are found in the Vat Room Deposit (Momigliano 1990) and are reported from the early deposit, beneath the floor in West Magazine 1 (Evans 1921, 172).

141–2 are made with a technique very similar to the Shallow Grooved Ware of the early part of the Old Palace period at Knossos. They are quite close in form to examples in a related ware from the Trapeza Cave in Lasithi (Pendlebury *et al.* 1936, fig. 14).

The clay and the forms are very similar to those of the Lasithi region and Myrtos-Pyrgos (Pendlebury *et al.* 1936, 59–69 fig. 14; Cadogan 1990). Dimopoulou and Rethemiotakis have found a workshop of the Old Palace period, producing a very similar class of ceramics at Kastelli-Pedhiada, a likely source for the Knossian pieces (Dimopoulou 1987; Rethemiotakis 1988; 1989; 1990).

Coarse Red

A small number of open and closed forms are made with a brick red coloured matrix, having inclusions of purple schist and tiny flecks of silver mica. 146 is in Group A and 591–7 are in Group E. 595 is an open bowl coated with a creamy slip and decorated in the Feather-wave Style, also found in Tempered Soft Buff Fabric. The fabric, surface treatment and style are well known from the early neopalatial period at Palaikastro, where 595 may have originated (Bosanquet and Dawkins 1923, 33 fig. 21). 596–7 are hand lamps very much like the Type 2 hand lamps in Gritty Soft Buff Fabric. 592–4 are curious, disc-shaped juglets without close parallel.

iv. Fine Orange Fabric

605, 968 and 880–1 are distinctive wheel-made forms, made with a hard but flaking, layered, orange coloured matrix, apparently quite well-levigated, with very discreet flecks of silver mica. The pedestalled forms 605 and 880 are quite foreign to Knossos, but there is little evidence to suggest their origin.

v. Red/Brown Fabric

747–8 and 785–7 from the Royal Pottery Stores are made from a soft, reddish-brown coloured matrix, with numerous sandy grits and tiny flecks of silver mica. 785 is similar to Fine Buff Shallow Bowls of Type 1. The jugs and goblets are quite distinctive, yet without close parallel.

vi. Gritty Orange/Buff Fabric

882–5 and 970 are wheel-made forms in a soft, orange to buff coloured matrix with numerous tiny rounded grits, and have a flaking surface. 883 is similar to Crude Cups of Type 4, otherwise this group is without close parallels.

vii. Gritty Brown Fabric

137 is made from a soft brown, layered matrix fired dark-brown at the core and with white grit inclusions. The three-handled jar is in every way a singleton, perhaps a survivor from an earlier period.

viii. Gritty Orange/Brown Fabric

147 is made from an orange-brown coloured matrix with rounded red inclusions. Quite distinct from the Knossian pottery in fabric and style, macroscopically it most closely resembles the MM pottery of W Crete.

ix. Cycladic Fabrics

Cycladic White Ware

606 and 666 are in a fine, soft, light-buff to orange-buff coloured matrix filled with silver mica. At the time of its discovery, Mackenzie likened 666 to the pottery of Melos, with which he was familiar (1902 PB (2), 66). 606 is decorated in the Black and Red Style of Phylakopi (Atkinson *et al.* 1904, pls. 20–1), also found at Kea (Overbeck 1989, 76 pl. 52 Group AG vase 10a) and Naxos (Renfrew 1972, pl. 13.1), but regarded as a Melian product by Barber (1978, 376).

607 and 608 are jug fragments in a hard, gritty, white clay, decorated with designs in a matt black paint and in a manner very similar to the Cycladic White style. Though Cycladic White Ware is characteristic both of Melos and Thera, and there are problems distinguishing the ceramics products of both islands (Jones 1986, 426, 429–30), Marthari might accept 607, with its quatrefoil disk-rosette decoration, as a Theran product (1993, 253). If so, it would join the MC jug from Lerna and help provide an equivalent Middle Helladic date to correspond to late MM II B or early MM III A for the Theran style (Zerner 1990, 31 fig. 44). The Cycladic jug fragments from MM III contexts at Kommos may also be Theran, and contribute to the image of links between Thera and central Crete early in the neopalatial period (Betancourt 1990, nos. 501, 592).

The Cycladic vase, from a MM I B level in Royal Road South, seems to be from a jug of similar type to 606 and 666, and so could be from the same source, though of an earlier date (Hood 1960, 23 fig. 24; 1966, 110).

Micaceous Buff

1012–20 are fragments of amphorae in a highly micaceous, buff fabric, with plain or self-smoothed surface and, in the case of 1012, with traces of thin, dull, dark-brown horizontal bands painted at the neck, FIG. 2.25 (MacGillivray 1984 *a*, 154 fig. 2). The macroscopic similarity of the fabric with that of 606 and 666 may indi-

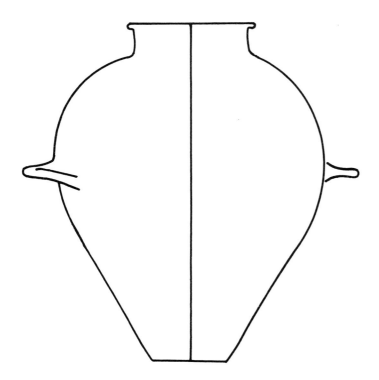

Fig. 2.25. Micaceous Buff amphora restoration.

cate a Melian origin, as Davis has shown for a very similar example from Kea (1986, 43, 108 U–73), though a similar type is found in Thera (Doumas 1983, 107 fig. 13d). Otherwise, the amphorae are of a type quite common in Middle Helladic Greece (Buck 1964, 248 Type C5).

Micaceous Brown
890 is a juglet in a gritty, brown, quite micaceous fabric, that resembles those of the central Cyclades, but the straight-sided form is unlike anything yet discovered in the islands. 973 is a large closed jar in a similar fabric but fired grey at the core.

Micaceous Red
974 is fragments of an amphora of the same type as 1012–20, but in a gritty, red, very micaceous fabric. A Cycladic origin, perhaps Naxos or Syros, may be postulated, although this is quite speculative until similar material is identified in the islands.

x. Near Eastern Fabric
1021 is the fragments of more than one closed jar in a very distinctive soft and porous pink matrix, with frequent rounded sand-like grits. One fragment with a handle comes from a wheelmade jar, with a maximum diameter of roughly 25.0 cm (FIG. 2.26). The exterior has a thin pink *engobe* and traces of finely incised hori-

zontal lines on the body. At the base of the handle three horizontal grooves are incised.

The jars are much too fragmentary to be compared with Amiran's typology of North Syrian or 'Canaanite' jars (1969, 140–2 pl. 43), although they are unlikely to have come from angular forms. The incisions near the handle are reminiscent of those on similar jars from the Royal Tombs of Byblos (Tufnell 1969, 15). The Group N context suggests they were imported either late in MM II B or early in MM III A, at the time Minoan pottery is found in some quantity in the Levant, see pp. 105–06.

PART 4. SYNTHESIS

There are 'archaeological' events at Knossos that can be linked to architectural periods. Trends in the arts, often reflected in pottery styles, by contrast cannot always be linked to those events responsible for the primary deposits so cherished by excavators. Nonetheless, the deposits can be used to monitor those changes in techniques and tastes across time that we treat as 'stylistic development'. The boundaries are not firm. Instead, they must be flexible enough to allow for the long-term popularity of some techniques, forms or designs, while admitting that others may be short-lived. The following conclusions isolate those wares, styles and forms described above within the periods of the Old Palace at Knossos, as first set out by Evans and largely re-affirmed by a century of Cretan excavations. The tables in FIGS. 2.27–30 chart the chronological distribution of the wares, styles and types described above. The aim here is to provide hypothetical 'type-fossils', to be used in comparison with other regions so that issues of influence, communication and chronology might be clarified and further tested as well as enhanced at Knossos.

i. Diagnostic Pottery of the MM I A Period
A number of wares, styles and types may be proposed as diagnostic of the MM I B period, because of their appearance in groups assigned to that stage of the palace's history in Chapter 1. However, as the line of argument here is necessarily circular, given the lack of certainty regarding their contexts, it is essential to emphasize the validity of the stylistic evaluation as well as the stratigraphical. In order to do this, the pottery of the periods preceding MM I B needs to be examined, if only to be certain that none of the types classified as characteristic of MM I B are not, in fact, survivors from an earlier stage.

Momigliano's re-investigation of the EM III–MM I A pottery deposits from Knossos dismisses the instances of stratigraphy associated with MM I A levels, and in doing so may overlook important evidence for a stratigraphic definition of MM I B. Mackenzie stated that he observed a level of early polychrome decorated pottery beneath the 'MM II' floor in the Monolithic

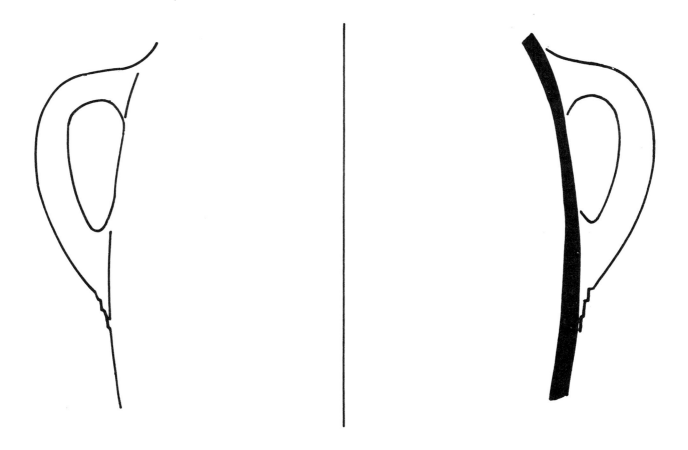

Fig. 2.26. 'Canaanite' jar fragment 1021.

FINE BUFF WARES	MM I A	MM I B	MM II A	MM II B	MM III A
Pared Ware	XXXX	XXX			
Barbotine Ware	XXXX	XXXX	XXX		
Egg-shell Ware			XXX		
Shallow Grooved Ware		XXX	?		
Precision Grooved Ware				XX	XX
Stamped and Impressed Ware			XXXX		
Precision Stamped Ware				XXXX	
Early Printed Ware		XXXX	XXXX		
Late Printed Ware				XXX	
Ridged Ware				X	XXX

Fig. 2.27. Chronological distribution of Fine Buff Wares.

PATTERN PAINTED STYLES	MM I A	MM I B	MM II A	MM II B	MM III A
White-banded Style	XXXX	XXXX	XXX		
Diagonal Red and White Style		XXXX			
Woven Style		XXXX			
Sunrise Style				XXXX	
Starburst Style				XXXX	
Wavy-line Style				XXX	
Spiral Band Style				XXX	
White-spotted Style				X	XXXX
Heavy Spiral Style				X	XXXX

Fig. 2.28. Chronological distribution of styles in Pattern Painted Ware.

FINE BUFF TYPES	MM I A	MM I B	MM II A	MM II B	MM III A
Shallow Bowl	1	1,2			
Rounded Tripod Bowl		1			
Rounded Goblet	1	1,2,3	?1] 2, 3		
Conical Goblet		1,2	3		
Tumbler	1	1,2	3, 4	4	
Straight-sided Cup		1,2,3,4,5,6	?2] 5,6	5,6,7,8,9,10,11,12	8,11,12,13
Convex-sided Cup	[?1	1			
Tall-rimmed Angular Cup		1,2,3	?1,2] 4,5,6		
Short-rimmed Angular Cup		1,2	?1] 2	3	
Squat Rounded Cup		1,2			
Rounded Cup	1	1,2,3,4	3,4	5,6,7	?5,7]
Shallow Angular Bowl		1	2		
Pyxis			1,2,3,4,5	6	
Angular Bridge-spouted Jar		1,2	1		
Squat Rounded Bridge-spouted Jar		1			
Baggy-shaped Bridge-spouted Jar				1	
Rounded Bridge-spouted Jar		2	1,3,4	5,6	
Jug with Cut-away Spout		1	2,3,4	4	?4
Jug with Horizontal Spout			1,2		3
Rhyton				1,2	1,2

Fig. 2.29. Chronological distribution of Fine Buff Ware Types.

CRUDE TYPES	MM II A	MM II B
Bowl Type 1		XXXXX
Bowl Type 2	XXXXX	XXXXX
Bowl Type 3	XXXXX	XXXXX
Bowl Type 4		XXXXX
Pyxis	XXXXX	XXXXX
Goblet	XXXXX	
Cup Type 1	XXXXX	XXXXX
Cup Type 2	XXXXX	
Cup Type 3		XXXXX
Cup Type 4		XXXXX
Amphoriskos		XXXXX
Juglet	XXXXX	XXXXX
Jug Type 1		XXXXX
Jug Type 2		XXXXX

Fig. 2.30. Chronological distribution of Fine Buff Crude Types.

Pillar Basement, see above pp. 45–6. He assigned this earliest floor in the building to the MM I A period. Momigliano rejected this date, and even the floor's existence, on the basis of comparisons with the material of the Old Palace period (1991, 163–6). The closest parallels for the early polychrome pottery, however, are in the material from the upper floor level, reported in House B below the West Court. This was assigned by Pendlebury to a late stage of the MM I A period and used to illustrate the decorated pottery of that phase (1930, 60 pl. 14; 1939, 105 fig. 16). Here again Momigliano dismissed the significance of the upper level, because it could no longer be verified and parallels for the polychrome pottery, presented by Pendlebury, were said to be with the Old Palace pottery (1991, 210–16). A third deposit, that found on the floor in House C below the West Court, was also assigned by Momigliano to the MM I A period even though it is stratified above an EM III or early MM I A building, see above p. 23.

In spite of the fact that the finds from these three areas have been mixed and cannot be verified at present, it is still possible to accept the statements made by Evans, Mackenzie and Pendlebury at the time of excavation, especially in view of the fact that much of the material they illustrate from these levels does not fit the stylistic definitions of either the early stages of MM I A or the MM I B period ceramics but may be seen to work as a stylistic bridge between the two. This study proposes to use the three groups mentioned above as a working definition of the ceramics of the late MM I A period, immediately preceding the foundation of the palace in MM I B (see also Cadogan *et al.* 1993, 25).

The most secure pottery groups of the early MM I A period to emerge from Momigliano's study are those from the Upper East Well and the floor deposit in House A below the West Court. There are also vases specifically said to come from the earlier floor in House B. Using these groups as representative of early MM I A ceramics, it becomes clear that much of the pottery found in the later deposits is very similar, and most likely represents close continuity or survivors from the earlier MM I A period. However, there are some features that show development toward the styles of MM I B.

The most obvious example of development is the footed goblet from House B decorated with horizontal lines on the body and diagonal strokes on the rim in orange and white paint (Pendlebury and Pendlebury 1930, pl. 14.17), which Momigliano rejects as MM I A, and likens to MM I B Goblets of Type 1 (1991, 235–6 pl. 54.121). The goblet cited does not fit the MM I B typology, but is very similar in form and decoration to goblets from the lowest level in the Monolithic Pillar Basement (Mackenzie 1906, pl. 7.11–16). It might be seen best as representing a stage of development between the footed goblets of early MM I A and those of the MM I B period and, given the contexts of the examples, be placed in the late MM I A period.

A new form in the late MM I A period is the wide, angular bridge-spouted jar, which is an obvious predecessor to the MM I B Angular Bridge-spouted Jar of Type 1 (Momigliano 1991, 258–60 fig. 36 Types 2–4; Mackenzie 1906, pl. 9.14). The complete examples are often decorated with vertical lines, but one has a zone of barbotine work with fine ridges (Momigliano 1991, 179, 183 pl. 29.16), which is quite different from both the 'rockwork' barbotine of late MM I A and the 'prickle' barbotine of MM I B, but is very similar to that on one of the goblet fragments from the lowest level in the Monolithic Pillar Basement (Mackenzie 1906, 248–9 pl. 7.13).

Many of the fragments of bridge-spouted jars from the Monolithic Pillar Basement and House B are decorated with patterns in orange and white that, following Mackenzie, might be termed the 'Polychrome Geometric Style' (1906, 246). The overall compositions are defined by vertical, horizontal and diagonal lines, and triangles, lozenges and arches, filled with cross-hatching, oblique strokes or dots, are the basic motifs. While there is rare (only two examples) use of polychrome decoration in early MM I A (Momigliano 1991, 265), there is no precedent for the full and somewhat complicated use in late MM I A. It is easily distinguished from the Pattern Painted Styles of the MM I B and MM II A periods, which employ abstract naturalistic motifs and rarely use dots or hatching to fill designs.

The Polychrome Geometric Style, then, may be taken to represent a distinctive ceramic style of the late MM I A period. With this definition we may include the controversial jug and miniature bridge-spouted jar from

House C, above p. 23, the rim fragment of an angular jar from the North Quarter of the City (Momigliano 1991, 180 pl. 31.36), and the fragments of jars and shallow bowls from the Prepalatial Houses to the S of the Palace (ibid., 203–4 pl. 40.14–18). The MM I A deposit beneath Vano XXV of the first palace at Phaistos may also be linked to this late stage of the period (Pernier 1935, 139–42 pl. XIV). At least one pot in this style was exported to Melos, where it may be one of the earliest Minoan artefacts at Phylakopi (Renfrew 1972, pl. 13. 4; Papagiannopoulou 1991, no. 383).

This definition also embraces the dark burnished and incised pyxides and lids from various deposits at Knossos, which, on stratigraphic and stylistic grounds, may now be placed in the late stages of the MM I A period (MacGillivray, Day *et al.* 1987; Momigliano 1991, 172 n.117). Although the decoration on the pyxides is incised, it very closely reflects the geometric patterns, and use of dots and oblique strokes as filling devices, in the Polychrome Geometric Style.

A comparison may also be made with the geometric designs and patterns on the contemporary pottery from Patrikies in the Mesara (Bonacasa 1968; Levi 1976, 747–56 pl. VIIi, l).

Illustrated with the polychrome pottery from House B are a few fragments decorated with abstract floral motifs, composed of a central dot surrounded by other dots of the same size or smaller (Pendlebury and Pendlebury 1930, pl. 14.3, 5, 13). These motifs are similar to those employed in the Woven Style and it would be tempting to see them as an incipient version of the predominantly MM I B style, but the possibility that the level contains later material does not preclude their being examples of the later style. The same may be said of a fragment with white and orange naturalistic sprays, which are very similar to those on **74** (ibid., pl. 14.1 and 7), and the rim fragments of two cups (ibid., pl. 14.13 and 15). A cup from the late MM I A deposit near Building 6 at Archanes-Phourni (Sakellarakis 1972, pl. Ea; 1991 101 fig. 74) comes very close to bridging the interval between the Polychrome Geometric and Woven Styles, as may convex cup **69** in Group A.

Although a much more detailed study is required, it is possible at present to suggest that the forms most likely to belong to the later part of the MM I A period are the wide footed goblet and wide, angular bridge-spouted jar; both have polychrome and a type of barbotine decoration. The most distinctive decorative style of the period is 'Polychrome Geometric', and 'ridged barbotine' patterns may also be characteristic. The full publication of the late MM I A group, from near Building 6 at Archanes-Phourni, should provide a wider range of forms and styles, as will the material from the lower floor in the Royal Road South Basements.

This definition of the late MM I A period ceramics allows for the isolation of type-fossils for the MM I B period to be put forward with some confidence, although further detailed study of the MM I A period may alter the following list, particularly as regards some of the handmade forms which occur only in Group A.

ii. Diagnostic Pottery of the MM I B Period

The pottery associated with the earliest stages of the palace has some features, which are carried through from the late stages of MM I A, as might be expected. The fact that there is a close progression in styles, such as the Polychrome Geometric to the Woven and in some of the 'proto-wheelmade' forms found in the deposits that we take to mark the end of MM I B, indicates a short time span for the interval from the first construction works in the palace, with which the Vat Room Deposit might be associated, to the events that caused the burnt deposit at the SW Palace Angle.

The pottery most diagnostic of the end of MM I B is: Conical Goblets of Type 2, Tall-rimmed Angular Cups of Types 1–2 and Angular Bridge-spouted Jars of Type 1b, in the Diagonal Red and White Style, and Straight-sided Cups of Types 2–3, Tall-rimmed Angular Cups of Type 1a, Shallow Angular Bowls of Type 1, Angular Bridge-spouted Jars of Type 2, Squat Rounded Bridge-spouted Jars and Rounded Bridge-spouted jars of Type 2 in the Woven Style. Also characteristic are the Jugs with Cut-away Spout of Type 1 and, perhaps, the Tall-rimmed Angular Cups of Types 1 to 3.

Forms thrown on the radial centred potter's wheel first appear in some quantity during this period, in types such as the Straight-sided Cup of Types 4, 5–6, the Shallow Bowl of Type 2, the Tall-rimmed Angular Cup of Type 3, the Short-rimmed Angular Cup of Types 1–2, the Squat Rounded Cup, the Rounded Cup of Types 3–4, the Rounded Goblet of Types 2–3, and the Rounded Bridge-spouted Jar of Type 3. This may coincide with the appearance of Evely's Type 2 wheelhead or bat made of fired clay found at Phaistos and Malia (1988, 89, 97–100 fig. 3).

Additions and corrections to this definition should come with the publication of the groups from the SW Palace Angle, and the Royal Road South Basements— Middle Floor (Cadogan *et al.* 1993, 25).

iii. Diagnostic Pottery of the MM II A Period

During the interval from the end of the MM I B period to the event, indicated by the burnt destruction deposits in the Royal Pottery Stores and East Central Enclave, a great many innovations may be observed in the techniques and styles of the ceramics. The most apparent change is the widespread adoption of the radial centred potter's wheel. Thrown pottery becomes the norm, especially in the case of small forms. With the technical change, came the confidence to experiment with new forms, the unprecedented and wide variety of which is particularly noticeable in the material in the North-West

Pit. The Flywheel disc and collar, Evely's Type 3c, found in MM contexts at Malia, would have served the purpose well (1988, 90, 100–1).

The most distinctive pottery in use at the time of the destruction is in Egg-shell Ware and Stamped and Impressed Ware using Rounded Cups of Type 3. Also diagnostic are Conical Goblets of Type 3, Tumblers of Type 3, Tall-rimmed Angular Cups of Types 4–6, Pyxides of Types 1–5, Rounded Bridge-spouted Jars of Types 3–4 and Jugs with Horizontal Spout of Type 2.

One of the most striking innovations is the introduction and apparently rapid and widespread adoption of the technique of 'throwing off the hump', to produce the limited range of small utilitarian forms here called Crude Ware. Though many of the forms in Crude Ware first appear now, the Goblet and Type 2 Cup seem to belong only in MM II A.

It should be possible to identify many more wares and styles, as the wealth and diversity of the ceramics from the North-West Pit demonstrates. For example, a 'polychrome reserved style' could be suggested for 203–20, for which there is a corresponding style at Phaistos. The problem would be supporting such a stylistic appraisal with stratigraphic certainty, currently lacking at Knossos.

iv. Diagnostic Pottery of the MM II B Period

The pottery in use at the time of the destruction of the palace is not found in secure contexts within the building. In order to construct the following summary it is necessary to rely on comparisons with material from primary destruction deposits in the town of Knossos, at Archanes and at Phaistos, and to accept that the event used to mark the end of the period, a violent earthquake, was felt throughout central Crete.

The wares and styles most diagnostic of the earthquake horizon are: Precision Stamped Ware and the Sunrise, Starburst, Spiral Band and Wavy-line Styles used most frequently on Straight-sided Cups of Types 9–10, Rounded Cups of Types 5–6 and Rounded Bridge-spouted Jars of Types 4–5. Also characteristic are the Pyxis of Type 6 and Short-rimmed Angular Cups of Type 3.

Many of the Crude types introduced in MM II A seem to continue, but Bowls of Types 1–4, Types 3–4 Cup and both Jug types appear to belong within this period.

It is quite likely that Ridged Ware and the White-spotted and Heavy Spiral styles were introduced before the end of MM II B, but they are more common in the next period.

v. Diagnostic Pottery of the MM III A Period

As with the previous period, there are no pure MM III A deposits from within the palace. The pottery in use immediately following the seismic event, that marks the end of the Old Palace period, is best understood from comparison with deposits in the town of Knossos and in the town and palace at Phaistos.

The Knossian potters seem to have carried on producing the fine wares and styles, current at the end of the Old Palace period, for at least another generation, until the event responsible for forming the primary deposits in the Early Town Houses, Group P, and deposits A and B in the Knossos Acropolis Houses. As the samples from the palaces of Knossos and Phaistos come from contexts associated with re-construction works, Groups E and N at Knossos and Vano 18 and 50 at Phaistos, it is hardly surprising that there be such close continuity from the end of MM II B. For example, Ridged Ware, White-spotted and Heavy Spiral styles form the bridge between the Old and New Palace periods. New forms seem to be the Conical Rhyton, Straight-sided Cup of Type 13 and Jug with Horizontal Spout of Type 3.

The Crude Types of MM II have given way to the distinctive conical cup and miniature forms of MM III and LM I. Perhaps the clearest indicator for the end of the MM III A period is the 'everted rim bowl', absent in Groups E and N, but present at the Knossos Acropolis Houses and at Phaistos (Warren and Hankey 1989, 58).

vi. The Passage of Time in Ceramics Terms

There has been an attempt to link changes in pottery styles with the passage of time, by assuming that each generation will produce its own style and this will be an 'improvement' upon the last (Popham 1990). Caution must be exercised, when attributing a chronological value to stylistic change. Significant changes in ceramic production and design could be placed in an evolutionary model, and used to indicate a long interval between archaeological events. The same innovations could equally signify an influx of new ideas and populations, reflecting a very short interval, during which new styles and techniques quickly dominate and force the abandonment of previous trends, thereby ending their development. We are limited to what we see. For example, the Polychrome Geometric Style of the late MM I A period may be viewed, on the basis of motifs, paint and forms, as a close predecessor for the Woven Style popular in the MM I B destruction deposits, and so we might suppose a short period of unbroken progression. Whereas the designs and forms of the MM II A deposits seem quite far removed from those of MM I B. For example, the appearance of Fine Buff Crude pottery and the widespread adoption of the radial centred potter's wheel (used to make such fine ceramics as the Egg-shell Ware, characteristic of the MM II A destruction deposits) could indicate a long interval between major events in the palace. Equally valid, however, would be the suggestion that the innovations were the result of a rapid influx of new technologies, in this case from Egypt. In contrast, some of the MM II B wares, for example Precision Stamped and Late Printed, may be regarded as the next generation along from the Stamped and Impressed and Early Printed wares of MM II A. This is particularly clear when comparing the motifs on cups **624–6** of MM II A with MM II B cups **293–8**. This short interval may be the reason for the continuation of some of the Crude Types, without perceptible change, from MM II A to the end of MM II B, for example: the Bowls of Types 2 and 3, the pyxides, the Cups of Type 1 and the Juglet. Likewise, the interval between the end of MM II B and the end of MM III A may have been short, as there is little change in the Ridged Ware and Precision Grooved Ware of both periods and the White-spotted and Heavy Spiral styles could also indicate a short period of unbroken stylistic development.

The interval that sees the greatest innovation in ceramic technique and design is the MM II A period. A detailed study of the pottery from the North-West Pit could show specific stages within the period, though without the stratigraphic framework necessary to confirm hypotheses that must remain stylistic. The North-West Pit could have held a gradual accumulation of debris, withdrawn from use over time, and so could represent a long interval. A similar situation was indicated by a series of well-stratified trodden earth surfaces on the N façade of Building 7 at Palaikastro, also of the MM II A period and most likely indicating a long unbroken interval at Palaikastro (MacGillivray, Sackett *et al.*, 1992, 133).

3

Historical implications

INTRODUCTION

As histories tend to be written around major events, so too does this historical chronology of the MBA in central Crete; although in this case the 'events' are archaeological, that is, significant changes as observed and evaluated by the analysis of physical remains. The changes we observe in the archaeological record are difficult to associate, with confidence, to social and/or political change. For example seismic activity of such intensity as to bring down a village, may have had little long-term effect upon the village's inhabitants, or, conversely, could have brought about significant reaction and change. The physical evidence may record a major architectural change, while the indicators of social change, for example burial, ritual practice, choice of styles etc. may seem unaffected. Nonetheless, my duty here is to establish a framework, within which to discuss the more complex issues of Cretan society at the time of the first palaces. The focus is on published sites in N central Crete and their relation to Knossos. I have decided not to include Kommos, Malia and sites to the E and W of the island, as the complexities of their local styles and stratigraphy are much better left in the hands of others. Andreou (1978), Betancourt (1990), Cadogan (1978a; 1990), Godart and Tzedakis (1992), Poursat (1987), Stürmer (1992), and Walberg (1983) have begun the task of forming the stylistic and chronological relationships, necessary to construct the larger image of Proto-palatial Crete.

PART 1. EVENTS IN THE EARLY PALACE AND TOWN AT KNOSSOS

Evans imagined that the architects for the Palace of Minos shaved off the tell, that had formed at the site over centuries of occupation, presumably having evacuated the town's occupants and destroyed their dwellings. Manteli and Evely observe that there was a thin layer of white material scattered over the top of the neolithic levels, perhaps associated with the first building operations in the area of the Throne Room (1995, 2–3). We might suggest the purely functional 'builder's plaster' as an explanation, but equally valid would be a process or ceremony to consecrate or purify the ground surface, prior to the construction of an important monument.

Stylistically, the earliest groups within the palace are the Vat Room Deposit and the similar deposit set in the floor beneath West Magazine 1. Although neither context is well defined, they may be foundation deposits set in position after the end of the MM I A period, as marked by the destruction deposits on the latest floors in West Court Houses B (upper floor) and C, both with pottery in the Polychrome Geometric Style of the late MM I A period.

The earliest architectural element to be incorporated into the palace is the NW Angle, the support wall of which was built during the EM III period (MacGillivray 1994).

The description of the Gypsades cistern and pits as repositories, into which pottery was placed at one time, is reminiscent of the Early Chamber beneath the West Court (Group A), Hogarth's Early Heap in the Town and Wardle's deposit N of the Villa Ariadne. The repositories in the town could have been used as Hogarth suggested and may have contained material from destruction deposits, such as those at the SW Palace Angle, the Room of the Jars in the Royal Pottery Stores (Group I), the vases in the Town Drain (Group O). Other contexts, which might be taken as fill of this period, are the material from the floor at 3.00 m in the Monolithic Pillar Basement (Group M) and the middle floor in the Royal Road S Basements. All certainly suggest an event in the site's history, though the nature of the event is far from clear. Nor is it obvious that a single event is represented. Nonetheless, these contexts have been grouped together here on the basis of ceramic parallels, to form a general picture of the pottery at the end of the MM I B period.

The presence of MM I B pottery beneath West Magazine 1, at the SW Angle, in the Vat Room Area, in the buildings of the Royal Pottery Stores and in the material from the Early Olive Press floor, seems to indicate that most, if not all, of the architectural elements that make up the W and E wings of the palace existed by the end of MM I B.

A significant event in the palace's history is indicated by burnt deposits in W Magazine 2, the Royal Pottery Stores, and the Early Olive Press floor. Similar events in Early SW House 1 and the NW Treasure House may be related and help to define a picture of general conflagration, that is taken to mark the end of the MM II A period.

Evans interpreted the presence of huge blocks from the SE Palace Angle in the House of the Fallen Blocks, and a similar stretch of fallen wall along the line of the South Enceinte, as firm proof of a seismic event of such destructive power, as to require the subsequent rebuilding of much of the palace. The process of cleaning and rebuilding effectively obscured the deposits that might have been formed by the event; but it created a number of contexts in and around the palace, where the debris, from the fallen structures and their contents, might be disposed of and used to level off areas for the next building stage. This would account for the filling in the Loomweight Basement and the West and South Polychrome deposits. The appearance of pottery in use at the time of the seismic event is best seen in small groups

formed in the town, at Trial KV and SEX F/FG, but also at Anemospilia near Archanes and especially in the major floor deposits at Phaistos.

The reconstruction following the earthquake, taken to mark the end of the MM II B period, represents the beginning of the neopalatial period, during which the palace at Knossos sees a large number of architectural innovations. Soon into this first stage of the rebuilding, there is evidence in the town for an event responsible for creating the primary floor deposits in the Town Houses (Group P) and Acropolis Houses deposit A and the re-deposited context of Hogarth's Later Heap. The event is used here to mark the end of the MM III A period and set quite soon, within a generation, of the end of the Old Palace period.

The deposits discussed in Chapter 1 are set out in the order of the chronological periods suggested here in FIG. 3.1.

Period	West Court	Palace West Wing	East Wing	Town
MM III A				Town Houses (P) Hogarth's Later Heap Acropolis A–B
	West Polychrome (E)		South Polychrome (N)	
MM II B	Early SW House 2		Loomweight Basement (K)	Trial KV—destruction SEX F/FG
				?Trial KV—silt
MM II A	Early SW House 1 NW Treasury (B–D)	West Magazine 2	Early Olive Press (L) Royal Pottery Stores (F, G, H, J)	RR/S: upper floor
MM I B	Group A	SW Palace Angle West Magazine 1 Vat Room Deposit Early Keep	Room of the Jars MPB/floor at 3 m (M)	Town Drain (O) RR/S: middle floor Hogarth's Early Heap Gypsades 'pits'
MM I A	House C House B—upper floor Houses A and B	NW Platform	MPB/Early Deposit	RR/S: lowest floor RR/S: early fill

Fig. 3.1. Chronological chart of main Middle Minoan groups at Knossos.

PART 2. NORTH CENTRAL CRETE

i. Juktas

Karetsou's excavations, in the architectural complex of the neopalatial period on the N tip of Mt. Juktas, have demonstrated that there was activity in the area during the MM I A period (1978, 232 pl. 160a). In 1978, she discovered a deposit of fill from the upper terrace, or Terrace I, quite near the 'Chasm' (1978, 247–9; 1981*b*). While the excavator argues that the earliest pottery is a mixture of MM I A, MM I B and MM II styles, it could equally be suggested, through comparison with Knossos Group A and related material, that the published Juktas pottery could be of one date, the MM I B period. This is indicated by the presence of Angular Bridge-spouted Jars of Types 1 and 2 in the Woven Style of Pattern Painted Ware (1978, figs. 11. 6, 7; 12. 4), and Shallow Grooved Ware (ibid., fig. 11. 2). Even the presence of a cup of MM I A type (ibid., fig. 11. 2) need not be a problem as these seem to continue in use, if not manufacture, into the MM I B period at Knossos, for example 145 in Group A. This would indicate that the construction of the terrace should coincide roughly with the foundation of the palaces at Knossos and Phaistos. The establishment of the building around the early terrace and chasm seems to have taken place at the end of MM II–III, according to the results of trials in 1988, and thus belongs to the neopalatial period (Tomlinson 1995, 60).

ii. Archanes

Phourni

The low hill at Phourni, immediately N of Juktas, was used for funerary practices from EM II to the end of the Bronze Age. There seem not to have been any primary inhumations during the Old Palace period, but there is one context that seems to have been formed early in the period and remained undisturbed.

A deposit comprising hundreds of small vases was found between Funerary Building 6 and the W outer wall of Tholos B (J. and E. Sakellarakis 1972). The pottery had been re-deposited, perhaps from the predecessor to Tholos B, Funerary Building 7 of the MM I A period. While some of the forms may be from the MM I A period, a small number of pieces, including a Tumbler of Type 1 (ibid., pl. 2a), a Tall-rimmed Angular Cup of Type 1 (ibid., pl. 5b), and a Straight-sided Cup of Type 2 in the Woven Style (ibid., pl. 5a) may provide a *terminus post quem* in the MM I B period, perhaps earlier than the groups taken to mark the end of the period at Knossos.

Anemospilia

The remains of a finely built structure, on the spur called Anemospilia on the N slopes of Juktas adjacent to a cluster of eroded rock shelters from which it takes its name, were cleared in 1979 (J. and E. Sakellarakis

1979, 1981, 1991). The building seems to have been destroyed at one time and not rebuilt, thereby leaving a very useful collection of finds in primary contexts. Among the types and styles linked to Knossos are a Rounded Cup of Type 6 in the Wavy-line Style (J. and E. Sakellarakis 1979, pl. 183b; 1991, 144 fig. 120), a Jug with Cut-away Spout of Type 4 (ibid., pl. 183), a Crude Juglet (ibid., pl. 183), a jug of the same type as 566 in Group E decorated in the Closed Heavy Spiral Style (ibid., 1979, pl. 183; 1991, fig. 120), and a large jug, with abstract floral motif painted opposite the handle, quite similar in form and decoration to 583–4 in Group E (ibid., 1991 fig. 120).

There can be little doubt that the primary deposits in the structure at Anemospilia were sealed by an event best explained as seismic. The excavators are quite clear in their reconstruction of events (ibid., 1981). The choice of contemporary events at neighboring Knossos and Phaistos is limited to two: the seismic event at the end of the MM II B period, and the event responsible for the primary contexts that mark the end of the MM III A period. The effects of an earthquake, observed at Knossos by Evans and at Phaistos by La Rosa, makes a strong case for the events at all three sites to be related in origin, and exactly contemporary. Given the very close similarity of the pottery with that of Groups E and N at Knossos and period 3 at Phaistos, there is a very strong likelihood that the primary deposits at Anemospilia were created at the end of the MM II B period, as suggested by the excavators.

iii. Gournes

Hatzidakis cleared what he regarded as a funerary structure at the coastal site of Gournes to the E of Knossos in 1914 (1915). The detailed publication of the pottery by Zois allows for a series of close correspondences with the pottery of Knossos to be observed (1969, 2–24). There are several pieces that belong in the MM I A period, for example a group of footed goblets with a type of barbotine decoration (ibid., nos. 7008–9) and a conical goblet in the Polychrome Geometric Style (ibid., no. 7010). A group of juglets is very similar to examples in the Vat Room Deposit (ibid., pls. 1–4; Momigliano 1991, no. 16) and thus early MM I B, but the latest pottery includes a Straight-sided Cup of Type 2 in the Woven Style (ibid., no. 7014a), Convex-sided Cups (ibid., pl. 34 nos. 7015, 7046), and Tall-rimmed Angular Cups of Type 1 (ibid., pl. 28 no. 7015) and Type 3 (ibid., nos. 7012–4), all forms found in the groups that mark the end of the MM I B period at Knossos.

PART 3. PHAISTOS

The stratigraphic sequence at Phaistos has been the subject of a great deal of discussion since Doro Levi's excavations of the 1950's produced a new wing of the

Old Palace (Levi 1976; 1980; Levi and Carinci 1988). Levi's synthesis of the results suggested an historical sequence, quite different to that proposed by Evans for Knossos and Pernier for the previous excavations at Phaistos (Levi 1960). The debate which followed Levi's proposal questioned the contents of some of his periods (Fiandra 1962; 1980; Zois 1965; Platon 1968; Warren and Hankey 1989, 47–9). The result is that there are two alternative systems of periods to distinguish the four major sequential phases of the MM period at Phaistos: that of the excavator, who calls his periods Ia, Ib, II and III, and that of the excavation architect who calls her periods 1, 2, 3 and 4 (Fiandra 1962). Unfortunately, the two systems are not compatible. As in Zois' and Warren and Hankey's, so in the present study the periods and their definitions as set forth by Fiandra are recognized as the most convincing for the Phaistos stratigraphy, and also the most relevant for the comparative material from Knossos and N central Crete.

The following definitions are based on the regrouping of stratified deposits, as given in preliminary reports and listed by Levi and Carinci (1988, 353–79) and Fiandra (1962; 1980). The contexts are arranged in chronological order in FIG. 3.2. The resulting architectural phasing seems to conform with the architectural and stylistic periods as originally set forth by

Pernier. Therefore, it has been necessary to ignore most of Levi's stylistic groupings (1976), as these are seen to conflict with the stratigraphic evidence.

MM I A

Pernier illustrates material from below the pavement in Vano XXV including a jug, juglet and the head of a terracotta figurine painted in tones very similar to those of the Knossos Polychrome Geometric Style (Pernier 1935, 139–42 pls. XIV, XV), and a jar from below the pavement in Vano XII (ibid., pl. XIII). He also illustrates a number of vases of similar date from a variety of locations generally given as below the floor levels of the palace (ibid., 133–8, figs. 58–9, pl. XIII). His conclusion that the material is from contexts earlier than the palace is significant, as it gives a *terminus post quem* for the building's construction, confirmed by Fiandra.

The group of pottery from Patrikies near Phaistos provides a wider variety of MM I A forms than is available from the palace deposits (Bonacasa 1968; Levi 1976, 747–56). Though the predominant form, the teapot, is rare outside of the Mesara, the decoration is closely related to the Polychrome Geometric Style of late MM I A at Knossos (Levi 1976, pl. VII i, l). Evans and Pernier had agreed on the MM I A date for the latest material

Period	Palace		Town
MM III A	Vani 18, 50 *calcestruzzo*	**4**	South West Court Vani 86, 87
MM II B	deposits throughout Vani 5–9, 66–7	**3**	
MM II A	Vani 11, 25, 49, 51–5, 65 drain fill: Vani 59, 60, 64 bench: Vano 63 Vani 24, 27 N Block West Wing	**2**	W. West Court Vani 81, 83, 95, 97–101, 102–03
MM I B	Vano 65—1st floor Vano 11—chest	**1**	W. West Court—Vani 99–101, 103
MM I A	Vano 25 beneath floor		Patrikies group

Fig. 3.2. Chronological chart of main Middle Minoan groups at Phaistos. Roman numerals of Levi's excavations here converted to Arabic.

from beneath the palace (Evans 1921, 144). We may now place it close to the end of the period, when the Polychrome Geometric Style was popular at Knossos.

Period 1

The beginning of Period 1 is marked by the construction of the South-West Block of the First Palace. Two groups may assigned to this early phase.

The first is sherd material from the foundation trench for the Façade (Fiandra 1962, 114–15, 117 pl. 19). Included are at least six examples of Barbotine Ware, two fragments of teapots, the shoulder of a closed vessel with remains of circular patterns (similar to F. 2171 from the Period 1 floor in Vano LXV, belonging to a later stage of this period), and a sherd in Early Printed Ware with white S motifs on a dark ground (ibid., pl. 19 top left).

The second is the contents of a chest, set into the floor of Vano 11, perhaps as a foundation deposit, that pre-dates the main Period 2 destruction deposit stratified above it (Levi 1976, 363–4). The whole vases include two rounded bridge-spouted jars with horizontal barbotine decoration (F. 61, 62), a spouted cup with similar decoration (F. 353), a rounded bridge-spouted jar in Early Printed Ware, with an S-pattern in white on the shoulder (F. 361), and a straight-sided cup similar to Knossos Type 2 (F. 362). The painted dot medallion opposite the spout on F. 62 is quite similar to the motif as employed in the Woven Style at Knossos, see above p. 59; FIGS. 2.2 (3); 2.3 (2).

Also belonging to this period, but apparently later, are the earliest deposits in Vani IC, C, CI and CIII in the houses W of the W Court (Levi 1976, 537–55). Pottery includes examples in Early Printed Ware (F. 5479a), Polychrome Reserved Style (F. 5330, 5957c) and in a style closely related to Knossian Woven Style (F. 5474, 5482, 5939, 5946).

A mature stage of Period 1 may be represented by a destruction deposit on the earliest floor in Vano LXV. The pottery includes examples in Barbotine Ware (F. 2116, 2169, 2170) and an example of Early Printed Ware (F. 2175) very similar to Knossos 632 in Group F.

Fiandra's definition of Period 1 generally conforms to Levi's phase Ia. A detailed re-examination should make it possible to subdivide the pottery further into early and late wares and styles. Examples from the early stage are closely related to Group A at Knossos and should be regarded as contemporary. Fiandra assigned this material to the MM I B period, as Evans had done for Group A at Knossos. The present study agrees that this period be taken to mark the beginning of the Old Palace period at both sites, and, as the pottery may be distinguished from that of the previous MM I A period and develops without break into MM II A wares and styles (in particular the Printed Ware and Woven Styles), that it continue to be called MM I B. There is no reason why Phaistos Period 1 and Knossos MM I B should be co-terminous, but, until the recently excavated Knossian deposits are fully published and compared with those from Phaistos, it seems most convenient to regard the periods as largely contemporary.

Period 2

The end of the second period is defined by the burnt destruction deposits in the early rooms beneath the SW façade of the New Palace in Vani 10, 11 and 25; the floors assigned by Levi to his phase Ib in the area of Vani IL, LI–LV, LXV. Also to the period belongs the material from the drain beneath Vani LIX, LX and LXIV, stratified beneath floor deposits of Period 3, the contents of the bench in Vani LXIII, and a group of floor deposits in the houses W of the W Court in Vani LXXXI, LXXXIII–XCV, XCVII–CI and CII–CIII.

Many of the pottery parallels between Phaistos and Knossos are cited in the descriptions of the wares and styles in Chapter 2. They are far too numerous to be repeated here in detail. For example, the deposit in Vano 11 includes Rounded Bridge-spouted jars of Type 4 (F. 414, 415, 428), one which is decorated with the eight-petalled rosette motif of Knossos Cup **617**, an angular cup in Shallow Grooved Ware (F. 397), a cup in Early Printed Ware (F. 418), a Tall-rimmed Angular Cup of Type 1 (F. 400), a Pedestalled Lamp of Type 1 (F. 381), and an angular cup decorated in stone-like veins (F. 396) very similar to Knossos jar **246**. In general, the pottery is most similar to that of the Royal Pottery Stores, Groups F–H, and Early Olive Press Floor, Group L, at Knossos. Fiandra used this material to define the ceramics of the MM II A period (1980), as Evans had done at Knossos. The present study proposes that it be taken to mark the end of the period.

Fiandra places the construction of the N block of the W Wing of the Old Palace to this period and vases published by Pernier from below Vano XXVII (1935 pl. 16 a, b), Vano XXIV (ibid., pl. 21b) and Vano XI (ibid., pl. 24b) tend to confirm this.

The end of this period at both Phaistos and Knossos is marked by burnt destruction deposits which preserved sealings and tablets in the Hieroglyphic and Linear A scripts at both palaces. The pottery styles from both sites are so similar as to suggest that the events were contemporary.

Period 3

The end of the third period is marked by a severe destruction in both blocks of the W Wing, which left upper and lower floor deposits *in situ* in almost all of the rooms. As Levi had separated these into two periods, Ib and II, it is necessary to combine many of his groups in the S block in order to gain a full understanding of the ceramics in use at the time of the destruction (Warren and Hankey 1989, 47–8).

Deposits are in the Corridoio LIII–LV and Sottoscale LI, LIII, LIV, LV, LVI, LVII, LVIII, LIX, LX, LXIV. The NW corner rooms, V–VII, were added to the N block of the W Wing during this period and, like the other rooms in the block and under the Grand Staircase, XXXIV, contained destruction deposits. To the SW of the palace, deposits were found in XXVII–XXVIII, XLVII, LXVII and LXVIII.

In many areas a layer of 'calcestruzzo' was laid over the levelled debris, apparently at one time but at differing absolute heights (Fiandra 1980, 170–6; Warren and Hankey 1989, 47).

The pottery from this final destruction horizon of the Old Palace at Phaistos provides the most comprehensive definition of central Cretan ceramics at the close of the Old Palace period. Fiandra, following Evans, placed the destruction at the end of the MM II B period (1962). Comparanda from the palace at Knossos are quite numerous and cited, with the wares and styles, in Chapter 2. They are from deposits formed in the palace during the event and early in the subsequent period, Groups E, K and N, and are thus a mixture of MM II B and MM III A wares and styles. However, the destruction deposit in Trial KV and the contents of the pit in Tomb XVII at Mavrospilio, though meagre, confirm Fiandra's dating to the MM II B period.

Period 4

Fiandra's Period 4 is roughly equivalent to Levi's phase III which comprises the whole of the MM III period and, because it includes material from the Kamilari tholos, extends into LM III. To an early stage of the period may be assigned the small deposit, formed during the earliest stages of the re-building of the palace in Vano 18 (Levi 1976, 374–7 fig. 586; Carinci 1989, 78). The pottery includes Straight-sided Cups like Knossos Types 8 and 10, decorated in the Spiral Band Style (F. 367, 373, 375), a Rounded Cup like Type 5, in the Heavy Spiral Style (F. 354) and another cup in the same style (F. 387). To this early stage of the period may also be assigned the votive or foundation deposit beneath Vano 50 (Levi 1976, 405–8 figs. 623–30). The pottery includes four Straight-sided Cups like Types 8 and 10, decorated in the Spiral Band Style (F. 707a–d) and a rounded cup like Type 5 in the Heavy Spiral Style (F. 490).

The Heavy Spiral Style at Knossos is placed late in the MM II B period and early in MM III A, see above p. 64; a conclusion supported by its appearance in primary deposits, after the events that mark the end of the Old Palace at Phaistos.

The early neopalatial building, S of the W Court, may have come into existence during this period and the floor deposits in Vani LXXXVI and LXXXVII may be earlier than those in the other rooms, which contained pottery of the MM III B period (Levi 1976, 489).

The comparanda at Knossos for the pottery from the early stages of this period come from the mixed groups of fill, deposited after the destruction of the Old Palace, Groups E and N, but also from the Early Town Houses, Group P, Hogarth's Heap, and the earliest deposits, A and B, in the Acropolis Houses, which conform to Evans' definition of the ceramics of the MM III A period.

This period, then, is very similar in its composition and nature at both sites. The pottery may be distinguished from the well-known styles of the MM III B period, best illustrated by Deposit C in the Acropolis Houses at Knossos (Catling *et al.* 1979, 34–9) and the floor deposits in Rooms LXXXIX–XCIII of the house S of the W Court at Phaistos. It is proposed here to retain Evans' designation of MM III A, at both Phaistos and Knossos, to comprise the first stage of re-building following what appears to have been a seismic event in central Crete.

The nature of the event that marks the horizon between periods 3 and 4 has been clarified further, in recent excavations by La Rosa, who has found traces of a seismic destruction at Phaistos (Tomlinson 1995, 63). This would conform with the evidence from Anemospilia and Knossos and contribute to the hypothesis of an earthquake at the end of the MM II B period.

PART 4. EGYPT AND THE LEVANT

i. Chronology and History of Egypt in the Middle Kingdom

The complexities of Egyptian chronology have all but obscured the field in recent years, for scholars reliant on the Egyptian accession dates for the stability of other chronologies. We have arrived at a time when we must decide to support the most convincing argument for the moment, accept a series of dates, and write history to the best of our ability, with the understanding that it could be overturned by the time it goes to press. I have decided to use Kitchen's 'best' dates (1989, 152–3; in press), which have become the most commonly used by Aegean scholars (Warren and Hankey 1989; Warren 1995; Kuhrt 1995, 161). As Kitchen's dates are revised, so too must those employed here.

The XIth Dynasty lasts the 143 years from 2116 to 1973 BC and seems to correspond largely with the MM I A period (Warren and Hankey 1989, 128–30). The XIIth Dynasty kings built for their capital the fortress city in the neighbourhood of modern Lisht at Itht-toui, 'The Controller of the Two Lands', between Herakleiopolis and Memphis. The dynasty begins with the accession of Amenemhat in 1973 who ruled until his death in 1944. The last nine years of his reign were shared with his son, Senusret—the Greek Sesostris—who ruled 1953–1908. The last three years of his 45 year reign were shared with his son Amenemhat II, who acceded to the throne in 1911. Amenemhat II's 35 year reign ended with his death in 1876. His successor, Senusret II became co-regent with his father in 1878 and ruled for 6 years until 1872. On his death, Senusret III ruled for 19 years until 1853. With his death came the ascendancy of Amenemhat III, whose 45 year reign marked a high point in the stability of the XIIth Dynasty's rule. He was succeeded in 1808 by Amenemhat IV who ruled for 9 years until his death in 1799. Sobeknefru's reign of 4 years ending in 1795 concludes the XIIth Dynasty. What follows in the XIIIth Dynasty is a different kind of administration without the strength of one long rule, but rather a time of internal struggle for power lasting a minimum of 150 years from 1795 to 1638 BC, when the Hyksos occupied the Delta. The Egyptian government certainly continued to operate, but the impression is one of a withdrawal from the Delta with consolidation and enlargement at Lisht after roughly 1650/40 BC (Quirke 1991, 123), until Ahmose conquered Avaris over a century later in 1540 and began the re-unification of the country under the XVIIIth Dynasty.

ii. Minoica in Egypt

The discovery of 'Aegean' pottery by Petrie in 1889 and 1890 at Kahun provided one of the most reliable historical links between the early Aegean cultures and Egypt even before the Bronze Age Cretans had been re-discovered (Petrie 1891). The resulting chronological impact has been the subject of a great deal of debate, as the historical sequence for the Aegean Bronze Age continues to rely heavily on links between the Cretans and their eastern neighbours. The comprehensive publication of Minoan pottery in Egypt by Kemp and Merrillees (1980) remains the most useful source, as it reviews find contexts and very much facilitates comparison with the Cretan material. In the following brief re-appraisal of the chronological value of the Cretan exports in Egypt, reference is made to their numbering system wherever possible.

Qubbet el-Hawa

The small, handmade jug, found with a group of disturbed material in a secondary use of shaft IV in Tomb 88 at Qubbet el-Hawa near Aswan, is unique in some respects, but has features that allow it to be placed with a great deal of confidence in the early part of the Cretan MBA (Edel in Kemp and Merrillees 1980, 176–219). The jug's overall shape has no close parallels, but the foot is quite similar to those on the Tall-rimmed Angular Cup Type 1b, Rounded Cup of Type 1b, Shallow Angular Bowl of Type 1 and Angular Bridge-spouted Jar of Type 1b, all handmade forms of the MM I B period at Knossos, though the piece is almost certainly not from Knossos. The decoration belongs to the very characteristic Alternating Red and White Floral Style of E Crete (Cadogan 1983, 515–16; 1990, 172–4; 1994, 65–6), a close parallel to the decoration is found on a tumbler like Knossos Type 1 from Malia (Demargne 1945, pl. IX no. 8658; Cadogan 1983, 516). The plastic flowers may be placed within a 'Plastic Style' of Palaikastro, though birds and animals are more common embellishments (Bosanquet and Dawkins 1923, 12, pls. VI.D, VII). The E Cretan style is contemporary with MM I B–II A at Knossos (MacGillivray and Driessen 1990, 398), and so, it seems, should be the Qubbet el-Hawa jug. The material found with the jug is largely early Middle Kingdom in date (Kemp and Merrillees 1980, 217–19), though the latest finds suggest a date early in the XIIth Dynasty providing for a likely overlap between the MM I B period and the early XIIth Dynasty (Warren and Hankey 1989, 130).

Haraga—Cemetery B

Tomb 326 at Haraga contained a number of Egyptian pots including two crinkle rim bowls/cups interpreted as local imitations of Minoan pots (Kemp and Merrillees 1980, 36–9 fig. 17 Ha. 13, 14). If the cups imitate Cretan originals, the prototypes would belong to the earlier part of the Old Palace period and it is more likely that they would be from E Crete than the centre; as for example the silver cups from Gournia House Tomb I (Boyd-Hawes et al. 1908, pl. C. 1–3). Davis assigns the Cretan cups to the MM I B period (1979, 37).

El Tôd

The 153 silver vessels in copper chests bearing the cartouche of Amenemhat II, found at El Tôd in 1936, have been compared with Minoan ceramics since their discovery and publication (Bisson de la Roque et al. 1953). The variety of opinion generated may reflect the variety of sources for a collection of vessels and other objects gathered together late in the king's reign, as Porada suggested (1982), recently revised by Maxwell-Hyslop (1995). The date of the context has been disputed, but Lilyquist has presented a convincing case for the integrity of its XIIth Dynasty deposition (1993).

Warren (1980, 495–6) and Warren and Hankey (1989, 131–5) summarize the conflicting views, and present a detailed and convincing argument both for a Minoan origin for some of the metalware and for a sound chronological correspondence. The Cretan ceramic examples they cite for the cups, however, are similar to Rounded Cups of Type 5 (ibid. 1989, pl. 5A, C). A more convincing parallel might be the Squat Rounded Cups of Type 1. The similarity between Tôd 70580, 70583 and **22, 44** and **45** suggests a chronological link for the silver cups with the end of the MM I B period. The vertical arcades on 70593, 70604–5, and rosette patterns on 70623, 70627, 70629 and 70630, however, are quite likely to have inspired the impressed and painted patterns on Egg-shell Ware cups of the MM II A period, for example **616, 617** and examples cited by Warren and Hankey (1989, 132–5), and so should be contemporary with a stage of MM II A.

Some of the silver jewellery and ingots have been shown to originate in the N Aegean, as they conform with the Thasos—Chalkidiki or Troadic fields as defined by lead isotope analysis (Menu 1994). Two of the cups analysed, however, are not made of silver from the same source and seem to lie outside the known fields, perhaps due to the alloying or mixing of metals from a variety of sources. As there is no source of silver in Crete, the expectation of Aegean scholars has been that Siphnos or the Laurion would have been the likely source for Cretan metal smiths. Matsas' discovery of a Minoan roundel and nodule at Mikro Vouni in Samothrace has done much to alter previous expectations, and provide the firm administrative evidence to support the conclusions of the lead isotope analysis (1991; 1995). They certainly prove that Cretans were active in the N Aegean. The Mikro Vouni documents were associated with material similar to the early sub-period of Troy VI and Matsas proposed a date in late MM II (1991) revised to MM II B–III A (1995). The first published C-14 dates of 2030–1785 and 2030–1876 BC, for bone samples associated with the roundel, may seem early (ibid. 1991, 168). In fact, the second date fits quite well with Kitchen's dates for the reign of Amenemhat II, the exact time that the silver used to create the ingots and bracelets in the Tôd treasure was probably produced and shipped south; this conforms well with a stylistic link between the Tôd cups and Knossian pottery in MM I B and MM II A. The second set of dates, however, bring the Minoan documents down to *c.* 1750 BC and beyond the date of Amenemhat II.

Lisht

Excavations on the W side of the N of the two pyramids at el-Lisht, that of Amenemhat I, produced a number of Minoan sherds from a fill context, that unfortunately cannot be placed with more precision than from the early XIIth to the late XIIIth Dynasty (Kemp and Merrillees 1980, 5–6). Among the published pottery are a few pieces, for which close parallels may be cited.

Li.1 is part of a handmade composite vase without close parallels in central Crete, but very much at home in the Alternating Red and White Floral Style of E Crete (Cadogan 1983, 515–16; 1990, 172–4; 1994, 65–6), as with the Qubbet el-Hawa jug, above. The upright branch pattern is quite close to that on a MM I B cup from Gournia (Boyd-Hawes *et al.* 1908, pl. C3), and so the vase's manufacture was probably during the MM I B period in E Crete.

Li. 3 is the handle of a rounded bridge-spouted jar of uncertain type. The type of handle, though, is unlikely to be earlier than the MM I B period and, given its similarity to the handles on Rounded Bridge-spouted Jars of Types 4 and 5, most likely to belong within the MM II period.

Kemp and Merrillees point out the likelihood that a seventh sherd, not in their inventory, could be Cretan (1980, 4 pl. 3 middle row, second from right). If so, it finds a close parallel in the decoration of Rounded Cup Type 3, **645**, from the MM II A context of Group F.

The Minoan pottery from Lisht, therefore, was manufactured during the MM I B and MM II A periods and may have arrived at the site over a period of several generations.

Kahun

The majority of the twenty sherds of Minoan pottery from Kahun comes from a dump, near the big houses on the N part of the site (Kemp and Merrillees 1980, 82–90).

A recent analysis of the Kahun sherds in the BM has shown that most were probably manufactured in the same workshops, producing the fine wares for Phaistos and the Mesara (Fitton *et al.* 1999). The chemical results, though at first surprising, may be confirmed by the following stylistic comparison with pottery from Phaistos and Knossos.

Among the numerous fragments of Middle Minoan pottery in Pattern Painted Ware said to be from Kahun are fragments of Rounded Bridge-spouted Jars (Ka. 1, 2, 3, 4, 8, 10, 11). The two most complete, Ka. 1 and 2, are closest in form to jars of Type 4 at Knossos, typical of the destruction deposits at the end of the MM II A period. The decoration on Ka. 1 very closely resembles that on **250** and the two could well be the products of the same workshop. The decoration of a sharp pointed petalled rosette on Ka. 2 is not common at Knossos, but very much a feature of Phaistos Period 2. Ka.6 and 7 are the spouts of 'teapots'; a form not known at Knossos, but quite common at Phaistos (Levi and Carinci 1988, pls. 44–6, e.g., F. 4789, 6187). The white painted pattern of a tiny dot rosette on Ka. 6 is one most often encountered on pottery of the MM II A period at Knossos, for example **655, 942–6, 994**, but is also quite common at Phaistos, the source of the examples above (Fitton *et al.* 1999).

The one fragment that may be Knossian, straight-sided cup Ka. 17, is quite similar in form and decoration to **637** in the MM II A Group F.

Kemp and Merrillees (1980, 87) point out that Kahun became prosperous, because it was well situated for the increased commerce with the Fayum, at a time when it was being developed for agriculture by the XIIth Dynasty kings. It has been suggested that the most likely time for the importation of the Minoan pots would have been during the town's floruit in the reign of Amenemhat III or soon thereafter (Fitton *et al.* 1999). A MM sherd from N Karnak, said to be from a Middle Kingdom level and compared to those from Kahun, may also belong to this period (Jacquet-Gordon 1991, 29).

Haraga

Excavations in the Middle Kingdom cemetery site at Haraga during the winter of 1913/14 produced about 20 fragments of MM pottery (Kemp and Merrillees 1980, 6–14). The fragments were found in debris in the area of cemeteries C, C2 and C3. The main bulk of the graves in the Haraga cemeteries date to the second half of the XIIth Dynasty and there has been a tendency to associate the imported ceramics with those from Kahun and link the notion of Aegean workers in the town with 'their' pottery (Evans 1928, 210). Among the sherds some are comparable to known types in Crete:

Ha. 4 is a body fragment of Barbotine Ware, quite common in Crete in the MM I B period, but probably still produced in MM II A at Knossos.

Ha. 5 may be the shoulder of a bridge-spouted jar in Stamped and Impressed Ware of the MM II A period at Knossos.

Ha.16 is a body fragment of a rounded bridge-spouted jar from just below the spout. Although the type cannot be ascertained, the decoration is quite similar to that on Rounded Bridge-spouted Jars of Type 4, 957–8, in Group L, and fragments of very similar bridge-spouted jars from Phaistos (Fiandra 1980, 186–7 pl. 45. 1, 10, 13). The Cretan contexts are both in the MM II A period.

Like Kahun, the Minoan pottery at Haraga could all have been manufactured in Crete during the MM II A period, and found its way to the site in the second half of the XIIth Dynasty. Dorothea Arnold dates the deposition of the rubbish deposits, that contained the Minoan sherds, to after the reign of Amenemhat III and decidedly before the middle of the XIIIth Dynasty (1990), so the early XIIIth Dynasty is the *terminus ad quem*.

Abydos

The importance of the Minoan jar in Abydos tomb 416 was recognised in 1907 by Evans, who used it to form a link between Knossos in the MM II period and XIIth Dynasty Egypt (Kemp and Merrillees 1980, 118–19 fig. 38 pl. 13).

The form of the jar conforms well with the MM II B Knossian Rounded Bridge-spouted Jar of Type 5. The main decorative motif is similar to that of the Starburst Style, but the central disc is red, as on 956, although the motif on the earlier, MM II A, jar stands alone. A white starburst with red centre on a sherd from Kommos is assigned to MM II B (Betancourt 1990, no. 419). The lozenge motif is similar to that on a cup from a MM II A context at Phaistos (Fiandra 1980, 180–1 pl. 36.5,6). The undulating design on a jar from Monastiraki is also similar and includes lozenges, though in white (Godart and Tzedakis 1992, 68 pl. LXXVI.1). However, the overall decoration is so close to that on K. 1010, a MM II B Straight-sided Cup of Type 9, that it probably comes from the same workshop.

Kemp and Merrillees' exhaustive attempt to fix a date for the contents of Tomb 416 concludes with 'The most positive thing that one can say is that had it been found at el-Haraga, it would fit very well indeed into the Middle Kingdom phase of culture there, always remembering that the term "Middle Kingdom" covers the Thir-

teenth Dynasty as well' (1980, 174). The Abydos jar, then, was probably manufactured during the MM II B period in central Crete and could have been brought to Egypt and deposited during the early part of the XIIIth Dynasty.

Tell el-Dab'a

The base and lower body fragments of a rounded cup in the Wavy-line Style of MM II B was found at Tell el-Dab'a in the secure context of stratum D/1, which is stratum G/4 on tell A (Bietak 1995, 19; Walberg 1991, 115–20; MacGillivray 1995, 81–4). The level covers the earliest years of the XIIIth Dynasty, *c.* 1790–1760 BC in the High Chronology. The cup is almost certainly a product of the workshop, that created the Rounded Cups of Type 6 in the Wavy-line Style, characteristic of the groups at the end of the Old Palace period in central Crete, which must then be placed during the early part of the XIIIth Dynasty.

iii Minoica in the Levant

Hazor

The body fragment of an open form, suspected to be Minoan, was found in Stratum 3 in Area C at Hazor in 1956 (Yadin *et al.* 1960, 91 pl. CXV.13). The sherd looks very much as though it could have come from a rounded open form, most likely a bowl, but little more can be said without a more detailed publication. The context is late MB II and so would belong to the time of the MM imports in Egypt and the Levant.

Beirut

Rescue excavations in the centre of Beirut at Kharji in 1954 uncovered a large MB and LB cemetery. In Grotta 4, chamber 1, was found a fine MM cup (Warren and Hankey 1989, 134–5 pl. 12a). The cup is not one of the types defined by the present study, but may be part of the period of experimentation evident in the wide variety of singular forms, that make up the fine wares from the North-West Pit at Knossos (Group D). A close parallel for the shape, though without the distinctive closed base, might be 234. The Group D material is essentially unstratified, but the majority of the fine wares can be referred to the MM II A and MM II B periods. The form is also quite similar to a cup of central Cretan manufacture found on a burnt floor of the MM II B or early MM III A period in Building 6 at Palaikastro (MacGillivray *et al.*, 1998). The most likely date for the Beirut cup, then, would be late MM II B or early MM III A.

Byblos

The excavation in 1922 of a large rock-cut chamber tomb or 'hypogeum' of 'Phoenician' type produced a group of undisturbed artefacts including an obsidian jar from the reign of Amenemhat III and two silver vases said to be of Aegean origin (Virolleaud 1922). One, a spouted jug, is not like those of central Crete (ibid., 285 fig. 5 pl. LXIV.10). The other, a rounded cup with embossed interlocking spirals, may be recognized as the inspiration for the painted design on Egg-shell Ware cup **620**, but even more so for the Precision Stamped Ware of the MM II B period at Knossos. The ceramic copies of the cup should be later than the Minoan pottery at Kahun and Haraga and after the end of Amenemhat III's reign. A full analysis of the latest possible date in Egyptian and Aegean terms would be necessary before attempting to make the link between the obsidian jar and MM II B at Knossos.

Rescue excavations in 1955 revealed a tomb first used in the EBA, then re-used in the MBA (Baramki 1973). Associated with the second interment is a Minoan bridge-spouted jar, similar in form to **1002** and decorated in the Wavy-line Style, with a pattern very much like **356**. The jar is almost certainly the product of the Knossian workshop producing the Wavy-line Style of the end of the MM II B period.

In his excavations in the town of Byblos, Dunand reports the discovery of seven fragments of MM pottery from a depth of about 2 metres in 'levée X' (1939, 191 pl. CLXXVII no. 2986; Schaeffer 1948, 66 fig. 74. 2–4). The fragments all belong to a rounded bridge-spouted jar, most similar in profile to Knossos Type 6. The decoration is difficult to decipher, but seems to be related to the Heavy Spiral Style with closed spirals. Form and decoration, then, indicate that the vase was manufactured in the late MM II B or early MM III A period, most likely at Knossos.

The Minoan pottery seems to indicate a link between Knossos and Byblos at the end of the Old Palace period.

Ugarit

The rim fragment of a Minoan cup was found in the ossuary tomb XXXVI (Schaeffer 1949, 256 fig. 109A). The fragment belongs to a rounded cup decorated in the Wavy-line Style and is almost certainly a Knossian product of the MM II B period.

A second Minoan cup from Ugarit was found in the dromos of Tomb LXXXVI (Schaeffer 1949, 256 fig. 109 pl. XXXVIII bottom). It has some of the features of the Wavy-line Style, including the pattern-painted base decorated in and out, the use of tiny white dots in the patterns and the cup's form, but the main motif, while constructed above and below an undulating line, incorporates an ivy pattern not seen in Crete until the LM I A period (Bernini 1995, 64 fig. 8E). One wonders if the cup could not have been painted over, at a time several generations subsequent to its manufacture.

In 1937 Schaeffer cleared a particularly rich group of finds from a built Tomb LVII of Middle Ugarit 2 date (1938, 222–50). While none of the pottery is obviously Minoan, two vases certainly imitate Cretan pro-

totypes. One is a rounded bridge-spouted jar of similar size and form to Cretan jars of the same type, but instead of the arched handle of Crete, the same position on the shoulder is occupied by double handles of Syro-Palestinian type (ibid., 242 fig. 35I pl. XXIV). The other is a red burnished jug, quite out of place in the local sequence and suspected of being imported, but very similar to **591** in Group E and examples from the context of Group N in PLATE 144 (ibid., fig. 35H pl. XXIV). A third vase in the tomb is a 'local' jug of a type very similar to the Dolphin Vase from Tomb 879 at Lisht, now known to have been manufactured in Gaza (ibid., fig. 35D pl. XXIV; McGovern *et al.* 1994).

Qatna

Excavations at Mishrifé-Qatna in 1924 produced the rim fragment of a Rounded Cup of Type 6 in the Wavy-line Style (Du Mesnil du Buisson 1926, 324 fig. 41). Unfortunately, the context at 'la falaise' is not recorded, but the MM II B cup's presence at the site of ancient Qatna provides evidence for Cretan ceramic products being traded in the interior of Syria, at the time of their popularity on the coast (Schaeffer 1948, 117).

PART 5. SYNTHESIS

Cretan relations with Egypt in the Middle Kingdom may be viewed as a society very much under the influence of the dominant power of its time. For this reason, I have decided to link the Minoan periods to specific Egyptian reigns where possible, both because I believe that significant changes in the rule of the most powerful state in the region must have had some effect on neighbouring states, but also because the shifting sands of Egyptian time seem to play less havoc with the Cretan periods, if they are linked to royal accessions. Thus, it can be suggested that the foundation of the palaces at Knossos and Phaistos be linked to the accession of Senusret I in 1953, 20 years into the XIIth Dynasty, allowing for the rule of Amenemhat I to overlap with the latest stages of the MM I A period.

The Cretan pottery in Egypt may indicate a shift in regional influence within the Cretan Old Palace period. The Lisht composite vase (Li. 1) and Qubbet el-Hawa jug are stylistically the earliest Cretan imports and both almost certainly products of E Cretan workshops of the MM I B period. The crinkle-rimmed cups from Haraga Tomb 326 would best be seen as imitations of metal or ceramic vases of the MM I B period in E Crete. A relationship between Palaikastro and Zakros and early XIIth Dynasty Egypt may be hypothesized, though little can be offered in terms of reciprocal goods until the Old Palace period levels are more fully explored at the Cretan sites. The distinctive styles of late MM I A and MM I B Knossos are found in the Cyclades and Greek mainland, but not in the Levant or Egypt.

The ceramic forms inspired by the silver wares in the Tôd treasure are found in MM I B and MM II A deposits at Knossos and Phaistos, and so the MM II A period should have begun by the end of the reign of Amenemhat II in 1876. As it seems that the Cretan pottery styles undergo a relatively minor development between the end of MM I A and the end of the MM I B period, I have chosen to place the events that mark the end of MM I B at the end of the reign of Senusret I in 1908. This would allow forty-five years, or between one and two generations, from the foundation of the major palace structure at Knossos to the time of the first major archaeological event at the end of MM I B.

A significant percentage of the Cretan ceramics found at Kahun and Haraga have been shown to have originated in the Mesara in the MM II A period, perhaps indicating a strong link between Phaistos and Egypt during the middle and later half of the XIIth Dynasty. As this was a period of well documented diplomatic ties between Egypt and her neighbours, it would be interesting to speculate on the influential role Phaistos and the Mesara might have played during this long period of stability in the eastern Mediterranean, especially during the reign of one of Egypt's strongest rulers, Amenemhat III, 1853–1808 BC. Knossos at this time seems to have continued to look N, as the Minoan pottery in the Cyclades again seems to resemble most closely that of Knossos.

The death of Amenemhat III initiated a time of weak rule and may have led a certain amount of instability, that may have encouraged the Hyksos conquest of the Delta, and enlargement of Lisht in the XIIIth and XIVth Dynasties (Kuhrt 1995, 176–7). The changes in the Delta must have had serious effects on the country's foreign diplomatic and trading relationships, and could be one of the factors responsible for the decline in the influence of Phaistos by the end of the Old Palace period, in favour of Knossos. The shift to N central Crete is suggested by the Abydos jar and Tell el-Dab'a cup of Knossian MM II B origin, both in late XIIth or early XIIIth Dynasty contexts after the reign of Amenemhat III. For this reason I have chosen to place the events that mark the end of the MM II A period, after the end of the reign of Amenemhat III and before the XIIIth Dynasty context of the el-Dab'a cup. The most suitable horizon is where Kitchen places the end of the XIIth Dynasty, in 1795; though anywhere within a range of ten to fifteen years after Amenemhat III could be argued. I propose to place the end of the MM II B period close to the time of the deposition of the el-Dab'a cup, roughly 1760. The relatively short stretch of 35 years would help explain the minor changes in Cretan ceramic technique and design from the end of MM II A to the end of MM II B. The major changes in technique, form and design in Minoan ceramics from the end of MM I B to the end of MM II A could be accounted for by the 113 year interval proposed here, thereby allowing for perhaps four to five generations of craftsmen and clients.

The nature of the events at the end of the MM II A period in Crete could indicate the end of a period of conflict on the island. The most convincing evidence for this is the sudden proliferation of fortifications and administrative posts and the improved military technologies, as suggested by the dagger types being produced in Crete (Wiener 1991; MacGillivray 1993).

Cretan exports to Egypt may be seen to fall away during the frequent changes of the rulers in the XIIIth and XIVth Dynasties and subsequent Second Intermediate Period. It may be that the lack of a strong figurehead in Egypt left the Cretans without a clear trading partner or diplomatic ally in the Nile. At roughly the same time, Knossian products and their copies began to appear on the Levantine coast, perhaps signalling the direction that the new balance of power in the eastern Mediterranean was taking. Sixteen years after the death of Amenemhat III, Hammurabi rose to power in Babylon and set about consolidating his realm. Hammurabi's accession in 1792 and his period of extensive conquests crowned with the capture of Mari in 1760, coincides quite closely with the proposed dates for the MM II B period in Crete (Kuhrt 1995, 108–9). This is also the date of the Dolphin vase, a Syro-Palestinian product of MB II A–II B date in the early to middle XIIIth Dynasty context of tomb 879 at Lisht, but partially decorated with Aegean-like dolphins (McGovern et al. 1994).

The Knossian exports to Byblos and Ugarit, the imitation of Minoan forms and the addition of Aegean design motifs to Syro-Palestinian vase forms, may now be placed against the background of the Mari letters. The Cretan products and their local imitations may be linked to the Kaptarite interpreters who lived at Ugarit and were paid in tin (Wiener 1991; Neimeier 1991, 191). In one letter, Zimri-lim offers to Hammurabi the gift of a weapon (*kakkum kaptaru*) partly covered with gold and the top inlaid with lapis lazuli (Dossin 1939, 111–12; Astour 1973, 19–20; Durand 1983, 258–61). We may now offer as examples the swords from the palace at Malia (Chapouthier and Charbonneaux 1928), and especially one from the Quartier Mu (Detournay et al., 147–9, frontispiece, fig. 219). The palatial context has been clarified by Pelon and placed at the end of MM II or beginning of MM III (Pelon 1983, 701–3). The Quartier Mu context is the major destruction at the end of MMII. Both contexts are near or at the end of the Old Palace period at Malia, which Cadogan and Poursat equate roughly with the end of MM II B at Knossos, and thus exactly contemporary with the last years of Zimri-lim, whose career ends in 1760. The Cretan link is further supported by the 'Canaanite' jar fragments, 1021, from Knossos. The associations outlined above are charted against the background of Egyptian chronology in FIG. 3.3.

The fall of Mari in 1760 saw the closing off of the routes to tin and copper sources for the W, and thus the collapse of what may have been a major part of the economic basis for the Cretan traders on the Syro-Palestinian coast. This could explain why the next area we find Minoan ceramics is at the SE Aegean sites of Trianda in Rhodes, the Seraglio in Kos, Miletos and Iasos (Furumark 1950; Davis 1982; Papagianopoulou 1985). The earliest stylistic dates for the pottery is MM II B or, more likely, early MM III A (Papagianopoulou 1985, 87 fig. 1). The Cretans, perhaps now under the central authority of Knossos, were forced to establish new trading posts near the sources of copper and tin but far from the reaches of the emerging Babylonian dynasty. The MM III A jug in the Creamy-bordered Style, found in a Period V tomb context at Troy, may reflect the Cretans' explorations of the NE Aegean coastline at this time (Korfmann in press). The date of the Minoan finds from Samothrace is relevant here, as they also could be part of the pattern of the search for new trade routes in the early neopalatial period (Matsas 1995).

Evidence for exchange between the Aegean and Egypt on a significant scale does not re-appear until Ahmose founds the XVIIIth Dynasty in *c.* 1540 BC thereby restoring order and stability. The Cretan palaces respond by re-opening communications, as reflected in the discovery of LM I B ceramics at Abydos and Amarna (Warren and Hankey 1989, 141–4),and the numerous Egyptian alabaster vases that begin to appear in and around Knossos (Warren 1991*b*).

While history may be a continuum it should not be treated as a linear development. Relations between towns, states, or regions at any given time must be examined within the context of that time, and not as logical steps towards the conclusions historians long to make. The influences apparent in the Old Palace period at Knossos may have been due to exchanges with a variety of regions, that altered over time.

The many changes apparent between the Old and New Palace period in Crete, then, may have been due less to the earthquake in central Crete around 1760 BC, than to a move away from the dominant political and social power of Egypt following the weakening of the central authority's control over the ports at the end of the XIIth Dynasty. The time of the XIII/XIVth Dynasty finds the Cretans exploring the Levantine coast, and setting up new trading relationships with the emerging powers in North Syria and Babylon. These come to an abrupt end with the violent campaigns of Hammurabi and the new frontiers being established in North Syria, very close to the end of the Old Palace period in Crete. The combined effects of the Cretan earthquake and the renewed search for raw materials that brought the Cretans into contact with the SW Anatolian cities at the time of Anitta, King of Kussara, in what may have been the formative years of the Hittite Old Kingdom (Kuhrt 1995, 225–8), must have had a profound influence on how the Minoans viewed their world. These factors could account for significant changes in art and architecture, as well as religion and philosophy; but this is more than sherds can tell.

Year	Dyn.	King	Minoica in Egypt	Egyptiaca in Crete	Minoica in Levant	Periods
1730						1730
1735						
1740						MM III A
1745						
1750	XIV					
1755					Beirut cup	
1760	XIII		el-Dab'a cup		Byblos cup, jars	1760
1765					Ugarit cups	
1770			Abydos jar		Qatna cup	
1775						MM II B
1780					Hazor bowl	
1785						
1790						
1795		Sobeknefru 1795	Kahun, Haraga	RR/S scarab		1795
1800		1799				
1805		Amenemhat IV				
1810		1808				
1815						
1820						
1825						
1830		Amenemhat III				
1835						
1840						
1845						
1850						MM II A
1855		1853				
1860						
1865		Senusret III			Karmi cup	
1870	XII					
1875		1872 II				
1880		1876 1878	Tôd silver ware			
1885						
1890						
1895		Amenemhat II				
1900						
1905		1908				1908
1910		1911				
1915						
1920						
1925						MM I B
1930		Senusret I				
1935			Haraga Tomb 326			
1940						
1945			Lisht jar, Li. 1			
1950						1953
1955		1953	Qubbet el-Hawa pot			

Fig. 3.3. Chronological links between Egypt and Crete in the Old Palace period. Minoica placed on stylistic criteria. Egyptian dates based on Kitchen in press.

References

ABBREVIATIONS

AA	Archäologischer Anzeiger.
AAA	Athens Annals of Archaeology/ Ἀρχαιολογικὰ Ἀνάλεκτα ἐξ Ἀθηνῶν.
Acts 1	The Mycenaeans in the Eastern Mediterranean. Acts of the International Archaeological Symposium, 27th March–2nd April 1972. Nicosia. 1973.
Acts 2	The Relations between Cyprus and Crete, ca. 2000–500 B.C. Acts of the International Archaeological Symposium, 16th–22nd April 1978. Nicosia. 1979.
ADelt	Ἀρχαιολογικὸν Δελτίον (Chr. = Χρονικά section, Mel. = Μελέται section).
AE	Ἀρχαιολογικὴ Ἐφημερίς.
Aegaeum	Annales d'archeologie égéenne de l'Université Liège.
AJA	American Journal of Archaeology.
AnnLiv	Annals of Archaeology and Anthropology. Liverpool.
Ant.Cretesi	Antichità Cretesi. Studi in onore di Doro Levi. (Cronache di archeologia 12–13, 1973–74). Catania. 1978.
AR	Archaeological Reports.
AS	Anatolian Studies.
ASAtene	Annuario della Scuola Archeologica di Atene.
AthMitt	Mitteilungen des Deutschen Archäologischen Instituts. Athenische Abteilung.
Atlas-Crete	The Aerial Atlas of Ancient Crete, Myers and Cadogan (eds.) London. 1992.
BCH	Bulletin de Correspondance Hellénique.
BdA	Bollettino d'Arte del Ministero della educazione nazionale.
Berytus	Berytus: Archaeological Studies.
BICS	Bulletin of the Institute of Classical Studies of the University of London.
BSA	Annual of the British School at Athens.
CAH³	Cambridge Ancient History, 3rd Edition. Cambridge. 1970–77.
CMS	Corpus der Minoischen und Mykenischen Siegel.
Cretological 1	Proceedings of the First International Cretological Congress. 2 vols. Herakleion. 1962.
Cretological 2	Proceedings of the Second International Cretological Congress. 2 vols. Athens. 1968.
Cretological 3	Proceedings of the Third International Cretological Congress. 3 vols. Athens. 1973.
Cretological 4	Proceedings of the Fourth International Cretological Congress. 4 vols. Athens. 1980.
Cretological 5	Proceedings of the Fifth International Cretological Congress. 3 vols. Herakleion. 1985.
Cretological 6	Proceedings of the Sixth International Cretological Congress. Chania. 1991.
Cretological 7	Proceedings of the Seventh International Cretological Congress. Chania. 1996.
CS	Cretan Studies.
Eilapini	Εἰλαπίνη. Τόμος τιμητικὸς γιά τὸν Καθηγητὴ Νικολάο Πλάτωνα. 2 vols. Herakleion. 1987.
Ergon	Τὸ Ἔργον τῆς Ἀρχαιολογικῆς Ἑταιρείας.
EtCret	Études Crétoises de l'école française d'Athènes.
Function-Palaces	Hägg and Marinatos 1987.
Function-Villa	Hägg 1997.
Iconographie	Darcque and Poursat 1985.
JAS	Journal of Archaeological Science.
ILN	The Illustrated London News.
IstMitt	Istanbuler Mitteilungen.
JdI	Jahrbuch des Deutschen Archäologischen Instituts.
JHS	Journal of Hellenic Studies.
JMA	Journal of Mediterranean Archaeology.
JMAA	Journal of Mediterranean Archaeology and Anthropology.
KrChron	Κρητικὰ χρονικά.
Kritiki Estia	Κρητικὴ Ἑστία.
Kritologia	Κρητολογία. Περιοδικὴ ἐπιστημονικὴ ἔκδοσις.
Labyrinth	Evely et al. 1994.
L'habitat	Darcque and Treuil 1990.
LCC	A Land Called Crete. A Symposium in Memory of Harriet Boyd Hawes, 1871–1945. (Smith College studies in history 45). Northampton, Mass. 1967.
Lyktos	Λυκτος.
MonAnt	Monumenti Antichi. Accademia nazionale dei Lincei.
OJA	Oxford Journal of Archaeology.
OpArch	Opuscula Archaeologica. Skrifter Utgivna av Svenska Institutet i Rom.
OpAth	Opuscula Atheniensia. Skrifter Utgivna av Svenska Institutet i Athen.
Origines	Aux origines de l'hellénisme. La Crète et la Grèce. Hommages à Henri van Effenterre. Paris. 1984.
PAE	Πρακτικὰ τῆς ἐν Ἀθήναις Ἀρχαιολογικῆς Ἑταιρείας. Proceedings of the Archaeological Society of Athens.

PdP	La Parola del Passato. Rivista di studi antichi.
PPS	Proceedings of the Prehistoric Society.
Problems	French and Wardle 1988.
RDAC	Report of the Department of Antiquities. Cyprus.
RevArch	Revue Archéologique.
Sanctuaries	Hägg and Marinatos 1981.
SIMA	Studies in Mediterranean Archaeology.
SMEA	Studi Micenei ed Egeo-Anatolici.
Society	Krzyszkowska and Nixon 1983.
TDAUP	Transactions of the Department of Archaeology, University of Pennsylvania.
TFMSA	University of Philadelphia Transactions of the Department of Archaeology, Free Museum of Science and Art.
Thalassocracy	Hägg and Marinatos 1984.
Thera	Kaloyeropoulou 1971.
TAW II	Doumas 1978–80.
TAW III	Hardy et al. 1990.
TUAS	Temple University Aegean Symposium.
Wace & Blegen	Zerner 1993.

REFERENCES

Åberg, N., 1933. *Bronzezeitliche und früheisenzeitliche Chronologie IV, Griechenland.* Stockholm.

Alexiou, S., 1967. 'Ἀρχαιότητες καὶ μνημεῖα κεντρικῆς καὶ Ἀνατολικῆς Κρήτης' *ADelt* 22 Chr. B2: 480–8.

———, 1968. 'Σπηλαιώδεις τάφοι Πόρου Ἡρακλείου' *AAA*: 250–5.

Amiran, R., 1969. *Ancient Pottery of the Holy Land.* Jerusalem.

Amouretti, M.-C., 1970. *Fouilles executées à Mallia. Le Centre politique.* II. *La Crypte hypostyle (EtCret 18).* Paris.

Andreou, S., 1978. *Pottery Groups from the Old Palace Period in Crete.* Ph.D. Cincinnati.

Arnold, D., 1990. '*The date of the Minoan sherd context at Haraga*'—private circulation.

———, 1993. *Techniques and Traditions of Manufacture in the Pottery of Ancient Egypt,* Fasc. 1 in Arnold and Bourriau 1993: 5–141.

Arnold, D. and Bourriau, J., 1993. (eds.) *An Introduction to Ancient Egyptian Pottery* (Deutsches archäologisches Instituts. Abteilung Kairo. Sonderschrift 17). Mainz.

Astour, M. C., 1973. 'Ugarit and the Aegean' in Hoffner, 1973: 17–27.

Åström, P., 1962. 'Remarks on Middle Minoan chronology' *Cretological* 1: 137–50.

———, 1968. 'New evidence for Middle Minoan chronology' *Cretological* 2: 120–7.

———, 1972a. *The Middle Cypriot Bronze Age. The Swedish Cyprus Expedition IV,* Pt. 1(b). Lund.

———, 1972b. 'Relative and absolute chronology, foreign relations, historical conclusions' in *The Swedish Cyprus Expedition IV,* Pt. 1(d): 675–781.

———, 1978. 'Methodological viewpoints on Middle Minoan chronology' *OpAth* 12: 87–90.

———, 1984. 'Middle Minoan chronology' in Åström et al.: 3–7.

———, 1987–89. (ed.) *High, Middle or Low? Acts of an International Colloquium on Absolute Chronology held at the University of Gothenburg 20th–22nd August 1987* I–III (SIMA Pocket-books 56, 57 and 80). Gothenburg.

Åström, P., Palmer, L. R. and Pomerance, L., 1984. *Studies in Aegean Chronology* (SIMA Pocket-book 25). Gothenburg.

Atkinson, T. D. et al., 1904. *Excavations at Phylakopi in Melos* (*JHS* Suppl. 4). London.

Banti, L., 1931. 'La grande tomba a tholos de Haghia Triada' *ASAtene* 13–14: 155–251.

———, 1940. 'Cronologia e ceramica del palazzo minoico di Festòs' *ASAtene* 1–2: 9–39.

Baramki, D., 1973. 'A tomb of the Early and Middle Bronze Age at Byblos' *Bulletin du Musée de Beyrouth* 26: 27–30.

Barber, R. L. N., 1974. 'Phylakopi 1911 and the history of the later Cycladic Bronze Age' *BSA* 69: 1–53.

———, 1978. 'The Cyclades in the Middle Bronze Age' *TAW* II(1): 367–79.

———, 1981a. 'A tomb at Ayios Loukas, Syros: some thoughts on Early–Middle Cycladic chronology' *JMAA* 1: 167–79.

———, 1981b. 'The Late Cycladic period: a review' *BSA* 76: 1–21.

———, 1984a. 'The status of Phylakopi in Creto-Cycladic relations' *Thalassocracy*: 179–82.

———, 1984b. 'The pottery of Phylakopi, First City, Phase ii (I–ii)' in MacGillivray and Barber 1984: 88–94.

———, 1987. *The Cyclades in the Bronze Age.* London.

Barber, R. L. N. and Hadjianastasiou, O., 1989. 'Mikre Vigla: a Bronze Age settlement on Naxos' *BSA* 84: 63–162.

Barber, R. L. N. and MacGillivray, J. A., 1980. 'The Early Cycladic period: matters of definition and terminology' *AJA* 84: 141–57.

Baurain, C., 1987. 'Les nécropoles de Malia' *Aegaeum* 1: 61–73.

Baurain, C. and Darcque, P., 1983. 'Un triton en pierre de Malia' *BCH* 107: 3–73.

Beale, T. W., 1978. 'Bevelled rim bowls and their implications for change and economic organization in the later Fourth Millennium B.C.' *Journal of Near Eastern Studies* 37: 289–313.

Benzi, M., 1984. 'Evidence for a Middle Minoan settlement on the Acropolis at Ialysos (Mt. Philerimos)' *Thalassocracy*: 89–92.

Bequignon, Y., 1933. 'Chronique des fouilles' *BCH* 57: 236–312.

Bernini, L. A., 1995. 'Ceramics of the early neo-palatial period at Palaikastro' *BSA* 90: 55–82.

Best, J. G. P. and de Vries, N. M. W., 1980. (eds.) *Interaction and Acculturation in the Mediterranean: Proceedings of the 2nd. International Congress of Mediterranean Pre- and Protohistory, Amsterdam 19–23 November 1980.* 2 vols. (1980, 1982). Amsterdam.

Betancourt, P. P., 1977. 'Some chronological problems in the Middle Minoan dark-on-light pottery of eastern Crete' *AJA* 81: 341–53.

———, 1978. 'A Middle Minoan Pottery Deposit' *Hesperia* 47: 155–64.

———, 1980. *Cooking Vessels from Minoan Kommos. A Preliminary Report.* Los Angeles.

———, 1983. *Minoan Objects Excavated from Vasilike, Pseira, Sphoungaras, Priniatikos Pyrgos, and other sites.* Philadelphia.

———, 1984a. *East Cretan White-on-Dark Ware.* Philadelphia.

———, 1984b. 'The Middle Minoan pottery of southern Crete and the question of a Middle Minoan thalassocracy' *Thalassocracy*: 89–92.

————, 1984c. Review of Walberg, G., *Provincial Middle Minoan Pottery* in *AJA* 88: 601-2.

————, 1985a. *The History of Minoan Pottery*. Princeton.

————, 1985b. 'Distinguishing Middle Minoan I B and II A at Kommos' *TUAS* 10: 11–15.

————, 1985c. 'The Middle Minoan pottery of Kommos' *Hydra* 1: 3–10.

————, 1986. 'The chronology of Middle Minoan plain cups in southern Crete' in Φιλία ἔπη εἰς Γεώργιον Ε. Μυλωνᾶν, διὰ τὰ 60 ἔτη τοῦ ἀνασκαφικοῦ τοῦ ἔργου 1st of 3 vols. (Βιβλιοθήκη τῆς ἐν Ἀθήναις Ἀρχαιολογικῆς Ἑταιρείας, Ἀρ. 103): 284–92. Athens.

————, 1990. *Kommos* II. *The Final Neolithic through Middle Minoan III Pottery*. Princeton.

Betancourt, P. P. and Davaras, C., 1988. 'Excavations at Pseira, 1985 and 1986' *Hesperia* 57: 207–25.

Betancourt, P. P., Gaisser, T. K., Koss, E., Lyon, R. F., Matson, F. R., Montgomery, S., Myer, G. H. and Swann, C. P., 1979. *Vasiliki Ware. An Early Bronze Age Pottery Style in Crete* (SIMA 56). Gothenburg.

Betancourt, P. P. and Weinstein, G. A., 1976. 'Carbon-14 and the beginning of the Late Bronze Age in the Aegean' *AJA* 80: 329–48.

Bietak, M., 1984. 'Problems of Middle Bronze Age chronology: new evidence from Egypt' *AJA* 88: 329–48.

Bikaki, A. H., 1984. *Ayia Irini: The Potter's Marks* (Keos IV). Mainz.

Bisson de la Roque, F., Contenau, G. and Chapoutier, F., 1953. *Le Trésor de Tôd*. Cairo.

Blackman, D. J. and Branigan, K., 1982. 'The excavation of an Early Minoan tholos tomb at Ayia Kyriaki, Ayiofarango, southern Crete' *BSA* 77: 1–57.

Blackman, D. J., Branigan, K. *et al.*, 1977. 'An archaeological survey of the lower catchment of the Ayiofarango valley' *BSA* 72: 13–84.

Boardman, J., 1961. *The Cretan Collection in Oxford*. Oxford.

————, 1963. *The Date of the Knossos Tablets* in Palmer and Boardman 1963.

Bonacasa, N., 1968. 'Patrikies—Una stazione medio-minoica fra Haghia Triada e Festòs' *ASAtene* 29–30: 7–54.

Borda, M., 1946. *Arte Cretese-Micenae nel Museo Pigorini di Roma*. Rome.

Bosanquet, R. C., 1902a. 'Excavations at Palaikastro I' *BSA* 8: 286–316.

————, 1902b. 'Excavations at Praesos I' *BSA* 8: 231–81.

————, 1904. 'Some 'Late Minoan' vases found in Greece' *JHS* 24: 317–29.

Bosanquet, R. C. and Dawkins, R. M., 1923. *The Unpublished Objects from the Palaikastro Excavations 1902–1906. Part 1* (BSA Supplementary vol. 1). London.

Boyd, H. A., 1905. 'Gournia. Report of the American Exploration Society's excavations at Gournia, Crete, 1904' *Transactions of the Department of Archaeology, Free Museum of Science and Art* 1: 177–88.

Boyd-Hawes, H., Williams, B. E., Seager, R. B. and Hall, E. H., 1908. *Gournia, Vasiliki and other Prehistoric Sites on the Isthmus of Hierapetra, Crete*. Philadelphia.

Branigan, K., 1966. 'Byblite daggers in Cyprus and Crete' *AJA* 70: 123–6.

————, 1967a. 'Further light on prehistoric relations between Crete and Syria' *AJA* 71: 117–21.

————, 1967b. 'The Early Bronze Age daggers of Crete' *BSA* 62: 211–39.

————, 1968a. *Copper and Bronzework in Early Bronze Age Crete* (SIMA 19). Lund.

————, 1968b. 'The Mesara tholoi and Middle Minoan chronology' *SMEA* 5: 12–30.

————, 1968c. 'Early Minoan metallurgy —a re-appraisal' *Cretological* 2(2): 30–4.

————, 1968d. 'Silver and lead in Prepalatial Crete' *AJA* 72: 219–29.

————, 1969a. 'The genesis of the Household Goddess' *SMEA* 8: 28–38.

————, 1969b. 'The earliest Aegean scripts—the Prepalatial background' *Kadmos* 8: 1–22

————, 1969c. 'A transitional phase in Minoan metallurgy' *BSA* 64: 185–203.

————, 1970a. *The Foundations of Palatial Crete*. London.

————, 1970b. *The Tombs of Mesara*. London.

————, 1971. 'Cycladic figurines and their derivatives in Crete' *BSA* 66: 57–78.

————, 1973. 'Radio-Carbon and the absolute chronology of the Aegean Bronze Age' *KrChron* 25: 352–74.

————, 1974. *Aegean Metalwork of the Early and Middle Bronze Age*. Oxford.

————, 1975. 'The tombs of the Mesara: new tombs and new evidence' *BICS* 22: 200–3.

————, 1981. 'Minoan Colonization' *BSA* 76: 23–34.

————, 1983. 'Craft specialization in Minoan Crete' *Society*: 23–32.

————, 1984a. 'Early Minoan society: the evidence of the Mesara tholoi revised' *Origines*: 29–37.

————, 1984b. 'Minoan community colonies in the Aegean?' *Thalassocracy*: 49–52.

————, 1987a. 'Body-counts in the Mesara tholoi' *Eilapini*: 299–309.

————, 1987b. 'Ritual interference with human bones in the Mesara tholoi' *Aegaeum* 1: 43–51.

————, 1987c. 'The economic role of the first palaces' *Function–Palaces*: 245–49.

————, 1988. 'Social security and the state in Middle Bronze Age Crete' *Aegaeum* 2: 11–16.

————, 1992. 'The early keep, Knossos: a reappraisal' *BSA* 87: 153–63.

Brown, A., 1983. *Arthur Evans and the Palace of Minos*. Oxford.

Brown, A. and Peatfield, A., 1987. 'Stous Anthropolithous: a Minoan site near Epano Zakro, Sitias' *BSA* 82: 23–33.

Buck, R. J., 1964. 'Middle Helladic matt-painted pottery' *Hesperia* 33: 231–308.

Cadogan, G., 1978a. 'Pyrgos, Crete, 1970–77' *AR* 1977–78: 70–84.

————, 1978b. 'Dating the Aegean Bronze Age without radio-carbon' *Archaeometry* 20: 209–14.

————, 1979. 'Cyprus and Crete c. 2000–1400 B.C.' *Acts* 2: 63–8.

————, 1980. 'Minoan Pyrgos' *Cretological* 4: 57–61.

————, 1983. 'Early Minoan and Middle Minoan chronology' *AJA* 87: 507–18.

————, 1986a. (ed.) *The End of the Early Bronze Age in the Aegean*. Leiden.

————, 1986b. 'Why was Crete different?' in Cadogan 1986a: 153–71.

————, 1988. 'Some Middle Minoan problems' *Problems*: 95–9.

————, 1990. 'Lasithi in the Old Palace period' *BICS* 37: 172–4.

————, 1994. 'An Old Palace period Knossos state?' *Labyrinth*: 57–68.

Cadogan, G., Day, P., Macdonald, C., MacGillivray, J. A., Momigliano, N., Whitelaw, T. and Wilson, D., 1993. 'Early and Middle Minoan pottery groups from Knossos' *BSA* 88: 21–8.

Carinci, F., 1983. 'Sulle suddivisioni del Medio Minoico III alcune osservazioni su un saggio di scavo a Cnosso' *Archeologia Classica* 35: 119–37.

————, 1989. 'The 'III fase protopalaziale' at Phaestos. Some observations' *Aegaeum* 3, 72–80.

Caskey, J. L., 1972. 'Investigations in Keos. Part II: A Conspectus of the Pottery' *Hesperia* 41: 357–90.

————, 1973. 'Ayia Irini in Keos. 1972' *ADelt* 28: 547–50.

————, 1979. 'Ayia Irini, Keos: the successive periods of occupation' *AJA* 83: 412.

Caskey J. L. and Huxley G. L., 1978. *Conical Cups. Questions and Answers, 1966*—privately printed.

Casson, S., 1927. (ed.) *Essays in Aegean Archaeology Presented to Sir Arthur Evans in Honour of his 75th Birthday*. Oxford.

Catling, E. A., H. W. and Smyth, D., 1979. 'Knossos 1975: Middle Minoan III and Late Minoan I houses by the acropolis' *BSA* 74: 1–80.

Catling, H. W., 1974. 'Archaeology in Greece, 1973–74' *AR* 20: 3–41.

————, 1982. 'Archaeology in Greece, 1981–82' *AR* 28: 3–62.

————, 1988. 'Archaeology in Greece 1987–88' *AR* 34: 3–85.

Catling, H. W. and Karageorgis, V., 1960. 'Minoika in Cyprus' *BSA* 55: 109–27.

Catling, H. W. and MacGillivray, J. A., 1983. 'An Early Cypriot III vase from the palace at Knossos' *BSA* 78: 1–8.

Chapouthier, F., 1936. *Deux Epées d'apparat découvertes en 1936 au Palais de Mallia* (*EtCret* 5). Paris.

Chapouthier, F. and Charbonneaux, J., 1928. *Fouilles executées à Mallia. Première Rapport (1922–1924)* (*EtCret* 1). Paris.

Chapouthier, F. and Demargne, P., 1942. *Fouilles executées à Mallia. Troisième Rapport. Exploration du Palais* (*EtCret* 6). Paris.

Chapouthier, F., Demargne, P. and Dessenne, A., 1962. *Fouilles executées à Mallia. Quatrième Rapport. Exploration du Palais* (*EtCret* 12). Paris.

Chapouthier, F. and Joly, R., 1936. *Fouilles executées à Mallia. Deuxième Rapport. Exploration du Palais (1925–1926)* (*EtCret* 4). Paris.

Charbonneaux, J., 1928. 'L'architecture et la céramique du palais de Mallia' *BCH* 52: 347–87.

Charvalia, G. and Antonopoulou, L., 1986. Τὰ Κρητικὰ Ὑφαντά (*Voroi Museum of Cretan Ethnology* 8). Athens.

Cherry, J. F., 1983. 'Evolution, revolution, and the origins of complex society in Minoan Crete' *Society*: 33–45.

————, 1986. 'Polities and palaces: some problems in Minoan State formation' in Renfrew and Cherry 1986, 19–45.

Coldstream, J. N. and Huxley, G. L., 1972. *Kythera: excavations and studies conducted by the University of Pennsylvania Museum and the British School at Athens*. London.

Crossland, R. A. and Birchall, A., 1974. (eds.) *Bronze Age Migrations in the Aegean*. New Jersey.

Damiani-Indelicato, S., 1982. *Piazza pubblica e palazzo nella Creta minoica*. Rome.

————, 1984a. 'A new kouloura at Phaistos' *AJA* 88: 229–30.

————, 1984b. 'Gournia, cité minoenne' *Origines*: 47–54.

Dandamayev, M. A. et al., 1982. (eds.) *Societies and Languages of the Ancient Near East: Studies in Honor of I. M. Diakonoff*. Warminster.

Darcque, P. and Poursat, J.-C., 1985. (eds.) *L'Iconographie minoenne: actes de la table ronde d'Athènes (21–22 avril 1983)* (BCH Supplément 11). Paris.

Darcque, P. and Treuil, R., 1990. (eds.) *L'habitat égéen préhistorique: actes de la Table Ronde internationale … (Athènes 23–25 juin 1987)* (BCH Supplément 9). Paris.

Daux, G., 1958. 'Chroniques des fouilles' *BCH* 82: 644–830.

————, 1960. 'Chroniques des fouilles en 1959' *BCH* 84: 617–869.

Davies, W. V. and Schofield, L., 1995. (eds.) *Egypt, the Aegean and the Levant: interconnections in the Second Millennium B.C.* London.

Davis, E. N., 1977. *The Vapheio Cups and Aegean Gold and Silver Ware*. New York.

————, 1979. 'The silver kantharos from Gournia' *TUAS* 4: 34–45.

Davis, J. L., 1982. 'The earliest Minoans in the southeast Aegean: a reconsideration of the evidence' *AS* 32: 33–41.

————, 1986. *Ayia Irini: Period V* (*Keos* v). Mainz.

Davis, J. L. and Cherry, J. F., 1979. (eds.) *Papers in Cycladic Prehistory* (U.C.L.A. Inst. of Archaeology Monograph 14). Los Angeles.

————, 1990. 'Spatial and temporal uniformitarianism in Late Cycladic I: perspectives from Keos and Melos on the prehistory of Akrotiri' *TAW* III(1): 185–200.

Dawkins, R. M., 1903a. 'Excavations at Palaikastro II' *BSA* 9: 274–341.

————, 1903b. 'Pottery from Zakro' *JHS* 23: 248–60.

————, 1904. 'Excavations at Palaikastro III' *BSA* 10: 192–226.

————, 1905. 'Excavations at Palaikastro IV' *BSA* 11: 258–92.

Dawkins, R. M. and Laistner, M. L. W., 1913. 'The excavation of the Kamares cave in Crete' *BSA* 19: 1–34.

Day, P., 1988. 'The production and distribution of storage jars in Neopalatial Crete' *Problems* 499–508.

Demargne, P., 1945. *Fouilles executées à Mallia. Exploration des nécropoles (1921–1933)* (*EtCret* 7). Paris.

Demargne, P. and Gallet de Santerre, H., 1953. *Fouilles executées à Mallia. Exploration des maisons et quartiers d'habitation (1921–1948), premier fascicule* (*EtCret* 9). Paris.

De Pierpont, G., 1987. 'Réflexions sur la destination des edifices de Chrysolakkos' *Aegaeum* 1: 79–94.

Deshayes, J., 1962. 'A propos du Minoen Ancien' *BCH* 86: 543–68.

Deshayes, J. and Dessenne, A., 1959. *Fouilles executées à Mallia. Exploration des maisons et quartiers d'habitation (1948–1954), deuxième fascicule* (*EtCret* 11). Paris.

Dessenne, A. 1951. *BCH* 75: 195f.

Detournay, B., Poursat, J.-C. and Vandenabeele, F., 1980. *Fouilles exécutées à Mallia. Le Quartier Mu II* (*EtCret* 26). Paris.

Dimopoulou, N., 1987. [Archaeological news from the Pediada] *Lyktos* 2: 30–41.

Dimopoulou-Rethemiotakis, N., 1988a. [Komopoli Archanon] *Kritiki Estia* 2: 321.

————, 1988b. [Poros] *Kritiki Estia* 2: 325–27.

Dossin, G., 1939. 'Les archives économiques du palais de Mari' *Syria* 20: 97–113.

Doumas, C., 1978–1980. (ed.) *Thera and the Aegean World. Papers presented at the Second International Scientific Congress, Santorini, Greece, August 1978.* 2 vols. London.

——, 1983. *Thera*. London.

Driessen, J. M., 1987. 'Earthquake resistant construction and the wrath of the 'Earth-Shaker'' *Journal of the Society of Architectural Historians* 46: 171–8.

Du Mesnil Du Buisson, Compte, 1926. 'Les ruines d'el-Mishrifé, au nord-est de Homs' *Syria* 7: 289–325.

Dunand, M., 1939. *Fouilles de Byblos* I. Paris.

Dunbabin, T. J., 1947. 'Antiquities of Amari' *BSA* 42: 184–93.

Durand, J.-M., 1983. *Textes administratifs des salles 134 et 160 du palais de Mari* (*Archives Royales de Mari* 21). Paris.

Edel, E., 1975. 'Der Funde eines Kamaresgefasses in einem Grabe der Qubbet el Hawa bei Assuan' in *Acts du XXXIXe Congres International des Orientalistes.* (*Egyptologie* I): 38–40. Paris.

——, 1908. 'A Kamares vase from Qubbet el-Hawa, near Aswan' in Kemp and Merrillees 1980, 176–219.

Emre, K., Hrouna, B., Mellink, M. and Özgüç, N., 1989. (eds.) *Anatolia and the Ancient Near East: Studies in Honor of Tahsin Özgüç.* Ankara.

Ehrich, R. W., 1965. (ed.) *Chronologies in Old World Archaeology.* Chicago.

Evans, A. J., 1900. 'Knossos, I. The Palace' *BSA* 6: 3–70.

——, 1901. 'The Palace of Knossos' *BSA* 7: 1–120.

——, 1902. 'The Palace of Knossos' *BSA* 8: 1–124.

——, 1903. 'The Palace of Knossos' *BSA* 9: 1–153.

——, 1904. 'The Palace of Knossos' *BSA* 10: 1–62.

——, 1905a. 'The Palace of Knossos and its dependencies' *BSA* 11: 1–26.

——, 1905b. *Preliminary scheme for the classification and approximate chronology of the periods of Minoan culture in Crete from the close of the Neolithic to the Early Iron Age*—privately printed.

——, 1906. *Essai de classification des époques de la civilisation minoenne.* London.

——, 1909. *Scripta Minoa* I. Oxford.

——, 1914. 'The Tomb of the Double Axes and associated group and Pillar Rooms with ritual vessels of the Little Palace at Knossos' *Archaeologia* 65: 1–94.

——, 1921. *The Palace of Minos at Knossos* I. London.

——, 1928. *The Palace of Minos at Knossos* II. London.

——, 1930. *The Palace of Minos at Knossos* III. London.

——, 1935. *The Palace of Minos at Knossos* IV. London.

Evans, J. D., 1964. 'Excavations in the Neolithic settlement at Knossos, 1957–60' *BSA* 59: 132–240.

——, 1968. 'Neolithic Knossos, Part II: summary and conclusions' *BSA* 63: 267–76.

——, 1971. 'Neolithic Knossos. The growth of a settlement' *PPS* 1971 Pt.2: 95–117.

——, 1972. 'The Early Minoan occupation of Knossos' *AS* 22: 115–28.

Evely, D., 1988. 'The potters' wheel in Minoan Crete' *BSA* 83: 83–126.

——, 1993. *Minoan Crafts: Tools and Techniques. An Introduction* I (SIMA 92:1). Gothenburg.

Evely, D., Hughes-Brock, H. and Momigliano, N., 1994. (eds.) *Knossos: a Labyrinth of History. Papers presented in Honour of Sinclair Hood.* Oxford.

Fairbanks, A., 1928. *Museum of Fine Arts, Boston. Catalogue of the Greek and Roman Vases, Preceding Athenian Black-figured Ware.* Cambridge, Mass.

Fiandra, E., 1962. 'I periodi struttivi del Primo Palazzo di Festòs' *Cretological* 1: 112–26.

——, 1973. 'Skutelia MM a Festòs' *Cretological* 3: 84–91.

——, 1980. 'Precisazioni sul MM II a Festòs' *Cretological* 4: 169–96.

——, 1990. 'Design and style of the MM and LM ceramics' *SMEA* 28: 117–24.

Fitton, L., Hughes, M. and Quirke, S., 1999. 'Northerners at Lahun: neutron activation analysis of Minoan and related pottery in the British Museum' in Quirke (ed.) *Lahun Studies*: 112–40.

Forsdyke, E. J., 1925. *Prehistoric Aegean Pottery* (*Catalogue of the Greek and Etruscan Vases in the British Museum* 1. (Pt 1). London.

——, 1927. 'The Mavro Spelio cemetery at Knossos' *BSA* 28: 243–96.

Foster, K. P., 1978. 'The Mount Holyoke collection of Minoan pottery' *TUAS* 3: 1–30.

——, 1979. *Aegean Faience of the Bronze Age,* London.

——, 1982. *Minoan Ceramic Relief* (SIMA 64). Gothenburg.

Frankfort, H., 1927. *Studies in Early Pottery of the Near East* II. London.

French, E., 1987. 'Using pottery for chronology' (*6th Int. Colloquium on Aegean Prehistory*). Athens.

——, 1993. 'Archaeology in Greece 1992–93' *AR* 39: 3–81.

——, 1994. 'Archaeology in Greece 1993–94' *AR* 40: 3–84.

French, E. B. and Wardle, K. A., 1988. (eds.) *Problems in Greek Prehistory: papers presented at the Centenary of the British School of Archaeology at Athens, Manchester April 1986.* Bristol.

Furness, A., 1953. 'The Neolithic pottery of Knossos' *BSA* 48: 94–134.

Furumark, A., 1941. *The Mycenaean Pottery.* Stockholm.

——, 1950. 'The settlement at Ialysos and Aegean history c. 1550–1400 B.C.' *OpArch* 6: 150–271.

Gale, N., 1991. (ed.) *Bronze Age Trade in the Mediterranean* (SIMA 90). Gothenburg.

Garstang, J., 1913. 'Note on a vase of Minoan fabric from Abydos (Egypt)' *AnnLiv* 5: 107–11.

Georgiou, H., 1973a. 'Minoan 'fireboxes' from Gournia' *Expedition* 15.4: 7–14.

——, 1973b. 'Aromatics in antiquity and in Minoan Crete. A review and reassessment' *KrChron* 25: 441–56.

——, 1983. 'Minoan coarse wares and Minoan technology' *Society*: 75–92.

——, 1986. *Ayia Irini: Specialized Domestic and Industrial Pottery* (*Keos* VI). Mainz.

Gesell, G., 1985. *Town, Palace and House Cult in Minoan Crete* (SIMA 67). Gothenburg.

Gill, M. A. V., 1965. 'The Knossos sealings: provenance and identification' *BSA* 60: 58–98.

——, 1967. 'On the authenticity of the Middle Minoan half-cylinder Oxford 1938. 790' *Kadmos* 6: 114–18.

Gillis, C., 1990. *Minoan Conical Cups* (SIMA 89). Gothenburg.

Godart, L. and Olivier, J.-P., 1978. *Fouilles executées à Mallia, Le Quartier Mu* I (*EtCret* 23). Paris.

Godart, L. and Tzedakis, Y., 1992. *Témoignages archéologiques et épigraphiques en Crète occidentale du néolitique au Minoen Récent III b (Incunabula Graeca 93)*. Rome.

Grace, V. R., 1940. 'A Cypriote tomb and Minoan evidence for its date' *AJA* 44: 10–52.

Graham, J. W., 1962. *The Palaces of Crete*. Princeton.

Hägg, R., 1984. 'Degrees and character of the Minoan influence on the Mainland' *Thalassocracy*: 119–21.

———, 1997. *The Function of the 'Minoan Villa'*, (*Skrifter Utgivna av Svenska Institutet i Athen* 46, Volume II). Stockholm.

Hägg, R. and Marinatos, N., 1981. (eds.) *Sanctuaries and Cults in the Aegean Bronze Age: proceedings of the First International Symposium of the Swedish Institute in Athens, 12th–13th May, 1980 (Skrifter Utgivna av Svenska Institutet i Athen 28)*. Stockholm.

———, 1984. (eds.) *The Minoan Thalassocracy: Myth and Reality: proceedings of the Third International Symposium at the Swedish Institute in Athens, 31st May–5th June, 1982 (Skrifter Utgivna av Svenska Institutet i Athen 32)*. Stockholm.

———, 1987. (eds.) *The Function of the Minoan Palaces: proceedings of the Fourth International Symposium at the Swedish Institute in Athens 10th–16th June, 1984 (Skrifter Utgivna av Svenska Institutet i Athen 35)*. Stockholm.

Halbherr, F., 1901. 'Three Cretan necropoleis' *AJA* 5: 259–93.

Halbherr, F., Stephani, E. and Banti, L., 1977. 'Haghia Triada nel Periodo Tardo Palaziale' *ASAtene* 39.

Hall, E. H., 1905. 'Early Painted Pottery from Gournia' *TFMSA* 1: 191–205.

———, 1907. 'The decorative arts of Crete in the Bronze Age' *TFMSA* 2: 5–50.

———, 1912. 'Excavations in eastern Crete. Sphoungaras' (*University of Pennsylvania. The University Museum Anthropological Publications* III): 39–73. Philadelphia.

Hallager, E. and Tzedakis, Y., 1988. 'The Greek-Swedish excavations at Kastelli, Khania, 1989–90' *AAA* 21: 15–55.

Hankey, V., 1980. 'Stone vessels at Myrtos Pyrgos' *Cretological* 4: 210–15.

Hankey, V. and Warren, P., 1974. 'The absolute chronology of the Aegean Late Bronze Age' *BICS* 21: 142–52.

Hansen, J. L., 1988. 'Agriculture in the prehistoric Aegean: data versus speculation' *AJA* 92: 39–52.

Hardy, D. *et al.*, 1990. (eds.) *Thera and the Aegean World III. Proceedings of the Third International Scientific Congress, Santorini, Greece, 3–9 September 1989*. 3 vols: 1, Archaeology; 2, Natural Sciences; 3, Chronology. London.

Hatzidakis, J., 1915. 'Πρωτομινωϊκοὶ τάφοι παρὰ τὸ χωρίον Γοῦρνες' *ADelt* 1: 58–63.

———, 1918. 'Gournes' *ADelt* 3, 45–57.

———, 1921. *Tylissos à l'Epoque Minoenne*. Paris.

———, 1934. *Les Villas Minoennes de Tylissos (EtCret 3)*. Paris.

Hawke Smith, C. F., 1976. 'The Knossos frescoes: a revised chronology' *BSA* 71: 65–76.

Hayes, W. C., 1970. 'Chronology I. Egypt to the end of the Twentieth Dynasty' *CAH³* (1): 173–93.

Helck, W., 1979. *Die Beziehungen Ägyptens und Vorderasiens zur Ägäis bis ins 7. Jahrhundert v. Chr.* Darmstadt.

Hennessy, J. B., 1967. *The Foreign Relations of Palestine during the Early Bronze Age*. London.

Hiller, S., 1993. 'Minoan and Minoanizing pottery on Aigina' in *Wace & Blegen*: 197–9.

Hoffner, H. A. Jnr., 1973. (ed.) *Orient and Occident. Essays presented to Cyrus H. Gordon on the occasion of his sixty-fifth birthday (Alter Orient und Altes Testament 22)*. Kevelaer.

Hogarth, D. G., 1900. 'Knossos II. Early town and cemeteries' *BSA* 6: 70–85.

———, 1901. 'Excavations at Zakro, Crete' *BSA* 7: 121–49.

Hogarth, D. G. and Welch, F. B., 1901. 'Primitive painted pottery in Crete' *JHS* 21: 78–98.

Hood, M. S. F., 1955. 'Archaeology in Greece' *JHS* 75: 3–19.

———, 1958. 'Archaeology in Greece, 1957' *AR* 1957: 3–25.

———, 1959. 'Archaeology in Greece, 1958' *AR* 1958: 3–22.

———, 1960. 'Archaeology in Greece, 1959' *AR* 1959–60: 3–26.

———, 1962. 'Stratigraphic Excavations at Knossos, 1957–61' *Cretological* 1: 92–8.

———, 1964. Letter to the Editor *Nestor* 2: 342–3.

———, 1966. 'The Early and Middle Minoan periods at Knossos' *BICS* 13: 110–11.

———, 1971a. *The Minoans*. London.

———, 1971b. 'An Early Helladic III import at Knossos and Anatolian connections' in *Mélanges de préhistoire, d'archéocivilisation et d'ethnologie offerts à Andre Varagnac*: 427–36. Paris.

———, 1978. *The Arts in Prehistoric Greece*. Harmondsworth.

———, 1986. 'Palatial Crete' at *Centenary Conference of the British School at Athens*. Athens.

———, 1994. 'Knossos: Soundings in the palace area, 1973–87' *BSA* 89: 101–2.

Hood, M. S. F., Huxley, G. and Sandars, N., 1959. 'A Minoan Cemetery on Upper Gypsades' *BSA* 53–54: 194–261.

Hood, M. S. F. and Smyth, D., 1981. *Archaeological Survey of the Knossos Area* (BSA Supplementary vol. 14). Oxford.

Hood, M. S. F. and Taylor, W., 1981. *The Bronze Age Palace at Knossos* (BSA Supplementary vol. 13). Oxford.

Hutchinson, R. W. 1954., 'Minoan Chronology reviewed' *Antiquity* 28: 153–64.

———, 1962. *Prehistoric Crete*. Harmondsworth.

Immerwahr, S. A., 1990. *Aegean Painting in the Bronze Age*. Philadelphia and London.

Jacquet-Gordon, H., 1991. *Bulletin de Liaison du Groupe internationale d'Études de la céramique égyptienne* 15: 29.

Johnston, A. W., 1973. 'A Catalogue of Greek Vases in Public Collections in Ireland' *Proceedings of the Royal Irish Academy* 73, Section C: 339–506.

Jones, R. E., 1986. *Greek and Cypriot Pottery*. Athens.

Jones, R. E. and Rutter, J. B., 1977. 'Resident Minoan potters on the Greek mainland? Pottery composition analysis from Ayios Stephanos' *Archaeometry* 19: 211–19.

Kaloyeropoulou, A., 1971. (ed.) *Acta of the 1st International Scientific Congress on the Volcano of Thera held in Greece 15th–23rd September 1969*. Athens.

Kanta, A., 1984. 'The Minoan settlement of the north part of the district of Apokoronas and Minoan Apatawa' *Origines*: 9–16.

———, 1988. 'Monastiraki', *Kritiki Estia* 2: 313.

———, 1992. 'Monastiraki', *Atlas-Crete*: 194–7.

Kantor, H. J., 1947. 'The Aegean and the Orient in the second millennium BC' *AJA* 51: 1–103.

——, 1965. 'The Relative chronology of Egypt and its foreign correlations before the Late Bronze Age' in Ehrich 1965: 1–46.

Karetsou, A., 1974. 'Ἱερὸν κορυφῆς Γιούχτα' *PAE*: 228–39.

——, 1975. 'Ἱερὸ κορυφῆς Γιούχτα' *PAE*: 330–42.

——, 1976. 'Τὸ ἱερὸ κορυφῆς Γιούχτα' *PAE*: 408–18.

——, 1977. 'Τὸ ἱερὸ κορυφῆς Γιούχτα' *PAE*: 419–20.

——, 1978. 'Τὸ ἱερὸ κορυφῆς Γιούχτα' *PAE*: 232–58.

——, 1980. 'Τὸ ἱερὸ κορυφῆς Γιούχτα' *PAE*: 337–53.

——, 1981*a*. 'Τὸ ἱερὸ κορυφῆς Γιούχτα' *PAE*: 405–8.

——, 1981*b*. 'The peak sanctuary of Mt. Juktas' *Sanctuaries*: 137–51.

Karo, G., 1908. 'Archäologische Funde im Jahre 1907. Kreta' *AA*: 120–6.

——, 1930–33. *Die Schachtgräber von Mykenai* I–II. Munich.

Kemp, B. J. and Merrillees, R. S., 1980. *Minoan Pottery in Second Millennium Egypt*. Mainz.

Kenna, V. E. G., 1960. *Cretan Seals*. Oxford.

——, 1968. 'Ancient Crete and the use of the cylinder seal' *AJA* 72: 321–36.

Kitchen, K. A., 1987. 'The basics of Egyptian chronology in relation to the Bronze Age' in Åström 1987–89 I: 37–55.

——, 1989. Supplementary notes on 'The basics of Egyptian chronology' in Åström 1987–89: 152–9.

——, in press. 'The historical chronology of Egypt: a current assessment' in Randsborg, K. (ed.) *Absolute Chronology. Archaeological Europe 2500–500 BC*, *Acta Archaeologia* 67 (1996) (Supplementa I).

Knapp, A. B., 1990. 'Ethnicity, entrepreneurship, and exchange: Mediterranean inter-island relations in the Late Bronze Age' *BSA* 85: 115–53.

Koehl, R. B., 1981. 'The functions of Aegean Bronze Age rhyta' *Sanctuaries*: 179–87.

Kopcke, G., 1987. 'The Cretan palaces and trade' *Function-Palaces*: 255–9.

——, 1990. *Handel* (*Archaeologia Homerica* M). Gottingen.

Korfmann, M., in press. 'Troia. Ausgrabungen 1996' *Studia Troica* 7.

Krzyszkowska, O. and Nixon, L., 1983 (eds.) *Minoan Society. Proceedings of the Cambridge Colloquium, 1981*. Bristol.

Kuhrt, A., 1995. *The Ancient Near East*. New York.

Laffineur, R., 1976. *Cyclades, Crete, Mycenes, Chypre*. Bruxelles.

——, 1988. 'Réflexions sur le trésor de Tôd' *Aegaeum* 2: 17–29.

Lamb, W., 1936. *CVA Great Britain* II, *Cambridge, Fitzwilliam Museum*. Oxford.

La Rosa, V., 1977. 'La ripresa dei lavori ad Haghia Triada: relazione preliminare sui saggi del 1977' *ASAtene* 39: App. 297–342.

——, 1987. 'Spigolature vecchie e nuove da Haghia Triada' *Eilapini*: 383–90.

Laviosa, C., 1964. 'Sull'origine degli idoletti fittili micenei' *ASAtene* 25–26: 7–24.

——, 1973. 'L'abitato prepalaziale di Haghia Triada' *ASAtene* 34–35: 503–13.

Lembesi, A., 1967. 'Ἀνασκαφὴ σπηλαιώδους τάφου εἰς Πόρον Ἡρακλείου' *PAE*: 195–209.

——, 1970. 'Ἀνασκαφικαὶ ἔρευναι εἰς Ἀνατολικὴν Κρήτην' *PAE*: 256–97.

——, 1971. 'Ἀνασκαφικαὶ ἔρευναι καὶ περισυλλογὴ ἀρχαίων εἰς Κεντρικὴν Κρήτην' *PAE*: 287–300.

——, 1976. 'A sanctuary of Hermes and Aphrodite in Crete' *Expedition* 18.3: 2–13.

——, 1981. 'Ἡ συνέχεια τῆς κρητομυκηναϊκῆς λατρείας. Ἐπιβιώσεις καὶ ἀναβιώσεις' *AE*: 1–24.

——, 1994. 'Σύμη Βιάννου. Ἱερὸ τοῦ Ἑρμῆ καὶ τῆς Ἀφροδίτης' *Ergon* 1993: 100–7.

Levi, D., 1951. 'Attività della Scuola Archeologica italiana di Atene nell' anno 1950' *BdA* 36: 335–58.

——, 1952. 'Attività della Scuola Archeologica italiana di Atene nell' anno 1951' *BdA* 37: 320–39.

——, 1953. 'Attività della Scuola Archeologica italiana di Atene nell' anno 1952' *BdA* 38: 252–69.

——, 1954. 'La campagna di scavi a Festòs nel 1953' *ASAtene* 14–16: 389–469.

——, 1955. 'Attività della Scuola Archeoligica italiana di Atene nell' anno 1954. I. Festòs' *BdA* 40: 141–64.

——, 1956*a*. 'Atti della Scuola' *ASAtene* 17–19: 292–303.

——, 1956*b*. 'Attività della Scuola Archeologica italiana di Atene nell' anno 1955' *BdA* 41: 238–70.

——, 1958*a*. 'L'archivo di cretule a Festòs' *ASAtene* 19–20: 7–192.

——, 1958*b*. 'Gli Scavi a Festòs nel 1956 e 1957' *ASAtene* 19–20: 193–362.

——, 1960. 'Per una nuova classificazione della civiltà Minoica' *PdP* 71: 81–121.

——, 1962*a*. 'La Tomba a tholos di Kamilari presso a Festòs' *ASAtene* 23–24: 7–148.

——, 1962*b*. 'Gli scavi a Festòs negli anni 1958–1960' *ASAtene* 23–24: 377–504.

——, 1964. *The Recent Excavations at Phaistos* (SIMA 11). Lund.

——, 1965. 'Le varietà della primitiva ceramica cretese' in *Studi in onore de Luisa Banti*: 223–39. Rome.

——, 1966. 'La conclusione degli scavi a Festòs' *ASAtene* 27–28: 313–99.

——, 1968. 'L'abitato di Festòs in località Chalara' *ASAtene* 29–30: 55–166.

——, 1976. *Festòs e la civiltà' Minoica* I (*Incunabula Graeca* 60). Rome.

——, 1980. *Festòs e la civiltà' Minoica* IIa (*Incunabula Graeca* 77). Rome.

——, 1987. 'La cretule' *Eilapini*: 395–405.

Levi, D. and Carinci, P., 1988. *Festòs e la civiltà' Minoica* IIb (*Incunabula Graeca* 77). Rome.

Levy, E., 1987. (ed.) *Le système palatial en Orient, en Grece et à Rome: actes du colloque de Strasborg, 19–22 juin 1985* (*Travaux du Centre … la Grece antique* 9). Leiden.

Lilyquist, C., 1993. 'Granulations and Glass: chronological and stylistic investigations at selected sites, ca. 2500–1400 BC' *Bulletin of the American Oriental Society* 29091: 29–94.

Lucas, A., 1962. *Ancient Egyptian Materials and Industries*. London.

Macdonald, C. F. and Driessen, J. M., 1988. 'The drainage system of the Domestic Quarter in the Palace at Knossos' *BSA* 83: 235–58.

MacGillivray, J. A. 1984*a*. 'Cycladic jars from Middle Minoan III contexts at Knossos' *Thalassocracy*: 153–8.

——, 1984*b*. 'The relative chronology of Early Cycladic III' in MacGillivray and Barber (eds.): 70–7.

———, 1984c. Review of Walberg 1983, *AJA* 88, 250.

———, 1987. 'Pottery workshops and the Old Palaces in Crete' *Function-Palaces*: 273–8.

———, 1990. 'The foundation of the Old Palaces in Crete' *Cretological* 6: 429–34.

———, 1994. 'The early history of the palace at Knossos' *Labyrinth*: 45–55.

———, 1995. 'A Minoan cup at Tell el-Dab'a' *Egypt and the Levant* 5: 81–4.

———, 1996. 'Late Minoan II and III pottery and chronology at Palaikastro: an introduction' in Hallager, E. (eds.) *Late Minoan III Pottery*: 193-207.

———, 1997. 'The Cretan countryside in the Old Palace Period' *Function-Villa*: 21–5.

MacGillivray, J. A. and Barber, R. L. N., 1984. (eds.) *The Prehistoric Cyclades: contributions to a Workshop on Cycladic Chronology (held in London on June 10th, 11th and 13th, 1983)*. Edinburgh.

MacGillivray, J. A., Day, P. and Jones, R. E., 1987. 'Dark-faced incised pyxides from Knossos: problems of date and origin' *Problems*: 91–4.

MacGillivray, J. A. and Driessen, J., 1990. 'Minoan settlement at Palaikastro' *L'habitat*: 395–412.

MacGillivray, J. A., Sackett, L. H., Driessen, J., Bridges, R. and Smyth, D., 1989. 'Excavations at Palaikastro, 1988' *BSA* 84: 417–45.

MacGillivray, J. A., Sackett, L. H., Driessen, J., and Hemingway, S., 1992. 'Excavations at Palaikastro, 1991' *BSA* 87: 121–52.

MacGillivray, J. A., Sackett, L. H., Driessen, J., Macdonald, C. and Smyth, D., 1988. 'Excavations at Palaikastro, 1987' *BSA* 83: 259–82.

MacGillivray, J. A., Sackett, L. H., Driessen, J. and Smyth, D., 1987. 'Excavations at Palaikastro, 1986' *BSA* 82: 135–54.

MacGillivray, J. A., Sackett, L. H., Driessen, J., Farnoux, A. and Smyth, D., 1991. 'Excavations at Palaikastro, 1990' *BSA* 86: 121–47.

MacGillivray, J. A. *et al.*, 1998. 'Excavations at Palaikastro, 1994, 1996' *BSA* 93.

Mackenzie, D., 1902 DB 1. Excavation Day-book. Ashmolean Museum. (Unpublished).

———, 1902 DB 2. Excavation Day-book. Ashmolean Museum. (Unpublished).

———, 1902 PB 1. Pottery notebook. British School at Athens. (Unpublished).

———, 1902 PB 2. Pottery notebook. British School at Athens. (Unpublished).

———, 1903. 'The pottery of Knossos' *JHS* 23: 157–205.

———, 1903 DB 1. Excavation Day-book. Ashmolean Museum. (Unpublished).

———, 1903 PB. Pottery notebook. British School at Athens. (Unpublished).

———, 1904 DB 1. Excavation Day-book. Ashmolean Museum. (Unpublished).

———, 1904 PB 2. Pottery notebook. (Unpublished).

———, 1906. 'The Middle Minoan pottery of Knossos' *JHS* 26: 243–67.

———, 1907 DB. Excavation Day-book. Ashmolean Museum. (Unpublished).

———, 1921 DB 1. Excavation Day-book, Ashmolean Museum. (Unpublished).

———, 1922 DB 1. Excavation Day-book, Ashmolean Museum. (Unpublished).

———, 1922 DB 2. Excavation Day-book. Ashmolean Museum.

Manning, S. W., 1995. *The Absolute Chronology of the Aegean Early Bronze Age: Archaeology, Radiocarbon and History* (Monographs in Mediterranean Archaeology I). Sheffield.

Manteli, K. and Evely, D., 1995. 'The Neolithic levels from the Throne Room system, Knossos' *BSA* 90: 1–16.

Mariani, L., 1895. 'Antichità Cretesi' *MonAnt* 6: 154–347.

———, 1901. 'The vases of Erganos and Courtes' *AJA* 5: 302–14.

Marinatos, N., 1983. 'The West House at Akrotiri as a cult center' *AthMitt* 98: 1–19.

———, 1984. 'The date-palm in Minoan iconography and religion' *OpAth* 15: 115–22.

———, 1987. 'Public festivals in the West Court of the palaces' *Function-Palaces*: 135–45.

Marinatos, N. and Hägg, R., 1983. 'Anthropomorphic cult images in Minoan Crete' *Society*: 185–201.

Marinatos, S. N., 1925. 'Μεσομινωϊκὴ οἰκία ἐν Κάτω Μεσαρᾷ' *ADelt* 9: 53–78.

———, 1974. *Thera* VII. Athens.

Marthari, M., 1984. 'The destruction of the town at Akrotiri, Thera, at the beginning of LC I: definition and chronology' in MacGillivray and Barber (eds.): 119–33.

———, 1987. 'The local pottery wares with painted decoration from the volcanic destruction level at Akrotiri, Thera, a preliminary report' *AA*: 359–79.

———, 1990. 'The chronology of the last phases of occupation at Akrotiri in the light of the evidence from the West House pottery groups' *TAW* III(3): 57–70.

———, 1993. 'The ceramic evidence for contacts between Thera and the Greek Mainland' *Wace & Blegen*: 249–62.

Matsas, D., 1991. 'Samothrace and the northeastern Aegean: the Minoan connection' *Studia Troica* I: 157–79.

———, 1995. 'Minoan long-distance trade: a view from the northern Aegean' *Aegaeum* 12: 235–47.

Matthäus, H., 1980. *Die Bronzegefässe der kretisch-mykenischen Kultur* (Prähistorische Bronzefund II. 1). Munich.

Matz, F., 1951. (ed.) *Forschungen auf Kreta 1942*. Berlin.

———, 1973a. 'The maturity of Minoan civilization' in *CAH*3 (II.i): 141–64.

———, 1973b. 'The zenith of Minoan civilization' in *CAH*3 (II.i): 557–81.

Maxwell-Hyslop, K. R., 1995. 'A note on the Anatolian connections of the Tôd Treasure' *AS* 45: 243–50.

McEnroe, J. C., 1982. 'A typology of Minoan Neopalatial houses' *AJA* 86: 3–19.

McGeorge, P. J. P., 1986. 'New data on average life expectancy in Minoan Crete' *Kritiki Estia* 1: 9–15.

———, 1987a. 'Biosocial evolution in Bronze Age Crete' *Eilapini*: 407–16.

———, 1987b. 'Mythical pygmies and giants: new data on the stature of the Minoans' *Kritiki Estia* 2: 9–18.

McGovern, P., Bourriau, J., Harbottle, G. and Allen, S. J., 1994. 'The archaeological origin and significance of the dolphin vase as determined by neutron activation analysis' *Bulletin of the American Schools of Oriental Research* 296: 31–43.

Mee, C. B., 1978. 'Aegean trade and settlement in Anatolia in the second millennium BC' *AS* 28: 121–56.

———, 1982. *Rhodes in the Bronze Age*. Warminster.

Mee, C. B. and Doole, J., 1993. *Aegean Antiquities on Mersey-*

side. Liverpool.

Melas, M.,1985. *The Islands of Karpathos, Saros and Kasos in the Neolithic and Bronze Age* (SIMA 68). Gothenburg.

Menu, M., 1994. 'Analyse du trésor de Tôd' *Bulletin de la Societé Française d'Egyptologie* 130: 29–45.

Mercando, L., 1980. 'Lampade, lucerne, bracieri di Festòs' *ASAtene* 52–53: 15–167.

Merrillees, R. S., 1972. 'Aegean Bronze Age relations with Egypt' *AJA* 76: 281–94.

Michael, H. N. and Betancourt, P. P., 1988. 'Further arguments for an early date' and 'Addendum' *Archaeometry* 30: 169–75 and 180–1.

Mirie, S., 1979. *Das Thronraumareal des Palastes von Knossos*. Bonn.

Momigliano, N., 1990. 'The development of the footed goblet ('egg-cup') from EM II to MM III at Knossos' *Cretological* 6, 477–87.

——— , 1991. 'MM IA pottery from Evans excavations at Knossos' *BSA* 85: 149–271.

——— , 1992. 'The 'Proto-palatial facade' at Knossos' *BSA* 87: 165–75.

Monaco, G., 1941. 'Scavi nella zona micenea di Jaliso (1935–1936)' *Clara Rhodos* 10: 41–178.

Money-Coutts, M., 1936. 'A stone bowl and lid from Byblos' *Berytus* 3: 129–36.

Montet, P., 1928. *Byblos et L'Égypte*. Paris.

Moody, J., 1987. *The Environmental and Cultural Prehistory of the Khania region of West Crete: Neolithic through Late Minoan III*. PhD, University of Minnesota.

Moody, J., Rackham, O. and Rapp, G., 1996. 'Environmental archaeology of prehistoric NW Crete' *JFA* 23: 273–97.

Morgan, L., 1983. 'Morphology, syntax and the issue of chronology' in MacGillivray and Barber (eds.): 165–78.

——— , 1988. *The Miniature Wall Paintings of Thera*. Cambridge.

Morricone, L., 1973. 'Coo—Scavi e scoperte nel 'Seraglio' e in località minori (1935–1943)' *ASAtene* 34–35: 139–396.

Mortzos, C. E., 1972. 'Partira'. Ἐπετήρις Ἐπιστημονικῶν Ἐρευνῶν 3: 386–419.

Mosso, A., 1907. *The Palaces of Crete and their Builders*. London.

——— , 1908. 'Ceramica neolithica di Phaestos e vasi dell'epoca minoica primitiva' *MonAnt* 19: 141–218.

Muhly, P., 1992. Μινωϊκὸς λαξευτὸς τάφος στὸν Πόρο Ἡρακλείου. Athens.

Myers, J. W., E. E. and Cadogan, G., 1992. (eds.) *The Aerial Atlas of Ancient Crete*. London.

Mylonas, G., 1972–73. *Grave Circle B at Mycenae*. Athens.

Myres, J. L., 1895. 'Prehistoric polychrome pottery from Kamarais, in Crete' *Proceedings of the Society of Antiquaries*: 351–6.

Newbury, P. E., 1893. *Beni Hasan* I. London.

Niemeier, W.-D., 1985. *Die Palaststilkeramik von Knossos. Stil, Chronologie und historischer Kontext* (Deutches Archäologisches Institut. Archäologische Forschungen 13). Berlin.

——— , 1986. 'Zur Deutung des Thronraumes im Palast von Knossos' *AthMitt* 101: 63–95.

——— , 1987. 'On the function of the 'Throne Room' in the palace at Knossos' *Function-Palaces*: 163–9.

——— , 1988. 'The 'Priest King' fresco from Knossos, a new reconstruction and interpretation' *Problems*: 235–44.

——— , 1991. 'Minoan artisans travelling overseas: the Alalakh frescoes and the painted plaster floor at Tel Kabri (Western Galilee)' *Aegaeum* 7: 189–200.

Nixon, L., Moody, J. and Rackham, O., 1988. 'A survey of Sphakia' *Kritiki Estia* 2: 292–5.

Noll, W., 1982. 'Mineralogie und Technik der Keramiken Altkretas' *Neues Jahrbuch fur Mineralogie* 143: 150–99.

Overbeck, J. C., 1982. 'The hub of commerce: Keos and Middle Helladic Greece' *TUAS* 7: 38–49.

——— , 1984. 'Stratigraphy and ceramic sequence in Middle Cycladic Ayia Irini, Kea' in MacGillivray and Barber 1984: 108–13.

——— , 1989. *Ayia Irini: Period IV Part 1: The Stratigraphy and the Find Deposits* (*Keos* VII). Mainz.

Overbeck, J. C. and G. F., 1979. 'Consistency and diversity in the Middle Cycladic era' in Davis and Cherry (eds.): 106–21.

Palmer, L., 1964. Letter to the Editor *Nestor* 2: 323–5.

——— , 1965. *Mycenaeans and Minoans*. Oxford.

——— , 1969a. *The Penultimate Palace of Knossos*. Rome.

——— , 1969b. *A New Guide to the Palace of Knossos*. London.

Palmer, L. and Boardman, J., 1963. *On the Knossos Tablets*. Oxford.

Palmer, L. and Raison, J., 1973. 'L''Insula Nord-ouest' du palais de Knossos: position des sols et stratigraphie' *Minos* 14: 17–38.

Panagiotaki, M., 1993a. 'Sealings from the Olive Press Room, Knossos: new information from the unpublished notes of Sir Arthur Evans' *BSA* 88: 29– 47.

——— , 1993b. 'The Temple Repositories of Knossos: new information from the unpublished notes of Sir Arthur Evans' *BSA* 88: 49–91.

Papagiannopoulou, A. G., 1985. 'Were the S. E. Aegean islands deserted in the MBA?' *AS* 35: 85–92.

——— , 1991. *The Influence of Middle Minoan Pottery on the Cyclades* (SIMA Pocket-book 96). Jonsered.

Papenfuss, D. and Strocka, V. M., 1982. (eds.) *Palast und Hutte: Beiträge zum Bauern und Wohnen im Altertum von Archäologen, Vor- und Frühgeschichtlern*. Mainz.

Parabeni, R., 1904. 'Ricerche nel sepolcreto di Haghia Triada presso Phestos' *MonAnt* 14: 677–756.

——— , 1913. 'Scavi nella necropoli preellenica de Festo. . . Siva' *Ausonia* 8: 14–31.

Payne, H. G. G., 1930. 'Archaeology in Greece, 1929–30' *JHS* 50: 236–52.

Peatfield, A., 1983. 'The topography of Minoan peak sanctuaries' *BSA* 78: 273–80.

Pelagatti, P., 1962. 'Osservazioni sui ceramisti del I Palazzo di Festòs' *Cretological* 1: 99–111.

Pelon, O., 1970. *Fouilles executées à Mallia. Exploration des maisons et quartiers d'habitation (1963–1966) troisième fascicule* (*EtCret* 16). Paris.

——— , 1980. 'Aspects de la vie religieuse minoenne à la lumière des recherches récentes au palais de Malia (Crete)' *Academie des Inscriptions et Belles Lettres. Comptes Rendus*: 658–70.

——— , 1982. 'L'Épée à l'acrobate et la chronologie Maliote' *BCH* 106: 165–90.

——— , 1983. 'L'Épée à l'acrobate et la chronologie Maliote (II)' *BCH* 107: 679–703.

——— , 1986. 'Un dépot de fondation au palais de Malia' *BCH* 110: 3–19.

———, 1987a. 'Particularités et développement des palais minoens' in Levy (ed.) *Le système palatial en Orient, en Grèce et à Rome*: 187–201. Leiden.

———, 1987b. 'Une figurine en bronze du musée d'Iraklion' *Eilapini*: 431–9.

———, 1988. 'L'autel minoen sur le site de Malia' *Aegaeum* 2: 31–46.

———, 1989. 'L'Anatolie à l'origine de l'architecture palatiale de Crète?' in Emre *et al.* 1989: 431–9.

Pelon, O. and Sturmer, V., 1989. 'Sur les pseudo-trompettes de Malia' *BCH* 113: 101–11.

Pendlebury, H. W. and J. D. S., 1930. 'Two protopalatial houses at Knossos' *BSA* 30: 53–73.

Pendlebury, H. W., J. D. S. and Money-Coutts, M. B., 1936. 'Excavations in the plain of Lasithi. I. The cave of Trapeza' *BSA* 36: 5–131.

———, 1938a. 'Excavations in the plain of Lasithi. II' *BSA* 38: 1–56.

———, 1938b. 'Excavations in the plain of Lasithi. III. Karphi: a city of refuge of the Early Iron Age in Crete' *BSA* 38: 57–145.

Pendlebury, J. D. S., 1930. *Aegyptiaca*. Cambridge.

———, 1933. *A Guide to the Stratigraphical Museum in the Palace at Knossos*. London.

———, 1939. *The Archaeology of Crete* (rep. 1965). London.

Pernier, L., 1902. 'Ricerche e scavi sulle acropoli di Phaestos' *MonAnt* 12: 7–132.

———, 1904. 'Scavi della Missione Italiana a Phaistos (1902–1903)' *MonAnt* 14: 313–492.

———, 1907. 'Scavi e scoperte periodo preelenico' *Ausonia* 2: 106–27.

———, 1935. *Il Palazzo Minoico di Festòs*, I: *Gli Strati piu antichi e il Primo Palazzo*. Rome.

Pernier, L. and Banti, L., 1951. *Il Palazzo Minoico di Festòs*, II: *Il Secondo Palazzo*. Rome.

Petrie, W. F., 1891. *Ilahun, Kahun and Gurob*. London.

Pierrat, G., 1994. 'A propos de la date et de l'origine du trésor de Tôd' *Bulletin de la Societe Française d'Egyptologie* 130: 18–27.

Pilali-Papasteriou, A., 1987. 'Ἱερὰ καὶ ἀποθῆκες στὴν Ἀνατολικὴ Κρήτη' *Eilapini*: 179–96.

Pini, I., 1968. *Beiträge zur minoischen Gräberkunde*. Wiesbaden.

Platon, N., 1947. 'Ἡ ἀρχαιολογικὴ κίνησις ἐν Κρήτῃ κατὰ τὰ ἔτη 1941–1947' *KrChron* 1: 631–40.

———, 1949a. 'Ἡ χρονολογία τῶν μινωϊκῶν ἀνακτόρων τῆς Φαιστοῦ' *KrChron* 3: 150–66.

———, 1949b. 'Nouvelle interpretation des idoles-cloches du Minoen Moyen I' *Mélanges Charles Picard*: 830–46.

———, 1954. 'Τὰ μινωϊκὰ οἰκιακὰ ἱερά' *KrChron* 7: 428–83.

———, 1955a. *A Guide to the Archaeological Museum of Heraclion*. Heraclion.

———, 1955b. 'Ἡ ἀρχαιολογικὴ κίνησις ἐν Κρήτῃ κατὰ τὸ ἔτος 1955' *KrChron* 8: 553–69.

———, 1956. 'La chronologie minoenne' in Zervos 1956: 509–12.

———, 1959. 'Ἀνασκαφὴ μεσομινωϊκοῦ ἱεροῦ εἰς Ρουσσὲς Χόνδρου' *PAE*: 208–9.

———, 1962. 'Συγκριτικὴ χρονολογία τῶν τριῶν μινωϊκῶν ἀνακτόρων' *Cretological* 1: 127–36.

———, 1967. 'Ἀνασκαφαὶ Ζάκρου' *PAE*: 162–94.

———, 1968. 'Τὰ προβλήματα χρονολογήσεως τῶν

μινωϊκῶν ἀνακτόρων' *AE*: 1–58.

———, 1971. *Zakros*. New York.

———, 1973a. 'La chronologie des receptacles de trésor du sanctuaire — The 'Temple Repositories' — et des autres depots contemporains du palais de Cnossos' *Cretological* 3: 241–53.

———, 1973b. 'La chronologia degli archivi di scrittura geroglifica a Creta' *AntCretesi* I: 12–20.

Pomerance, L., 1984. 'The mythogenesis of Minoan chronology' in Åström *et al.*: 8–14.

Popham, M. R., 1964. *The Last Days of the Palace at Knossos* (SIMA 5). Lund.

———, 1970a. *The Destruction of the Palace at Knossos* (SIMA 12). Gothenburg.

———, 1970b. 'Late Minoan chronology' *AJA* 74: 226–8.

———, 1974. 'Trial KV (1969), a Middle Minoan building at Knossos' *BSA* 69: 181–94.

———, 1977. 'Notes from Knossos, Part 1' *BSA* 72: 185–95.

———, 1984. *The Minoan Unexplored Mansion at Knossos* (BSA Supplementary vol. 17). Oxford.

———, 1990. Pottery styles and chronology' *TAW* III(3): 27–8.

Porada, E., 1982. 'Remarks on the Tôd treasure in Egypt' in Dandamayev *et al.* 1982: 285–303.

Pottier, E., 1907. 'Documents céramiques du Musée du Louvre' *BCH* 31: 115–38.

Poursat, J.-C., 1966. 'Un sanctuaire Minoen Moyen II' *BCH* 90: 514–51.

———, 1972. 'Mallia' *BCH* 96: 957–61.

———, 1973a. 'Découvertes récentes à Malia: le Quartier Mu (1966–1971)' *Cretological* 3: 274–8.

———, 1973b. 'Mallia' *BCH* 97: 580–3.

———, 1975. 'Fouilles récentes à Mallia (Crete): l'art palatial minoen à l'époque de Camares' *Gazette des Beaux-Arts* 86: 89–98.

———, 1984. 'Poissons minoens à Mallia' *Origines*: 25–8.

———, 1987. 'Le début de l'époque protopalatial à Malia' *Eilapini*: 461–6.

Quirke, S., 1991a. 'Royal power in the 13th Dynasty' in Quirke 1991b: 123–39.

———, 1991b. (ed.) *Middle Kingdom Studies*. New Malden.

———, 1999. (ed.) *Lahun Studies*. London.

Raison, J., 1988. *Le Palais du Second Millenaire à Knossos*, I. *Le Quartier Nord* (EtCret 28). Paris.

Renfrew, C., 1972. *The Emergence of Civilization*, London.

———, 1978. 'Phylakopi and the Late Bronze I period in the Cyclades' *TAW* II(1): 403–21.

Renfrew, C. and Cherry, J. F., 1986. (eds.) *Peer Polity Interaction and Socio-Political Change: Excavations and Studies conducted by the University of Pennsylvania Museum and the British School at Athens*. Cambridge.

Rethemiotakis, G., 1988. [Kastelli] *Kritiki Estia* 2: 327–8.

———, 1989. 'Καστέλλι Πεδιάδος' *ADelt* 44, Chr. B.2: 428–9.

———, 1990. *Cretological* 6: 243–4.

Rice, P. M., 1976. 'Rethinking the ware concept' *American Antiquity* 41: 538–43.

———, 1984. 'Change and conservatism in pottery producing systems' in Van Der Leeuw and Pritchard (eds.): 231–88.

———, 1987. *Pottery Analysis: A Sourcebook*. Chicago.

Riley, J., 1983. 'The contribution of ceramic petrology to our understanding of Minoan society' *Society*: 283–92.

Rutkowski, B., 1968. 'The origin of the Minoan coffin' *BSA* 63: 219–27.

———, 1972. *Cult Places in the Aegean World*. Bratislava.

———, 1981. *Frühgriechische Kultdarstellungen*. Berlin.

———, 1986. *The Cult Places of the Aegean*. New Haven and London.

———, 1988. 'Minoan peak sanctuaries: the topography and architecture' *Aegeaum* 2: 71–99.

Sackett, L. H. and Popham, M., 1965. 'Excavations at Palaikastro, VI' *BSA* 60: 248–314.

———, 1970. 'Excavations at Palaikastro, VII' *BSA* 65: 203–42.

Sakellarakis, J. and E., 1972. Ἀποθέτης κεραμεικῆς τῆς τελευταίας φάσεως τῶν προανακτορικῶν χρόνων εἰς Ἀρχάνας' *AE* Chron: 1–11.

———, 1979. Ἀνασκαφὴ Ἀρχανῶν' *PAE*: 331–92.

———, 1981. 'Drama of Death in a Minoan Temple' *National Geographic* 159: 205–22.

———, 1982. Ἀνασκαφὴ Ἀρχανῶν' *PAE*: 467–530.

———, 1983. Ἀνασκαφὴ Ἀρχανῶν' *PAE*: 367–414.

———, 1991. *Archanes*. Athens.

Saltz, D. L., 1977. 'The chronology of the Middle Cypriot period' *RDAC*: 51–70.

Sampson, A., 1980. Μινωϊκὰ ἀπὸ τὴν Τῆλο' *AAA* 13: 68–73.

Sapouna-Sakellaraki, E., 1971. *Μινωϊκὸν Ζῶμα*. Athens.

Schaeffer, C. F. A., 1938. 'Les fouilles de Ras Shamra-Ugarit neuvième campagne (printemps 1937)' *Syria* 19: 193–334.

———, 1948. *Stratigraphie comparée et chronologie de l'Asie Occidentale (IIIe et IIe millénaires)*. Oxford.

———, 1949. *Ugaritica* II. Paris.

Schlager, N., 1987. 'Untersuchungen zur prähistorischen Topographie im äussersten Südosten Kretas: Zakros bis Xerokampos' *Kolloquium zur Ägäischen Vorgeschichte* (Schriften des Deutschen Archäologen-Verbandes 9): 75–7.

———, 1991. *Archäologische Gelandeprospektion Südostkreta erste Ergebnisse* (Österreichisches Archäologisches Instituts Berichte und Materialien 2). Wien.

Schmid, M. E., 1983. 'Les portes multiples au 'Megaron' du palais de Malia' *BCH* 107: 705–16.

———, 1985. 'Esquisse du trace d'un ensemble architectural de l'epoque minoenne: Malia, le Quartier Mu' *Le dessin d'architecture dans les sociétés antiques*: 63–73.

Schoep, I., 1994. 'Home sweet home: some comments on the so-called house models from the prehellenic Aegean' *OpAth* 20: 189–210.

Seager, R. B., 1905. 'Excavations at Vasiliki, 1904' *TFMSA* 1: 207–21.

———, 1907. 'Report of excavations at Vasiliki, Crete, in 1906' *TFMSA* 2: 111–32.

———, 1910. *Excavations on the Island of Pseira, Crete*. Philadelphia.

———, 1912. *Explorations in the Island of Mochlos*, Boston and New York.

———, 1916. *The Cemetery of Pachyammos, Crete*. Philadelphia.

Smith, S., 1945. 'Middle Minoan I and II and Babylonian Chronology' *AJA* 49: 1–24.

Soles, J., 1979. 'The early Gournia Town' *AJA* 83: 151–6.

———, 1991. 'The Gournia palace' *AJA* 95: 17–78.

Spence, Y., 1990. 'Was there a guarded southern entrance way to the First Palace at Mallia?' *BSA* 85: 369–74.

Speziale, A., 1993. 'Considerazioni sulle lucerne medio minoiche da Festòs' *Sileno* 19: 539–49.

Stewart, J. R., 1962. 'The tomb of the seafarer at Karmi in Cyprus' *OpAth* 4: 197–204.

Strøm, I., 1980. 'Middle Minoan Crete: a re-consideration of some its external relations' in Best and De Vries 1980: 105–23. Amsterdam.

Stürmer, V., 1992. *MM III: Studien zum Stilwandel der minoischen Keramik* (Archaeologica Heidelbergensia vol. 1). Mainz.

———, 1993. 'La céramique de Chrysolakkos: catalogue et réexamen' *BCH* 117: 123–87.

Taramelli, A., 1901 'A visit to the grotto of Kamares on Mount Ida' *AJA* 4: 437–51.

Themelis, P., 1969. Μινωϊκὰ ἐξ Ὀλυμπίας' *AAA*: 248–56.

Tomlinson, R. A., 1995. 'Archaeology in Greece 1994–95' *AR* 41: 1–74.

———, 1996. 'Archaeology in Greece 1995–1996' *AR* 42: 1–47.

Tsipopoulou, M., 1988a. Ἁγία Φωτιά Σιτείας τό νεό εὕρημα' *Problems*: 31–47.

———, 1988b. [Petras] *Kritiki Estia* 2: 336–8.

Tufnell, O., 1969. 'The pottery from the Royal Tombs I–III at Byblos' *Berytus* 18: 5–34.

Tzedakis, I., 1984. 'Le passage au Minoen ancien en Crete occidentale' *Origines*: 3–7.

Tzedakis, I. and Chrysoulaki, S., 1989. 'Routes minoennes: un rapport préliminaire. Défense de la circulation ou circulation de la défense?' *BCH* 113: 43–75.

Van As, A., 1984. 'Reconstructing the potter's craft' in Van Der Leeuw and Pritchard (eds.) 131–59.

Vandenabeele, F., 1985. 'La chronologie des documents en Lineaire A' *BCH* 109: 12–15.

Van der Leeuw, S. E. and Pritchard, A. C., 1984. (eds.) *The Many Dimensions of Pottery. Ceramics in Archaeology and Anthropology*. Amsterdam.

Van Effenterre, H., 1948. *Nécropoles du Mirabello (EtCret 8)*. Paris.

———, 1980a. *Le Palais de Mallia et la cité minoenne*. Rome.

———, 1980b. 'Jalons pour une nouvelle histoire des premiers palais' *Cretological* 3: 137–49.

———, 1987. 'A propos de l'approvisionment en eau des sites et palais minoens' *Eilapini*: 479–83.

Van Effenterre, H. and M., 1963. *Fouilles executées à Mallia. Etude du Site (1956–1957) et Exploration des Nécropoles (1915–1928) (EtCret 13)*. Paris.

———, 1969. *Fouilles executées à Mallia Le Centre politique I. L'Agora (1960–1966) (EtCret 17)*. Paris.

Vasilakis, A., 1990. 'Prehistoric sites in the neighbourhood of the Odigitria Monastery, South Crete' *Kritiki Estia* 3: 11–79.

Virolleaud, C., 1922. 'Découverte à Byblos d'un hypogée de la douzième dynastie égyptienne' *Syria* 3: 273–90.

Walberg, G., 1976. *Kamares. A Study of the Character of Palatial Middle Minoan Pottery (Boreas 8)*. Uppsala.

———, 1981a. 'Mittleminoische Keramik. Methode und Probleme' *AA*: 1–14.

———, 1981b. 'The identification of Middle Minoan painters and workshops' *AJA* 85: 73–5.

———, 1983. *Provincial Middle Minoan Pottery*. Mainz.

———, 1984. 'The Tôd treasure and Middle Minoan absolute chronology' *OpAth* 15: 173–7.

———, 1986. *Tradition and Innovation. Essays in Minoan Art*. Mainz.

———, 1987. 'Early Cretan tombs: the pottery' *Aegaeum* 1: 53–60.

———, 1988. 'Was Evans right? Further notes on Middle Minoan absolute chronology' *OpAth* 17: 199–201.

———, 1991. 'The finds at Tell el-Dab'a and Middle Minoan chronology' *Ägypten und Levante* 2: 115–18.

———, 1992. *Middle Minoan III—A Time of Transition* (SIMA 97). Jonsered.

Ward, W. A., 1971. *Egypt and the East Mediterranean World. Studies in Egyptian Foreign Relations during the First Intermediate Period*. Beirut.

———, 1981. 'The scarabs from Tholos B at Platanos' *AJA* 85: 70–3.

Warren, P. W., 1967. 'A stone vase-maker's workshop in the Palace at Knossos' *BSA* 62: 195–201.

———, 1969. *Minoan Stone Vases*. Cambridge.

———, 1972. *Myrtos: Early Bronze Age Settlement* (*BSA* Suppl. 6). Oxford.

———, 1980. 'Problems of chronology in Crete and the Aegean in the third and earlier second millennium B.C.' *AJA* 84: 487–99.

———, 1981. 'Knossos: Stratigraphical Museum excavations, 1978–1980. Part 1' *AR* 27: 73–92.

———, 1985a. 'The fresco of the garlands from Knossos' *Iconographie*: 187–207.

———, 1985b. 'Minoan pottery from Egyptian sites' (Review of Kemp and Merrillees (1980) *The Classical Review* 35: 147–51.

———, 1987. 'Absolute dating of the Aegean Late Bronze Age' *Archaeometry* 29: 205–11.

———, 1988. 'Further arguments against an early date' *Archaeometry* 30: 176–9.

———, 1991a. 'A new Minoan deposit from Knossos, c. 1600 BC, and its wider relations' *BSA* 86: 317–40.

———, 1991b. 'A merchant class in Bronze Age Crete? The evidence of Egyptian stone vases from the city of Knossos' in Gale 1991: 295–301.

———, 1994. 'The Minoan roads of Knossos' *Labyrinth*: 189–210.

———, 1995. 'Minoan Crete and Pharonic Egypt' in Davies and Schofield 1995: 1–18.

Warren, P. M. and Hankey, V., 1989. *Aegean Bronze Age Chronology*. Bristol.

Watrous, V., 1982. *Lasithi* (*Hesperia* Suppl. 18). Princeton.

———, 1994. 'Review of Aegean Prehistory III: Crete from the earliest prehistory through the Protopalatial period' *AJA* 98: 695–753.

Weingarten, J., 1983. *The Zakro Master and his Place in Prehistory* (SIMA Pocket-book 26). Gothenburg.

———, 1986a. 'Some unusual Minoan clay nodules' *Kadmos* 25: 1–21.

———, 1986b. 'The sealing structures of Minoan Crete: MM II Phaistos to the destruction of the palace at Knossos. Pt. I: The evidence until the LM I B destructions' *OJA* 5: 279–98.

———, 1987a. 'Seal use at LM I B Ayia Triada: a Minoan elite in action. Pt. I. administrative considerations' *Kadmos* 26, 38–43.

———, 1987b. 'Addendum: some unusual clay nodules' *Kadmos* 26: 38–43.

———, 1988. 'The sealing structures of Minoan Crete: MM II Phaistos to the destruction of the palace at Knossos. Pt. II: the evidence from Knossos until the destruction of the palace' *OJA* 7: 1–17.

———, 1989. 'Old and new elements in the seals and sealings of the Temple Repository, Knossos' *Aegaeum* 3: 39–47.

———, 1990. 'Three upheavals in Minoan sealing administration: a comprehensive analysis of function' *Aegaeum* 4: 105–14.

———, 1994. 'Sealings and sealed documents at Bronze Age Knossos' *Labyrinth*: 171–88.

Wiener, M., 1987. 'Trade and rule in Palatial Crete' *Function-Palaces*: 261–6.

———, 1990. 'The isles of Crete?' *TAW* III(1): 128–60.

———, 1991. 'The nature and control of Minoan foreign trade' in Gale 1991: 325–50.

Wilson, D. E., 1984. *The E. M. IIA West Court House, Knossos* (Ph.D. dissertation, University of Cincinnati, University Microfilms no. 84-20922).

———, 1985. 'The pottery and architecture of the EM II A West Court House at Knossos' *BSA* 80: 281–364.

———, 1994. 'Knossos before the palaces: an overview of the Early Bronze Age (EM I–EM II)' *Labyrinth*: 23–44.

Wilson, D. E. and Day, P. M., 1994. 'Ceramic regionalism in prepalatial central Crete: the Mesara imports at EM I to EM II A Knossos' *BSA* 89: 1–87.

Wotzka, H. P., 1990. 'The abuse of User. A note on the egyptian statuette from Knossos' *BSA* 85: 449–53.

Xanthoudides, S., 1924. *The Vaulted Tombs of the Mesara*. London.

Xenaki-Sakellariou, A., 1985. *Les Tombes à Chambre de Mycènes*. Paris.

Yadin, Y., Aharoni, Y., Amiran, R., Dothan, T., Dunayevsky, I. and Perrot, J., 1960. *Hazor* II. Jerusalem.

Yule, P., 1978. 'On the date of the 'Hieroglyphic Deposit' at Knossos' *Kadmos* 17: 1–7.

———, 1980. *Early Cretan Seals: A Study of Chronology*. Mainz.

———, 1983. 'Notes on scarabs and Aegean chronology' *BSA* 78: 359–67.

———, 1987. 'Early and Middle Minoan foreign relations: the evidence from the seals' *SMEA* 26: 161–77.

Zerner, C. W., 1993 (ed.) *Wace and Blegen. Pottery as Evidence for Trade in the Aegean Bronze Age, 1939-1989: proceedings of the International Conference held at the American School of Classical Studies at Athens December 2-3, 1989*. Amsterdam.

Zervos, C., 1956. *L'Art de la Crete*. Paris.

Zois, A. A., 1965. 'Phaistiaka' *AE*: 27–109.

———, 1968. *Der Kamares Stil. Werden und Wesen*. Tubigen.

———, 1969. Προβλήματα χρονολογίας τῆς μινωϊκῆς κεραμεικῆς. Γούρνες, Τύλισος, Μάλια (Βιβλιοθήκη τῆς Ἀρχαιολογικῆς Ἑταιρείας, ἀρ. 66). Athens.

———, 1976. Βασιλική I. Νέα ἀρχαιολογική ἔρευνα εἰς τὸ Κεφάλι πλησίον τοῦ χωρίου Βασιλικὴ Ἱεραπέτρας (Βιβλιοθήκη τῆς Ἀρχαιολογικῆς Ἑταιρείας, ἀρ. 83). Athens.

———, 1982. 'Gibt es vorläufer der minoischen Palästen auf Kreta? Ergebnisse neuer Untersuchungen' in Papenfuss and Strocka 1982: 207–15.

Appendix I. Catalogue

The following catalogue is organised in the order of the groups described in Chapter 1. The ceramics are subdivided on the basis of macroscopic observations of fabric begining with the most frequent, Fine Buff Ware, then by manufacturing technique, surface treatment and the type that corresponds in general to the typology set out in Chapter 2.

Conventions

Measurements (given in centimetres)

H.	—	height
D.	—	diameter
max.	—	maximum
pres.	—	preserved

Locations

AM	—	Ashmolean Museum
BM	—	British Museum
HM	—	Herakleion Museum
KSM	—	Knossos Stratigraphical Museum

Other

Para.	—	Close parallels for form and decoration
F.	—	Close parallels from Phaistos (see p. 19)
#	—	Knossos Stratigraphical Museum box number.

GROUP A: THE EARLY CHAMBER BENEATH THE WEST COURT

FABRIC: FINE BUFF

Technique: Handmade—Pared Ware

Surface: Plain

Rounded Goblet—Type 1

1. (K.289) PLATE 33 Intact. H. 5.7, D. rim 8.0, base 4.5 cm. Shallow groove below rim. KSM B I 7 #220. SMP 9551.
2. (K.290) PLATE 33 Intact. H. 6.0, D. rim 8.5, base 4.3 cm. KSM B I 7 #220. SMP 9552.
3. (K.291) PLATE 33 Complete; recomposed. H. 6.0, D. rim 8.0, base 4.0 cm. KSM B I 7 #220. SMP 9553.
4. (K.292) PLATE 33 Intact. H. 5.5, D. rim 8.0, base 4.5 cm. KSM B I 7 #217. SMP 9554.
5. (K.294) PLATE 33 Large rim fragment missing. H. 6.0, D. rim 8.5, base 5.0 cm. KSM B I 7 #220. SMP 9555.
6. (K.295) PLATE 33 Large rim fragment missing. H. 6.0, D. rim 7.5, base 4.0 cm. KSM B I 7 #217. SMP 9556.

7. (K.296) Intact. Evans 1921, 187 fig. 136b. Not located.

Straight-sided Cup—Type 1

8. (K.297) PLATE 31 ?Intact. Evans 1921, 187 fig. 136l. Not located.
9. (K.298) PLATE 33 Rim chipped. H. 4.7, D. rim *c.* 9.0, base 6.0 cm. KSM B 17 #217. SMP 9557.
10. (K.299) PLATES 1, 33 Rim chipped. H. 5.5, D. rim 10.0, base 6.6 cm. KSM B I 7 #217. SMP 9558.
11. (K.300) PLATE 33 Intact. H. 4.5, D. rim 9.5, base 5.3 cm. KSM B I 7 #215. SMP 9559.
12. (K.301) PLATE 33 Rim fragment missing. H. 5.5, D. rim 10.5, base 6.5 cm. KSM B I 7 #220. SMP 9560.
13. (K.302) PLATE 33 One-third of rim missing. H. 5.0, D. rim 9.5, base 6.0 cm. KSM B I 7 #220. SMP 9561.
14. (K.303) PLATE 33 Few rim fragments missing. H. 5.0, D. rim 9.5, base 5.5 cm. KSM B I 7 #220. SMP 9562.

Surface: Dark-on-buff spray or smear

Rounded Goblet—Type 1

15. (K.288) PLATE 33 Intact. H. 6.5, D. rim 8.0, base 4.5 cm. Thin brown paint smeared on rim and dripped down side. KSM B I 7 #215. SMP 9563.
16. (K.293) PLATE 33 Rim chipped. H. 6.5, D. rim 8.5, base 4.3 cm. Smear of thin reddish-brown paint at rim. KSM B I 7 #219. SMP 9564.

Surface: Monochrome coated

Tumbler—Type 1

17. (K.248) Large rim and side fragment missing. H. 3.0, D. rim 4.2, base 2.2 cm. Exterior coated brown, fired red and dark-brown in places. KSM B I 7 #217. SMP 9565.

Technique: Handmade, plain

Surface: Buff, undecorated

Shallow Bowl—Type 1

18. (K.308) Complete; recomposed. H. 3.2, D. rim 9.4, base 5.0 cm. KSM B I 7 #219. SMP 9566.

Surface: Dark-on-buff painted

Tall-rimmed Angular Cup—Type 2

19. (K.240) PLATES 1, 33 Base, lower side and one-third of rim missing. H. pres. 6.0, D. rim 11.5 cm. Four wide vertical bands descending from rim to horizontal band on lower side all in dark-brown paint. KSM B I 7 #219. SMP 9567.

Surface: Reserved buff with added white

Straight-sided Cup—Type 2

20. (K.273) PLATES 31, 34 Rim chipped. H. 4.4, D. rim 8.0, base 5.5 cm. Both sides dipped in lustrous grey-brown paint leaving handle and central section buff outlined in white. Evans 1921, 187 fig. 136k; Pendlebury 1939, pl. VII3b. HM 4402.

Tall-rimmed Angular Cup—Type 1a

21. (K.214) Rim and side fragment with handle. Part of body, rim and handle painted lustrous brown and outlined in white. Interior also has reserved zone but not outlined in white. KSM B I 7 #222. SMP 9568.

Rounded Cup—Type 1a

22. (K.221) PLATES 1, 34 Three fragments of rim and side missing; restored in plaster. H. 5.8, D. rim *c.* 9.0, base 4.0 cm. Exterior has thick uneven rim band in dark-brown with outline in white at bottom. Interior has thick uneven rim band in semilustrous black. KSM B I 7 #219; handle in #1853. SMP 9569.

Jug with cut-away spout—Type 1

23. (K.360) PLATE 34 Spout, handle and a few base and side fragments missing. H. pres. 7.3, D. base 6.5 cm. Top and bottom coated in semilustrous dark grey-brown leaving horizontal reserved zone in centre outlined in white. KSM B I 6 #180. SMP 9570.

Surface: Monochrome coated

Shallow Bowl—Type 1

24. (K.309) Fragment of base, side and one-third of rim. H. 3.8, D. rim 16.0, base 5.0 cm. Coated in dull reddish-brown throughout. KSM B I 7 #220. SMP 9571.

Tripod Bowl

25. (K.319) PLATES 31, 34 Intact. H. 4.5, D. rim 6.0, base 3.5 cm. Coated throughout in dark-brown paint. Evans 1921, 187 fig. 136m. HM 4409.

Straight-sided Cup—Type 2

26. (K.254) PLATE 34 Rim chipped. H. 4.6, D. rim 8.3, base 5.5 cm. Coated in semilustrous black throughout, now worn. KSM B I 7 #217. SMP 9572.

27. (K.255) PLATE 34 H. 5.0, D. rim 7.5, base 5.3 cm. Coated in semilustrous black throughout, worn. KSM B I 7 #217. SMP 9573.

28. (K.256) PLATE 34 Rim chipped. H. 4.5, D. rim 7.5–8.0, base 5.5 cm. Coated dark-brown, worn. KSM B I 7 #217. SMP 9574.

29. (K.257) PLATE 34 One-third of rim missing. H. 4.4, D. rim 7.5, base 5.3 cm. Coated semilustrous dark-brown throughout, worn. KSM B I 7 #219. SMP 9575.

30. (K.258) PLATE 34 One-third of rim missing. H. 4.5, D. rim 7.5, base 5.5 cm. Coated semilustrous grey-brown throughout, worn. KSM B I 7 #220. SMP 9576.

Tall-rimmed Angular Cup—Type 1

31. (K.230) PLATES 1, 35 Rim chipped, restored. H. 4.1, D. rim 6.0, base 2.5 cm. Coated dark-brown throughout. KSM B I 7 #219. SMP 9577.

32. (K.231) PLATES 1, 35 Single rim fragment missing. Restored in plaster. H. 4.7, D. rim 8.0, base 4.0 cm. Coated semilustrous brown throughout. KSM B I 7 #217. SMP 9578.

33. (K.232) PLATE 35 Part of handle, base and one-third of rim and side missing. Partially restored in plaster. H. 4.5, D. rim 8.0, base 3.5 cm. Coated throughout in semilustrous black, worn. KSM B I 7 #215, 220. SMP 9579.

34. (K.1011) PLATE 31 Large fragment of rim and side missing. Evans 1921, 187 fig. 136i. Not located.

Rounded Cup—Type 2

35. (K.227) PLATE 35 Fragment of side missing. H. 6.0, D. rim 7.2, base 3.0 cm. Coated throughout in semilustrous dark-brown to black paint. KSM B I 7 #220. SMP 9580.

Angular Bridge-spouted Jar—Type 1a

36. (K.359) PLATE 35 Half of rim, much of side and one handle missing. H. 10.3, D. rim *c.* 11.0, base 5.0 cm. Exterior roughly finished and scraped, coated with thin, dull dark-brown paint, now flaking away. Interior has thick uneven rim band and large drops of dark paint. KSM B I 7 #186. SMP 9581.

Surface: Monochrome coated; white decorated

Straight-sided Cup—Type 2

37. (K.264) PLATE 36 One-third of rim and most of handle missing. H. 4.8, D. rim 8.0, base 5.4 cm. Coated dark-brown throughout. Exterior has wide horizontal band at base and six pendant semicircles at the rim. KSM B I 7 #215, 220. SMP 9582.

38. (K.265) PLATE 35 Three joined fragments of rim, side, base and handle. H. 4.5, D. rim 8.0, base 5.0 cm. Coated grey-brown throughout. Exterior has five large pendant semicircles at rim. KSM B I 7 #220. SMP 9583.

39. (K.266) PLATE 31 Intact? Exterior has groups of semi-circles at base and rim. Evans 1921, 187 fig. 136e; Pendlebury 1939, pl. XVII3c. Not located.

40. (K.271) PLATE 35 Handle missing. H. 4.4, D. rim 8.0, base 5.0 cm. Coated semilustrous dark-brown throughout. Exterior has three groups of three vertical bars. KSM B I 7 #217. SMP 9584.

41. (K.272) PLATE 35 Half of rim, side and base missing. H. 4.0, D. rim 8.5, base 5.5 cm. Coated lustrous grey-brown throughout. Exterior has four? groups of three vertical lines. KSM B I 7 #219. SMP 9585.

Convex-sided Cup

42. (K.353) PLATES 1, 36 Handle and three-quarters of rim missing. H. 5.5, D. rim 7.5, base 5.0 cm. Coated semilustrous grey-brown throughout. Exterior has three closed spirals with traces of a cross in the centre. KSM B I 6 #186. SMP 9586.

Tall-rimmed Angular Cup—Type 1a

43. (K.215) PLATE 32 Handle missing. Exterior has large closed spiral. Not located.

Rounded Cup—Type 1a

44. (K.222) PLATE 36 Three small fragments of rim and body missing. H. 5.2, D. rim 8.5, base 4.2 cm. Coated in semilustrous black throughout. Exterior has two horizontal lines on side, three diagonal strokes on top of handle. KSM B I 7 #219. SMP 9587.

Rounded Cup—Type 1b

45. (K.220) PLATES 1, 36 Two rim fragments missing. Restored in plaster. H. 5.4, D. rim 8.0, base 5.2 cm. Coated dull reddish-brown, except for handle. Exterior has two horizontal lines on side and three groups of five diagonal strokes joining top horizontal line to rim. KSM B I 7 #218. SMP 9588.

Rounded Bridge-spouted Jar—Type 2

46. (K.323) PLATE 32 Intact? Exterior has part of foliate band, horizontal, on side. Not located.

47. (K.327) PLATE 1 Six recomposed fragments of rim, shoulder and side with one handle and five non-joining fragments. H. pres. 5.0, D. rim *c.* 8.0 cm. Exterior coated semilustrous dark-brown, mostly worn; horizontal band at rim and ?near base, large spots on side. Interior has uneven dark rim band and paint drops. KSM B I 7 #219.

Jug with cut-away spout—Type 1

48. (K.331) PLATES 1, 37 Part of handle missing, restored in plaster. H. 11.0, D. base 7.5 cm. Exterior coated in grey-black semilustrous paint, worn; traces of closed spiral on front. Andreou 1978, fig. 5.6. KSM B I 7 #220. SMP 9589.

Surface: Monochrome coated; white and red/orange decorated

Tripod Bowl

49. (K.318) PLATES 1, 37 Intact. H. 4.5, D. rim 6.0, base 3.5 cm. Coated throughout in dull reddish-brown. Exterior has diagonal pattern of four groups of two orange lines alternating with single white lines and four diagonal spaces with groups of three white horizontal strokes at top and bottom. KSM B I 7 #218. SMP 9590.

Shallow Angular Bowl—Type 1

50. (K.306) PLATES 1, 32, 37 Two recomposed non-joining parts of base and rim with side and one handle. Restored in plaster. H. 5.6, D. rim 14.0, base 6.5 cm. Interior has ten tiny pierced buttons arranged in a circle around a central bowl. Coated thin semilustrous dark-brown throughout. Interior has white diagonal slashes at rim, red slashes at spouts, horizontal white band with superimposed red dots with rows of white dots above and below outlined in orange on side below rim. Exterior has row of white dots framed with orange bands above and below on upper side. Inscribed 'K.04 W Sq. T.P.3'. Zervos 1956, fig. 321. HM 4376.

51. (K.330) PLATE 45 Single rim fragment. D. rim *c.* 15 cm. Coated dull reddish-brown throughout. Interior has white horizontal band below rim and traces of white slashes near spout. Exterior has thick orange band and two white bands below rim. KSM B I 7 #219. SMP 9591.

Tumbler—Type 1

52. (K.250) PLATES 1, 37 Half of rim and side missing. H. 5.8, D. rim 6.5, base 2.9 cm. Interior plain with thick rim band. Exterior coated in thin reddish-brown and has floral motifs alternating in white and orange framed by white and orange bands with thick white band at base. KSM B I 6 #209; KSM B I 7 #218. SMP 9592.

53. (K.348) PLATES 1, 37 Most of rim and side and small part of base missing. H. 5.8, D. rim 8.0, base 3.7 cm. Bottom plain. Sides coated dull reddish-brown. Exterior has zone of wavy lines alternating? with floral (daisy?) pattern framed in two orange bands and white band at base. KSM B I 6 #186. SMP 9593.

Tumbler—Type 2

54. (K.251) PLATES 31, 38 Fragment comprising base and lower side. H. 10.4, D. base 4.1 cm. Coated throughout in metallic black. Exterior has horizontal zone of white crescents with red band and one or two rows of white dots above and white and red bands below; white band at base. Evans 1921, 187 fig. 136a. HM 4408.

Conical Goblet—Type 2

55. (K.219) PLATES 1, 38 Eleven fragments of rim, side and foot; partially recomposed. H. *c.* 21.0, D. rim 9.5, base 10.0 cm. Coated throughout in thin, semilustrous dark-brown. Top of foot and exterior decorated with pairs of red and white lines spiralling from top to bottom. KSM B I 6 #183, 186; KSM B I 7 #219.

Straight-sided Cup—Type 2

56. (K.259) PLATES 2, 36 Rim fragment missing; restored. H. 4.3, D. rim 8.0, base 5.5 cm. Interior 'dipped' on both sides leaving buff area across centre. Exterior coated dark-brown, fired red in places. Exterior has two panels marked out by pairs of white vertical lines. Panels have rosettes of an orange dot in the centre with four white dots evenly spaced around it. KSM B I 7 #217. SMP 9594.

57. (K.260) PLATE 36 Intact. H. 4.8, D. rim 7.7, base 5.0 cm. Coated throughout in semi-lustrous black, worn. Exterior has two horizontal zones of thick white wavy lines separated by a horizontal red band. KSM B I 7 #217. SMP 9595.

58. (K.261) PLATE 36 Half of rim and side missing. H. 4.5, D. rim 8.0, base 6.0 cm. Coated throughout in semilustrous dark-brown. Exterior has decoration like 57. KSM B I 7 #220. SMP 9596.

59. (K.350) PLATE 2 Intact. H. 4.4, D. rim 8.0, base 5.5 cm. Coated semilustrous grey-brown throughout. Exterior decorated like 57 and 58. KSM B I 6 #183. SMP 9597.

60. (K.262) PLATE 36 Fragment of half of rim, side and base; handle missing. H. 4.3, D. rim 8.0 cm. Coated semilustrous dark-brown throughout. Exterior has two horizontal zones with rows of overlapping white semicircles separated by a red band. KSM B I 7 #217. SMP 9598.

61. (K.263) PLATE 36 Most of handle and two rim fragments missing. H. 4.8, D. rim 8.0, base 5.2 cm. Coated and decorated like 60. KSM B I 7 #219. SMP 9599.

62. (K.351) Small rim and base fragments missing. H. 4.4, D. rim 8.0, base 5.5 cm. Coated semilustrous grey-brown throughout. Exterior decorated like 60 and 61. KSM B I 7 #183. SMP 9600.

63. (K.267) PLATE 35 Handle missing. H. 4.5, D. rim 8.0, base 5.5 cm. Coated semilustrous dark-brown throughout, worn in places. Exterior has two zones defined by three sets of two or three vertical orange lines with two thick white curved lines in both zones. KSM B I 7 #217. SMP 9601.

64. (K.268) PLATE 35 Handle, much of rim missing. H. 4.5, D. rim 8.5, base 5.5 cm. Coated red-brown throughout. Exterior decorated like 63. KSM B I 7 #219, 220. SMP 9602.

65. (K.269) PLATE 35 Fragment of rim, side and base. H. 4.0, D. rim 8.0, base 5.5 cm. Coated and decorated like 63. KSM B I 7 #217.

66. (K.270) PLATE 35 One-quarter of rim, side and base missing.

H. 4.2, D. rim 8.0, base 5.0 cm. Coated semilustrous dark-brown throughout. Exterior has two pairs of vertical white lines defining two zones each having three thick red vertical lines each with a pair of thin white lines superimposed. KSM B I 7 #217. SMP 9604.

67. (K.352) PLATE 36 Much of rim and side missing. H. 4.5, D. rim 7.5, base 5.5 cm. Coated semilustrous dark-brown throughout, worn. Exterior has three white leaf patterns with hatching between pairs of orange vertical lines. KSM B I 6 #186. SMP 9605.

Straight-sided Cup—Type 3

68. (K.274) PLATES 2, 31 Few rim and side fragments missing. Restored in plaster. H. 7.5; D. rim 13.3; base 9.7 cm. Exterior has wide orange band with three added white Xs connected by white dots outlined in white at centre and rows of white arcades at rim and base. Evans 1921, 187 fig. 136g; Pendlebury 1939, pl. XVII3a. HM 4400.

Convex-sided Cup

69. (K.275) PLATES 32, 38 Few rim, side and base fragments missing. Restored in plaster. H. 5.7, D. rim 7.1, base 4.8 cm. Coated dull brown throughout. Exterior has white horizontal wavy line at centre outlined with two pairs of white lines and a red/orange line at rim and base. HM 4404.

Tall-rimmed Angular Cup—Type 1b (with crinkled rim)

70. (K.213) PLATES 2, 38 Two joining fragments of rim, side and base, with lower handle attachment. H. 4.5, D. base 3.0 cm. Coated semilustrous dark-brown throughout. Exterior has row of reverse 3s in white below rim, white bands on lower side and base, and orange bands at rim and centre. KSM B I 7 #219, 222. SMP 9606.

Tall-rimmed Angular Cup—Type 2

71. (K.344) PLATES 2, 38 Two non-joining parts of rim and side with complete handle. H. 5.0, D. rim 11.0 cm. Coated semilustrous grey-brown throughout. Exterior has diagonal pattern of a pair of orange lines outlined by pairs of white lines on both sides. KSM B I 6 #183, 186. SMP 9607.

72. (K.345) PLATES 2, 38 Two non-joining parts of rim and side. H. 4.8, D. rim 11.0 cm. Surface and decoration as 71. KSM B I 6 #183, 186; KSM B I 7 #218. SMP 9608.

Squat Rounded Bridge-spouted Jar

73. (K.322) PLATES 2, 32, 39 Top of one handle missing, restored in plaster. H. 9.0, D. rim 7.5, base 7.7 cm. Interior of rim and exterior coated dark-brown. Exterior has 9 orange vertical lines alternating with 9 white foliate bands from base to rim. Inscribed 'K.04 W Sq T.P.4'. Zervos 1956, fig. 364 left. HM 4396.

74. (K.326) PLATE 2 Several joining fragments of rim and shoulder with trace of handle and spout. H. 6.5, D. rim 8.0 cm. Interior of rim and exterior coated semilustrous grey-brown. Exterior has thick orange band below rim and on lower side, four groups of floral/reed sprays each having three orange leaves in the centre with groups of three white leaves above and below evenly spaced around shoulder, and traces of a rosette composed of one orange dot surrounded by six white dots below handle. Pendlebury 1939, 108 fig. 17.13. KSM B I 6 #183, 186; KSM B I 7 #220. SMP 9609.

Angular Bridge-spouted Jar—Type 2

75. (K.324) PLATES 2, 32, 39 Tip and half of spout, most of rim and base and much of side and handles missing. Restored. H. 16.6, D. rim 13.5, base 8.5 cm. Interior of spout and rim and exterior coated semilustrous dark-brown. Exterior has large panel on lower shoulder and upper side with ?four groups of zig-zags—one orange between two white—with two rosettes composed of eight connected white dots with one orange dot at the centre below the handles, outlined in white with thick orange bands at rim and lower side and thick white band near base. Pendlebury 1939, pl. XVII2c. HM 4390.

Rounded Bridge-spouted Jar—Type 2

76. (K.321) PLATES 2, 39 Tip of spout, several large rim and body fragments and both handles missing. Restored in plaster. H. 10.0, D. rim 10.0, base 5.5 cm. Interior of rim and exterior coated semilustrous grey-brown. Exterior has four thick evenly spaced vertical white bands outlined in orange and bordered by pairs of white lines, and a horizontal band at the rim and two near the base. Spout outlined in white. KSM B I 6 #180; KSM B I 7 #218. SMP 9610.

77. (K.325) PLATES 31, 39 Recomposed fragments of base and lower side. H. 13.0, D. base 10.5 cm. Exterior coated semilustrous dark-brown and has four thick roughly vertical orange bands bordered by pairs of white lines alternating with pattern of small white dots between large orange dots and ordered by interconnected C pattern. Evans 1921 187, fig. 136h; Pendlebury 1939, 108 fig. 17.10; Zois 1965 pls. 20, 21. HM 4395.

Large Jug

78. (K.332) PLATE 39 Nine non-joining fragments of spout and shoulder with complete handle. Exterior coated semilustrous black and has alternating thick white with orange border and orange with white border in ?spiral from base. KSM B I 7 #215, 218, 219.

Technique: Wheelmade

Surface: Monochrome coated

Shallow Bowl—Type 2

79. (K.310) One-third of rim missing. H. 4.5, D. rim 20.0, base 6.5 cm. Coated dull red-brown throughout. Cut-away marks on the base. KSM B I 7 #220. SMP 9611.

Straight-sided Cup—Type 4

80 (K.280) PLATE 40 Small rim fragment missing. H. 6.0, D. rim 8.0, base 4.5 cm. Coated semilustrous dark-brown throughout. KSM B I 7 #217. SMP 9612.

81. (K.281) PLATES 31, 39 Intact. H. 5.8, D. rim 9.3, base 4.7 cm. Coated lustrous metallic black throughout. Evans 1921, 187 fig. 136f. HM 4406.

82. (K.282) PLATE 40 One-third of rim missing. Restored in plaster. H. 6.0, D. rim 8.7, base 4.0 cm. Coated semilustrous black throughout. KSM B I 7 #215, 220. SMP 9613.

83. (K.283) PLATE 40 Small rim fragment missing. H. 4.5, D. rim 8.5, base 5.0 cm. Coated semilustrous dark-brown throughout. KSM B I 7 #217. SMP 9614.

84. (K.284) PLATE 40 Intact. H. 5.6, D. rim 9.0, base 5.0 cm. Coated semilustrous dark-brown throughout. KSM B I 7 #222. SMP 9615.

85. (K.285) PLATE 40 Two-thirds of rim missing. H. 6.0, D. rim 9.0, base 4.0 cm. Coated in thin brown paint throughout. String-marks on base. KSM B I 7 #220. SMP 9616.

86. (K.286) PLATE 40 Half of rim missing. H. 6.0, D. rim 9.0, base 4.5 cm. Coated in thin brown paint throughout. String-marks on base. KSM B I 7 #220. SMP 9617.

Straight-sided Cup—Type 5

87. (K.278) PLATE 40 Two small body fragments missing, restored in plaster. H. 6.6, D. rim 9.7, base 6.0 cm. Coated semilustrous dark-brown throughout. KSM B I 7 #219. SMP 9618.

Straight-sided Cup—Type 6

88. (K.279) PLATE 40 Most of rim missing. H. 8.5, D. rim 10.5, base 5.5 cm. Coated brown throughout. Horizontal grooves on sides. KSM B I 7 #219. SMP 9619.

Tall-rimmed Angular Cup—Type 3

89. (K.233) PLATES 3, 35 Rim and side fragment missing. Restored in plaster. H. 5.1, D. rim 8.0, base 3.5 cm. Coated brown all over except part of handle; mottled. KSM B I 7 #219. SMP 9620.

90. (K.234) PLATE 35 One-third of rim and side missing. H. 4.8, D. rim 8.0, base 3.8 cm. Coated metallic grey-brown all over except part of handle. String marks on base. KSM B I 7 #220. SMP 9621.

91. (K.235) PLATES 3, 35 Top of handle, parts of rim, base and lower side missing. Restored in plaster. H. 4.6, D. rim 8.0, base 3.0 cm. Coated semilustrous black throughout. KSM B I 7 #219. SMP 9622.

92. (K.236) Three joining fragments of rim side and base. H. 5.0, D. rim 8.0, base 3.3 cm. Coated brown throughout. String marks on base. KSM B I 7 #219. SMP 9623.

93. (K.237) PLATE 35 Three small rim fragments, part of side and most of base missing. Restored in plaster. H. 5.0, D. rim 8.0, base 4.0 cm. Coated brown all over except part of handle, mottled in places. Three thin horizontal grooves on side. KSM B I 7 #219. SMP 9624.

94. (K.238) PLATE 35 Three joining fragments of rim side and base with handle. Partially restored in plaster. H. 5.0, D. rim 8.5, base 3.8 cm. Coated semilustrous red-brown all over except handle. KSM B I 7 #215, 219, 220. SMP 9625.

95. (K.239) PLATES 3, 40 Two non-joining rim and side fragments. H. 4.6, D. rim 8.5 cm. Coated semilustrous dark-brown throughout. Exterior has incised horizontal or perhaps spiralling lines or grooves. KSM B I 7 #219. SMP 9626.

Large Angular Cup

96. (K.343) PLATES 3, 40 Rim and side fragment. H. 6.0, D. rim 12.0 cm. Coated semilustrous dark-brown throughout. Horizontal grooves on upper side. KSM B I 6 #186. SMP 9627.

Large Angular Cup with strainer

97. (K.218) PLATES 3, 32, 41 Two large non-joining parts of rim, side and base with top of handle, rim fragment in HM has complete strainer (PLATE 32). H. 11.0, D. rim 13.0, base 8.0 cm. Coated semilustrous dark red-brown throughout. Horizontal grooves at centre of upper side. KSM B I 6 #182; KSM B I 7 #215, 219. HM 5756. SMP 9628.

Short-rimmed Angular Cup—Type 1

98. (K.241) PLATES 3, 33 Rim chipped, most of handle missing. H. 5.3, D. rim 10.0, base 4.5 cm. Coated dull brown throughout. KSM B I 7 #218. SMP 9629.

Short-rimmed Angular Cup—Type 2a

99. (K.242) PLATES 3, 41 Two rim fragments missing. H. 6.8, D. rim 12.0, base 5.0 cm. Coated dark-brown throughout. Andreou 1978, fig. 5.5. KSM B I 7 #220. SMP 9630.

Short-rimmed Angular Cup—Type 2b

100. (K.243) PLATES 3, 41 Two-thirds of rim and half of side missing. Partially restored in plaster. H. 7.7, D. rim 12.0, base 4.5 cm. Coated dull red-brown throughout. String marks on base. KSM B I 7 #220. SMP 9631.

101. (K.244) PLATE 32 Intact? Not located.

Angular Cup with crinkled rim

102. (K.216) PLATE 41 Joining fragments of rim with handle. H. 6.0 cm Coated semilustrous grey-brown throughout. KSM B I 7 #215.

103. (K.217) Five non-joining parts of rim, side and handle. H. 7.0 cm. Coated dull red-brown throughout, worn. KSM B I 7 #215, 219, 220, 222.

Squat Rounded Cup—Type 1

104. (K.224) PLATES 3, 42 Most of rim, side and handle missing. Restored in plaster. H. 5.4, D. rim 6.5, base 2.5 cm. Coated semilustrous dark-brown throughout. KSM B I 7 #219. SMP 9632.

105. (K.225) Two fragments of rim, side and complete base. H. 6.0, D. rim 7.5, base 3.5 cm. Coated lustrous dark-brown throughout. KSM B I 7 #215.

106. (K.226) PLATES 3, 42 Most of rim and side missing. H. 7.0, D. rim 7.5, base 4.1 cm. Coated semilustrous dark-brown throughout, worn. Traces of four horizontal grooves below rim. String marks on base. KSM B I 6 #179; KSM B I 7 #220. SMP 9633.

Squat Rounded Cup—Type 2

107. (K.223) PLATES 3, 42 Much of rim missing. Restored in plaster. H. 7.5, D. rim 7.5, base 4.5 cm. Coated dull dark-brown all over except top of handle. KSM B I 7 #220. SMP 9634.

Rounded Cup—Type 4

108. (K.229) PLATES 4, 42 Fragments of base and lower side missing. Restored in plaster. H. 6.0, D. rim 8.8, base 3.5 cm. Coated dull brown throughout. String marks on base. KSM B I 7 #219. SMP 9635.

Rounded Cup—Type 3

109. (K.228) PLATES 4, 41 Few rim and body fragments missing; restored in plaster. H. 7.5, D. rim 9.0, base 4.3 cm. Coated semilustrous brown throughout. String marks on base. KSM B I 7 #220. SMP 9636.

Surface: Monochrome coated; white decorated

Rounded Goblet—Type 2

110. (K.287) PLATES 4, 33 Few small rim and side fragments missing. H. 7.8, D. rim 8.0, base 4.5 cm. Coated metallic grey-brown in and out but foot plain. Exterior has thick white horizontal band below rim. KSM B I 7 #215, 219, 222. SMP 9637.

Rounded Goblet—Type 3

111. (K.342) PLATES 4, 42 Seven joined fragments of rim and side, foot missing. H. 7.8, D. rim 12.0 cm. Coated dull red-brown throughout. Interior has thin line at rim. Exterior has three evenly spaced horizontal bands: at rim, middle and lower side. KSM B I 6 #183, 186. SMP 9638.

Straight-sided Cup—Type 5

112. (K.276) PLATES 4, 42 Handle and numerous rim, side and base fragments missing. H. 5.0, D. rim 9.5, base 6.3 cm. Coated semilustrous dark-brown throughout. Thick horizontal band at centre. KSM B I 7 #215, 219, 220, 222. SMP 9639.

Straight-sided Cup—Type 6

113. (K.277) PLATES 4, 42 Five joined fragments of rim and side with complete handle. H. 5.0, D. rim 9.0 cm. Coated semilustrous dark-brown throughout. One side only of exterior has vertical line at handle and horizontal bands at rim and ?centre of side. KSM B I 7 #219. SMP 9640.

Tall-rimmed Angular Cup—Type 3

114. (K.212) PLATES 4, 43 Few rim and body fragments and top of handle missing. Restored in plaster. H. 3.9, D. rim 7.0, base 2.4 cm. Coated thin brown throughout, mottled red-brown and worn. Exterior has traces of sponge print decoration on upper and lower side. KSM B I 7 #219, 222. SMP 9641.

Large Bevelled Cup with pulled rim-spout

115. (K.211) PLATES 4, 43 Handle, most of rim and much of side missing. H. 7.0, D. base 6.3 cm. Coated semilustrous brown throughout, worn in places. Exterior has wide horizontal bands at base and centre of side. KSM B I 6 #186; KSM B I 7 #219. SMP 9642.

Surface: Monochrome coated; white and red/orange decorated

Shallow Bowl—Type 2

116. (K.304) Five joined fragments of rim and side. D. rim 17.0 cm. Coated semilustrous black throughout. Exterior has thick horizontal white bands at rim and middle of side, and groups of three red and white vertical lines alternating in the zones between the bands. KSM B I 7 #219, 222. SMP 9643.

Straight-sided Cup—Type 5

117. (K.347) PLATES 4, 43 Fragment of rim and side. H. 5.3, D. rim 11.0 cm. Coated semilustrous dark-brown throughout. Wide horizontal bands of white painted barbotine at rim and ?middle of side with thin orange lines above and below. KSM B I 6 #186. SMP 9644.

Straight-sided Cup—Type 6

118. (K.346) PLATES 4, 43 Fragment of rim and side. H. 7.5, D. rim 9.0, base 5.0 cm. Coated semilustrous dark-brown throughout. Exterior has white hollow swastika encircled by yellow/orange loop within a white loop or spiral pattern. KSM B I 6 #186. SMP 9645.

119. (K.362) PLATE 4 Fragment of rim, side and base. H. 7.5, D. rim 9.0, base 5.5 cm. Coated semilustrous black throughout. Exterior has horizontal red line at middle with white lines above and below and rows of white semicircles at rim and base. KSM B I 6 #201. SMP 9646.

Cup—uncertain type

120. (K.305) PLATES 5, 43 Fragments of base and lower side. H. 6.0, D. base 5.0 cm. Coated semilustrous black throughout. Exterior has a row of tiny white dots at base and perhaps lower side above red lines, alternating red outlined in white and yellow/orange dots framed by white connected arcades on foot, and two pairs of white strokes on bottom. KSM B I 6 #186; KSM B I 7 #219. SMP 9647.

Squat Rounded Cup—Type 1

121. (K.205) PLATES 5, 31, 43 Few side and base fragments and lower part of handle missing. Restored in plaster. H. 7.0, D. rim 9.7, base 5.0 cm. Coated dark-brown throughout. Exterior has white ovals with pairs of volutes and orange-filled ?palm tree motifs above and below alternating with orange crosses encircled in white on the side, an orange line with white arcades on upper side and a white line with vertical strokes at rim. Evans 1921, 187 fig. 136p; Walberg 1976, fig. 21. HM 4398.

122. (K.206) PLATES 5, 44 Seven non-joining fragments of rim, side and base. H. 7.5, D. rim 9.0, base 5.0 cm. Coated semilustrous brown throughout. Exterior has white horizontal ladder pattern at middle and four evenly spaced white circles filled with alternating yellow and orange horizontal lines above and below. KSM B I 7 #219. SMP 9648.

Squat Rounded Cup—Type 2

123. (K.207) PLATES 5, 31, 44 Half of rim and side fragment missing. Restored in plaster. Unjoined rim fragments in KSM. H. 9.9, D. rim 8.3, base 5.5 cm. Interior sprayed with paint. Interior of rim and exterior coated semilustrous black. Exterior has pairs of connected white spirals in a zone framed by horizontal white and red lines on side, white vertical strokes on moulding, white lines below rim and at base, and double white cross on bottom. Evans 1921, 187 fig. 136g; Zois 1965, pl. 29. KSM B I 7 #219. HM 4397. SMP 9649.

Rounded Cup with sharply offset rim

124. (K.210) PLATES 5, 44 Several rim and side fragments and handle missing. Restored. H. 5.0, D. rim 12.0, base 4.0 cm. Coated thin semilustrous brown throughout, worn. Interior has pendant white arcades at rim and eight orange with white outline ovals evenly spaced around side. Exterior has an orange line outlined by white lines at middle and white line at base. KSM B I 7 #219, 222. SMP 9650.

Rounded Cup—Type 3 with pulled out rim

125. (K.208) PLATES 5, 44 Three-quarters of rim, handle part of side and centre of base missing. Restored. H. 6.6, D. rim 8.0, base 3.7 cm. Coated brown throughout, worn. Exterior has horizontal red line below rim and six panels outlined with red vertical lines and three of which are filled with white. HM 4401.

126. (K.209) PLATES 5, 31, 44 One-third of rim and handle missing. Restored in plaster. H. 8.3, D. rim 12.5, base 5.2 cm. Coated dull brown throughout. Exterior has thick white horizontal band at middle with red line superimposed and four groups of white semicircles three above and below evenly spaced around the body, red line below rim with groups of four vertical white strokes above, and white band near base with diagonal strokes below. Evans 1921, 187 fig. 136o. HM 4399.

Rounded Bridge-spouted Jar—Type 3

127. (K.329) PLATE 45 Fragment of side with half of handle. Exterior coated semilustrous black and has white circle filled with horizontal lines and three white crosses with tiny dots under handle, and a white and orange stroke on top of handle. KSM B I 7 #219. SMP 9651.

Bridge-spouted Jar

128. (K.328) PLATE 45 Fragment of shoulder. Exterior coated semilustrous black and has one horizontal and four vertical rows of barbotine, and a cross of red and orange outlined with tiny white dots. Pendlebury 1939, 108 fig. 17.18. KSM B I 7 #218. SMP 9652.

FABRIC: FINE SOFT BUFF

Technique: Wheelmade

Surface: Burnished

Pyxis

129. (K.320) PLATES 5, 45 Few side and base fragments missing. Restored in plaster. H. 9.6, D. rim 12.5, base 9.5 cm. Exterior lightly smoothed or burnished to give low lustre. KSM B I 7 #218, 219, 220. SMP 9653.

FABRIC: HARD GRITTY BUFF

Technique: Handmade

Surface: Plain

Lid

130. (K.337) PLATE 45 Intact. D. 15.0 cm. KSM B I 7 #217. SMP 9654.

Surface: Dark-on-buff

Lid

131. (K.338) PLATE 45 Two-thirds of rim missing. H. 2.5, D. 19.0 cm. Underside of rim coated black. Top has black loops at rim, bar below handle which is outlined and has two spots on top. KSM B I 7 #220. SMP 9655.

Three-handled Jar

132. (K.334) PLATE 45 Rim and part of one handle missing. H. 11.2, D. base 6.0 cm. Exterior lightly burnished and has three groups of three vertical black lines between handles. KSM B I 7 #218, 219. SMP 9656.

Surface: Slipped and burnished

Three-handled Jar

133. (K.333) PLATES 31, 46 Intact. H. 10.4, D. rim 5.6, base 4.3 cm. Exterior lightly slipped brown and well burnished. Evans 1921, 187 fig. 136n. HM 4410.

Surface: Monochrome coated; white and red decorated

Large Jug

134. (K.361) PLATE 6 Most of rim, lower body, base and handle missing. H. 26.0, D. rim 9.5 cm. Interior of spout and exterior coated thin semilustrous black now worn off in most places. Exterior has white horizontal bands at rim and base of neck. Large circular pattern with white dot filled with vertical red lines around which about fifteen tassels revolve is in middle of side. KSM B I 6 #183, 186. SMP 9657.

Technique: Wheelmade

Surface: Plain

Shallow Bowl

135. (K.311) Fragment of rim, side and base. H. 4.0, D. rim 17.0 cm. Traces of burning on interior. KSM B I 7 #215.

136. (K.312) Fragment of rim, side and base. H. 5.7, D. rim 22.0, base 10.5 cm. Traces of burning on interior of base. KSM B I 7 #219. SMP 9658.

FABRIC: GRITTY BROWN

Technique: Handmade

Surface: Plain

Three-handled Jar

137. (K.335) PLATE 46 One-third of rim and most of side and base missing. H. 8.5, D. rim 7.5 cm. Exterior blackened in places. KSM B I 7 #215, 219. SMP 9659.

FABRIC: FINE RED

Technique: Wheelmade

Surface: Plain

Tumbler—as Type 1

138. (K.249) Rim chipped. H. 5.0, D. rim 6.0, base 3.0 cm. Mottled in places. KSM B I 7 #215. SMP 9660.

139. (K.252) PLATE 6 Rim fragment with complete handle. H. 5.0, D. rim 6.0 cm. KSM B I 7 #219. SMP 9661.

Surface: Monochrome coated

Shallow Bowl

140. (K.307) PLATE 6 Fragment of rim, side and base. H. 3.5, D. rim 11.0, base 5.0 cm. Coated dull red-brown throughout. KSM B I 7 #215, 220.

Tumbler

141. (K.349) PLATES 6, 46 Fragment of base and side. H. 2.8, D. base 3.7 cm. Exterior slipped black and has deep horizontal grooves cut into side. KSM B I 6 #186. SMP 9662.

Angular Cup

142. (K.253) PLATES 6, 46 Three non-joining fragments of rim and side with handle. H. 4.7, D. rim 8.0 cm. Exterior slipped red-brown and has three horizontal grooves at middle. KSM B I 6 #179; KSM B I 7 #219. SMP 9663.

Surface: Monochrome coated; white decorated

Tumbler

143. (K.247) PLATES 6, 46 Much of rim missing. Restored. H. 7.0, D. rim 6.0, base 2.5 cm. Coated red-brown throughout. Exterior has six wide vertical lines framing two zones filled with three pairs of interconnecting C-pattern and two zones of pairs of thin lines. Andreou 1978, fig. 5.1. KSM B I 7 #220. SMP 9664.

144. (K.246) PLATE 46 Rim chipped, few small body fragments missing. H. 4.6, D. rim 4.5, base 1.9 cm. Coated red-brown throughout. Interior has thin horizontal band at rim. Exterior has three wide horizontal bands at rim, middle and base and in top zone has six rosettes of six or seven tiny dots. KSM B I 7 #218. SMP 9665.

145. (K.245) PLATES 32, 46 Rim chipped. H. 6.5, D. rim 5.8, base 2.3 cm. Coated red-brown throughout. Interior has thin horizontal band at rim. Exterior has three wide horizontal bands at rim, middle and base and top zone has four rosettes of eleven dots. Inscribed: 'WS T.P.4 K.04'. Zois 1965, pl. 28. HM 4407.

FABRIC: COARSE RED

Technique: Handmade

Surface: Plain

Large Spouted Jar

146. (K.363) PLATE 47 Few rim fragments missing. H. 24.0, D. rim 14.0, base 10.3 cm. Exterior blackened in places. Mackenzie 1904 DB (1), 27. KSM B I 6 #209. SMP 9666.

FABRIC: GRITTY ORANGE-BROWN

Technique: Wheelmade

Surface: White decorated.

Bowl

147. (K.313) PLATES 6, 47 One-third of rim missing. H. 4.5, D. rim 13.2, base 4.2 cm. Exterior blackened in places. Interior has floral pattern in the form of cross with branch motifs between arms and band at rim. KSM B I 7 #218. SMP 9667.

FABRIC: SOFT GRITTY BUFF

Technique: Wheelmade

Surface: Monochrome coated

Hand Lamp—Type 1

148. (K.340) PLATE 47 Tip of handle missing. H. 3.0, D. rim 8.0, base 6.0 cm. Coated thick red-brown throughout, now worn.

Interior of spout burnt. String marks on base. KSM B I 7 #215, 219. SML 954.

149. (K.356) PLATE 47 Rim fragment and most of handle missing. H. 3.5, D. rim 7.5, base 7.0 cm. Coated red-brown throughout, now flaking away. Spout burnt. KSM B I 6 #186. SML 955.

150. (K.357) PLATE 6 Handle missing. H. 3.4, D. rim 7.0, base 6.0 cm. Coated red-brown throughout, now flaking away. Spout burnt. KSM B I 6 #179. SML 956.

151. (K.358) Rim chipped, spout and most of handle missing. H. 3.2, D. rim 7.0, base 5.0 cm. Coated red-brown throughout. KSM B I 6 #183. SML 957.

Pedestalled Lamp—Type 1

152. (K.341) PLATES 6, 47 Few small fragments of rim and bowl and foot missing. H. rest. 21.5, D. rim 30.0 cm. Interior of pedestal plain but for horizontal band near foot. Top and exterior coated semilustrous red-brown. Spouts blackened. KSM B I 7 #222, 215. SML 94.

GROUP B: THE AREA OF THE POLYCHROME JUG

FABRIC: FINE BUFF

Technique: Handmade

Surface: Monochrome coated

Straight-sided Cup—Type 2

153. (K.1078) PLATE 48 Handle missing? Evans 1903, 119 fig. 74i. Not located.

Large Jug

154. (K.891) PLATES 48, 49 Most of spout missing. Restored in plaster. H. 33.5, D. rim 10.0, base 9.5 cm. Interior of rim and exterior coated semilustrous dark grey brown, badly worn away. Evans 1903, 119 fig. 74b. KSM A II 9 #92. SMP 9668.

Surface: Monochrome coated; white or polychrome decoration

Straight-sided Cup—Type 2

155. (K.892) PLATE 49 Rim, side and base fragment. H. 3.1, D. rim 5.0, base 4.0 cm. Coated semilustrous dark grey-brown throughout. Exterior has wide orange diagonal band with three thin and one wide white band on either side. KSM A II 9 #93.

156. (K.893) PLATE 49 Rim fragment. D. rim 8.0 cm. Coated semilustrous dark-brown. Exterior has rosette composed of red dot in centre with four white dots around it connected to other rosettes by triple white S-curves. KSM A II 9 #93.

Rounded Bridge-spouted Jar—Type 1

157. (K.889) PLATES 48, 49 Handles missing, restored in plaster. H. 7.6, D. rim 7.0, base 8.7 cm. Exterior coated dull dark-brown and has four large white interconnected spirals running continuously around the side. Evans 1903, 119 fig. 74c. HM 5759.

Technique: Wheelmade

Surface: Plain

Crude Goblet

158. (K.894) PLATE 48 Rim chipped. H. 4.0, D. rim 8.5, base 4.0 cm. ?Evans 1903, 119 fig. 74d. KSM A II 9 #93.
159. (K.895) PLATE 48 Evans 1903, 119 fig. 74d. Not located.
160. (K.896) PLATE 48 Evans 1903, 119 fig. 74d. Not located.

Surface: Monochrome coated

Crude Bowl—Type 2

161. (K.899) PLATE 48 Evans 1903, 119 fig. 74h. Not located.

Surface: Monochrome coated; white decorated

Rounded Goblet—Type 2

162. (K.897) PLATE 48 Evans 1903, 119 fig. 74e. Not located.
163. (K.898) PLATE 48 Evans 1903, 119 fig. 74e. Not located.

FABRIC: SOFT GRITTY BUFF

Technique: Wheelmade

Surface: Slipped and burnished

Small Angular Jug

164. (K.890) PLATES 48, 49 Spout and most of handle missing. H. 13.5, D. base 4.5 cm. Exterior coated red-brown and sides lightly burnished. String marks on base. Evans 1903, 119 fig. 74g. KSM A II 9 #93. SMP 9669.

FABRIC: TEMPERED BUFF

Technique: Handmade

Surface: Monochrome coated; polychrome decorated

Large Bridge-spouted Jar

165. (K.888) Tip of spout and few small body and base fragments missing. Restored in plaster. H. 23.3, D. rim 14.5, base 11.0 cm. Exterior coated semilustrous black and has radiating floral designs on front and back and tree-designs below handles. Mackenzie 1903 PB (3) #7; Evans 1921, pl. III; Betancourt 1985a, 99 fig. 72. HM 2680.

FABRIC: UNCERTAIN

Oval-mouthed Amphora

166. (K.900) PLATE 48 Exterior has two wide horizontal bands in dark paint on the buff ground of the side. Evans 1903, 118 fig. 73a. Not located.

Large spouted Jar

167. (K.901) PLATE 48 Evans 1903, 118 fig. 73b. Not located.

Large Jar

168. (K.902) PLATE 48 Exterior has trickle pattern. Evans 1903, 11 fig. 73c. Not located.

GROUP C: THE PORCELAIN DEPOSIT

FABRIC: FINE BUFF

Technique: Wheelmade

Surface: Buff reserved with added white

Tumbler—Type 4

169. (K.904) PLATE 50 Rim and side fragments with complete handle in Ash. H. *c.* 12.0, D. rim 11.5 cm. Interior spotted black. Exterior has three zones of horizontal grooves evenly spaced on side, left buff. Thick white horizontal bands outlined in black below rim and at middle; thick black bands outlined in white on upper side and near base. KSM A II 17 #106. AM AE 967.

Surface: Monochrome coated; polychrome decorated

Tall-rimmed Angular Cup—Type 4

170. (K.903) PLATES 7, 50 Fragment of rim and side. H. 6.5, D. rim 9.0 cm. Coated semilustrous black throughout. Interior has white rim band. Exterior has remains of unity pattern centred on large white cross with added groups of three orange lines and floral patterns in spaces. KSM A II 17 #106. Para: F. 426.

GROUP D: THE NORTH-WEST PIT

FABRIC: FINE BUFF

Technique: Handmade

Surface: Dark-on-buff, smeared

Small Amphora

171. (K.885) PLATE 54 Rim chipped; one handle missing, restored in plaster. H. 13.2, D. rim 5.0, base 4.7 cm. Exterior has rough dark-brown band on side between handles. Inscribed 'K.03 NWKA'. HM 4389.

Surface: Reserved buff

Tall-rimmed Angular Cup—Type 1a

172. (K.1020) PLATE 52 Fragment of base and lower side. Sides dipped in dark-brown paint leaving buff zone in centre. Mackenzie 1904 PB (2), 6; Mackenzie 1906, pl. VIII.19. HM 5196.

Surface: Monochrome coated; white decorated

Straight-sided Cup—Type 2

173. (K.910) PLATE 54 Three fragments of rim, side and base missing. Restored. H. 4.3, D. rim 7.5, base 5.4 cm. Coated semilustrous dark-brown throughout. Exterior has border at rim base and handle framing design of two pairs of sprays flanking dot rosette. KSM A II 10 #94. SMP 9670.

174. (K.912) PLATE 54 Handle and half vase missing. H. 4.2, D. rim 7.0, base 6.0 cm. Coated red-brown throughout. Exterior has border at rim, base and handle framing four evenly spaced flowers. KSM A II 11 #96.

Surface: Monochrome coated; polychrome decorated

Tumbler—Type 1

175. (K.1076) PLATE 7 Single fragment of rim and side. H. pres. 4.6, rest. 5.2, D. rim 6.0 cm. Exterior and interior of rim coated semilustrous black. Exterior has wide orange bands at rim lower middle and toward base, lower bands outlined in white. Horizontal zone of ?scorpion designs below rim band. HM 5757.

176. (K.907) PLATE 56 Most of rim and side missing, restored in plaster. H. 7.2, D. rim 7.1, base 3.5 cm. Coated dark-brown throughout. Exterior has two horizontal white and one orange line near the base and alternating pairs of orange and white diagonal lines between rim and orange line. HM 4378.

177. (K.1075) PLATE 7 Single fragment of rim and side. H. pres. 5.4, rest. 6.8, D. rim 8.4 cm. Interior of rim and exterior coated lustrous grey-brown; top of rim white; exterior has at least two wide red horizontal bands outlined in white at rim and lower side and white s-pattern with floral loop in horizontal zone. HM 5757.

Straight-sided Cup—Type 2

178. (K.911) PLATE 54 Much of rim and half of base missing. H. 5.0, D. rim 8.0, base 5.5 cm. Coated semilustrous dark-brown throughout. Exterior has orange border at rim, base and handle framing three evenly spaced orange flowers. KSM A II 11 #96.

179. (K.913) PLATE 54 Handle and large rim and side fragment missing. H. 3.5, D. rim 6.0, base 4.5 cm. Coated semilustrous dark-brown throughout. Exterior has two pairs of diagonal orange lines each bordered by pairs of white lines. KSM A II 11 #96.

180. (K.914) PLATE 54 Handle and two large rim and side fragments missing. H. 5.0, D. rim 8.0, base 5.5 cm. Coated semilustrous dark-brown throughout. Exterior has wide orange band at middle and rows of white semicircles at rim and base. KSM A II 10 #94.

181. (K.915) PLATE 54 Handle and most of rim and side missing. H. 5.0, D. rim 8.0, base 5.8 cm. Coated semilustrous dark-brown throughout. Exterior has three zones of diagonal orange dots framed by smaller white dots and four thick white lines. KSM A II 11 #96.

182. (K.916) PLATE 54 Rim, side and base fragment. H. 4.5, D. rim 8.0, base 5.2 cm. Coated semilustrous dark-brown throughout. Exterior has three zones with pairs of vertical orange lines connected by diagonal white slashes and framed by pairs of vertical white lines. KSM A II 10 #94.

183. (K.917) PLATE 54 Fragment of base and side. H. 4.7, D. base 5.5 cm. Coated semilustrous dark-brown throughout. Exterior has thick orange band at middle outlined in white and rows of white dots intersected with orange lines at rim and base. KSM A II 10 #94.

184. (K.918) PLATE 54 Fragment of rim, side, base. H. 4.4, D. rim 7.0, base 5.5 cm. Coated semilustrous dark-brown throughout. Exterior has three large orange circles with four white semicircles inside making reserved lozenge. KSM A II 10 #94.

185. (K.919) PLATE 54 Fragment of rim, side, base. H. 5.0, D. rim 8.0, base 5.0 cm. Coated semilustrous grey-brown throughout. Exterior has wide diagonal orange band outlined in white and part of ?chevron design with white dots at tips of points. KSM A II 10 #94.

186. (K.920) PLATE 54 Fragment of rim, side, base. H. 4.2, D. rim 8.0, base 5.5 cm. Coated semilustrous dark-brown throughout. Exterior has white spots placed at random. KSM A II 10 #94.

187. (K.921) PLATE 54 Fragment of rim, side, base. H. 4.5, D. rim 8.0, base 5.0 cm. Coated semilustrous dark-brown throughout. Exterior has trace of white semi-circle with white star pattern with orange dot at centre within; perhaps one of three alternating designs. Rough version of 611. KSM A II 10 #94.

188. (K.922) PLATE 54 Rim fragment. Coated semilustrous dark-brown throughout. Exterior has trace of white criss-cross pattern with orange dots at joints. KSM A II 10 #94.

Straight-sided Cup—Type 3

189. (K.924) PLATE 54 Many rim, side and base fragments missing. Restored in plaster. H. 8.4, D. rim 14.0, base 10.5 cm. Coated semilustrous dark-brown to black throughout. Exterior has six thick white vertical bands outlined in orange and framed by pairs of white lines. KSM A II 10 #94. HM 5757. SMP 9671.

190. (K.925) PLATE 7 Handle and most of rim and side missing. H. 8.5, D. rim 15.0, base 12.0 cm. Coated semilustrous grey-brown throughout. Exterior has eight vertical orange lines and alternating zones of white chevrons with dots on the points and pairs of white dot rosettes with orange dots at the centre. KSM A II 11 #96.

191. (K.923) PLATES 7, 55 Six non-joined fragments of rim and side with handle stub. H. 9.0, D. rim 15.5 cm. Coated semilustrous dark-brown throughout. Exterior has thick white rim band and pattern of alternating white floral spray and pairs of dot rosettes with tiny orange dot at centre surrounded by tiny white dots then large orange dots and tiny white dots and encircled in orange. Evans 1921, 184 fig. 133d. KSM A II 11 #96. AM AE 954.2; 1910.167b.

Tall-rimmed Angular Cup—Type 1a

192. (K.929) PLATE 55 Handle and much of rim and base missing. H. 5.0, D. rim 8.0, base 5.0 cm. Coated semilustrous dark-brown throughout. Exterior has thick orange bands at rim and base with white lines above and below. Side has alternating patterns of large white dot and dot rosette with large orange dot at centre surrounded by tiny white dots and large orange dots. KSM A II 10 #94.

Angular Bridge-spouted Jar—Type 2

193. (K.953) PLATE 51 Rim fragment. Interior has smear of black at rim with drops on inside. Exterior coated semilustrous dark-brown to black and has thick horizontal red band at rim and red diagonal bands with superimposed white dots on shoulder marking zones with white border and white open spiral with large blobs at top and bottom. Evans 1903, 17 fig. 6e. AM AE 1032.1.

194. (K.1014) PLATE 51 Rim fragment. Exterior has thick horizontal orange band below rim and white and orange spiral and ?floral decoration on shoulder. Evans 1903, 17 fig. 6k. Not located.

195. (K.1038) Fragment of shoulder. Trace of thick horizontal rim band on interior. Exterior coated thin semilustrous brown and has thick orange band near rim with white line below and four orange semicircles in circular pattern forming lozenge in reserve with dot rosette in white inside. Evans 1921, 262 fig. 194h. AM AE 952.

196. (K.954) PLATES 53, 55 Five non-joining fragments of rim and lower side. Interior has thin brown spots where paint has

dripped. Exterior coated dark-brown to black and has alternating white and orange floral design around side with orange band at rim, thin white band below design and wide orange and white bands toward base. Evans 1921, 184 fig. 133b; Evans 1935, 100 fig. 66e. AM AE 954.4,5; 1938.441. HM 5757.

197. (K.1026) PLATE 52 Fragment of lower side. Exterior dark-brown and has two thick orange bands at right angles outlined in white with added white crosses and a single dot rosette of alternating large and tiny dots. Mackenzie 1904 PB (2), 3; Mackenzie 1906, pl. VIII.9. HM 5196.

Teapot
198. (K.1077) PLATE 7 Two non-joining fragments of side with handle stubs and spout. H. 6.9, D. rim 7.5 cm. Interior has dark rim band with pairs of white diagonal strokes. Exterior coated lustrous crackling black with white rim band, white fish on shoulder with red eyes and gills and white screen pattern on spout. AM AE 1027. HM 5757.

Jug with cut-away spout—Type 1
199. (K.958) PLATE 51 Intact. H. *c.* 10.0 cm. Exterior coated dark-brown and has thick white horizontal band at neck and large white cross on side in a white circle with a red dot at the centre. Evans 1903, 17 fig. 6r. AM AE 917.

Small Rounded Jug
200. (K.960) PLATES 51, 55 Seven recomposed fragments of spout, neck and side. Restored in plaster. H. 15.0 cm. Exterior coated semilustrous dark-brown, now flaking. Decorated in two large zones with thin barbotine lines in circular pattern with added white dots alternating with pairs of tiny white dots making large rosette design. Both sides separated by thin barbotine line with added white dots and outlined in red and white lines which also runs around neck below two white lines below spout which has eye-boss painted red. Inscribed 'K.03 N.W.K.A.'. Evans 1903, 17 fig. 6l. HM 4374. Para: F. 2171.

Footed Rectangular Box
201. (K.949) PLATES 51, 55 Two non-joining fragments of base and side with three of the four pods. Restored. H. 5.4, W. 13.3 by 12.5 cm. Coated semilustrous dark-brown throughout. Two faces have pendant barbotine lines alternating with white dots and red lines; other two have a pair of white ovals outlined with barbotine and then white dots. Evans 1903, 17 fig. 6s. HM uncatalogued.

Technique: Wheelmade

Surface: Dark-on-buff smear
Conical Cup
202. (K.909) Intact. H. 5.5, D. rim 9.4, base 4.3 cm. Uneven semilustrous black uneven rim band and dripped on side. Inscribed 'K.03 NWKA'. HM 4394.

Surface: Buff reserved with added polychrome
Short-rimmed Angular Cup—Type 2
203. (K.1017) PLATE 52 Rim fragment. Interior has dark band with added white dots and superimposed red line at rim. Exterior has similar decoration at rim, above angle and in vertical line connecting other two. Mackenzie 1904 PB (2), 2; Mackenzie 1906, pl. VIII.5. HM 5196.

204. (K.1018) PLATE 52 Rim fragment. Interior coated black with white band at rim and spray of white paint. Exterior has dark horizontal lines at rim and angle and dark lines criss-crossing between, all with added white dots. Mackenzie 1904 PB (2), 3; Mackenzie 1906, pl. VIII.8. HM 5196.

205. (K.1019) PLATE 52 Two non-joining rim fragments. Interior has orange band at angle and dark vertical bands below rim with alternating added white and yellow dashes. Exterior has orange band at angle and thick dark band at rim with added white floral design. Mackenzie 1904 PB (2), 5; Mackenzie 1906, pl. VIII.15,16. HM 5196.

206. (K.1029) PLATE 52 Fragment of side. Interior coated black. Exterior has dark bands outlined in white at rim and angle and dark dots outlined and spotted white on side. Row of barbotine at angle. Mackenzie 1904 PB (2), 4; Mackenzie 1906, pl. VIII.13. HM 5196.

207. (K.1032) PLATE 52 Fragment of lower side. Interior coated black. Exterior has dark vertical bands—one bordered with an orange band, other with tiny white dots. Mackenzie 1904 PB (2), 5–6; Mackenzie 1906, pl. VIII.18. HM 5196.

Crinkly-rimmed Cup
208. (K.1023) PLATE 52 Rim fragment. Interior coated black. Exterior has alternating vertical patterns of a solid band with added S motif alternating yellow and orange and dark crosses with added white crosses. Mackenzie 1904 PB (2), 2; Mackenzie 1906, pl. VIII.4. HM 5196.

Rounded Cup—Type 3
209. (K.1027) PLATE 52 Large fragment of base and lower side. Interior and exterior decorated dark ?sponge pattern outlined with tiny white dots and superimposed with yellow 8s, and dark crosses with added red crosses. Mackenzie 1904 PB (2), 3–4; Mackenzie 1906, pl. VIII.11. HM 5196.

Rounded Cup—Type 4
210. (K.935) PLATES 52, 53, 56 Three non-joining fragments of base and lower side. Interior sprayed with dark-brown spots and red and white flecks. Exterior has two white rings on underside and dark leaves with added white dots and yellow chevrons connected by alternating yellow and red horizontal lines on side. Mackenzie 1904 PB (2), 1; Mackenzie 1906, pl. VIII.1; Forsdyke 1925, 89 fig. 112 A536. AM AE 1042.1, 2. BM A 536.

Cylindrical Spouted Jar
211. (K.947) PLATES 52, 56 Nine non-joined fragments of rim, side and base with traces of spout and handle. H. 8.7, D. rim 8.8, base 6.8 cm. Interior coated semilustrous red to dark-brown. Exterior has dark band at rim with added red and white dashes, two dark floral patterns with added white dots connected by a red line. Mackenzie 1904 PB (2), 3; Mackenzie 1906, pl. VIII.10; Forsdyke 1925, 89 fig. 112 A537. KSM A II 2 #58; KSM A II 10 #94; KSM A II 11 #95. AM AE1060.1,3; 1938.579,580. HM 5196; HM 5756. BM A 537 1. SMP 9672.

Angular Bridge spouted Jar—Type 2
212. (K.1034) PLATE 52 Fragment of lower body. Exterior has irregular angular dark pattern outlined in white and one dark dot. Mackenzie 1904 PB (2), 6; Mackenzie 1906, pl. VIII.21. HM 5196.

Rounded Bridge-spouted Jar

213. (K.1033) PLATE 52 Shoulder fragment with complete spout, rim chipped. Exterior has thick dark band at rim with added white dots and vertical bands on side and around spout outlined in white and orange. Mackenzie 1904 PB (2), 6; Mackenzie 1906, pl. VIII.20. HM 5196.

214. (K.956) PLATES 56, 60 Two non-joining fragments of rim with handle stubs. D. rim *c.* 7.5 cm. Interior has thin black rim band. Exterior has wide dark rim band with added white dots with tassels and red line bisecting, dark band at handle joint and dark circle with traces of white and yellow decoration on shoulder. KSM A II 2 #61. AM AE 1041.5.

215. (K.1030) PLATE 52 Fragment of lower body. Exterior has diagonal row of white dots bisected in red and outlined in white on a dark ground with reserved zone to one side. Mackenzie 1904 PB (2), 4–5; Mackenzie 1906, pl. VIII.14. HM 5196.

216. (K.1031) PLATE 52 Fragment of lower body. Interior has drip pattern in dark paint. Exterior has rows of dark paint barbotine on a buff ground alternating with rows of white dots bisected red on a dark ground. Mackenzie 1904 PB (2), 5; Mackenzie 1906, pl. VIII.17. HM 5196.

217. (K.1022) PLATE 52 Shoulder fragment. Exterior has dark circles on a buff ground—one filled with cross hatching and outlined in red, the other divided by an eight-sided white star into alternating zones of brown and red. Mackenzie 1904 PB (2), 1–2; Mackenzie 1906, pl. VIII.3. HM 5196.

218. (K.1024) PLATE 52 Fragment of shoulder. Exterior has dark band with added white dots below rim and a horizontal row of dark dots with large white dots added. Mackenzie 1904 PB (2), 2–3; Mackenzie 1906, pl. VIII.6. HM 5196.

219. (K.1025) PLATE 52 Fragment of lower side. Exterior has pendant or random curved dark lines with added white dots. Mackenzie 1904 PB (2), 3; Mackenzie 1906, pl. VIII.7. HM 5196.

220. (K.1028) PLATE 52 Fragment of lower side. Exterior has alternating dark and buff zones, the former with white floral design, the latter with dark vertical bands with alternating white and yellow dashes—both like **205**. Mackenzie 1904 PB (2), 4; Mackenzie 1906, pl. VIII.12. HM 5196.

Surface: Monochrome coated; white decorated

Rounded Cup—Type 3

221. (K.941) PLATES 51, 56 Handle and most of rim and side missing. Restored. H. 6.4, D. rim 9.5, base 4.5 cm. Coated thin semilustrous brown throughout. Exterior has horizontal bands below rim and on lower side, and a row of odd floral motifs. Evans 1903, 17 fig. 6b. HM 4504.

Flask

222. (K.961) PLATE 56 Recomposed part of one side with base, handle stub and hole for spout. H. 13.0, D. max. 11.0 cm. Exterior coated semilustrous dark-brown to black and has three large concentric circles on either side. KSM A II #96. SMP 9673.

Surface: Monochrome coated; white decorated—printed decoration

Straight-sided Cup—Type 10

223. (K.1035) Four fragments of base and side. D. base 8.0 cm. Coated dark-brown throughout. Exterior has creamy-white band at middle with single row of printed dark crescents added and two rows of printed white crescents above and below. Similar to **293**. KSM A II 11 #95. AM AE 1061.6, 12.

Surface: Monochrome coated; polychrome decorated

Shallow Bowl with internal handle

224. (K.945) PLATE 56 Much of rim missing. H. 2.0, D. rim 14.0, base 7.0 cm. Coated semilustrous black throughout. Underside has white bands below rim and near base and white cross on bottom. Top has wide red band below rim, white filled semicircles on rim, open running spirals on side and pair of concentric white circles in centre. KSM A II 3 #80; KSM A II 11 #95; KSM A II #114. HM 5757. SMP 9674.

Tumbler—Type 3

225. (K.906) PLATE 56 Intact. H. 6.5, D. rim 6.0, base 2.8 cm. Coated dark-brown throughout. Interior has row of red vertical strokes connected by cream or yellow diagonal strokes and horizontal row of tiny white dots below. Exterior has red horizontal lines below rim and at middle dividing zones with rows of reverse 3s in white—one at rim and pairs on upper and lower side. Inscribed 'K.03 NWKA'. HM 4377.

Rounded Goblet—Type 3

226. (K.1016) PLATE 51 Fragment of foot and lower side. Exterior appears to have barbotine on lower side, horizontal bands near base and radiating lines on foot. Evans 1903, 17 fig. 6q. Not located.

Conical Goblet—Type 3

227. (K.908) PLATE 51 Rim, base, foot and much of side missing. Restored. Coated dark-brown throughout. Exterior has large white flowers with red centres and zones of diagonal barbotine lines painted red. Evans 1903, 17 fig. 6f; Evans 1921, 268 fig. 199b. AM AE 955.

Straight-sided Cup—Type 4

228. (K.926) PLATE 57 Most of rim missing. Restored in plaster. H. 6.5, D. rim 10.0, base 5.0 cm. Coated red-brown throughout. Exterior has three pairs of vertical white lines each outlined in orange. KSM A II 10 #94. SMP 9675.

Straight-sided Cup—Type 6

229. (K.928) PLATES 7, 57 Large fragment of rim. H. 9.0, D. rim 11.0 cm. Coated metallic grey-brown throughout. Exterior has zone of white crescents at middle outlined in orange and white, and white filled semicircles at rim and base. KSM A II 2 #53.

230. (K.927) PLATES 7, 27 Two non-joining fragments of rim, side and base. H. 10.2, D. rim 12.0, base 7.0 cm. Interior has dark-brown smear at rim and drips throughout. Exterior coated dark-brown and has ?three white plant motifs with added red dots on stem. KSM A II 11 #95.

Tall-rimmed Angular Cup—Type 3

231. (K.933) PLATES 7, 57, 60 Half recomposed and restored in HM, handle and base fragments in AM, rim in KSM. H. 5.6, D. rim 8.4, base 3.0 cm. Coated in semilustrous dark-brown to black throughout. Exterior has alternating zones of vertical white ladder designs and red and white dot designs on upper side and horizontal white lines at base and on lower side. KSM A II 11 #96. AM 1910.167c. HM 4580. SMP 9676.

232. (K.1039) Fragment of base and lower side. H. 5.0, D. base 4.0 cm. Coated red-brown throughout. Exterior has white horizontal lines at base and below angle, white chevrons at

angle below orange line and red line near rim with red diagonal strokes below with white dots at tips. AM AE 951.

Short-rimmed Angular Cup

233. (K.930) PLATE 60 Rim and side fragment in AM, rims in BM and KSM. H. 4.0, D. rim 11.0 cm. Coated semilustrous dark-brown to black throughout. Interior has groups of white diagonal lines at rim making triangles, see **234**. Exterior has impressed trefoil pattern filled with white paint with white arcades below and at rim above rows of tiny white dots, traces of arcades on side below angle are similar. Forsdyke 1925, 89 fig. 112 A528. KSM A II #144a. AM AE 936. BM A 528.2.

234. (K.931,1043) PLATES 8, 51 Recomposed base and lower side fragments and rim fragment. Joined on paper. H. 9.8, D. rim 12.4, base 3.7 cm. Coated black throughout. Rim: Interior has vertical white lines in triangular design at rim with white flayed duck motif in spaces. Exterior has row of tiny white dots at rim and white curvilinear pattern with white dot and pointilles filling and added red dots. Base: Exterior has white lines with tassles on bottom, vertical white wavy lines on foot, white loop design around red dot below row of tiny white dots on lower side and red band with added white chevrons below angle. Inscribed 'NWKA K.04 4'. Evans 1903, 17 fig. 6h; Evans 1921, 246 fig. 186g; Evans 1928, 215 pl. IXb. HM 4387.

235. (K.932) PLATE 8 Four non-joining fragments of rim, side and base. H. 6.3, D. rim 10.5, base 4.0 cm. Coated semilustrous black throughout. Interior has yellow/orange cross designs with red centres and tiny white crosses between the points interconnected by white S-curves. Exterior has tiny pendant white semicircles at rim, continuous white feather-like motifs adorned with white dots and red and orange dashes within two thick red bands and two white bands on lower side. KSM AII 10 #94.

Rounded Cup—Type 3

236. (K.942) PLATE 8 Fragment of half of rim and side. Recomposed. H. 5.0, D. rim 11.0 cm. Coated semilustrous dark-brown throughout. Interior has white filled semi-circles at rim. Exterior has white filled semi-circles at rim and white open spirals adorned with dots and diagonal strokes between two thick red bands, one with added white dots, on side. KSM A II #144a. Para: F. 430.

Rounded Cup—Type 5

237. (K.936) PLATE 57 Three fragments of side. D. max. 17.0 cm. Coated semilustrous dark-brown throughout. Exterior has zone of stamped concentric circles in two rows painted white between two horizontal red grooves below a row of white interconnected spirals on upper side and white groove below rim. AM 1910.169h. KSM A II #95.

238. (K.1044) Two rim fragments. D. rim c. 11.0 cm. Interior has thick black band with added white band at rim and black flecks on side. Exterior coated semilustrous black and has white filled pendant semicircles with red vertical lines added at rim. KSM A II 11 #95. AM AE 950.

Rounded Cup—Type 6

239. (K.937) PLATE 58 Five fragments in AM, four in KSM. Complete profile. D. rim 11.0, base 5.0 cm. Coated semilustrous burgundy throughout. Interior has white vertical slashes at rim and wavy line near base. Exterior has white filled triangles at rim, two white lines below rim zone of white scale pattern

with alternating white dot rosettes and red floral design with two wavy lines below and white S pattern above red band at base. Evans 1921, 595 fig. 437a,b. KSM A II 11#95. AM AE 832.1,5,6,7.

Rounded Cup—Type 5

240. (K.938) PLATE 58 Three fragments of base and lower side. D. base 5.0 cm. Coated semilustrous dark red-brown throughout. Exterior has two thick and thin white bands at base and lower side, red band above and interconnecting spirals with thick white wavy border beneath on side. KSM A II 11 #95. AM AE 832, 832.4.

241. (K.939) PLATE 58 Three fragments of side. Coated semilustrous dark-brown throughout. Horizontal zone of closed white spirals with thick white wavy border below and pairs of white lines below rim and above base. KSM A II 11 #95. AM AE 832.3.

Rounded Cup—Type 6

242. (K.940) PLATE 58 Five fragments of rim and side. Coated dark-brown throughout. Interior has white pendant semicircles at rim and dense white spotting on side. Exterior has white wavy line pattern with alternating tiny white dots in diagonal rows and white dot rosettes with red centres. KSM A II 11 #95; KSM A II #128.

Straight-sided Jar

243. (K.948) PLATES 8, 53, 59 Two non-joining fragments of rim and base. H. 10.0, D. rim 12.0, base 6.4 cm. Coated semilustrous dark-brown to black throughout. Exterior has white floral pattern with red strokes in leaves and red dots on stem. Evans 1935, 101 fig. 66d. AM AE 954.7, 1938.442.

244. (K.1037) Fragment of lower side. Interior has drips of dark paint. Exterior coated semilustrous dark-brown to black and has floral design in white with red filling of the leaves and red dots on the stem. Evans 1921, 184 fig. 133f. AM AE 954.3.

Closed Jar

245. (K.950) PLATE 51 Most of rim missing. Appears to have alternating zones of white and orange diagonal strokes on ridges in side. Evans 1903, 17 fig. 6d. Not located.

Angular ?spouted Jar

246. (K.952) PLATES 51, 59, 60 Fragments of base and lower side, top half missing. H. 9.5, D. max.14.5, base 4.5 cm. Interior has thick uneven black circular streaks from painting while pot turned. Exterior coated semilustrous black and has red and orange stone veining pattern outlined in white. Evans 1903, 17 fig. 6n. KSM A II 11 #95. AM AE 956. HM 5757. Para: F. 396.

Rounded Bridge-spouted Jar—Type 3

247. (K.955) PLATE 59 Few fragments of side and base missing. Recomposed. H. 12.0, D. rim 8.8, base 6.7 cm. Interior has dark rim band. Exterior coated black and has white pendant loops within two vertical lines with traces of added red either side of spout and white curvilinear lines on side below handle; decoration very worn. Diagonal grooves on lower side may belong to part of the forming process of the vase. Mackenzie 1903 PB (3) # 8. HM no number.

Rounded Bridge-spouted Jar

248. (K.1040) Fragment of shoulder. Exterior coated semilustrous brown and has orange stone veining like decoration outlined in white. Evans 1921, 178 fig. 127c. AM AE 941.

249. (K.1041) PLATE 53 Fragment of lower side. Exterior coated semilustrous dark-brown and has red dot rosette with yellow centre and yellow and white three-dot rosettes surrounding it in a white circle all in a circular depression in the side of the jar. Evans 1935, 101 fig. 66c. AM 1938.443.

Jug with Cut-away Spout—Type 3

250. (K.959) PLATES 8, 59 Several small fragments of spout, neck and body missing. H. 13.7, D. base 4.5 cm. Interior of spout coated dark-brown. Exterior coated dark-brown and thick orange bands at base of neck and middle of side, four white lines on shoulder with vertical stripes in alternating groups and large white crescents on lower side. KSM A II #127. SMP 9677.

?Jug

251. (K.1042) PLATE 53 Fragment of base and side. Exterior coated dark and has alternating white and ?orange floral patterns. Not located.

FABRIC: SOFT BUFF

Technique: Wheelmade

Surface: Monochrome coated; polychrome decorated

? Loop-handled Bowl

252. (K.943) PLATE 59 Two non-joining rim fragments. D. rim *c.* 9.0 cm. Coated dark-brown throughout. Exterior has two or three groups of three pendant white lines. Interior has red and white pendant lines, white interlocking S-pattern and a white line of alternating triangles. KSM A II 10 #94.

253. (K.944) PLATE 59 Fragment of base and side. Coated dark-brown throughout. Exterior has white band at base and three pendant white lines on side. Interior has remains of cross-hatched lozenge in white with red border. KSM A II 10 #94.

Angular Cup

254. (K.934) PLATE 60 Fragments of side with handle stub. Partially restored. Coated semilustrous dark-brown to black throughout. Exterior has horizontal row of white chevrons at angle and four dot white rosettes connected by double S-curves on side framed by rows of tiny white dots bordered by red bands and two white bands on lower body. Forsdyke 1925, 85 pl. VIII. KSM A II #144a. BM A 510.

FABRIC: TEMPERED BUFF

Technique: Handmade

Surface: Dark-on-buff

Closed Jar or Jug

255. (K.963) PLATE 60 Three non-joining fragments of side. Exterior has thick dark band on lower side and irregular dark dots on upper side. KSM A II 10 #94. Para: F. 717, 5293.

Surface: Buff reserved with added polychrome

? Offering Table

256. (K.1021) PLATE 52 Fragment of bowl. Underside has dark band at rim and dark floral motif outlined in red and white. Mackenzie 1904 PB (2), 1; Mackenzie 1906, pl. VIII.2. HM 5196.

Surface: Monochrome coated; polychrome decorated

Offering Table

257. (K.946) PLATE 60 Rim fragments, partially restored in plaster. H. 2.4, D. rim 26.0 cm. Coated in thick semilustrous black throughout. Top of rim has interlocking S-spirals, side of rim has thin red line and diagonal white slashes, underside has thick horizontal white bands. Interior has thick red band at rim and floral pattern in white with red dot in centre. Evans 1921, 267 fig. 198d; Åberg 1933, 151 fig. 269. KSM A II 11 #95. AM 1938.448.

258. (K.1015) PLATE 51 Recomposed part of pedestal. Exterior appears dark coated and has light band near base and light curvilinear designs on side. Evans 1903, 17 fig. 6p. Not located.

Cylindrical Spouted Jar

259. (K.1012) PLATES 51, 60 Three fragments of base and side. H. 10.5, D. base 10.0 cm. Coated semilustrous black throughout. Exterior covered with barbotine spikes except for oval areas with red outlines and orange filling. Dot rosettes in white at random on barbotine surface. Clay in lower body mixed with angular temper to height of *c.* 6.0 cm above base, then clay becomes finer. Incorrectly assigned to pits SE of palace—Evans 1935, 106. Evans 1903, 17 fig. 6i; Evans 1935, 107 fig. 73c. AM AE 1062.1–4. Para: F. 263, 2173, 3001.

260. (K.1013) PLATE 51 Fragment of rim and handle. Exterior has horizontal lines of barbotine at rim and middle bisecting verticals, zones thus formed filled with large light cross with ?red dot at centre. Evans 1903, 17 fig. 6g. Not located.

Large flat Bowl or Lid

261. (K.1036) PLATE 51 Large fragment of bowl with possible handle. Interior has large light Maltese crosses in red circles. Evans 1903, 17 fig. 6m. AM AE 1029.

GROUP E: THE WEST POLYCHROME DEPOSITS

FABRIC: FINE BUFF

Technique: Wheelmade

Surface: Dark on Buff —sprayed

Deep Rounded Bowl

262. (K.566) PLATE 68 Three non-joining fragments of rim and base. H. 5.0, D. rim 14.0, base 5.6 cm. Dense splattering of brown throughout. KSM B I 19 #322, 323.

Surface: Dark on buff—sprayed; white decorated

Straight-sided Cup—Type 6

263. (K.471) PLATE 68 One rim and a few body fragments missing. Restored. H. 8.0, D. rim 10.5, base 5.8 cm. Coated with spray of brown on buff throughout. Exterior has three white wavy lines running continuously around the side. Inscribed 'K.30 N.8'. HM 8845.

264. (K.472) Two non-joining rim fragments. D. rim 9.5 cm. Coated with spray of brown on buff throughout. Exterior is decorated in the same manner as 263. KSM B III 8 #418.

265. (K.473) PLATE 68 Two large rim and many side fragments missing. Restored. H. 8.5, D. rim 10.5, base 6.2 cm. Coated with spray of brown on buff throughout. Exterior has thick brown wavy line outlined in white running continuously around the side. HM 8846.

266. (K.474) Three non-joining fragments of rim, side and base. H. 8.0, D. rim 12.0, base 7.0 cm. Coated with spray of brown on buff throughout. Exterior is decorated in the same manner as 265. KSM B III 8 #416, 417.

Surface: Dark on buff; decorated

Large Bowl

267. (K.568) PLATE 68 Two non-joining parts of rim and side with complete lug. H. 8.0, D. rim 24.0 cm. Exterior has two thick dark-brown horizontal bands on the side. Interior has featherwave pattern throughout. KSM B I 14 #259; KSM B I 19 #327.

268. (K.569) PLATE 68 Two non-joining fragments of rim and base. H. 5.2, D. rim 18.0, base 8.0 cm. Thin smear of brown paint throughout. Thick dark-brown horizontal bands: one at base and two on sides at exterior, with two on side and one at rim on interior. KSM B I 20 #330; KSM B III 8 #418.

Surface: Monochrome coated; white decorated

Straight-sided Cup—Type 5

269. (K.469) PLATE 69 Large part of rim and base. H. 6.5, D. rim 10.0, base 5.5 cm. Coated metallic grey-brown throughout. Exterior has white horizontal lines at rim and base and three wavy lines running continuously around side. KSM B I 19 #323.

270. (K.470) PLATES 66, 69 Two joining fragments of rim, side and base. H. 7.0, D. rim 11.0, base 7.0 cm. Coated semilustrous grey-brown throughout, worn. Exterior has three wavy lines running continuously around side. KSM B III 8 #417, 418.

Straight-sided Cup—Type 6

271. (K.475) Three non-joining fragments of rim, side and base. H. 7.8, D. rim 12.0, base 6.0 cm. Coated semilustrous red-brown throughout. Exterior has three white wavy lines running continuously around side. KSM B I 20 #330; KSM B III 8 #417.

272. (K.562) PLATES 9, 69 Three fragments of rim, side and base. Restored in plaster. H. 8.2, D. rim 11.0, base 6.5 cm. Coated brown throughout, mottled in places. Exterior has horizontal bands at rim and base and four evenly spaced white circles in double wavy lines above and below. Inscribed 'K.30 N.8'. HM 8847.

Straight-sided Cup—Type 10

273. (K.483) PLATE 9 Two large non-joined fragments of rim, side

and base. H. 8.5, D. rim 10.0, base 5.0 cm. Coated brown throughout, worn. Exterior has pairs of vertical lines with at least one foliate band. KSM B I 19 #323, 326. Para: F. 1453a.

Straight-sided Cup—Type 7

274. (K.446) PLATE 69 Large fragment of rim and side, recomposed. H. 6.0, D. rim 9.0, base 6.0 cm. Coated grey-brown throughout. Exterior has large rosette in ?spiral design. KSM B I 19 #325, 327.

Straight-sided Cup—Type 8

275. (K.447) PLATE 69 Fragment of rim, side and base. H. 7.5, D. rim 10.5, base 7.5 cm. Coated grey-brown throughout. Exterior decorated like 274. KSM B I 20 #344, 348.

Straight-sided Cup—?Type

276. (K.448) PLATES 9, 69 Rim and side fragment. H. 6.0, D. rim 8.0 cm. Coated dark-brown throughout. Exterior has thick band at rim and spiralling rosette with open centre on side. KSM B I 14 #259.

Straight-sided Cup—Type 10

277. (K.449) PLATE 69 Rim, side and base fragment. H. 8.3, D. rim 11.5, base 8.0 cm. Coated semilustrous dark grey-brown throughout. Exterior has large rosette in ?spiral. KSM B I 14 #257.

Straight-sided Cup—Type 6

278. (K.464) PLATES 9, 69 Two non-joining fragments of rim and base. D. rim 8.5, base 5.8 cm. Coated semilustrous dark-brown throughout. Interior has uneven rim band. Exterior has filled semicircles at rim and base and ?jug motif on side. KSM B I 19 #329; KSM B I 20 #333.

Straight-sided Cup—Type 8

279. (K.453) PLATE 73 Rim, side and base fragment. H. 7.7, D. rim 10.0, base 7.0 cm. Coated semilustrous dark-brown throughout. Exterior has two horizontal lines at middle, open running spirals below rim and repeating S-pattern above base. KSM B I 20 #349

Straight-sided Cup—Type 9

280. (K.477) PLATE 9 Two fragments of base and lower side. H. 6.3, D. base 5.0 cm. Coated brown throughout. Exterior has three horizontal lines at middle and at least one 'sunrise' motif below rim. KSM B I 20 #340, 345.

Straight-sided Cup—Type 5

281. (K.481) PLATE 70 Rim fragment. H. 5.6, D. rim 9.0 cm. Coated semilustrous black throughout. Exterior has the same decoration as 280. KSM B I 20 #342.

282. (K.479) Fragment of base and side. H. 6.0, D. base 7.6 cm. Coated dark-brown to black throughout. Exterior has three horizontal lines at middle, at least one 'sunrise' motif near rim and repeating S-pattern above base. KSM B I 20 #347.

Straight-sided Cup—?Type

283. (K.482) PLATE 70 Fragment of rim and side. H. 5.0, D. rim 7.5 cm. Thin coat of grey-brown throughout, flaking. Exterior has two horizontal lines at middle, a row of filled semicir-

cles below and a 'sunrise' motif above near rim. KSM B I 14 #259, 260.

Straight-sided Cup—Type 9

284. (K.480) PLATES 9, 70 Fragment of base and lower side. H. 5.7, D. base 5.0 cm. Coated dark-brown to black throughout. Exterior has two horizontal lines at the middle with a 'sunrise' motif above and a row of white dots below and filled semicircles near base. KSM B I 21 #354, 355, 356.

Rounded Cup—Type 5

285. (K.407) PLATE 9 Two non-joining fragments of rim and lower side with handle stub. H. *c.* 6.5, D. rim 11.0 cm. Coated grey-brown throughout. Exterior has filled semicircles at rim, row of dots on upper side and arcades on lower side to base. KSM B I 19 #322, 326, 329.

286. (K.408) PLATE 9 Three non-joining fragments of rim, side and base. H. 7.0, D. rim 11.5, base 4.5 cm. Coated dark-brown throughout. Interior has thin horizontal rim band. Exterior has *c.* ten vertical stripes from thin rim band to underside. KSM B III 8 #418.

Pyxis—Type 5

287. (K.619) Fragment of rim, side and half of base with complete horizontal lug. H. 3.5, D. rim 8.0, base 5.5 cm. Coated dull dark-brown throughout. Exterior has horizontal bands at base and below rim. KSM B I 21 #355.

288. (K.620) Fragment of rim, side and base. H. 3.3, D. rim 9.0, base 6.0 cm. Coated dull dark-brown throughout. Exterior has three horizontal bands on side and radiating stokes on rim. KSM B I 21 #353.

Pyxis—Type 6

289. (K.621) Fragment of rim, side and base. H. 6.2, D. rim 10.0, base 6.5 cm. Interior of rim and exterior coated dull dark-brown. Exterior has three horizontal bands on side. KSM B I 20 #345, 347.

Rounded Bridge-spouted Jar—Type 4

290. (K.627) PLATES 9, 70 Four non-joining fragments of rim, side and complete base. H. 14.5, D. rim 6.0, base 5.6 cm. Interior has thick uneven smear at rim and drips of red-brown paint. Exterior coated red-brown and has pattern of dots in interconnected circles with sprays of petals. KSM B I 20 #341, 345.

291. (K.628) PLATES 9, 70 Two non-joining fragments of lower side near base. Interior has large drip of paint. Exterior coated brown and has traces of decoration similar to 290. KSM B I 20 #338, 345.

Kalathos

292. (K.696) PLATE 10 Two non-joining fragments of rim, side and base with part of one horizontal handle. H. 6.0, D. rim 24.5, base 13.5 cm. Coated metallic grey-brown throughout. Exterior has wide band at base and three bands on top of rim. KSM B I 20 #338, 348

Surface: Monochrome coated; print decorated

Straight-sided Cup—Type 10

293. (K.563) PLATES 10, 70 Half of rim and side and handle missing. H. 7.7, D. rim 10.5, base 6.4 cm. Coated semilustrous

dark-brown to black throughout. Exterior has wide cream/buff band at middle with dark-brown printed crescents superimposed and two rows of printed white crescents above and below. Inscribed 'K.30 N.18'. HM 8848.

294. (K.486) PLATE 71 Recomposed rim, side and base base fragments, partially restored in plaster. H. 7.6, D. rim 9.0, base 6.5 cm. Coated dark-brown throughout. Exterior decorated like 293. KSM B I 19 #326, 328. SMP 9678.

295. (K.487) PLATES 67, 71 Rim, side and base fragment. H. 8.3, D. rim 13.0, base 8.0 cm. Coated semilustrous black throughout. Exterior decorated like 293. KSM B I 20 #330, 338, 346, 347, 350. SMP 9679.

296. (K.488) Rim, side and base fragment. H. 7.5, D. rim 11.0, base 7.5 cm. Coated dark-brown throughout. Exterior decorated like 293. KSM B I 20 #330; KSM B III 8 #418.

297. (K.490) PLATE 70 Two rim fragments, much of base and handle stub. Restored in plaster. H. 7.5, D. rim 10.5, base 6.0 cm. Coated dark-brown throughout. Exterior has thick cream/buff band at middle with printed brown crescents in two rows added and two rows of white printed crescents at base and probably at rim; unlike restoration. True H. should be 6.0 and D. rim *c.* 7.5 cm. AM AE 1061.5. HM 8849.

298. (K.489) PLATE 71 Three non-joining fragments of rim, side and base. D. rim 11.0, base 9.0 cm. Coated dark-brown throughout. Exterior has thick buff/cream band at middle with single row of printed brown circles added and two rows of printed white crescents above and below and printed dark circles on the buff/cream coated underside. KSM B I 14 #258, 260.

Surface: Monochrome coated; white spotted

Deep Rounded Bowl

299. (K.567) PLATE 68 Two non-joining rim fragments with complete loop handle. H. 5.0, D. rim 10.0 cm. Coated semilustrous dark-brown throughout. Exterior covered with white spots. KSM B I 19 #329.

Straight-sided Cup—Type 8

300. (K.491) PLATE 71 Half of rim and side missing. Restored in plaster. H. 7.7, D. rim 9.7, base 5.0 cm. Coated semilustrous dark-brown throughout. ?Traces of white spotting on interior. KSM B I 19 #323, 325. SMP 9680.

301. (K.492) PLATE 71 One-third of rim, several side and base fragments and handle missing. Restored in plaster. H. 8.2, D. rim 10.0, base 5.8 cm. Coated dark-brown throughout. Thin white line on rim. Exterior white spotted at random. KSM B I 21 #345, 355, 356. SMP 9681.

302. (K.493) PLATE 71 Few rim and body fragments and upper part of handle missing. Restored in plaster. H. 9.0, D. rim 10.5, base 5.8 cm. Coated metallic grey-black throughout, but very worn. KSM B I 20 #335, 336.

Straight-sided Cup—Type 7

303. (K.494) PLATE 71 Few small rim and side fragments and upper part of handle missing. Restored. H. 7.0, D. rim 9.5, base 5.4 cm. Coated dark-brown throughout. Exterior has careful white spotting on side and underside. KSM B I 19 #328. SMP 9683.

304. (K.495) PLATE 71 Half of rim and side and handle missing. Partially restored in plaster. H. 6.8, D. rim 9.5, base 5.5 cm. Coated brown to red-brown throughout. Interior has rough white spotting. KSM B I 19 #325.

305. (K. 496) PLATE 71 One-third of rim and side and handle missing. Coated grey-brown and white spotted throughout. KSM B I 19 #322, 323.

Surface: Monochrome coated; polychrome decorated

Small Bowl with handles

306. (K.564) PLATES 10, 68 Two non-joining fragments of rim, side and base with one complete double loop handle. H. 5.5, D. rim 11.5, base 8.5 cm. Coated dull dark-brown throughout. Exterior has horizontal orange bands at rim and base, white open running spirals on side, and white slashes on top of handle. KSM B I 14 #257.

307. (K.565) PLATE 68 Rim fragment with complete loop handle at rim. H. 3.5 cm. Coated semilustrous dark-brown throughout. Thick orange band with added white wavy line at rim, white foliate band on side and white slashes on rim and top of handle. KSM B I 14 #256.

Tumbler—Type 4

308. (K.432) PLATE 72 Rim and most of upper side missing. Restored in plaster. H. 14.5, rest. 16.2, D. base 4.9 cm. Coated semilustrous dark-brown to black throughout. Exterior has vertical zones of orange branch designs with white dots outlined in white dots alternating with white filled wavy lines from rim to base, and a white band of cross-hatching between two zweipass designs on underside. Evans 1935, 130 pl. XXXA; Zervos 1956, fig. 364 centre. HM 8874.

Miniature Straight-sided Cup

309. (K.468) PLATE 10 Most of handle and part of rim missing. H. 3.5, D. rim 6.0, base 4.4 cm. Coated dark-brown throughout. Interior has thin white rim band. Exterior has orange and white horizontal bands at the middle, white open running spirals at the rim and scale pattern at the base, and a crude rosette on the bottom. KSM B I 19 #329.

Straight-sided Cup—Type 5

310. (K.442) PLATES 10, 72 Two-thirds of rim and side and most of handle missing. Partially restored in plaster. H. 5.4, D. rim 8.5, base 7.0 cm. Coated semilustrous dark-brown throughout. Exterior has a thick orange band outlined in white at the middle, white repeating S-pattern at rim and open running white spirals and horizontal white band at base. Underside has white cross and lozenge in centre. KSM B I 20 #330, 344, 345, 347. SMP 9684.

311. (K.439) PLATES 10, 62, 72 Fragment of base missing. One fragment not joined. Restored in plaster. H. 6.0, D. rim 10.5, base 7.5 cm. Coated grey-brown throughout. Exterior has white closed running spirals in middle with orange lines above and below and white repeating S-patterns at rim and base. KSM B I 19 #322, 323, 326, 328. AM AE 823. SMP 9685.

312. (K.440) PLATE 10 Five non-joining fragments of rim, side and base. H. 5.8, D. rim 12.0, base 7.5 cm. Coated dark-grey-brown throughout. Exterior has white foliate band at middle with orange and white horizontal lines above and below and repeating S-pattern at rim and base. KSM B I 19 #322, 326, 329. Para: F. 5184.

313. (K.441) Two non-joining rim and side fragments with trace of handle stub. H. 6.8, D. rim 9.0 cm. Coated dark-brown throughout. Exterior decorated as 312. KSM B I 19 #327, 328.

Straight-sided Cup—Type 6

314. (K.433) PLATE 10 Five fragments of rim, side and base. H. 7.5, D. rim 12.0, base 6.0 cm. Coated dark grey-brown throughout. Exterior has white foliate band at middle, orange and white horizontal lines above and below and rows of white dots with added red dots at rim and base. KSM B I 14 #259; KSM B I 19 #324, 326, 329. Para: F. 4657b.

Straight-sided Cup—Type 10

315. (K.434) PLATE 72 Handle and most of rim and side missing. H. 7.8, D. rim 10.0, base 5.5 cm. Coated dull red-brown throughout. Exterior has white foliate band at middle with horizontal white lines above and below and rows of white dots with added red dots at rim and base. KSM B I 14 #260, 262; KSM B I 19 #326, 329.

316. (K.435) Three non-joining fragments of rim and base. H. 9.5, D. rim 10.0, base 6.5 cm. Coated dark-brown throughout. Interior has thin white rim band. Exterior has white foliate band at middle, orange horizontal line above and white above and below, and rows of white dots with added red dots above and below. KSM B I 20 #343, 345.

317. (K.436) Two non-joining fragments of rim and base. H. 9.0, D. rim 9.0, base 5.6 cm. Coated semilustrous dark-brown throughout. Interior has thin white rim band. Exterior is decorated like 314. KSM B I 20 #345.

Straight-sided Cup—Type 6

318. (K.437) Fragment of rim, side and base. H. 6.0, D. rim 8.0, base 6.0 cm. Coated dark-brown throughout. Exterior decorated like 314. KSM B I 20 #342.

Straight-sided Cup—Type 9

319. (K.443) Handle and most of rim and side missing. H. 7.0, D. rim 8.0, base 5.2 cm. Coated metallic grey-brown throughout. Exterior has white foliate band at rim, red horizontal line outlined in white at middle and repeating S pattern on lower side. Evans 1928, fig. 200e. KSM B I 19 #327. AM AE 824.1.

320. (K.457) PLATES 10, 72 Fragment of rim, side and base with handle stubs. H. 6.6, D. rim 9.0, base 6.0 cm. Coated semilustrous dark grey-brown throughout. Interior has thin white rim band. Exterior has orange band with added white wavy line at middle, white foliate band at rim and large white filled semicircles on lower side with horizontal white line at base. KSM B I 20 #347, 349.

321. (K.458) PLATE 72 Most of rim, side and base missing. H. 6.4, D. rim 8.5, base 6.0 cm. Coated dark grey-brown throughout. Exterior decorated like 320 but without trace of added white wavy line on orange band at middle. KSM B I 19 #324, 328.

Straight-sided Cup—Type 10

322. (K.459) Two non-joining rim, side and base fragments. H. 7.5, D. base 5.2 cm. Coated dark-brown throughout. Exterior has an orange band at middle, white foliate band at rim and three white horizontal bands on lower side. KSM B I 20 #342, 347.

Straight-sided Cup—Type 7

323. (K.460) PLATES 10, 72 Large fragment of rim, side and base with handle stub. H. 5.8, D. rim 8.0, base 4.8 cm. Coated dark-brown throughout. Interior has thin white rim band. Exterior orange horizontal band at middle, white foliate band

at rim and row of white dots outlined in white on lower side. KSM B I 20 #335, 336; KSM B I 21 #352.

Straight-sided Cup—?Type

324. (K.462) PLATE 72 Large rim fragment with complete handle. H. 5.4, D. rim 8.0 cm. Coated dark grey-brown throughout. Orange horizontal band outlined in white at middle, white foliate band at rim and white horizontal line on lower side. KSM B I 19 #323, 328.

325. (K.463) PLATES 10, 72 Three non-joining fragments of rim and upper side. H. 6.0, D. rim 11.0 cm. Coated semilustrous black throughout. Exterior has thick horizontal orange band at middle with added red dots and outlined in white, white foliate band at rim and trace of white repeating S-pattern on lower side. KSM B I 20 #343, 345.

Straight-sided Cup—Type 9

326. (K.461) PLATES 11, 72 Rim, side and base fragment. H. 7.0, D. rim 12.5, base 5.5 cm. Coated semilustrous dark-brown throughout. Exterior has horizontal zone of white reverse C pattern bordered in white with white and orange lines above and below, rows of white dots near rim and base and white lines at rim and base. KSM B I 19 #328.

327. (K.438) PLATES 11, 72 Few small fragments of rim, side, handle and base missing. Restored in plaster. H. 8.0, D. rim 12.0, base 5.5 cm. Coated black throughout but badly worn. Exterior has large white open running spirals in middle with orange and white horizontal lines above and below and repeating S-pattern at rim and base. KSM B I 19 #324. SMP 9686.

328. (K.444) Fragment of base and lower side. H. 3.7, D. base 5.5 cm. Coated semilustrous dark-brown throughout. Exterior has thick orange band with added red dots and outlined in white at base and zone of chevrons above. Overall decoration most likely similar to **997**. KSM B I 19 #323.

Straight-sided Cup—Type 7

329. (K.450) PLATE 73 Rim, side and base fragment with handle stubs. H. 5.5, D. rim 10.0, base 8.0 cm. Coated dark-brown throughout. Exterior has thick orange band with added white wavy line at middle, row of open running spirals at rim and three white horizontal lines at base. KSM B III 8 #416.

Straight-sided Cup—?Type

330. (K.451) PLATES 11, 73 Two non-joining fragments of rim with upper handle stub. H. 7.3, D. rim 9.0 cm. Coated dark grey-brown throughout. Exterior has thick orange band at middle, row of white open running spirals at rim and filled white semicircles near base. KSM B I 19 #324, 329.

Straight-sided Cup—Type 10

331. (K.452) PLATE 11 Three non-joining fragments of base and lower side with lower handle stub. H. 7.0, D. base 4.5 cm. Coated dark grey-brown throughout. Exterior has thick orange band outlined in white at middle, repeating S-pattern on lower side and open running spirals at rim. KSM B I 20 #345, 347, 349.

Straight-sided Cup—Type 9

332. (K.454) PLATE 73 Two non-joining rim, side and base fragments. H. 6.7, D. rim 8.5 cm. Coated semilustrous dark-brown throughout. Exterior has thick red band at middle, white open running spirals with partial white filling at rim and white horizontal line at base. KSM B I 19 #329.

Straight-sided Cup—Type 8

333. (K.455) PLATES 11, 73 Two non-joining rim and base fragments. H. 7.5, D. rim 11.0, base 5.5 cm. Coated dark grey-brown throughout. Exterior has white horizontal line at middle, white open running spiral at rim, white line outlined in orange on lower side and repeating S-pattern at base. KSM B I 14 #257; KSM B I 20 #347.

Straight-sided Cup—?Type

334. (K.456) PLATES 11, 73 Six non-joining rim and side fragments. H. 6.0, D. rim 12.0 cm. Coated dark grey-brown throughout. Thick red band with added white S-pattern outlined in white at middle, open running spirals with partial white filling at rim, and white line on lower side. KSM B I 14 #260; KSM B I 19 #326, 327, 329.

Straight-sided Cup—Type 9

335. (K.484) PLATE 11 Two non-joining fragments of rim and base. H. 6.5, D. rim 8.0, base 5.3 cm. Coated semilustrous dark-brown to black throughout. Interior has thin white rim band. Exterior has thick orange band outlined in white and white band at middle and white zig-zags at rim and lower side and white line at base. KSM B I 20 #330, 346.

336. (K.478) PLATES 11, 70 Two non-joining fragments of base and lower side. H. 6.2, D. base 5.0 cm. Coated semilustrous dark grey-brown throughout. Exterior has two white horizontal lines at middle, white S-pattern on lower side and ?alternating 'sunrise' motif and groups of five vertical orange bars at rim. K SM B I 19 #325.

337. (K.465) PLATE 11 Four non-joining fragments of rim, side and base. H. 6.5, D. rim 9.0, base 5.0 cm. Coated thin dark-brown throughout. Exterior has two horizontal white lines at middle, S-pattern and white line at base and ?alternating 'sunrise' and white flower with orange centre at rim. KSM B I 19 #322, 326, 329.

Straight-sided Cup—Type 10

338. (K.445) PLATES 11, 71 Over half of rim, side and handle missing. Partially restored in plaster. H. 8.4, D. rim 10.0, base 5.7 cm. Coated brown throughout and mottled in places. Exterior has two large white rosettes in spirals on either side and traces of an orange petaloid loop at front between them and white stripe on bottom. KSM B I 20 #340, 345, 347, 350. SMP 9687.

339. (K.485) PLATE 11 Complete base with half of lower side and non-joining rim fragment. H. 7.0, D. rim 11.0, base 6.2 cm. Coated semilustrous dark-brown throughout. Exterior has trace of white diagonal palm motifs on either side of handle, large circular white design opposite handle and thick orange zone between the white designs. KSM B I 19 #324, 326, 327, 329.

Rounded Cup—Type 6

340. (K.381) PLATES 12, 73 Five non-joining rim and side fragments with complete handle. H. 4.0, D. rim 13.0 cm. Coated semilustrous grey-brown throughout. Interior had diagonal white slashes at rim. Exterior has thick orange band with added white S-pattern below rim, white dots and slashes at rim and white scale pattern filled with 'sunrise' motif on side. KSM B I 19 #324; KSM B I 20 #347, 349; KSM B I 21 #353.

341. (K.364) PLATES 12, 73 Two non-joining rim and side frag-

ments. D. rim 8.0 cm. Coated semilustrous black throughout. Interior has row of white pendants at rim. Exterior has vertical slashes at rim and white wavy line decoration with alternating white dot circle and orange loaf with added red dot in centre and four white dots. KSM B I 19 #327, 329.

342. (K.365) PLATES 12, 65, 73 Rim fragment. D. rim 11.0 cm. Coated semilustrous black throughout. Interior has white diagonal slashes at rim. Exterior has white wavy line pattern with alternating white dot circle and orange loaf with four white dots. KSM B I 20 #337; KSM B III 8 #416.

343. (K.366) PLATES 65, 73 Two non-joining fragments of rim and side with upper and lower parts of handle. D. rim 11.0 cm. Coated semilustrous dark-brown throughout. Interior has white diagonal slashes at rim. Exterior has white wavy line pattern filled with orange loaves with added red dots and four white dots. KSM B I 20 #342.

344. (K.367) PLATE 73 Large rim and side fragment. D. rim 12.0 cm. Coated semilustrous dark-brown throughout. Interior has white vertical slashes at rim. Exterior has white wavy line pattern with alternating white dot circle and orange loaf with white dot circle. KSM B I 20 #347, 348, 350.

345. (K.368) PLATE 73 Large rim fragment. D. rim 11.0 cm. Coated semilustrous dark-brown throughout, now worn. Interior has white diagonal slashes at rim. Exterior has white wavy line pattern with alternating white dot circle and orange loaf with added red dot and four white dots. KSM B I 19 #324, 328.

346. (K.369) PLATES 12, 62, 73 Two non-joining rim fragments. D. rim 11.0 cm. Coated semilustrous grey-brown throughout. Interior has thin white horizontal rim band. Exterior has white wavy line pattern with alternating white dot circle and pair of white diagonal strokes crossed by pair of orange strokes. KSM B I 19 #326, 328.

347. (K.370) PLATE 73 Rim fragment. D. rim 12.0 cm. Coated dark grey-brown throughout. Interior white filled semicircles at rim. Exterior has white wavy line pattern with alternating white dot circle and red dot with orange loaves above and below and four white dots. KSM B I 20 #342.

348. (K.371) PLATES 12, 74 Rim fragment. D. rim 11.0 cm. Coated semilustrous black throughout. Interior has white diagonal slashes at rim. Exterior has white wavy line pattern with alternating double row of white dots and orange loaf on vertical white strokes. KSM B I 19 #328.

349. (K.372) PLATE 74 Two non-joining rim fragments. D. rim 11.0 cm. Coated semilustrous black throughout. Interior has white diagonal slashes at rim. Exterior has white wavy line pattern with alternating double diagonal rows of white dots and pair of vertical orange loaves with four white dots. KSM B I 20 #342, 347.

350. (K.373) PLATE 74 Rim fragment. D. rim 11.0 cm. Coated semilustrous black throughout. Interior has white diagonal slashes at rim. Exterior has white wavy line pattern with alternating double diagonal rows of white dots and double horizontal orange loaves with seven white dots. KSM B I 20 #347.

351. (K.374) PLATES 12, 74 Rim fragment. D. rim 14.0 cm. Coated semilustrous dark-brown throughout. Interior has white diagonal slashes at rim. Exterior has white wavy line pattern with alternating double rows of white dots and double orange loaves on white vertical stroke. KSM B I 19 #328.

352. (K.375) PLATES 12, 74 Large rim and side fragment. D. rim 12.0 cm. Coated thick dark-brown throughout. Interior has white filled semicircles at rim. Exterior has white wavy line pattern with alternating double rows of diagonal white dots and diagonal white stroke with pair of orange loaves either side. KSM B I 20 #347; KSM B III 8 #416.

353. (K.376) PLATE 74 Rim fragment. D. rim 10.0 cm. Coated semilustrous dark-brown throughout. Interior has white diagonal slashes at rim. Exterior has white wavy line pattern with alternating triple diagonal rows of white dots with red loaf with four added white dots. KSM B I 19 #329.

354. (K.377) PLATES 12, 65, 74 Rim fragment. D. rim 9.0 cm. Coated dark-brown throughout. Interior has thin white horizontal rim band. Exterior has white wavy line pattern with pair of white loaves in open areas and orange loaves where wavy lines meet. KSM B III 8 #416.

355. (K.378) PLATE 74 Four non-joining fragments of rim and side. D. rim 12.0 cm. Coated semilustrous black throughout. Interior has white decoration at rim. Exterior has white wavy line pattern with alternating diagonal row of thick white dots and pair of vertical orange loaves with added diagonal red loaf. KSM B I 20 #344, 347.

356. (K.379) PLATES 12, 74 Two non-joining fragments of rim with upper part of handle. D. rim 11.0 cm. Coated semilustrous dark-brown throughout. Interior has thick white rim band. Exterior has thick orange rim band with added red dots and white wavy line pattern filled with floral motif. KSM B I 14 #256, 257.

357. (K.380) PLATE 74 Large fragment of rim and side with handle stubs. D. rim 13.0 cm. Coated dark-brown throughout. Interior has white diagonal slashes at rim. Exterior has white wavy line pattern filled with orange loaf outlined in white with added red dot. KSM B I 19 #327.

358. (K.382) PLATE 74 Rim fragment. D. rim 11.0 cm. Coated dark-brown throughout. Interior has diagonal white slashes at rim. Exterior has white wavy line/scale pattern with curving orange line down the side across it. KSM B I 19 #322, 323.

359. (K.383) PLATE 74 Two non-joining body fragments. D. max. 12.0 cm. Coated semilustrous black throughout. Exterior has white wavy line pattern with alternating diagonal row of white dots and large orange oval outlined in white, orange semicircles outlined in white where wavy lines meet. KSM B I 20 #347.

360. (K.384) PLATE 74 Two non-joining fragments of base and lower side. D. base 5.0 cm. Coated grey-brown throughout. Interior has trace of white decoration. Exterior has white scale pattern with pendant white strokes and orange band at base. KSM B I 20 #339, 342.

361. (K.385) PLATES 13, 65, 74, 75 Base and lower side fragment. D. base 4.5 cm. Coated dark red-brown throughout. Interior has orange cross in centre base with four bat designs around. Exterior has groups of three or four white vertical lines on lower side and zone of white spirals across middle of base with white dots to one side. KSM B I 21 #350; KSM B III 8 #416.

362. (K.386) PLATES 13, 74, 75 Base and lower side fragment. D. base 4.0 cm. Coated semilustrous black throughout. Interior has white lozenge design with four ovals with orange loaves and four white dots completing circle and two concentric circles of white dots at centre base. Exterior has white and orange concentric circles on base and groups of three vertical white lines on lower side. KSM B I 20 #333, 340, 342.

363. (K.387) PLATES 74, 75 Two non-joining base and lower side fragments. D. base 4.0 cm. Coated dull brown throughout. Interior has white diagonal slashes on lower side. Exterior has white wavy line pattern with diagonal white criss-cross filled with orange loaves and orange band at base with added white strokes. KSM B I 20 #345, 347.

364. (K.388) PLATES 13, 74, 75 Large base fragment. D. base 4.2 cm. Coated semilustrous grey-brown throughout. Interior has large orange cross with open bat design in two concentric white

dot circles. Exterior has white five-sided star with added orange star in centre of base. KSM B I 19 #324.

365. (K.389) PLATES 13, 74, 75 Base fragment. D. base 3.5 cm. Coated semilustrous black throughout. Interior has white flower with orange dot at centre in white dot circle and wavy line. Exterior has three white dot circles with pattern of alternating orange dot and white dot circle between first and second from centre. KSM B I 20 #344.

366. (K.390) PLATES 13, 74, 75 Base fragment. D. base 4.5 cm. Coated semilustrous black throughout. Interior has orange cross with double outline in white. Exterior has five orange stripes on base. KSM B I 20 #347.

367. (K.391) PLATES 13, 74, 75 Small base fragment. D. base c. 3.5 cm. Coated black throughout. Interior has orange dot with added white flower in centre. Exterior has orange circle with white outline on base. KSM B I 20 #345.

368. (K.392) PLATES 13, 74, 75 Small base fragment. D. base c. 3.5 cm. Coated grey-brown throughout. Interior has orange cross with white bat design around it in base. Exterior has white dot circles at centre and edge of base with white ovals in space between. KSM B I 20 #347.

Miniature Rounded Cup

369. (K.415) PLATE 14 Fragment of rim, side and base. H. 4.0, D. rim 7.0, base 3.0 cm. Coated semilustrous dark-brown to black throughout. Exterior has thick orange rim band and two rows of white wavy lines on side, white line at base. KSM B I 19 #329.

Rounded Cup—Type 5

370. (K.413) PLATE 14 Two non-joining fragments of rim and side with complete handle. H. 5.0, D. rim 10.0 cm. Coated grey-brown throughout. Interior has thick white horizontal rim band. Exterior has thick orange band at rim with added white wavy line and orange band on lower side; two white wavy lines on side and white line near base. KSM B I 19 #322, 328; KSM B I 20 #335.

371. (K.412) PLATE 14 Four non-joining rim and body fragments with upper and lower handle attachments. H. 4.0, D. rim 11.5 cm. Coated semilustrous dark-brown to black throughout. Interior has thin white horizontal rim band. Exterior has thick red/orange rim band and white wavy ladder pattern on side above horizontal white line. KSM B I 19 #324, 325; KSM B I 20 #335, 350; KSM B I 21 #357.

372. (K.410) PLATE 14 Four non-joining fragments of rim and side. H. 5.7, D. rim 12.0 cm. Coated semilustrous black throughout. Interior has trace of white rim band. Exterior has thick orange bands outlined in white with added red dots at rim and lower side and white foliate band on side. KSM B I 14 #257; KSM B I 20 #334, 347.

373. (K.411) PLATE 14 Four non-joining fragments of rim and upper side. H. 4.0, D. rim 14.0 cm. Coated dull brown throughout. Interior has white rim band. Exterior thick orange rim band and two rows of white dots bisected by orange lines with white horizontal lines below. KSM B I 14 #260; KSM B I 19 #324, 326, 327.

374. (K.404) PLATES 14, 62 Two non-joining fragments of rim and side with handle. H. 5.7, D. rim 13.0 cm. Coated semilustrous grey-brown throughout. Exterior has thick orange band at rim with added white wavy line and white line on side with large diagonal strokes above. KSM B I 19 #324, 326, 328.

375. (K.405) PLATE 14 Four non-joining fragments of rim, side and base (not ill.). H. 9.0, D. rim 16.0, base 7.0 cm. Coated

dark-brown throughout. Exterior has thick orange band below rim and white petals on side continuing to base. KSM B I 19 #323, 327, 328.

376. (K.406) PLATE 14 Five non-joining fragments of rim, side and base with top part of handle. H. 8.0, D. rim 13.5, base 5.0 cm. Coated semilustrous dark grey/brown throughout. Interior has white filled semicircles at rim. Exterior has thick orange band (?with added white wavy line) below rim, white diagonal lines on side connected by groups of five or six white strokes and pair of vertical white lines on lower side. KSM B I 19 #322, 323, 324, 327.

Miniature Bridge-spouted Jar

377. (K.635) PLATE 75 Spout, handles and many rim and side fragments missing. Restored in plaster. H. 7.0, D. base 3.1 cm. Exterior coated black and has horizontal red and white bands on side and red and white radiating lines on rim. Inscribed 'K.30 N.11'. HM 8878.

378. (K.636) PLATES 64, 75 Tip and half of spout, one handle and much of rim and side missing. Restored. H. 11.7, D. rim 7.0, base 5.2 cm. Interior of spout and exterior coated red-brown and has complex open rosettes alternating with racquet pattern on side above three sharp wavy lines, all white, with loop in orange below wavy lines. Inscribed 'K.30 N.11'. Evans 1935, 137 fig. 107. HM 8881.

Rounded Bridge-spouted Jar—Type 5

379. (K.561) PLATES 15, 62, 75 Four non-joining fragments of rim and side with complete handle and spout. H. 12.0, D. rim 9.0 cm. Interior has uneven brown smear at rim. Exterior coated semilustrous dark-brown, worn, and has large white foliate band at middle with orange and white lines above and below, white with added red dots below rim and on lower side and white lines at rim and lower side. Inscribed 'MM III'. KSM B I 19 #326, 328.

380. (K.622) PLATE 76 Seven non-joining fragments of rim and side with complete spout and one handle. D. rim 9.5 cm. Very similar to **379**. KSM B I 20 #322, 345, 350.

381. (K.623) Seven non-joining fragments of rim and side with part of spout. D. rim 9.0 cm. Very similar to **379** but has orange line on lower side. KSM B I 19 #324, 326, 328, 329.

382. (K.624) PLATES 15, 76 Spout, most of rim and side and one handle missing. H. 10.5, D. rim 7.5, base 5.6 cm. Interior has brown smear at rim. Exterior coated semilustrous dark-brown, now worn, and has large white foliate band at middle, orange and white lines above and below and white dots on lower side and at rim. KSM B I 20 #342.

383. (K.625) PLATES 15, 76 Three non-joining fragments of rim with spout and handles. D. rim 9.0 cm. Interior has thick dark smear at rim. Exterior coated semilustrous metallic dark-brown and has a thick orange band outlined in white with added red dots below spout and handles and white open running spirals at rim. Lower panel probably as on **384**. KSM B I 20 #346, 347.

384. (K.626) PLATE 76 Rim fragment with handle stub. Exterior coated semilustrous dark-brown and decorated as **383** with a row of white chevrons at middle but no trace of added red dots. KSM B I 20 #345, 347.

385. (K.630) PLATE 15 Numerous non-joining fragments of rim and side with most of spout and one complete handle. H. 12.0, D. rim 9.0 cm. Interior has smear at rim and drips of dark paint on side. Exterior coated dark grey-brown and has large white zone of S-pattern at middle with alternating white

'sunrise' and orange coralline motif with added red dots outlined in white at rim and two thick white wavy lines on lower
side and white band at base. KSM B I 14 #259; KSM B I 21
#354, 355, 356.

386. (K.631) PLATE 77 Rim fragment. D. rim *c.* 7.5 cm. Interior
has dark smear at rim. Exterior coated dark-brown and has
alternating white 'sunrise' motif and groups of three vertical
red lines at rim above horizontal white line. KSM B I 20 #349,
350.

387. (K.632) PLATE 77 Two non-joining rim fragments with complete handle. D. rim 10.0 cm. Interior has dark smear at rim.
Exterior coated dark-brown and has traces of white pendant
'sunrise' motif above horizontal white line. KSM B I 14 #259.

388. (K.633) PLATES 66, 76 Large fragment of rim and side with
chipped spout. D. rim *c.* 9.0 cm. Interior has dark smear at
rim. Exterior coated dark-brown and large white ?spirals on
sides and orange pendant loop with three white petals at front
below spout. KSM B I 20 #332, 333.

Rounded Bridge-spouted Jar—Type 6

389. (K.629) PLATE 77 Spout, handles most of rim and shoulder
missing. Restored in plaster. H. 14.2, rest. 16.5, D. base 6.5
cm. Interior has drips of dark paint on side. Exterior coated
semilustrous dark grey-brown and has four large white circles
with white horizontal bands with fins and added red strokes
on side, orange wavy line below, white spiral and loop pattern
near base and white band at base. Inscribed 'K.30 N.8'. Evans
1935, 131 fig. 99; Åberg 1933, 191 fig. 355. HM 8880.

Baggy-shaped Bridge-spouted Jar

390. (K.637) PLATES 15, 77 Three non-joining fragments of upper
side with spout. D. max 16.5 cm. Interior has trace of smear
at rim. Exterior coated dull grey-brown and has thick orange
bands outlined in white below rim and at widest point, and
large white open running spirals on shoulder. KSM B I 14
#259, 262.

391. (K.638) PLATES 15, 67, 77 Two fragments of rim and shoulder.
D. rim *c.* 12.0 cm. Interior has dark smear at rim. Exterior
coated semilustrous dark-brown and has two horizontal white
lines on shoulder with zone of white open spirals with dots
above and red dots in linear white pattern below on side. KSM
B I 21 #354; KSM B III 8 #416.

Spouted Jar

392. (K.639) PLATES 16, 77 Six non-joining fragments of upper
and lower side. D. max. 13.0 cm. Exterior coated semilustrous
black and has horizontal white branch zone at middle with
row of tiny white dots above and below and white bat motif
with orange vertical lines (trace of added white wavy line) between on shoulder and lower side. KSM B I 14 #259; KSM B
I 20 #337, 345, 347, 348.

Juglet

393. (K.660) PLATES 66, 78 Fragment of base and side. H. 5.8, D.
base 4.0 cm. Exterior coated semilustrous dark-brown and
has three white and one red band in grooves at base, white S-
pattern with connecting strokes (similar to 376) on lower side
and part of orange coralline motif outlined in white at widest
part of side. KSM B I 20 #330, 350.

394. (K.661) PLATE 78 Fragment of base and side. H. 7.0, D. base
4.0 cm. Exterior coated metallic dark grey-brown and has white
band at base and vertical dentate band with orange line in middle on both sides. KSM B I 20 #330.

Conical Rhyton

395. (K.669) PLATES 16, 66, 78 Two large fragments of rim and
side. H. 24.0, D. rim 8.0 cm. Interior of rim has smear of dark
paint. Exterior coated semilustrous dark-brown to black and
has a zone of white concentric circles with orange and white
lines and white zig-zags above and below and four rows of open
spirals made of tiny white dots and two rows of tiny white dots
at rim and groups of three thin alternating with one thick white
line on lower side. KSM B I 20 #330, 336, 347.

396. (K.670) PLATES 16, 65, 78 Four non-joining fragments of rim
and side, one rim lug. H. 12.0, D. rim 7.5 cm. Interior has
dark smear at rim. Exterior coated semilustrous dark-brown
and has two large orange and white rosettes in two white concentric circles on side, vertical white foliate band opposite handle which is outlined in orange and white, white foliate band
on rim and orange paint on rim lug. KSM B I 20 #347; KSM
B I 21 #355; KSM B III 8 #416.

397. (K.671) Rim fragment with lug. Top of rim has red coralline
motif outlined in white, complex decoration in red and white
on side. Evans 1935, 130 pl. XXXc. Not located.

Globular Rhyton

398. (K.672) PLATES 62, 78 Fragment of bottom. D. hole 1.6 cm.
Interior has drips of red-brown paint and white band at rim.
Exterior coated semilustrous dark-brown and has thick orange
band with added red dots at rim, two white bands and start of
white diagonal lines on side. KSM B I 14 #259; KSM B I 19
#326, 329.

399. (K.673) PLATES 65, 78 Fragment of bottom. D. hole 0.7 cm.
Exterior coated semilustrous dark-brown and has two white
bands near hole and start of vertical white lines on side. KSM
B III 8 #416.

Large Bowl

400. (K.571) PLATE 78 Two non-joining framents of rim, side and
base with part of one loop handle. H. 7.5, D. rim 20.0, base
10.0 cm. Coated thin semilustrous grey-brown throughout,
worn. Interior has large white foliate band at middle with red
band outlined in white at rim and base and large angular white
marks on bottom. Exterior has trace of white ?wavy line pattern on side. KSM B I 20 #339.

401. (K.601) PLATE 79 Half of rim and side missing. H. 5.7, D. rim
28.0, base 9.0 cm. Coated semilustrous dark-brown throughout. Interior has thick orange band below rim and white open
running spirals on top of rim. KSM B I 14 #261.

Technique: Handmade

Large closed Jar

402. (K.684) PLATES 16, 79 Fragment of lower side. H. 15.0, D.
max. 25.0 cm. Exterior coated dark-brown and has large white
floral design with orange detail on side. Evans 1935, 136 fig.
106. KSM B I 20 #330, 343; KSM sherd collection 'MM
II B'.

Technique: Wheelmade, ridged and grooved

Surface: Monochrome coated; plain or white spotted
Straight-sided Cup—Type 13

403. (K.502) PLATES 17, 49 Rim, side and base fragments, partially

restored in plaster. H. 13.2, D. rim 12.0, base 7.5 cm. Coated semilustrous black throughout. Blunt grooves above and below flange. Traces of white spotting below rim and on interior. KSM B I 14 #259, 260; KSM B I 19 #322, 327. SMP 9688.

Straight-sided Cup—Type 12

404. (K.500) PLATES 17, 79 Two non-joining fragments of rim, side and base with lower handle stub. H. 7.5, D. rim 11.5, base 8.0 cm. Coated semilustrous metallic black throughout. Interior white spotted. Exterior has three ridges on lower side and white spotting below rim. KSM B I 21 #351, 355

405. (K.497) PLATE 17 Rim, upper side and handle missing. H. 6.7, D. base 5.6 cm. Coated semilustrous dark grey-brown to black throughout. Interior has crude white spotting. Exterior has three evenly spaced horizontal ridges on side. KSM B I 20 #330.

406. (K.498) PLATES 17, 79 Fragment of rim and side with lower handle stub. H. 5.8, D. rim 9.2 cm. Coated dark-brown throughout, mottled in places. Interior carefully white spotted. Exterior has three evenly spaced horizontal ridges on side. KSM B I 14 #259.

407. (K.499) PLATES 17, 79 Fragment of base and lower side. H. 5.7, D. base 7.0 cm. Coated semilustrous grey-black throughout. Interior white spotted. Exterior has five evenly spaced horizontal ridges on side. KSM B I 20 #348.

Straight-sided Cup—Type 8

408. (K.501) PLATES 17, 79 Two non-joining fragments of rim and base. H. *c.* 10.0, D. rim 12.0 cm. Coated semilustrous black throughout. Exterior has two groups of five horizontal grooves on side. KSM B I 19 #327.

Short-rimmed Angular Cup—Type 3

409. (K.427) PLATES 17, 79 Handle and most of rim and side missing. Partially restored in plaster. H. 10.0, D. rim 11.0, base 4.5 cm. Coated semilustrous dark grey-brown throughout. Interior white spotted with thin white rim band. KSM B I 19 #323, 327.

410. (K.428) PLATE 79 Rim and handle missing. H. 8.5, D. base 4.5 cm. Coated grey-brown throughout, worn. Probably white spotted. KSM B I 19 #326.

411. (K.429) PLATES 17, 80 Rim, handle and most of side missing. H. 9.8, D. max.11.2, base 5.0 cm. Coated semilustrous dark grey-brown throughout. KSM B I 19 #322, 323, 329.

412. (K.430) PLATES 17, 80 Large rim and side fragment. H. 9.5, D. rim 13.5 cm. Coated semilustrous dark grey-brown throughout. Interior white spotted. Exterior has two groups of three horizontal grooves on side. KSM B I 19 #326.

Rounded Cup—Type 7

413. (K.422) PLATES 18, 80 Handle and most of rim and side missing. Partially restored in plaster. H. 6.4, D. rim 9.8, base 5.0 cm. Coated semilustrous dark-brown to black throughout. Interior white spotted. Exterior has three thin horizontal grooves on upper side and white spotting below rim. KSM B I 19 #323, 327. SMP 9690.

414. (K.421) PLATES 18, 80 One-third of rim and side missing. Partially restored. H. 6.8, D. rim 9.0, base 4.6 cm. Coated dull brown throughout. Interior carefully white spotted. Exterior has four thin horizontal grooves on side and white spotting below rim. KSM B I 14 #258, 261. SMP 9691.

415. (K.423) PLATES 18, 80 Handle, half of rim and much of side missing. H. 6.6, D. rim 10.0, base 4.0 cm. Coated semilustrous black throughout. Interior white spotted. Exterior has three horizontal grooves on lower side above foot. KSM B I 19 #322, 323, 326, 327, 329.

416. (K.424) PLATE 18 Two non-joining rim and side fragments. H. 4.0, D. rim 10.0 cm. Coated semilustrous dark grey-brown throughout. Interior white spotted. Exterior has horizontal groove with thick white band on lower side and dense white spotting at rim. KSM B I 19 #324, 326; KSM B I 20 #345.

Rounded Cup—Type 5

417. (K.417) PLATE 18 Three non-joining fragments of rim, side and base. H. 7.0, D. rim 14.0, base 5.5 cm. Coated lustrous black throughout. Three deep horizontal grooves at widest point. KSM B I 19 #324, 327, 329.

418. (K.416) Large rim, side and base fragment. H. 8.0, D. rim 13.5, base 5.5 cm. Coated semilustrous black throughout. Interior sprayed with red and white dots. Exterior has five horizontal grooves at widest point. KSM B I 20 #350.

419. (K.418) PLATE 18 Large fragment of rim and side with upper part of handle. H. 6.5, D. rim 14.0 cm. Coated dull dark-brown throughout. Exterior has two or three horizontal grooves at widest point and dense white spotting below rim and on top of handle. KSM B I 19 #323.

420. (K.419) Eight non-joining fragments of rim and side with handle. H. 7.0, D. rim 16.0 cm. Coated semilustrous dark-brown to black except on handle and interior zone where cup escaped dipping. Interior has red and white paint spray. Exterior has four horizontal grooves on side and white spotting below rim. KSM B I 14 #259, 260; KSM B I 19 #324, 326, 327, 329.

421. (K.420) Fragment of rim, side and base. H. 5.4, D. rim 11.0, base 5.0 cm. Coated dull red-brown throughout. Exterior has thin horizontal grooves on lower side. KSM B III 8 #417.

Large spouted Jar

422. (K.693) PLATE 80 Five non-joining fragments of rim and shoulder with handle stub. D. rim 13.5 cm. Interior of rim and exterior coated semilustrous black. Exterior has evenly spaced horizontal grooves 2.0 cm apart from rim to lower side. KSM B I 20 #338, 339.

Surface: Monochrome coated; polychrome decorated

Straight-sided Cup—Type 11

423. (K.506) PLATE 81 Four non-joining fragments of rim, side and base with complete handle. H. 5.8, D. rim 9.5, base 7.2 cm. Coated semilustrous dark-brown throughout. Exterior has three horizontal ridges at upper middle, below which is zone of white with thick orange band with added white S-pattern; white spotting below rim and on top of handle. KSM B I 20 #330, 338, 345, 347, 350.

424. (K.507) Three non-joining fragments of base and lower side. D. base 7.3 cm. Coated semilustrous grey black throughout. Exterior as **423**. KSM B I 20 #336, 345.

425. (K.508) PLATE 81 Two non-joining fragments of rim, side and base. H. 5.8, D. rim 9.2, base 7.2 cm. Coated semilustrous grey black throughout. Exterior as **423**. KSM B I 20 #335, 345, 347.

426. (K.509) PLATES 18, 81 Large fragment of rim, side and base with lower part of handle. H. 5.7, D. rim 9.5, base 7.8 cm. Coated semilustrous grey black throughout. Exterior as **423**. KSM B I 20 #345, 347.

Straight-sided Cup

427. (K.466) PLATES 18, 69 Two non-joining fragments of rim, side and base. H. 7.0, D. rim 8.0, base 4.5 cm. Coated semilustrous dark-brown throughout. Interior has thin white rim band. Exterior has three evenly spaced horizontal grooves with white lines, two opposing white zones of S-pattern at middle, orange with added red dots in opposing white arches at rim and base and white band at base. KSM B I 14 #257; KSM B I 19 #329.

Angular Cup

428. (K.425) PLATES 18, 81 Two non-joining fragments of rim and side. H. 5.4, D. rim 12.0 cm. Coated semilustrous brown throughout. Interior white spotted. Exterior has incised double zig-zag on lower side between two thick orange bands with added white S-pattern and white spotting below rim. KSM B I 20 #330.

429. (K.426) PLATES 18, 81 Two non-joining fragments of rim and side with handle stub. H. 6.0, D. rim 9.6 cm. Coated semilustrous grey-brown throughout. Interior white spotted. Exterior has fine groove and thick orange band at angle and white spotting above and below. KSM B I 19 #326, 329.

Technique: Wheelmade, Stamped

Surface: Monochrome coated; plain or white decorated

Rounded Cup

430. (K.401) PLATES 19, 82 Two fragments of rim with complete handle. D. rim 11.0 cm. Coated semilustrous black throughout. Interior sprayed with red and white paint. Exterior has horizontal grooves below rim and at widest point and stamped circles on upper side. KSM B I 20 #339, 348.

431. (K.402) PLATE 82 Rim fragment. D. rim 10.0 cm. Coated semilustrous red-brown throughout. Horizontal row of stamped circles below rim. KSM B I 19 #322.

432. (K.403) PLATE 82 Rim fragment. D. rim 12.0 cm. Coated grey-brown throughout. Horizontal groove and row of stamped circles below rim. KSM B I 21 #354.

Surface: Monochrome coated; polychrome decorated

Straight-sided Cup—Type 7

433. (K.503) PLATES 19, 82 Four non-joining fragments of rim, side and base. H. 6.0, D. rim 10.5, base 7.5 cm. Coated semilustrous dark grey-brown throughout. Exterior has white filled horizontal groove below rim, three rows of stamped 'star' motif on lower side and white foliate band at rim. KSM B I 19 #323.

Straight-sided Cup

434. (K.504) PLATES 19, 82 Large rim and side fragment. H. 4.8, D. rim 9.0 cm. Coated semilustrous dark grey-brown throughout. Exterior has horizontal zone of white filled stamped open running spirals on side between red filled grooves and white foliate band at rim and base. KSM B I 20 #335, 336; KSM B I 21 #354.

435. (K.505) PLATE 82 Three non-joining fragments of rim and upper side. H. 5.5, D. rim 11.0 cm. Coated semilustrous dark grey-brown throughout. Interior has thin spray of white and orange paint. Exterior white filled horizontal groove below rim,

three rows of stamped open spirals below and row of white with added red dots at rim. KSM B I 20 #336; KSM #1844. (Unprovenanced.)

Rounded Cup—Type 5

436. (K.393) PLATE 83 Two non-joining rim and side fragments. H. 7.5, D. rim 11.0 cm. Coated semilustrous grey-brown throughout. Interior has flecks of red and white paint. Exterior has red filled horizontal groove on upper side with three rows of stamped concentric circles below, orange band with added red dots near base, white foliate band below rim and red band at rim. KSM B I 20 #345, 347.

437. (K.394) PLATES 19, 83 Two non-joining rim and side fragments with part of handle. H. 8.0, D. rim 11.0 cm. Coated semilustrous dark grey-brown throughout. Exterior has orange filled horizontal grooves on upper side framing white zig-zag pattern, two rows of stamped concentric circles at widest point, two white lines on lower side and one white rim band. KSM B I 19 #326, 327.

438. (K.395) PLATE 83 Two non-joining fragments of rim and side. D. rim 16.0 cm. Coated dark red-brown throughout. Exterior has horizontal grooves on upper side and below rim framing zone with white wavy line, three rows of stamped concentric circles on side and orange filled semicircles at rim. KSM B I 20 #345.

439. (K.396) PLATE 83 Two non-joining fragments of rim and side. Coated semilustrous dark-brown throughout. Interior has white diagonal slashes at rim. Exterior has row of white stamped open running spirals, orange horizontal groove on upper side with row of white circles with dot circles inside and white branch pattern at rim. KSM B I 19 #326.

440. (K.397) PLATE 83 Three non-joining fragments of rim and side with handle stub. D. rim 13.0 cm. Coated semilustrous dark grey-brown throughout. Exterior has red filled horizontal grooves on upper side and below rim, white dentate band at rim, reverse Z pattern on shoulder and trace of stamped circles or spirals on side. KSM B I 19 #327, 328.

441. (K.398) PLATE 83 Two non-joining rim and side fragments. D. rim 11.0 cm. Coated thick dull dark-brown throughout. Exterior has horizontal groove on upper side, stamped concentric circles on side, white with added red dots on shoulder and pendant white wavy line at rim. KSM B I 19 #322, 328.

442. (K.399) PLATE 83 Rim fragment. D. rim *c.* 17.0 cm. Coated semilustrous black throughout. Interior has white spray of paint. Exterior has row of stamped concentric circles on side, orange bands with added red wavy lines on upper side and below rim framing white open running spirals, and white arches at rim. KSM B I 21 #350.

443. (K.400) PLATE 83 Rim fragment. D. rim *c.* 12.5 cm. Coated dark-brown throughout. Exterior has orange filled horizontal grooves on upper side and below rim, row of stamped concentric circles on side, white wavy line at rim and crossing white wavy lines with orange vertical strokes and filled with white dots on shoulder. KSM B I 21 #347.

444. (K.1045) PLATE 67 Body fragment. Coated grey-brown throughout. Exterior has at least two rows of stamped shells at widest point with red filled horizontal groove below and white concentric dots on lower side. Evans 1935, 118 fig. 84a,b. AM 1938.567.

Rounded Bridge-spouted Jar

445. (K.634) PLATE 83 Numerous non-joining fragments of rim and side. Interior has thick dark smear. Exterior coated

semilustrous dark-brown and has at least three rows of stamped concentric circles at widest point, orange bands with added red dots above and below and white decoration in shoulder and rim zone difficult to understand. KSM B I 20 #339, 341, 345, 349, 350.

Technique: Wheelmade—cone thrown

Surface: Plain or Dark smeared

Crude Bowl—Type 1

446. (K.578) PLATE 84 Intact. H. 3.5, D. rim 10.0, base 5.0 cm. Interior coated dull red-brown. Exterior sprayed from rim. KSM B I 14 #260.

447. (K.579) PLATE 84 Rim chipped. H. 2.7, D. rim 9.5, base 5.0 cm. Traces of dark-brown spray at interior. KSM B I 20 #346.

448. (K.580) PLATE 84 Rim fragment missing. H. 2.6, D. rim 9.5, base 5.0 cm. Interior sprayed dark-brown. KSM B I 20 #347.

449. (K.581) PLATE 84 Rim chipped. H. 2.7, D. rim 9.0, base 6.0 cm. Interior sprayed red-brown. KSM B I 20 #338.

450. (K.582) PLATE 84 Intact. H. 2.4, D. rim 9.0, base 5.7 cm. Coated dull red-brown throughout. KSM B I 19 #329.

Crude Bowl—Type 2

451. (K.572) PLATE 84 Rim slightly chipped. H. 2.7–3.4, D. rim 10.2, base 4.5 cm. Sprayed red-brown throughout. KSM B I 14 #261.

452. (K.573) PLATE 84 Rim chipped, cracked. H. 2.5, D. rim 8.5, base 3.7 cm. Plain. KSM B I 14 #262.

453. (K.574) PLATE 84 Rim chipped. H. 2.2, D. rim 9.3, base 3.6 cm. Plain. KSM B I 20 #332.

454. (K.575) PLATE 84 Rim chipped. H. 2.0–2.8, D. rim 9.0, base 3.8 cm. Plain. KSM B I 14 #260.

455. (K.576) PLATE 84 Rim chipped. H. 2.5–3.2, D. rim 8.7–9.3, D. base 4.5 cm. Coated dull red-brown throughout. KSM B I 20 #348.

456. (K.577) PLATE 84 Rim chipped. H. 4.0, D. rim 10.0, base 5.0 cm. Plain. KSM B I 14 #257.

Crude Bowl—Type 3

457. (K.583) PLATE 84 Rim chipped and flaking. H. 2.0, D. rim 9.5, base 5.2 cm. Interior and one side of exterior sprayed red-brown. KSM B I 20 #348.

458. (K.584) PLATE 84 Intact. H. 1.6, D. rim 8.5, base 5.0 cm. Plain. Traces of burning in two places at rim. KSM B I 19 #329.

459. (K.585) PLATE 84 Rim chipped. H. 2.1, D. rim 9.0, base 4.7 cm. Sprayed dull brown throughout. KSM B I 14 #260.

460. (K.586) PLATE 84 Intact. H. 3.2, D. rim 8.7, base 5.0 cm. Coated semilustrous dark-brown throughout. KSM B I 14 #257.

461. (K.587) PLATE 84 Rim chipped. H. 3.0, D. rim 10.5, base 4.5 cm. Coated dull red-brown to dark-brown throughout. KSM B III 8 #417.

462. (K.588) PLATE 85 Complete. H. 2.6, D. rim 10.4 base 5.0 cm. Plain, blackened in places. KSM B I 20 #345.

463. (K.589) PLATE 85 Two rim fragments missing. H. 2.6, D. rim 9.3, base 4.5 cm. Coated dark-brown throughout. KSM B I 20 #330; KSM B I 21 #354.

Crude Bowl—Type 4

464. (K.590) PLATE 85 Large rim fragment missing. H. 3.3, D. rim 8.5, base 3.3 cm. Interior has brown band at rim. KSM B I 20 #342.

465. (K.591) PLATE 85 One-third of rim and side missing. H. 3.2, D. rim 10.0, base 4.0 cm. Coated semilustrous dark grey-brown throughout. KSM B I 20 #330.

466. (K.592) PLATE 85 One-third of rim and side missing. H. 3.4, D. rim 9.5, base 5.5 cm. Coated dull red-brown throughout. KSM B I 14 #257.

Surface: Dipped dark

Crude Bowl—Type 3

467. (K.593) PLATE 85 Small rim fragment missing. H. 3.5, D. rim 9.5, base 4.4 cm. Part of rim, interior and exterior dipped brown. KSM B I 14 #260.

468. (K.594) PLATE 85 Fragment of rim, side and base. H. 3.2, D. rim 12.5, base 4.5 cm. Half dipped in dark grey-brown paint. KSM B I 20 #342.

469. (K.595) PLATE 85 Half of rim, side and base. H. 4.5, D. rim 13.0, base 5.5 cm. More than half dipped in semilustrous dark-brown paint. KSM B I 19 #323.

Crude Pyxis

470. (K.597) PLATE 85 Small rim and side fragments missing. H. 4.8, D. rim 9.0, base 5.2 cm. Coated dull red-brown throughout. KSM B I 20 #330.

471. (K.598) PLATE 85 Rim fragment missing. H. 4.6, D. rim 8.0 base 5.0 cm. Few flecks of dark-brown paint in and out. KSM B III 8 #417.

Crude Cup—Type 1

472. (K.510) PLATE 86 Intact. H. 6.0, D. rim 8.5, base 4.3 cm. Interior splashed brown. Exterior has thin smear of red on one side. KSM B I 19 #329.

473. (K.511) PLATE 86 Intact. H. 5.2–6.4, D. rim 7.4–8.0, base 4.5 cm. Interior and exterior splashed with brown paint on one side. KSM B I 19 #327.

474. (K.512) PLATE 86 Rim chipped. H. 5.5–5.8, D. rim 6.8–8.0, base 4.3 cm. Coated dull dark-brown throughout. KSM B I 19 #327.

475. (K.513) PLATE 86 Rim chipped. H. 5.4, D. rim 7.5, base 3.8 cm. Faint red spots on exterior. KSM B I 20 #337.

476. (K.514) PLATE 86 Rim chipped. H. 6.7, D. rim 7.5, base 4.0 cm. Exterior has thick band of dull red-brown paint at rim. KSM B I 20 #342.

477. (K.515) PLATE 86 Rim fragment missing. H. 5.5, D. rim 9.0, base 4.5 cm. Coated dull orange to red-brown throughout. KSM B III 8 #417.

478. (K.516) Much of rim and side missing. H. 7.0, D. rim 9.0, base 4.0 cm. Interior has thin rim band and drips of dark-brown paint. Exterior has thick uneven rim band in dull dark-brown. KSM B I 20 #335.

479. (K.517) PLATE 86 Half of rim and side missing. H. 5.0, D. rim 8.0, base 4.5 cm. Coated dull dark-brown throughout. KSM B I 21 #352.

480. (K.518) PLATE 86 Half of rim and side missing. H. 5.2–6.0, D. rim 8.0, base 4.5 cm. Coated dull dark-brown throughout. KSM B I 21 #354.

481. (K.519) PLATE 86 One-third of rim and side missing. H. 6.0, D. rim 7.5, base 4.0 cm. Coated dull brown throughout. KSM B I 20 #342.

482. (K.520) PLATE 86 One-third of rim and side missing. H. 5.2, D. rim 7.5, base 4.5 cm. Interior splashed with thin red-brown paint. KSM B I 20 #348.

483. (K.521) PLATE 86 Small rim fragment missing. H. 4.8–5.7, D. rim 8.0–8.7, base 4.0 cm. Plain. KSM B I 20 #336.

484. (K.522) PLATE 86 Small rim fragment missing. H. 5.5, D. rim 8.0–8.7, base 4.0 cm. Few small splashes of thin dark-brown paint at rim in and out. KSM B I 14 #256.

485. (K.523) Half of rim and side missing. H. 5.5–6.0, D. rim 8.0, base 4.3 cm. Coated dull red-brown throughout. KSM B I 21 #355.

486. (K.524) One-third of rim, side and base missing. H. 5.6, D. rim 8.0, base 4.8 cm. Coated dull red-brown throughout. KSM B I 21 #354.

487. (K.525) Rim fragment missing. H. 5.7, D. rim 7.5–8.0, base 3.5 cm. Plain. KSM B I 20 #341.

488. (K.526) PLATE 86 Rim chipped. H. 6.0, D. rim 6.5–7.0, base 3.3 cm. Misfired. Plain. KSM B I 20 #346.

489. (K.527) PLATE 86 One-third of rim and side missing. H. 5.2–5.7, D. rim 7.3, base 4.0 cm. Plain. KSM B I 20 #343.

490. (K.528) PLATE 86 Half of rim and side missing. H. 5.8, D. rim 8.5, base 4.0 cm. Plain. KSM B III 8 #417.

491. (K.529) PLATE 86 Two rim fragments missing. H. 5.8, D. rim 8.0, base 3.0 cm. Coated dull red-brown to dark-brown throughout. KSM B I 20 #337.

Crude Cup—Type 3

492. (K.530) PLATE 86 Most of rim and handle missing. H. 6.0, D. rim 7.0, base 4.0 cm. Coated dull red-brown throughout. KSM B I 14 #262.

493. (K.531) PLATES 19, 86 Rim chipped. H. 5.7–6.0, D. rim 7.5–8.5, base 4.0 cm. Coated dull orange throughout. KSM B I 20 #337.

494. (K.532) PLATE 86 Half of rim, side and base missing. H. 6.0, D. rim 9.0, base 5.4 cm. Coated throughout in dull red brown. KSM B I 21 #352.

495. (K.533) PLATE 686 Most of rim, side and base missing. H. 6.0, D. rim 9.0, base 5.0 cm. Coated dull red-brown throughout. KSM B I 21 #355.

496. (K.534) PLATE 86 Most of rim, side and base missing. H. 6.5, D. rim 9.0, base 6.0 cm. Plain. KSM B I 21 #351.

497. (K.535) PLATE 86 Most of rim, side and handle missing. H. 6.3, D. rim 8.0, base 4.1 cm. Wide uneven dark-brown smear at rim in and out. KSM B I 21 #352.

498. (K.536) Rim chipped, handle missing. H. 6.5, D. rim 8.0, base 3.5 cm. Thick dull brown rim band in and out. KSM B I 14 #256.

499. (K.537) Small rim fragment missing. H. 6.5, D. rim 8.5–10.5, base 4.2–5.0 cm. Coated thin dull red-brown throughout. KSM B I 20 #337.

500. (K.538) Most of rim and side and handle missing. H. 6.5, D. rim 10.0, base 5.7 cm. Plain. KSM B I 21 #351.

Crude Cup—Type 4

501. (K.539) PLATE 87 Much of rim and side missing. H. 6.0, D. rim 7.0, base 3.4 cm. Thick brown rim band in and out and on top of handle. KSM B I 20 #330.

502. (K.540) PLATES 19, 87 Rim fragment missing. H. 5.6, D. rim 7.8–8.8, base 4.7 cm. Splashes of red-brown paint in and out. KSM B I 20 #337.

503. (K.541) PLATE 87 Most of rim and side missing. H. 6.8, D. rim 9.0, base 4.7 cm. Crumbling orange fabric. Plain. Interior blackened by burning. KSM B III 8 #417.

504. (K.542) Half of rim, side and handle missing. H. 5.3, D. rim 7.5, base 3.5 cm. Coated red-brown throughout. KSM B I 21 #352.

505. (K.543) Rim fragment and handle missing. H. 5.6, D. rim 8.5, base 5.3 cm. Coated red-brown throughout. KSM B I 20 #330.

506. (K.544) PLATE 87 Rim chipped, handle missing. H. 5.3, D. rim 7.5, base 4.2 cm. Semifine orange/brown fabric. Plain. KSM B I 14 #260.

507. (K.545) PLATE 87 Rim fragment and handle missing. H. 5.7, D. rim 9.0, base 5.0 cm. Plain. KSM B I 20 #342.

508. (K.546) PLATE 87 Rim fragment and handle missing. H. 5.8, D. rim 8.0, base 4.0 cm. Lightly sprayed with brown paint throughout. KSM B I 14 #260.

509. (K.547) PLATE 87 Rim fragment missing. H. 5.0, D. rim 8.7, base 3.8 cm. Coated dark red-brown throughout. KSM B III 8 #417.

510. (K.548) PLATE 87 Half of rim and most of handle missing. H. 5.6, D. rim 9.0, base 4.0 cm. Coated semilustrous dark-brown throughout. KSM B I 20 #339.

511. (K.549) PLATE 87 Most of rim and side and handle missing. H. 5.5, D. rim 9.0, base 3.8 cm. Coated semilustrous dark-brown throughout. KSM B III 8 #417.

512. (K.550) PLATE 87 Rim chipped, handle missing. Distorted during firing. H. 5.3, D. rim 9.0, base 4.5 cm. Coated semilustrous dark-brown throughout. KSM B III 8 #418.

513. (K.551) PLATE 87 Half of rim and handle missing. H. 5.5, D. rim 8.0, base 3.5 cm. Dull red-brown uneven rim bands in and out. KSM B I 20 #345.

514. (K.552) PLATE 87 Rim fragment and handle missing. H. 6.0, D. rim 9.0, base 3.7 cm. Plain. KSM B I 20 #341.

515. (K.553) PLATE 87 Rim fragment and handle missing. H. 5.6, D. rim 7.6, base 3.5 cm. Coated dull dark-brown throughout. KSM B I 20 #348.

516. (K.554) PLATE 87 Rim fragment and handle missing. H. 4.7, D. rim 7.7–8.0, base 4.4 cm. Coated dull red-brown throughout. KSM B I 20 #342.

Crude Cup with spout

517. (K.555) PLATE 87 Half of rim and one handle missing. H. 5.6, D. rim 8.0, base 3.5 cm. Plain. KSM B I 20 #345.

518. (K.1046) PLATE 61 Intact. Not located.

Amphoriskos

519. (K.654) PLATE 88 Rim chipped. H. 6.3, D. rim 3.4, base 3.8 cm. Plain. KSM B I 20 #346.

520. (K.655) PLATE 88 Fragment of side with handle. Plain. KSM B III 8 #417.

Crude Juglet

521. (K.640) PLATES 19, 88 Handle missing. H. 7.4, D. rim 4.0, base 3.7 cm. Interior of rim and one side exterior sprayed dark-brown. KSM B I 14 #257.

522. (K.641) PLATE 88 Handle and most of rim missing. H. 8.0, D. base 3.4 cm. Exterior has traces of dark paint. KSM B I 14 #257.

523. (K.642) PLATE 88 Most of rim and side missing. H. 5.5, D. base 3.9 cm. Coated dull red-brown. KSM B I 20 #346.

524. (K.643) PLATE 88 Most of rim and handle missing. H. 5.0, D. base 5.0 cm. Exterior has dark band below rim and dark-brown circle on front. KSM B I 20 #344.

525. (K.644) PLATE 88 Handle and half of rim missing. H. 4.7, D. rim 3.8 cm. Interior of spout and exterior coated dull red-brown. KSM B I 14 #256.

526. (K.645) PLATE 88 Half of spout and body and handle missing. H. 5.3, D. base 4.5 cm. Interior of rim and exterior coated dark-brown, worn. KSM B I 20 #336.

Crude Jug—Type 1

527. (K.646) PLATES 19, 88 Spout chipped. H. 7.8, D. base 4.0 cm. Plain. KSM B I 20 #335.
528. (K.647) PLATE 88 Spout chipped, handle missing. H. 7.0, D. base 3.0 cm. Plain. Groove in centre of handle. KSM B I 20 #337.

Crude Jug—Type 2

529. (K.648) PLATE 89 Spout and most of handle missing. H. 10.5, D. base 5.0 cm. Exterior has rough incised horizontal lines on shoulder, lower side dipped in dark-brown paint. KSM B I 20 #334.
530. (K.649) PLATE 89 Spout chipped, handle and two body fragments missing. H. 10.7, base 5.5 cm. Lower part dipped in dark-brown paint. KSM B I 20 #336.

FABRIC: FINE SOFT BUFF

Technique: Handmade

Surface: Buff reserved with added white

Large Jar

531. (K.683) PLATE 89 Three non-joining fragments of neck, shoulder and lower side. H. *c.* 27.0 cm. Exterior has three pairs of wide dark-brown bands outlined in white, one on shoulder and two on lower side, and a large dark dot with white dot at centre outlined in white in middle of either side. KSM B I 14 #259, 260.

Surface: Monochrome coated; white decorated

Large Spouted Jar

532. (K.689) PLATE 89 Five non-joining fragments of rim and side including spout. D. rim 15.0 cm. Interior has smears of red paint near rim. Exterior coated semilustrous red-brown and has two horizontal rim bands, a zone of large white open running spirals on shoulder and two wavy lines on lower side. KSM B I 20 #336, 339, 340, 345, 347; KSM B I 21 #353.
533. (K.690) PLATE 89 Three non-joining rim and side fragments. Interior of rim and exterior coated dark-brown. Exterior has horizontal band below rim, row of S-pattern and zone of large white open running spirals on shoulder. KSM B I 20 #341, 346, 348.

Oval mouthed Amphora

534. (K.687) PLATE 89 Two large joining fragments of neck and shoulder with handle stub. H. 13.0 cm. Interior of spout and exterior coated dark-brown. Exterior has horizontal zone of S-pattern and large open running spirals on shoulder. KSM B I 20 #333, 334, 336, 341, 352.

Technique: Wheelmade

Surface: Plain.

Pyxis

535. (K.615) PLATE 90 Three non-joining fragments of rim and side with complete handle. H. 7.5, D. rim 9.0 cm. Plain. KSM B I 14 #258, 262.
536. (K.616) PLATE 90 Fragment of top with complete handle. D. max. 8.0 cm. Traces of red paint on handle. KSM B I 14 #258.
537. (K.617) PLATE 90 Rim and side fragment with handle stub. H. 6.0, D. rim 13.0 cm. Possible traces of light-brown coat on exterior. KSM B I 14 #259. Para: Catling 1982, 53 fig. 116.
538. (K.618) PLATE 90 Fragment of one-quarter of lid with complete handle. D. 11.0 cm. Top lightly smoothed. KSM B I 14 #256.

Surface: Ripple burnished

Ovoid Rhyton

539. (K.674) PLATES 21, 90 Fragment of bottom. H. 6.4, D. max 7.5 cm. Exterior has three horizontal bands at bottom and zone of ripple burnish pattern in semilustrous light-brown. Similar to **1005**. KSM B I 14 #257.

Surface: Buff reserved with added white and orange

Jug

540. (K.676) PLATES 61, 62, 90 Large fragment of shoulder and spout with complete handle. H. 8.0 cm. Exterior has dark band on rim of spout, dark wavy zone at base of neck and shoulder with orange band on flange and white dots above white wavy line on shoulder, dark band outlined in orange with added white S-pattern on body, fingerprints of sloppy potter in dark-brown on handle. KSM B I 19 #326, 328.
541. (K.677) PLATE 90 Four non-joining fragments of shoulder, middle and lower side. Exterior has two wide vertical brown bands, one with added white floral band, other with white arches both outlined in orange, crude horizontal stripes on shoulder and lower side, and group of brown dots on one side and large ?flower on other in middle. KSM B I 20 #330, 345, 347.

Surface: Polychrome decorated 'creamy-bordered'

Jug

542. (K.656) PLATE 90 Handle and tip of spout missing. Restored in plaster. H. 17.2, D. base 3.9 cm. Exterior below neck coated semilustrous black, worn. Neck flange red. Front of spout coated soft creamy-white except for lugs painted orange with red dot on top. Back of spout ?dark but worn. Body has white horizontal bands on shoulder and lower side and white open running spirals with orange dots at centre. Evans 1935, pl. XXIXD. HM 9168.
543. (K.657) PLATE 91 Fragment of spout. Vase restored in plaster based on **542**. Exterior of spout same as **542** but with red floral pattern on front of spout. Evans 1935, pl. XXIXF. HM 9169.
544. (K.658) PLATE 91 Fragment of neck with complete ring at base. Exterior of body coated semilustrous black and has thin white horizontal line on shoulder. Neck coated creamy-white with added red floral pattern like **543** on front. Ring coated orange with added red dots. AM AE 1035.
545. (K.659) PLATE 91 Fragment of neck with ring at base, handle stub and part of rim lug. Exterior as **544** and rim lug coated orange. AM 1938.569.

FABRIC: TEMPERED SOFT BUFF

Technique: Handmade

Surface: *Plain*

Amphoriskos

546. (K.675) PLATE 91 Half of body with one lug and part of vertical handle. H. 11.2 cm. Plain. KSM B I 14 #256. Para: F. 5291.

Technique: Wheelmade

Surface: *Dark on buff; print decorated*

Bowl

547. (K.570) PLATE 91 Two joining rim fragments. D. rim 19.0 cm. Self-slipped pink and printed with odd wavy pattern throughout. KSM B I 19 #324. AM AE 814.

Surface: *'Creamy-bordered'*

Bowl

548. (K.607) PLATES 63, 91 Two non-joining fragments of rim and side. D. rim int. 28.0 cm. Rim cut away to form points or petals which are impressed with concentric circles and coated creamy-white. Rest of vase coated semilustrous dark-brown. Interior has dark-red band with added white spots inside rim and trace of white decoration on side. Exterior white spotted. KSM B I 20 #332.

549. (K.608) PLATE 91 Rim fragment. D. rim int. 20.0 cm. Rim cut away to form petals incised and coated creamy-white. Rest of vase coated dark-brown. Interior has red band at rim with added white spots. Exterior has thick white horizontal bands at rim and lower side and four large white circles. KSM B I 14 #259.

550. (K.1047) Two non-joining rim fragments. Top of rim has moulded plastic argonauts coated creamy-white. Rest of vase coated light red-brown, worn. Evans 1935, 128 fig. 97 pl. XXXD. AM 1938.571. HM 8920.

551. (K.1048) Fragment of moulded flower. Coated creamy-white with red at centre. Evans 1935, 124 fig. 95 pl. XXIXC. Not located.

Surface: *Dark on buff; ripple burnished*

Bowl

552. (K.610) PLATE 91 One-third of rim, most of bowl and base missing. D. rim 27.0 cm. Top of rim rim has three circular bands and radiating ripple burnishing. Interior has featherwave pattern. Underside of rim has ripple burnishing and exterior coated dark-brown, worn. KSM B I 14 #256, 259, 261, 262. SMP 9692.

553. (K.611) PLATES 63, 92 Two large non-joining rim and side fragments. D. rim 33.0 cm. Interior has ripple burnishing on rim, band below rim and featherwave pattern in bowl in orange to red-brown paint. Exterior has ripple burnishing below rim and bowl coated orange. KSM B I 20 #332, 333, 345.

554. (K.612) PLATE 92 Two non-joining fragments of rim and side. D. rim 36.0 cm. Decorated like 553 in light-brown. KSM B I 14 #260, 262.

555. (K.613) PLATE 92 Four non-joining fragments of rim and bowl. D. rim 34.0 cm. Decorated like 553 but in dark-brown and exterior of bowl has featherwave pattern. KSM B I 20 #330; KSM B I 21 #355.

Large Basin

556. (K.701) PLATE 92 Large rim fragment. H. 10.0, D. rim 27.0 cm. Smear of light-brown on rim and interior. Exterior has featherwave pattern at rim and part of ripple burnish zone at middle. KSM B I 20 #333; KSM B III 8 #418.

Large Jar

557. (K.686) PLATE 92 Numerous non-joining fragments of shoulder and side. Exterior has three wide zones of ripple burnishing separated by wide dark horizontal bands outlined in white with traces of white spotting. KSM B I 19 #327; KSM B I 20 #330, 332, 333, 338, 339, 340, 346, 349, 350; KSM sherd collection 'MM III A'.

FABRIC: TEMPERED BUFF

Technique: Handmade

Surface: *Dark on buff*

Large Jar

558. (K.688) PLATE 92 Most of upper side and top missing. H. pres. 31.0 cm. Exterior has irregular drip pattern in dark-brown from shoulder to base. KSM B III 8 #416, 417. SMP 9693.

559. (K.685) PLATE 93 Four non-joining fragments of shoulder and side. H. 18.0 cm. Interior and exterior of neck coated lustrous metallic grey brown. Exterior has zones of horizontal bands on upper and lower side, dark floral motifs on shoulder and crude wavy lines at middle. KSM B I 19 #326; KSM B I 20 #337, 339, 341, 345, 347, 350.

Askos

560. (K.682) PLATE 93 Large fragment of top with complete handle and spout. Exterior has dark band on top of handle and spout, thick band at neck and dark pattern with added white on body. KSM B I 20 #347.

Pyxis

561. (K.698) Fragment of one-quarter of rim and side with complete lug. H. 4.8, D. rim 11.5, base 12.5 cm. Stained red throughout, similar to red used in wall painting. Traces of white plaster on exterior. KSM B I 21 #356.

Technique: Wheelmade

Surface: *Dark on buff*

Footed Bowl

562. (K.600) PLATE 93 Two-thirds of rim missing. H. 11.0, D. rim 21.5, base 9.5 cm. Sprayed with dark-brown paint throughout. KSM B I 14 #261.

Shallow Basin

563. (K.699) PLATE 93 Fragment of one-quarter of rim. H. 4.5, D. rim 23.0 cm. Interior of rim and exterior coated dull red-

brown. Underside plain. KSM B I 20 #347.

564. (K.700) PLATE 93 Fragment of one-third of rim and side. H. 5.5, D. rim 25.5 cm. Interior and exterior side coated red-brown. Underside plain. KSM B I 20 #342.

Surface: Monochrome coated; white or polychrome decorated

Jug

565. (K.662) PLATES 19, 93, 94 Numerous non-joining fragments of body; three in AM, others in KSM. Partially recomposed. H. 15.0, D. base 5.7 cm. Interior has large drip of dark red-brown paint. Exterior coated thin semilustrous dark-brown to black and has open floral pattern in white filled with orange in places. KSM B I 14 #257, 259, 261; KSM B I 19 #322. AM AE 960.

566. (K.664) PLATES 20, 94 Six non-joining fragments of body and upper side with spout and half of handle. H. *c.* 18.0 cm. Interior of spout and exterior coated semilustrous dark-brown and top of spout has white line, with 'eye' on side of spout, thick red band at base of neck, white open running spirals on shoulder above white S-pattern bordered in red and large zone of white wavy lines on lower side. KSM B I 14 #257, 258, 259, 260, 262.

567. (K.663) PLATES 20, 94 Three large body fragments. H. *c.* 18.0 cm. Interior of spout and exterior coated semilustrous black. Exterior has groups of four white horizontal lines on shoulder and lower side and a white wavy line at middle white and red petals with added white dots above and below. KSM B I 14 #256.

568. (K.665) PLATES 19, 62, 94 Five fragments of body with handle stub and neck flange. Exterior coated red-brown and has white foliate bands with added red lines along the middle in arching patterns on side and white horizontal band at flange. KSM B I 19 #322, 323, 325, 326, 327, 328.

569. (K.681) Numerous fragments of body and spout missing. Restored in plaster. H. 42.5, D. base 8.0 cm. Exterior lightly self-slipped and has traces of red curving bands at front and back and thick red band at base. Inscribed 'K.30 N.8'. HM 8834.

Flask

570. (K.666) PLATES 20, 94 Two non-joining fragments of side. D. 19.0 cm. Exterior coated semilustrous dark-brown and has large white flower of eight petals in reserve with smaller pointed petals and orange dot at centre ?on either side and large white S-pattern at edge. KSM B I 20 #334; KSM B I 21 #352.

571. (K.667) PLATES 20, 94 Body fragment. D. 17.0 cm. Exterior coated dull brown and has trace of white flower on side and white foliate band at edge. KSM B I 20 #346.

572. (K.668) PLATE 94 Fragment of top edge with spout, handle and trace of other handle. D. body 12.0 cm. Exterior coated dark-brown and has white line at rim, white band at neck and trace of white circular design on side. KSM B I 21 #355.

'Egg-tray'

573. (K.702) PLATE 95 Fragment of one-quarter of rim with trace of three holes and one stub of foot. D. tray 28.0, holes 4.5–5.0 cm. Coated dark-brown throughout. Top has white band on rim and white circle around central hole. KSM B I 19 #328. Form: Evans 1928, 307 fig. 178.

Bowl

574. (K.599) PLATES 63, 95 Pedestal and many rim and body fragments missing. Partially restored in plaster. H. 6.8, D. rim

19.5 cm. Coated black throughout. Interior has two large open opposing white loop patterns with two spirals and a large red dot in each. Underside has three large circles in white. Evans 1935, 130 pl. XXXB. HM 8916.

575. (K.602) PLATE 95 Much of rim and base missing. H. 4.5, D. rim 27.0 cm. Coated dull red-brown throughout. Top has white band at edge and open running spirals on top of rim. Side of rim has white filled semicircles. Trace of white decoration on underside. KSM B I 20 #332; KSM B I 21 #345, 346.

576. (K.603) PLATE 95 Half of rim and side, base and pedestal missing. H. 4.0, D. rim 29.0 cm. Coated dull brown throughout. Top of rim has white open running spirals, interior of bowl white spotted. KSM B III 8 #418.

577. (K.604) PLATES 63, 95 Rim fragment. D. rim 24.5 cm. Coated semilustrous grey-brown throughout. Interior has white open running spirals on rim and white band below. Exterior has four large white circles on underside. KSM B I 20 #332.

578. (K.605) PLATES 63, 95 Rim fragment. D. rim 26.0 cm. Coated dull brown throughout. Interior has white foliate band bordered in white on top of rim. Exterior has large white circles on underside. KSM B I 20 #333.

579. (K.606) PLATE 95 Large rim fragment. D. rim 30.0 cm. Coated grey-brown throughout. Interior has white foliate band bordered red and white on top of rim. Outer edge of rim has white dots. Exterior has four large white circles and white bands at rim and base of underside. KSM B I 20 #333. Para: F. 5186.

580. (K.609) Rim fragment. D. rim 28.0 cm. Coated dull dark-brown and white spotted throughout. KSM B I 21 #353.

Kalathos

581. (K.697) PLATE 96 Large fragment of rim, side and base with handle stub. H. 8.5, D. rim 24.0, base 16.0 cm. Top of rim and exterior coated dull red-brown. White open running spirals on side. KSM B I 20 #348.

Large Bridge-spouted Jar

582. (K.694) PLATE 96 Ten non-joining fragments of rim and side with part of one handle and spout. D. rim 13.0 cm. Interior sprayed dark-brown. Interior of rim and exterior coated semilustrous dark-brown. Exterior white spotted and top of rim coated white. KSM B I 20 #345; KSM B I 21 #355; KSM B III 8 #418.

Large Jug

583. (K.678) PLATES 61, 62, 96 Five non-joining fragments of spout, shoulder and base with complete handle. D. rim 10.0, base 7.0 cm. Interior of rim and exterior coated dark red-brown. White band on interior of rim. Exterior has white band below rim, orange band at base of neck, three diagonal white strokes on top of handle and large white flower motifs with added orange on front and back of body. KSM B I 19 #325, 328; KSM B I 20 #336, 341.

584. (K.679) PLATES 63, 96 Fragment of rim and shoulder with complete handle. D. rim 9.0 cm. Decoration same as 583 but has white band at base of neck instead of orange. KSM B I 20 #330, 349, 350.

Large Spouted Jar

585. (K.691) PLATE 96 Numerous non-joining fragments of rim, side and base with complete handle. D. rim 15.0, base 8.2 cm. Interior of rim has smear of brown paint. Exterior coated semilustrous dark-brown and has large white foliate band at

middle with rows of white dots with added red dots bordered by red and white lines above and below and thick white horizontal bands on lower side. KSM B I 14 #259; KSM B I 19 #322, 323, 324, 326, 328, 329.

586. (K.692) PLATE 96 Two non-joining fragments of side. H. 22.0 cm. Interior has large drops of brown paint. Exterior coated dark-brown and has large zone of white running spirals in middle bordered by thick horizontal orange bands with added white S-pattern and white foliate bands above and below. KSM B I 14 #256, 259.

FABRIC: FINE RED

Technique: Wheelmade

Surface: Monochrome coated; white decorated

Straight-sided Cup

587. (K.467) PLATES 21, 97 Two non-joining rim fragments. H. 4.8, D. rim 11.0 cm. Surface slipped red throughout and has thin white rim band on interior and pendant white filled semicircles at rim and pair of white wavy lines on side of exterior. KSM B I 20 #330, 339.

588. (K.476) PLATES 21, 97 Rim, side and base fragment. H. 7.0, D. rim 11.0, base 6.5 cm. Coated dark-brown fired black with lustrous metallic sheen on exterior. Exterior has two thick white horizontal bands at base and group of three white pendant semicircles at rim. KSM B III 8 #417.

Rounded Cup

589. (K.414) PLATE 21 Rim fragment. H. 4.0, D. rim 10.0 cm. Coated dull light red-brown throughout. Interior has thin white rim band. Exterior has horizontal band below rim and large closed spirals in white on side. KSM B I 19 #322, 323.

590. (K.409) PLATE 21 Four non-joining fragments of rim and side. H. 7.0, D. rim 13.0 cm. Coated brown throughout. Exterior has thick orange rim band and large white open running spirals on side above white wavy line. KSM B I 19 #323, 326, 329.

FABRIC: COARSE RED

Technique: Wheelmade

Jug

591. (K.680) PLATE 97 Tip of spout and numerous fragments of neck and body missing. Restored in plaster. H. 26.5, D. base 7.8 cm. Exterior slipped red-brown. KSM B III 8 #416, 417. Para: F. 48.

Juglet

592. (K.651) PLATE 97 Handle and two rim fragments missing. H. 3.5, D. rim 4.0, base 6.2 cm. Surface plain. Inscribed 'K.30 N.8'. HM 8935.

593. (K.652) PLATES 64, 97 Most of rim and spout missing. H. 4.5, D. max. 9.0, base 6.5 cm. Surface plain. AM 1938.600.

594. (K.653) Fragment of half of vase with complete handle. D. max. 12.0, base 6.0 cm. Surface plain. KSM B I 20 #348.

Bowl

595. (K.614) PLATE 97 Four non-joining fragments of rim and side, pedestal missing. D. rim 28.0 cm. Coated with lustrous cream slip and decorated with dark-brown feather wave pattern throughout. Evans 1935, 123 fig. 93. KSM B I 19 #329; KSM B I 20 #330, 345, 346, 348. AM 1938.598.

Hand Lamp—Type 2

596. (K.703) PLATE 98 Handle missing, chipped. H. 3.0, D. 10.5, base 5.5 cm. Plain. Spout burnt. KSM B I 19 #329.

597. (K.704) PLATE 98 Handle missing, rim chipped. H. 3.8, D. 10.5, base 6.0 cm. Plain. Spout burnt. String marks on base. KSM B I 20 #334.

FABRIC: SOFT GRITTY BUFF

Technique: Wheelmade

Surface: Monochrome coated

Hand Lamp—Type 2

598. (K.705) PLATE 98 Handle and most of spout missing, rim chipped. H. 3.5, D. 10.0, base 4.5 cm. Spout burnt. KSM B I 20 #345.

599. (K.706) PLATE 98 Half, including handle missing. H. 3.0, D. 10.5, base 5.0 cm. Traces of light-brown paint throughout. KSM B I 21 #352.

600. (K.707) PLATE 98 Half, including handle missing. H. 3.5, D. 11.5, base 7.0 cm. Plain. KSM B I 19 #325.

601. (K.708) PLATE 98 One-third of side, spout and tip of handle missing. H. 3.7, D. 10.0, base 6.2 cm. Traces of red-brown throughout. KSM B I 20 #337.

Hand Lamp

602. (K.709) PLATE 98 Half of side, spout and tip of handle missing. H. 4.3, D. 10.0, base 5.0 cm. Coated dark red-brown throughout. Traces of burning on interior. KSM B I 20 #330.

603. (K.710) PLATE 98 Most of side and handle missing. H. 3.5, D. base 5.0 cm. Coated thin matt black throughout. KSM B I 20 #330.

FABRIC: COARSE RED/BROWN

Hand Lamp

604. (K.711) PLATE 98 Rim and spout fragment. Lightly burnished throughout. KSM B I 14 #260.

FABRIC: FINE ORANGE

Technique: Wheelmade

Footed Goblet

605. (K.431) PLATES 21, 63, 99 Most of rim missing, restored in plaster. H. 14.0, D. rim 9.5, base 4.7 cm. Exterior coated thick lustrous red-brown and burnished. KSM B I 20 #330. SMP 9695.

FABRIC: CYCLADIC WHITE

?Jug

606. (K.1049) PLATE 99 Two non-joining fragments of shoulder. Fine soft light-buff fabric. Exterior has horizontal buff reserved zones with interlocking S-pattern and vertical strokes and thick band of deep burnished red outlined in black. KSM B I 20 #330.

607. (K.1050) PLATE 99 Shoulder fragment. Hard gritty white fabric. Exterior has dot rosette in matt black paint on plain surface. KSM B I 20 #330.

608. (K.1051) PLATE 99 Shoulder fragment. Hard gritty white fabric. Exterior has angular pattern filled with hatching in dark-brown paint on plain surface. KSM B I 20 #330.

GROUP F: ROYAL POTTERY STORES, THE SOUTH-WEST ROOM

FABRIC: FINE BUFF

Technique: Handmade

Surface: Monochrome coated; polychrome decorated

Conical Goblet—Type 1

609. (K.719) PLATES 22, 102 Base and most of rim missing. H. 6.0, D. rim 6.0 cm. Coated semilustrous grey-brown throughout, except perhaps foot left plain. Exterior has pairs of red and white lines spiralling up side from foot to rim. KSM L III 1 #998, 1197.

610. (K.720) PLATE 102 Fragment of lower side and foot. H. 5.7, D. base 5.0 cm. Foot plain. Top coated semilustrous dark-brown in and out. Exterior has pairs of orange and white lines spiralling up side from base. KSM M III 2 #1197.

Straight-sided Cup—Type 2

611. (K.729) PLATE 102 Handle and over half of rim and side missing. Restored. H. 4.5, D. rim 8.0, base 5.0 cm. Coated brown throughout. Exterior has three white stars in semicircles with red dots at the centre. KSM L III 1 #998.

612. (K.730) PLATE 102 Fragment of rim, side and base. H. 4.3, D. rim 8.0, base 6.0 cm. Coated semilustrous dark grey-brown throughout. Exterior has thick horizontal orange band outlined in white at middle and rows of white dots at rim and base. KSM L III 1 #998.

Tall-rimmed Angular Cup—Type 1

613. (K.733) PLATES 22, 102 Two non-joining fragments of rim and side with handle stub. H. 4.7, D. rim 6.5 cm. Coated semilustrous dark-brown throughout. Exterior has pairs of diagonal lines of barbotine framed by pairs of orange and white lines on either side. KSM M III 2 #1197.

Squat Jar

614. (K.6) PLATES 22, 101 Most of rim, most of lower side and base missing. Also, perhaps, spout and handles, if such existed. H. 15.0, D. rim 10.0, base c. 8.5 cm. Exterior coated dull brown and has pairs of horizontal white lines below rim and above base and four large dot rosettes of three large orange dots at centre with three tiny white dot groups in circles of tiny white dots contained within closed white spirals alternating with four diagonal panels each with a row of tiny white dots with groups of three or four alternating orange and white dots on either side in a white frame. Mackenzie 1902 PB (2), 70 K.6; Åberg 1933, 148 fig. 262. HM 2675.

Technique: Wheelmade; 'Egg-shell ware'

Surface: Polychrome decorated

Straight-sided Cup—?Type 5

615. (K.12) PLATES 22, 100 Numerous rim and side fragments with handle stub at rim. D. rim 9.0; H. pres. 4.0 cm. Coated black throughout. Thin white horizontal band at interior. Exterior has white filled semicircles at rim from which hang white pendant lines. Inscribed 'K.02 12'. Mackenzie 1902 PB (2), 72, K12. HM 5186.

Rounded Cup—Type 4

616. (K.18) PLATE 103 All but one rim fragment, much of upper side and handle missing. Restored in plaster. H. 7.4, D. rim 12.0, base 4.4 cm. Coated dark-brown throughout. Stamped row of circles on side white filled and white and red pointed pattern framing them, stamped white filled arcades on lower side in white flower petal pattern starting in centre of base which has white dot with added red dot in centre. Incorrectly restored. Inscribed 'NEKA K.02 18'. Mackenzie 1902 PB (2), 67, 73; Evans 1921, 241 fig. 181. KSM M III 2a #1198. HM 2693.

617. (K.19) PLATE 103 Handle, much of rim and many side fragments missing. Restored in plaster. H. 7.0, D. rim 13.0, base 5.5 cm. Interior has even spray of brown paint on sides and thick brown rim band outlined in white. Exterior coated semilustrous metallic dark-brown and has white flowers with petals in reserve on either side and on base within white spiral pattern with added red vertical lines, and a red line and row of white dashes below rim. Mackenzie 1902 PB (2), 73; Mackenzie 1903, pl. V.1; Evans 1921, 241 pl. IIa. HM 2690.

Rounded Cup—Type 3

618. (K.20) PLATE 103 Several rim and side fragments and most of base missing. Restored in plaster. H. 8.0, D. rim 12.5, base 4.4 cm. Interior has even spray of brown paint on sides and thick brown rim band outlined in white. Exterior coated semilustrous metallic dark-brown and has white zig-zag pattern at rim, seven white flowers with red dots at their centres, a row of white dashes, a red line and four white lines on lower side. Mackenzie 1903, pl. V.2; Evans 1921, 241 pl. IIc. KSM M III 2 #1194. HM 2692.

619. (K.21) PLATE 103 Many rim and body fragments and base missing. Restored in plaster. H. 8.4, D. rim 13.5, base 4.5 cm. Coated semilustrous dark-brown throughout. Interior has traces of red paint at rim. Exterior has thick white horizontal bands with added red interlocking S-pattern at rim, middle and base and vertical white lines in between. Mackenzie 1903, pl. V.3; Evans 1921, 241 pl. IIb. KSM L III 1 #996. HM 2691.

620. (K.37) PLATES 22, 103 Numerous non-joining fragments of rim, side and base with handle in KSM; recomposed body in Liverpool. H. 8.0, D. rim 12.0, base 4.5 cm. Coated lustrous black throughout. White vertical slashes at interior of rim. Exterior has horizontal red lines at rim and base and three rows

of red dots interconnected by white curving lines. Mee and Doole 1993, # 284. KSM L III 1 #996; KSM M III 2 #1197. Liverpool 55.66.74.

621. (K.17) PLATES 100, 103 Numerous non-joining fragments of rim and side with handle in KSM; AM largely restored in plaster. H. 8.6, D. rim 12.0 cm. Evenly sprayed brown throughout. Interior of rim has dark-brown band outlined in white. Exterior has dark-brown stone veining pattern outlined in white. Mackenzie 1902 PB (2), 73; Evans 1921, fig. 178. KSM M III 2 #1194, 1197, 1198. AM AE 947.

622. (K.9) PLATES 100, 104 Numerous non-joining fragments of rim, side and base with complete handle. H. 7.0, D. rim 9.0, base 4.6 cm. Coated thin semilustrous dark-brown throughout. Interior has thin white rim band. Exterior has white filled semicircles and horizontal line at rim, white pairs of linked closed spirals and ?zweipass design in orange circle on side, two white lines at base and underside has white circle at edge with double crosses in centre and red dots where white lines cross. Mackenzie 1902 PB (2), 70 K.9; Åberg 1933, 152 fig. 270. KSM L III 1 #996, 998; KSM M III 2 #1194, 1197. AM AE 1204.0. HM uncatalogued.

623. (K.39) PLATE 104 Six non-joining rim and base fragments. Interior sprayed with red-brown and white paint. Exterior coated semilustrous red-brown and has ?floral designs in white with orange filling. KSM L III 1 #997; KSM M III 2 #1197.

Technique: Wheelmade

Surface: Dark on buff; printed

Straight-sided Cup—Type 6

624. (K.1) PLATE 104 Most of rim missing. Restored in plaster. H. 8.7, D. rim 12.0, base 7.3 cm. Self-slipped. Pattern of brown crescents printed throughout including base and handle top. Inscribed 'K 02 NEKA' and 'Kam. dep. NE Shoot'. Mackenzie 1902 PB (2), 68 K.1; Mackenzie 1903, 176 fig. 3.1. HM 2700.

625. (K.2) PLATE 104 Most of rim and side missing. Restored in plaster. H. 8.4, D. rim 11.8, base 6.8 cm. Self-slipped. Decorated as 624. Inscribed 'K.02 NEKA' and 'Kam dep' 'NE Shoot'. Mackenzie 1902 PB (2), 68 K.2; Mackenzie 1903, 176 fig. 3.2; Zervos 1956, fig. 375b. HM 2701.

626. (K.45) PLATE 104 Rim, handle and much of side missing. H. 7.4, D. base 6.0 cm. Self-slipped. Decoration as 624. KSM L III 1 #998; KSM L III 16 #1077.

627. (K.3) Recomposed base and lower side. D. base 8.2 cm. Interior coated black and has white flecks. Exterior has thick dark-brown bands at rim and base with two rows of added white printed crescents leaving zone in reserve at middle which has ?two rows of dark printed crescents, base plain with seven rows of dark printed crescents. Similar to 297. Inscribed 'Kam dep NE Shoot'. Mackenzie 1902 PB (2), 68-9; Mackenzie 1903, 176 fig. 3.3; Evans 1921, 244 fig. 184a. AM AE 1061.3. HM 2702.

Surface: Monochrome coated; white printed

Straight-sided Cup—Type 6

628. (K.4) PLATE 104 Most of rim and upper side missing. Restored in plaster. H. 8.6, D. rim 12.0, base 7.0 cm. Coated semilustrous dark-brown throughout. Exterior has five rows of white circular sponge prints, also occur on handle and underside. Inscribed 'K.02 NEKA'. Mackenzie 1902 PB (2), 69

K.4; Mackenzie 1903, 176 fig. 3.4; Evans 1921, 244 fig. 184b. KSM M III 2 #1198. HM 2699.

629. (K.8) Two non-joining fragments of rim and base. Coated black throughout. Exterior has large white dots printed or painted on side. Similar to 628. Inscribed 'NE Shoot' and 'K8'. Mackenzie 1902 PB (2), 71 K.8. HM 2703; HM 5188.

630. (K.13) PLATE 100 Three non-joining fragments of rim and base. D. base 5.8 cm. Interior has dark spray and uneven rim band. Exterior coated dark-brown and has large white dots like 628. Inscribed 'K. d. NE Shoot', 'K 02 13'. Mackenzie 1902 PB (2), 71. HM 5188.

Rounded Cup—Type 3

631. (K.712) PLATE 105 Six non-joining fragments of rim, side and base. H. 7.0, D. rim 13.0, base 5.0 cm. Coated semilustrous dark-brown throughout. Interior sprayed with white dots. Exterior has printed white pattern of irregular shapes. KSM L III 1 #998; KSM M III 2 #1197.

Bridge-spouted Jar

632. (K.744) PLATE 105 Two ?joining fragments of lower side. Exterior coated dark-brown and has white printed decoration with forms similar to those on 631. Forsdyke 1925, 88 fig. 112. KSM L III 1 #996; KSM M III 2 #1197. BM A 527. Para: F. 2175.

Surface: Monochrome coated; white decorated

Tumbler—Type 3

633. (K.716) PLATE 105 Two non-joining fragments of rim and upper side. D. rim 8.0 cm. Coated semilustrous grey-brown throughout. Interior has thin white band at rim. Exterior has vertical lines. KSM L III 1 #996, 1197.

634. (K.717) PLATE 105 Two non-joining fragments of rim and base. D. rim 6.0, base 2.1 cm. Interior has wide uneven brown band with thin added white line at rim. Exterior coated dull dark-brown and has vertical lines from rim to base. KSM L III 1 #996, 998.

635. (K.718) PLATE 105 Three non-joining fragments of rim and base with complete handle. H. 3.6, D. rim 5.0, base 2.2 cm. Coated semilustrous dark-brown throughout. Exterior has vertical lines from rim to base. Thin white strokes on top of handle. KSM L III 1 #998.

Straight-sided Cup—Type 6

636. (K.721) PLATE 105 Most of rim and side missing. H. 8.4, D. rim 13.0, base 7.3 cm. Coated semilustrous black throughout. Interior has rim band. Exterior has thick bands at rim and base and group of three in middle of side. KSM L III 1 #998; KSM M III 2 #1197, 1198.

Straight-sided Cup

637. (K.725) PLATES 22, 105 Rim fragment. D. rim 12.0 cm. Interior has wide brown band at rim. Exterior coated semilustrous grey-brown and has large spiral on side. KSM M III 2 #1197.

Straight-sided Cup—Type 6

638. (K.726) PLATE 106 Fragment of base and lower side. H. 4.1, D. base 6.2 cm. Interior sprayed with brown paint. Exterior coated dark-brown and has four evenly spaced horizontal bands of filled semicircles alternating pendant and upward and cross on underside. KSM L III 1 #998.

639. (K.727) PLATES 22, 106 Handle and most of rim missing. H. 9.0, D. rim 11.0, base 6.3 cm. Treated like **638**. KSM #1853.

Straight-sided Cup

640. (K.728) PLATE 106 Fragment of base and lower side. H. 6.5, D. base 8.8 cm. Interior sprayed with brown paint. Exterior coated semilustrous dark-brown and has pair of horizontal bands at base, trace of large circular or ovoid discs on side and double white cross in circle on underside. KSM L III 1 #998; KSM M III 2 #1197; KSM L III 15 #1071.

641. (K.723) PLATE 106 Two non-joining rim and side fragments. H. 6.0, D. rim 8.0 cm. Coated semilustrous dark-brown throughout. Exterior has two horizontal bands on lower side and three rows of painted dots on upper side. KSM L III 1 #996; KSM M III 2 #1197.

Rounded Cup—Type 4

642. (K.38) PLATE 106 Several non-joining fragments of rim, side and base. H. *c.* 7.5, D. rim *c.* 11.0, base 4.5 cm. Interior sprayed black with drips in places. Exterior coated lustrous black and has thin horizontal line at rim and base and pendant scale pattern on side. KSM L III 1 #996, 998; KSM M III 2 #1197. HM 5186.

Rounded Cup—Type 3

643. (K.42) PLATE 22 Handle, base and much of rim and side missing. H. 7.5, D. rim 12.0 cm. Interior sprayed and has dark-brown band at rim. Exterior coated semilustrous dark-brown and has at least two large dots in circles in middle of side. KSM L III 1 #996; KSM M III 2 #1194, 1197.

644. (K.43) Large fragment of rim, side and base with handle. H. 8.0, D. rim 14.0, base 4.5 cm. Coated semilustrous dark-brown throughout. Interior has thin rim band. Exterior has horizontal bands at rim and base and two at middle of side. Trace of curved design on lower side. KSM L III 1 #998; KSM M III 2 #1197.

645. (K.713) PLATE 106 Four non-joining fragments of rim and lower side with handle stub at rim. D. rim 13.0 cm. Interior has thick uneven rim band and drips of brown paint. Exterior coated semilustrous metallic dark grey-brown and has vertical lines from rim to base. KSM L III 1 #996; KSM M III 2 #1197.

646. (K.714) PLATE 107 Four non-joining fragments of rim and side. D. rim 12.0 cm. Coated semilustrous dark-brown and sprayed with white paint throughout. KSM L III 1 #996.

Pedestalled Bowl

647. (K.736) PLATES 22, 107 Several non-joined rim and side fragments. H. 7.0, D. rim 21.0, base 5.0 cm. Coated semilustrous dark-brown throughout. Interior has horizontal bands at base and middle and painted dots on upper side. Exterior has four evenly spaced horizontal bands on lower side and careful white spotted decoration below rim. Evans 1921, fig. 127f. KSM L III 1 #996. AM AE 942. HM 5186, 5189. SMP 9712. Para: Pelon 1982 fig. 8.

Pyxis—Type 1

648. (K.739) PLATE 107 Three non-joining rim, side and base fragments. H. 6.5, D. rim 10.0, base 5.5 cm. Interior has thick uneven rim band and drips of brown paint. Exterior coated semilustrous dark-brown and has wide horizontal band at middle of side. KSM M III 2 #1197.

649. (K.740) PLATE 107 Three non-joining rim fragments. D. rim

10.0 cm. Interior has uneven brown rim band and white on top of rim. Exterior coated semilustrous dark-brown and has traces of four ?spirals on side. KSM L III 16 #1077; KSM M III 2 #1197.

Surface: Monochrome coated; polychrome decorated

Tumbler—Type 3

650. (K.16) PLATE 107 Three large rim and body fragments missing. Restored. H. 6.5, D. rim 6.0, base 2.2 cm. Coated semilustrous black throughout. Exterior has open white crisscross pattern with framing red dots each with five white crosses attached on side, and white star with red dot at centre on underside. Inscribed 'K.02 NEKA'. Similar to **807**. Mackenzie 1902 PB (2), 72; Mackenzie 1903, 177 pl. VI.1; Betancourt 1985a, pl. 8H. HM 2684.

Conical Goblet—Type 3

651. (K.14) PLATES 22, 100, 108 Two fragments of rim and side restored in plaster, foot missing. H. pres. 8.0, rest. 13.0; D. rim 9.2 cm. Interior sprayed brown and white. Exterior coated dark-brown and has two horizontal zones of continuous antithetic J-spirals (abstract ivy-leaves) framed in red and white horizontal lines. Inscribed 'K.02 NEKA 14'. Mackenzie 1902 PB (2), 72; Zervos 1956, fig. 369 right. HM 2696.

652. (K.15) PLATE 108 Base, one-quarter of rim and several side fragments missing. Restored in plaster. H. 10.0, D. rim 9.0 cm. Interior sprayed red, brown and white and has thick brown rim band. Exterior coated dark-brown and has seven evenly spaced horizontal red lines and spaces between decorated with alternating rows of white dots and white zig-zag pattern with tiny white crosses with added red dots at cross. Inscribed 'K.02 NEKA'. Mackenzie 1902 PB (2), 72; Mackenzie 1903, 177 pl. VI.2. HM 2695.

Straight-sided Cup—Type 5

653. (K.722) PLATES 23, 107 Non-joining fragments of rim and side and part of handle. H. 5.8, D. rim 12.0, base 11.0 cm. Coated dark-brown throughout. Exterior has thick orange bands with added white crescents at rim and base and white design on side. KSM L III 1 #996, 998; KSM M III 2 #1197.

Straight-sided Cup—Type 6

654. (K.46) PLATES 23, 108 Two non-joining fragments of base and lower side. H. 7.4, D. base 6.4 cm. Coated red-brown throughout. Exterior has orange spiral design repeated from rim and base outlined in white. KSM L III 1 #996, 998; KSM M III 2 #1197.

Straight-sided Cup—?Type

655. (K.724) PLATES 23, 108 Rim fragment. H. 6.2, D. rim 12.0 cm. Coated grey-brown throughout. Exterior has dot rosette of orange dot surrounded by tiny white dots encircled in white and ?interconnected with another rosette. KSM M III 2 #1197.

Tall-rimmed Angular Cup—Type 4

656. (K.732) PLATES 23, 108 Two large rim and side fragments and top of handle missing. Restored in plaster. H. 6.5, D. rim 9.0, base 3.5 cm. Coated semilustrous dark-brown throughout. Exterior has red horizontal band below rim and white wavy line above, thick white vertical bands with added red lines connected by diagonal white lines on side and white band above base. KSM L III 1 #996; KSM L III 16 #1075.

Tall-rimmed Angular Cup—Type 6

657. (K.734) PLATES 23, 108 Most of rim and side missing, non-joining handle fragment. H. 7.1, D. rim 14.0, base 4.4 cm. Coated semilustrous dark-brown throughout. Interior has white rim band and well-formed dot in centre of base. Exterior has large white S-spiral pattern with traces of added red or orange and white and orange petals. KSM L III 1 #996, 998; KSM M III 2 #1197.

658. (K.735) PLATES 23, 100, 109 Fragment of base and lower side. ?Rim fragment in PLATE 100. H. 4.7, D. base 3.9 cm. Coated semilustrous dark-brown throughout. Exterior has white pendant patterns and part of orange loop. KSM L III 1 #998; KSM M III 2 #1197. SMP 9697.

Angular Cup with offset rim

659. (K.731) PLATE 23 Four non-joining fragments of rim, side and base. H. 6.8, D. rim 15.0, base 4.5 cm. Coated semilustrous grey-brown throughout. Exterior has thick white band outlined in orange below rim and white and orange bands at base. KSM L III 1 #996, 998. HM 5186, 5188. SMP 9698.

Miniature Rounded Cup

660. (K.715) PLATE 109 Two non-joining fragments of rim and lower side. D. rim 8.0 cm. Interior sprayed brown and white and has thick brown rim band. Exterior coated brown and has thick orange zig-zag pattern outlined in white with red dots at the top and tiny white crosses in open areas near base. KSM M III 2 #1194.

Rounded Cup—Type 4

661. (K.41) PLATES 23, 109 Five non-joining fragments in KSM, three in HM, of rim, side and base with most of handle. H. 8.0, D. rim 12.5, base 4.5 cm. Coated semilustrous dark-brown throughout. Exterior has thick vertical orange bands with pendant white festoons between them on side, double white cross in circle on underside. KSM L III 1 #996, 998; KSM M III 2 #1197. HM 5186. SMP 9696.

Shallow Angular Bowl—Type 2

662. (K.737) PLATES 23, 109 Two non-joining fragments of rim with complete handle. H. 3.2, D. rim *c.* 14.0 cm. Coated semilustrous grey-brown throughout. Interior has dot rosette with orange dot at centre, surrounded by tiny white then large orange then tiny white dots in a field of large white dots. Exterior has white pendant arches from rim and white strokes on handle. KSM M III 2 #1197.

Angular Spouted Cup

663. (K.742) PLATE 109 Two non-joining fragments of side. Coated semilustrous dark-brown to black throughout. Exterior has pairs of orange dots alternating with groups of five diagonal white slashes following horizontal ridges. KSM L III 1 #996; KSM Sherd Collection 'MM II A'. Para: F. 2172.

Pyxis Lid

664. (K.741) PLATE 107 Fragment of one-quarter of lid. D. *c.* 9.0 cm. Coated brown throughout. Top has white cross outlined in orange across double white cross. KSM M III 2 #1197.

Rounded Bridge-spouted Jar—Type 4

665. (K.743) PLATE 109 Four non-joining fragments of rim and side. D. rim 9.0 cm. Interior has dark smear at rim and drops of paint throughout. Exterior coated semilustrous dark grey-brown and has white horizontal lines and large white with added red dots in between. KSM L III 1 #996; KSM M III 2 #1197.

FABRIC: CYCLADIC

Closed Jar

666. (K.1052) PLATE 110 Fragment of base. D. base 7.0 cm. Soft orange buff fabric with numerous inclusions. Handmade. Exterior has cross-hatched lozenges and pairs of vertical lines in dull orange paint. Mackenzie suggested a Melian origin. Mackenzie 1902 PB (2), 66. KSM L III 1 #998.

FABRIC: FINE SOFT BUFF

667. (K.5) PLATES 23, 110 Few small rim and side fragments missing, restored in plaster. Spout, part of handle and rim and base fragments in KSM. H. 12.5, D. rim 11.0, base 9.5 cm. Wheelmade. Interior has thin dark rim band. Exterior has rim band and arched lines in dull dark-brown paint outlined in white. Inscribed 'NEKA K.02. K5.' Mackenzie 1902 PB (2), 69–70; Zervos 1956, fig. 377. KSM L III 1 #996. HM 2685. SMP 9699.

FABRIC: SEMIFINE BUFF

Jug with Trefoil Spout

668. (K.745) PLATES 24, 110 Four non-joining fragments of upper part of handle, neck and upper and middle side. H. 15.0, D. max. 12.0 cm. Wheelmade. Interior of spout and exterior coated semilustrous dark-brown. Exterior has thick white bands outlined in red at base of neck and middle of side. KSM L III 1 #996; KSM L III 16 #1075.

FABRIC: FINE RED

Rounded Cup

669. (K.35) PLATE 110 Numerous fragments of rim and side missing, few rim fragments in KSM. Restored in plaster. H. 8.3–9.0, D. rim 12.5, base *c.* 3.5 cm. Wheelmade, surface lightly burnished lustrous red-brown. Interior has large white flower in centre of base. Exterior has four large white flowers on side and white diagonal strokes at rim. KSM M III 2 #1197. AM 1938.562.

FABRIC: TEMPERED BUFF

Offering Table

670. (K.738) PLATE 110 Rim fragment. D. rim 23.5 cm. Tempered buff fabric, handmade. Coated semilustrous metallic black throughout. Underside has large white open running spirals with orange loop. Top of rim has white wavy line. Interior has

large white floral pattern with red dot. KSM L III 1 #996; KSM M III 2 #1197.

GROUP G: ROYAL POTTERY STORES, THE AREA OF THE LIME KILN

FABRIC: FINE BUFF

Technique: Handmade—Pared Ware

Rounded Goblet—Type 1

671. (K.748) PLATE 111 Rim chipped. H. 6.0, D. rim 7.8, base 4.8 cm. Trace of paring on lower side. Thin red-brown paint throughout, badly worn. KSM L III 16 #1072.

Technique: Handmade

Amphora

672. (K.815) PLATE 111 Intact. H. 7.4, D. rim 3.7, base 4.0 cm. Plain. Inscribed 'NE Shoot'. Mackenzie 1902 PB (2), 45. KSM L III 16 #1074.

Tumbler—Type 1

673. (K.746) PLATE 111 Rim chipped. H. 2.6, D. rim 3.7, base 1.7 cm. Coated dark-brown throughout. Exterior has spray of white paint on one side. KSM L III 16 #1074.

Surface: Monochrome coated; polychrome decorated

Straight-sided Cup—Type 2

674. (K.760) PLATE 102 Intact. H. 4.7, D. rim 7.7, base 5.7 cm. Coated semilustrous dark grey-brown throughout. Exterior has two groups of three vertical orange lines and large white diagonal double cross with white dot rosettes either side. KSM L III 16 #1074. SMP 9700.

675. (K.761) PLATE 102 Rim, side and base fragment. H. 4.5, D. rim 8.0, base 5.0 cm. Coated semilustrous dark-brown throughout. Exterior has thick horizontal orange band at middle with three added white zig-zags and white semicircles at rim and base. KSM L III 16 #1075.

Technique: Wheelmade

Surface: Plain

Amphora

676. (K.816) PLATE 111 Rim chipped. H. 11.3, D. rim 5.4, base 5.4 cm. Plain with curious false handles on shoulder. String-marks on base. Inscribed 'NE Shoot'. Mackenzie 1902 PB (2), 45. KSM L III 16 #1074. SMP 9701.

Surface: Monochrome coated

Short-rimmed Angular Cup—Type 2

677. (K.771) PLATE 112 Rim fragment missing. H. 7.0, D. rim 10.5, base 4.5 cm. Coated dull red-brown all over except handle. Inscribed 'E of L kiln. NE Sh'. KSM L III 16 #1074. SMP 9702.

678. (K.772) PLATE 112 Intact. H. 7.1, D. rim 12.0, base 4.7 cm. Coated semilustrous dark-brown throughout. Inscribed 'NE Sh'. KSM L III 16 #1074. SMP 9703.

679. (K.773) PLATE 112 Intact. H. 6.6, D. rim 11.5, base 4.2 cm. Coated semilustrous dark-brown throughout. Inscribed 'Sh'. KSM LIII 16 #1074. SMP 9704.

680. (K.774) PLATE 112 Complete, recomposed. H. 6.2, D. rim 11.5, base 4.5 cm. Coated semilustrous dark-brown throughout. Inscribed 'NE Sh'. KSM L III 16 #1074. SMP 9705.

681. (K.775) PLATE 112 Handle and half of rim missing. H. 6.7, D. rim 12.5, base 4.5 cm. Coated thin dull brown throughout. KSM L III 16 #1074.

Surface: Monochrome coated; white decorated

Rounded Goblet—Type 2

682. (K.749) PLATE 111 Large rim fragment missing. H. 7.4, D. rim 7.5, base 4.5 cm. Foot plain with drips of dark-brown paint from upper side coated in and out. Exterior has thick white band on side. KSM L III 16 #1077.

Pyxis—Type 3

683. (K.806) PLATE 112 Two side fragments missing, restored in plaster. H. 6.3, D. rim 9.5, base 4.0 cm. Interior has dark-brown smear at rim. Exterior coated semilustrous black and has white band at rim and lower side, and white strokes on lugs. Inscribed 'NE'. Mackenzie 1902 PB (2), 45. KSM L III 16 #1074. SMP 9706.

Pyxis Lid ?

684. (K.807) PLATE 112 Lid. Tip of handle missing. D. 8.8 cm. Coated semilustrous black throughout. Top has white horizontal band at handle. Inscribed 'NE Sh'. Probably belongs with 683. KSM L III 16 #1074.

Jug with Horizontal Spout—Type 1

685. (K.810) PLATE 112 Most of spout and handle missing. Boss at handle attachment inside rim. H. 9.2, D. rim 4.0, base 3.8 cm. Interior of rim and exterior coated metallic black. Inscribed 'NE Sh'. KSM L III 16 #1074.

686. (K.811) PLATES 24, 112 Rim chipped. H. 10.0, D. rim 3.5, base 2.9 cm. Interior of rim and exterior coated brown and sprayed with white paint on one side. Inscribed 'NE Sh'. KSM L III 16 #1074.

Jug with Cut-away Spout—Type 4

687. (K.814) PLATE 113 Spout chipped, one handle missing. H. 14.2, D. base 3.5 cm. Exterior coated dark-brown and has three white horizontal bands at middle of side. Stringmarks on base. KSM L III 16 #1072. SMP 9707.

Rounded Bridge-spouted Jar—Type 4

688. (K.817) PLATE 113 Fragment of base and side. D. base 6.4 cm. Exterior coated semilustrous dark-brown to black and has part of large white six-sided star with dot at centre on side. KSM L III 16 #1075.

Technique: Wheelmade—cone thrown

Crude Goblet

689. (K.751) PLATE 113 Foot chipped. H. 4.7, D. rim 9.0, base 4.5

cm. Plain. KSM L III 16 #1077.

690. (K.752) PLATE 113 Rim chipped. H. 4.0, D. rim 8.7, base 4.3 cm. Plain. KSM L III 16 #1077.

691. (K.753) PLATE 113 Base chipped. H. 4.7, D. rim 8.0, base 4.0 cm. Plain. Inscribed 'NE Sh'. KSM L III 16 #1074.

692. (K.754) PLATE 113 Rim chipped. H. 5.0, D. rim 8.5, base 4.0 cm. Plain. Inscribed 'Sh'. KSM L III 16 #1074.

693. (K.755) PLATE 113 Rim and base chipped. H. 5.2, D. rim 8.2, base 4.0 cm. Plain. Inscribed 'NE Sh'. KSM L III 16 #1074.

694. (K.756) PLATES 24, 113 Base chipped. H. 5.3, D. rim 8.5, base 4.5 cm. Plain. Inscribed 'NE Sh'. KSM L III 16 #1074.

695. (K.757) PLATE 113 Base chipped. H. 5.2, D. rim 8.5, base 4.8 cm. Plain. Inscribed 'NE Sh'. KSM L III 16 #1074.

696. (K.758) PLATE 113 Intact. H. 5.3, D. rim 9.5, base 5.0 cm. Plain. Inscribed 'NE Sh'. KSM L III 16 #1074.

697. (K.759) PLATE 113 Rim chipped. H. 5.3, D. rim 8.7, base 4.5 cm. Plain. Inscribed 'NE Sh'. KSM L III 16 #1074.

698. (K.750) PLATE 111 Intact. H. 5.0, D. rim 8.2, base 4.0 cm. Coated dull dark-brown throughout, mottled in places. Inscribed 'NE Sh'. KSM L III 16 #1074.

Crude Cup—Type 1

699. (K.762) PLATE 113 Rim chipped. H. 6.2, D. rim 8.5, base 3.7 cm. Coated semilustrous dark-brown throughout, one side mottled. Inscribed 'NE Sh'. KSM L III 16 #1074.

700. (K.763) PLATE 113 Rim chipped. H. 6.0, D. rim 9.0, base 4.9 cm. Coated thin dull red-brown throughout. Inscribed 'NE Sh'. KSM L III 16 #1074.

Crude Cup—Type 2

701. (K.764) PLATES 24, 114 Intact. H. 6.0, D. rim 8.5, base 4.4 cm. Coated dull red-brown throughout. KSM L III 16 #1074.

702. (K.765) PLATE 114 Base chipped. H. 6.0, D. rim 9.0, base 5.0 cm. Coated dull red-brown throughout. Inscribed 'NE Sh'. KSM L III 16 #1074.

703. (K.766) PLATE 114 Rim chipped. H. 6.0, D. rim 9.0, base 4.8 cm. Coated dull light-brown throughout. Inscribed 'NE Sh'. KSM L III 16 #1074.

704. (K.767) PLATE 114 Rim chipped. H. 6.0, D. rim 9.0, base 4.7 cm. Coated semilustrous dark-brown except on part of handle. Inscribed 'NE Sh'. KSM L III 16 #1074.

705. (K.768) PLATE 114 Rim chipped. H. 6.6, D. rim 9.0, base 4.7 cm. Coated dull dark-brown throughout. Inscribed 'NE Sh'. KSM L III 16 #1074.

706. (K.769) PLATE 114 Rim chipped. H. 5.8, D. rim 9.0, base 4.5 cm. Coated dull dark-brown and mottled throughout. Inscribed 'NE Sh'. KSM L III 16 #1074.

707. (K.770) PLATE 114 Intact. H. 5.5, D. rim 8.5, base 4.5 cm. Coated dull red-brown throughout. Inscribed 'NE Sh'. KSM L III 16 #1074.

Crude Bowl—Type 2

708. (K.776) PLATE 114 Rim chipped. H. 2.3, D. rim 11.0, base 5.5 cm. Coated dull red-brown throughout. KSM L III 16 #1077.

709. (K.777) PLATE 114 Rim chipped. H. 2.8, D. rim 11.0, base 5.3 cm. Coated dull brown throughout. KSM L III 16 #1077.

710. (K.778) PLATE 114 Rim chipped. H. 2.8, D. rim 11.5, base 5.8 cm. Coated dull brown throughout. KSM L III 16 #1077.

711. (K.779) PLATE 114 Rim chipped. H. 3.2, D. rim 11.5, base 4.6 cm. Coated dull brown throughout. Inscribed 'NE Sh'. KSM L III 16 #1074.

712. (K.780) PLATE 114 Intact. H. 3.0, D. rim 11.5, base 6.0 cm. Coated semilustrous brown all over except one part of rim

where held during painting. Inscribed 'NE Sh'. KSM L III 16 #1074.

713. (K.781) PLATE 114 Rim chipped. H. 2.5, D. rim 10.6, base 5.2 cm. Coated dull red-brown throughout. Inscribed 'NE Sh'. SM L III 16 #1074.

714. (K.782) PLATES 24, 114 Intact. H. 3.3, D. rim 12.0, base 5.8 cm. Coated brown throughout. Inscribed 'NE Sh'. KSM L III 16 #1074.

715. (K.783) PLATE 114 Intact. H. 2.9, D. rim 12.2, base 5.2 cm. Coated semilustrous dark-brown throughout. Inscribed 'NE Sh'. KSM L III 16 #1074.

716. (K.784) PLATES 24, 114 Recomposed, rim chipped. H. 3.0, D. rim 11.0, base 4.8 cm. Coated semilustrous dark-brown throughout. KSM L III 16 #1074.

Crude Bowl—Type 3

717. (K.785) PLATE 114 Rim chipped. H. 2.0, D. rim 8.5, base 4.4 cm. Coated dark-brown throughout. KSM L III 16 #1077.

718. (K.786) PLATE 114 Rim chipped. H. 1.8, D. rim 8.5, base 4.8 cm. Coated red-brown throughout. KSM L III 16 #1077.

719. (K.787) PLATE 114 Intact. H. 2.0, D. rim 9.5, base 4.0 cm. Coated dull red-brown throughout. KSM L III 16 #1077.

720. (K.788) PLATE 114 Rim chipped. H. 2.4, D. rim 9.7, base 5.5 cm. Coated semilustrous dark-brown throughout. KSM L III 16 #1077.

721. (K.789) PLATE 115 Rim chipped. H. 2.5, D. rim 8.5, base 4.0 cm. Coated dark-brown throughout. KSM L III 16 #1077.

722. (K.790) PLATE 115 Small rim fragment missing. H. 2.0, D. rim 8.4, base 4.8 cm. Coated red-brown throughout. KSM L III 16 #1077.

723. (K.791) PLATE 115 Rim fragment missing. H. 2.3, D. rim 8.5, base 4.5 cm. Coated red-brown throughout. KSM L III 16 #1077.

724. (K.792) PLATE 115 Rim chipped. H. 2.7, D. rim 9.5, base 5.0 cm. Coated brown throughout. Inscribed 'NE Sh'. KSM L III 16 #1074.

725. (K.793) PLATES 24, 115 Rim chipped. H. 3.1, D. rim 10.2, base 5.3 cm. Coated semilustrous dark-brown throughout. KSM L III 16 #1074.

726. (K.794) PLATE 115 Rim chipped. H. 2.0, D. rim 7.5, base 4.0 cm. Coated red-brown throughout. Inscribed 'NE Sh'. KSM L III 16 #1074.

727. (K.795) PLATE 115 Intact. H. 2.0, D. rim 8.0, base 4.0 cm. Coated brown to dark-brown throughout. Inscribed 'NE Sh'. KSM L III 16 #1074.

728. (K.796) PLATE 115 Rim chipped. H. 2.5, D. rim 9.0, base 5.0 cm. Coated brown throughout. Inscribed 'NE Sh'. KSM L III 16 #1074.

729. (K.797) PLATE 115 Intact. H. 2.8, D. rim 9.8, base 4.2 cm. Coated red to dark-brown throughout. Inscribed 'NE Sh'. KSM L III 16 #1074.

730. (K.798) PLATE 115 Rim chipped. H. 2.4, D. rim 10.2, base 6.0 cm. Coated brown throughout. KSM L III 16 #1077.

731. (K.799) PLATE 115 Rim chipped. H. 3.0, D. rim 9.5, base 4.8 cm. Coated dark red-brown throughout. KSM L III 16 #1077.

732. (K.800) PLATES 24, 115 Rim chipped. H. 3.0, D. rim 11.0, base 5.8 cm. Coated dark red-brown throughout. Inscribed 'NE Sh'. KSM L III 16 #1074.

Shallow Bowl

733. (K.801) PLATE 115 Rim chipped. H. 2.2, D. rim 11.0 cm. Coated dull red-brown throughout. Inscribed 'NE Sh'. KSM L III 16 #1074.

Deep Bowl

734. (K.802) PLATE 115 Rim chipped. H. 3.8, D. rim 8.0, base 3.5 cm. Plain. KSM L III 16 #1072.

Crude Pyxis

735. (K.803) PLATES 24, 115 Rim chipped. H. 3.3, D. rim 8.2, base 6.0 cm. Coated dark red-brown throughout. KSM L III 16 #1074.

Crude Juglet

736. (K.808) PLATE 116 Rim fragment missing. H. 6.8, D. rim 4.0, base 4.5 cm. Plain. KSM L III 16 #1072.

737. (K.809) PLATE 116 Half of rim missing. H. 8.1, D. rim 3.5, base 4.0 cm. Interior of rim and exterior coated semilustrous dark-brown; shallow horizontal grooves on neck. Inscribed 'NE Sh'. KSM L III 16 #1074.

FABRIC: SEMIFINE BUFF

Technique: Handmade

Surface: Dark on buff; reserved

Large Jar

738. (K.818) PLATE 116 Four non-joining fragments of neck, side and base with stubs for one horizontal handle. D. base 7.5 cm. Exterior has four broad horizontal dark-brown bands outlined in white evenly spaced on side from neck to base. KSM L III 16 #1072.

739. (K.821) PLATE 116 Four non-joining fragments of shoulder and lower side. Exterior has dark-brown circular pattern with added white. KSM L III 16 #1073.

Surface: Monochrome coated; white decorated

Oval-mouthed Amphora

740. (K.819) PLATE 116 Partially recomposed with numerous non-joining body fragments. Handles missing. H. 44.0, D. base 15.0 cm. Interior of spout and exterior coated semilustrous dark-brown mottled in places. Exterior has white horizontal band at base of neck from which white vertical lines descend to base. KSM L III 1 #996; KSM L III 16 #1073, 1075. SMP 9708.

741. (K.820) PLATE 116 Three large non-joining fragments of spout and shoulder with both handles. Rim 8.5 × 11.0 cm. Interior of spout and exterior coated brown. Exterior like 740. KSM L III 16 #1073,1075. SMP 9709.

FABRIC: TEMPERED BUFF

Technique: Wheelmade

Surface: Dark on buff

Lid

742. (K.823) PLATE 117 Rim chipped. D. 12.5 cm. Top has two groups of three lines beside handle, pairs of curved lines at edge and six strokes on handle in dark-brown paint on buff surface. KSM L III 16 #1074.

Large Basin

743. (K.822) Three large non-joining fragments of rim, side and base with one complete horizontal handle. H. 11.5, D. rim 52.0, base 49.0 cm. Exterior has two thick dark-brown bands at rim and base with reserved zone in middle outlined in white. KSM L III 16 #1072.

Surface: Monochrome coated; white decorated

Lid

744. (K.824) PLATE 117 Most of rim missing. D. 16.5 cm. Top coated red-brown and has two thick white circles. Inscribed 'NE Sh'. KSM L III 16 #1074.

745. (K.825) PLATE 117 Half of rim and large top fragment missing. D. 18.0 cm. Coated dull red-brown throughout. KSM L III 16 #1074.

Surface: Monochrome coated; polychrome decorated

Offering Table

746. (K.805) PLATES 24, 117 Rim Fragment. H. 4.5, D. rim 22.5 cm. Coated black throughout. Top of rim has white filled semicircles. Interior has large white and orange floral pattern. Exterior has large white interlocking circles. Inscribed 'NE Shoot'. KSM L III 16 #1074.

FABRIC: RED-BROWN

Technique: Wheelmade

Jug with Pinched Spout

747. (K.812) PLATE 117 Spout chipped. H. 9.5, D. base 5.0 cm. Gritty fabric. Plain. KSM L III 16 #1072.

748. (K.813) PLATE 117 Most of spout and handle missing. H. 9.4, D. base 5.5 cm. Gritty fabric. Exterior coated dull red-brown. KSM L III 16 #1072.

FABRIC: FINE RED

Technique: Wheelmade

Tumbler

749. (K.747) PLATE 111 Rim chipped. H. 4.3, D. rim 3.8, base 2.0 cm. Coated dull red-brown throughout. KSM L III 16 #1074.

FABRIC: SOFT GRITTY BUFF

Technique: Wheelmade

Surface: Monochrome slipped and burnished

Bowl with tripartite division

750. (K.804) Most of rim missing. H. 3.0, D. rim 9.5, base 4.8 cm. Coated dull red-brown throughout. Interior sprayed with white paint. KSM L III 16 #1072.

Hand Lamp—Type 1

751. (K.826) Handle and two rim fragments missing. H. 3.0, D. rim 9.0, base 4.5 cm. Coated semilustrous red-brown throughout. Burnt at spout. Inscribed 'NE Sh'. KSM L III 16 #1074.

752. (K.827) Handle and part of spout missing. H. 4.1, D. rim 12.0, base 6.0 cm. Coated dark red-brown throughout, badly worn. One side burnt. KSM L III 16 #1075.

Pedestalled Lamp—Type 1

753. (K.828) Rim and spout fragment. D. rim 19.0 cm. Coated red-brown throughout. Spout burnt. KSM L III 16 #1075.

GROUP H: ROYAL POTTERY STORES, THE SMALL EAST ROOM

FABRIC: FINE BUFF

Technique: Handmade

Surface: Monochrome coated

Rounded Cup—Type 1a

754. (K.831) PLATE 118 Rim chipped, hole in base. H. 5.6, D. rim 9.0, base 5.0 cm. Coated dark-brown throughout. KSM L III 15 #1071.

Angular Bridge-spouted Jar—Type 1a

755. (K.861) PLATE 118 Spout and rim chipped. Handles missing. H. 10.0, D. rim 10.3, base 5.7 cm. Interior has dark smear at rim and drips of paint on sides. Outside coated thin light-brown, underside plain. Mackenzie 1902 PB (2), 53.3. KSM L III 15 #1071. SMP 9710.

Technique: Wheelmade

Surface: Monochrome coated

Tall-rimmed Angular Cup—Type 3

756. (K.830) PLATE 118 Rim chipped, handle missing. H. 4.6, D. rim 8.0, base 3.5 cm. Coated semilustrous dark-brown throughout. KSM L III 15 #1071.

Pyxis—Type 4

757. (K.856) PLATE 118 Fragment of rim, side and half of base. H. 5.5, D. rim 12.0, base 9.0 cm. Interior has thin dark smear at rim. Top of rim and exterior coated dark-brown. KSM L III 15 #1071.

Large Pyxis—as Type 4

758. (K.857) PLATE 118 One-third of rim and side and most of base missing. H. 6.5, D. rim 19.5, base 17.0 cm. Interior has dark smear at rim. Top of rim and exterior coated black, flaking away. Mackenzie 1902 PB (2), 53.4. KSM L III 15 #1071. SMP 9711.

Surface: Monochrome coated; white decorated

Short-rimmed Angular Cup—Type 1

759. (K.829) PLATE 118 Rim chipped. H. 3.7, D. rim 7.2, base 3.5 cm. Coated dark red-brown all over except handle, which is plain. Exterior has horizontal lines at rim and angle with groups of three diagonal strokes in between. KSM L III 15 #1071.

Pyxis—Type 4

760. (K.855) PLATE 118 Fragment of one-quarter of rim side and base. H. 5.2, D. rim 11.0, base 7.5 cm. Interior has dark smear at rim. Top of rim and exterior coated brown. Exterior has horizontal bands below rim and on lower side and vertical stroke on handle. KSM L III 15 #1071.

Tray

761. (K.858) PLATE 118 Half of rim missing. H. 1.5, D. 13.0 cm. Coated semilustrous dark-brown to black throughout. Interior has three concentric circles. KSM L III 15 #1071.

Surface: Monochrome coated; polychrome decorated

Pyxis—Type 3

762. (K.854) Rim and side fragment. H. 5.5, D. rim 9.0 cm. Interior has dark smear at rim. Top of rim and exterior coated dull brown. Exterior has horizontal orange band at angle and two white bands at middle of side. KSM L III 15 #1071.

Technique: Wheelmade—cone thrown

Surface: Plain

Crude Goblet

763. (K.832) PLATE 119 Base chipped. H. 4.9, D. rim 8.0, base 3.7 cm. KSM L III 15 #1071.

764. (K.833) PLATE 119 Intact. H. 4.0, D. rim 8.7, base 3.3 cm. KSM L III 15 #1071.

765. (K.834) PLATE 119 Rim chipped. H. 5.0, D. rim 8.5, base 5.0 cm. KSM L III 15 #1071.

Surface: Monochrome coated

Crude Cup—Type 2

766. (K.836) PLATE 119 Large rim fragment missing. H. 5.8, D. rim 9.5, base 4.1 cm. Coated light-brown throughout. KSM L III 15 #1071.

767. (K.837) PLATE 119 Large rim fragment missing. H. 5.3, D. rim 9.0, base 5.2 cm. Coated red-brown throughout. KSM L III 15 #1071.

768. (K.838) PLATE 119 Half of rim missing. H. 6.0, D. rim 9.0, base 5.0 cm. Coated red-brown throughout. KSM L III 15 #1071.

769. (K.839) PLATE 119 Half of rim missing. H. 5.5, D. rim 9.0, base 4.5 cm. Coated red-brown throughout. KSM L III 15 #1071.

770. (K.840) PLATE 119 Handle missing, rim chipped. H. 6.3, D. rim 9.0, base 4.7 cm. Coated red-brown throughout. KSM L III 15 #1071.

771. (K.841) PLATE 119 Handle missing, rim chipped. H. 6.0, D. rim 8.5, base 4.6 cm. Coated dark-brown throughout. KSM L III 15 #1071.

Crude Bowl—Type 2

772. (K.842) PLATE 119 Rim fragment missing. H. 1.8, D. rim 11.5, base 5.5 cm. Coated dark-brown throughout. KSM L III 15 #1071.

773. (K.843) PLATE 119 Rim chipped. H. 3.0, D. rim 10.5, base 4.6 cm. Coated brown all over except two places potter missed. KSM L III 15 #1071.

774. (K.844) PLATE 119 Rim chipped. H. 2.8, D. rim 11.0, base 4.6 cm. Coated red-brown throughout. KSM L III 15 #1071.

775. (K.845) PLATE 119 Intact. H. 2.7, D. rim 11.5, base 5.5 cm. Coated semilustrous dark-brown throughout. KSM L III 15 #1071.

776. (K.846) PLATE 119 Rim chipped. H. 3.0, D. rim 11.5, base 5.5 cm. Coated light-brown throughout. KSM L III 15 #1071.

Crude Bowl—Type 3

777. (K.848) PLATE 120 Rim chipped. H. 2.2, D. rim 8.5, base 4.8 cm. Coated brown all over except one place on rim where held by potter. KSM L III 15 #1071.
778. (K.849) PLATE 120 Rim fragment missing. H. 2.3, D. rim 8.5, base 4.5 cm. Coated brown throughout. KSM L III 15 #1071.
779. (K.850) PLATE 120 Rim fragment missing. H. 2.2, D. rim 9.4, base 4.0 cm. Coated dark red-brown throughout. KSM L III 15 #1071.
780. (K.851) PLATE 120 Rim fragment missing. H. 2.3, D. rim 9.5, base 3.5 cm. Coated dark-brown throughout. KSM L III 15 #1071.
781. (K.852) PLATE 120 Rim chipped. H. 2.5, D. rim 10.0, base 5.2 cm. Coated red-brown throughout. KSM L III 15 #1071.
782. (K.853) PLATE 120 Rim chipped. H. 3.0, D. rim 10.5, base 4.8 cm. Coated dark-brown throughout. KSM L III 15 #1071.

FABRIC: TEMPERED BUFF

Lid

783. (K.859) Fragment of rim and top with complete knob. H. 2.5, D. 16.0 cm. Surface plain. Two white concentric bands on top around knob. KSM L III 15 #1071.
784. (K.860) Fragment of rim and top with complete knob. H. 2.8, D. 21.0 cm. Top and knob coated dark, now worn away. Side has dark bands at rim and top leaving reserved zone in middle. KSM L III 15 #1071.

FABRIC: RED-BROWN

Technique: Wheelmade—cone thrown

Surface: Plain

Shallow Bowl—as Type 1

785. (K.847) PLATE 120 Three small rim fragments missing. H. 3.3, D. rim 13.2, base 6.5 cm. Plain red surface. KSM L III 15 #1071.

Open Spouted Goblet

786. (K.835) PLATE 120 Intact. H. 5.7, D. rim 5.0, base 4.5 cm. KSM L III 15 #1071.
787. (K.882) PLATE 120 Intact. H. 5.8, D. rim 6.3, base 3.6 cm. Inscribed 'NE Sh'. SMP 1983.

GROUP I: ROYAL POTTERY STORES, THE ROOM OF THE JARS

FABRIC: FINE BUFF

Technique: Handmade

Surface: Monochrome coated

Tall-rimmed Angular Cup—Type 1b

788. (K.864) PLATE 123 Half of rim and side missing. H. 6.2, D. rim 9.0, base 4.0 cm. Coated semilustrous dark-brown throughout. KSM L III 8 #1052.

Surface: Monochrome coated; white decorated

Straight-sided Cup—Type 2

789. (K.862) PLATE 123 Two rim fragments missing. H. 4.6, D. rim 8.0, base 5.5 cm. Coated semilustrous dark-brown throughout. Exterior has horizontal band below rim. KSM L III 8 #1052.
790. (K.863) PLATE 123 Two rim fragments missing. H. 4.5, D. rim 7.5, base 5.2 cm. Coated semilustrous dark-brown throughout. Exterior has horizontal band at middle. KSM L III 8 #1052.

FABRIC: UNCERTAIN

Technique: uncertain

Surface: Monochrome coated; white decorated

Tall Amphora

791. (K.865) PLATE 121 Recomposed. Exterior has broad white horizontal band at middle of side and base. Evans 1921, 572 fig. 416a. ?HM.
792. (K.866) PLATE 121 Recomposed. Exterior has broad white horizontal band at middle. ?HM.
793. (K.867) PLATE 122 Recomposed. Both handles and most of rim missing. Exterior has three broad white horizontal bands on shoulder and side. ?HM.

Elongated Jar

794. (K.868) PLATE 122 Recomposed. Exterior has broad white horizontal band at middle. ?HM.

GROUP J: ROYAL POTTERY STORES, GENERAL

FABRIC: FINE BUFF

Technique: Handmade

Surface: Monochrome coated

Tall-rimmed Angular Cup—Type 1b

795. (K.873) PLATE 124 Rim chipped. Mackenzie 1903, 180 fig. 6.4. Not located.

Angular Bridge-spouted Jar—Type 1

796. (K.883) PLATE 123 Base chipped, two small body fragments missing. H. 13.0, D. rim 10.0, base 5.8 cm. Interior has dark band at rim and drips on sides. Exterior coated semilustrous dark-brown. Inscribed 'NE'. Mackenzie 1902 PB (2), 46. HM 4351.

Surface: Monochrome coated; polychrome decorated

Straight-sided Cup—Type 2

797. (K.871) PLATE 124 Rim chipped. H. 4.2, D. rim 7.4, base 5.2 cm. Coated dark-brown throughout. Exterior has pairs of red vertical lines alternating with diagonal white slightly rounded ladder pattern. Inscribed 'NE Sh. 5'. Mackenzie 1903, 180 fig. 6.5. HM 4383.

Technique: Wheelmade; 'Egg-shell ware'

Straight-sided Cup—?Type

798. (K.44) Rim fragment. D. rim *c.* 12.0 cm. Interior has spray of light-brown paint and thin rim band. Exterior has four rows of light-brown printed crescents. AM AE 1061.7. HM 5187.

Rounded Cup—Type 4

799. (K.31) Rim fragment. Coated brown throughout, mottled in places. Decorated with stamped semicircles formed by edge of shell. Evans 1921, 242 fig. 182a. AM AE 937.

800. (K.32) Rim fragment. Coated brown throughout. Decorated with stamped reverse-S pattern below rim and two rows of stars on lower side. Evans 1921, 242 fig. 182b. AM AE 935.

801. (K.33) Large rim fragment. Restored in plaster. H. 8.4 cm. Coated dark-brown throughout. Side impressed into double arcade pattern into which is painted white lily in upper register and orange with added red dot at top of lower one. Evans 1921, 242 figs. 183a.l, 194d. AM 1938.561.

Technique: Wheelmade

Surface: Monochrome coated

Short-rimmed Angular Cup—Type 2

802. (K.878) PLATES 124, 125 Intact. H. 6.5, D. rim 11.0, base 5.0 cm. Coated thin red throughout. Inscribed 'K 02 NE Sh 2'. Mackenzie 1903, 180 fig. 6.2. HM 4392.

803. (K.879) PLATE 125 Complete, recomposed. H. 6.4, D. rim 11.5, base 4.7 cm. Coated dull red-brown throughout. Inscribed 'K.02 NE Sh'. HM 4391.

Surface: Monochrome coated; white decorated

Short-rimmed Angular Cup—Type 1

804. (K.880) PLATE 123 Few small fragments of base and lower side missing. Restored in plaster. H. 5.0, D. rim 9.0, base 3.0 cm. Coated dull red-brown all over except for handle. Exterior has pair of horizontal lines at rim and angle. Inscribed 'NE Sh'. Mackenzie 1902 PB (2), 47. HM 4354.

Rounded Cup—Type 3

805. (K.1053) PLATE 124 Recomposed. Exterior appears white sprayed. Mackenzie 1902 PB (2), 45; Mackenzie 1903, 180 fig. 6.1; Forsdyke 1925, 86 fig. 107. BM A 514.

Pyxis—Type 3

806. (K.884) PLATE 123 Large fragment of one-third of rim, side and base, restored in plaster. H. 5.5, D. rim 8.5, base 3.0 cm.

Interior has dark smear at rim and drips on sides. Exterior coated dark-brown and has thick white bands below rim and at angle. Inscribed 'K.02 NEKA' 'K.02 K d.' Mackenzie 1902 PB (2), 45. HM 4385.

Surface: Monochrome coated; polychrome decorated

Tumbler—Type 3

807. (K.34) H. 6.5 cm. Coated black throughout. Exterior has large open white criss-cross pattern with red dots each surrounded by six white crosses in open spaces. Underside has white star with red dot at centre. Similar to 650. Evans 1935, 99 fig. 64a. AM AE 944.

Open Spouted Bowl

808. (K.30) PLATES 25, 125 Almost half of side and rim and all of base missing. Restored in plaster. H. 7.5, D. rim 14.5, base 6.0 cm. Coated dull brown throughout. Interior has alternating red and orange vertical bars with white dots between at rim. Exterior has three rows of barbotine below rim and two at angle, red horizontal band at rim, white reverse-S pattern bordered above and below by red line with tassels with white at the ends in middle, red and white horizontal lines on lower side. Inscribed 'K.02 NEKA'. Pendlebury 1939, pl. XVII.2.a. HM 2674.

Small Jar

809. (K.36) PLATE 125 One handle, small fragments of rim and foot missing. Restored in plaster. H. 9.5, D. rim 7.5, base 3.8 cm. Interior of rim and exterior coated semilustrous dark-brown and exterior has thick horizontal orange band below handles. Three moulded beetles set on shoulder between handles. Evans 1921, fig. 180. HM 2686.

Technique: Wheelmade—cone thrown

Crude Cup—Type 2

810. (K.876) PLATES 124, 125 Intact. H. 5.0, D. rim 8.5, base 5.0 cm. Plain. Inscribed 'NE Sh'. Mackenzie 1903, 180 fig. 6.7. HM 5762.

Crude Cup—Type 4

811. (K.881) PLATES 124, 125 Intact. H. 5.5, D. rim 8.0, base 3.5 cm. Thick uneven red-brown rim band with drips in places. Inscribed 'NE Sh', '3'. Mackenzie 1903, 180 fig. 6.3. HM 5760.

Crude Cup—Type 2

812. (K.874) PLATES 123, 124 Intact. H. 5.3, D. rim 9.0, base 5.0 cm. Coated thin red-brown throughout. Inscribed 'NE Sh 6'. Mackenzie 1903, 180 fig. 6.6. HM 5711.

Crude Goblet

813. (K.875) PLATE 124 Mackenzie 1903, 180 fig. 6.8. Not located.

GROUP K: THE LOOMWEIGHT BASEMENT

FABRIC: FINE BUFF

Technique: Handmade

Miniature Cup

814. (K.154) PLATE 127 Intact. H. 3.5, D. rim 3.8, base 3.0 cm. Plain. Long strand of clay folded over rim to act as lug. KSM M III 2 #1190.

Technique: Wheelmade

Surface: Dark on buff

Miniature Straight-sided Cup

815. (K.134) PLATE 127 Most of handle and half of rim missing. H. 3.0, D. rim 4.5, base 2.0 cm. Thin dark-brown rim band in and out. KSM M III 2 #1192.

Miniature Pedestalled Cup

816. (K.135) PLATES 126, 127 Rim chipped and base missing. H. 3.4, D. rim 4.2 cm. Interior of rim and exterior to base of handle coated red-brown. KSM M III 2 #1189.

Surface: Monochrome coated; white decorated

Tumbler—Type 3

817. (K.129) Intact. H. 6.6 cm. Coated black throughout. Exterior has three evenly spaced vertical foliate bands from base to rim. Evans 1921, 255 fig. 191; Brown 1983, 88 fig. 43a. AM AE 1241.

Rounded Cup

818. (K.132) PLATE 25 Several non-joining fragments of rim and side with complete handle—not joining. H. 9.5, D. rim 20.5 cm. Coated lustrous metallic black and white spotted throughout. KSM M III 2 #1190, 1192.

Miniature Amphora

819. (K.28) PLATES 126, 127 Small rim fragment missing. H. 7.6, D. rim 3.4, base 2.3 cm. Interior of rim and exterior coated semilustrous black. Exterior has horizontal bands at base, on lower side and below rim, two concentric circles on shoulder and a filled semicircle below each handle. Inscribed 'K.02 K.28'. Mackenzie 1902 PB (2), 79; Evans 1921, 255 fig. 191. HM 2688.

820. (K.29) PLATES 126, 127 Recomposed, complete. H. 6.9, D. rim 4.2, base 2.1 cm. Interior of rim and exterior coated semilustrous black. Interior has thin rim band. Exterior has horizontal band at base, two rows of pendant filled semicircles on lower side and large pendant filled semicircles on shoulder. Inscribed 'K.02 K.29'. Mackenzie 1902 PB (2), 79; Evans 1921, 255 fig. 191; Panagiotaki 1993a, 45 fig. 10b. HM 2689.

821. (K.155) PLATE 126 Evans 1921, 255 fig. 191. Not located.

822. (K.156) Intact. H. 7.8 cm. Exterior coated black and has horizontal band at neck and six vertical lines evenly spaced from neck to base. Forms pair with 823. Brown 1983, 88 fig. 43a. AM 1938.585.

823. (K.157) PLATES 126, 127 Both handles and fragments of rim missing. Restored. H. 7.8, D. base 2.2 cm. Exterior coated black and decorated like 822. KSM M III 2 #1190.

Surface: Monochrome coated; polychrome decorated

Cup

824. (K.131) PLATES 25, 127 Rim fragment. D. rim 13.0 cm. Coated lustrous metallic black throughout. Interior has white diagonal slashes at rim. Exterior has traces of white circular decoration with added red vertical stripes. KSM M III 2 #1190.

Jug with Horizontal Spout—Type 1

825. (K.163) Recomposed, rim chipped. H. 8.9 cm. Interior of rim and exterior coated black. Exterior has orange band on flange at neck, white horizontal band on neck and traces of white decoration on body. Evans 1921, 255 fig. 191; Brown 1983, 88 fig. 43a. AM 1938.586.

Technique: Wheelmade—cone thrown

Crude Cup—Type 3

826. (K.147) Rim chipped. H. 6.8, D. rim 9.5, base 4.5 cm. Coated dull red-brown throughout. KSM M III 2 #1191.

827. (K.148) Complete, recomposed. H. 5.5, D. rim 9.0, base 4.2 cm. Coated dull red-brown throughout. Mottled. KSM M III 2 #1192.

828. (K.141) PLATE 128 Large fragment of rim and side missing. H. 5.4, D. rim 9.0, base 4.2 cm. Coated thin brown throughout. KSM M III 2 #1191.

829. (K.142) PLATE 128 Small rim fragment missing. H. 5.8, D. rim 8.5, base 4.5 cm. Coated dull red-brown throughout. KSM M III 2 #1191.

830. (K.143) PLATE 128 Small rim fragment missing. H. 5.5, D. rim 8.5, base 4.3 cm. Coated thin metallic grey-brown throughout, worn away. KSM M III 2 #1192.

831. (K.144) PLATE 128 One-third of rim missing. H. 6.0, D. rim 8.5, base 4.5 cm. Coated dull dark-brown throughout. KSM M III 2 #1191.

832. (K.145) PLATE 128 One-third of rim and side missing. H. 5.5, D. rim 9.0, base 4.7 cm. Coated lustrous metallic grey-brown throughout. KSM M III 2 #1192.

833. (K.146) PLATE 128 Three-quarters of rim and side missing. H. 6.3, D. rim 9.0, base 4.5 cm. Coated dull red-brown throughout. KSM M III 2 #1192.

Crude Cup—Type 4

834. (K.149) PLATE 128 Intact. H. 5.0, D. rim 8.5, base 5.0 cm. Coated brown throughout. KSM M III 2 #1191.

835. (K.150) PLATE 128 One-third of rim and top of handle missing. H. 5.0, D. rim 8.0, base 5.0 cm. Coated semilustrous brown throughout, worn away. KSM M III 2 #1192.

836. (K.151) PLATE 128 Handle and rim fragment missing. H. 5.0, D. rim 9.0, base 4.0 cm. Coated semilustrous grey-brown throughout. KSM M III 2 #1192.

837. (K.152) PLATE 128 Handle and fragment of rim missing. H. 4.5, D. rim 8.5, base 3.8 cm. Coated brown throughout. KSM M III 2 #1191.

Crude Cup—Type 4 with folded over rim

838. (K.139) PLATE 128 Rim chipped. H. 5.0, D. rim 8.0, base 4.5 cm. Plain. KSM M III 2 #1191.

839. (K.140) PLATE 128 Rim chipped. H. 5.7, D. rim 9.0, base 4.0 cm. KSM M III 2 #1192.

Crude Juglet

840. (K.171) PLATES 126, 129 Complete, recomposed. H. 6.3, D. rim 4.0, base 4.0 cm. Interior of spout and exterior splattered with red-brown paint. Evans 1921, 255 fig. 191. KSM M III 2 #1190.

841. (K.172) PLATE 129 Rim chipped. H. 8.1, D. rim 4.0, base 3.7 cm. Exterior splattered orange. KSM M III 2 #1192.

842. (K.158) PLATE 129 Intact. H. 6.0, D. rim 3.5, base 3.0 cm. Interior of rim and exterior coated dull brown. KSM M III 2 #1190.

843. (K.159) PLATE 129 Rim chipped. H. 7.0, D. rim 3.0, base 3.5 cm. Interior of rim and exterior coated dull dark-brown. KSM M III 2 #1190.

844. (K.160) PLATE 129 Rim chipped. H. 7.7, D. rim 3.2, base 3.5 cm. Interior of rim and exterior coated dull dark-brown. KSM M III 2 #1190.

845. (K.161) PLATE 129 Appears to be intact. ?Monochrome coated exterior. Not located.

846. (K.162) PLATE 129 Rim chipped. H. 7.5, D. rim 3.0, base 3.5 cm. Interior of rim and exterior coated dull dark-brown. KSM M III 2 #1192.

847. (K.164) PLATE 129 Rim and most of handle missing. H. 7.3, D. base 3.3 cm. Exterior coated dull dark-brown. KSM M III 2 #1190.

848. (K.165) PLATE 129 Handle missing. H. 5.8, D. rim 3.3, base 3.9 cm. Interior of rim and exterior coated thin brown. KSM M III 2 #1190.

849. (K.166) PLATE 129 Handle missing. H. 5.8, D. rim 3.3, base 4.5 cm. Faint traces of six horizontal incised lines on body. Interior of rim and exterior coated thin brown. KSM M III 2 #1190.

850. (K.167) PLATE 129 Handle missing. H. 6.0, D. rim 3.4, base 4.3 cm. Coated thin brown throughout. KSM M III 2 #1190.

851. (K.168) PLATE 129 Handle missing. H. 6.0, D. rim 3.0, base 3.8 cm. Traces of four thinly incised horizontal lines on shoulder. Interior of rim and exterior coated thin brown. KSM M III 2 #1190.

852. (K.169) PLATE 129 Handle and half of rim missing. H. 6.2, D. rim 3.5, base 4.0 cm. Interior of rim and exterior coated dull red-brown. KSM M III 2 #1190.

853. (K.170) Handle and most of rim missing. H. 5.5, D. rim 2.5, base 3.5 cm. Interior of rim and exterior coated dull red-brown. KSM M III 2 #1190.

Crude Bowl—Type 2

854. (K.174) PLATE 129 Rim slightly chipped. H. 2.2, D. rim 11.9, base 6.2 cm. Coated dull red-brown throughout. KSM M III 2 #1190.

855. (K.175) PLATE 129 Rim fragment missing. H. 3.9, D. rim 11.0, base 6.0 cm. Coated dull red-brown throughout. KSM M III 2 #1191.

856. (K.176) PLATE 129 Rim chipped. H. 2.5, D. rim 10.0, base 3.7 cm. Coated dark red-brown throughout. KSM M III 2 #1192.

857. (K.177) PLATE 129 Rim chipped. H. 2.8, D. rim 10.0, base 5.7 cm. Coated metallic grey-brown throughout. KSM M III 2 #1191.

858. (K.178) PLATE 129 Rim chipped. H. 2.5, D. rim 9.7, base 5.0 cm. Traces of thin red-brown paint throughout. KSM M III 2 #1192.

859. (K.179) PLATE 129 Intact. H. 3.0, D. rim 10.5, base 5.0 cm. Coated metallic grey-brown throughout. KSM M III 2 #1191.

860. (K.180) PLATE 129 Rim slightly chipped. H. 3.4, D. rim 9.0, base 5.0 cm. Plain. One side pulled down and burnt, probably used as lamp. KSM M III 2 #1190.

Crude Bowl—Type 3

861. (K.181) PLATE 130 One-third of rim missing. H. 3.0, D. rim 10.2, base 5.0 cm. Coated dull red-brown over most of surface. KSM M III 2 #1190.

862. (K.182) PLATE 130 Rim and side fragment missing. H. 2.5, D. rim 10.5, base 5.7 cm. Coated semilustrous dark-brown throughout. KSM M III 2 #1191.

863. (K.183) PLATE 130 Rim and side fragment missing. H. 3.0, D. rim 9.5, base 5.3 cm. Coated thin brown throughout. KSM M III 2 #1191.

864. (K.184) PLATE 130 Rim slightly chipped. H. 3.2, D. rim 9.5, base 5.3 cm. Coated dull dark-brown throughout. KSM M III 2 #1192.

865. (K.185) PLATE 130 Rim slightly chipped. H. 2.6, D. rim 10.0, base 5.0 cm. Coated dull red-brown throughout. KSM M III 2 #1191.

866. (K.186) PLATE 130 Rim chipped. H. 3.0, D. rim 9.5, base 5.0 cm. Coated dull red-brown throughout. KSM M III 2 #1191.

867. (K.187) PLATE 130 Rim fragment missing. H. 2.5, D. rim 9.0, base 5.0 cm. Coated thin light-brown throughout. Impression of rim of other pot on base. KSM M III 2 #1190.

868. (K.188) PLATE 130 Rim chipped. H. 2.5, D. rim 8.0, base 4.5 cm. Coated thin dull red-brown throughout. KSM M III 2 #1191.

869. (K.189) PLATE 130 Rim chipped. H. 2.0, D. rim 7.0, base 4.7 cm. Coated thin dull red-brown throughout. KSM M III 2 #1192.

870. (K.190) PLATE 130 Rim fragment missing. H. 2.8, D. rim 10.0, base 6.0 cm. Coated thin dull red-brown throughout, mottled in places. KSM M III 2 #1191.

FABRIC: SEMIFINE BUFF

Technique: Handmade

Large Jar

871. (K.201) PLATE 130 Four non-joining fragments of side. Exterior has dark-brown connected oval pattern with added white. Similar to 739. KSM M III 2 #1191.

872. (K.202) PLATE 130 Five non-joining fragments of shoulder, side and base. D. base 10.0 cm. Interior has red smear on neck. Exterior has dark-red ?oval or circular pattern with added white, ? similar to 871. KSM M III 2 #1191.

Jug

873. (K.196) PLATE 131 Fragment of neck and spout with upper part of handle. H. 17.2 cm. Interior of spout and exterior coated dull dark-brown. Applied horizontal rings at on lower neck. KSM M III 2 #1190.

FABRIC: FINE SOFT BUFF

Technique: Wheelmade

Bridge-spouted Jar

874. (K.133) PLATES 25, 131 Four non-joining fragments of rim and lower side with spout. D. rim 7.0 cm. Exterior has alternating vertical zones of dark paint with added white 'drops' and buff reserved zones with dark-brown 'drops'. Similar to 1004. KSM M III 2 #1190, 1192, 1196.

FABRIC: TEMPERED BUFF

Technique: Handmade

Large Deep Basin

875. (K.195) PLATE 131 Three large rim and side fragments with one handle. H. 18.0, D. rim 36.0 cm. Interior has thick uneven rim band. Exterior coated in thin, dull dark-brown paint and has large white star pattern in middle of both sides. Similar to **1004**. KSM M III 2 #1191.

Large Spouted Jar

876. (K.197) Tip of spout and numerous body fragments missing. Restored. Exterior has two large horizontal zones of white foliate bands bordered above and below by rows of white with added red dots bordered in white and red, traces of thick white horizontal bands on lower side. Mackenzie 1903, 178 fig. 5; Evans 1921, 255 fig. 191. ?HM.

877. (K.198) Few body fragments missing. Exterior has large horizontal zone of white open running spirals at middle bordered above and below by zones of white crescents bordered orange bands with added red dots. Mackenzie 1903, 177 fig. 4; Evans 1921, 257 fig. 192a. HM display.

Large Jug

878. (K.199) PLATES 25, 131 Recomposed part of shoulder and side and eleven non-joining fragments. H. 26.5 cm. Exterior coated semilustrous black and has decoration like **877** except for having red instead of orange bands and no added red dots. Mackenzie 1902 DB (2), 1; Mackenzie 1902 PB (2), 11. KSM M III 2 #1189. SMP.2023.

Technique: Wheelmade

Large Bowl

879. (K.193) PLATES 26, 131 One-third of rim and side and over half of base missing. Restored in plaster. H. 14.0, D. rim 29.0, base 9.0 cm. Coated thin, dull dark-brown throughout. Top of rim has broad white bands. Exterior has large white open running spirals with petaloid loops above and below and white band at base. KSM M III 2 #1194. SMP 2024.

FABRIC: FINE ORANGE

Technique: Wheelmade

Pedestalled Cup

880. (K.130) PLATES 26, 127 Rim and handle missing. H. 7.5, D. base 2.9 cm. Interior of rim and exterior coated red-brown. KSM M III 2 #1190.

Shallow Bowl/Cup

881. (K.191) PLATE 130 Intact. H. 3.8, D. rim 8.0, base 3.4 cm. Plain. KSM M III 2 #1192.

FABRIC: GRITTY ORANGE-BUFF

Technique: Wheelmade

Lid

882. (K.138) PLATES 26, 127 Rim fragment missing. H. 2.0, D. 7.7 cm. Top has even brown spray with added white and orange rockwork pattern. KSM M III 2 #1190.

Crude Cup—as Type 4

883. (K.153) PLATE 128 Handle missing, rim chipped. H. 5.5, D. rim 7.3, base 3.6 cm. Plain. KSM M III 2 #1192.

Jug

884. (K.137) PLATE 131 Fragment of upper side with complete spout and handle. H. 10.0 cm. Interior of spout and exterior coated dull black. Thin white band on rim of spout. Exterior has thick white horizontal band on neck. KSM M III 2 #1192.

Tray

885. (K.192) PLATE 132 One-third preserved. H. 1.7, D. rim 19.0, base 17.5 cm. Coated dull red-brown throughout. Interior has two large white concentric circles one at rim other in centre. KSM M III 2 #1192.

FABRIC: SOFT GRITTY BUFF

Technique: Wheelmade

Surface: Monochrome coated

Tray

886. (K.194) Six non-joining fragments of rim, side and base. H. 7.8, D. rim 26.0, base 21.0 cm. Coated with thick white paint, similar to creamy bordered ware and house models. KSM M III 2 #1190.

Hand Lamp—Type 2

887. (K.203) Single fragment of rim with complete handle. Coated dull orange throughout. KSM M III 2 #1191.

Pedestalled Lamp—Type 2

888. (K.204) PLATE 26 Three non-joining fragments of rim and foot. H. c. 23.0, D. rim 24.0 cm. Coated red all over except interior of pedestal. KSM M III 2 #1192.

OTHER FABRICS

Miniature Spouted Cup

889. (K.136) PLATE 127 Handle missing, rim chipped. H. 3.0, D. rim 4.0, base 1.3 cm. Fine grey fabric, wheelmade. Exterior coated black. KSM M III 2 #1190.

Juglet

890. (K.173) PLATE 132 Small rim fragment missing. H. 6.9, D. max 6.8, base 6.1 cm. Gritty brown very micaceous fabric. Wheelmade. Plain. KSM M III 2 #1190. SMP 9713.

Large Jar

891. (K.200) Complete. Half in AM and half in HM. Coarse red-brown fabric. Exterior coated thick semilustrous black and has six large white palm trees with added red detail on body and white bands at rim and neck. Evans 1921, 254 fig. 190; Betancourt 1985a, pl. 12 I. AM AE 1654. HM 7691.

GROUP L: THE FLOOR BENEATH THE ROOM OF THE OLIVE PRESS

FABRIC: FINE BUFF

Technique: Handmade—Pared Ware

Rounded Goblet—Type 1

892. (K.110) PLATE 132 Rim and base fragments missing. H. 7.0, D. rim 8.0, base 5.0 cm. Interior has thin brown rim band. Exterior has smear of brown paint all over. KSM M II 5 #1180.

893. (K.111) PLATE 132 Intact. H. 7.5, D. rim 8.0, base 4.5 cm. Thin red-brown smears at rim in and out. KSM M II 5 #1180.

894. (K.112) PLATE 132 Intact. H. 6.8, D. rim 8.0, base 4.5 cm. Traces of thin brown paint in and out but not underside. KSM L III 1 #997.

895. (K.113) PLATE 132 Rim chipped. H. 7.0, D. rim 8.0, base 4.2 cm. Plain. KSM L III 1 #997.

896. (K.114) PLATE 132 Rim chipped. H. 7.0, D. rim 8.0, base 4.5 cm. One area of rim coated red-brown in and out. KSM L III 1 #997.

897. (K.115) PLATE 132 Rim chipped. H. 5.5–7.0, D. rim 7.5–8.0, base 4.5 cm. Traces of thin brown paint throughout. KSM L III 1 #997.

Tumbler—Type 1

898. (K.107) PLATE 132 Intact. H. 6.5, D. rim 8.0, base 3.5 cm. Interior has accidental smear of red-brown paint at rim. Exterior has thick horizontal red-brown band below rim and one thick diagonal band at rim. KSM L III 1 #997.

Technique: Handmade

Conical Goblet—Type 1

899. (K.85) Large rim fragment. H. 4.5, D. rim 6.5 cm. Coated dark-brown throughout. Exterior has alternating pairs of red and white spiralling lines, similar to 55. KSM L III 1 #997.

Straight-sided Cup—Type 1

900. (K.99) PLATE 133 Large fragment of rim, side and base with complete handle. H. 6.0, D. rim 10.0, base 6.0 cm. Interior has accidental drip of light-brown paint near handle. Exterior has brown paint applied with brush to side but not handle or underside. KSM M II 5 #1181.

Small Angular Cup

901. (K.96) Large fragment of rim and side with complete handle. H. 4.3, D. rim 8.5 cm. Carelessly coated thin dark-brown throughout. KSM M II 5 #1178, 1180, 1181.

Rounded Cup—Type 1b

902. (K.100) PLATE 133 Large rim fragment missing. H. 5.5, D. rim 8.3, base 4.5 cm. Thick red-brown rim band in and out. KSM M II 5 #1173, 1174.

Angular Bridge-spouted Jar—Type 1

903. (K.105) PLATE 133 Most of lower side and base missing. H. 9.8, D. rim 10.0, base 4.5 cm. Thick brown band at rim and spout in and out. KSM M II 5 #1176, 1177, 1178, 1179, 1180.

904. (K.106) PLATE 27 Three non-joining fragments of rim, spout and complete base. H. 13.0, D. rim 12.0, base 6.0 cm. Interior has dark uneven rim band. Exterior coated dull dark-brown throughout. KSM M II 5 #1178, 1180.

905. (K.74) PLATES 27, 133 One-third of rim and side missing, base chipped. One rim fragment in AM. Restored. H. 13.5, D. rim 9.0, base 6.0 cm. Interior has uneven dark rim band and accidental drips of paint. Exterior coated semilustrous black and has three zones of two orange diagonal lines with pairs of white lines either side from white base band to rim. KSM M II 5 #1175, 1181–2; KSM M III 2 #1195; KSM L III 1 #997. AM 1910.167i. SMP 9714.

Technique: Wheelmade

Surface: Monochrome coated

Straight-sided Cup

906. (K.101) Two large non-joining fragments of rim, side, base and handle. H. 6.4, D. rim 8.8, base 4.5 cm. Coated throughout in dull brown paint. KSM M II 5 #1173.

Tall-rimmed Angular Cup—Type 5

907. (K.97) PLATES 27, 133 One-third of rim and side missing. Restored in plaster. H. 6.3, D. rim 11.0, base 4.2 cm. Coated metallic black throughout. KSM M II 5 #1173, 1174, 1176. SMP 9715.

908. (K.98) PLATE 133 Large fragment of rim, side and base. H. 6.4, D. rim 13.0, base 5.3 cm. Coated thin dark-brown throughout. KSM M II 5 #1179, 1181.

Short-rimmed Angular Cup—Type 2

909. (K.91) PLATES 27, 134 Two-thirds of rim missing. Partially restored in plaster. H. 6.8, D. rim 11.0, base 4.0 cm. Coated dull red-brown all over except for area of handle where potter held to paint. KSM M II 5 #1176, 1177, 1178, 1180, 1181. SMP 9716.

910. (K.92) PLATE 134 Most of rim and side missing. Partially restored in plaster. H. 7.0, D. rim 10.5, base 4.0 cm. Coated dull red-brown all over except for area of handle where held by potter. KSM M II 5 #1176, 1180.

911. (K.93) PLATE 134 Three-quarters of rim and half of body missing. H. 6.5, D. rim 11.0, base 4.0 cm. Coated dark-brown throughout. KSM M II 5 #1178, 1179, 1180, 1181.

912. (K.94) PLATE 134 Large fragment of rim, side and base with complete handle. H. 6.5, D. rim 11.0, base 4.0 cm. Coated dull dark-brown all over except for area of handle where held by potter. KSM M II 5 #1176, 1178, 1179.

913. (K.86) PLATES 27, 134 Several small rim and side fragments missing. Restored. H. 7.7, D. rim 13.5, base 4.7 cm. Coated red-brown throughout. KSM M II 5 #1173, 1176, 1177, 1178, 1180, 1181. SMP 9717.

914. (K.87) PLATES 27, 134 Most of rim, side and part of handle missing. H. 7.5, D. rim 17.0, base 5.5 cm. Coated red-brown throughout. KSM M II 5 #1177, 1178, 1180.

915. (K.88) Several non-joining fragments of rim, side and handle with complete base. D. rim 17.0, base 5.8 cm. Coated dark-brown throughout. KSM M II 5 #1176, 1178, 1180, 1182.

916. (K.89) Four fragments of rim and base with complete handle. D. rim 16.0, base 5.3 cm. Coated dark-brown throughout. KSM M II 5 #1178, 1180, 1181; KSM L III 1 #997.

917. (K.90) Large fragment of base and lower side with handle stub. H. 5.5, D. max.13.0, base 4.7 cm. Coated black throughout. KSM M II 5 #1180, 1181.

Surface: Monochrome coated; white decorated

Rounded Goblet—Type 2

918. (K.108) PLATE 132 Rim chipped. H. 7.7, D. rim 8.0, base 4.5 cm. Interior and exterior of upper part coated semilustrous dark-brown. Foot plain but has drips of dark paint from upper part and smear on underside. Exterior has thick white horizontal band on side. KSM L III 1 #997.

919. (K.109) PLATE 132 Two-thirds of rim missing. H. 7.5, D. rim 9.0, base 5.0 cm. Interior and exterior of upper part coated dull brown. Underside plain. Interior has two diagonal white strokes at rim. Exterior has thick white horizontal band on side. KSM M II 5 #1180.

Straight-sided Cup

920. (K.95) PLATES 27, 133 Half of rim missing. Restored. H. 7.0, D. rim 9.0, base 4.8 cm. Interior has thick dark rim band. Exterior coated dull brown and has traces of white decoration on lower side. KSM M II 5 #1173, 1174, 1177. SMP 9718.

Rounded Cup—Type 3

921. (K.82) PLATES 27, 134 Large fragment of rim and side with complete strap handle. H. 5.0, D. rim 8.0 cm. Coated thin dark-brown throughout. Interior has rim band. Exterior has horizontal band below rim and vertical stripes on side. Panagiotaki 1993a, 45 fig. 10b. KSM M II 5 #1182.

Rounded Cup—Type 4

922. (K.81) PLATES 27, 134 Three non-joining fragments of rim, lower side and base. H. 7.0, D. rim 12.0, base 5.0 cm. Interior has uneven dark band at rim and drips on sides. Exterior coated semilustrous dark red-brown and has bands at rim and base and traces of large circular pattern with inturned teeth in three places on side. KSM M II 5 #1174, 1182; KSM L III 1 #997.

Pyxis

923. (K.116) PLATE 135 Large fragment of base and side. H. 5.5, D. base 9.0 cm. Interior smeared and sprayed with dark paint. Exterior coated semilustrous metallic grey-brown and has horizontal bands at base and in group of three at middle of side. KSM M II 5 #1182; KSM M III 2 #1190, 1195.

Pyxis—Type 2

924. (K.117) PLATES 28, 135 Most of base and rim missing. H. 5.8, D. rim 10.3, base 7.5 cm. Interior has uneven dark rim band and drips of paint. Exterior coated dark-brown and has horizontal bands at rim, middle and base. KSM M II 5 #1182; KSM L III 1 #997.

Surface: Monochrome coated; polychrome decorated

Rounded Goblet—Type 3

925. (K.49) PLATE 135 Three fragments of lower side. Restored in plaster. H. rest. 6.7, D. rim rest. 9.5 cm. Coated semilustrous dark-brown throughout. Interior has complicated pattern in white. Exterior has three horizontal white lines with added red strokes alternating with yellow diagonal slashes partly outlined in white. Evans 1903, 20 fig. 8 pl. II.1. HM 2698.

Shallow Angular Bowl—Type 2

926. (K.47) PLATE 135 Three large rim fragments, one handle and half of base missing. Restored in plaster. H. 5.3, D. max.17.0, base 5.3 cm. Interior has large brown splashes on sides and rows of barbotine with white semicircles on spouts. Exterior has barbotine row at angle, reserved bands outlined in white on lower side, base coated brown and has white cross on underside in centre, upper side coated semilustrous dark-brown and has eight barbs each side coated red and surrounded by tiny white dots and three pairs of pendants white lines on each spout. Evans 1903, pl. II.2; Evans 1935, 134 fig. 102; Betancourt 1985a, pl. 9G. HM 2694.

927. (K.48) Most of rim missing. Restored in plaster. Similar to 926 but lacks the reserved bands on lower side. Mackenzie 1903 PB (3) # 9; Evans 1935, 135 fig. 105. AM 1930.645.

Jug with Horizontal Spout—Type 2

928. (K.102) PLATES 28, 135 Two-thirds of rim, handle and few small body fragments missing. Restored in plaster. H. 12.3, D. rim 4.7, base 3.5 cm. Interior of rim and exterior coated dark-brown. Exterior has white horizontal band at base of neck and three white and three red alternating vertical lines on side. KSM L III 1 #997. SMP 9719.

Small Rounded Bridge-spouted Jar

929. (K.75) PLATES 28, 136 Spout, base and most of side missing. H. 7.0, D. rim 7.5 cm. Interior has thin rim band and large drips of dark paint. Exterior coated black and has orange rim band with added white dots and large white zig-zag pattern on side. KSM M III 2 #1195, 1196.

Rounded Bridge-spouted Jar—Type 4

930. (K.50) PLATE 136 Large fragment of half of rim, spout, side and base with one handle. Restored in plaster. H. 14.0, D. rim 9.3, base 6.0 cm. Interior has few drips of dark paint near rim. Exterior coated dark-brown and has large white foliate band with added orange dots and horizontal lines at middle with rows of white dots in pairs of lines and red dots connected with white S-spirals above and below, and three horizontal white bands near base. Evans 1921, 268 fig. 199e. AM AE 912.

931. (K.51) PLATES 28, 136 One-quarter of rim and few body fragments missing. Restored in plaster. H. 14.5, D. rim 8.5, base 6.0 cm. Similar to 930 but red added to foliate band not orange. KSM M II 5 #1175, 1196. SMP 9720.

932. (K.52) PLATE 136 One handle, most of rim and several side fragments missing. Partially restored in plaster. H. 14.5, D. rim 9.0, base 6.0 cm. Similar to 930 but pink added to foliate band and orange used instead of red elsewhere. KSM M II 5 #1175; KSM M III 2 #1192, 1194, 1195, 1196; KSM #1852. SMP 9721.

933. (K.53) PLATE 136 Spout and many body fragments missing. Restored in plaster. H. 14.5, D. rim 9.0, base 5.0 cm. Similar to 930. KSM M II 5 #1175, 1182; KSM M III 2 #1195, 1196; KSM L III 1 #997. SMP 9722.

934. (K.54) PLATE 136 Spout, one handle and much of rim and side missing. H. 14.5, D. rim 9.0, base 5.0 cm. Similar to 930. KSM M II 5 #1175, 1176, 1180, 1181, 1182; KSM M III 2 #1195, 1196; KSM L III 1 #997. SMP 9723.

935. (K.55) PLATE 137 Large fragment of base and lower side. H. 13.5, D. base 6.0 cm. Similar to 930. KSM M III 2 #1190, 1194, 1195, 1196. SMP 9724.

936. (K.56) PLATE 137 Large fragment of rim and side with complete handle. H. 9.5, D. rim 10.0 cm. Similar 930. KSM M II 5 #1175, 1182; KSM M III 2 #1196; KSM L III 1 #997.

937. (K.57) Numerous non-joining fragments of body with both handles. Similar to 930. KSM M III 2 #1195, 1196.

938. (K.58) PLATE 137 Large fragment of rim and upper side. H. 7.5, D. rim 9.0 cm. Similar to **930**. KSM M II 5 #1182; KSM M III 2 #1196.

939. (K.59) PLATE 137 Two non-joining fragments of rim and upper side. H. 5.3, D. rim 9.0 cm. Similar to **930**. KSM M II 5 #1173, 1174; KSM M III 2 #1196.

940. (K.60) PLATE 137 Seven non-joining fragments of lower side. Similar to **930**. KSM M II 5 #1175, 1180; KSM M III 2 #1198; KSM L III 1 #997.

941. (K.61) PLATE 137 Two non-joining fragments of rim and lower side. Similar to **930**. KSM M II 5 #1182; KSM L III 1 #997.

942. (K.62) PLATES 28, 138 Numerous rim and body fragments missing. Restored in plaster. H. 15.0, D. rim 8.0, base 5.9 cm. Interior has dark uneven band at rim and spout. Exterior coated dark-brown and has large white dots surrounded by tiny white dots in white circles interconnected by orange and white lines. KSM M II 5 #1175, 1180, 1181, 1182; KSM M III 2 #1195, 1196; KSM L III 1 #997. SMP 9725.

943. (K.63) PLATE 138 Spout, most of rim, one handle and many fragments of body missing. Rim fragment in AM? Partly restored in plaster. H. 15.0, D. rim 8.0, base 6.0 cm. Similar to **942**. KSM M II 5 #1175, 1182; KSM M III 2 #1195, 1196. AM AE 1032.3. SMP 9726.

944. (K.64) PLATE 138 Large non-joining fragments of rim with spout and lower side. H. 4.0, D. rim 8.5 cm. Similar to **942** but has added red on orange bands. KSM M III 2 #1195.

945. (K.65) PLATE 138 Three fragments of rim with spout and one handle. D. rim 9.0 cm. Similar to **944**. KSM M II 5 #1175, 1182; KSM M III 2 #1195; KSM L III 1 #997.

946. (K.66) PLATE 138 Three fragments of rim with complete spout. H. 10.0, D. rim 9.0 cm. Similar to **944**. KSM M II 5 #1174, 1175, 1182; KSM M III 2 #1195; KSM L III 1 #997.

947. (K.67) PLATES 28, 139 Most of rim and one handle missing. Restored in plaster. H. 14.0, D. rim 8.0, base 5.0 cm. Interior has thick black rim band. Exterior coated black and has three zones of white chevrons bordered in white and three horizontal orange bands with added red dots. KSM M II 5 #1175, 1182; KSM M III 2 #1195, 1196; KSM M II 3 #1133. SMP 9727.

948. (K.68) PLATE 139 Tip of spout and numerous body fragments missing. Restored in plaster. H. 15.5, D. rim 8.5, base 6.0 cm. Similar to **947**. KSM M II 5 #1173, 1174, 1175, 1178, 1182; KSM M III 2 #1196; KSM L III 1 #997. SMP 9728.

949. (K.69) PLATE 139 Large fragment of base and lower side. Partially restored. H. 10.0, D. base 6.0 cm. Similar to **947**. KSM M II 5 #1175, 1182; KSM M III 2 #1195; KSM L III 1 #997. SMP 9729.

950. (K.70) PLATE 139 Large fragment of lower side. H. 11.5 cm. Similar to **947**. KSM M III 2 #1195, 1196.

951. (K.71) PLATE 139 Three non-joining fragments of rim with complete spout and one handle. H. 7.5, D. rim 9.5 cm. Similar to **947**. KSM M II 5 #1173, 1175, 1182; KSM M III 2 #1196.

952. (K.72) PLATE 139 Large fragment of side with complete spout. H. 7.5 cm. Similar to **947**. KSM M III 2 #1195, 1196.

953. (K.73) PLATES 28, 140 Half of rim, one handle and base missing. Partially restored. H. 12.0, D. rim 9.5 cm. Interior has dark uneven rim band. Exterior coated dark-brown throughout and has large white closed spirals with orange petals with added red dots at middle and and connected white circles with petaloid loops above and ?below. KSM M II 5 #1182; KSM M III 2 #1195, 1196. SMP 9730.

954. (K.76) PLATES 29, 140 Large fragment of two-thirds of rim with complete spout. H. 4.5, D. rim 8.5 cm. Interior has dark uneven rim band. Exterior coated black and has white decoration of ?large white circles or spirals at middle, zone of white vertical lines with triangles either side above handle at rim and white loop with added orange and red. KSM M II 5 #1175, 1182.

955. (K.77) PLATES 29, 140 Two large non-joining fragments of rim with half of spout and complete handle. H. 6.5, D. rim 9.0 cm. Interior has wide dark-brown band at rim. Exterior coated black and has traces of white wavy line decoration at rim and on spout and thick white wavy band outlined in orange at middle. KSM M II 5 #1182; KSM M III 2 #1195.

956. (K.78) PLATE 140 Six non-joining fragments of side and rim with part of spout. D. rim 9.0 cm. Interior has thick brown rim band. Exterior coated dark-brown and has thick white band at rim and at least two large white flowers with red dots at centres. KSM M III 2 #1195, 1196. Para: F. 4864a.

957. (K.79) PLATE 140 Six non-joining fragments of rim and side with complete spout and handle. D. rim 9.0 cm. Interior has thick red-brown rim band. Exterior coated red-brown and has two opposing wavy lines of white semicircles bisected by orange lines at middle and orange dot with white loops above and below beneath handle. KSM M II 5 #1182; KSM M III 2 #1195, 1196.

958. (K.80) PLATE 140 Two non-joining fragments of rim and side. H. 3.8, D. rim *c.* 12.0 cm. Similar to **957**. KSM M II 5 #1182; KSM M III 2 #1195, 1196.

Technique: Wheelmade—cone thrown

Crude Bowl—Type 2

959. (K.123) Half of rim and side missing. H. 3.5, D. rim 13.5, base 6.5 cm. Coated red-brown throughout. KSM M II 5 #1178, 1180.

960. (K.124) Fragment of rim, side and base. H. 2.0, D. rim 12.5, base 5.0 cm. Coated thin brown throughout. KSM M II 5 #1181.

Crude Bowl—Type 3

961. (K.120) Large fragment of rim, side and base. H. 2.0, D. rim 10.3, base 5.5 cm. Coated brown throughout. KSM M II 5 #1176.

962. (K.122) Fragment of base with one-third of side and rim. H. 1.6, D. rim 8.0, base 4.2 cm. Coated thin brown throughout. KSM M II 5 #1173.

963. (K.121) H. 2.8, D. rim 9.0, base 5.0 cm. Coated red-brown throughout. KSM M II 5 #1173.

OTHER FABRICS

Shallow Bowl

964. (K.125) Fine, red-brown clay. Most of rim missing. H. 3.7, D. rim 17.0, base 5.0 cm. Coated brown throughout. KSM M II 5 #1180.

Tumbler

965. (K.84) PLATE 29 Rim and much of upper side missing. H. 5.8, rest. 7.0, D. base 2.5 cm. Fine porous grey-green fabric. Wheelmade. Interior has dark rim band outlined in white. Exterior has dark-brown open buckle motif outlined in white on either side on reserved ground. KSM L III 1 #997.

Angular Cup

966. (K.83) PLATES 29, 134 Large fragment of side. H. 5.5, D. max 12.0 cm. Fine hard red-brown fabric. Wheelmade. Five horizontal grooves cut at middle. Coated thin dark-brown through-

out. KSM M III 2 #1195; O II 3 #1387.

Juglet

967. (K.104) PLATE 135 Spout, handle and much of side missing. H. 5.8, D. base 3.6 cm. Semifine brown fabric. Wheelmade. Plain. KSM M II 5 #1176, 1180, 1181.

Jug with Cut-away Spout—as Type 4

968. (K.103) PLATE 29 Four non-joining fragments of neck, side and base. H. rest. 21.0, D. base 4.5 cm. Fine orange fabric. Wheelmade. Interior of spout and exterior coated dull dark-brown, fired grey-brown in places and flaking away. Exterior has thick white horizontal bands at base and neck and in group of three at middle. KSM M III 2 #1191, 1195; O II 3 #1387.

Large Shallow Bowl

969. (K.126) Rim chipped. H. 4.0, D. rim 15.0, base 8.0 cm. Gritty grey-green fabric. Wheelmade. Plain. KSM L III 1 #997.

970. (K.127) Much of rim and side missing. H. 4.5, D. rim 20.0, base 11.0 cm. Gritty orange-buff fabric. Wheelmade. Plain. KSM M II 5 #1180.

Hand Lamp—Type 1

971. (K.119) Two-thirds of body, handle and most of spout missing. H. 3.2, D. rim 9.0, base 8.0 cm. Soft Gritty Buff fabric. Wheelmade. Traces of red slip and burnish. Spout burnt. KSM M II 5 #1181.

Cooking pot

972. (K.128) PLATE 29 Five large fragments of rim, side and base with two pods. H. 23.5, D. rim 22.0, base 12.0 cm. Gritty red-brown fabric. Handmade. Plain. Lower exterior and one side blackened through use. KSM M II 5 #1173, 1174.

Large Jar

973. (K.1054) Large fragment of rim and shoulder. H. 14.0, D. rim 11.0 cm. Gritty brown very micaceous fabric fired grey at core. Handmade. Plain. Three shallow horizontal grooves on upper shoulder. Possibly central Cycladic. KSM M II 5 #1162, 1169, 1173, 1174.

Amphora

974. (K.1055) Several non-joining fragments of rim and side with complete handle. Gritty red micaceous fabric. Handmade. Plain. Possibly central Cycladic. KSM M II 5 #1135, 1162, 1166, 1169, 1171, 1174.

GROUP M: THE MONOLITHIC PILLAR BASEMENT

FABRIC: FINE BUFF

Technique: Wheelmade

Surface: Dark on buff; polychrome decorated

Squat Rounded Cup—Type 1

975. (K.22) PLATES 142, 143 Handle and several fragments of rim and lower side missing. H. 8.1, D. rim 9.5, base 4.5 cm. Inte-rior coated semilustrous dark-brown with white pendant semi-circles at rim above thin red line. Exterior has dark-brown interlocking S-pattern on buff ground bordered by thin orange line and thick dark band with alternating S and oval pattern both with added orange filling at rim and base. Inscribed 'SE K Area K.02'. Mackenzie 1902 PB (2), 75 K.22; Mackenzie 1903, pl. VI.4. HM 2698.

Surface: Monochrome coated; polychrome decorated

Rounded Goblet—Type 3

976. (K.1058) PLATE 29 Foot, half of rim and most of lower side missing. H. pres. 7.5, D. rim 8.6 cm. Interior coated dark-brown. Exterior coated dark-brown and has eight horizontal rows of alternating orange and white printed crescents. Mackenzie 1904 PB (2), 14; Mackenzie 1906, pl. IX.7; Momigliano 1991, pl. 22.4. HM 5200 display.

Tumbler

977. (K.1056) PLATES 142, 143 Fragment of base and lower side. H. 6.9, D. rim 4.6 cm. Coated dark-brown throughout. Exterior has alternating vertical lines of prickle barbotine, red and white dots and white lines. Inscribed 'S E K Area'. HM 3875.

Rounded Cup—Type 4

978. (K.24) PLATE 142 Most of rim and side missing. Appears to have dark coated exterior with thick white vertical bands with added red wavy lines. Not located.

Angular Cup

979. (K.23) PLATES 142, 143 Base, part of handle and rim fragment missing. Restored. H. rest. 9.0, D. base 10.0 cm. Coated semilustrous dark-brown throughout. Interior has zone of vertical white bars with added red dots with alternating red and yellow S between bordered by white connected semi-circles above and below. Exterior has foliate band at middle red band below rim and above base and same pattern as on interior repeated on upper and lower side. Mackenzie 1902 PB (2), 75 K.23; Evans 1921, 242 fig. 183a4. HM 2697.

980. (K.1057) Four non-joining fragments of rim, lower side and base. H. pres. 5.7, rest. *c.* 12.0, D. rim 15.0 cm. Coated semilustrous black throughout. Interior has tiny white dot rosettes inside cream circles with added red dots near rim. Exterior has repeated vertical zones of cream bands with added red dots outlined in red with added orange dots, white zig-zag on right and tiny dot rosettes connected by S-pattern of tiny white dots on left side. Mackenzie 1902 PB (2), 77; Mackenzie 1903, pl. VII.5. KSM O II 3 #1387,1391. AM 1938.576,.589,.817.

Spouted Jar

981. (K.957) PLATES 142, 143 Rim fragment with spout. H. 5.5, D. rim 12.0 cm. Interior has red-brown rim band. Exterior coated red-brown and has horizontal rows of white linked circles at rim spout and upper side. Interior of spout has white semicircles and spots on rim and white radiating motif in bowl. AM 1938.587.

FABRIC: ?TEMPERED BUFF

Offering table

982. (K.26) Fragment of pedestalled foot with base of bowl. Exte-

rior appears dark coated and has horizontal rows of barbotine alternating with red and yellow stripes and rows of white dots all enclosed in white linked semicircles on two sides and white ivy leaf design filled with red and orange alternating in between. Mackenzie 1902 PB (2), 79 K.26; Evans 1921, opp. 231 pl. Ib; Evans 1935, 114 fig. 8oc. Not located.

983. (K.27) Mackenzie 1902 PB (2), 77. Not located.

FABRIC: GRITTY RED-BROWN

Angular Cup

984. (K.886) PLATES 142, 143 Handle missing. Restored in plaster. H. c. 8.0 cm. Handmade. Plain surface with white horizontal lines—one at rim, two at middle and three at angle; two rows of white with added red dots between horizontal lines. HM 4353.

GROUP N: THE SOUTH POLYCHROME DE-POSITS

FABRIC: FINE BUFF

Technique: Wheelmade

Surface: Dark on buff; Decorated

Bowl

985. (K.980) PLATE 30 Fragment of half of rim and base with two lugs. H. 6.5, D. rim 13.0, base 4.5 cm. Interior has dark band at rim and lower side and large painted ripple pattern on buff ground below rim. Exterior has thick dark bands at rim, middle and base leaving reserved zones. KSM R V #1566, 1568.

Jug

986. (K.972) PLATE 147 Spout, handle and half of body missing. Partly restored. H. 13.1, D. base 4.1 cm. Exterior body coated dull red-brown, spout left in reserve. KSM R IV 5 #1533, 1546.

Surface: Monochrome coated

Rounded Cup—Type 5

987. (K.966) PLATE 147 Half of rim and side and lower part of handle missing. H. 7.3, D. rim 13.0, base 4.7 cm. Coated red-brown throughout. Five horizontal grooves cut into middle of side. KSM R V 2 #1557, 1558, 1567, 1589.

Surface: Monochrome coated; white decorated

Jug with Cut-away Spout—Type 4

988. (K.974) PLATE 147 Part of spout, two handles, many body fragments and base missing. Restored in plaster. H. 17.5, D. base c. 4.0 cm. Interior of spout and exterior coated red-brown throughout. Exterior has white horizontal bands—one at neck, three at middle and ?one near base. KSM R IV 5 #1535; KSM R V 2 #1555; KSM R V 6 #1582, 1585. SMP 9731.

Surface: Monochrome coated; white spotted

Tumbler—Type 4

989. (K.970) PLATE 147 Most of rim and upper side missing. H. 11.0, D. rim 11.5, base 4.0 cm. Coated semilustrous black and white spotted throughout. KSM R V 6 #1582, 1585, 1586, 1587, 1589.

Straight-sided Cup—Type 7

990. (K.967) PLATE 147 Few small rim and side fragments and half of handle missing. Restored in plaster. H. 6.3, D. rim 9.5, base 6.9 cm. Coated semilustrous dark-brown throughout. Exterior and top of handle carefully spotted white. KSM R IV 6 #1538. SMP 9732.

Short-rimmed Angular Cup—Type 3

991. (K.968) PLATE 148 Foot, handle and much of rim missing. Restored in plaster. H. rest. 8.3, D. rim 10.2 cm. Coated semilustrous black throughout. Interior spotted white. KSM R V 2 #1555, 1558. SMP 9733.

992. (K.969) PLATES 30, 148 Half of rim and handle and few small body and base fragments missing. Restored in plaster. H. 9.1, D. rim 10.0, base 4.5 cm. Coated black throughout. Interior white spotted. KSM R IV 6 #1539, 1540. SMP 9734.

Jug

993. (K.973) PLATE 147 Spout, handle and many body and base fragments missing. Partly restored in plaster. H. 12.0, D. base 3.5 cm. Interior of spout and exterior coated dark red-brown. Exterior has thick orange bands at base of neck and middle and white spotting all over. KSM R V 2 #1554, 1557, 1558.

Surface: Monochrome coated; polychrome decorated

Straight-sided Cup—Type 7

994. (K.559) PLATE 30 Three non-joining fragments of rim, side and base with lower handle stub. H. 5.0, D. rim 10.0, base 8.0 cm. Coated semilustrous dark grey-brown throughout. Interior has white band at rim. Exterior has white figure-of-eight with circles of tiny white dots and orange flower on left side. KSM R V 5 #1580; KSM R V 6 #1587, 1588.

Straight-sided Cup

995. (K.558) PLATES 30, 148 Fragment of rim and side. H. 7.5, D. rim 11.0 cm. Coated semilustrous dark-brown throughout. Interior has white band at rim. Exterior has horizontal orange band with added red dots at middle and white chevrons at rim and ?base. KSM R IV 4 #1530; KSM R V 6 #1586.

Straight-sided Cup—Type 10

996. (K.556) PLATE 148 Most of rim, side and handle missing. Restored in plaster. H. 7.8, D. rim 9.4, base 5.1 cm. Coated light red-brown throughout. Exterior has large white rosette with open circle at centre enclosed in large white circle either side and odd orange filled ?foliate design above closed spiral at front opposite handle. Evans 1928, 371 fig. 206c. HM 7696.

997. (K.557) PLATES 30, 148 Half of rim, top of handle and most of base missing. Partly restored in plaster. H. 7.5, D. rim 10.5, base 6.0 cm. Coated dark grey-brown throughout. Exterior has horizontal orange bands with added red dots and outlined in white at middle and base, white open running spirals at rim

and white chevrons on lower side. KSM R IV 1 #1524; KSM R IV 6 #1539, 1540, 1542. SMP 9735.

Rounded Cup—Type 6

998. (K.964) PLATE 148 One rim fragment, few body fragments, part of base and handle. Restored in plaster. H. 6.2, D. rim 12.5, base 4.5 cm. Coated dull brown throughout. Interior has diagonal white slashes at rim and white rosette pattern with red dot at centre in base. Exterior has wavy line pattern alternating orange and pink with white dots with added orange dashes at joints and filled with tiny white flowers. Underside has white rosette in reserve with red circle separating inner from outer rosette. Evans 1928, pl. Ixa; Evans 1935, 132 fig. 100. HM 8406.

999. (K.965) PLATE 30 Five non-joining fragments of rim, side and base with lower handle stub. H. 6.0, D. rim 10.5, base 4.5 cm. Coated dark-brown throughout. Exterior white wavy line pattern filled with alternating circles of tiny white dots and orange loaves with four white dots. KSM R IV 5 #1533.

Rounded Bridge-spouted Jar

1000. (K.976) PLATE 149 Several non-joining fragments of rim and side with part of one handle. Restored in plaster. H. rest. 14.3, D. rim 8.2 cm. Interior has many dark-brown drips. Exterior coated dark-brown and has large white rosette with open circle at centre in white circle surrounded by white dots with multiple petals and orange loops on back and same repeated without rosette at spout, three white wavy lines on lower side. Mackenzie 1922 DB (1), 80; Evans 1928, 215 pl. Ixf. HM 7694.

1001. (K.978) PLATE 30 Numerous non-joining fragments of rim and side. H. 7.0, D. rim 9.5 cm. Interior has thick dark smear at rim. Exterior coated semilustrous black and has large white open running spirals with white petals filled with orange and red on shoulder and uncertain white decoration on lower side. KSM R IV 1 #1524; KSM R V 2 #1559; KSM R V 5 #1571, 1573, 1575, 1576, 1580, 1581; KSM R V 6 #1583, 1585, 1587, 1589.

Rounded Bridge-spouted Jar—Type 6

1002. (K.977) PLATES 30, 149 Spout, one-third of rim, one handle and several body fragments missing. Restored in plaster. H. 15.0, D. rim 9.8, base 6.6 cm. Interior has dark smear at rim. Exterior coated dark-brown, worn away, and has large white floral design with orange flower on front and back and thick white band at base. KSM R IV 5 #1534. SMP 9736.

Flask

1003. (K.975) PLATE 149 Spout, handle, base and several body fragments missing. H. 22.5, rest. 28.0 cm. Exterior coated semilustrous dark-brown and has large red swastika with white multiple petaloid designs on both flat sides. Mackenzie 1922 DB (1), 80; Evans 1928, 215 pl. Ixe; Zervos 1956, fig. 323. HM 7695.

FABRIC: FINE SOFT BUFF

Technique: Wheelmade

Surface: Dark on buff; reserved

Bridge-spouted Jar

1004. (K.979) PLATE 149 Large fragment of base. H. 6.8, D. base 5.0

cm. Exterior has alternating vertical zones with dark drops on reserved ground and white drops on a dark coated zone, similar to **874**. KSM R IV 6 #1547.

Globular Rhyton

1005. (K.983) PLATES 30, 149 Fragment of upper part of body with base of neck. Exterior has brown ripple burnished zone on shoulder and brown bands on neck and upper side. Similar to **539**. KSM R IV 5 #1536.

Surface: Monochrome coated

Tumbler

1006. (K.971) PLATE 147 Three-quarters of rim and upper side missing. H. 10.3, D. rim 9.0, base 5.1 cm. Interior of rim and exterior coated dull red-brown. KSM R IV 5 #1534.

Surface: Monochrome coated; polychrome decorated

Straight-sided Cup

1007. (K.560) PLATES 30, 149 Large fragment of base and side. H. 7.5, D. rim 9.6, base 6.0 cm. Coated dull dark-brown throughout. Exterior white foliate band bordered above and below by dark-red lines below rim and pairs of horizontal white lines at middle and base. Underside has double white cross with dark-red band in one bar. KSM R V 2 #1558; KSM R V 5 #1570; KSM R V 6 #1585.

FABRIC: TEMPERED SOFT BUFF

Technique: Handmade

Amphoriskos

1008. (K.981) PLATE 150 Large fragment of upper half with one handle and one lug. H. 10.7, D. rim 3.4 cm. Plain. KSM R IV 5 #1532. Para: F. 5157, 5291.

Lid

1009. (K.982) PLATE 150 Chipped and worn. H. 1.0, D. 4.8 cm. Plain. KSM R V 2 #1558. Para: F. 2693, 6269.

FABRIC: TEMPERED BUFF

Technique: Handmade

Amphora

1010. (K.984) PLATES 145, 150 Numerous fragments of side and shoulder missing. Restored in plaster. H. rest. 43.0, D. base 11.5 cm. Exterior has large dark-brown multiple petals in S-shaped design on both sides. Evans 1928, 304 fig. 176. HM 7739.

Open Spouted Pithos

1011. (K.985) Numerous fragments of rim and body missing. Restored in plaster. Interior has thick dark band at rim. Exterior coated dark-brown and has large white rosette with red dot at centre in elaborated design of white filled semicircles, raquet pattern, closed spirals, multiple petals and large red dots above horizontal white bands at lower side and base. Mackenzie 1922 DB (1), 80; Evans 1928, 215 pl. Ixd. HM display.

FABRIC: MICACEOUS BUFF; CYCLADIC

Technique: Handmade

Amphora

1012. (K.1060) PLATE 150 Seven non-joining fragments of rim, shoulder and lower side with one complete and half of other handle. H. rest. 36.0, D. rim 12.0 cm. Exterior has two thin dull dark-brown horizontal bands at neck, otherwise plain. MacGillivray 1984a, 154 fig. 2. KSM R IV 1 #1524; KSM R V 2 #1559, 1560; KSM R V 5 #1575.

1013. (K.1061) PLATE 150 Five non-joining fragments of shoulder, lower side and base with one complete and half of other handle. Plain. KSM R V 5 #1570, 1579, 1581.

1014. (K.1062) Fragments of body and handles. Plain. KSM R IV 1 #1524; KSM R V 2 #1553, 1559.

1015. (K.1063) PLATE 150 Two non-joining fragments of shoulder and complete handle. Plain. KSM R IV 6 #1541; KSM R V 5 #1575.

1016. (K.1064) PLATE 150 One complete handle. Plain. KSM R V 5 #1570.

1017. (K.1065) PLATE 150 One complete handle. Plain. KSM R V 5 #1581.

1018. (K.1066) PLATE 150 Fragment of half of handle. Plain. KSM R V 5 #1573.

1019. (K.1067) PLATE 150 Fragment of base. D. base c. 6.0 cm. Plain. KSM R V 5 #1573.

1020. (K.1068) PLATE 150 Fragment of lower side. Plain. ?Potter's mark. KSM R IV 6 #1543.

FABRIC: GRITTY PINK; NEAR EASTERN

Canaanite Jars

1021. (K.1069) PLATE 150 Seven non-joining fragments, probably from more than one pot, including complete handle. Pink very porous clay with rounded ?sand grits. Three incised horizontal grooves below handle. Traces of finely incised horizontal lines on body. Surface plain. KSM R IV 6 #1542, 1546; KSM R V 2 #1555; KSM R V 5 #1571, 1579, 1580.

GROUP O: THE TOWN DRAIN

FABRIC: FINE BUFF

Technique: Proto-wheelmade

Surface: Monochrome coated

Straight-sided Cup—Type 2

1022. (K.1070) PLATE 152 Intact. Coated black throughout. HM 9107.

1023. (K.1071) PLATE 152 Recomposed, complete. Coated dark-brown all over except handle. HM 8393.

1024. (K.1072) PLATE 152 Handle missing. Restored in plaster. H. 5.6, D. rim 9.6, base 7.0 cm. Coated semilustrous black throughout. HM 8394.

Technique: Handmade

Tall-rimmed Angular Cup—Type 2

1025. (K.1001) PLATE 152 Handle and two small rim fragments missing. Restored. H. 6.8, D. rim 13.0, base 6.0 cm. Coated dark-brown throughout. HM 8389.

Technique: Proto-wheelmade

Surface: Monochrome coated; polychrome decorated
Straight-sided Cup—Type 2

1026. (K.986) PLATE 153 Handle and one-third of rim and side missing. Restored. Coated black throughout. Exterior has white dot rosette at front and red crosses outlined in white at sides. HM 8391.

1027. (K.987) PLATE 153 One rim fragment missing. Restored in plaster. H. 5.3, D. base 5.4 cm. Coated dark-brown throughout. Exterior has alternating red diagonal band and white interlocking hook pattern. HM 8395.

Technique: Wheelmade

Surface: Monochrome coated

Miniature Tripod Cup

1028. (K.994) PLATE 153 Intact. Rim pulled to form spout. Three bosses on base form feet. H. 4.0, D. base c. 3.0 cm. Coated dark-brown throughout. HM 8399.

Tall-rimmed Angular Cup

1029. (K.995) PLATE 153 Handle and half of rim and side missing. Restored in plaster. H. 4.8, D. rim 8.2, base 3.6 cm. Coated thin brown throughout. HM 8397.

1030. (K.997) PLATES 151, 153 Handle and three-quarters of rim missing. Restored in plaster. H. 5.8, D. base 4.3 cm. Coated dull dark-brown throughout. HM 8395.

Rounded Cup—as Type 5

1031. (K.992) PLATE 153 Half of rim and side missing. H. 6.8, D. base 5.0 cm. Coated dark-brown throughout. Blunt incised not quite vertical lines in side. HM 8390.

Surface: Monochrome coated; white decorated

Tall-rimmed Angular Cup, crinkled rim—Type 3

1032. (K.998) PLATES 151, 154 Rim fragment missing. Restored in plaster. H. 6.1, D. base 3.9 cm. Coated black throughout. Exterior has white sponge printed patterns. HM 8386.

Surface: Monochrome coated; polychrome decorated
Tall-rimmed Angular Cup

1033. (K.996) PLATES 151, 154 Two fragments of rim missing. Restored in plaster. H. 5.0, D. rim 10.3, base 4.5 cm. Coated dull brown throughout. Exterior has barbotine floral patterns outlined in orange with red detail alternating upper and lower side with dot rosettes in white. Evans 1928, 369 fig. 205; Evans 1935, 106 pl. XXVIIc. HM 8388.

Jug with Cut-away Spout—Type 2

1034.(K.1003) PLATE 154 Complete, recomposed. H. 9.2, D. base 5.7 cm. Interior of rim and exterior coated dark-brown. Exterior has thin red horizontal lines at base of neck and widest point of body and rows of white dots below rim and on shoulder. HM 8384.

GROUP P: THE EARLY TOWN HOUSES

FABRIC: FINE BUFF

Technique: Handmade

Miniature Bridge-spouted Jar

1035.(K.1004) PLATE 154 Fragment of three-quarters of rim with one handle. Restored in plaster. H. rest. 6.3, D. rim 4.8 cm. Exterior coated dark grey-brown and has zone of white open running spirals at middle with white lines above and groups of white strokes on rim with three plastic shells at back, central shell red. Evans 1928, 371 fig. 206f. HM 7752.

Technique: Wheelmade

Rhyton

1036.(K.1006) PLATES 154, 155 Intact. H. 9.5, D. rim 7.0, base 4.0 cm. Interior and exterior of rim have thick brown band with drips in places. Base pierced with hole 0.5 cm when manufactured. HM 8401.

Surface: Monochrome coated

Straight-sided Cup—Type 12

1037.(K.988) PLATE 154 Half of rim and side missing. Restored in plaster. H. 6.9, D. rim 10.0, base 6.0 cm. Coated semilustrous dark-brown to black throughout. Two evenly spaced ridges in side. HM 8392.

Short-rimmed Angular Cup

1038.(K.1000) PLATES 155, 156 Few small fragments of rim and side missing. Restored in plaster. H. 8.8, D. rim 11.0, base 5.0 cm. Coated semilustrous brown throughout. HM 8398.

Rounded Cup—Type 5

1039.(K.993) Large fragment of rim, side and base. Restored. Evans 1928, 371 fig. 206b. Not located.

Jug with Horizontal Spout—Type 3

1040.(K.1007) PLATE 156 Front of spout chipped. H. 15.3, D. base

4.5 cm. Interior of rim and exterior coated dull dark-brown. HM 8382.

Surface: Monochrome coated; white decorated

Straight-sided Cup—Type 9

1041.(K.1073) PLATE 152 Intact. H. 6.9, D. rim 9.0, base 6.0 cm. Coated dull burgundy and carelessly sprayed white throughout. HM 8396.

Jug with Horizontal Spout—Type 3

1042.(K.1008) PLATES 155, 156 Intact. H. 11.0, D. rim 4.0, base 3.3 cm. Interior of rim and exterior coated semilustrous dark-brown. Exterior has three horizontal grooves cut into middle, white spotting on shoulder and thin white line at rim. HM 8383.

Surface: Monochrome coated; polychrome decorated

Straight-sided Cup—Type 7

1043.(K.989) Fragment of base and lower side. ?Restored. Evans 1928, 371 fig. 206d. Not located.

Straight-sided Cup—Type 12

1044.(K.990) PLATE 156 Most of rim, side and handle missing. Restored in plaster. H. 7.3, D. rim 10.0, base 5.7 cm. Coated semilustrous dark-brown throughout. Exterior has four horizontal ridges at middle with orange band on top ridge and white spotting below rim. KSM P III 5 #1484. SMP 9737.

Rounded Cup—Type 5

1045.(K.999) PLATES 155, 156 Few fragments of rim and base missing. Restored in plaster. H. 7.0, D. rim 11.0, base 5.0 cm. Coated semilustrous dark-brown throughout. Exterior has two horizontal grooves cut into middle painted orange and white spotting below rim. HM 8387.

OTHER FABRICS

Large three handled Jug

1046.(K.1009) PLATE 155 Intact. Probably tempered buff. Exterior appears dark coated and has thick orange band at middle with pairs of white bands below and at base, white spotting on shoulder and handles and orange band at base of neck. Evans 1928, 371 fig. 206e. Not located.

Bridge-spouted Jar—Type 6

1047.(K.1005) PLATE 156 Tip of spout, one handle and few body fragments missing. Restored in plaster. H. 15.0, D. rim 8.3, base 5.2 cm. Gritty red fabric, slightly micaceous. Wheelmade. Traces of red coat on exterior. HM 8381.

Footed Goblet

1048.(K.1002) Large fragment of base and lower side. Incorrectly restored into amphora. Probably like **605**. Evans 1928, 371 fig. 206a. Not located.

Hand Lamp

1049.(K.1074) PLATE 155 Handle missing. Traces of burning at spout. HM 8402.

Appendix II. Guide to material consulted in the Knossos Stratigraphical Museum

i. SHERD MATERIAL ASSIGNED TO THE POTTERY GROUPS IN CHAPTER 1:

A II 2 #49–51, 53, 56–75 'N.W. Area. Kouloura or Lakkos' (GROUP D)

A II 3 #80, 82 'N.W.K.A. Room and Area of Bronze Vessels' (GROUP D)

A II 9 #92–3 'Area of Polychrome two-handled spouted jug' (GROUP B)

A II 10 #94 'Area S. of polychrome two-handled spouted jug' (GROUP D)

A II 11 #95–6 'W. Border of Area' (GROUP D)

A II 17 #106 'Porcelain Deposit' (GROUP C)

A II 21 #112 'W. Rooms' (GROUP D)

A II #125–6 'N. W. Kamares Area' (GROUP D)

A II #127–8 'Area of N. W. Treasure House' (GROUP D)

A II #144a 'Area of Walls' (GROUP D)

B I 6 #178–191 'Test Pit 3. 2nd M.' (GROUP A)

B I 7 #215, 217–220, 222 'Test Pit 4' (GROUP A)

B I 14 #256–262 'Test Pit 11' (GROUP E)

B I 19 #322–9 'E. Kouloura I' (GROUP E)

B I 20 #330–350 'Middle Kouloura II' (GROUP E)

B I 21 #351–6 'W. Kouloura III' (GROUP E)

B III 8 #416–8 'Trench E. of later houses' (GROUP E)

L III 1 #996, 998 'SW Room' (GROUP F)

L III 1 #997 'SW Room' (GROUP L)

L III 8 #1027–52 'Room of Jars' (GROUP I)

L III 15 #1071 'Small rooms E. of Lime Kiln' (GROUP H)

L III 16 #1072–5 'Lot from area of Lime Kiln (N.E. Shoot)' (GROUP G)

M II 5 #1171–2 'Olive Press T. P. 2nd meter Selected' (GROUP L)

M II 5 #1173–82 'Olive Press Area Test Pit 2 3rd and 4th M.' (GROUP L)

M III 2 #1189–94 'Loom-weight Area S. of Area of Spiral Fresco' (GROUP K)

M III 2 #1194 'Loom-weight Area...' Fine sherds only (GROUP F)

M III 2 #1195–6 'Loom-weight Area...' (GROUP L)

M III 2 #1197–8 'Loom-weight Area...' (GROUP F)

O II 3 #1385–6, 1388–1403 'Area of Monolithic Pillars' (GROUP M)

O II 3 #1387 '? Monolithic Pillar Basement' (mixed elements of GROUPS L and M)

P III 5 #1482–4 'Area of the drain running N.' (GROUP P)

P III 6 #1485 'House B. From the direction of outlet of drain' (GROUP P)

P III 7 # 1486–7 'Where drain ends' (GROUP P)

R IV 2–6 #1527–51 'The House of the Fallen Blocks and Area' (GROUP N)

R V 2, 4–6 #1553–60, 1565–1589 'The House of Sacrifice' (GROUP N)

V. 1933 T.P.1 #1811–19 'T.P. 1 Taverna House Foundations' (GROUP P)

ii. SHERD MATERIAL LISTED AS BELONGING TO ONE OF THE POTTERY GROUPS, BUT DOES NOT JOIN:

A II #52, 54–5 'N.W.Area...Upper Deposit (Kouloura)' LM pottery which doesn't join GROUP D.

A II 17 #107 'Porcelain Deposit'. Mixed neolithic to LM pottery which doesn't join GROUP C.

B I 7 #221, 223 'T. P. 4 2nd M.' contain a mixture of MM, LM and Geometric pottery. Some fragments may belong to GROUP A but later mixing makes these boxes useless for the present study.

L III 15 #1070 'Small rooms E. of Lime Kiln' contain a mixture of ceramic periods and thus not included with GROUP H.

iii. SHERDS FROM THE POTTERY REFERENCE COLLECTION (?ORGANISED BY J. D. S. PENDLEBURY) WHICH JOIN EXAMPLES IN THE CATALOGUE:

'MM II A'	—	663
'MM II B'	—	402
'MM III A'	—	557
'MM III'	—	379

Appendix III. List of inscriptions on the pottery

GROUP A

50	—	'K.04 W Sq. T.P.3'
73	—	'K.04 W Sq. T.P.4'
145	—	'WS T.P.4 K.04'

GROUP D

171	—	'K.03 NWKA'
200	—	'K.03 N.W.K.A.'
202	—	'K.03 NWKA'
225	—	'K.03 NWKA'
234	—	'NWKA K.04 4'

GROUP E

263	—	'K.30 N.8'
272	—	'K.30 N.8'
293	—	'K.30 N.18'
377	—	'K.30 N.11'
378	—	'K.30 N.11'
379	—	'MM III'
389	—	'K.30 N.8'
569	—	'K.30 N.8'
592	—	'K.30 N.8'

GROUP F

615	—	'K.02 12'
616	—	'NEKA K.02 18'
624	—	'K 02 NEKA' and 'Kam. dep. NE Shoot'
625	—	'K.02 NEKA' and 'Kam. dep.' 'NE Shoot'
627	—	'Kam dep NE Shoot'
629	—	'NE Shoot' and 'K8'
630	—	'K. d. NE Shoot' and 'K 02 13'
650	—	'K.02 NEKA'
651	—	'K.02 NEKA 14'
652	—	'K.02 NEKA'
667	—	'NEKA K.02. K.5.'

GROUP G

672	—	'NE Shoot'
676	—	'NE Shoot'
677	—	'E of L kiln. NE Sh'
678	—	'NE Sh'
679	—	'Sh'
680	—	'NE Sh'
683	—	'NE'
684	—	'NE Sh'
685	—	'NE Sh'
686	—	'NE Sh'
691	—	'NE Sh'
692	—	'Sh'
693	—	'NE Sh'
694	—	'NE Sh'

695	—	'NE Sh'
696	—	'NE Sh'
697	—	'NE Sh'
698	—	'NE Sh'
699	—	'NE Sh'
700	—	'NE Sh'
702	—	'NE Sh'
703	—	'NE Sh'
704	—	'NE Sh'
705	—	'NE Sh'
706	—	'NE Sh'
707	—	'NE Sh'
711	—	'NE Sh'
712	—	'NE Sh'
713	—	'NE Sh'
714	—	'NE Sh'
715	—	'NE Sh'
724	—	'NE Sh'
726	—	'NE Sh'
727	—	'NE Sh'
728	—	'NE Sh'
729	—	'NE Sh'
732	—	'NE Sh'
733	—	'NE Sh'
737	—	'NE Sh'
744	—	'NE Sh'
746	—	'NE Shoot'
751	—	'NE Shoot'

GROUP H

787	—	'NE Sh'

GROUP J

796	—	'NE'
797	—	'NE Sh.5'
802	—	'K 02 NE Sh 2'
803	—	'K.02 NE Sh'
804	—	'NE Sh'
806	—	'K.02 NEKA' and 'K.02 K d.'
808	—	'K.02 NEKA'
810	—	'NE Sh'
811	—	'NE Sh', '3'
812	—	'NE Sh 6'

GROUP K

819	—	'K.02 K.28'
820	—	'K.02 K.29'

GROUP M

975	—	'SE K Area K.02'

Appendix IV. Correspondence of 'K' inventory numbers with the Catalogue

1	—	624	51	—	931	101	—	906	151	—	836
2	—	625	52	—	932	102	—	928	152	—	837
3	—	627	53	—	933	103	—	968	153	—	883
4	—	628	54	—	934	104	—	967	154	—	814
5	—	667	55	—	935	105	—	903	155	—	821
6	—	614	56	—	936	106	—	904	156	—	822
7			57	—	937	107	—	898	157	—	823
8	—	629	58	—	938	108	—	918	158	—	842
9	—	622	59	—	939	109	—	819	159	—	843
10			60	—	940	110	—	892	160	—	844
11			61	—	941	111	—	893	161	—	845
12	—	615	62	—	942	112	—	894	162	—	846
13	—	630	63	—	943	113	—	895	163	—	825
14	—	651	64	—	944	114	—	896	164	—	847
15	—	652	65	—	945	115	—	897	165	—	848
16	—	650	66	—	946	116	—	923	166	—	849
17	—	621	67	—	947	117	—	924	167	—	850
18	—	616	68	—	948	118			168	—	851
19	—	617	69	—	949	119	—	971	169	—	852
20	—	618	70	—	950	120	—	961	170	—	853
21	—	619	71	—	951	121	—	963	171	—	840
22	—	975	72	—	952	122	—	962	172	—	841
23	—	979	73	—	953	123	—	959	173	—	890
24	—	978	74	—	905	124	—	960	174	—	854
25			75	—	929	125	—	964	175	—	855
26	—	982	76	—	954	126	—	969	176	—	856
27	—	983	77	—	955	127	—	970	177	—	857
28	—	819	78	—	956	128	—	972	178	—	858
29	—	820	79	—	957	129	—	817	179	—	859
30	—	808	80	—	958	130	—	880	180	—	860
31	—	799	81	—	922	131	—	824	181	—	861
32	—	800	82	—	921	132	—	818	182	—	862
33	—	801	83	—	966	133	—	874	183	—	863
34	—	807	84	—	965	134	—	815	184	—	864
35	—	669	85	—	899	135	—	816	185	—	865
36	—	809	86	—	913	136	—	889	186	—	866
37	—	620	87	—	914	137	—	884	187	—	867
38	—	642	88	—	915	138	—	882	188	—	868
39	—	623	89	—	916	139	—	838	189	—	869
40			90	—	917	140	—	839	190	—	870
41	—	661	91	—	909	141	—	828	191	—	881
42	—	643	92	—	910	142	—	829	192	—	885
43	—	644	93	—	911	143	—	830	193	—	879
44	—	798	94	—	912	144	—	831	194	—	886
45	—	626	95	—	920	145	—	832	195	—	875
46	—	654	96	—	901	146	—	833	196	—	873
47	—	926	97	—	907	147	—	826	197	—	876
48	—	927	98	—	908	148	—	827	198	—	877
49	—	925	99	—	900	149	—	834	199	—	878
50	—	930	100	—	902	150	—	835	200	—	891

201	—	871	264	—	37	327	—	47	390	—	366
202	—	872	265	—	38	328	—	128	391	—	367
203	—	887	266	—	39	329	—	127	392	—	368
204	—	888	267	—	63	330	—	51	393	—	436
205	—	121	268	—	64	331	—	48	394	—	437
206	—	122	269	—	65	332	—	78	395	—	438
207	—	123	270	—	66	333	—	133	396	—	439
208	—	125	271	—	40	334	—	132	397	—	440
209	—	126	272	—	41	335	—	137	398	—	441
210	—	124	273	—	20	336			399	—	442
211	—	115	274	—	68	337	—	130	400	—	443
212	—	114	275	—	69	338	—	131	401	—	430
213	—	70	276	—	112	339			402	—	431
214	—	21	277	—	113	340	—	148	403	—	432
215	—	43	278	—	87	341	—	152	404	—	374
216	—	102	279	—	88	342	—	111	405	—	375
217	—	103	280	—	80	343	—	96	406	—	376
218	—	97	281	—	81	344	—	71	407	—	285
219	—	55	282	—	82	345	—	72	408	—	286
220	—	45	283	—	83	346	—	118	409	—	590
221	—	22	284	—	84	347	—	117	410	—	372
222	—	44	285	—	85	348	—	53	411	—	373
223	—	107	286	—	86	349	—	141	412	—	371
224	—	104	287	—	110	350	—	59	413	—	370
225	—	105	288	—	15	351	—	62	414	—	589
226	—	106	289	—	1	352	—	67	415	—	369
227	—	35	290	—	2	353	—	42	416	—	418
228	—	109	291	—	3	354			417	—	417
229	—	108	292	—	4	355			418	—	419
230	—	31	293	—	16	356	—	149	419	—	420
231	—	32	294	—	5	357	—	150	420	—	421
232	—	33	295	—	6	358	—	151	421	—	414
233	—	89	296	—	7	359	—	36	422	—	413
234	—	90	297	—	8	360	—	23	423	—	415
235	—	91	298	—	9	361	—	134	424	—	416
236	—	92	299	—	10	362	—	119	425	—	428
237	—	93	300	—	11	363	—	146	426	—	429
238	—	94	301	—	12	364	—	341	427	—	409
239	—	95	302	—	13	365	—	342	428	—	410
240	—	19	303	—	14	366	—	343	429	—	411
241	—	98	304	—	116	367	—	344	430	—	412
242	—	99	305	—	120	368	—	345	431	—	605
243	—	100	306	—	50	369	—	346	432	—	308
244	—	101	307	—	140	370	—	347	433	—	314
245	—	145	308	—	18	371	—	348	434	—	315
246	—	144	309	—	24	372	—	349	435	—	316
247	—	143	310	—	79	373	—	350	436	—	317
248	—	17	311	—	135	374	—	351	437	—	318
249	—	138	312	—	136	375	—	352	438	—	327
250	—	52	313	—	147	376	—	353	439	—	311
251	—	54	314			377	—	354	440	—	312
252	—	139	315			378	—	355	441	—	313
253	—	142	316			379	—	356	442	—	310
254	—	26	317			380	—	357	443	—	319
255	—	27	318	—	49	381	—	340	444	—	328
256	—	28	319	—	25	382	—	358	445	—	338
257	—	29	320	—	129	383	—	359	446	—	274
258	—	30	321	—	76	384	—	360	447	—	275
259	—	56	322	—	73	385	—	361	448	—	276
260	—	57	323	—	46	386	—	362	449	—	277
261	—	58	324	—	75	387	—	363	450	—	329
262	—	60	325	—	77	388	—	364	451	—	330
263	—	61	326	—	74	389	—	365	452	—	331

453	—	279	516	—	478	579	—	447	642	—	523
454	—	332	517	—	479	580	—	448	643	—	524
455	—	333	518	—	480	581	—	449	644	—	525
456	—	334	519	—	481	582	—	450	645	—	526
457	—	320	520	—	482	583	—	457	646	—	527
458	—	321	521	—	483	584	—	458	647	—	528
459	—	322	522	—	484	585	—	459	648	—	529
460	—	323	523	—	485	586	—	460	649	—	530
461	—	326	524	—	486	587	—	461	650		
462	—	324	525	—	487	588	—	462	651	—	592
463	—	325	526	—	488	589	—	463	652	—	593
464	—	278	527	—	489	590	—	464	653	—	594
465	—	337	528	—	490	591	—	465	654	—	519
466	—	427	529	—	491	592	—	466	655	—	520
467	—	587	530	—	492	593	—	467	656	—	542
468	—	309	531	—	493	594	—	468	657	—	543
469	—	269	532	—	494	595	—	469	658	—	544
470	—	270	533	—	495	596			659	—	545
471	—	263	534	—	496	597	—	470	660	—	393
472	—	264	535	—	497	598	—	471	661	—	394
473	—	265	536	—	498	599	—	574	662	—	565
474	—	266	537	—	499	600	—	562	663	—	567
475	—	271	538	—	500	601	—	401	664	—	566
476	—	588	539	—	501	602	—	575	665	—	568
477	—	280	540	—	502	603	—	576	666	—	570
478	—	336	541	—	503	604	—	577	667	—	571
479	—	282	542	—	504	605	—	578	668	—	572
480	—	284	543	—	505	606	—	579	669	—	395
481	—	281	544	—	506	607	—	548	670	—	396
482	—	283	545	—	507	608	—	549	671	—	397
483	—	273	546	—	508	609	—	580	672	—	398
484	—	335	547	—	509	610	—	552	673	—	399
485	—	339	548	—	510	611	—	553	674	—	539
486	—	294	549	—	511	612	—	554	675	—	546
487	—	295	550	—	512	613	—	555	676	—	540
488	—	296	551	—	513	614	—	595	677	—	541
489	—	298	552	—	514	615	—	535	678	—	583
490	—	297	553	—	515	616	—	536	679	—	584
491	—	300	554	—	516	617	—	537	680	—	591
492	—	301	555	—	517	618	—	538	681	—	569
493	—	302	556	—	996	619	—	287	682	—	560
494	—	303	557	—	997	620	—	288	683	—	531
495	—	304	558	—	995	621	—	289	684	—	402
496	—	305	559	—	994	622	—	380	685	—	559
497	—	405	560	—	1007	623	—	381	686	—	557
498	—	406	561	—	379	624	—	382	687	—	534
499	—	407	562	—	272	625	—	383	688	—	558
500	—	404	563	—	293	626	—	384	689	—	532
501	—	408	564	—	306	627	—	290	690	—	533
502	—	403	565	—	307	628	—	291	691	—	585
503	—	433	566	—	262	629	—	389	692	—	586
504	—	434	567	—	299	630	—	385	693	—	422
505	—	435	568	—	267	631	—	386	694	—	582
506	—	423	569	—	268	632	—	387	695		
507	—	424	570	—	547	633	—	388	696	—	292
508	—	425	571	—	400	634	—	445	697	—	581
509	—	426	572	—	451	635	—	377	698	—	561
510	—	472	573	—	452	636	—	378	699	—	563
511	—	473	574	—	453	637	—	390	700	—	564
512	—	474	575	—	454	638	—	391	701	—	556
513	—	475	576	—	455	639	—	392	702	—	573
514	—	476	577	—	456	640	—	521	703	—	596
515	—	477	578	—	446	641	—	522	704	—	597

705 — 598	768 — 705	831 — 754	894 — 158
706 — 599	769 — 706	832 — 763	895 — 159
707 — 600	770 — 707	833 — 764	896 — 160
708 — 601	771 — 677	834 — 765	897 — 162
709 — 602	772 — 678	835 — 786	898 — 163
710 — 603	773 — 679	836 — 766	899 — 161
711 — 604	774 — 680	837 — 767	900 — 166
712 — 631	775 — 681	838 — 768	901 — 167
713 — 645	776 — 708	839 — 769	902 — 168
714 — 646	777 — 709	840 — 770	903 — 170
715 — 660	778 — 710	841 — 771	904 — 169
716 — 633	779 — 711	842 — 772	905
717 — 634	780 — 712	843 — 773	906 — 225
718 — 635	781 — 713	844 — 774	907 — 176
719 — 609	782 — 714	845 — 775	908 — 227
720 — 610	783 — 715	846 — 776	909 — 202
721 — 636	784 — 716	847 — 785	910 — 173
722 — 653	785 — 717	848 — 777	911 — 178
723 — 641	786 — 718	849 — 778	912 — 174
724 — 655	787 — 719	850 — 779	913 — 179
725 — 637	788 — 720	851 — 780	914 — 180
726 — 638	789 — 721	852 — 781	915 — 181
727 — 639	790 — 722	853 — 782	916 — 182
728 — 640	791 — 723	854 — 762	917 — 183
729 — 611	792 — 724	855 — 760	918 — 184
730 — 612	793 — 725	856 — 757	919 — 185
731 — 659	794 — 726	857 — 758	920 — 186
732 — 656	795 — 727	858 — 761	921 — 187
733 — 613	796 — 728	859 — 783	922 — 188
734 — 657	797 — 729	860 — 784	923 — 191
735 — 658	798 — 730	861 — 755	924 — 189
736 — 647	799 — 731	862 — 789	925 — 190
737 — 662	800 — 732	863 — 790	926 — 228
738 — 670	801 — 733	864 — 788	927 — 230
739 — 648	802 — 734	865 — 791	928 — 229
740 — 649	803 — 735	866 — 792	929 — 192
741 — 664	804 — 750	867 — 793	930 — 233
742 — 663	805 — 746	868 — 794	931 — 234
743 — 665	806 — 683	869	932 — 235
744 — 632	807 — 684	870	933 — 231
745 — 668	808 — 736	871 — 797	934 — 254
746 — 673	809 — 737	872	935 — 210
747 — 749	810 — 685	873 — 795	936 — 237
748 — 671	811 — 686	874 — 812	937 — 239
749 — 682	812 — 747	875 — 813	938 — 240
750 — 698	813 — 748	876 — 810	939 — 241
751 — 689	814 — 687	877	940 — 242
752 — 690	815 — 672	878 — 802	941 — 221
753 — 691	816 — 676	879 — 803	942 — 236
754 — 692	817 — 688	880 — 804	943 — 252
755 — 693	818 — 738	881 — 811	944 — 253
756 — 694	819 — 740	882 — 787	945 — 224
757 — 695	820 — 741	883 — 796	946 — 257
758 — 696	821 — 739	884 — 806	947 — 211
759 — 697	822 — 743	885 — 171	948 — 243
760 — 674	823 — 742	886 — 984	949 — 201
761 — 675	824 — 744	887	950 — 245
762 — 699	825 — 745	888 — 165	951
763 — 700	826 — 751	889 — 157	952 — 246
764 — 701	827 — 752	890 — 164	953 — 193
765 — 702	828 — 753	891 — 154	954 — 196
766 — 703	829 — 759	892 — 155	955 — 247
767 — 704	830 — 756	893 — 156	956 — 214

957	—	981	988	—	1037	1019	—	205	1049	—	606
958	—	199	989	—	1043	1020	—	172	1050	—	607
959	—	250	990	—	1044	1021	—	256	1051	—	608
960	—	200	991			1022	—	217	1052	—	666
961	—	222	992	—	1031	1023	—	208	1053	—	805
962			993	—	1039	1024	—	218	1054	—	973
963	—	255	994	—	1028	1025	—	219	1055	—	974
964	—	998	995	—	1029	1026	—	197	1056	—	977
965	—	999	996	—	1033	1027	—	209	1057	—	980
966	—	987	997	—	1030	1028	—	220	1058	—	976
967	—	990	998	—	1032	1029	—	206	1059		
968	—	991	999	—	1045	1030	—	215	1060	—	1012
969	—	992	1000	—	1038	1031	—	216	1061	—	1013
970	—	989	1001	—	1025	1032	—	207	1062	—	1014
971	—	1006	1002	—	1048	1033	—	213	1063	—	1015
972	—	986	1003	—	1034	1034	—	212	1064	—	1016
973	—	993	1004	—	1035	1035	—	223	1065	—	1017
974	—	988	1005	—	1047	1036	—	261	1066	—	1018
975	—	1003	1006	—	1036	1037	—	244	1067	—	1019
976	—	1000	1007	—	1040	1038	—	195	1068	—	1020
977	—	1002	1008	—	1042	1039	—	232	1069	—	1021
978	—	1001	1009	—	1046	1040	—	248	1070	—	1022
979	—	1004	1010			1041	—	249	1071	—	1023
980	—	985	1011	—	34	1042	—	251	1072	—	1024
981	—	1008	1012	—	259	1043	—	234	1073	—	1041
982	—	1009	1013	—	260	1044	—	238	1074	—	1049
983	—	1005	1014	—	194	1045	—	444	1075	—	177
984	—	1010	1015	—	258	1046	—	518	1076	—	175
985	—	1011	1016	—	226	1047	—	550	1077	—	198
986	—	1026	1017	—	203	1048	—	551	1078	—	153
987	—	1027	1018	—	204						

Appendix V. Museum Concordances

HERAKLEION MUSEUM

2674	—	808	4391	—	803	5196	—	208	8385	—	1030
2675	—	614	4392	—	802	5196	—	209	8386	—	1032
2680	—	165	4394	—	202	5196	—	211	8387	—	1045
2684	—	650	4395	—	77	5196	—	212	8388	—	1033
2685	—	667	4396	—	73	5196	—	213	8389	—	1025
2686	—	809	4397	—	123	5196	—	215	8390	—	1031
2688	—	819	4398	—	121	5196	—	216	8391	—	1026
2689	—	820	4399	—	126	5196	—	217	8392	—	1037
2690	—	617	4400	—	68	5196	—	218	8393	—	1023
2691	—	619	4401	—	125	5196	—	219	8394	—	1024
2692	—	618	4402	—	20	5196	—	220	8395	—	1027
2693	—	616	4404	—	69	5196	—	256	8395	—	1030
2694	—	926	4406	—	81	5200	—	976	8396	—	1041
2695	—	652	4407	—	145	5711	—	812	8397	—	1029
2696	—	651	4408	—	54	5756	—	97	8398	—	1038
2697	—	979	4409	—	25	5756?	—	211	8399	—	1028
2698	—	925	4410	—	133	5757	—	175	8401	—	1036
2698	—	975	4504	—	221	5757	—	177	8402	—	1049
2699	—	628	4580	—	231	5757	—	189	8406	—	998
2700	—	624	5186	—	615	5757	—	196	8834	—	569
2701	—	625	5186	—	642	5757	—	198	8845	—	263
2702	—	627	5186	—	647	5757	—	224	8846	—	265
2703	—	629	5186	—	659	5757	—	246	8847	—	272
3875	—	977	5186	—	661	5759	—	157	8848	—	293
4351	—	796	5187	—	798	5760	—	811	8849	—	297
4353	—	984	5188	—	629	5762	—	810	8874	—	308
4354	—	804	5188	—	630	7691	—	891	8878	—	377
4374	—	200	5188	—	659	7694	—	1000	8880	—	389
4376	—	50	5189	—	647	7695	—	1003	8881	—	378
4377	—	225	5196	—	172	7696	—	996	8916	—	574
4378	—	176	5196	—	197	7739	—	1010	8920	—	550
4383	—	797	5196	—	203	7752	—	1035	8935	—	592
4385	—	806	5196	—	204	8381	—	1047	9107	—	1022
4387	—	234	5196	—	205	8382	—	1040	9168	—	542
4389	—	171	5196	—	206	8383	—	1042	9169	—	543
4390	—	75	5196	—	207	8384	—	1034			

ASHMOLEAN MUSEUM

AE 814	—	547	AE 832.7	—	239	AE 947	—	621	AE 955	—	227
AE 823	—	311	AE 912	—	930	AE 950	—	238	AE 956	—	246
AE 824.1	—	319	AE 917	—	199	AE 951	—	232	AE 960	—	565
AE 832	—	240	AE 935	—	800	AE 952	—	195	AE 967	—	169
AE 832.1	—	239	AE 936	—	233	AE 954.2	—	191	AE 1027	—	198
AE 832.3	—	241	AE 937	—	799	AE 954.3	—	244	AE 1029	—	261
AE 832.4	—	240	AE 941	—	248	AE 954.4	—	196	AE 1032.1	—	193
AE 832.5	—	239	AE 942	—	647	AE 954.5	—	196	AE 1032.3	—	943
AE 832.6	—	239	AE 944	—	807	AE 954.7	—	243	AE 1035	—	544

AE 1041.5 — **214**	AE 1062. — **259**	1938.442 — **243**	1938.580 — **211**
AE 1042.1 — **210**	AE 1204.0 — **622**	1938.443 — **249**	1938.585 — **822**
AE 1042.2 — **210**	AE 1241 — **817**	1938.448 — **257**	1938.586 — **825**
AE 1060.1 — **211**	AE 1654 — **891**	1938.561 — **801**	1938.587 — **981**
AE 1060.3 — **211**	1910.167b — **191**	1938.562 — **669**	1938.589 — **980**
AE 1061.3 — **627**	1910.167c — **231**	1938.567 — **444**	1938.598 — **595**
AE 1061.5 — **297**	1910.167i — **905**	1938.569 — **545**	1938.600 — **593**
AE 1061.6 — **223**	1910.169h — **237**	1938.571 — **550**	1938.817 — **980**
AE 1061.7 — **798**	1930.645 — **927**	1938.576 — **980**	
AE 1061.12 — **223**	1938.441 — **196**	1938.579 — **211**	

BRITISH MUSEUM

A 510 — **254**	A 52 — **632**	A 536 — **210**
A 514 — **805**	A 528.2 — **233**	A 537.1 — **211**

LIVERPOOL MUSEUM

55.66.74 — **620**

Appendix VI. List of cross-museum joins

No.	HM	Ashmolean	BM	KSM
97	5756			B I
123	4397			B I
169		AE 967		A II
189	5757			A II
191		AE 954.2		A II
		1910.167b		
196	5757	AE 954.4,5 1938.441		
210		AE 1042.1,2	A536	
211	5196 5756?	AE 1060.1,3 1938.579,580	A537.1	A II
214		AE 1041.5		A II
223		AE 1061.6, 12		A II
224	5757			A II
231	4580	1910.167c		A II
233		AE 936	A528.2	A II
237		1910.169h		A II
238		AE 950		A II
239		AE 832.1,5, 6,7		A II
240		AE 832, AE 832.4		A II
241		AE 832.3		A II
246	5757	AE 956		A II
254			A510	A II
257		1938.448		A II
297	8849	AE 1061.5		
311		AE 823		B I
319		AE 824.1		B I
547		AE 814		B I

No.	HM	Ashmolean	BM	KSM
550	8920	1938.571		
565		AE 960		B I
616	2693			M III
618	2692			M III
619	2691			L III
621		AE 947		M III
622	?	AE 1204.0		L III M III
627	2702	AE 1061.3,5		
628	2699			M III
632			A527	L III M III
642	5186			L III M III
647	5186 5189	AE 942		L III
659	5186 5188			L III
661	5186			L III M III
667	2685			L III
669		1938.562		M III
798	5187	AE 1061.7		
891	7691	AE 1654		
905		1910.167i		M II M III L III
943		AE 1032.3		M II M III
980		1938.576,589, 817		O II

Appendix VII. Publications Concordance

EVANS, 1902–3

fig. 8 — 925
pl. II.1 — 925
pl. II.2 — 926

EVANS, 1904

fig. 6 b — 221	fig. 6 k — 194	fig. 65 — 201	fig. 74 d — 159
fig. 6 d — 245	fig. 6 m — 261	fig. 73 a — 166	fig. 74 d — 160
fig. 6 e — 193	fig. 6 n — 246	fig. 73 b — 167	fig. 74 e — 162
fig. 6 f — 227	fig. 6 p — 258	fig. 73 c — 168	fig. 74 e — 163
fig. 6 g — 260	fig. 6 q — 226	fig. 74 b — 154	fig. 74 g — 164
fig. 6 h — 234	fig. 6 r — 199	fig. 74 c — 157	fig. 74 h — 161
fig. 6 i — 259	fig. 61 — 200	fig. 74 d — 158	fig. 74 i — 153

EVANS, 1921

fig. 127 c — 248	fig. 136 k — 20	fig. 184 a — 627	fig. 194 h — 195
fig. 127 f — 647	fig. 136 l — 8	fig. 184 b — 628	fig. 198 d — 257
fig. 133 b — 196	fig. 136 m — 25	fig. 186 g — 234	fig. 199 b — 227
fig. 133 d — 191	fig. 136 n — 133	fig. 190 — 891	fig. 199 e — 930
fig. 133 f — 244	fig. 136 o — 126	fig. 191 — 817	fig. 416 a — 791
fig. 136 a — 54	fig. 136 p — 121	fig. 191 — 819	fig. 437 a — 239
fig. 136 b — 7	fig. 178 — 621	fig. 191 — 820	fig. 437 b — 239
fig. 136 e — 39	fig. 180 — 809	fig. 191 — 821	pl. I b — 982
fig. 136 f — 81	fig. 181 — 616	fig. 191 — 825	pl. II a — 617
fig. 136 g — 68	fig. 182 a — 799	fig. 191 — 840	pl. II b — 619
fig. 136 g — 123	fig. 182 b — 800	fig. 191 — 876	pl. II c — 618
fig. 136 h — 77	fig. 183 a.1 — 801	fig. 192 a — 877	pl. III — 165
fig. 136 i — 34	fig. 183 a.4 — 979	fig. 194 d — 801	

EVANS, 1928

fig. 176 — 1010	fig. 206 b — 1039	fig. 206 f — 1035	pl. IX e — 1003
fig. 200 e — 319	fig. 206 c — 996	pl. IX a — 998	pl. IX f — 1000
fig. 205 — 1033	fig. 206 d — 1043	pl. IX b — 234	
fig. 206 a — 1048	fig. 206 e — 1046	pl. IX d — 1011	

EVANS, 1935

fig. 64 a — 807	fig. 84 a — 444	fig. 100 — 998	pl. XXIX D — 542
fig. 66 c — 249	fig. 84 b — 444	fig. 102 — 926	pl. XXIX F — 543
fig. 66 d — 243	fig. 93 — 595	fig. 105 — 927	pl. XXX A — 308
fig. 66 e — 196	fig. 95 — 551	fig. 107 — 378	pl. XXX B — 574
fig. 73 c — 259	fig. 97 — 550	pl. XXVII C — 1033	pl. XXX C — 397
fig. 80 c — 982	fig. 99 — 389	pl. XXIX C — 551	pl. XXX D — 550

MACKENZIE, 1902 DB (2)

1	—	878

MACKENZIE, 1902 PB (2)

11	—	878	68 K.2	—	625	72 K.12	—	615	77	—	980
45	—	683	68 K.3	—	627	71 K.13	—	630	79 K.26	—	982
45	—	806	69 K.4	—	628	72 K.14	—	651	79 K.27	—	983
46	—	796	69 K.5	—	667	72 K.15	—	652	79 K.28	—	819
47	—	804	70 K.6	—	614	72 K.16	—	650	79 K.29	—	820
66	—	666	71 K.8	—	629	75 K.22	—	975			
68 K.1	—	624	70 K.9	—	622	75 K.23	—	979			

MACKENZIE, 1903

fig. 3.1	—	624	fig. 6.1	—	805	fig. 6.7	—	810	pl. VI.2	—	652
fig. 3.2	—	625	fig. 6.2	—	802	fig. 6.8	—	813	pl. VI.4	—	975
fig. 3.3	—	627	fig. 6.3	—	811	pl. V.1	—	617	pl. VII.5	—	980
fig. 3.4	—	628	fig. 6.4	—	795	pl. V.2	—	618	pl. VII.15	—	978
fig. 4	—	877	fig. 6.5	—	797	pl. V.3	—	619			
fig. 5	—	876	fig. 6.6	—	812	pl. VI.1	—	650			

MACKENZIE, 1903 PB

p. 3 no 7	—	165
p. 3 no 8	—	247
p. 3 no 9	—	927

MACKENZIE, 1904 DB (1)

p. 27	—	146

MACKENZIE, 1904 PB (2)

p. 1	—	210	p. 3	—	219	p. 4	—	220	p. 5	—	207
p. 1	—	256	p. 3	—	204	p. 4	—	206	p. 6	—	172
p. 1	—	217	p. 3	—	197	p. 4	—	215	p. 6	—	213
p. 2	—	208	p. 3	—	211	p. 5	—	205	p. 6	—	212
p. 2	—	203	p. 3	—	209	p. 5	—	216	p. 14	—	976
p. 2	—	218									

MACKENZIE, 1906

pl. VIII.1	—	210	pl. VIII.7	—	219	pl. VIII.13	—	206	pl. VIII.19	—	172
pl. VIII.2	—	256	pl. VIII.8	—	204	pl. VIII.14	—	215	pl. VIII.20	—	213
pl. VIII.3	—	217	pl. VIII.9	—	197	pl. VIII.15	—	205	pl. VIII.21	—	212
pl. VIII.4	—	208	pl. VIII.10	—	211	pl. VIII.16	—	205	pl. IX.7	—	976
pl. VIII.5	—	203	pl. VIII.11	—	209	pl. VIII.17	—	216			
pl. VIII.6	—	218	pl. VIII.12	—	220	pl. VIII.18	—	207			

PENDLEBURY, 1939

fig. 17.10	—	77	fig. 17.18	—	128	pl. XVII 2c	—	75	pl. XVII 3b	—	20
fig. 17.13	—	74	pl. XVII 2a	—	808	pl. XVII 3a	—	68	pl. XVII 3c	—	39

ÅBERG, 1933

fig. 262	—	614	fig. 270	—	622
fig. 269	—	257	fig. 355	—	389

ANDREOU, 1978

fig. 5.1	—	143
fig. 5.5	—	99
fig. 5.6	—	48

BROWN, 1983

fig. 43 a	—	817
fig. 43 a	—	822
fig. 43 a right	—	825

FORSDYKE, 1925

fig. 107	—	805	fig. 112	—	211	pl. VIII	—	254
fig. 112	—	210	fig. 112	—	233			

ZERVOS, 1956

fig. 321	—	50	fig. 364 left	—	73	fig. 369 right	—	651	fig. 377	—	667
fig. 323	—	1003	fig. 364 centre	—	308	fig. 375 b	—	625			

Index

Cyclades 58, 69, 71, 106
    Knossian imports 69, 107
Cycladic fabrics. *See* minority fabrics: Cycladic fabrics
Cyprus
    Cypriot Red Polished III amphora 46
    Enkomi 57

D

dadoes 41
daggers 107
dais 39, 41, 42
Day-Books. *See* excavation notebooks
deep bowl 157
destruction by fire. *See* fire
Diagonal Red and White Style 26, 34, 35, 36, 43, 45, 59, 67, 72, 77, 94
Dolphin Vase, Lisht 106, 107
Dove Pit 45
dove vase 45
drain 49, 50. *See also* Town Drain
Dunand, M. 106
dies 57

E

Early Keep 34, 72
    date 34
Early Magazine A. *See* Magazines
Early Olive Press 59, 97. *See also* Room of the Olive Press
    floor 101
Early Printed Ware 26, 37, 46, 58, 66, 71, 75, 96, 101
    decorative motifs 58
Early South-West Houses. *See* South-West Houses
Early Town
    historical events 97–8
    Hogarth's Early Heap. *See* Hogarth, D. G.
    Hogarth's Later Heap. *See* Hogarth, D. G.
    Houses 49, 95, 102
        excavations 49
        Group P deposit 50–1, 171. *See also* Groups: P
    Town Drain. *See* Town Drain
Early West Magazine 2. *See* Magazines
earthquake. *See* seismic event
    horizon 95
East Central Enclave 39–45, 94
    Area of the Spiral Fresco 39–42
    Court of the Stone Spout 44, 45
    East Corridor 45
    Enamel Deposit. *See* Enamel Deposit
    excavations 39
    Loomweight Basement. *See* Loomweight Basement
    Room of the Olive Press. *See* Room of the Olive Press
    Room of the Stone Pier. *See* Room of the Stone Pier
    School Room Area 44, 45
    sequence of deposits 45
East Corridor 45
egg-cup 66
Egg-shell Ware 26, 37, 51, 56, 57, 75, 76, 95, 103, 106, 151–2, 160
    definition of 56
    technique of manufacture 56
'egg-tray' 149
Egypt 102–05, 106–08
    Abydos 62, 107
        Cretan import 105, 108
    Amarna
        Cretan imports 108
    El Tôd
        Minoan imports 103–04

Haraga 43, 56, 57, 103–05, 106
    Minoan imitations 103–05
    Minoan imports 104–05, 107
Kahun 80, 103, 106
    Minoan imports 104, 107
links with Phaistos 107
Lisht 103, 107
    Minoan imports 104, 106
Middle Kingdom chronology and history 102–03
Minoan imports 103–05, 106–08
Qubbet el-Hawa 104
    Minoan imports 103, 106
Tell el-Dab'a 63, 76, 107
    Minoan imports 105
Egyptian
    influence 82, 85, 96
    scarab 51
El Tôd, Egypt
    Cretan imports 103–04
    Cretan influence 103–04
el-Lisht. *See* Lisht
Enamel Deposit 41, 42, 45
    date of 42
    excavations 42
    stratigraphy 42
enamelled plaques 42
Enceinte walls 30–2
    abandonment 34
    construction 30–2
    date 30–2
    Southern 30–2, 98
        destruction 30–2
    Western 29, 30–2
Enkomi, Cyprus 57
Evans, A. J. 15–16, 17, 18, 19, 20, 21, 22, 23, 24, 25, 26, 27, 28, 29, 30, 31, 32, 33, 34, 35, 36, 37, 38, 39, 40, 41, 42, 43, 44, 45, 46, 47, 48, 49, 50, 51, 52, 53, 56, 57, 64, 65, 86, 88, 90, 93, 97, 98, 99, 100, 101, 102, 105
Evans, J. D. 22
Evans Archive, use of 18
Evely, D. 94, 95, 97
everted rim bowls 43, 52, 95
excavation notebooks, use of 18
excavators' inscriptions, use of 18
exports. *See* Cretan exports

F

fabric. *See also* coarse fabrics; fine fabrics; gritty fabrics; micaceous fabrics; minority fabrics
    Fine Buff Crude Ware. *See* Crude Ware
    Fine Buff Ware. *See* Fine Buff Ware
    macroscopic analysis 55
    Momigliano's Fabric I 55
    Wilson's Buff Fabric 55
faience
    enamelled plaques 42
    juglet 41
    Town Mosaic 42
Fayum 104
Feather-wave Style 88, 89
Fiandra, E. 16, 100, 101, 102
figurines
    terracotta 100
    bulls 36
Fine Buff Ware 26, 28, 33, 36, 41, 55–82, 90, 95, 96, 122–8, 129–30, 130–5, 135–47, 151–4, 155–7, 158–9, 159–62, 164–6, 167, 168–9, 170–1
    Kommos 55

PLATE 1

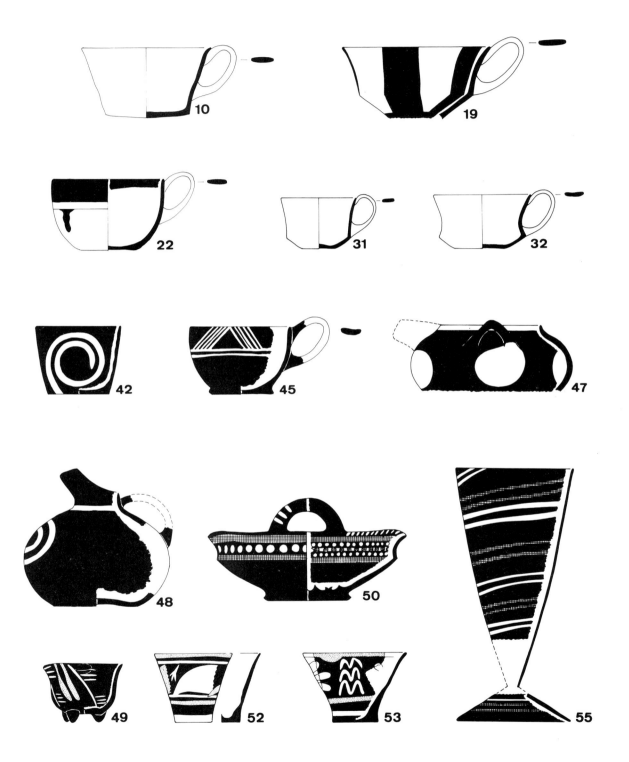

Group A, Fine Buff pottery. 1:3

PLATE 2

Group A, Fine Buff pottery. 1:3

PLATE 3

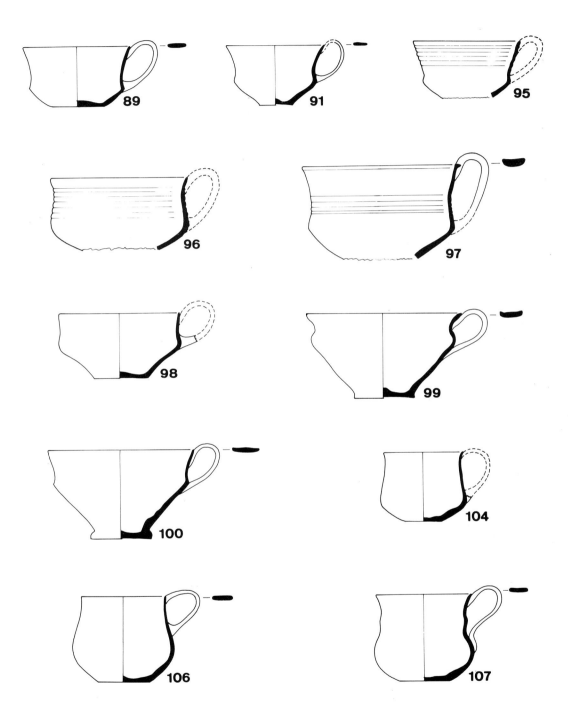

Group A, Fine Buff pottery. 1:3

PLATE 4

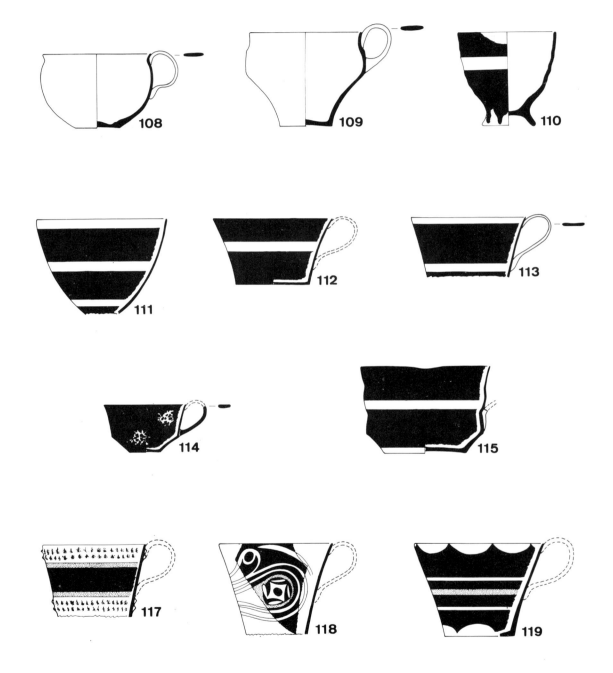

Group A, Fine Buff pottery. 1:3

PLATE 5

Group A, Fine Buff (120–6) and Soft Buff (129) pottery. 121 at 1:2, others 1:3

PLATE 6

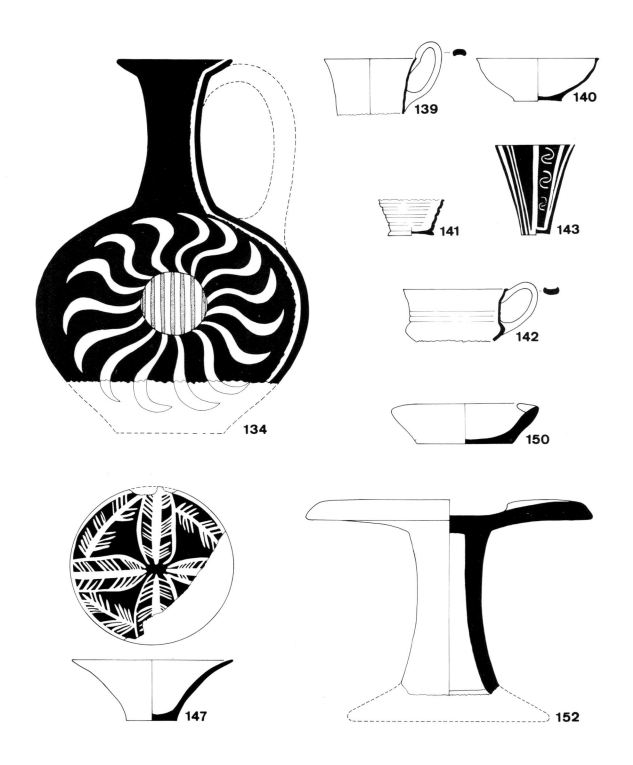

Group A, pottery in Minor Fabrics. 1:3

PLATE 7

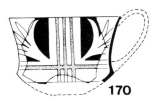

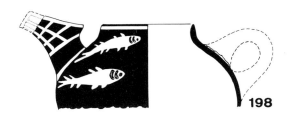

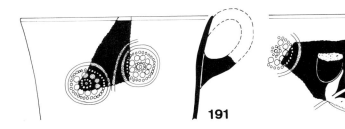

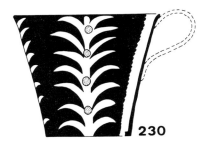

Group C (170) and Group D, Fine Buff pottery. 175 and 177 at 1:2, others 1:3

PLATE 8

234

236

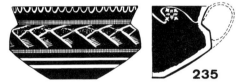

235

243

250

Group D, Fine Buff pottery. 1:3

PLATE 9

Group E, Fine Buff pottery. 1:3

PLATE 10

292

293

306

309

310

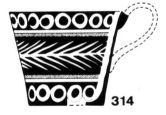

311

312

314

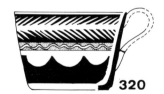

320

323

325

Group E, Fine Buff pottery. 1:3

PLATE 11

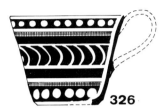

326

327

330

331

333

334

335

336

337

338

339

Group E, Fine Buff pottery. 1:3

PLATE 12

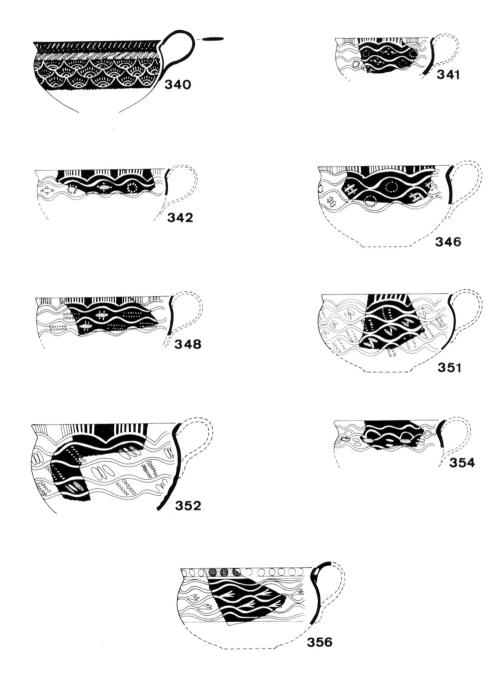

Group E, Fine Buff Rounded Cups of Type 6. 1:3

PLATE 13

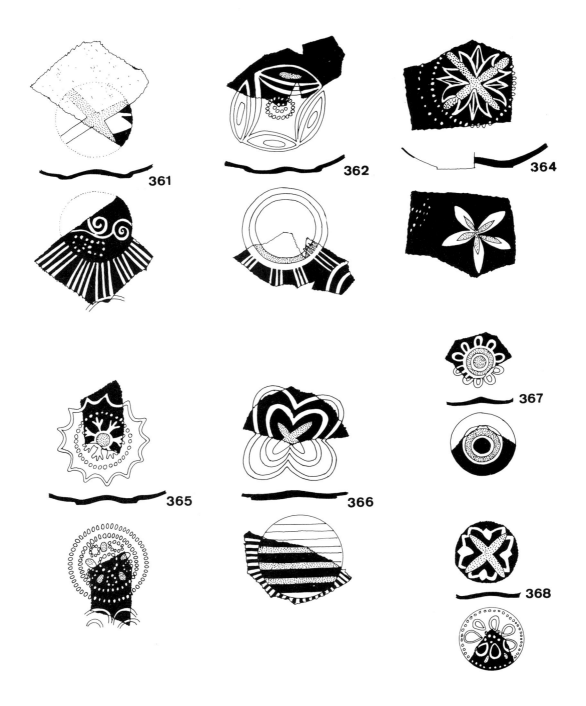

Group E, Fine Buff bases of Rounded Cups of Type 6. 1:3

PLATE 14

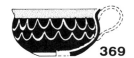

369

370

371

372

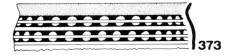

373

374

375

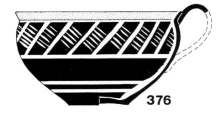

376

Group E, Fine Buff Rounded Cups of Type 5. 1:3

PLATE 15

379

382

383

385

390

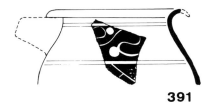

391

Group E, Fine Buff Bridge-spouted Jars. 1:3

PLATE 16

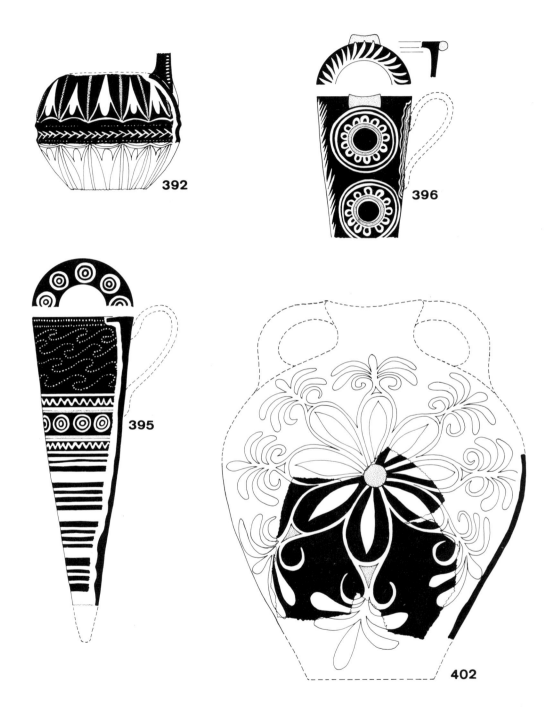

Group E, Fine Buff pottery. 1:3

PLATE 17

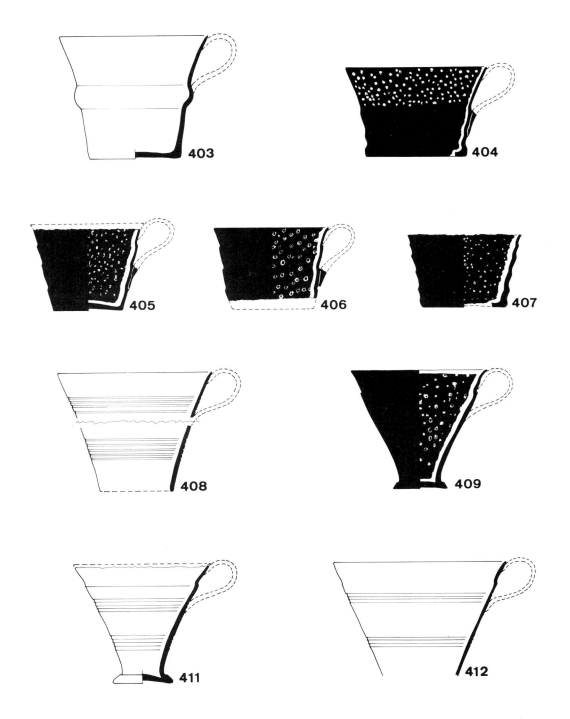

Group E, Fine Buff Cups. 1:3

PLATE 18

Group E, Fine Buff Cups. 1:3

PLATE 19

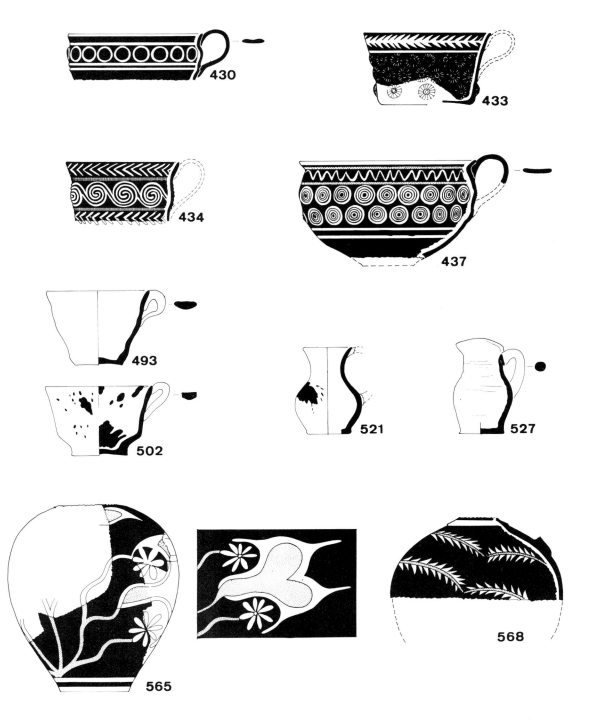

Group E, Fine (430–527) and Tempered (565, 568) Buff pottery. 1:3

PLATE 20

566

567

570

571

Group E, Tempered Buff pottery. 1:3

PLATE 21

539

587

588

589

590

605

Group E, pottery in Minor Fabrics. 1:3

PLATE 22

Group F, Fine Buff pottery. 1:3

PLATE 23

Group F, Fine and Fine Soft (667) Buff pottery. 1:3

PLATE 24

Group F (668) and Group G, Fine (686–735) and Tempered (746) Buff pottery. 1:3

PLATE 25

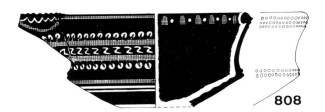

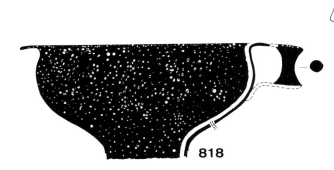

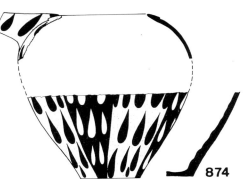

Group J (808) and Group K, Fine (818, 824), Semifine (874) and Tempered (878) Buff pottery. 1:3

PLATE 26

879

880

882

888

Group K, pottery in Minor Fabrics. 1:3

PLATE 27

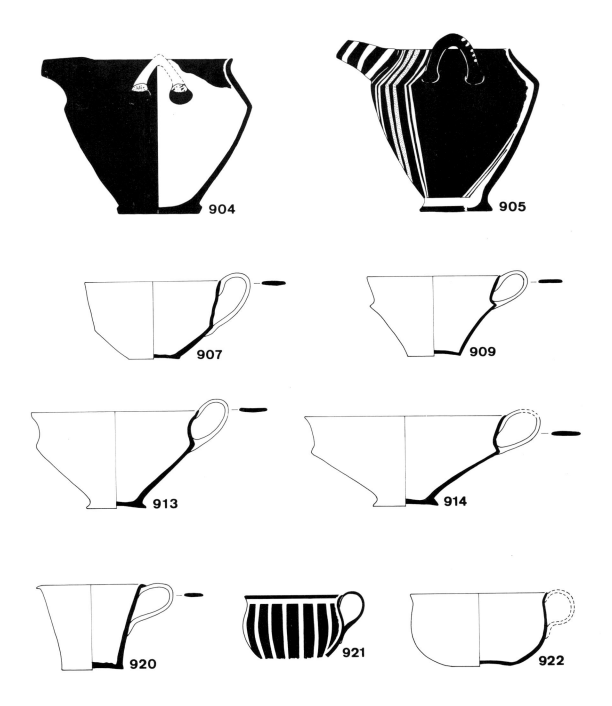

Group L, Fine Buff pottery. 1:3

PLATE 28

924

928

929

931

942

947

953

Group L, Fine Buff pottery. 1:3

PLATE 29

954

965

955

966

968

972

976

Group L, pottery in Fine Buff (954) and Minor Fabrics; Group M (976). 1:3

PLATE 30

Group N, pottery in Fine Buff and Minor Fabrics. 1:3

PLATE 31

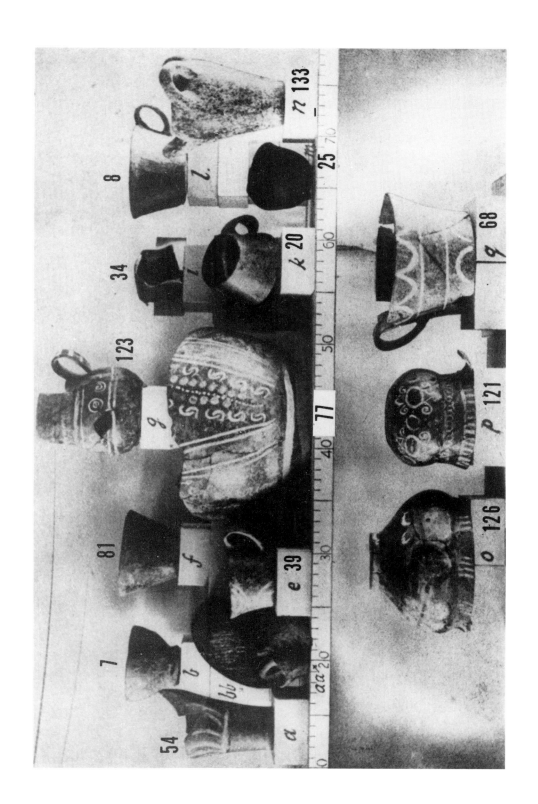

Group A, selection of pottery (Evans 1904, 15 fig. 4; 1921, 187 fig. 136).

PLATE 32

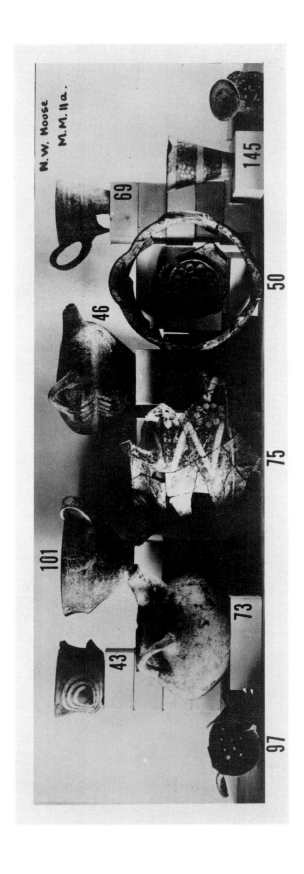

Group A, selection of pottery (Courtesy Ashmolean Museum).

PLATE 33

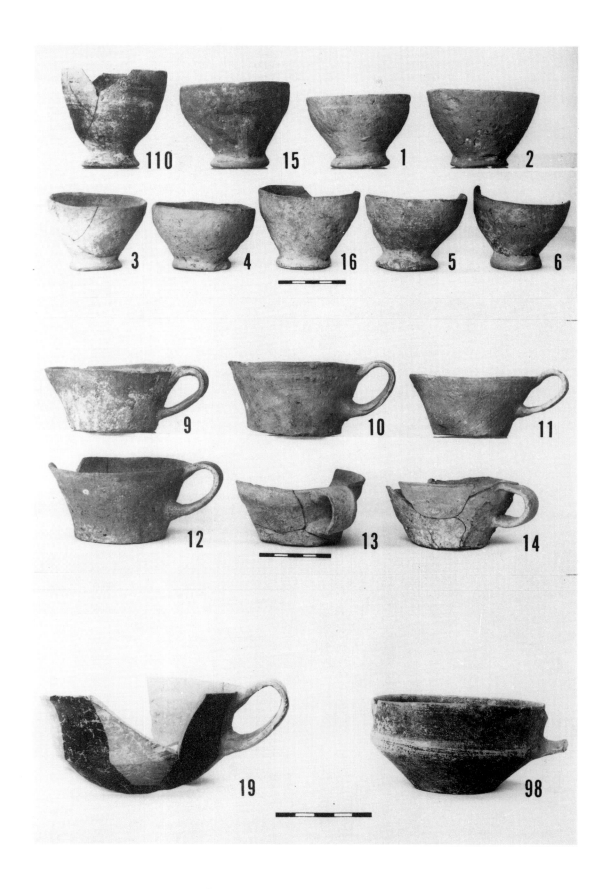

Group A, Fine Buff Goblets and Cups.

PLATE 34

Group A, Fine Buff pottery.

PLATE 35

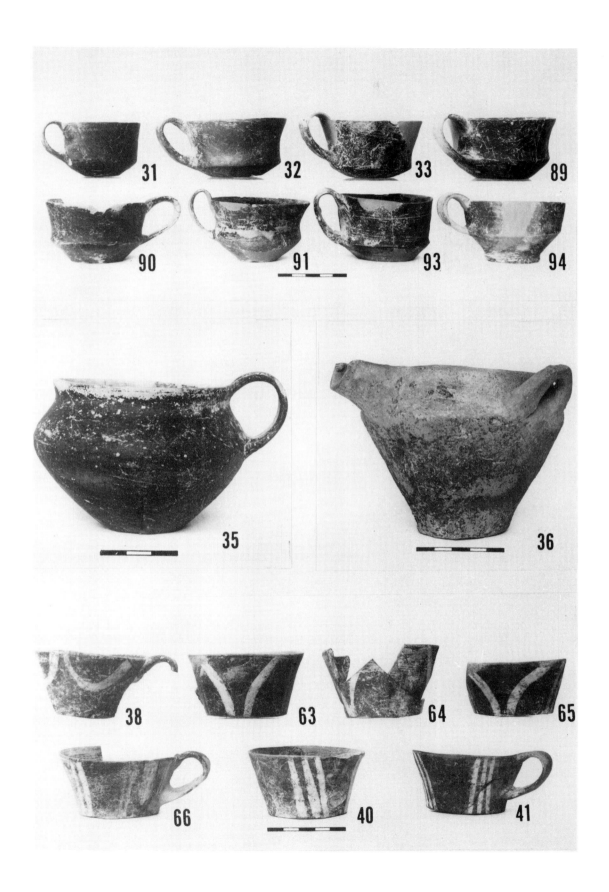

Group A, Fine Buff pottery.

PLATE 36

Group A, Fine Buff Cups.

PLATE 37

Group A, Fine Buff pottery.

PLATE 38

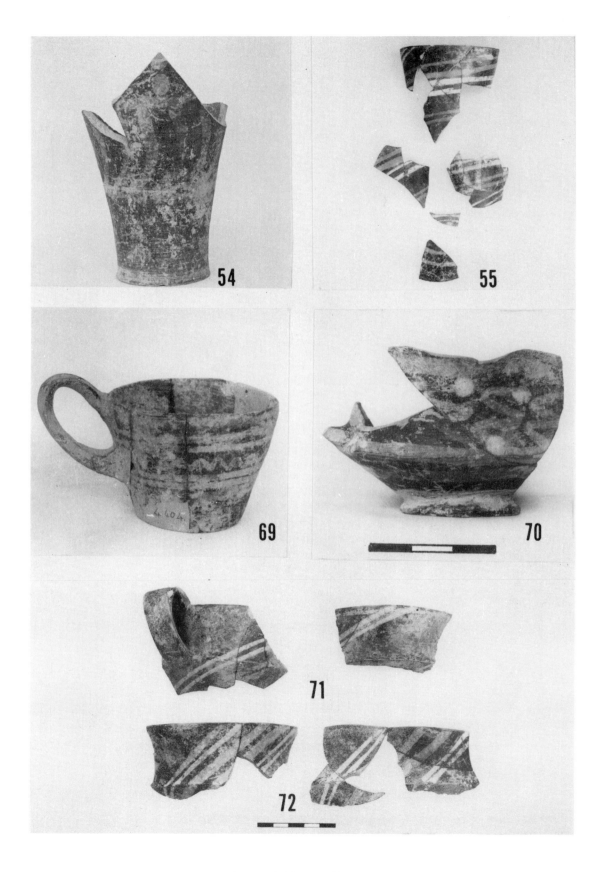

Group A, Fine Buff pottery.

PLATE 39

Group A, Fine Buff pottery.

PLATE 40

Group A, Fine Buff pottery.

PLATE 41

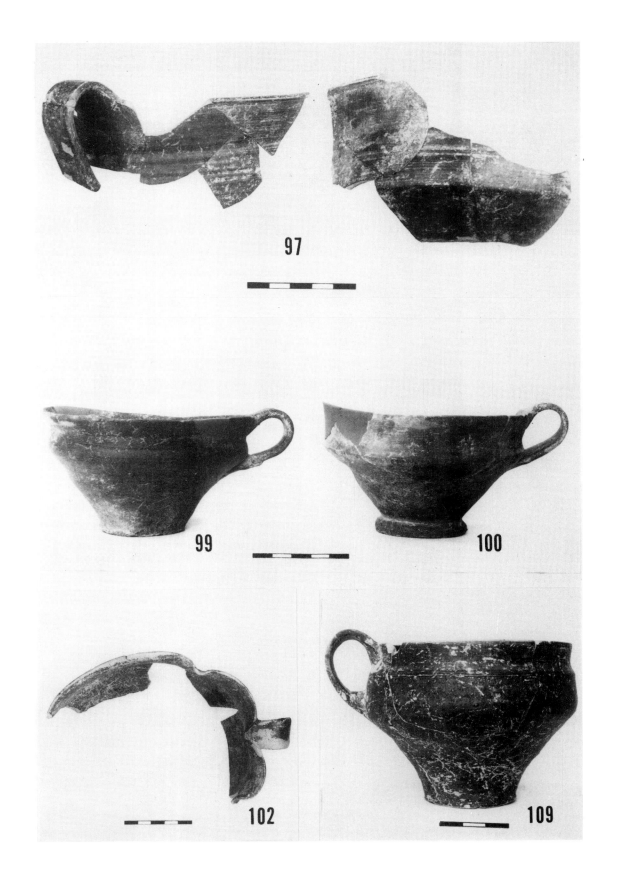

97

99

100

102

109

Group A, Fine Buff Cups.

PLATE 42

Group A, Fine Buff Cups.

PLATE 43

114

115

118

117

120

121

Group A, Fine Buff Cups.

PLATE 44

Group A, Fine Buff Cups.

PLATE 45

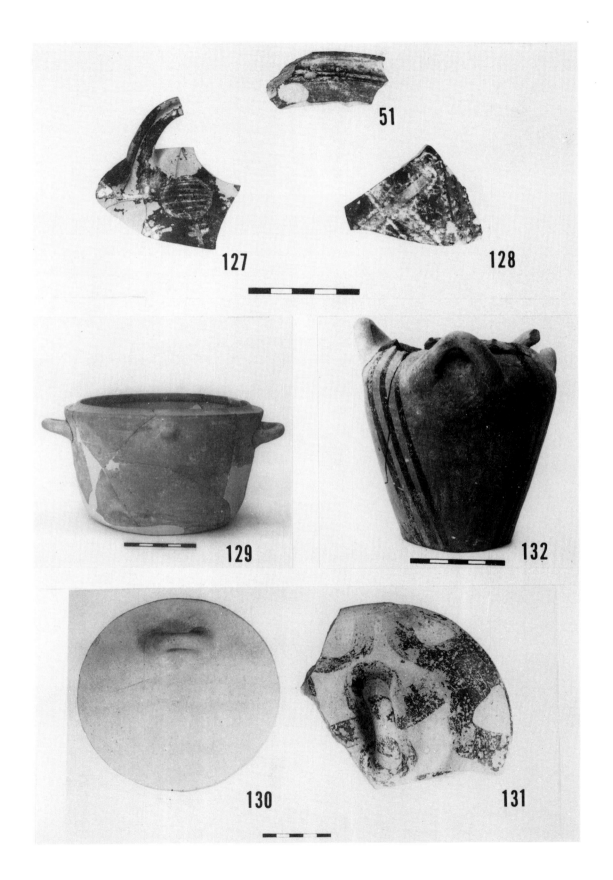

Group A, pottery in Fine Buff (51, 127–8) and Minor Fabrics.

PLATE 46

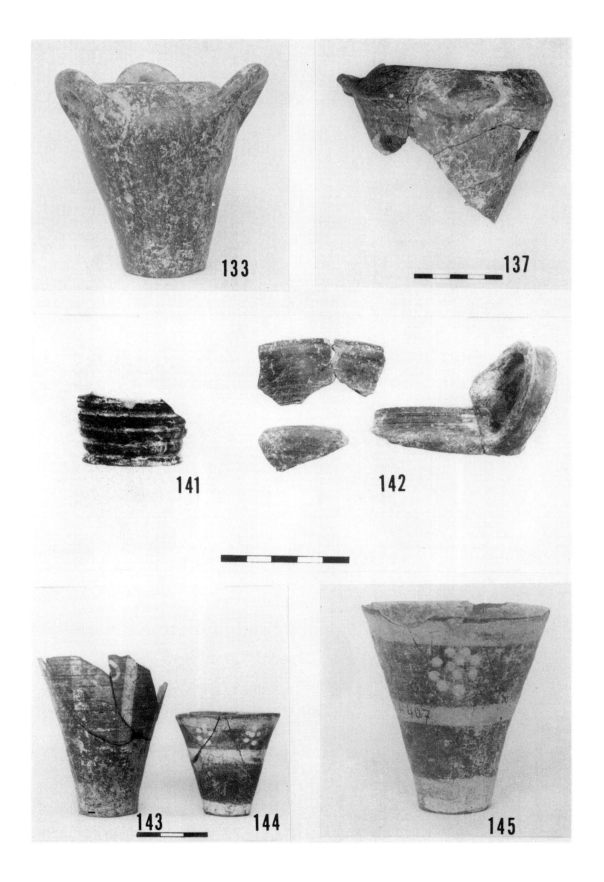

Group A, pottery in Minor Fabrics.

PLATE 47

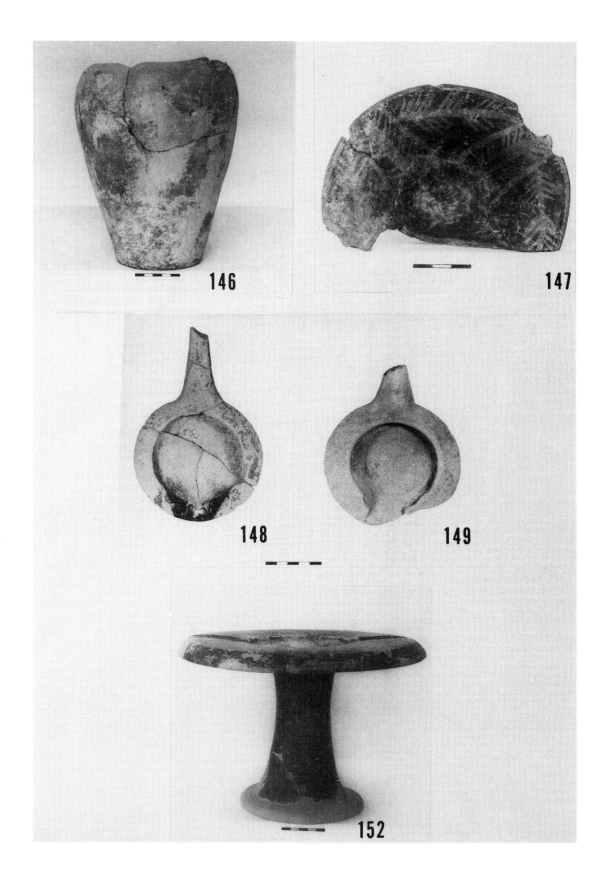

146

147

148

149

152

Group A, pottery in Minor Fabrics.

PLATE 48

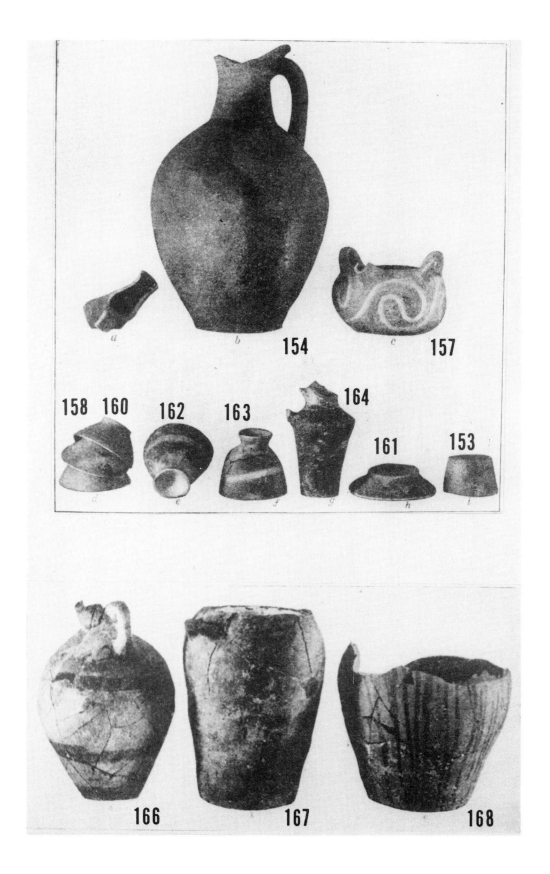

Group B, selection of pottery (Evans 1904).

PLATE 49

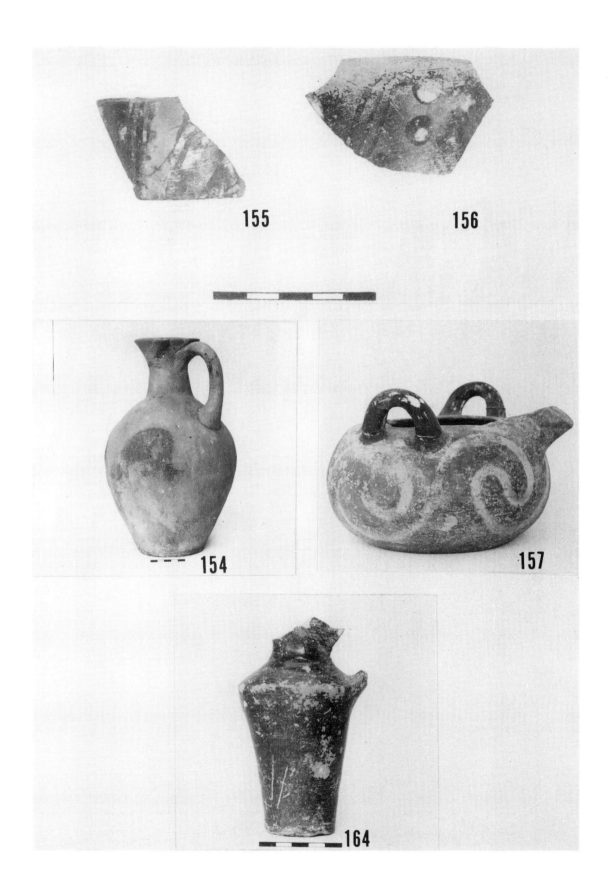

Group B, selection of pottery.

PLATE 50

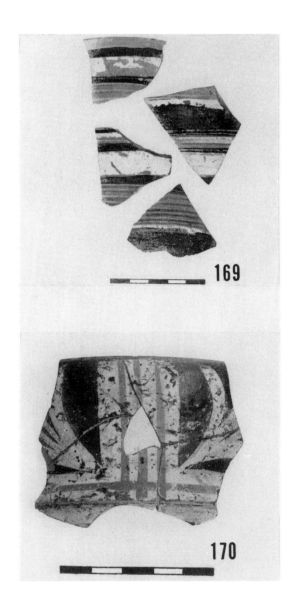

Group C, Fine Buff Ware Cups.

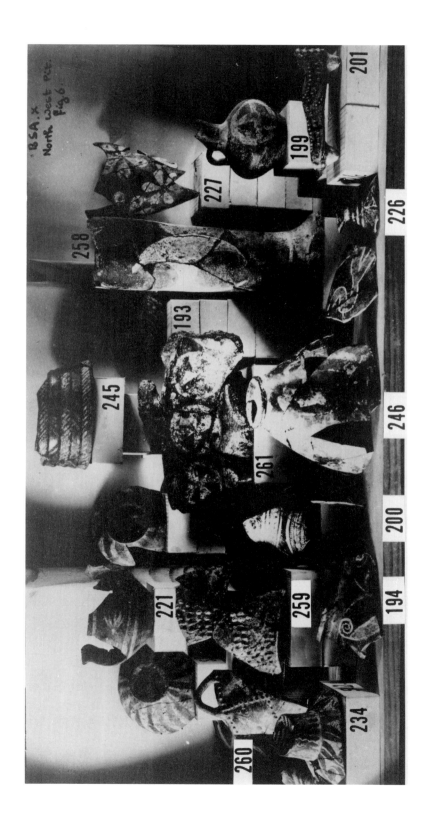

PLATE 51

Group D, selection of pottery (Evans 1904 fig. 6).

PLATE 52

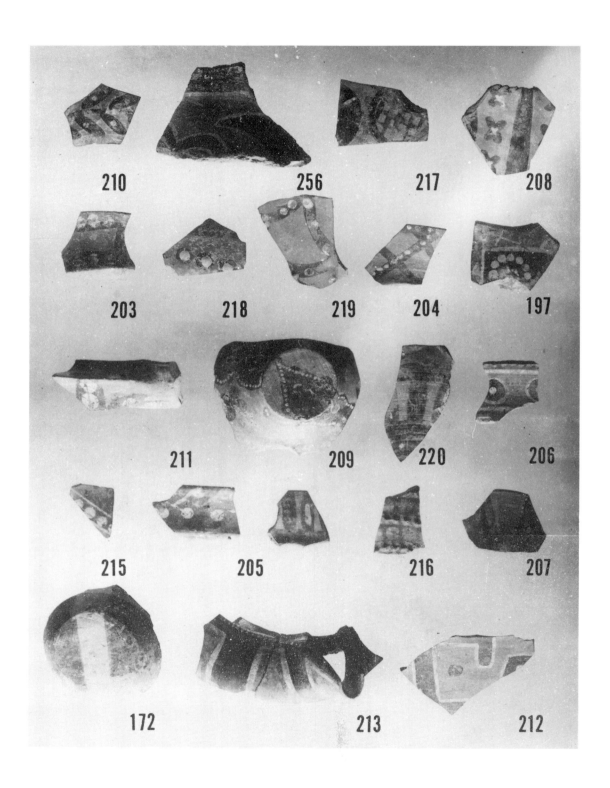

Group D, selection of Pattern Painted pottery (Courtesy Ashmolean Museum).

PLATE 53

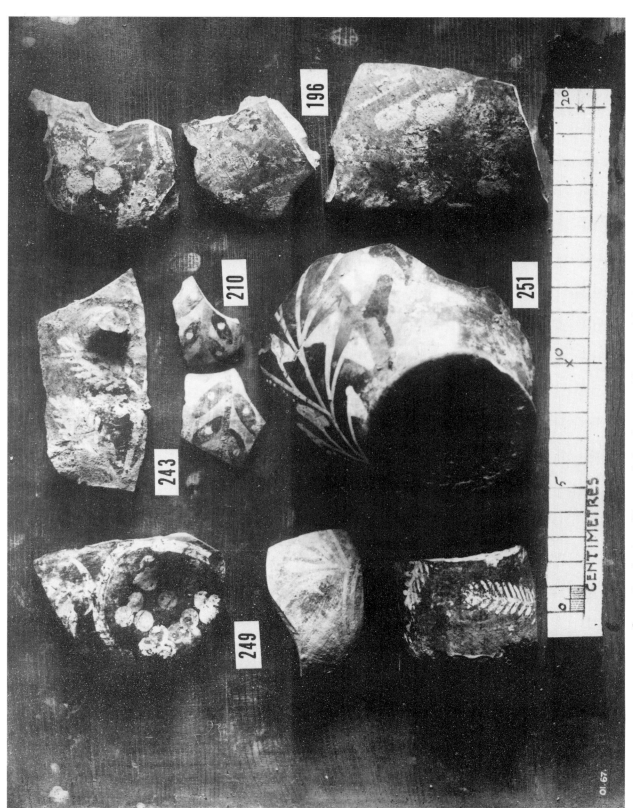

Group D, selection of Pattern Painted pottery (Courtesy Ashmolean Museum).

PLATE 54

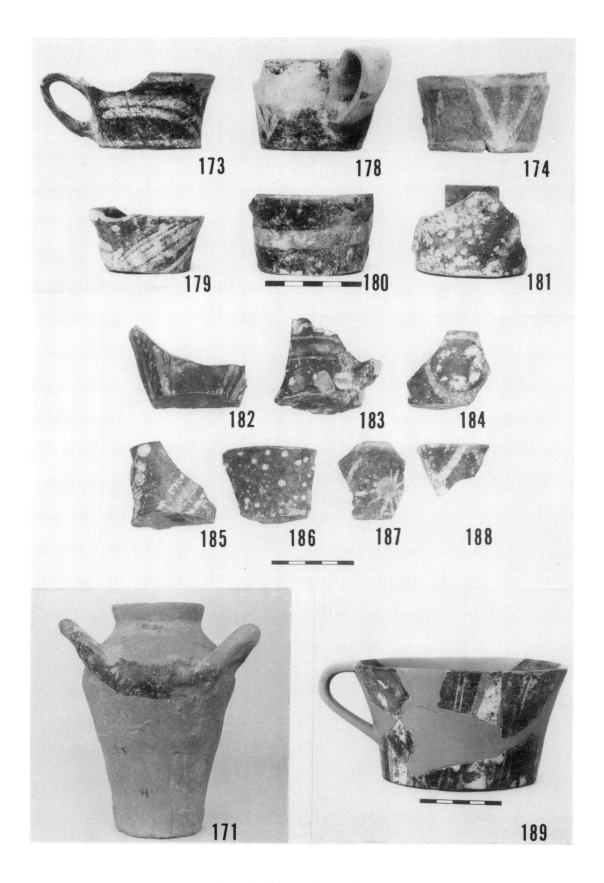

Group D, Pattern Painted pottery.

PLATE 55

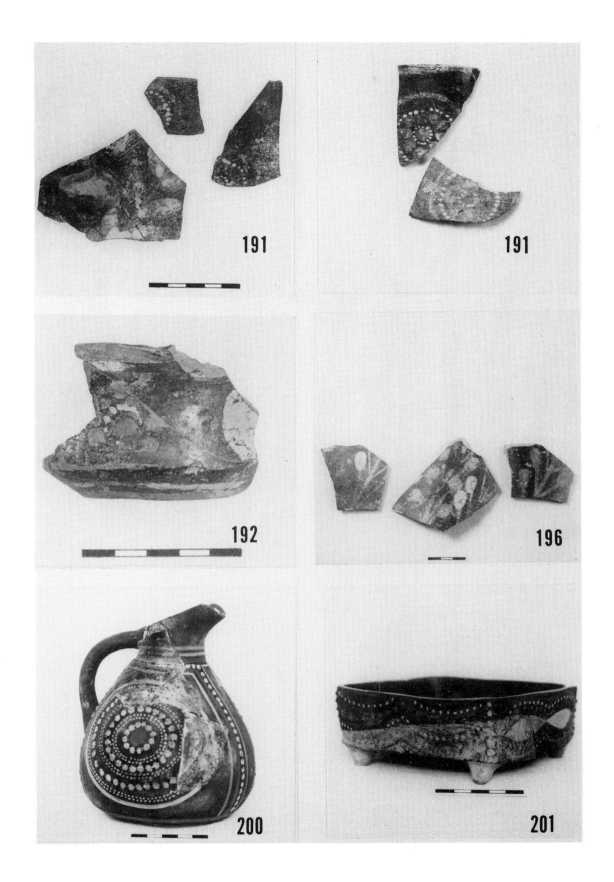

Group D, pottery in the Woven Style.

PLATE 56

Group D, Pattern Painted pottery.

PLATE 57

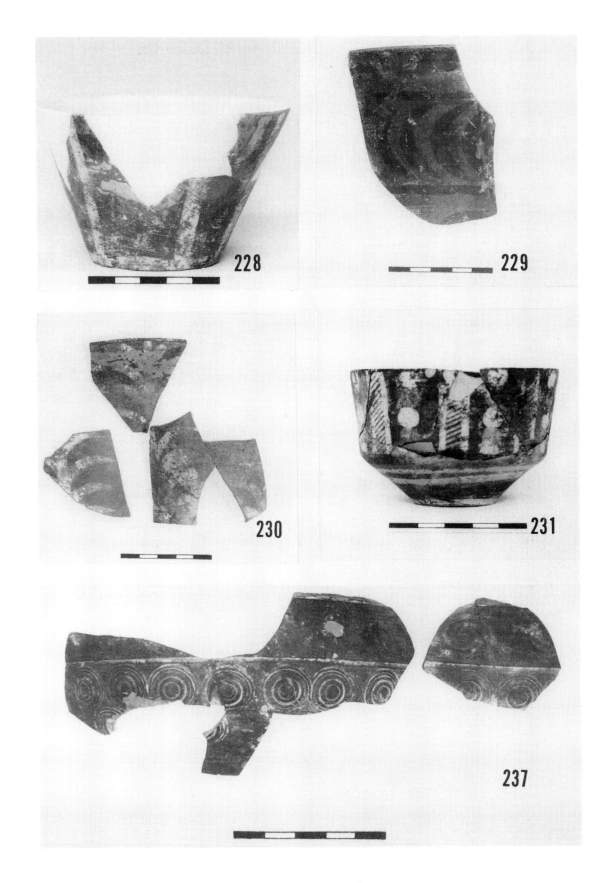

Group D, Pattern Painted pottery.

PLATE 58

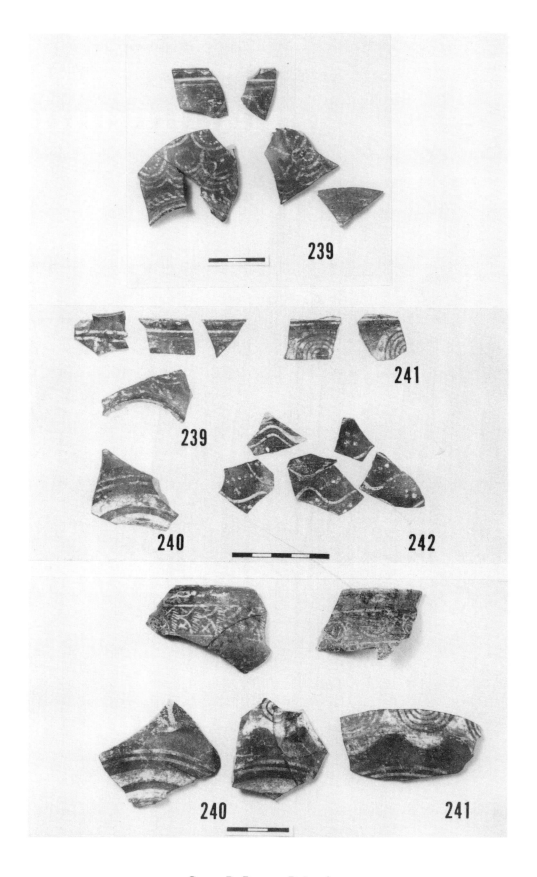

Group D, Pattern Painted pottery.

PLATE 59

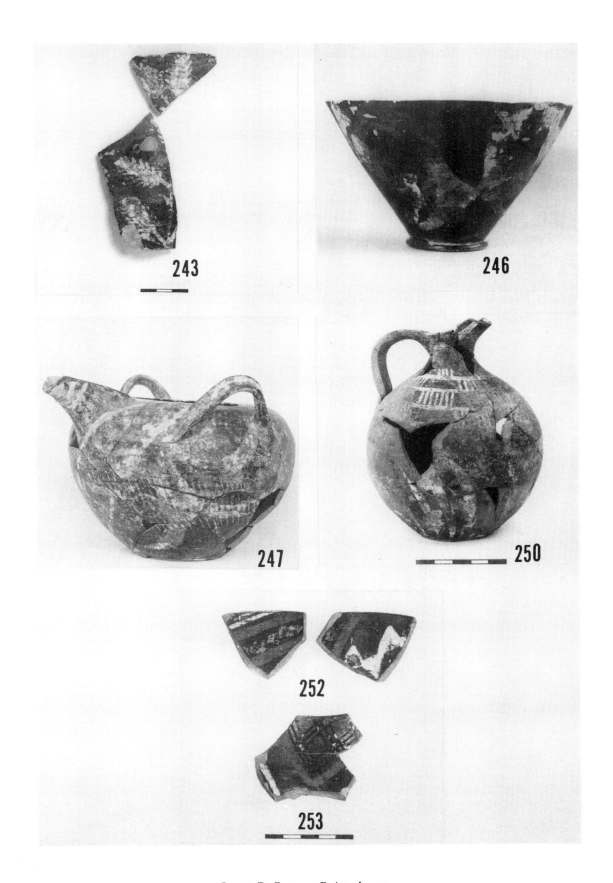

243

246

247

250

252

253

Group D, Pattern Painted pottery.

PLATE 60

Group D, pottery in Minor Fabrics.

PLATE 61

Group E, selection of pottery (Courtesy Ashmolean Museum).

PLATE 62

Group E, selection of pottery (Courtesy Ashmolean Museum).

PLATE 63

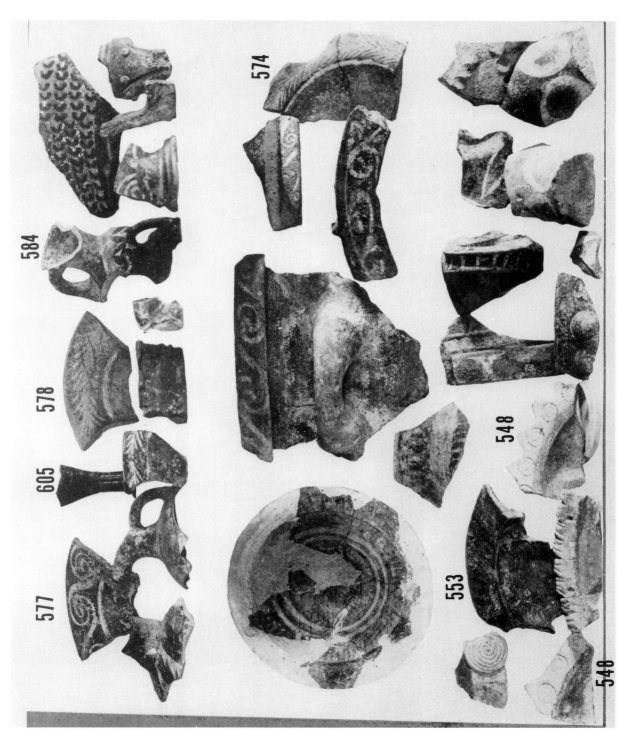

Group E, selection of pottery (Courtesy Ashmolean Museum).

PLATE 64

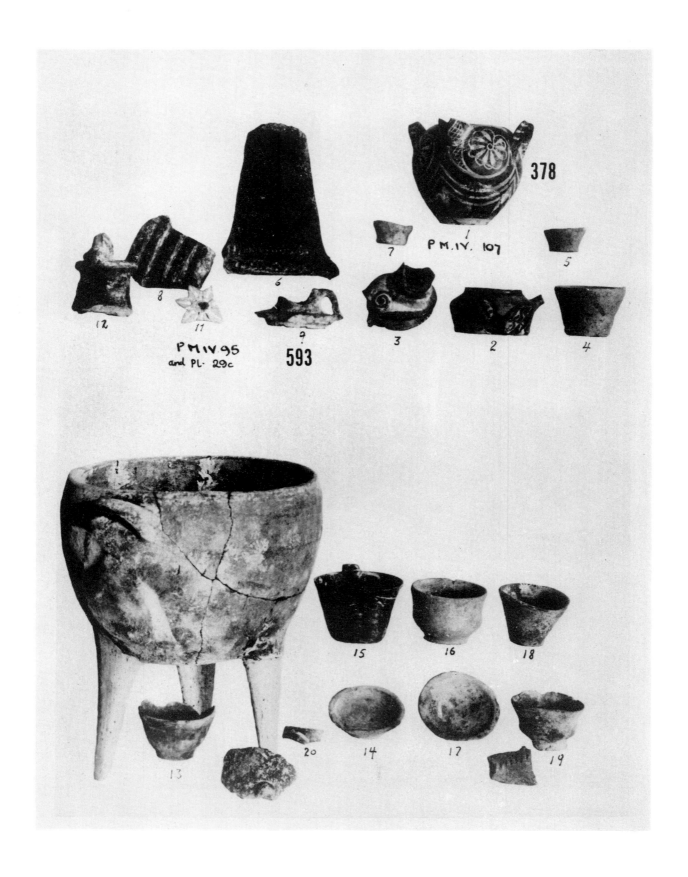

Group E, selection of pottery (Courtesy Ashmolean Museum).

PLATE 65

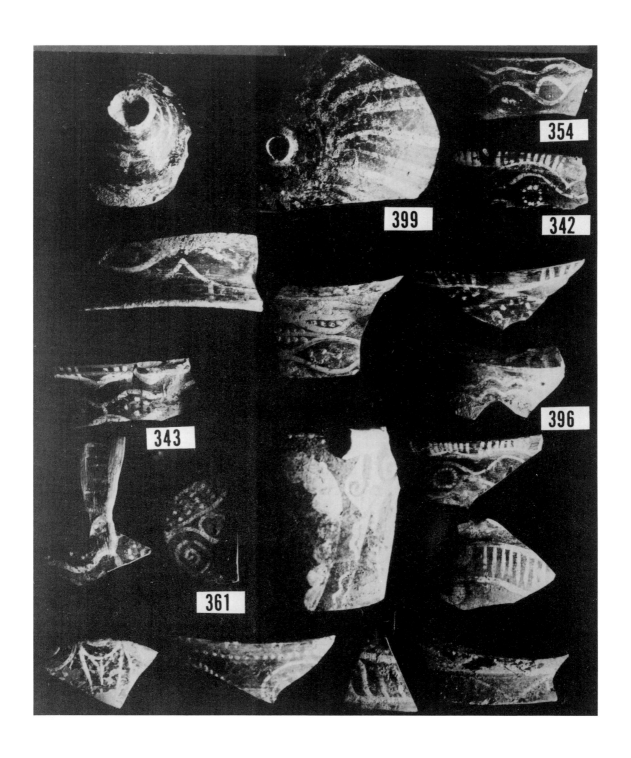

Group E, selection of pottery (Courtesy Ashmolean Museum).

PLATE 66

Group E, selection of pottery (Courtesy Ashmolean Museum).

PLATE 67

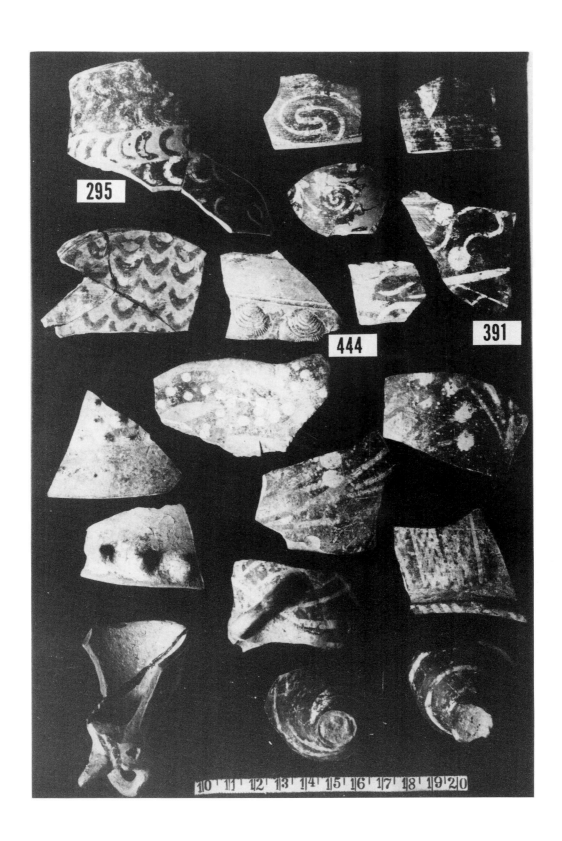

Group E, selection of pottery (Courtesy Ashmolean Museum).

PLATE 68

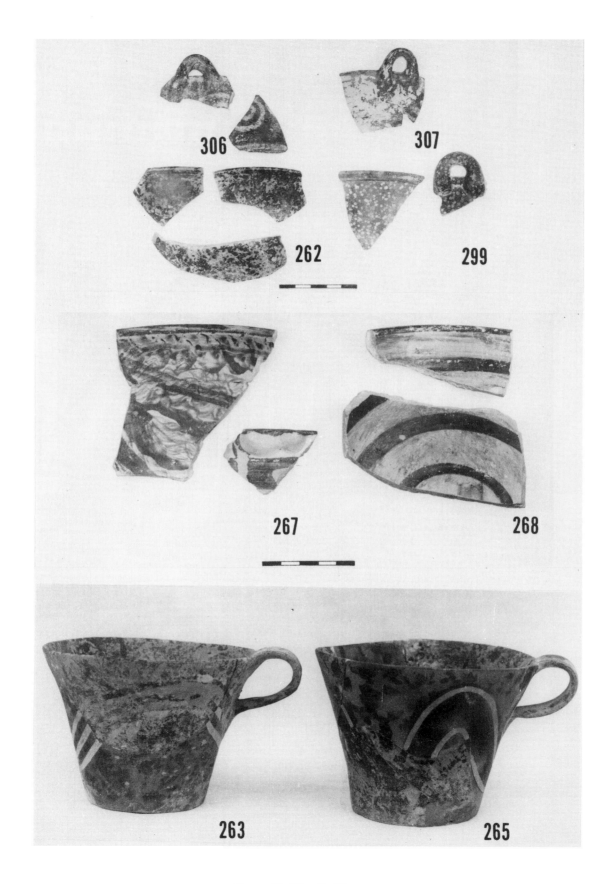

Group E, Fine Buff pottery.

PLATE 69

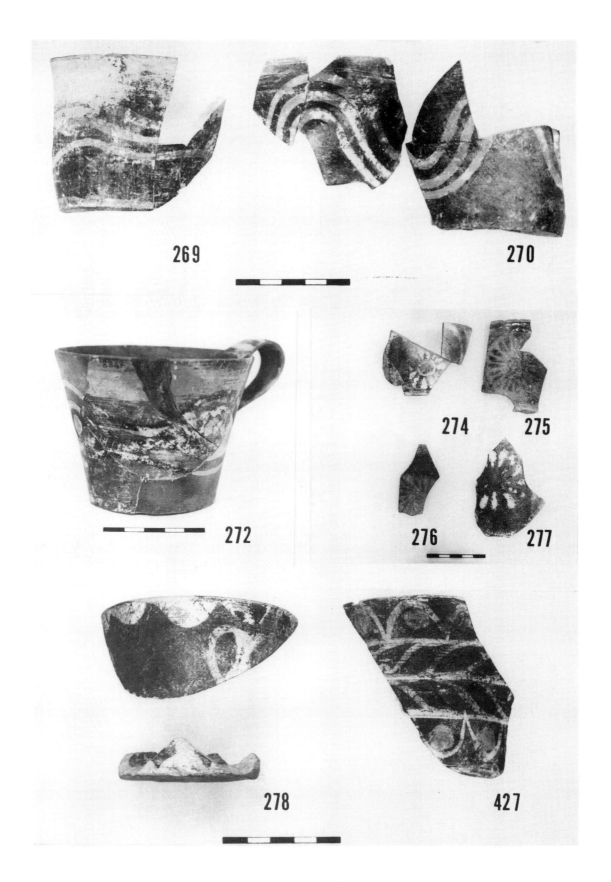

Group E, Fine Buff pottery.

PLATE 70

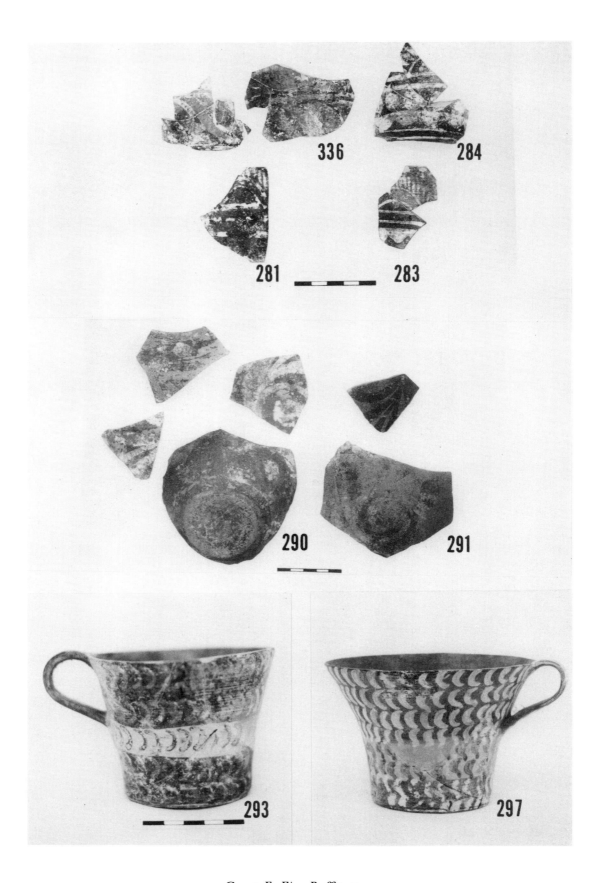

Group E, Fine Buff pottery.

PLATE 71

Group E, Fine Buff pottery.

PLATE 72

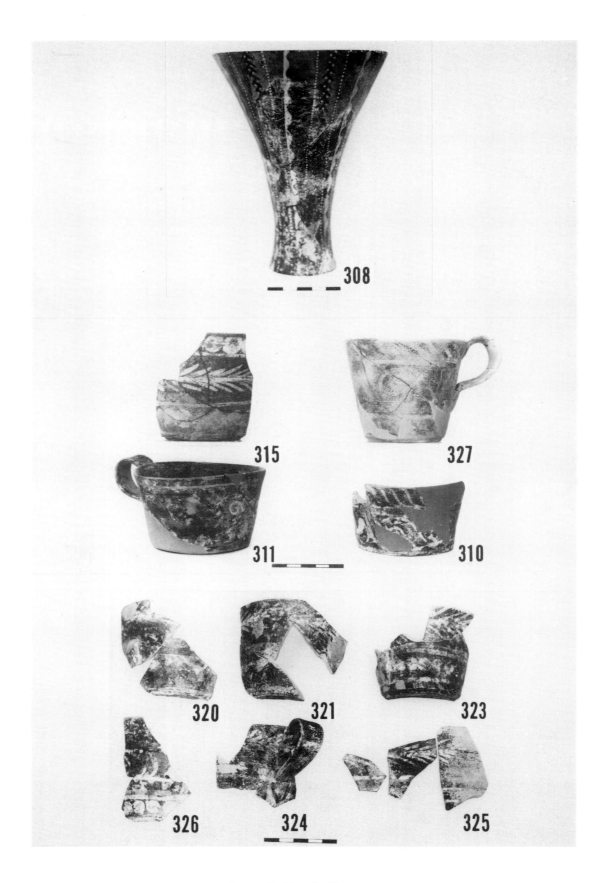

Group E, Fine Buff pottery.

PLATE 73

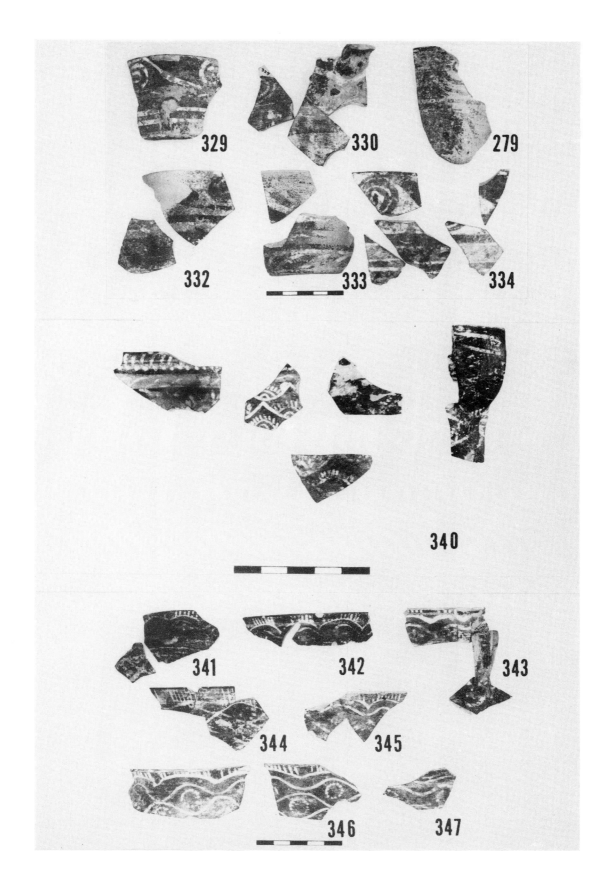

Group E, Fine Buff pottery.

PLATE 74

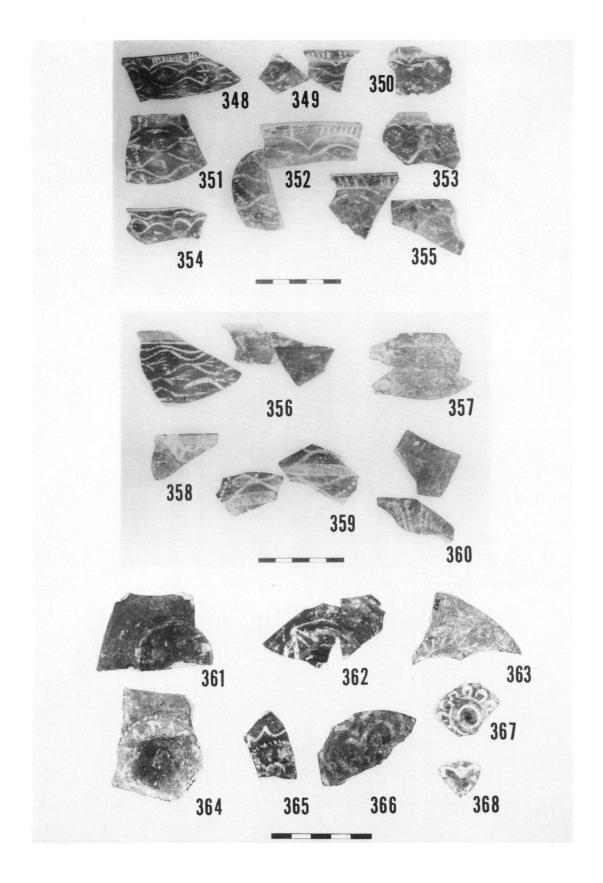

Group E, Fine Buff pottery in the Wavy-line Style.

PLATE 75

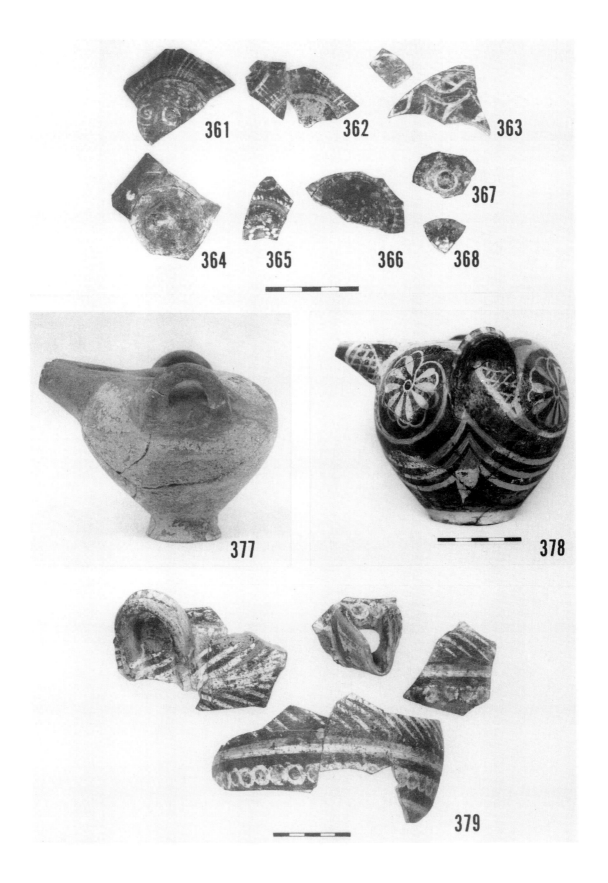

Group E, Fine Buff pottery.

PLATE 76

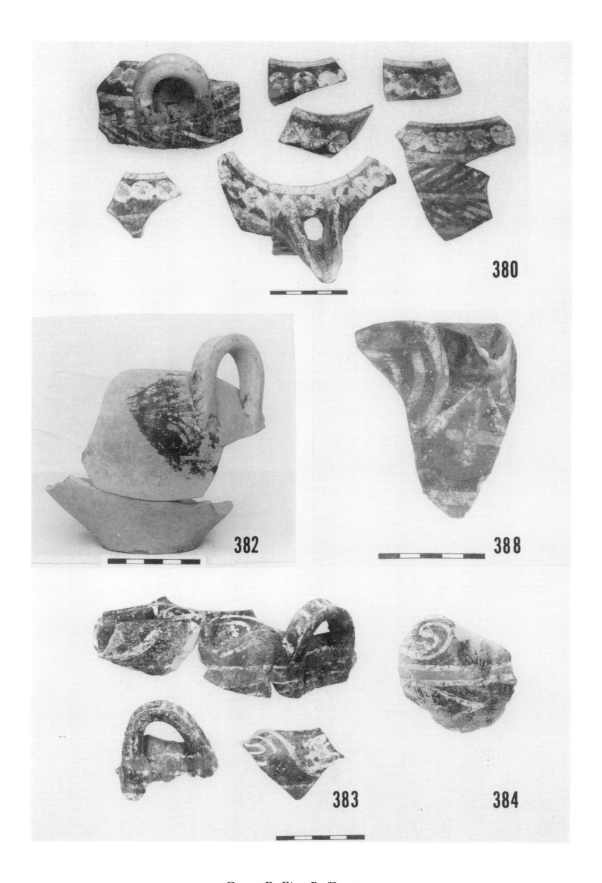

Group E, Fine Buff pottery.

PLATE 77

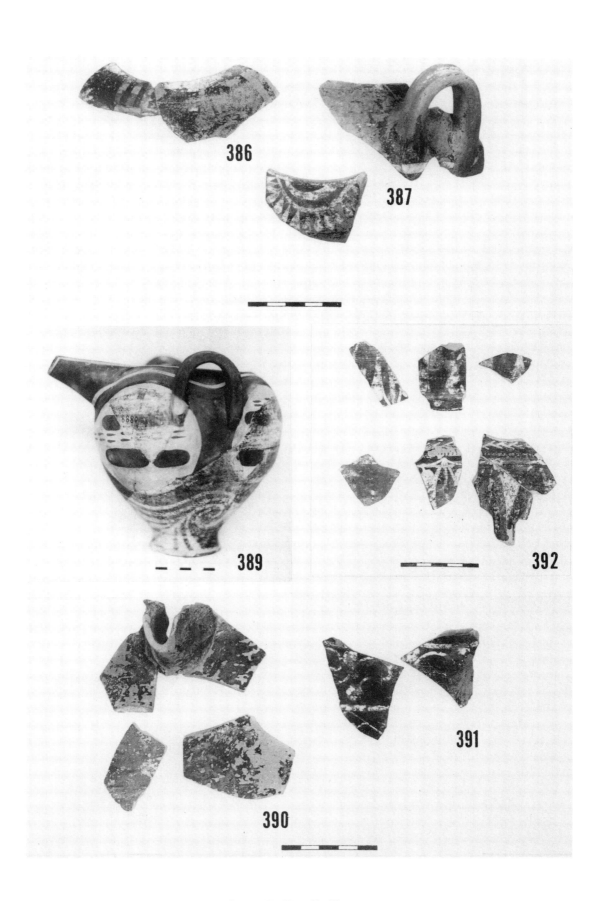

Group E, Fine Buff pottery.

PLATE 78

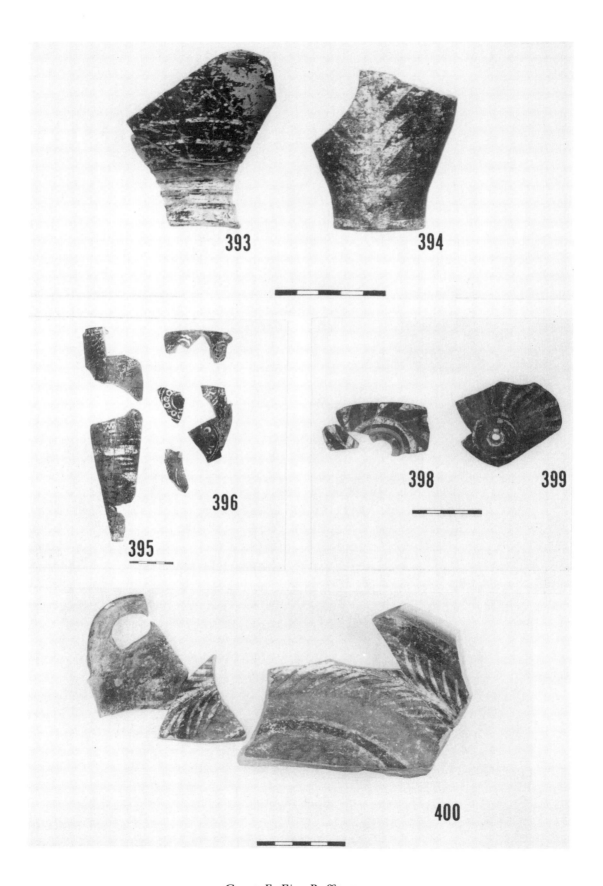

Group E, Fine Buff pottery.

PLATE 79

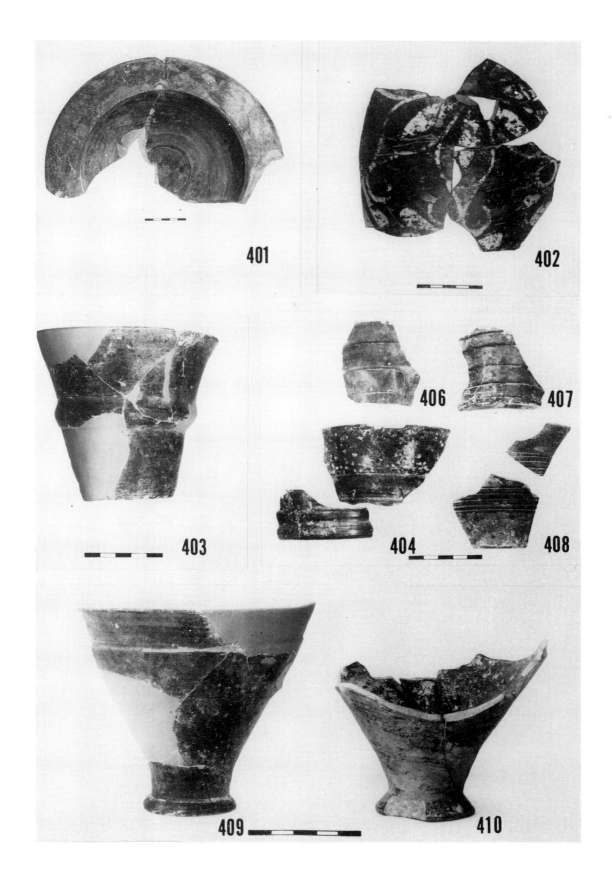

Group E, Fine Buff pottery.

PLATE 80

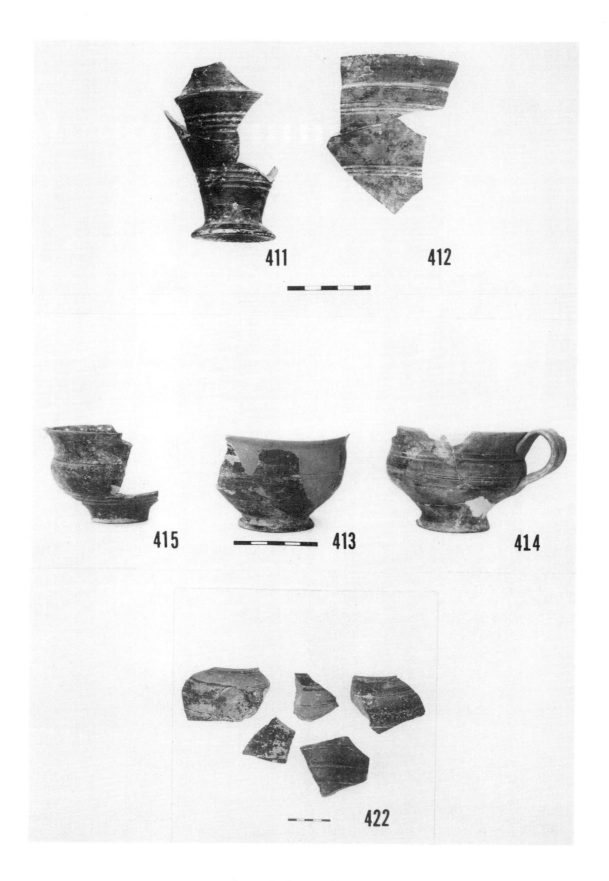

Group E, Fine Buff pottery.

PLATE 81

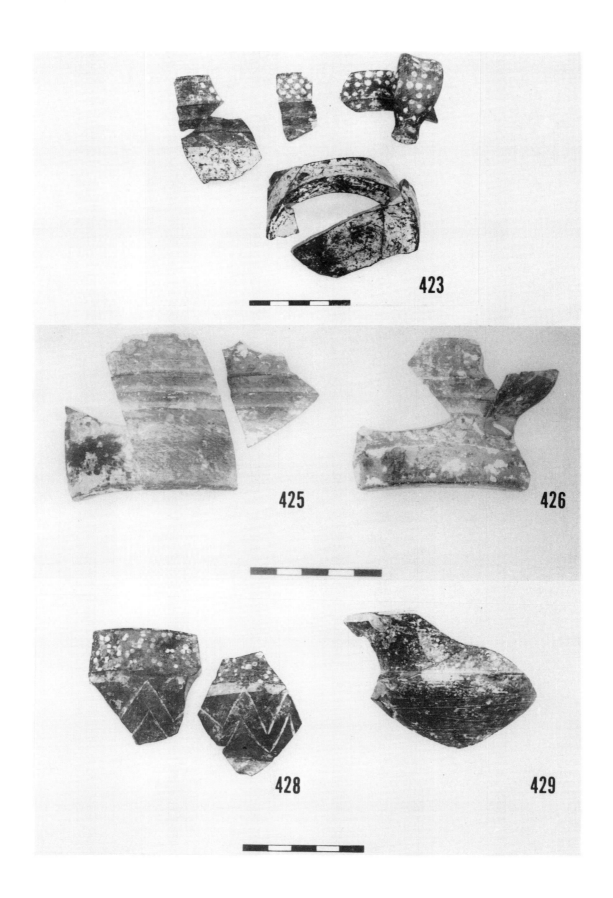

Group E, Fine Buff pottery.

PLATE 82

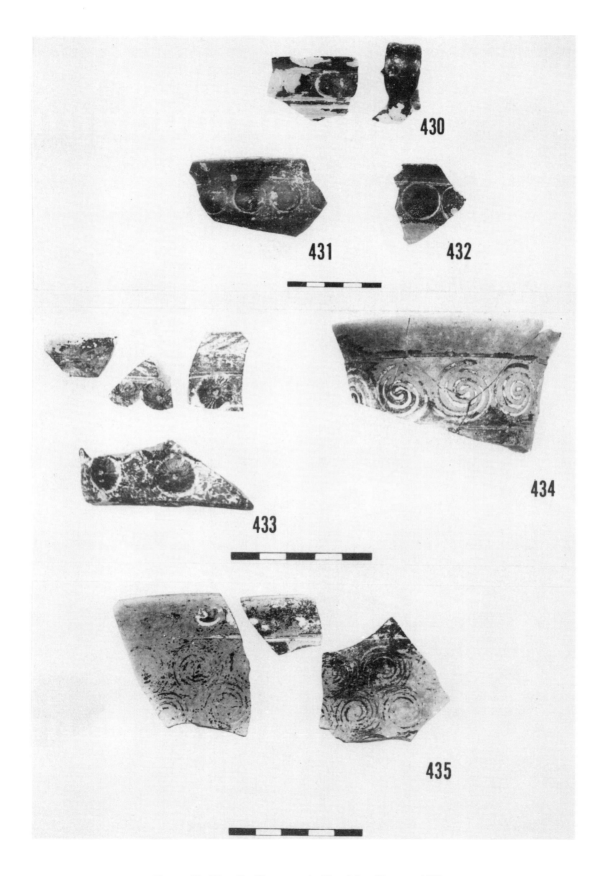

Group E, Fine Buff pottery in Precision Stamped Ware.

PLATE 83

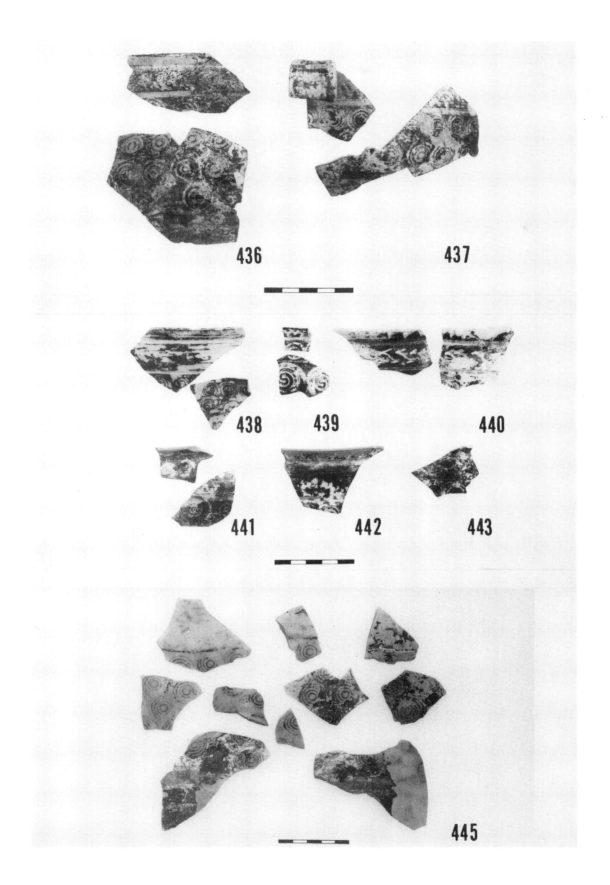

436 437

438 439 440

441 442 443

445

Group E, Fine Buff pottery in Precision Stamped Ware.

PLATE 84

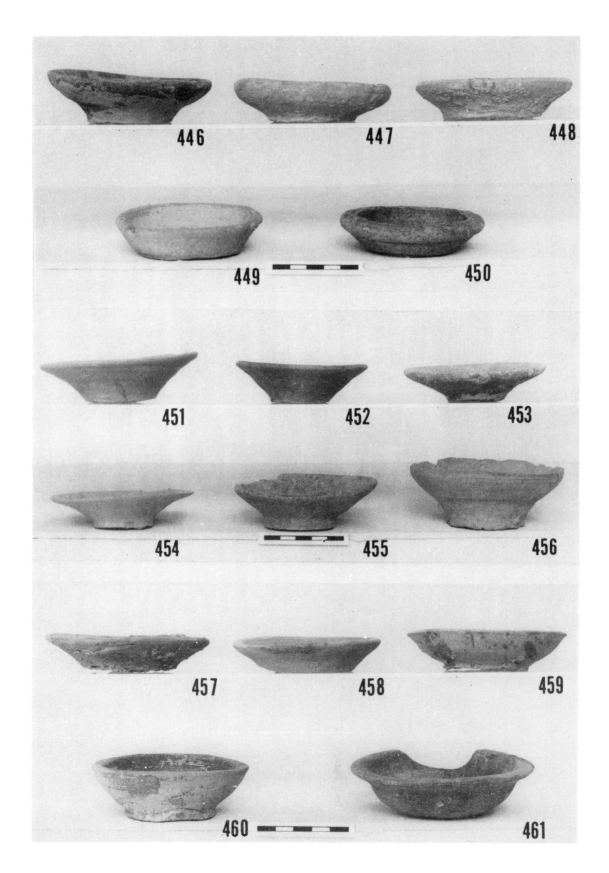

Group E, Fine Buff Crude Ware.

PLATE 85

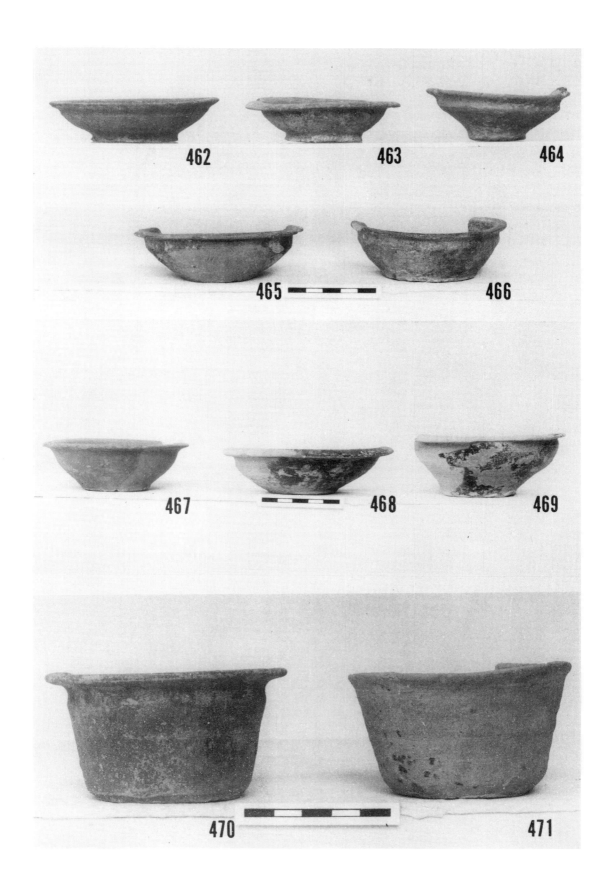

Group E, Fine Buff Crude Ware.

PLATE 86

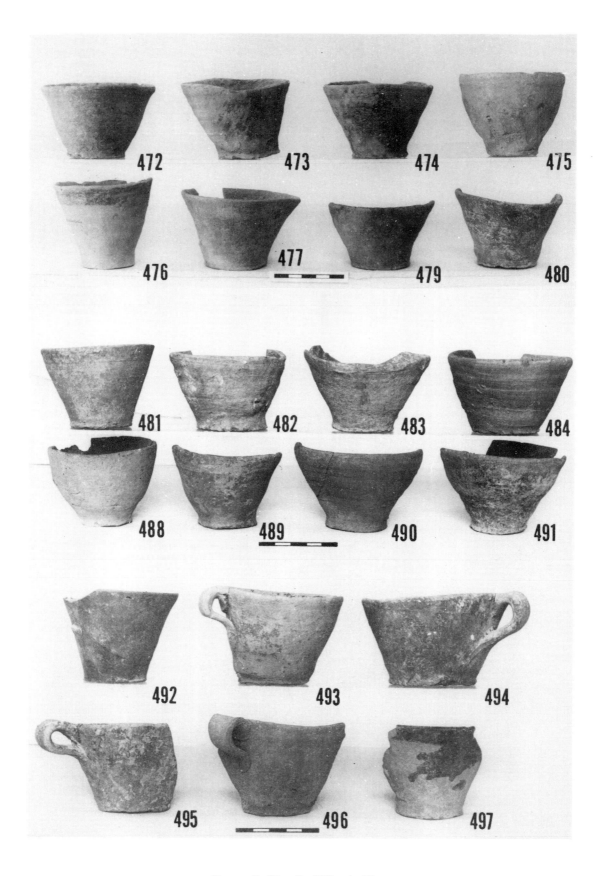

Group E, Fine Buff Crude Ware.

PLATE 87

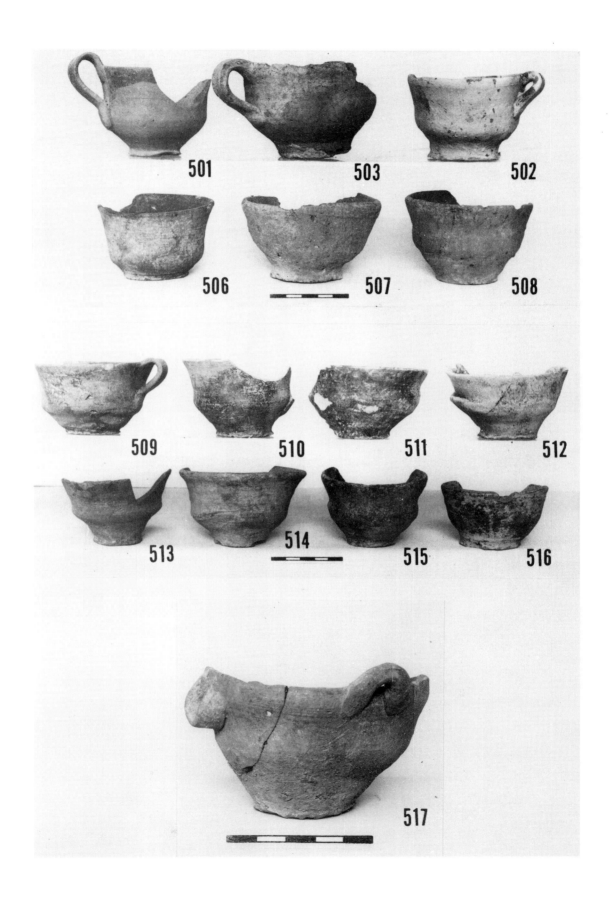

Group E, Fine Buff Crude Ware.

PLATE 88

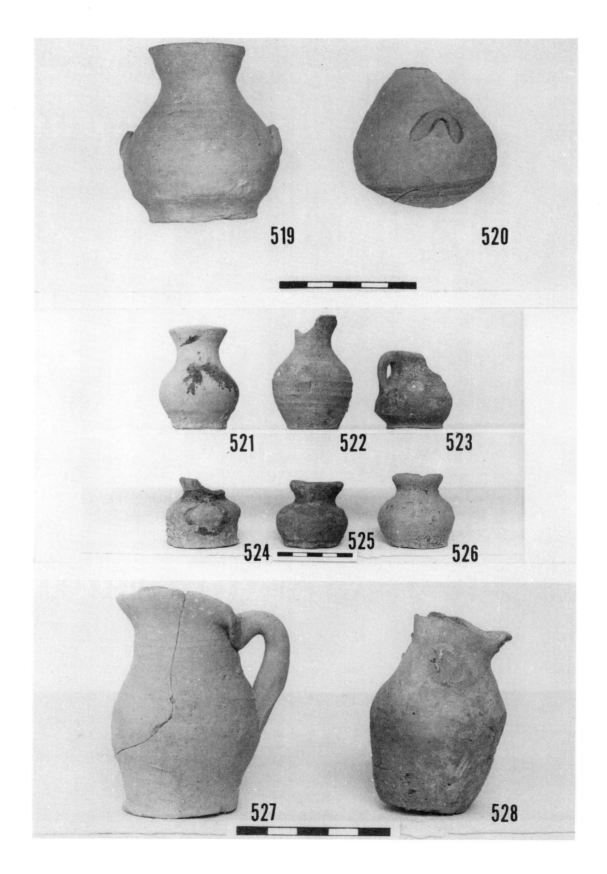

519   520

521   522   523

524   525   526

527   528

Group E, Fine Buff Crude Ware.

PLATE 89

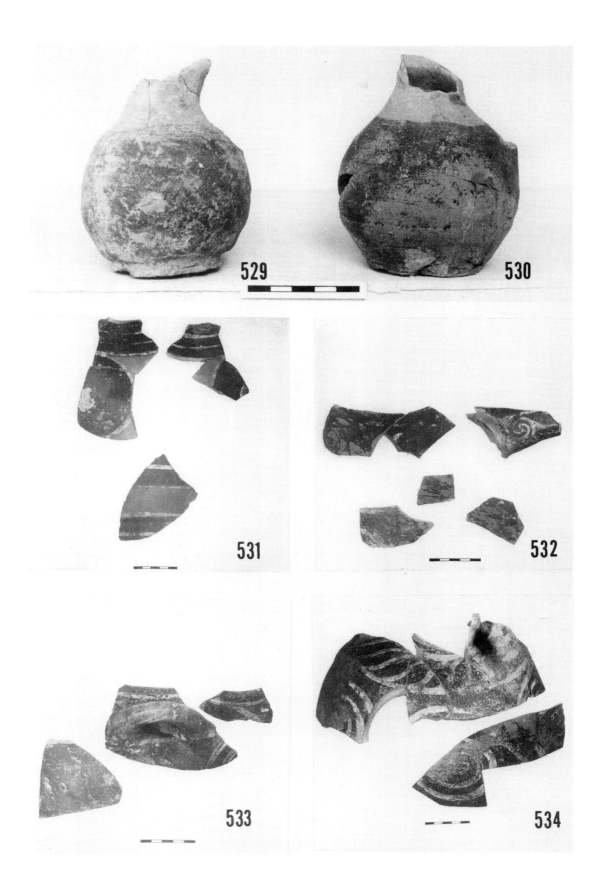

Group E, Fine Buff Crude Ware and Fine Soft Buff pottery.

PLATE 90

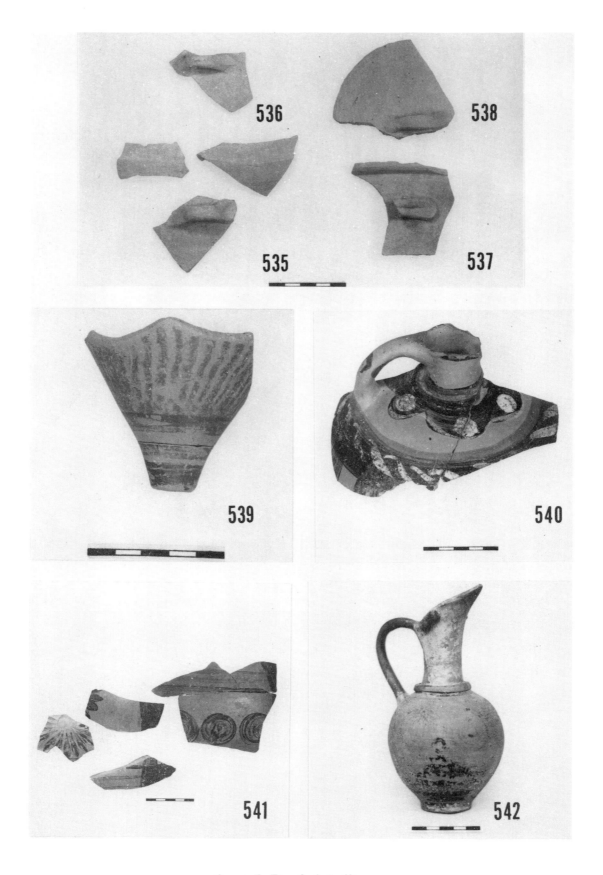

Group E, Fine Soft Buff pottery.

PLATE 91

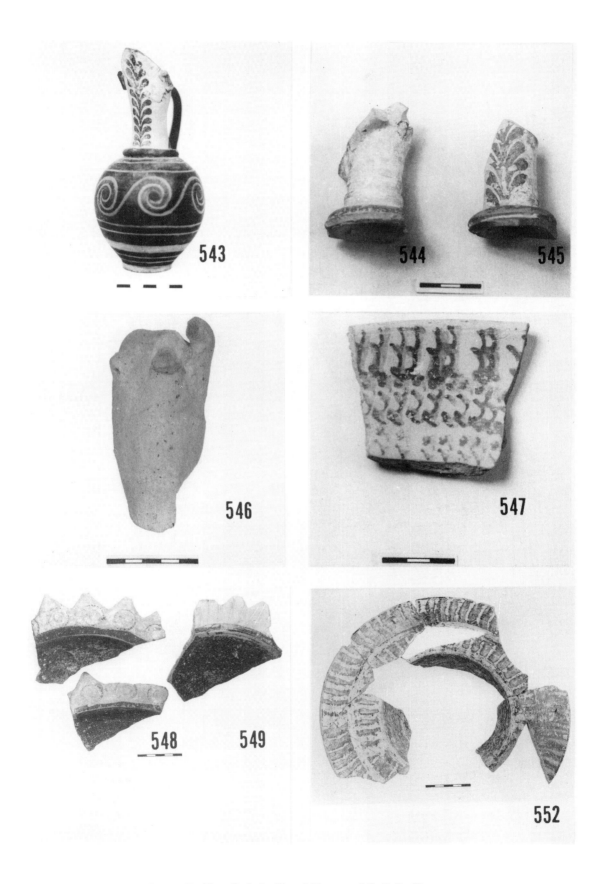

Group E, Fine Soft Buff and Tempered Soft Buff pottery.

PLATE 92

Group E, pottery in Minor Fabrics.

PLATE 93

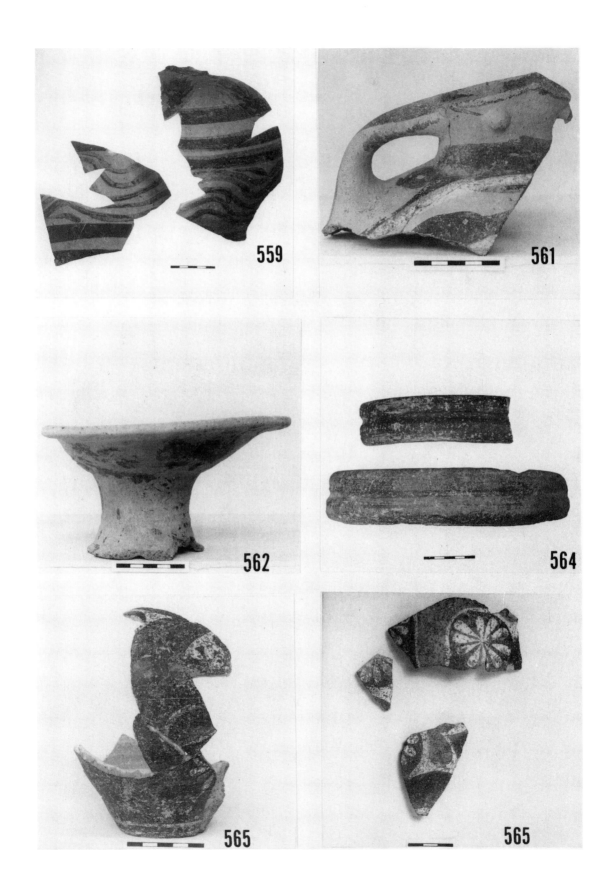

559

561

562

564

565

565

Group E, Tempered Soft Buff pottery.

PLATE 94

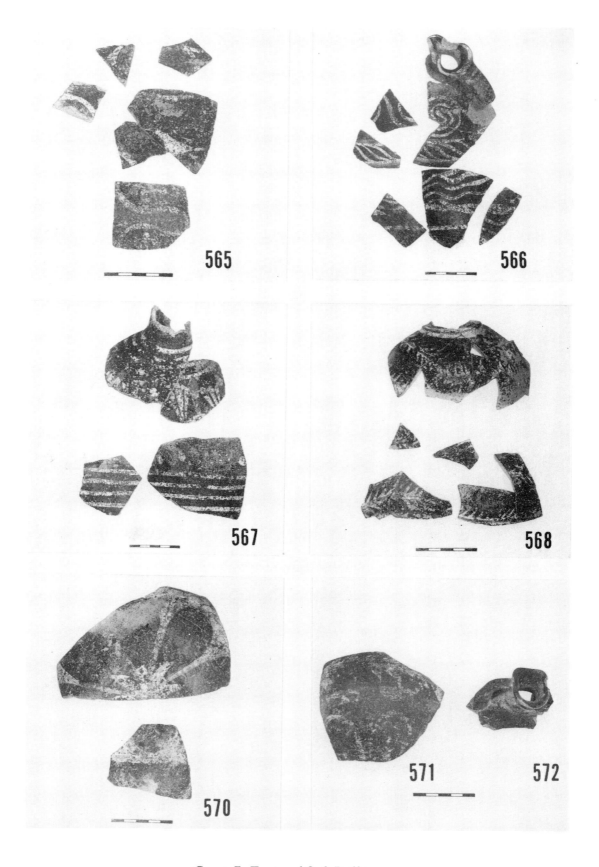

565

566

567

568

570

571   572

Group E, Tempered Soft Buff pottery.

PLATE 95

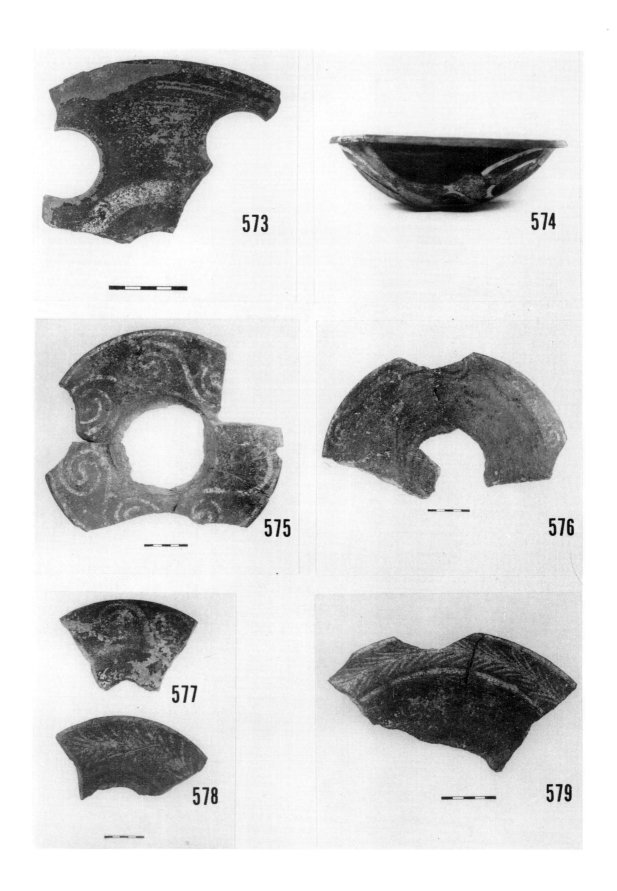

Group E, Tempered Soft Buff pottery.

PLATE 96

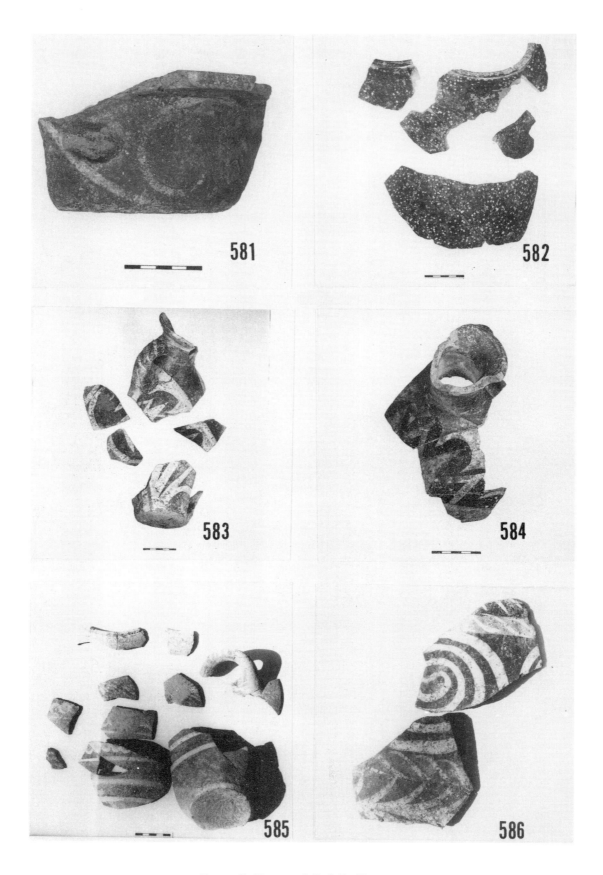

Group E, Tempered Soft Buff pottery.

PLATE 97

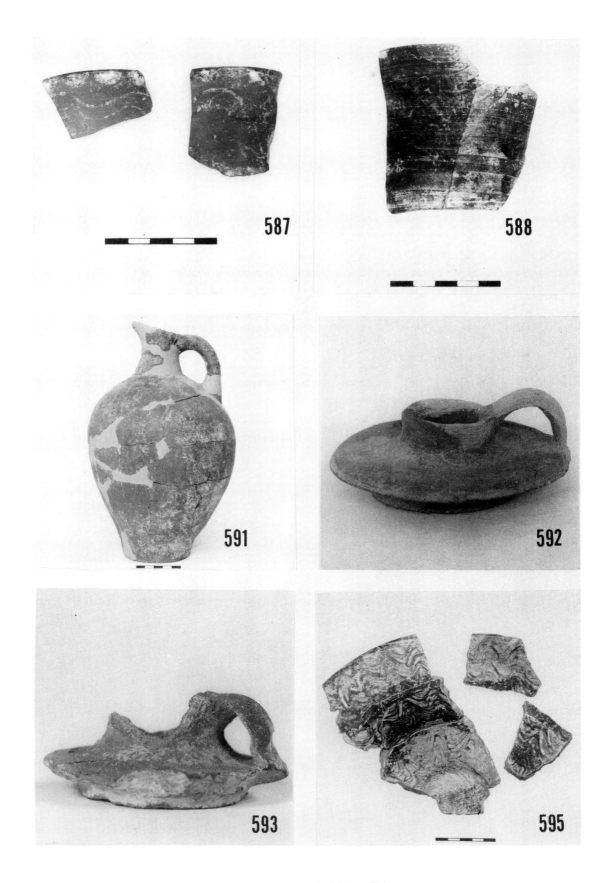

587
588
591
592
593
595

Group E, pottery in Minor Fabrics.

PLATE 98

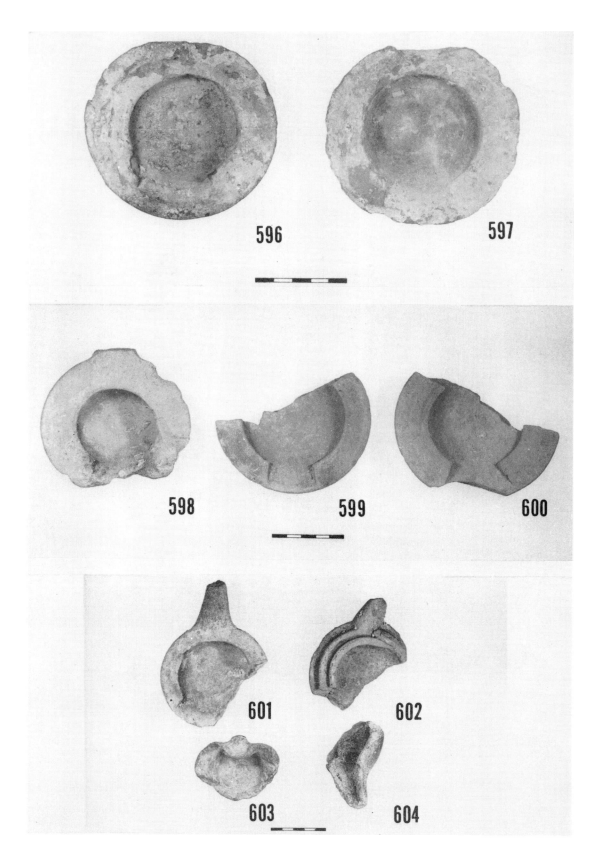

596

597

598

599

600

601

602

603

604

Group E, Coarse Red and Soft Gritty Buff pottery.

PLATE 99

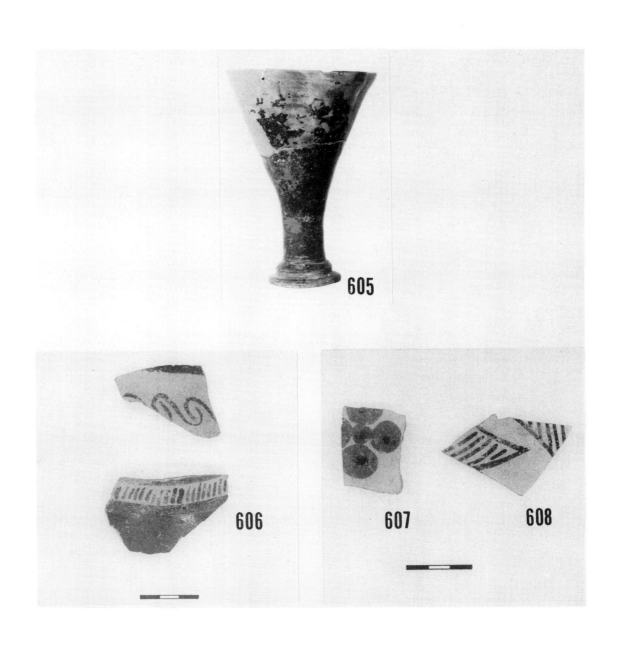

Group E, pottery in Minor Fabrics.

PLATE 100

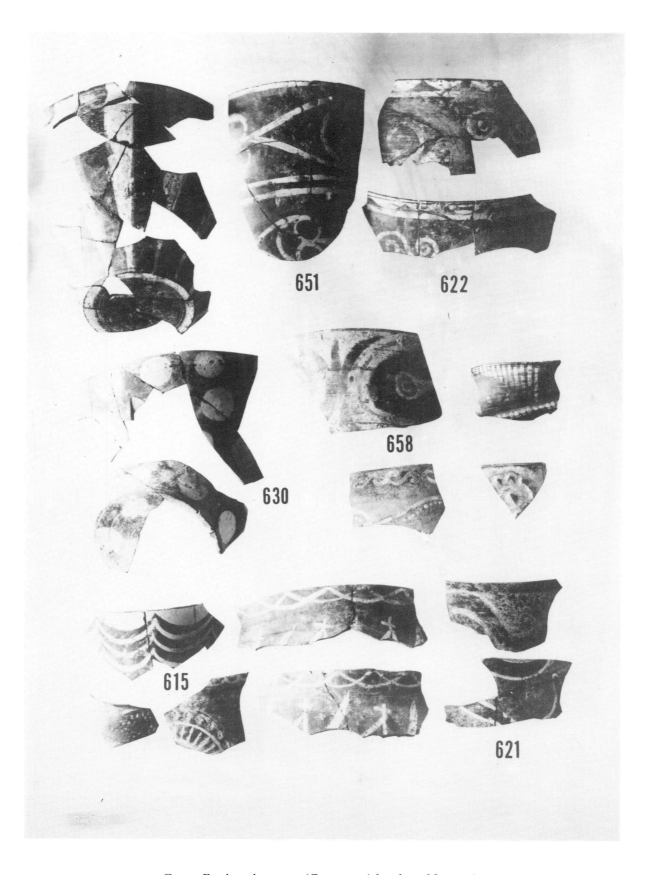

Group F, selected pottery (Courtesy Ashmolean Museum).

PLATE 101

Group F, jar **614** in the Woven Style.

PLATE 102

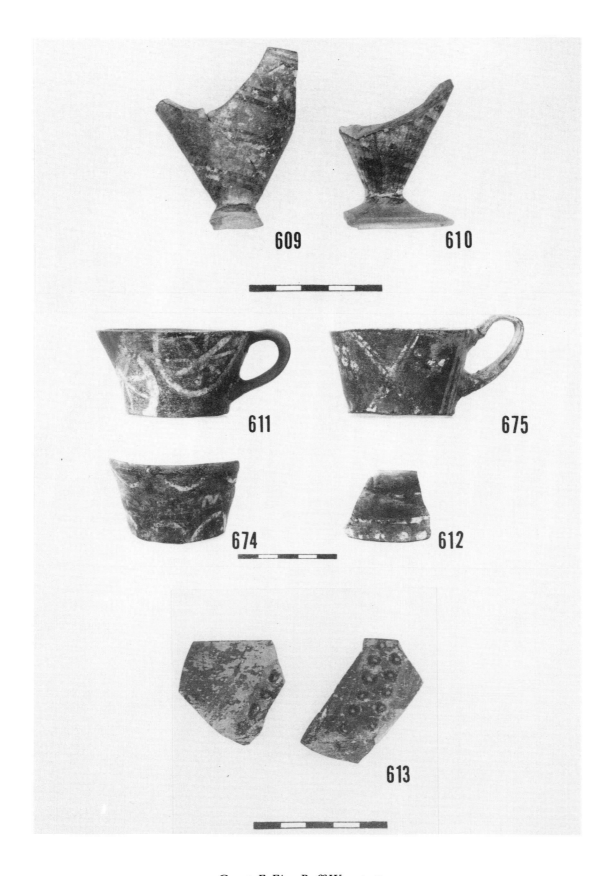

Group F, Fine Buff Ware pottery.

PLATE 103

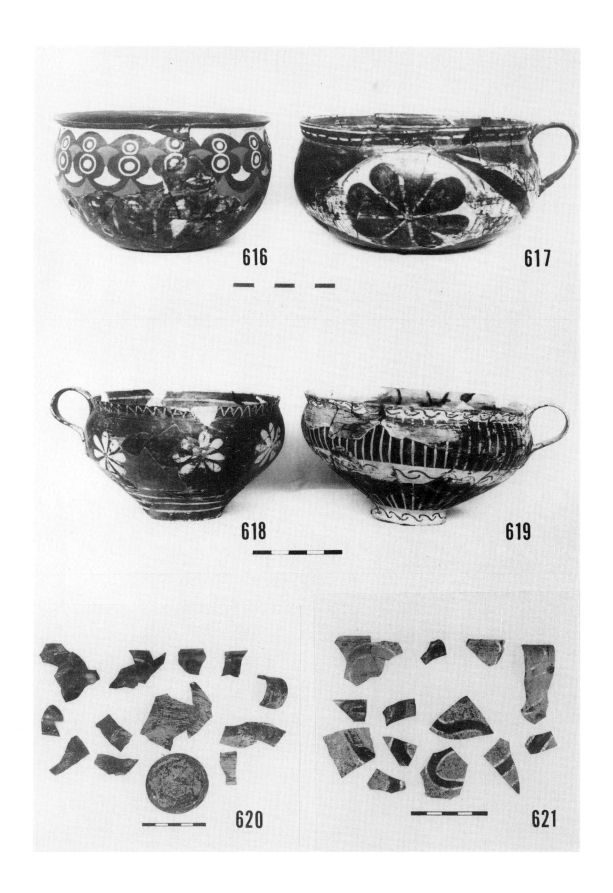

616 617

618 619

620 621

Group F, Fine Buff Egg-shell Ware pottery.

PLATE 104

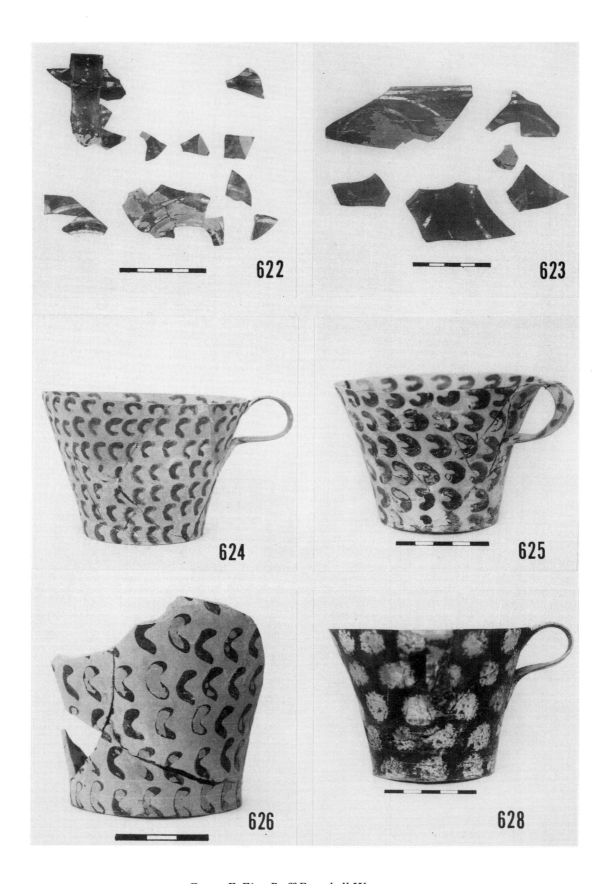

Group F, Fine Buff Egg-shell Ware pottery.

PLATE 105

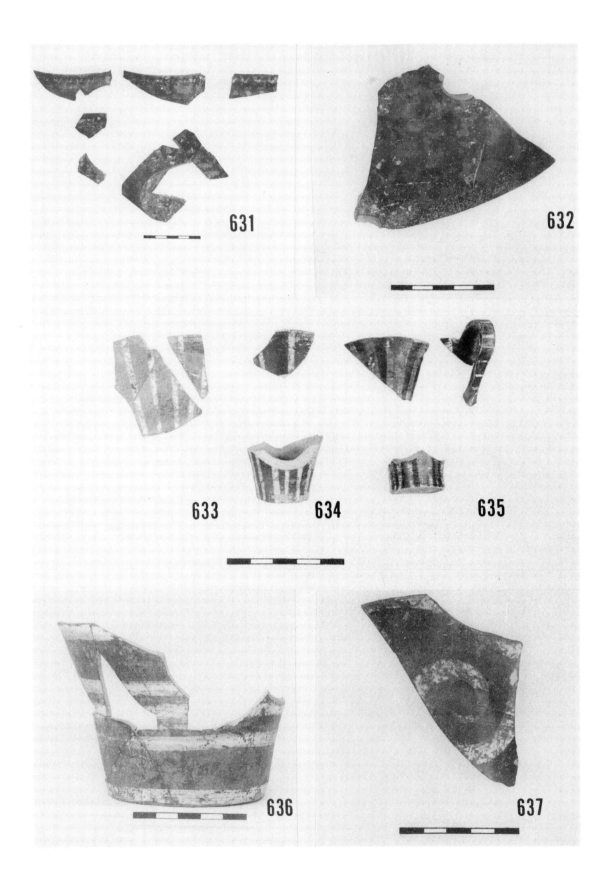

631 632 633 634 635 636 637

Group F, Fine Buff Ware pottery.

PLATE 106

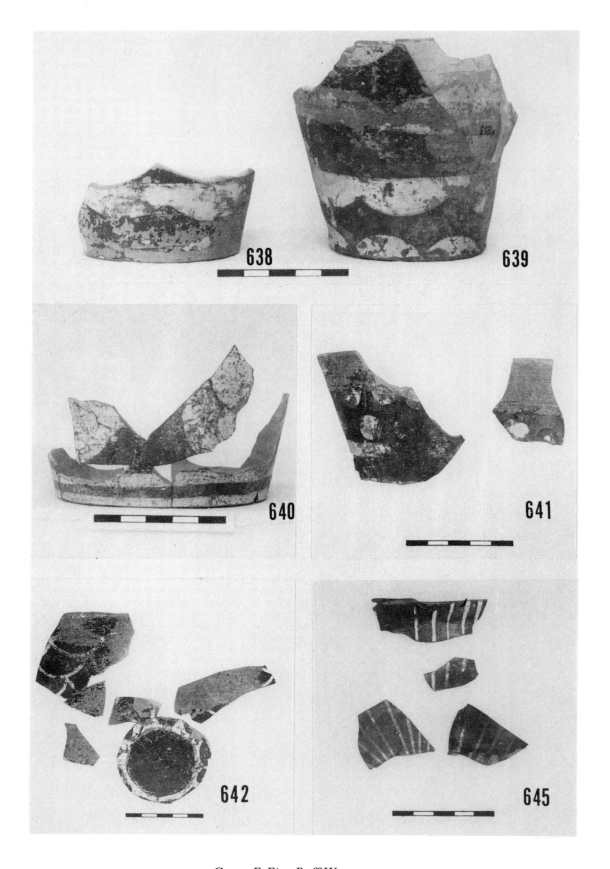

Group F, Fine Buff Ware pottery.

PLATE 107

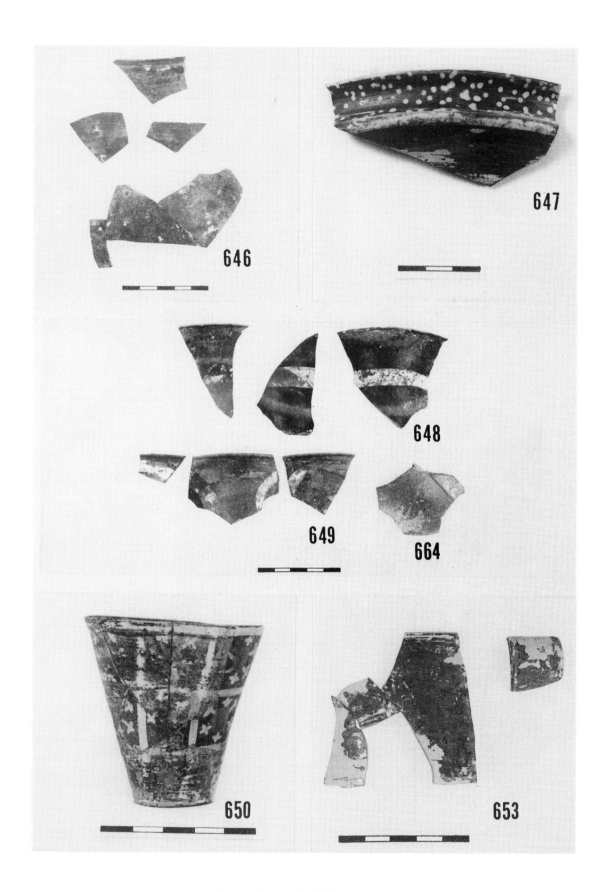

Group F, Fine Buff Ware pottery.

PLATE 108

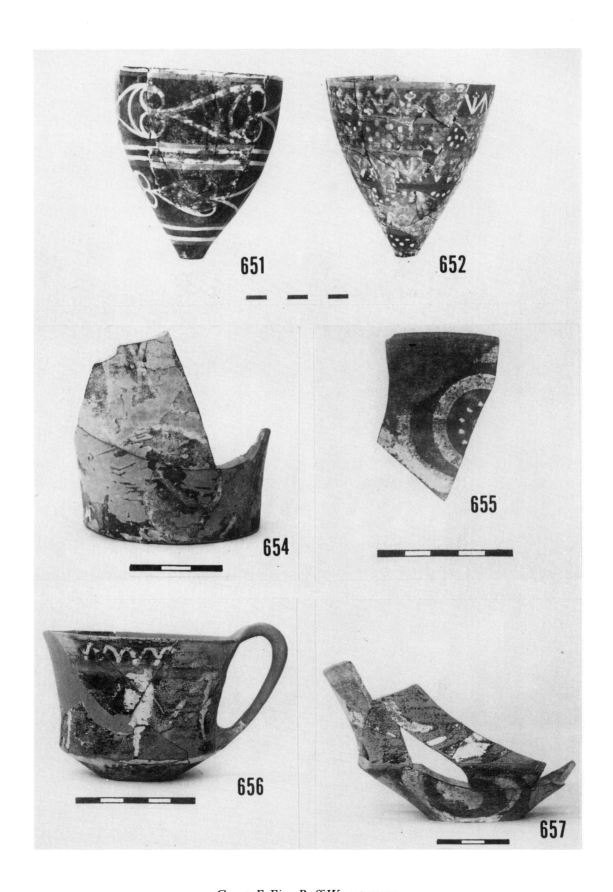

651   652

654

655

656

657

Group F, Fine Buff Ware pottery.

PLATE 109

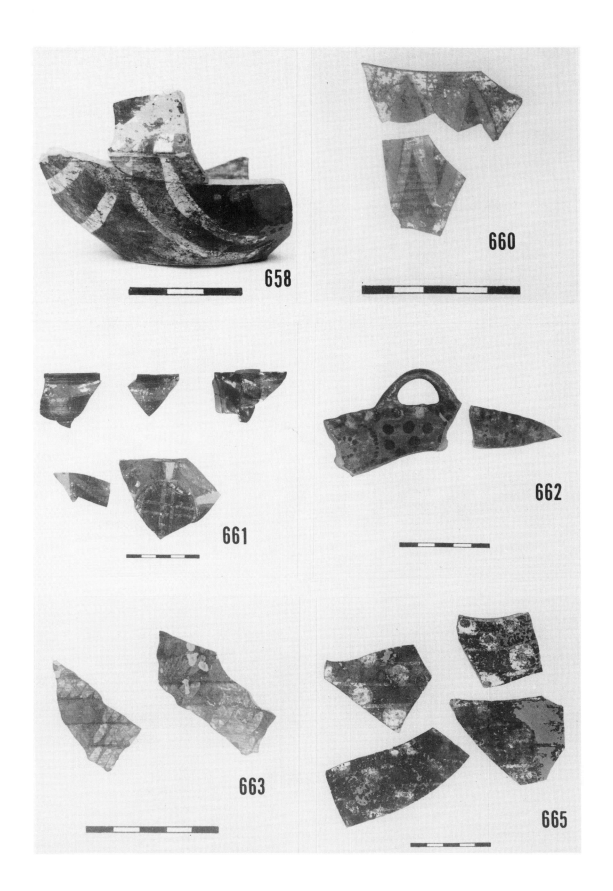

658

660

661

662

663

665

Group F, Fine Buff Ware pottery.

PLATE 110

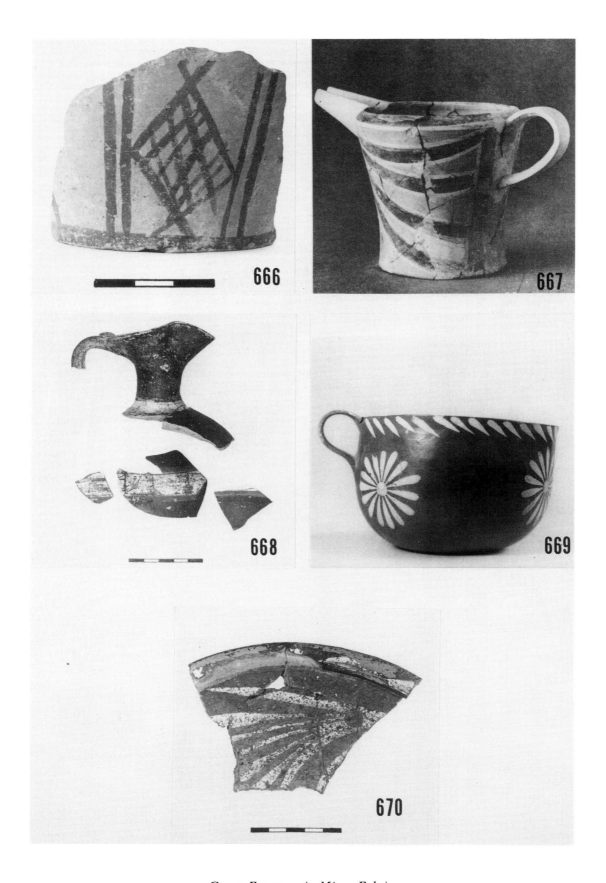

666 667 668 669 670

Group F, pottery in Minor Fabrics.

PLATE III

Group G, Fine Buff Ware pottery.

PLATE 112

Group G, Fine Buff Ware pottery.

PLATE 113

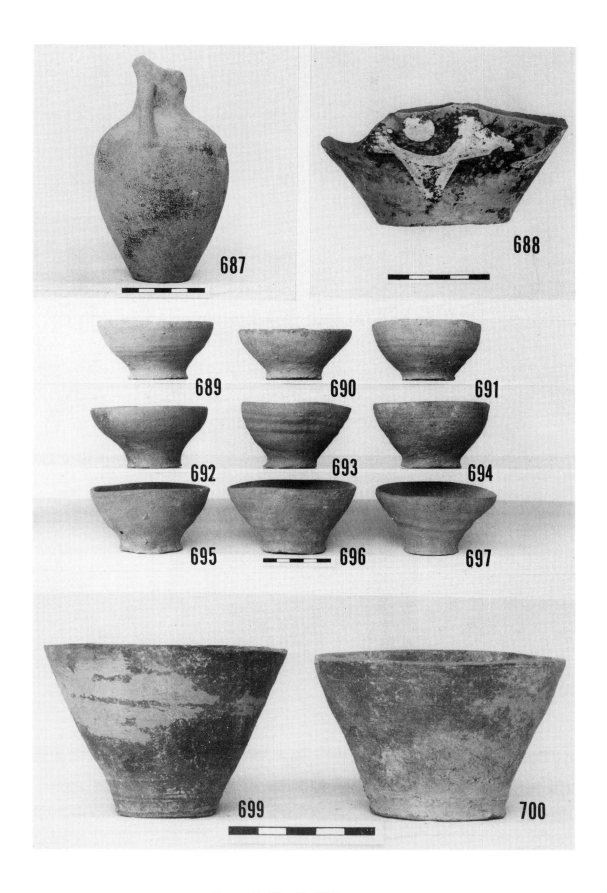

Group G, Fine Buff Ware pottery.

PLATE 114

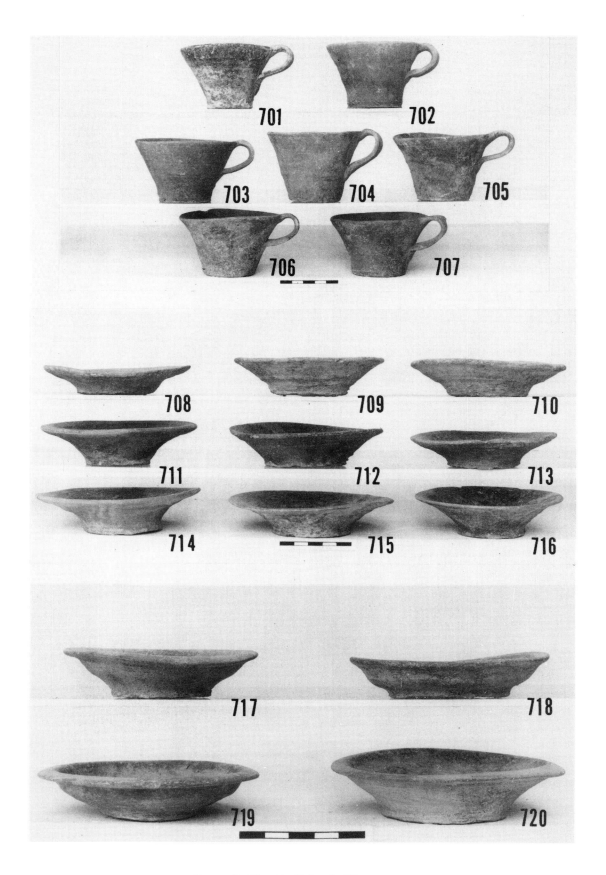

Group G, Fine Buff Crude Ware pottery.

PLATE 115

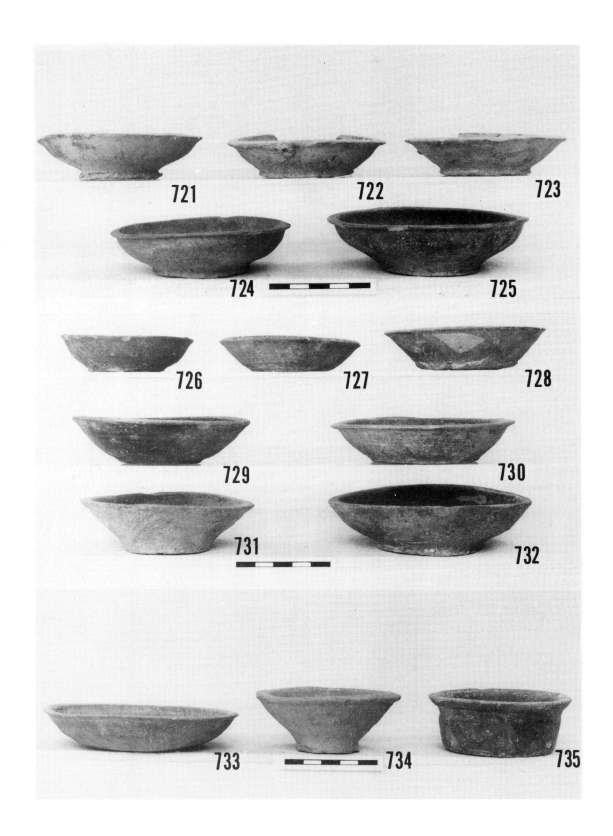

Group G, Fine Buff Crude Ware pottery.

PLATE 116

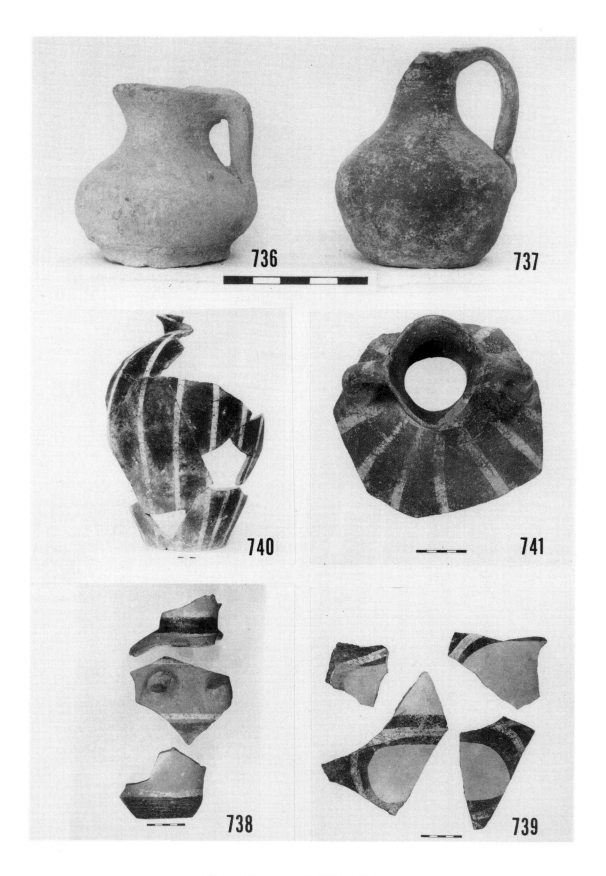

Group G, pottery in Minor Fabrics.

PLATE 117

Group G, pottery in Minor Fabrics.

PLATE 118

Group H, Fine Buff Ware pottery.

PLATE 119

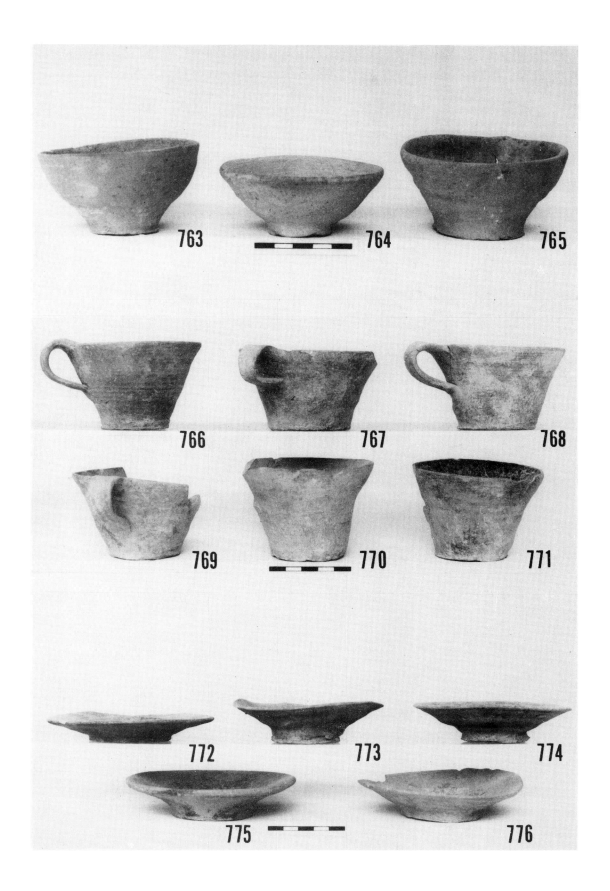

Group H, Fine Buff Crude Ware pottery.

PLATE 120

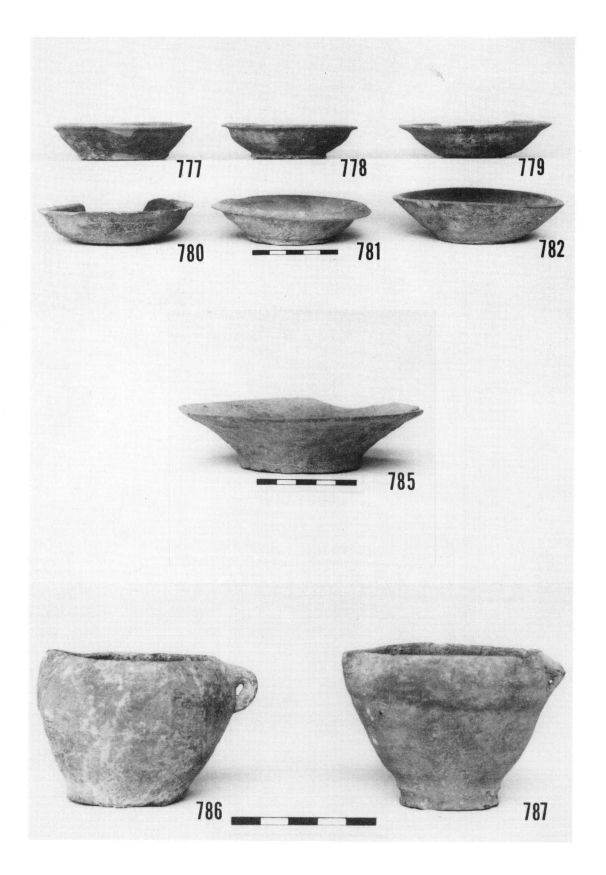

Group H, Fine Buff Crude Ware pottery.

PLATE 121

Group I, Large Jars (Courtesy Ashmolean Museum).

PLATE 122

Group I, Large Jars (Courtesy Ashmolean Museum).

PLATE 123

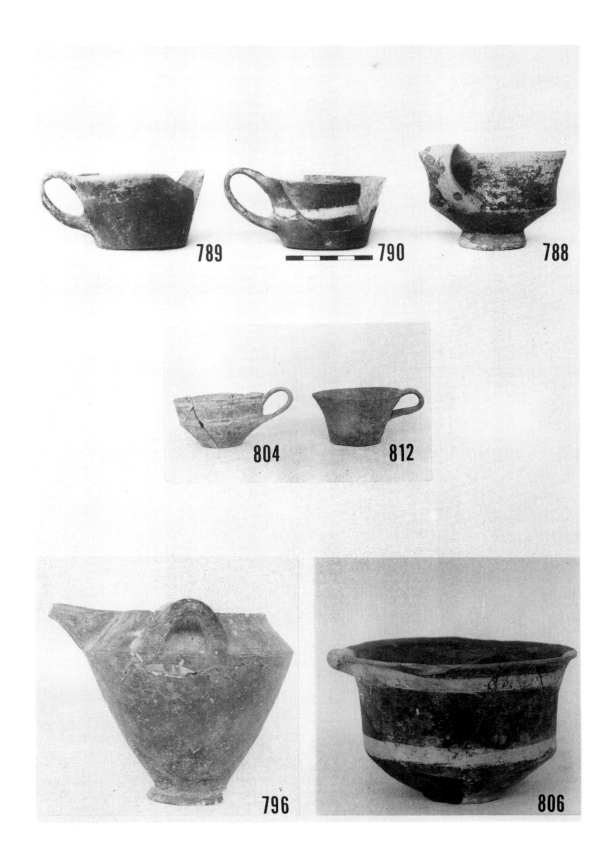

Group I, Fine Buff Ware pottery.

PLATE 124

Group J, selection of pottery (Courtesy Ashmolean Museum).

PLATE 125

Group J, Fine Buff Ware pottery.

PLATE 126

Group K, selection of pottery (Courtesy Ashmolean Museum).

PLATE 127

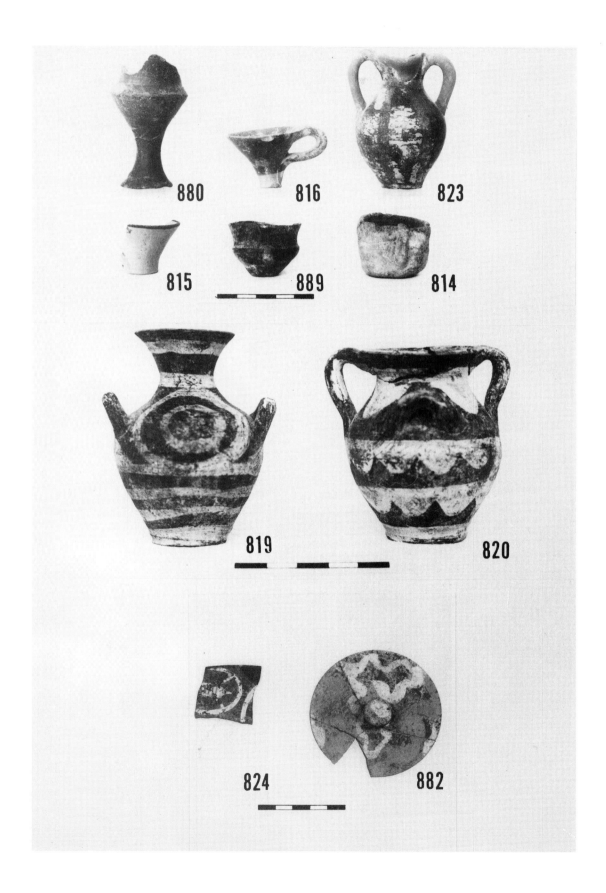

Group K, selection of pottery wares.

PLATE 128

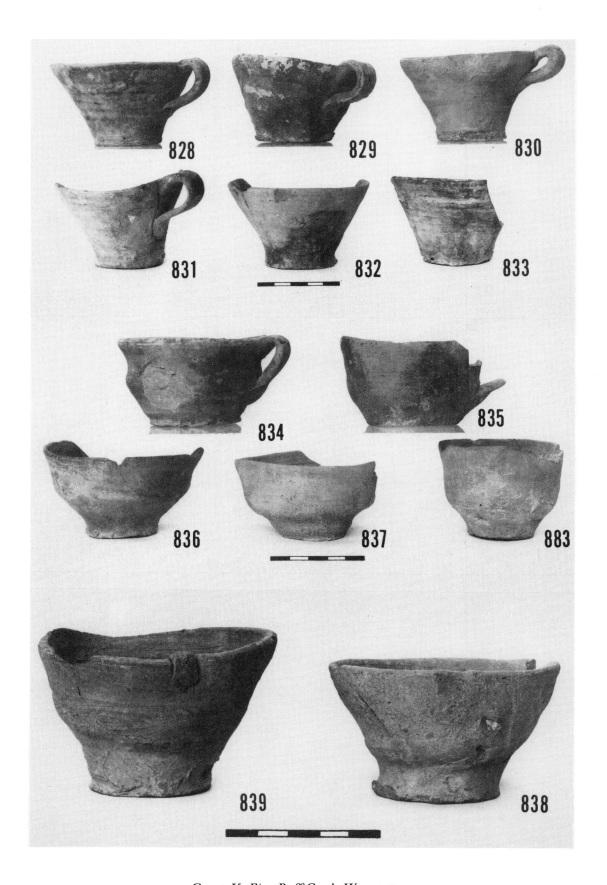

Group K, Fine Buff Crude Ware pottery.

PLATE 129

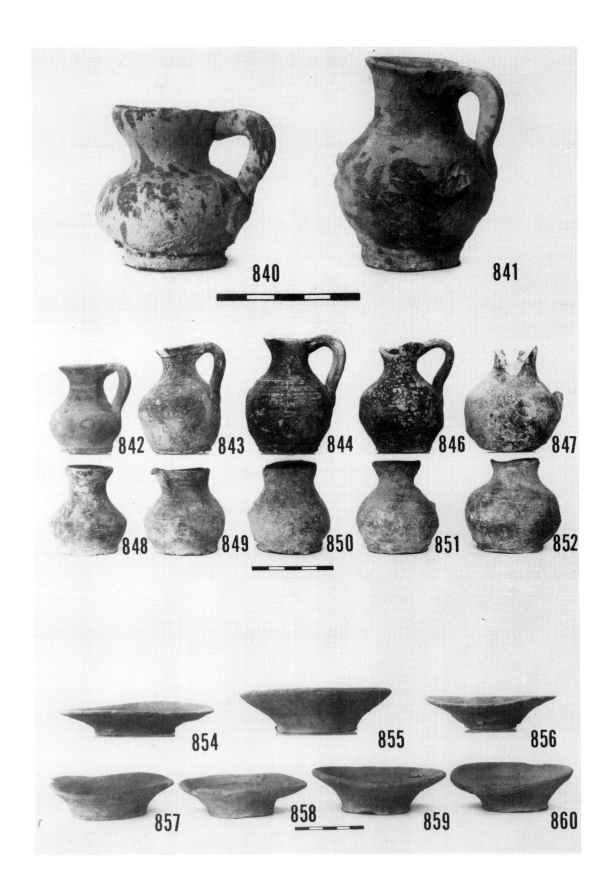

Group K, Fine Buff Crude Ware pottery.

PLATE 130

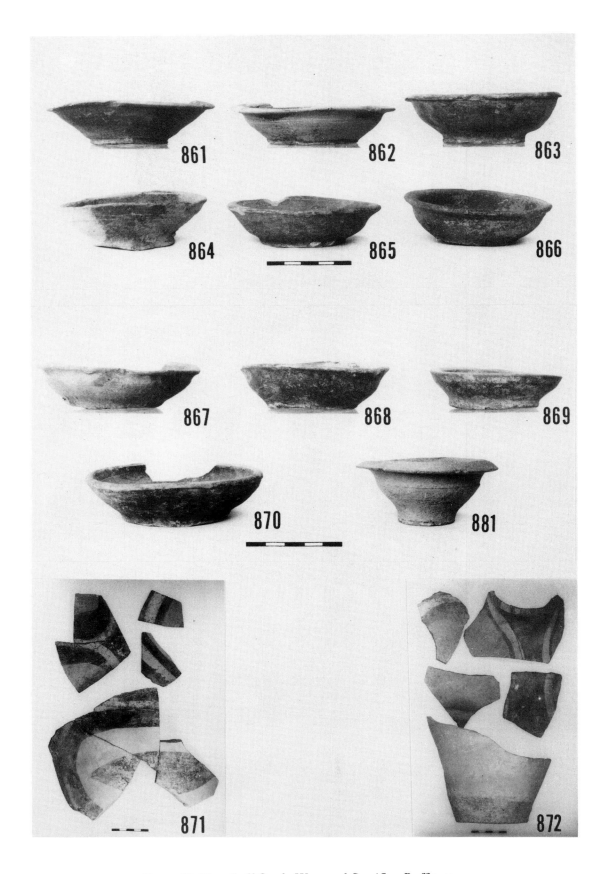

Group K, Fine Buff Crude Ware and Semifine Buff pottery.

PLATE 131

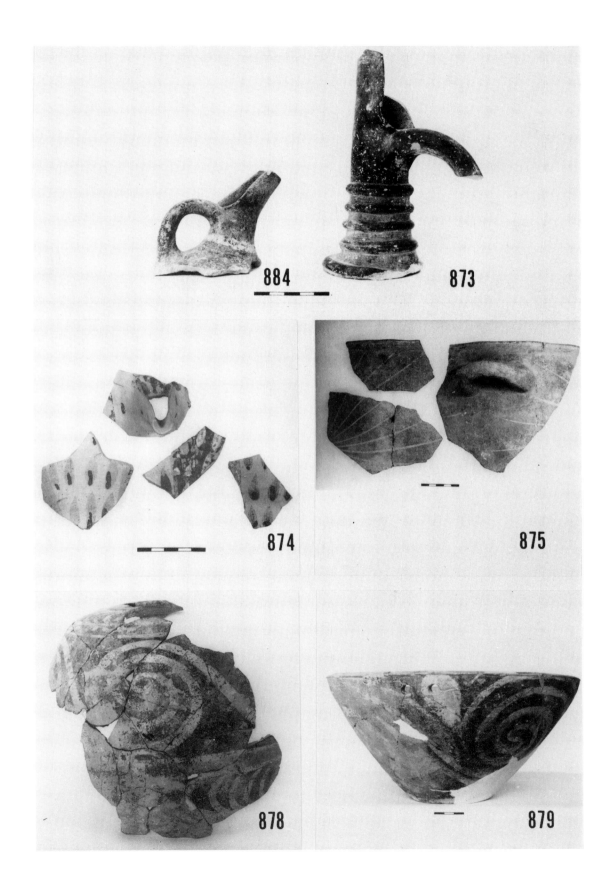

Group K, pottery in Minor Fabrics.

PLATE 132

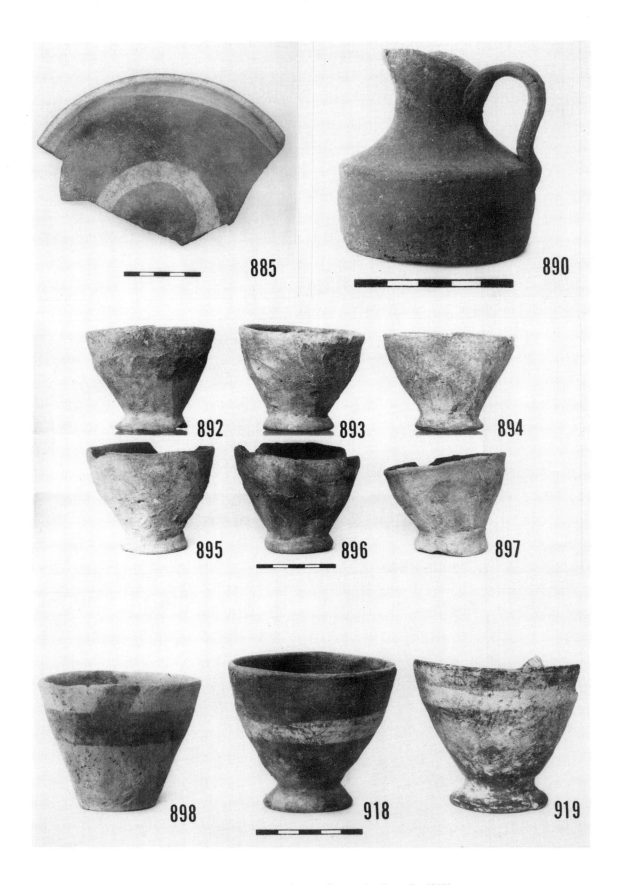

Group K, pottery in Minor Fabrics; Group L, Fine Buff Ware pottery.

PLATE 133

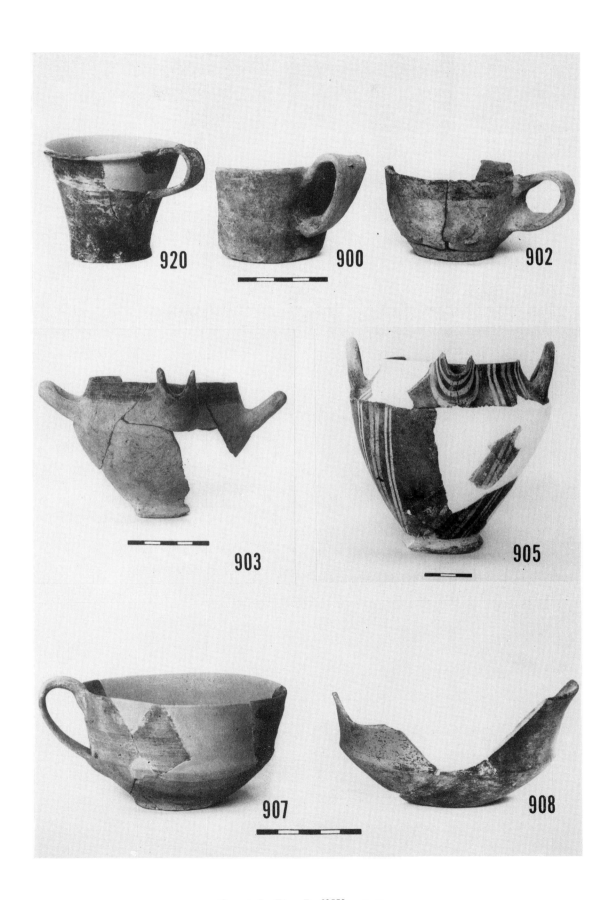

Group L, Fine Buff Ware pottery.

PLATE 134

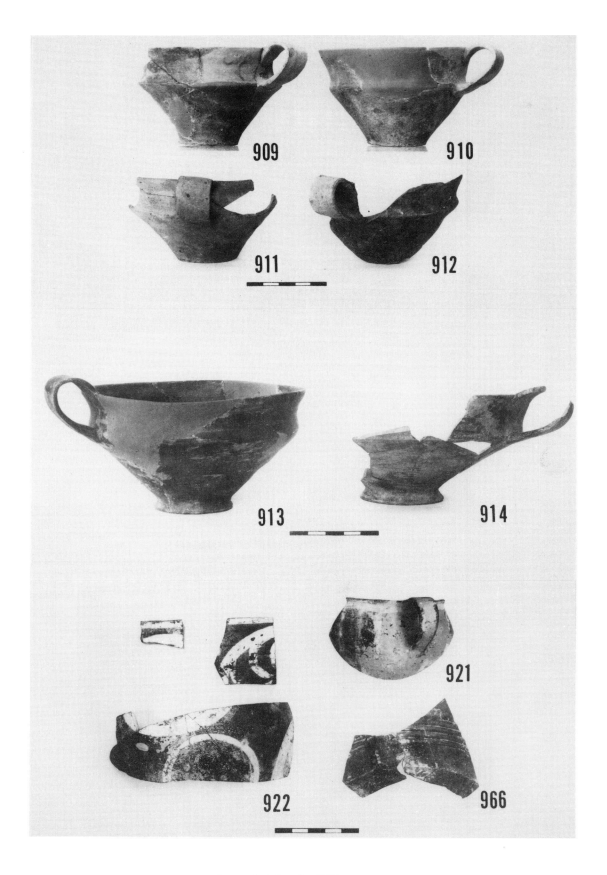

Group L, Fine Buff Ware pottery.

PLATE 135

923   924

925   926

928   967

Group L, Fine Buff Ware pottery.

PLATE 136

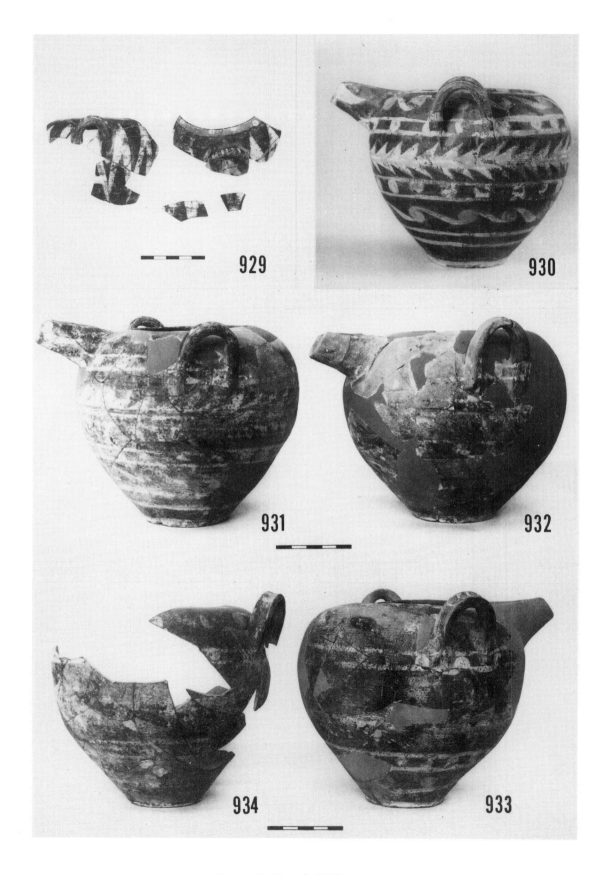

929

930

931

932

934 933

Group L, Fine Buff Ware pottery.

PLATE 137

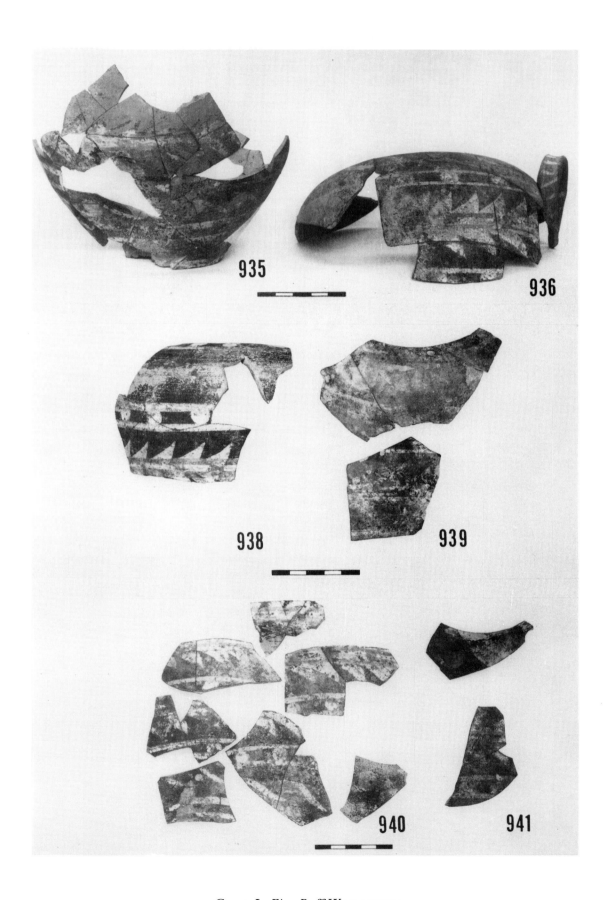

Group L, Fine Buff Ware pottery.

PLATE 138

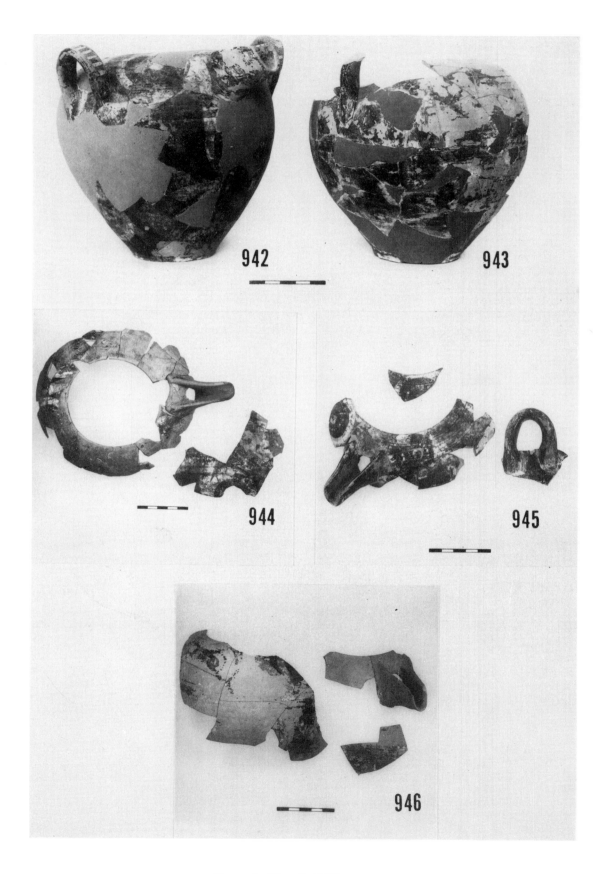

942   943

944   945

946

Group L, Fine Buff Ware pottery.

PLATE 139

947

948

949

950

951

952

Group L, Fine Buff Ware pottery.

PLATE 140

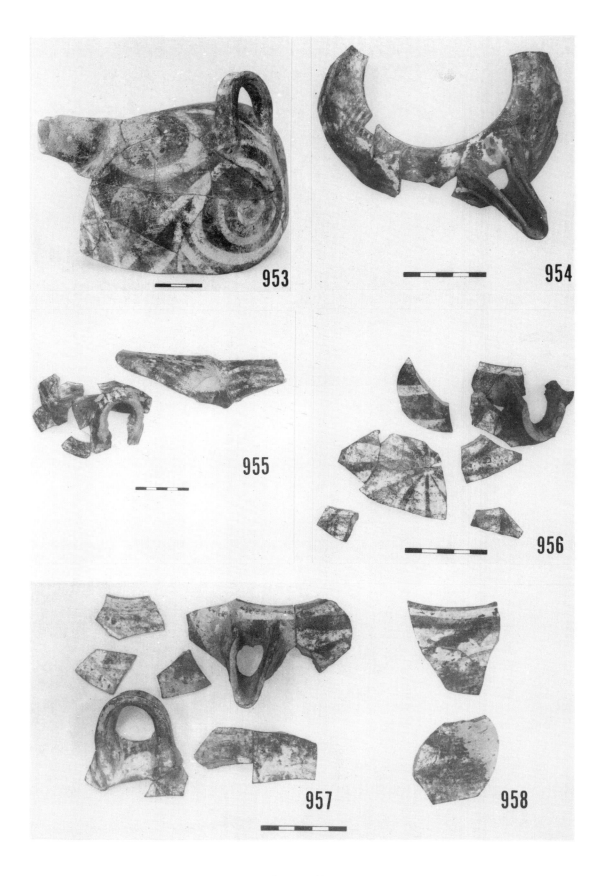

953   954   955   956   957   958

Group L, Fine Buff Ware pottery.

Room of the Stone Pier, selected pottery (Courtesy Ashmolean Museum).

PLATE 141

PLATE 142

Group M, selected pottery (Courtesy Ashmolean Museum).

PLATE 143

Group M, selected pottery.

PLATE 144

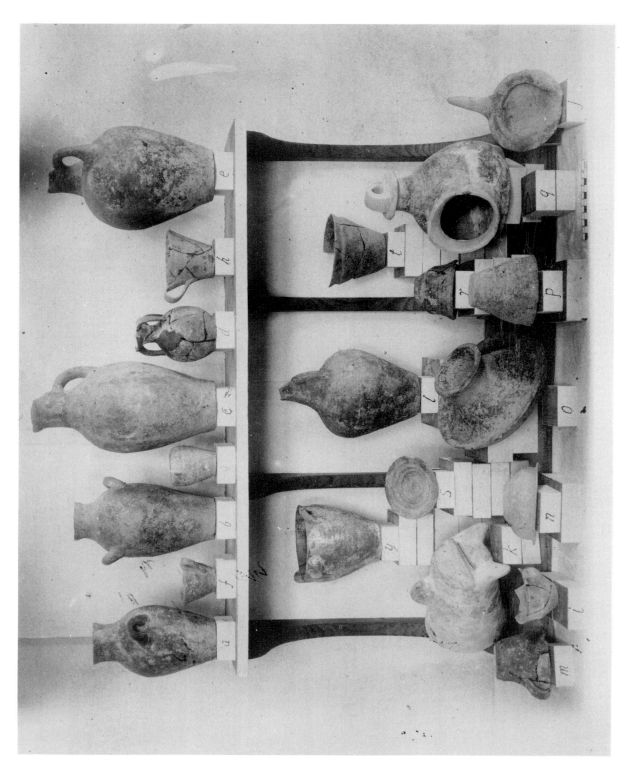

Group N, selected pottery (Courtesy Ashmolean Museum).

PLATE 145

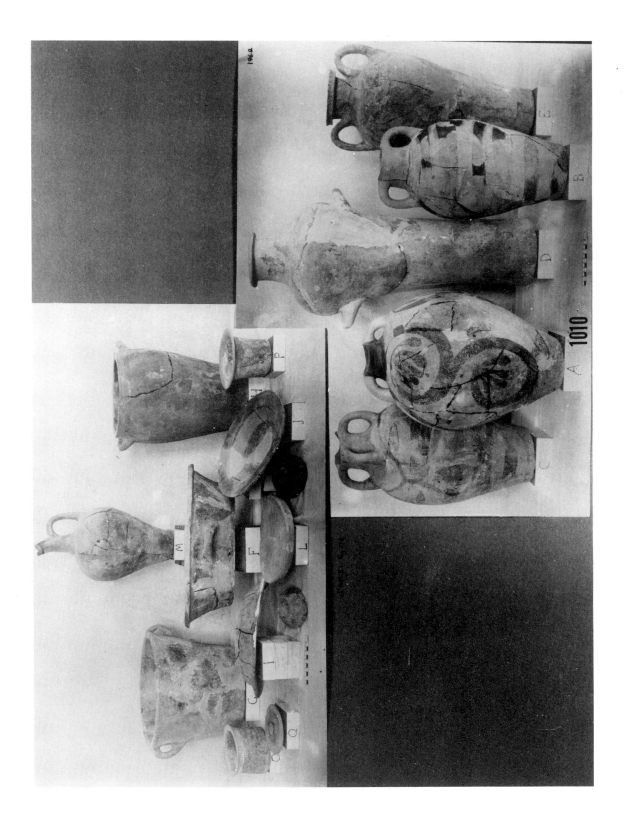

Group N, selected pottery (Courtesy Ashmolean Museum).

PLATE 146

Group N, selected Bowls (Courtesy Ashmolean Museum).

PLATE 147

Group N, Fine Buff Ware pottery.

PLATE 148

Group N, Fine Buff Ware pottery.

PLATE 149

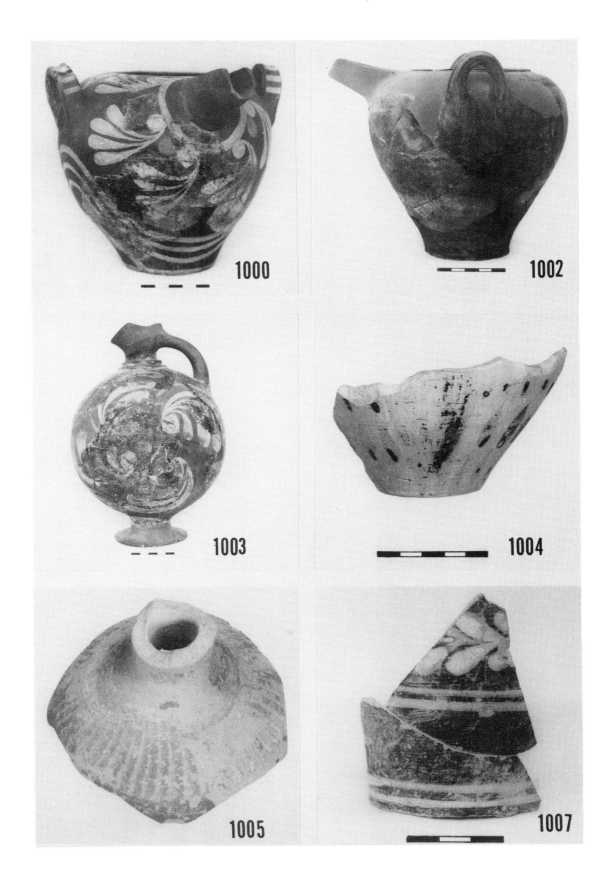

1000

1002

1003

1004

1005

1007

Group N, Fine Buff Ware and pottery in Minor Fabrics.

PLATE 150

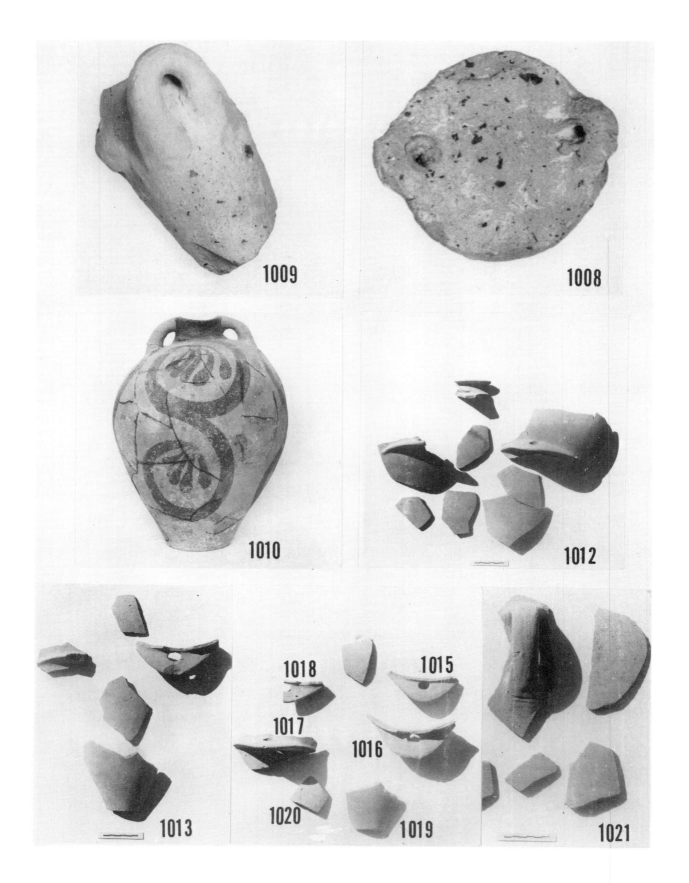

1009

1008

1010

1012

1018

1015

1017

1016

1013

1020

1019

1021

Group N, pottery in Minor Fabrics.

PLATE 151

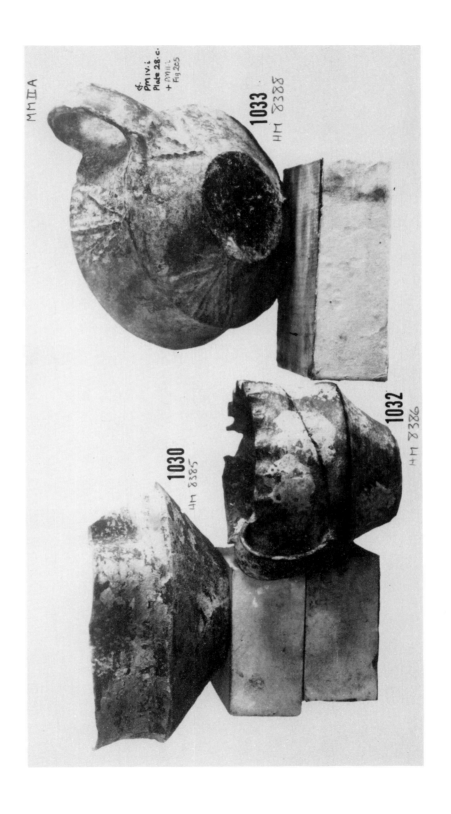

Group O, Fine Buff Ware Cups (Courtesy Ashmolean Museum).

PLATE 152

Group O, Fine Buff Ware Cups.

PLATE 153

1026   1027

1028   1029

1030   1031

Group O, Fine Buff Ware Cups

PLATE 154

Groups O and P, Fine Buff Ware pottery.

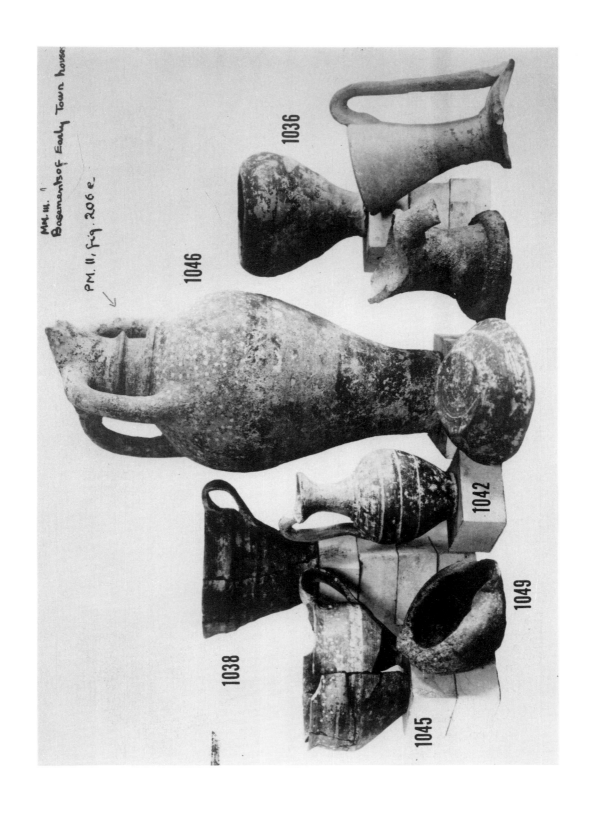

PLATE 155

Group P, selection of pottery (Courtesy Ashmolean Museum).

PLATE 156

Group P, pottery in Fine Buff and other fabrics.